EIGHTH EDITION

ASSESSMENT PROCEDURES FOR COUNSELORS AND HELPING PROFESSIONALS

EIGHTH EDITION

ASSESSMENT PROCEDURES FOR COUNSELORS AND HELPING PROFESSIONALS

Robert J. Drummond

Late of University of North Florida

Carl J. Sheperis

Lamar University

Karyn Dayle Jones

University of Central Florida

PEARSON

Boston   Columbus   Indianapolis   New York   San Francisco   Hoboken
Amsterdam   Cape Town   Dubai   London   Madrid   Milan   Munich   Paris   Montréal   Toronto
Delhi   Mexico City   São Paulo   Sydney   Hong Kong   Seoul   Singapore   Taipei   Tokyo

Vice President and Editorial Director: Jeffery W. Johnston
Vice President and Publisher: Kevin M. Davis
Editorial Assistant: Marisia Styles
Executive Field Marketing Manager: Krista Clark
Senior Product Marketing Manager: Christopher Barry
Project Manager: Lauren Carlson
Procurement Specialist: Deidra Skahill
Senior Art Director: Diane Ernsberger
Cover Designer: Cenveo
Cover Art: Purestock/Getty Images
Full-Service Project Management: Kailash Jadli, iEnergizer Aptara®, Ltd.
Composition: iEnergizer Aptara®, Ltd.
Printer/Binder: Courier - Westford
Cover Printer: Phoenix Color - Hagerstown
Text Font: Palatino

Credits and acknowledgments for material borrowed from other sources and reproduced, with permission, in this textbook appear on the appropriate page within the text.

Every effort has been made to provide accurate and current Internet information in this book. However, the Internet and information posted on it are constantly changing, so it is inevitable that some of the Internet addresses listed in this textbook will change.

Library of Congress Cataloging-in-Publication Data
Drummond, Robert J.
    Assessment procedures for counselors and helping professionals / Robert J. Drummond, Carl J. Sheperis, Karyn D. Jones.—Eighth edition.
      pages cm
    ISBN 978-0-13-285063-6—ISBN 0-13-285063-X
    1. Psychological tests. 2. Educational tests and measurements. 3. Counseling. I. Sheperis, Carl. II. Jones, Karyn Dayle. III. Title.
    BF176.D78 2016
    150.28'7—dc23
                                                                                            2015009259

10 9 8 7 6 5 4 3 2 1

PEARSON

ISBN 10:   0-13-285063-X
ISBN 13: 978-0-13-285063-6

The eighth edition is dedicated to my children who bring light to my world: Ellis, Jake, Joe Lee, Emily, and Laura Beth

— CJS

PREFACE

In *Assessment Procedures for Counselors and Helping Professionals*, our goal is to help current and future school counselors, marriage and family therapists, mental health counselors, career counselors, and other helping professionals become better consumers of the various methods and procedures used in the process of assessment. Assessment occurs in many settings, such as schools, mental health clinics, career counseling centers, substance abuse treatment centers, private practice, psychiatric hospitals, and vocational rehabilitation centers. Assessment is an integral part of the counseling process in which the counselor and client work together to gain a better understanding of the client's problems. We believe that effectiveness and accuracy in assessment are essential to effective counseling. Throughout the text, we stress that assessment is more than simply giving tests. Assessment involves collecting and integrating information about an individual from *multiple methods* and *multiple sources*. Throughout this textbook, our aim is to provide students with an overview of the many approaches to assessment so they can become competent and ethical practitioners in our multicultural society.

This textbook has three goals. The first goal is to supply foundational information about assessment, which includes an overview of the various methods and sources of assessment information. In addition, students must learn some basic principles of measurement in order to understand the applications and issues in assessment. Thus, we also provide foundational information about statistical concepts, test scores, and the psychometric aspects of assessment (e.g., validity and reliability). The second goal of this textbook is to present an overview of the general areas in which assessment is commonly utilized, such as in assessing intellectual ability, achievement, aptitude, career interests and skills, and personality. The third goal is to provide students with information about specific assessment applications and issues, such as clinical assessment, communicating assessment results, assessment with diverse populations, and ethical and legal issues.

To meet these goals, the textbook is divided into three parts that provide a balance of theory and practice information as well as coverage of the assessment instruments and strategies commonly used in school counseling, clinical mental health counseling, and vocational or career counseling settings. These sections include Principles and Foundations of Assessment, Overview of Assessment Areas, and Applications and Issues.

PRINCIPLES AND FOUNDATIONS OF ASSESSMENT

Part One of this textbook, Principles and Foundations of Psychological and Educational Assessment, focuses on the underlying principles and foundations of all forms of psychological and educational assessment. We designed this section to provide counselors with the essential concepts of measurement and evaluation that they need to engage in the assessment process. Chapter 1 introduces assessment and provides historical information that has influenced assessment practice. Chapter 2 focuses on the assessment process, emphasizing the importance of collecting data by using multiple methods from multiple sources. The chapter provides detailed information about formal and informal data-collection methods (e.g., interviews, tests, observations) as well as the sources of assessment information (e.g., the client, parents, significant others, teachers, health professionals). Chapter 3 presents basic statistical concepts associated with tests and assessment. Chapter 4 presents information about types of scores and standards for scoring and interpreting assessment instruments. Chapters 5 and 6 supply information about the key psychometric considerations that are essential in assessment: reliability and validity. Chapter 7 integrates the elements of the assessment process by presenting information about selecting, administering, scoring, and reporting assessment results.

ASSESSMENT AREAS

Part Two of the textbook, Overview of Assessment Areas, builds on the Principles and Foundations section by exploring specific assessment areas. Chapter 8 supplies information about assessing intellectual ability, including the major theories of intelligence, the major tests of intelligence (e.g., the Wechsler scales, the Stanford–Binet, the Kaufman tests), and special issues in intelligence testing. Chapter 9 covers assessment of achievement, including achievement test batteries, individual achievement tests, diagnostic achievement tests, subject-area tests, and other types of achievement tests. Chapter 10 presents information about aptitude assessment. Extensive changes in U.S. social and economic conditions may result in more counselors working with clients on career-related issues; thus, Chapter 11 provides important information about career and employment assessment. The last chapter in this section, Chapter 12, focuses on personality assessment and the many types of personality instruments and techniques.

APPLICATIONS AND ISSUES

The chapters in Part Three, Applications and Issues Related to Assessment, center on the applications and issues related to specific assessment areas. The main focus is the effective, competent, and ethical application of assessment methods in various settings and with diverse populations. For example, a primary purpose of assessment is for diagnosing client issues and problems. Thus, Chapter 13 focuses exclusively on clinical assessment and the use of assessment procedures to diagnose mental disorders, develop treatment plans, monitor counseling progress, and evaluate outcome. Chapter 14 presents information about assessment issues in education, such as the assessment activities of school counselors, the types of assessment instruments used in schools, assessing specific learning disabilities and giftedness, test preparation and performance, environmental assessment in the schools, and assessment competencies for school counselors. Because assessment strategies are applied to diverse populations, Chapter 15 supplies important information about multicultural assessment, including social and cultural factors related to assessing individuals, groups, and specific populations, as well as the competencies and standards required for assessing individuals from diverse backgrounds. Chapter 16 presents information about communicating assessment results. Finally, Chapter 17 focuses on the important ethical and legal issues related to assessment.

CHANGES IN THE EIGHTH EDITION

First published in 1988, this textbook has become a classic among assessment textbooks designed specifically for counselors. The eighth edition hosts extensive changes in the content of the text; we have updated all of the chapters and strived to provide the most accurate, up-to-date assessment information. At the same time, we have endeavored to maintain the original appeal of the text by retaining an easy-to-read format and continuing to emphasize assessment information that is most useful and relevant for school counselors, marriage and family therapists, mental health counselors, and other helping professionals. Throughout the text, we provide information and examples about widely used assessment instruments in order to help students become familiar with these well-known tests. This edition has been completely revised to align with the 2014 standards for educational and psychological testing.

Key revisions in this edition include the following:

- Chapter 1, Introduction to Assessment, consists of revised and expanded information about assessment in counseling. This introductory chapter provides an overview of the purpose for assessment as well as new information about the assessment process.
- Chapter 2, Methods and Sources of Assessment Information, has been revised to describe current information about the multiple methods and sources of data collection used in the assessment process. This chapter encompasses information about formal and informal assessment instruments and strategies divided into three broad categories: interviews, tests, and observation. Information about the importance of using collateral sources in assessment is also presented.
- The chapters on statistical concepts, understanding scores, and reliability and validity (Chapters 3, 4, 5, and 6) have been extensively reorganized and revised. Chapter 5 provides expanded information on sources of measurement error.
- Chapter 7 summarizes the assessment process by focusing on the procedures for selecting, administering, scoring, and interpreting assessment results. It includes information about the steps involved in selecting appropriate assessment instruments and strategies; the various sources of information about instruments; the process of evaluating assessment instruments; and procedures for administration, scoring, and interpretation.
- We have updated and improved all of the chapters in Part Two, Overview of Assessment Areas, to include the most current information about specific assessment strategies and instruments. All chapters in this section (Chapters 8 through 12) supply up-to-date information about the most widely used instruments and strategies. For example, Chapter 8, Assessment of Intelligence and General Ability, includes information about the latest revisions of key intelligence tests as well as expanded information on the contemporary and emerging theories of intelligence.
- Chapter 13, Clinical Assessment, has been restructured to include a broad presentation of the *Diagnostic and Statistical Manual of Mental Disorders*, Fifth Edition (DSM-5) and its use in clinical assessment. In addition, we have added new information about the mental status exam, suicide risk assessment, and behavioral observation used in clinical assessment.
- We have updated Chapter 14, Assessment in Education, including updated information about school assessment programs. We have also added specific information about the common assessment activities performed by school counselors and updated

information about conducting needs assessments, assessing specific learning disabilities, assessing giftedness, and environmental assessment in the schools.

- Chapter 15, Assessment Issues with Diverse Populations, has been extensively revised. We expanded the discussion of measurement bias to align with the concept of fairness in testing, as described in the 2014 edition of the *Standards for Educational and Psychological Testing.* We restructured the section on assessing individuals with disabilities to encompass assessment of individuals with visual impairment, hearing impairment, intellectual disability, and other disabilities.
- Chapter 16, Communicating Assessment Results, has also been extensively revised. Because counselors often orally communicate assessment results to clients, parents, and other professionals, we expanded the section on the use of feedback sessions to report results. Furthermore, we updated and improved the information provided about written assessment reports.
- In Chapter 17, Ethical and Legal Issues in Assessment, we have updated the overview of ethical codes from professional organizations relevant to assessment. We also have updated and expanded the section on statutes and regulations that have implications for assessment.

ACKNOWLEDGMENTS

I would like to thank my publisher, Kevin Davis, for believing in me and giving me the chance to revise such an esteemed book. This book influenced me during my graduate training, and now I have the privilege to revise it for the eighth edition. Thanks to the late Robert Drummond for his many contributions to the assessment world and for authoring such a foundational textbook. I would also like to thank Melinda Rankin for her excellent copyediting skills. She has an amazing eye for detail and a gentle way of helping me to see my own writing errors. Finally, I would like to thank the following colleagues, whose reviews improved this edition: Donald Deering, Oakland University and University of Phoenix; Josué R. Gonzalez, Clinical Psychologist—San Antonio, Texas; Dawn C. Lorenz, Penn State University; Diane Kelly-Riley, Washington State University; and Anthony Tasso, Farleigh Dickinson University.

CJS

ABOUT THE AUTHORS

Robert J. Drummond

Dr. Robert Drummond passed away on March 14, 2005. He was a retired professor and counselor educator at the University of North Florida for 20 years. He was foremost in the field of assessment, and he specialized in educational and psychological testing, career development, models for evaluation, educational research, and personality theory and measurement. Dr. Drummond wrote the first edition of this text in 1988. Now in its eighth edition, the book remains a popular assessment textbook in counseling.

Carl J. Sheperis

Dr. Carl J. Sheperis serves as Chair of the Department of Counseling and Special Populations at Lamar University. He is a past president of the Association for Assessment and Research in Counseling, associate editor for quantitative research for the *Journal of Counseling and Development*, and a director for the National Board for Certified Counselors. He has worked with the American Counseling Association as the chair of the Research & Knowledge Committee and has served as the editor of the *Journal of Counseling Research and Practice*.

In addition to this textbook, Dr. Sheperis is an author of *Research in Counseling: Quantitative, Qualitative, and Mixed Methods*; *Clinical Mental Health Counseling: Fundamentals of Applied Practice*; *DSM Disorders in Children and Adolescents*; and *The Peace Train*. He is also published in various textbooks, academic journals, and reference volumes. A frequent speaker and presenter at professional conferences and workshops as well, Carl Sheperis has appeared at such recent events as the American Counseling Association World Conference, The International Autism Conference, the Association for Counselor Education and Supervision Conference, the National Assessment Conference, and the National Head Start Conference.

Karyn Dayle Jones

Dr. Karyn Dayle Jones is an associate professor in counselor education at the University of Central Florida. She has over 20 years of experience in the counseling profession and has been a counselor educator for over 15 years. Jones is coauthor of *Introduction to the Profession of Counseling*, has authored or coauthored several book chapters and refereed publications, and has made numerous professional presentations. Her primary areas of research are assessment and diagnosis. She is the past president of the Association for Humanistic Counseling, a division of the American Counseling Association. Jones is a Florida Licensed Mental Health Counselor and a National Certified Counselor, and she has worked as a counselor in mental health agencies, schools, and private practice.

BRIEF CONTENTS

CONTENTS

Introduction to Assessment

Imagine being asked by a child welfare agency to conduct an assessment that would determine a child's potential for transitioning from foster care status to adoption within a family. As part of the assessment, you might visit the home of the potential parents to determine the appropriateness of the environment and to have a realistic sense of the family functioning. You would also have to evaluate the social and emotional development of the child and the readiness for adoption. For example, it would be necessary to consider the child's ability to bond with a new family, any developmental issues that may be present, and any potential barriers that might impact the success of the adoption process. In order to gather enough information to make this type of determination, you might interview the parents, observe the child playing and interacting, and conduct evaluation using standardized assessment instruments (e.g., the Bayley Scales of Infant and Toddler Development). Consider how important this assessment process would be to the children and the parents. The overall assessment process would be quite involved, and the results would have incredibly high stakes. The final assessment report would include information about any developmental concerns, an evaluation of the family environment, an interpretation of standardized scores, and a final recommendation based on the data. Based on the assessment results, the child welfare agency would make a decision about finalizing the adoption.

It is a privilege to play such a role in people's lives, and the privilege should be honored with careful attention to best practices and a wealth of knowledge about the assessment process. Although the results of assessment do not always lead to happy outcomes, this example provides some insight into where your journey through this book will lead. Assessment has long been regarded as a fundamental component of all helping professions and the cornerstone of the counseling process. Simply put, assessment is the process of gathering information about a client and determining the meaning of that information. It is through assessment that counselors can uncover the nature of a client's problems or issues; the magnitude of these problems and how they are impacting the client's life; how the client's family, relationships, or past experiences are affecting the current problem; the client's strengths and readiness for counseling; and whether counseling can be beneficial to the client. Assessment is also critical for establishing the goals and objectives of counseling and for determining the most effective interventions. Assessment occurs in all counseling settings, including schools, mental health clinics, career counseling centers, substance abuse treatment centers, private practice, psychiatric hospitals, and vocational rehabilitation centers. In practice, counselors are *always* assessing. Assessment is an ongoing, fluid, and dynamic process that continues throughout the course of the helping relationship.

Although students in the helping professions often initially question the need for assessment training, competency in assessment is integral to successful counseling practice (Whiston, 2012).

The purpose of this textbook is to help current and future school counselors, mental health counselors, career counselors, marriage and family therapists, and other helping professionals recognize the integral role between assessment and counseling, understand the process of assessment, develop an awareness of the applications of assessment, and understand the legal and ethical issues specific to assessment. We believe that competency in assessment is essential to positive outcomes in counseling. In order to be competent in assessment, you will need to seek supervised practice opportunities in addition to learning the content in this textbook. Each chapter in this book will help you build upon your ability to integrate assessment into your practice as a professional counselor.

Throughout the textbook, we use the term *assessment* rather than *testing*. It is important to understand that testing is just one component of the assessment process and that the scope of assessment activities is far beyond the exclusive use of standardized tests. Although we will present information about important and widely used educational and psychological tests throughout the text, we stress that assessment is more than simply giving tests. Assessment involves collecting and integrating information about an individual from *multiple methods* (e.g., interviews, observations, tests) and *multiple sources* (e.g., the client, family members, teachers, physicians). Corroborating data from multiple assessment methods and sources helps create a more comprehensive and accurate understanding of the client and his or her presenting concerns.

After studying this chapter, you should be able to:

- Define *assessment*.
- Describe the various purposes of assessment.
- Describe the broad categories of data collection methods and the various sources of assessment information.
- Explain the importance of integrating multiple methods and multiple sources of assessment information.
- List and describe the steps in the assessment process.
- Describe the competencies required by counselors for the effective use of assessment instruments.
- Describe the historical context of assessment.
- Describe the application of computer technology in the field of assessment.

WHAT IS ASSESSMENT?

Before we can talk about the assessment process, it is important to understand our definition of assessment. The term *assessment* refers to any systematic procedure for collecting information that is used to make inferences or decisions about the characteristics of a person (American Educational Research Association (AERA), American Psychological Association (APA), & National Council on Measurement in Education (NCME), 2014). Assessment encompasses a broad array of data collection methods from multiple sources to yield relevant, accurate, and reliable information about an individual. In counseling and other helping professions, assessment is considered a *process*, because it is the *continual practice* of gathering information. Some hold to a traditional (yet erroneous) belief that assessment is limited to the first meeting with an individual; in reality, assessment is an ongoing process that may begin even before the first face-to-face contact with the individual and that continues throughout the course of the helping relationship.

Many disciplines employ the activity of assessment, including psychology, counseling, education, social work, health, military, and business and industry. Educators and other school personnel use assessment to identify learning or behavioral or emotional problems in students and to determine appropriate interventions and educational plans. Psychologists and other mental health professionals utilize assessment to help in diagnosing mental disorders, treatment planning, and monitoring and evaluating treatment progress. Career counselors engage in assessment to evaluate individuals' vocational interests and aptitudes. Because numerous types of professionals engage in assessment, we will refer to those individuals as *counselors, test users, assessors, examiners*, or simply *professionals* throughout the textbook. Similarly, we will refer to individuals who participate in the assessment process as *clients, test takers, assessees*, or *examinees*.

Assessment is often equated with *testing*, and the two terms are often confused or erroneously used interchangeably. Even today, many published textbooks hardly distinguish between assessment and testing. As Cohen, Swerdlik, and Sturman (2012) noted, *testing* has been a catch-all phrase for the entire testing process rather than just the administration of a test. However, assessment goes beyond merely giving tests. It is a comprehensive process that involves the integration of information from multiple data collection methods (e.g., interviews, tests, observations). Therefore, tests are now considered to be one aspect of the overall assessment process (American Educational Research Association (AERA) et al., 2014). The fact that assessment can proceed effectively without testing helps to distinguish between these two activities (Weiner, 2013).

The methods for collecting assessment information can be grouped into three broad categories: interviews, tests, and observations. Each category comprises a wide array of formal and informal instruments and strategies, such as unstructured interviews, rating scales, standardized tests, projective drawings, checklists, questionnaires, and so on. Assessment also involves obtaining information from various sources, which may include the client, family members, spouses or partners, teachers, physicians, mental health professionals, and other professionals. The assessment process varies from assessment to assessment, depending upon the purpose for assessment, the setting in which the assessment takes place, the needs of the client, and the availability and utility of the methods and sources of information (Weiner, 2013). We emphasize the importance of using multiple methods in most assessments, because the results of a single assessment instrument should never be the sole determinant of important decisions about clients.

The Purposes of Assessment

Now that we have defined assessment, it is important to explore the rationale for conducting assessment in counseling and other helping professions. Why do counselors assess? The short answer to this question is to gather information about a client. However, the information that counselors need to collect about a client depends a great deal on the *purpose* or *reason for assessment*. The research literature contains at least four general purposes of assessment, including screening, identification and diagnosis, intervention planning, and progress and outcome evaluation (Erford, 2012; Sattler & Hoge, 2006; Selborn, Marion, & Bagby, 2013).

SCREENING *Screening* is a quick process, usually involving a single procedure or instrument, used to determine whether an individual has a high risk of having a specific problem and needs more in-depth assessment at that time. The screening process is not comprehensive, and the instruments used for screening are often held to lower standards of psychometrical soundness (Erford, 2012). Screening does not necessarily detect a specific problem or disorder an individual might have or how serious it might be; rather, it provides counselors with preliminary information that identifies those individuals with a high probability of having a particular problem. If an individual is identified as having a high risk for a disorder through the screening process, then further assessment is warranted. For example, many colleges have depression screening days in which students are given the opportunity to complete a questionnaire or instrument that detects a risk for depression. If the results of the instrument indicate a high risk for depression, then the student is referred to the counseling center for further evaluation and, if needed, counseling.

IDENTIFICATION AND DIAGNOSIS In counseling, assessment is often conducted as a means of *identifying* or *diagnosing* problems, symptoms, or disorders. *Diagnosis* can be defined as a "detailed analysis of an individual's strengths and weaknesses, with the general goal of arriving at a classification decision" (Erford, 2006, p. 2). The assessment process for diagnosis typically encompasses the use of a series of instruments and strategies to identify a client's problem areas that need to be targeted for intervention. Many counselors are required to diagnose individuals using a classification system called the *Diagnostic and Statistical Manual of Mental Disorders, Fifth Edition,* (DSM-5; American Psychiatric Association (APA), 2013). *Mental disorders* are behavioral or psychological patterns that impair an individual's cognitive, emotional, or behavioral functioning. In mental health counseling settings, depression and anxiety are examples of problems commonly diagnosed using the DSM-5. In school settings, identifying students who may be experiencing delays or learning problems is an important objective of assessment.

INTERVENTION PLANNING *Intervention planning* (i.e., treatment planning) involves deciding on a course of action that facilitates client change and helps improve the client's outcome. In most cases, an individual is referred for counseling because he or she is struggling and needs specific psychological, educational, or behavioral interventions to improve his or her situation (Lichtenberger, Mather, Kaufman, & Kaufman, 2005). In these cases, the purpose of assessment is to gather information to determine the most effective interventions that address and resolve the client's specific areas of concern. There are innumerable interventions that a counselor can choose from, and the interventions decided upon are based on the client's problems and the reason for referral. In addition, the setting in which the assessment takes place (such as a school, hospital, community mental health agency, private practice, or vocational center) will influence the types of interventions recommended (Lichtenberger et al., 2005).

PROGRESS AND OUTCOME EVALUATION Once interventions have been implemented, counselors may use various assessment instruments and strategies to monitor a client's progress and evaluate outcome. By periodically monitoring a client's progress, counselors can determine if the interventions are positively impacting the client. If an intervention is having no positive effects, then counselors may reevaluate the client and make new intervention plans. When an intervention program is completed, counselors may conduct an outcome evaluation to determine if the particular intervention was effective and if the client achieved his or her goals at the end of counseling. The first step in *progress and outcome evaluation* is establishing a *baseline measure* of the client's condition. This usually takes place during the initial meeting for assessment and can involve the use of formal or informal assessment instruments or strategies. For example, an informal method would be to ask the client to rate his or her feelings of depression on a scale from 0 to 10, with 0 indicating a complete absence of depressive symptoms and 10 indicating feeling intensely depressed. An example of a formal assessment instrument designed specifically for progress and outcome evaluation is the Outcome Questionnaire (OQ-45), which measures adult clients' psychological symptoms (e.g., depression, anxiety), interpersonal functioning, and social role functioning. The assessment methods used to collect baseline data are periodically readministered to monitor the client's progress over the course of intervention. To assess the outcome of the intervention, the same instruments are also administered after the client has completed the intervention. Results from the outcome assessment are analyzed to determine if there has been a change from the baseline score.

Multiple Methods and Multiple Sources

You are likely beginning to see that assessment is a complex but essential process. Counselors using best practices conduct assessment by using multiple methods and multiple sources. Imagine having a complex jigsaw puzzle that you need to put together without having an idea of what the puzzle is supposed to look like when it is completed. You might attempt to use different approaches to determine some direction for solving the puzzle, you might get others to give you input about the process and outcome, and you might apply some problem-solving methods to the task. Conducting a thorough assessment is a similar process. As counselors and helping professionals, we often are unaware of what the end picture will look like for a client, but we have to begin to piece together the parts that will aim toward a solution to the presenting problems.

Selecting and utilizing *multiple methods* of data collection, which may be referred to as a multimodal approach to assessment, is essential in order to have checks and balances for information gathered. The methods utilized to collect assessment information can be broadly categorized as interviews, tests, and observations. Within each category is a wide array of *formal* (e.g., standardized tests, structured interviews, formal observation) and *informal* (e.g., unstructured interviews, projective techniques, checklists, questionnaires, anecdotal reports) instruments and strategies. The sources of assessment information may include the client, parents, spouses or partners, teachers, physicians, and mental health professionals, to name just a few. Figure 1.1 illustrates the various methods and sources that may be utilized in the assessment process. In most assessments, using multiple methods and multiple sources is important for obtaining information that is thorough enough to produce an in-depth understanding of the individual. Counselors should never rely solely on the results of a single assessment instrument or strategy to make important decisions about clients. In this section, we will present an overview of the methods (i.e., interviews, tests, observations) and sources of assessment information. Chapter 2 more fully describes each of these assessment methods and sources.

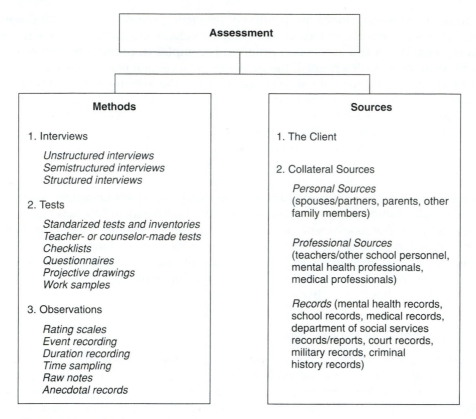

FIGURE 1.1   Multiple methods and multiple sources of the assessment process.

It may seem like an obvious point, but meeting face-to-face (or via camera) with a client is critical for gaining a complete picture from the assessment process. The *interview* is a face-to-face meeting of the assessment professional and the client. Interviewing may include such diverse techniques as unstructured interactions, semistructured interactions, and highly formal structured interactions. Its primary purpose is to gather background information relevant to the reason for assessment. The interview can be considered the single most important method of gathering information about the client's presenting problem and background information. Without interview data, information from tests and observations is without context and meaningless. In many settings, the interview is the primary (and sometimes only) assessment method used to collect data.

Tests are instruments designed to measure specific attributes of an individual, such as knowledge or skill level, intellectual functioning, aptitude, interests or preferences, values, personality traits, psychological symptoms, level of functioning, and so on. Counselors may use data collected from formal and informal tests, checklists, questionnaires, or inventories for several purposes, such as screening for emotional, behavioral, or learning problems; classifying or diagnosing certain attributes, problems, or disorders; selecting or placing individuals into training, educational or vocational programs, or employment opportunities; assisting in planning educational or psychological interventions; or evaluating the effectiveness of specific interventions or educational programs. Test results are particularly useful in assessment, because they may reveal vital diagnostic information that would not have been uncovered through other assessment methods.

Observation is an assessment method that involves watching and recording the behavior of an individual in a particular environment. It is a way of seeing what a person actually does, rather than relying on others' perceptions of behavior. Observation is useful for collecting information about an individual's emotional responses, social interactions, motor skills, and job performance and for identifying specific patterns of behavior. Observation can be formal, involving the use of standardized rating scales and highly structured procedures, or informal, with the counselor taking raw notes regarding a client's verbal and nonverbal behavior during the assessment.

In addition to multiple methods, counselors use *multiple sources* of information. The client is usually the primary source of information during the assessment process. Other sources of information (called *collateral sources*) include *personal sources*, such as parents, spouses or partners, and others close to the individual being evaluated, and *professional sources*, such as teachers, physicians, mental health professionals, and other professionals. Information from collateral sources is valuable, because it is typically more objective and reliable than information obtained directly from examinees. Another source of assessment information comes from client *records*, such as school grades or attendance, previous psychological or educational assessment reports, mental health treatment plans or summaries, court documents, records from social services agencies, and so on.

There is no set standard as to the number of methods or sources that should be used in assessment. The methods and sources chosen for the assessment process typically depend upon the nature of the referral questions, the reason for assessment, and available assessment resources. The client interview is considered the cornerstone of assessment and is employed in almost all cases. However, utilizing additional methods and sources of information leads to a more complete and accurate picture of the individual being evaluated. For example, say that a mental health counselor working in an outpatient counseling center conducts unstructured interviews with clients to determine the reason they are seeking counseling and to collect relevant background information. The counselor also asks clients to complete a self-report checklist of psychological symptoms. From the checklist, the counselor discovers that a particular client has many symptoms of depression, which the client did not disclose during the interview. In this example, the use of the checklist provided essential information that was not uncovered by the interview alone. The client profile also might be more clearly detailed with the administration of some standardized tests; however, the counselor might not have access to these tests in his work setting.

The Assessment Process

Now that we have defined assessment and discussed methods and sources, it is important to reemphasize that the assessment process is more than simply giving a test. Assessment is a complex, problem-solving process that necessitates collecting and analyzing information about an individual in order to make decisions or inferences about that person. The first and most important step in the assessment process is to identify the client's problem(s) to be addressed and the reason for assessment (Urbina, 2014). A clear sense of why an assessment is being conducted helps counselors select the methods and sources of information that will provide an adequate basis for arriving at useful conclusions and recommendations (Weiner, 2013). In most instances, the process of assessment ends with a verbal or written report that contains the assessment results and recommendations. In between the beginning and end points of the assessment process are other additional actions directed at collecting relevant client information. Although the process of assessment might appear overwhelming now, it can be broken down into the following four manageable steps (Hardwood, Beutler, & Groth-Marnat, 2011):

1. *Identify the Problem* The first step in the assessment process is identifying the presenting problem—that is, the reason that the individual is being assessed. Because assessment is so clearly linked to counseling, the reason for assessment and the reason for counseling are often one and the same. Reasons for assessment and/or counseling can stem from a variety of problems or concerns, such as academic or vocational performance, cognitive abilities, behavioral problems, or emotional and social functioning (Lichtenberger et al., 2005). In order to proceed to the next step in the assessment process, the counselor must have a clear idea about what the problem is and the reasons for which the client is being seen.

   Clients may be self-referred for assessment, or they may be referred by another source, such as a family member, teacher, judge, physician, or human resources manager. Referral sources can help clarify the nature and severity of the client's problem through the specific questions they want answered about the client. Thus, referral questions are often directly linked to the problem being addressed in assessment. The following are examples of referral questions that help define the client's problem:

   • Does this student have a learning disability? If so, does he or she qualify for special education or related services?
   • Is this child ready to begin kindergarten?
   • Does this child's problematic behavior indicate a diagnosis of Attention Deficit/ Hyperactivity Disorder (ADHD)?
   • Is this individual suicidal?
   • Does this adult have Posttraumatic Stress Disorder (PTSD)?
   • Does this parent have a mental disorder that might interfere with parenting?
   • What are this individual's vocational interests?
   • How well can this employee be expected to perform if promoted to a management position?

2. *Select and Implement Assessment Methods* After counselors determine the nature of the problem that needs to be appraised in the assessment process, the next step involves selecting and implementing methods for collecting data (e.g., interviews, tests, observation) and determining the sources of assessment information. Counselors choose from among numerous formal and informal assessment instruments and strategies based on the reason for referral, the context in which the assessment takes place, and the adequacy of the instruments and procedures they will use. Interviews are used in almost every assessment to obtain background information about an individual, including family history, work and education background, social history, and other relevant cultural and environmental factors. Counselors may administer tests to evaluate a person's cognitive functioning, knowledge, skills, abilities, or personality traits. Observation may be used to record or monitor a client's behavior in a particular setting. Collateral information also may be obtained from family members, spouses or partners, and others close to the individual being evaluated. Although there are no set guidelines for which or how many assessment

instruments or strategies to use, in general, the more methods used to collect data, the more accurate and objective the information obtained.

3. *Evaluate the Assessment Information* A key task for counselors is evaluating assessment information, which involves scoring, interpreting, and integrating information obtained from all assessment methods and sources to answer the referral question. To be competent in evaluating assessment information, counselors need knowledge and skills in basic statistical concepts, psychometric principles, and the procedures for interpreting assessment results. Evaluating assessment information is a difficult step, because the counselor is often confronted with a dizzying array of information gathered during the assessment process. To organize this data, counselors can use the following steps (Kamphaus & Frick, 2010; Sattler & Hoge, 2006):

   a. Document any significant findings that clearly identify problem areas.
   b. Identify convergent findings across methods and sources.
   c. Identify and explain discrepancies in information across methods and sources.
   d. Arrive at a tentative formulation or hypothesis of the individual's problem.
   e. Determine the information to include in the assessment report.

4. *Report Assessment Results and Make Recommendations* The final step in the assessment process is reporting results and making recommendations. This involves (a) describing the individual being assessed and his or her situation, (b) reporting general hypotheses about the individual, (c) supporting those hypotheses with assessment information, and (d) proposing recommendations related to the original reason for referral (Kaufman & Lichtenberger, 2002; Ownby, 1997; Sattler, 2008). The general hypotheses are the counselor's descriptive or clinical impressions of the individual that are based on multiple methods and sources of assessment data. When reporting these hypotheses, make sure to provide enough assessment data to support your conclusion.

   Making recommendations involves identifying specific ways to resolve the presenting problem or referral question by addressing the assessment's key findings about the individual (Lichtenberger et al., 2005). Counselors recommend strategies and interventions that are designed to facilitate change and improve outcomes based on the individual and his or her assessment results (Kaufman & Lichtenberger, 2002). Because individuals are referred for assessment for a variety of reasons, recommendations vary depending on the referral questions. In addition, the setting in which the assessment takes place (such as a school, hospital, mental health clinic, college, or vocational training center) will influence the type and number of recommendations (Kaufman & Lichtenberger, 2002). For example, in school settings, most referrals for assessment involve students' problems that affect their academic performance. In this situation, recommendations typically focus on behavioral interventions, instructional strategies, or other appropriate educational services (Lichtenberger et al., 2005). Assessments at mental health centers are requested generally for diagnosing mental disorders, treatment planning, and monitoring treatment progress; thus, recommendations may include a variety of clinical interventions and techniques.

Competencies Required for Assessment

Just like professional counseling, you need both knowledge and skills to be competent in assessment. Although a course in measurement and assessment might provide you with the foundational knowledge of assessment, you would need supervised practice to be competent. Because some people have underestimated the complexity of assessment, practiced beyond the scope of their training, or attributed too much meaning to a single test score, the public has developed a degree of skepticism in relation to assessment. As a result, several governing bodies and professional associations related to assessment have set explicit guidelines for the selection, use, administration, and interpretation of assessment instruments. Those guidelines can be translated into the following competencies:

1. Understand the basic statistical concepts and define, compute, and interpret measures of central tendency, variability, and relationship.
2. Understand basic measurement concepts, such as scales of measurement, types of reliability, types of validity, and norm groups.
3. Compute and apply measurement formulas, such as the standard error of measurement and Spearman–Brown prophecy formula.
4. Read, evaluate, and understand instrument manuals and reports.
5. Follow exactly as specified the procedures for administering, scoring, and interpreting an assessment instrument.
6. List and describe major assessment instruments in their fields.
7. Identify and locate sources of information about assessment instruments.
8. Discuss as well as demonstrate the use of different systems of presenting data in tabular and graphic forms.
9. Compare and contrast different types of scores and discuss their strengths and weaknesses.
10. Explain the relative nature of norm-referenced interpretation in interpreting individual scores.
11. Help teach clients to use tests as exploratory tools and in decision making.
12. Present results from assessment instruments both verbally (using feedback sessions) and in written form.
13. Pace a feedback session to enhance the client's knowledge of the test results.
14. Use strategies to prepare clients for testing to maximize the accuracy of the test results.
15. Explain assessment results to clients thoughtfully and accurately, but in language they understand.
16. Use effective communication skills when presenting assessment results to individuals, groups, parents, students, teachers, and professionals.
17. Shape the client's reaction to and encourage appropriate use of assessment information.
18. Be alert to the verbal and nonverbal cues expressed by the client throughout the assessment process.
19. Use appropriate strategies with clients who perceive assessment results as negative.
20. Be familiar with the interpretation forms and computerized report forms so as to guide the client to the information and explanation.
21. Be familiar with the legal, professional, and ethical guidelines related to assessment.
22. Be aware of the client's rights and the professional's responsibilities as a test administrator and counselor.
23. Have knowledge of the current issues and trends in assessment.

The Association for Assessment in Counseling (now the Association for Assessment and Research in Counseling) published *Responsibilities of Users of Standardized Tests*

(Association for Assessment in Counseling, 2003), which describes the qualifications that professionals must have in order to provide valuable, ethical, and effective assessment services to the public. Qualifications to use standardized tests depend on at least four factors:

1. *Purposes of Testing* A clear purpose for using an assessment instrument should be established. Because the purpose of an instrument directly affects how the results are used, qualifications beyond general competencies may be needed to interpret the results.
2. *Characteristics of Tests* Counselors should understand the strengths and limitations of each instrument used.
3. *Settings and Conditions of Test Use* Counselors should evaluate the levels of knowledge and skill required for using a particular assessment instrument prior to implementing the instrument.
4. *Roles of Test Selectors, Administrators, Scorers, and Interpreters* The education, training, and experience of test users determine which instruments they are qualified to administer and interpret.

HISTORICAL PERSPECTIVES

Part of being competent in assessment involves having a working knowledge of the history of assessment. Assessment is not a new concept. Even though the test movement in the United States began only at the turn of the 20th century (see Table 1.1), tests actually have been used for thousands of years. Around 2200 B.C., the Chinese used essay examinations to help select civil service employees. The philosophies of Socrates and Plato emphasized the importance of assessing an individual's competencies and aptitudes in vocational selection. Throughout the centuries, philosophers and educators have devised certain scales or items to provide teachers and parents with useful information to help their children. Anthony Fitzherbert (1470–1538) identified some items to screen individuals with retardation from those without—for example, being able to count to 20 pence, being able to tell one's age, and being able to identify one's father or mother.

Juan Huarte (1530–1589) was probably the first author to suggest formal intelligence testing. His book title was translated as *The Trial of Wits: Discovering the Great Differences of Wits among Men and What Sorts of Learning Suit Best with Each Genius.* Jean Esquirol (1772–1840), a French physician, proposed that there are several levels of intellectual deficiencies and that language is a valid psychological criterion for differentiating among levels. Eduardo Seguin (1812–1880) also worked with individuals with intellectual disabilities and believed that these people should be trained in sensory discrimination and in the development of motor control.

The Victorian era marked the beginning of modern science and witnessed the influence of Darwinian biology on the studies of individuals. In 1879 in Leipzig, Wilhelm Wundt (1832–1920) founded the first psychological laboratory. His work was largely concerned with sensitivity to visual, auditory, and other sensory stimuli and simple reaction time. He followed scientific procedures and rigorously controlled observations. He influenced the measurement movement by using methodology that required precision, accuracy, order, and reproducibility of data and findings. The interest in the exceptional individual broadened to include personality and behavior. Sigmund Freud, Jean Martin Charcot, and Philippe Pinel were interested in individuals with personal and social

TABLE 1.1 Major Events in the Test Movement

1900–1909

- Jung Word Association Test
- Binet and Simon Intelligence Scale
- Standardized group tests of achievement
- Stone Arithmetic Test
- Thorndike Handwriting, Language, Spelling, and Arithmetic Tests
- Spearman's measurement theory
- Pearson's theory of correlation
- Thorndike's textbook on educational measurement
- Goddard's translation of Binet into English

1910–1919

- Army Alpha and Army Beta Tests
- Stenquist Test of Mechanical Abilities
- Porteous Maze Test
- Seashore Measures of Musical Talents
- Spearman's Factors in Intelligence
- Stanford–Binet Intelligence Scale
- Otis Absolute Point Scale
- Stern's concept of mental quotient
- Woodworth Personal Data Sheet

1920–1929

- Founding of the Psychological Corporation
- Goodenough Draw-a-Man Test
- Strong Vocational Interest Blank
- Terman, Kelley, and Ruch's Stanford Achievement Test
- Clark's Aptitude Testing
- Spearman's *The Abilities of Man: Their Nature and Measurement*
- Morrison's School Mastery Tests
- Rorschach Ink Blot Test
- Hartshorne and May's Character Education Inquiry
- Kohs's Block Design Test

1930–1939

- Thurstone's primary mental abilities
- Buros's First Mental Measurements Yearbook
- Johnson's test-scoring machine

- Graduate Record Examinations
- Wechsler Bellevue Intelligence Scale
- 1937 revision of the Stanford–Binet Intelligence Scale
- Murray's Thematic Apperception Test
- Bernreuter Personality Inventory
- Leiter International Performance Scale
- Kuder Preference Scale Record
- Lindquist's Iowa Every-Pupil Test
- Bender Visual Motor Gestalt Test
- Marino's Sociometric Techniques
- Piaget's Origins of Intelligence
- Tiegs and Clark's Progressive Achievement Test
- Gesell Maturity Scale

1940–1949

- Minnesota Multiphasic Personality Inventory
- Wechsler Intelligence Scale for Children
- U.S. Employment Service's General Aptitude Test Battery
- Cattell Infant Intelligence Scale

1950–1959

- Lindquist's electronic test scoring
- *Technical Recommendations for Psychological Tests and Diagnostic Techniques*
- *Technical Recommendations for Achievement Tests*
- Guilford's *The Nature of Human Intelligence*
- Stevenson's *The Study of Behavior: Q-Technique and Its Methodology*
- Osgood's semantic differential
- National Defense Education Act
- Frederikson's In-Basket Assessment Technique
- Bloom's Taxonomy of Educational Objectives

1960–1969

- National Assessment of Educational Progress
- Wechsler Preschool and Primary Scale of Intelligence
- 1960 revision of the Stanford–Binet Intelligence Scale
- *Standards for Educational and Psychological Testing*

TABLE 1.1 Major Events in the Test Movement (*Continued*)

- Jensen's *How Much Can We Boost IQ and Scholastic Achievement?*
- Civil Rights Act of 1964
- Kuder Occupational Interest Survey
- Cattell's Theory of Fluid and Crystallized Intelligence
- Bayley Scales of Infant Development

1970–1979

- Family Educational Rights and Privacy Act of 1974
- New York State Truth in Testing Act
- Education of All Handicapped Children Act (became the Individuals with Disabilities Education Act [IDEA])
- Self-Directed Search
- System of Multicultural Pluralistic Assessment
- Wechsler Intelligence Scale for Children—Revised
- Revision of the *Standards for Educational and Psychological Testing*
- Rokeach Value Survey
- Peabody Picture Vocabulary Test
- Millon Clinical Multiaxial Inventory
- McCarthy Scales of Children's Abilities
- Use of computers in testing

1980–1989

- Thorndike, Hagen, and Stattler's revision of the Stanford–Binet Intelligence Scale
- Carl D. Perkins Vocational Education Act of 1984
- Kaufman Assessment Battery for Children
- Revision of the *Standards for Educational and Psychological Testing*
- Minnesota Multiphasic Personality Inventory, Second Edition
- Wechsler Adult Intelligence Scale—Revised
- Nader & Nairn's *The Reign of ETS: The Corporation that Makes Up Minds* (Ralph Nader's report on the Educational Testing Service)

- Differential Ability Scales
- Naglieri Nonverbal Ability Test
- Test of Nonverbal Intelligence 1–3
- Bayley Scale of Infant Development
- Computer-adaptive and computer-assisted tests

1990–2000

- Americans with Disabilities Act of 1990
- Health Insurance Portability and Accountability Act of 1996
- Herrnstein and Murray's *The Bell Curve*
- Sixteen Personality Factor Questionnaire, Fifth Edition
- Wechsler Adult Intelligence Scale, Third Edition
- Revision of the *Standards for Educational and Psychological Testing*
- Wechsler Individual Achievement Test
- Stanford–Binet Intelligence Scale, Fifth Edition
- Goleman's *Emotional Intelligence: Why It Can Matter More than IQ*
- Baron's Emotional Quotient Inventory
- Internet-based tests

2001–Present

- No Child Left Behind Act of 2001
- Individuals with Disabilities Education Improvement Act of 2004
- Newly revised Strong Interest Inventory
- Wechsler Intelligence Scale for Children, Fifth Edition
- Wechsler Preschool and Primary Scale of Intelligence, Third Edition
- Kaufman Brief Intelligence Test, Second Edition
- Wechsler Adult Intelligence Scale, Fourth Edition
- Standards for Educational and Psychological Testing (2014)
- International Test Commission Standards

judgment problems. Early interest in measuring intelligence also dates back to the late 19th century, when Sir Francis Galton (1822–1911), cousin to Charles Darwin, applied Darwin's evolutionary theory to attempt to demonstrate a hereditary basis for intelligence. In 1905, French psychologist Alfred Binet (1857–1911) constructed the first intelligence test (the Binet–Simon scale) that measured children's cognitive ability to learn school-type tasks or *educational attainments*, focusing on language, memory, judgment, comprehension, and reasoning (Binet & Simon, 1916). Binet claimed that his scale provided a crude means of differentiating between those children who could function in the regular classroom and those who could not.

The assessment of children rapidly expanded to the assessment of adults when the United States entered World War I in 1917 (Anastasi & Urbina, 1997). During this time, the armed services developed a group intelligence test called the Army Alpha to use in the selection and classification of military personnel. The original purpose of the army test was to identify those recruits whose lower intelligence would create problems for the military organization. A similar test was created for use with illiterate or non-English-speaking recruits, called the Army Beta. At the end of World War I, there was also an interest in screening recruits for psychosis and other emotional disabilities. The army once again developed a new test, called the Woodworth Personal Data Sheet, which was a forerunner of modern personality tests.

The successful use of tests by the armed services led to widespread adoption of tests in education and industry. Other factors also contributed to the acceptance of tests. Growth in population, free public education, compulsory school attendance laws, and the increase in students going on to institutions of higher education all were factors that changed the philosophy and practice of testing.

In addition, the egalitarian, political, and philosophical movements that championed integration, women's rights, rights of individuals with disabilities, and cultural group heritage influenced how people viewed tests. Tests were criticized for cultural bias, gender bias, unfairness to minority groups, and unfairness to groups with disabilities. These criticisms led to improved review procedures for the selection of test items and the selection of norming samples.

In recent years, however, the prevailing educational policy in the United States has changed from an open, humanistic education to back-to-basics and accountability-based approaches. The current use of high-stakes tests in the U.S. educational system can impact a student's educational paths or choices, such as whether a student is promoted or retained at a grade level, graduated, or admitted into a desired program.

Despite the changes in the social and political climate, the use of tests in the United States increased dramatically in the 20th and 21st centuries and continues to grow. It is estimated that Americans take anywhere from 143 million to nearly 400 million standardized tests yearly for education alone, 50 million to nearly 200 million job tests for business and industry, and several million more for government and military jobs (Sacks, 1999). The test industry has been greatly affected by technology. Computer-based tests represent a great advancement from the time when test usage was time-consuming and laborious in terms of administering, scoring, and interpreting tests, as well as writing up test results (Cohen et al., 2012). Today, most test publishers offer computer software for administering, scoring, and/or interpreting tests. Technological advances make the use of tests in the assessment process more convenient and affordable, further increasing the growth in test usage.

ASSESSMENT AND TECHNOLOGY

The assessment process has changed dramatically since the development of Wundt's first laboratory in 1879. Although observation is still an important component of the assessment process, we have now developed more efficient means to administer assessments, collect information, analyze data, and write reports. To say the least, counselors have seen tremendous growth in the use of technology in assessment. In today's world of counseling practice, computers are an essential component of the assessment process, and many assessment instruments can be administered via the Internet.

Computer-Based Assessment

The use of computers has been viewed as a way to enhance and advance the field of assessment. In all areas of assessment (e.g., personality, intellectual ability, achievement, career and employment assessment), computer-based assessment instruments and strategies are available. With dynamic visuals, sound, user interactivity, and near-real-time score reporting, computer-based assessment vastly expands assessment possibility beyond the limitations of traditional paper-and-pencil instruments (Scalise & Gifford, 2006). Although initially computers were used only in the processing of test data, computer-based assessment now encompasses a broad range of operations and procedures, such as the following:

- *Computer Administration of Assessment Instruments* Administering tests, questionnaires, and interviews via the computer is one of the most common computer assessment applications. This response format has many advantages over traditional paper-and-pencil methods, such as increased delivery, potential time savings, and the ability for items to be adapted or tailored based on the test taker's response to a previous item.
- *Automated Test Scoring* Computer-based assessment provides automated scoring of responses, thereby giving test takers almost immediate feedback and their overall score. Computer scoring reduces the possibility that respondents would make errors while filling out handwritten answer sheets and eliminates the errors that clinicians and technicians would make while hand-scoring items.
- *Computer-Generated Reports and Narratives* Computer-based assessment instruments often provide computer-generated reports or narratives. These reports are automated interpretations that are generated based on user input and resulting test scores (Butcher, 2013). The reports may contain very complex and detailed statements or summary statements.
- *Computer-Adaptive Tests* Computer-adaptive tests are specifically tailored to an individual's ability level. The computer quickly determines the examinee's ability level and then tailors the questions to that level. The first question is usually selected close to the passing level. If the test taker answers the question correctly, then a more difficult item is presented next. Using a computer-adaptive test, test takers have a more personalized assessment experience in a controlled environment. Computer-adaptive tests also provide sensitivity to the needs of users with disabilities, helping ensure equality and fairness in testing.
- *Computer Simulations* Computer simulation is the technique of representing real-world experiences through a computer program. Interactive software programs allow individuals to explore new situations, make decisions, acquire knowledge

based on their input, and apply this knowledge to control the ever-changing simulation state. Simulations have been in use for many years to assess performance in different environments. In the military, simulation has long been used for assessing the readiness of individuals to perform military operations, and devices used for computer simulations range from plastic mock-ups to laptop computers to full-motion aircraft simulators. In education, simulations can be used to investigate problem-solving skills, allowing students to explore a range of options in a particular problem scenario. Scenario-based testing is also used for some counseling-related exams, such as the Clinical Mental Health Counseling Exam (CMHCE).

Computer technology also helps facilitate and improve all phases of measurement practices. The increased availability of powerful computers and computer software in recent decades has greatly enhanced the ease of evaluating the reliability (consistency) and validity (accuracy) of test results. Such statistical operations are routinely carried out with computer software programs such as SPSS and SAS.

Despite the many advantages of using computer-based assessment, there are several limitations as well. For example, computer-based test interpretations or narrative reports should not be viewed as stand-alone clinical evaluations (Butcher, 2013). Computer-based interpretations are unable to take into account the uniqueness of the test taker and incorporate such elements as a client's personal history, life events, or current stressors. Therefore, computerized reports are considered broad, general descriptions that should not be used without the evaluation of a skilled counselor. Whether or not a counselor chooses to use a computer-based test interpretation, it is the counselor who is ultimately accountable for the accuracy of interpretations.

Internet-Based Assessment

The Internet is also changing the current landscape and the future of assessment by providing a profusion of assessment instruments with 24–7 access, ease of use, immediate scoring, and a more limited need for test administrators, leading to convenience, cost effectiveness, and efficient testing. It is difficult to estimate the number of assessment-related websites currently available on the Internet, other than to say that the number is large and increasing (Buchanan, 2002). Internet-based assessment websites vary in content, quality, and function. Some seek to adhere to high standards of professionalism of assessment, whereas others appear unprofessional and unconcerned with ethical and security issues. The motivation for development of many of these sites is easy to understand. Commercial assessment sites can make more money, because the Internet offers easy access to large numbers of participants. Researchers benefit from Internet-based assessment because they have access to large numbers of participants; the costs associated with traditional assessment methods, such as publishing and distributing paper surveys, mailing materials to study participants, and data collection and entry, are eliminated; and the costs to develop, publish, and maintain web-based surveys are significantly lower.

The expansion of assessment instruments on the Internet has brought about a number of issues. Concerns about the reliability and validity of the data collected through the Internet remain, although previous research indicates no significant difference between traditional and Internet-based testing. Another concern is that although many people have access to the Internet, not everyone does, which can be a confounding variable in a research study in terms of population sample. Questions regarding test security remain, and it is difficult to positively identify a person taking an online assessment if the test is not taken at a special site. Another issue involves providing feedback or results to participants—specifically, the inability to have human contact with a clinician or researcher while the participant is receiving and processing test results.

CONTROVERSIAL ISSUES IN ASSESSMENT

A field as complex and long-standing as assessment cannot exist without controversy. As you might guess, some of the controversy has been among assessment professionals themselves, and other controversies have been between the public and the assessment community. Some of the issues involved are recurrent and will be discussed again in other chapters. It is imperative that counselors who conduct assessment be aware of ongoing controversies and the impact on their scope of practice with regard to assessment. Controversy can drive changes in practice. As such, counselors should maintain awareness of legal and ethical guidelines related to the assessment process and should be certain to apply those guidelines to their practice. The following statements reflect some of the current issues, complaints, and controversies:

- Assessment is an invasion of privacy.
- There is too much reliance on test scores for decision making, without enough consideration for an individual's background history.
- Tests are biased; they are unfair and discriminate against diverse groups.
- Tests may be self-incriminating, and individuals should have the right to rebuttal.
- Intelligence tests are not measuring the right constructs.
- We cannot rely on grades and diplomas; we must have demonstration of competencies on objective tests.
- Multiple-choice tests need to be replaced by authentic and performance assessment.
- There is too much pressure on students, teachers, and parents because of high-stakes testing.

Summary

Many disciplines (e.g., psychology, counseling, education, social work, health, military, business or industry) employ the activity of assessment for such purposes as screening, identification and diagnosis, intervention planning, and progress evaluation. The assessment process encompasses multiple data collection methods from multiple sources to yield relevant, accurate, and reliable information about an individual. A key task of assessment professionals is to analyze and integrate information obtained from all assessment methods and sources to answer the referral question. Professionals must then make recommendations that are relevant to the assessment results and the referral question.

Having knowledge of the history of assessment can help with understanding current assessment issues and practices. The testing movement is about 100 years old. Some tests were constructed in the 19th century, but the majority of test development occurred in the 20th century. Many of the innovations and changes of the test movement resulted from major national crises and social and political movements. The use of computer-based and Internet-based assessment continues to become more prevalent in the assessment field.

Moving Forward

This textbook is divided into three parts (Part I, Principles and Foundations of Assessment; Part II, Overview of Assessment Areas; and Part III, Applications and Issues) that provide a balance of theory and practice information as well as coverage of the assessment instruments and strategies commonly used in the various areas of counseling (e.g., school counseling, clinical mental health counseling, vocational or career counseling settings). Although each section has a different focus, it is important to remember that all of the components of the textbook are interrelated and that each section builds upon your ability to be competent in the area of assessment. Chapter 1 introduced you to the principles and foundations of assessment. You will continue to explore this area in Chapters 2 through 7. Chapters 8 through 12 provide an overview of assessment areas, and the remainder of the book focuses on applications and issues. As you read each chapter, contemplate questions for discussion, and complete related activities, you should consider how each chapter fits within the framework we have provided and work to integrate the information into your epistemology of counseling practice.

Questions for Discussion

1. What tests have you taken during your lifetime? For what purposes were they given? How were the test results used? What type of feedback did you get about the results?
2. Do you believe assessment is an integral part of the counseling process? Why or why not?
3. Explain the importance of integrating multiple methods and multiple sources of assessment information.
4. Should knowledge of the historical foundations of testing be a competency required by workers in the helping professions? Why or why not?
5. In what ways are computer-based assessment instruments and traditional assessment instruments alike? In what ways are they different?

Suggested Activities

1. Interview individuals who are working in the helping professions to find out what assessment instruments or strategies they regularly use.
2. Review media sources (e.g., websites, newspapers), and identify three events that have occurred over the last 5 years that have impacted assessment.
3. Discuss the assessment issue you think is most important for counselors to address.

References

American Educational Research Association (AERA), American Psychological Association (APA), & National Council on Measurement in Education (NCME). (2014). *Standards for educational and psychological testing*. Washington, DC: Authors.

American Psychiatric Association (APA). (2013). *Diagnostic and statistical manual of mental disorders* (5th ed., text revision). Washington, DC: Author.

Anastasi, A., & Urbina, S. (1997). *Psychological testing* (7th ed.). Upper Saddle River, NJ: Prentice Hall.

Association for Assessment in Counseling. (2003). *Responsibilities of users of standardized tests (RUST)*. Alexandria, VA: Author.

Binet, A., & Simon, T. (1916). *The development of intelligence in children* (E. Kit, Trans.). Baltimore, MD: Williams & Wilkins.

Buchanan, T. (2002). Online assessment: Desirable or dangerous? *Professional Psychology: Research and Practice, 33*, 148–154.

Butcher, J. N. (2013). Computerized psychological assessment. In J. R. Graham & J. A. Naglieri (Eds.), *Handbook of psychology: Assessment psychology* (2nd ed., pp. 165–191). Hoboken, NJ: John Wiley & Sons.

Cohen, R. J., Swerdlik, M. E., & Sturman, E. D. (2012). *Psychological testing and assessment: An introduction to tests and measurement* (8th ed.). Boston, MA: McGraw-Hill.

Erford, B. T. (Ed.). (2006). *The counselor's guide to clinical, personality, and behavioral assessment.* Boston, MA: Houghton Mifflin/Lahaska Press.

Erford, B. T. (2012). *Assessment for counselors.* Boston, MA: Houghton Mifflin Company.

Hardwood, T.M, Beutler, L. E., & Groth-Marnat, G. (2011). *Integrative assessment of adult personality* (2nd ed.). New York, NY: Guilford Press.

Kamphaus, R. W., & Frick, P. J. (2010). *Clinical assessment of child and adolescent personality and behavior* (3rd ed.). New York, NY: Springer.

Kaufman, A. S., & Lichtenberger, E. O. (2002). *Assessing adolescent and adult intelligence* (2nd ed.). Boston, MA: Allyn & Bacon.

Lichtenberger, E. O., Mather, N., Kaufman, N. L., & Kaufman, A. S. (2005). *Essentials of assessment report writing.* Hoboken, NJ: John Wiley and Sons.

Ownby, R. L. (1997). *Psychological reports: A guide to report writing in professional psychology* (3rd ed.). New York, NY: Wiley.

Sacks, P. (1999). *Standardized minds: The high price of America's testing culture and what we can do to change it.* New York, NY: Da Capo Press.

Sattler, J. M. (2008). *Assessment of children: Cognitive foundations* (5th ed.). San Diego, CA: Jerome M. Sattler Publisher Inc.

Sattler, J. M., & Hoge, R. D. (2006). *Assessment of children: Behavioral, social, and clinical foundations* (5th ed.). San Diego, CA: Jerome M. Sattler Publisher Inc.

Scalise, K., & Gifford, B. (2006). Computer-based assessment in e-learning: A framework for constructing "intermediate constraint" questions and tasks for technology platforms. *Journal of Technology, Learning, and Assessment.* Retrieved from http://www.jtla.org

Selborn, M., Marion, B. E., & Bagby, R. M. (2013). Psychological assessment in adult mental health settings. In J. R. Graham, J. A. Naglieri, & I. B. Weiner (Eds.), *Handbook of psychology: Assessment psychology* (2nd ed., Vol. 10, pp. 241–260). Hoboken, NJ: John Wiley & Sons.

Sturman, E. D., Cohen, R. J., & Swerdlik, M. E. (2013). *Psychological testing and assessment: An introduction to tests and measurement* (8th ed.). Boston, MA: McGraw-Hill.

Urbina, S. (2014). *Essentials of psychological testing.* (2nd ed). Hoboken, NJ: John Wiley & Sons.

Weiner, I. B. (2013). The assessment process. In J. R. Graham & J. A. Naglieri (Eds.), *Handbook of psychology: Assessment psychology* (2nd ed., Vol. 10, pp. 3–25). Hoboken, NJ: John Wiley & Sons.

Whiston, S. C. (2012). *Principles and applications of assessment in counseling* (4th ed.). Belmont, CA: Brooks/Cole.

2 Methods and Sources of Assessment Information

The assessment process involves collecting relevant, accurate, and reliable information about an individual that can be used to make inferences or decisions about that person. To collect data that is thorough enough to produce an in-depth understanding of a client, counselors typically use multiple methods for collecting assessment information. These methods can be grouped into three broad categories: interviews, tests, and observations. Each category contains a wide array of formal and informal instruments and strategies, such as unstructured interviews, rating scales, standardized tests, projective drawings, checklists, questionnaires, and so on. Assessment also involves obtaining information from various sources, which may include the client, family members, spouses or partners, teachers, physicians, and other professionals. This chapter provides an overview of methods used in the assessment process and the sources of assessment information.

After studying this chapter, you should be able to:

- Identify and describe the data collection methods used in assessment.
- Identify and describe the various sources of assessment information.
- Explain the difference between formal and informal assessment instruments and strategies.
- Explain the importance of using multiple methods and multiple sources of information in assessment.
- Describe the initial interview and explain its purpose in the assessment process.
- Explain the differences among structured, semistructured, and unstructured interviews.
- Describe the categories and characteristics of tests used in the assessment process.
- Define *observation* and describe the various observation strategies and approaches used in the assessment process.

ASSESSMENT METHODS AND SOURCES

The assessment process utilizes diverse data collection methods from different sources to obtain relevant client information that serves as a basis for formulating conclusions and recommendations. The methods of data collection can be broadly categorized as interviews, tests, or observations. In each of these three categories, counselors may choose from a multitude of formal and informal instruments and strategies to collect information. Although the client is usually the primary source of information, information also may be obtained from relatives, friends, teachers, health professionals, and other relevant collateral sources. Information may also come from documents, such as medical records, school records, and written reports of earlier assessments.

The methods and sources of information can vary considerably from assessment to assessment, depending upon the purpose for assessment, the setting in which the assessment takes place, the needs of the client, and the availability and utility of the methods and sources of information (Weiner, 2013). Some assessments may be based entirely on information obtained from interviews, particularly if a client is quite forthcoming and open to the assessment process. If a client is reluctant to disclose information, then the assessment may primarily include information from collateral sources and records. In a clinical setting, it is often difficult to predict which methods and sources of information will prove most critical or valuable in the assessment process before meeting the client. Behavioral observation and standardized testing can both provide excellent information. Each may prove more useful than the other in certain cases. For example, a classroom assessment of disruptive behavior might best be served by observation strategies, whereas an assessment of pathology might be best served by standardized testing. In some cases, standardized test results could provide information that might not be evident through observation or interview (Weiner, 2013). As an example, imagine conducting a risk assessment for a college student who threatened a professor. Observation or interview alone would probably not provide enough information to arrive at a reliable estimate of the danger or lack thereof. In this case, the addition of data from a standardized assessment of psychopathology (e.g., Minnesota Multiphasic Personality Inventory [MMPI-2] and the Millon Clinical Multiaxial Inventory [MCMI-III]) would allow for a more thorough analysis of the individual's potential for harm.

Regardless of whether observation or standardized assessment is used, the initial interview is almost always required in the assessment process to obtain relevant background information about the client and the client's perceptions of his or her problems and strengths. When working with children, it is important to also interview parents or guardians, teachers, and other caregivers who can provide relevant information that will aid in your assessment of the child. We recommend for most assessments that counselors use more than one method and source of assessment information. Corroborating information from a number of methods and sources helps create a more comprehensive and accurate understanding of the client and his or her presenting concerns. We caution counselors against using the results of a single assessment instrument or strategy to make important decisions about clients.

We also recommend that counselors collect assessment data across settings when possible. Consider a child who is displaying disruptive behavior problems in school. Although a parent can provide the best insight about a child's behavior in many cases, it would also be important to have the teacher's perspective on this particular behavior. Imagine that you conduct observations in clinic, home, and school settings and discover that the behavior only occurs in a single teacher's classroom. The intervention you design would be setting specific, and you would attempt to determine the purpose (i.e., function) of the behavior in that setting. If at the onset you accept the behavior to be global and fail to evaluate behavior across settings, then you might limit the potential for success.

Formal and Informal Assessment Instruments and Strategies

Our examples thus far have demonstrated the complexity of assessment and the potential consequences of obtaining limited data. However, it is important to note that the complexity of the assessment process depends on the purpose of assessment. In some cases, counselors use an informal assessment process to gain some basic information. Assessment methods that are *informal* include the use of instruments and strategies that are developed *without* proven reliability and validity. There is no standardization of administration, scoring procedures, or interpretation. Furthermore, informal methods typically draw upon a counselor's professional judgment for determining hypotheses about the client, interpreting instrument results, and making recommendations. There are a variety of informal assessment procedures that counselors may use, including unstructured interviews, informal observation, projective drawings, checklists, work samples, teacher- or counselor-made tests, and questionnaires. An example of an informal assessment is the use of a feeling chart that describes the differences in emotional states to help clients identify their own emotional responses.

Methods of assessment that are categorized as *formal* generally involve the use of assessment instruments that are standardized. These formal assessment methods have structured materials, uniform administration procedures, and consistent methods for scoring and interpretation. A standardized instrument has undergone extensive instrument development, which involves the writing and rewriting of items, hundreds of administrations, the development of reliability and validity data, administrations to what are sometimes very large groups (i.e., thousands) of examinees, and the development of clearly specified administration and scoring procedures (Salkind, 2012). The primary purpose for standardizing an assessment instrument is to make sure that all the variables that are under the control of the examiner are as uniform as possible so that everyone who takes the test will be taking it in the same way (Urbina, 2014). Formal assessment instruments can include standardized psychological or educational tests, structured interviews, or structured behavior observations. As counselors, we use standardized tests for a variety of reasons. Counselors often use instruments such as the Beck Depression Inventory (Beck, Steer, & Brown, 1996) to diagnose and classify levels of depression in clients. The Beck Depression Inventory (BDI-II) is the most frequently used standardized instrument for the assessment of depression and provides a score that can indicate the severity of depression. Although this is a formal assessment instrument, it contains only 21 items and takes approximately ten minutes to complete.

An instrument that is standardized implies a level of technical quality or that the instrument is psychometrically sound. *Psychometrics* can be defined as the field of study concerned with educational and psychological measurement. An instrument that has *psychometric soundness* generally has proven *reliability* (or consistency of scores) and *validity* (the accuracy to measure what the instrument is designed to measure) and is standardized on a relevant *norm group* (i.e., a reference group of people who participated in the standardization of the test to which researchers and professionals can compare the performance of their subjects or clients). Psychometric aspects of assessment instruments will be discussed further in Chapters 4, 5, and 6.

Although throughout this textbook we have categorized assessment methods into three general categories (interviews, tests, and observations), it is important to remember that within each category there are many instruments and procedures that can be classified

TABLE 2.1 Examples of Formal and Informal Assessment Instruments and Strategies

Method	Formal	Informal
Interviews	Structured interviews Semistructured interviews	Unstructured interviews Semistructured interviews
Tests	Standardized tests and inventories	Teacher- or counselor-made tests Checklists Questionnaires Projective drawings Work samples
Observations	Rating scales Event recording Duration recording	Raw notes Anecdotal records

as either formal or informal (see Table 2.1). Using a combination of formal and informal assessment tools is recommended to provide an in-depth evaluation of clients, but the right mix of formal and informal assessment methods will vary from assessment to assessment. Chapter 7 will provide information on the process of selecting appropriate assessment instruments and strategies.

THE INITIAL INTERVIEW

Now that we have reviewed the elements of the assessment process, it is important to conduct a more in-depth exploration of each element. As we stated earlier, interviews are typically included in all forms of assessment and are one of the most important means of collecting information in the assessment process. The practice of interviewing covers a broad range, from totally unstructured interactions to semistructured interactions to highly formal structured interviews. The primary purpose of interviews is to gather background information relevant to the client's current problems. Obtaining background information often helps counselors understand the context for the client's current concerns, determine the longevity of problems and symptoms, and tailor plans for interventions to the client's specific context (Erford, 2013).

The interview generally begins prior to other assessment methods, and interview information often serves as a basis for selecting other instruments and strategies in the assessment process. Although counselors gather the majority of interview data at the onset of assessment, interview data is continually collected throughout the assessment and/or counseling process (Hardwood, Beutler, & Groth-Marnat, 2011). Interview data is integrated with other assessment data to describe the individual, make predictions or decisions about the individual, or both. The *initial interview* is considered the cornerstone of assessment: without interview data, there is no context in which to interpret results from other assessment methods.

During the initial interview, a client might discuss some symptoms of depression. In order to understand the symptoms more clearly, a counselor might use an informal assessment process, such as the SAD PERSONS Scale. This instrument is an informal scale that provides a rating of suicide potential based on categories such as sex, age, depression, and previous attempts at suicide. If the client has a moderate or high score on the SAD PER-SONS Scale, then the counselor might decide to use the BDI-II to corroborate the information and determine a more formal assessment of depression severity. The questions from the SAD PERSONS Scale could be woven into the interview process seamlessly.

Degrees of Structure in Interviews

The degrees of structure in interviews vary. Interviews can have little structure, allowing counselors to freely drift from one topic to the next, or be highly structured and goal oriented. The degree of structure depends on the purpose of the interview, the population (e.g., child, adult), the setting (e.g., school, research institute, outpatient counseling center, psychiatric hospital), and the skill of the counselor (e.g., ability to relate data to a decision tree for the diagnostic process). Based on the degree of structure, interviews can be categorized as *structured*, *semistructured*, or *unstructured*. Each approach has benefits and drawbacks, but the primary purpose of all three types is to obtain relevant background information about the individual being interviewed (see Table 2.2 for a summary of interview types).

STRUCTURED INTERVIEWS Structured interviews are the most rigorous and the least flexible interview format. As a formal assessment procedure, structured interviews consist of specific questions formulated ahead of time. They are commercially available standardized instruments that have specific instructions and guidelines for administering, scoring, and interpreting results. Using a structured interview, counselors are required to ask each client exactly the same questions in the same manner and not deviate from the text. Although all counselors can use structured interviews, they are especially helpful to those counselors who are beginning to learn the process of interviewing. The advantages of structured interviews are that (a) they ensure that specific information will be collected from all interviewees; (b) they do not require as much training, because interviewers simply read from a list of questions in a prescribed order; and (c) because of the standardization, they substantially improve the reliability of the assessment process (Erford, 2006). Because of the

TABLE 2.2 Summary of Interview Types

Unstructured interviews	Very flexible
	Informal (nonstandardized)
	Interviewer may follow a general format
	Widely used
Semistructured interviews	More flexible
	Not completely standardized
	Interviewers may probe and expand interviewee responses
Structured interviews	Less flexible
	Formal (standardized)
	No deviation in procedure
	Often used in research settings

consistency of the information obtained through structured interviews, they are invaluable tools in research settings. Because counselors are not allowed to deviate from the text, the use of structured interviews is often criticized for potentially damaging rapport with a client and preventing the therapeutic alliance between counselor and client from being established (Craig, 2005). It is important to note that structured interviews can be quite time-consuming. As such, counselors in clinical settings may see structured interviews as impractical because of time constraints.

SEMISTRUCTURED INTERVIEWS Although counselors might find structured interviews impractical because of the time requirement, there is still a need for interview tools that have structure and provide a means for gathering detailed information. Like structured interviews, semistructured interviews consist of a scripted set of questions; however, interviewers are allowed a degree of flexibility in the process. Interviewers may deviate from the text, change the wording of questions, or change the order in which questions are asked (Opie, 2004). Furthermore, interviewers are allowed to probe and expand on the interviewee's responses (Craig, 2009; Hersen & Turner, 2012). Semistructured interviews may be either standardized or nonstandardized instruments.

UNSTRUCTURED INTERVIEWS As an informal assessment strategy, the unstructured interview is the most frequently used type of interview among practicing counselors and psychologists (Sommers-Flanagan & Sommers-Flanagan, 2008). It is considered unstructured because it does not rely on a set of specified questions. The counselor is free to ask questions about whatever he or she considers to be relevant, and there is no predetermined order to questions. However, unstructured interviewing is not an agendaless process (Erford, 2013). Interviewers typically assess several general domains, including the presenting problem, family background, social and academic history, medical history, and previous counseling or psychiatric experiences (see Table 2.3). Counselors need to have a clear idea of why the individual is being interviewed ahead of time, because the kinds of questions asked depend on the types of decisions to be made after the interview.

Unstructured interviews have many similarities with counseling or psychotherapy (Jones, 2010). Both interviewers and counselors must establish rapport between themselves and interviewees or clients, which requires interviewers and counselors to be warm, genuine, respectful, and empathic. Interviewers and counselors must establish an atmosphere of safety and acceptance in order for interviewees or clients to feel comfortable with self-disclosure. In addition, interviewers and counselors both need effective listening skills, such as effective questioning, probing, and reflecting skills. Unlike counseling sessions, however, the primary goal of the interview is to obtain relevant client information. Although the interview can certainly be a therapeutic experience for the client, that is secondary to gathering information needed for determining the client's problems or concerns and formulating hypotheses about the client.

The unstructured interview has several advantages compared to other types of interviews: The interviewer is free to pursue important but unanticipated topics, the interviewee has more choice in deciding what to talk about, and there is more opportunity for building rapport, which is important to the success of counseling. Because of the flexibility of this method, counselors are able to adapt the interview to pursue certain problems or topics in depth while limiting focus on topics deemed unproblematic. A primary limitation of this method involves reliability and validity: Because every counselor's

TABLE 2.3 General Domains of Unstructured Interviews

I. *Identifying information*	Name, address, phone number, age, gender, date of birth, workplace, relationship status, and referral source
II. *Presenting problem*	The client's primary problems or concerns
III. *Family history*	Information about the client's family background, including information about first-degree relatives (parents or siblings), the composition of the family during the client's childhood and adolescence, and the quality of relationships with family members both past and present
IV. *Relationship history*	The client's current living situation, current and previous marital or nonmarital relationships, children, and social support
V. *Developmental history*	Significant developmental events that may influence current problems or circumstances
VI. *Educational history*	Schools attended, educational level attained, and any professional, technical, and/or vocational training
VII. *Employment history*	Current employment status, length of tenure on past jobs, military service (rank and duties), job performance, job losses, leaves of absence, and occupational injuries
VIII. *Medical history*	Previous and current medical problems (major illnesses and injuries), medications, hospitalizations, and disabilities
IX. *Previous psychiatric or counseling experiences*	Previous psychiatric or counseling services in inpatient or outpatient settings; also, any psychiatric medications

interview is different in terms of which questions are asked and how questions are worded, it is difficult to evaluate the reliability or validity of the information obtained during the interview.

Interview Guidelines

Successful interviews rely on the interviewer's ability to communicate and understand the communications of interviewees (Sattler & Hoge, 2006). Professionals should consider the following general guidelines before and during an interview (Groth-Marnat, 2009; Morrison, 2008; Young, 2012):

1. Be concerned about the physical setting or environment for the interview. Interviews will be better if the environment is quiet and comfortable. If the room is noisy or has poor lighting, then it may detract from the quality of the information gained. Seating should be arranged so that the interviewer and the interviewee are appropriately spaced, with no physical barriers (such as desks) between seats.
2. Explain the purpose of the interview and how the session will proceed. Explain how the interview information will be used.
3. Describe the confidential nature of the interview and the limits of confidentiality. In addition, explain that the client has the right not to discuss any information he or she does not wish to disclose.
4. When conducting a standardized semistructured or structured interview, abide by the published administration procedures.

5. When conducting an unstructured interview, begin with open-ended questions, and use more direct (closed) questions to fill in gaps. Avoid "why" questions, because they may increase interviewee defensiveness.
6. Be alert to the nonverbal as well as verbal behavior of the interviewee. How a person says something may be as important as what is said.

TESTS

Although assessment is an accepted practice in all helping professions, testing can be a controversial process and creates a level of suspicion in the public eye. The use of tests in the United States increased dramatically during the 20th century and continues to grow into the new millennium. It is estimated that Americans take anywhere from 143 million to nearly 400 million standardized tests yearly for education alone, 50 million to nearly 200 million job tests for business and industry, and several million more for government and military jobs (Sacks, 2001). Many test results can have a large impact on an individual's life path. These types of tests are often referred to as *High Stakes*. When tests impact the potential to obtain a job, graduate from public school, or become admitted into college, or affect other large life events, the scrutiny of testing becomes even more significant. We discuss these issues in more depth in Chapters 15 and 17.

As a counselor using testing as part of the assessment process, it is important to understand the elements of a test and have competency in the administration of tests. A *test* may be defined simply as a measurement process. In the helping professions, educational and psychological tests are used to provide a measure of various individual attributes, such as cognitive functioning, knowledge, skills, abilities, or personality traits. Test data is integrated into the overall assessment in a way that helps counselors better understand clients and make decisions in their best interests. Tests are utilized in assessment for a variety of purposes, including screening for emotional, behavioral, or learning problems; classifying an individual into a certain descriptive category (e.g., introvert); selecting or placing individuals into certain training, educational, or vocational programs; assisting in the diagnosis of a mental disorder; assisting in intervention or treatment planning; evaluating the effectiveness of a particular intervention or course of action (i.e., progress and outcome evaluation); and hypothesis testing in research studies.

Literally thousands of tests are available in education and psychology, and it is nearly impossible for counselors to be familiar with every test. Tests may differ on a number of features, such as content, format, administration procedures, scoring and interpretation procedures, and cost (Cohen, Swerdlik, & Sturman, 2012). The *content* (subject matter) of a test varies depending on the purpose or focus of the particular test. Some tests are comprehensive, with content covering a broad range of subject areas. For example, the California Achievement Test (CAT/6) measures several areas of achievement, including reading, language, math, study skills, science, and social studies. In contrast, some tests have a more narrow focus and contain content only on a single subject area, such as the SAT Subject Test in Biology.

The *format* of a test pertains to the type, structure, and number of items on the test. Test items can be classified as either selected-response or constructed-response items. *Selected-response items* (also called *forced-choice items*) require respondents to indicate which of two or more statements is correct. Multiple-choice, true/false, and matching items are all examples of selected-response items. *Rating scales* are also considered a type of selected-response format in which items are answered using a scale of successive intervals (rating scales are discussed in more detail in the Observation section later in this chapter). In contrast to selected-response items, *constructed-response items* require test takers to supply their own responses (rather than selecting a given response). These include fill-in-the-blank items, sentence completion, essay questions, verbal responses, performance tasks, portfolios, drawings, and so on. Selected-response items are typically preferred over constructed-response items, because they cover a broader range of content and can be answered and scored more quickly. However, selected-response items constrain test takers to a single appropriate answer and are subject to guessing, whereas constructed-response items allow individuals to demonstrate more in-depth understanding and more freedom and creativity in their responses. Figure 2.1 provides examples of some selected-response and constructed-response formats. Tests vary widely in the number of items and the length of test-taking time: a test can consist of 10 or 15 items and take 10 minutes to complete, it can encompass hundreds of items and take several hours to complete, or it can consist of anything in between.

Although it is important to understand all elements of testing, it is an ethical requirement that counselors only use tests for which they received training and that counselors

Format Type	Sample Item				
Selected response					
True/false	I have the time of my life at parties.		True		False

Multiple choice	At a grocery store, a customer hands the cashier a $20 bill to pay for a bottle of soda that costs $1.36. How much change should the cashier give back to the customer?
	
	    A. $17.64
	    B. $18.36
	    C. $18.64
	    D. $18.74
	    E. $19.36				

Rating scale	I value work environments that are flexible and do not require a specific time schedule				
	Strongly Disagree ☐	Disagree ☐	Neither Agree nor Disagree ☐	Agree ☐	Strongly Agree ☐
Constructed response					
Sentence completion	I often wish _____				
Verbal responses	Spell this word for me: solemn.				
Drawings	Draw as good a person as you can.				

FIGURE 2.1 Examples of item-response formats.

have competency in the administration of tests (American Counseling Association, 2014). Test administration procedures vary widely. Tests can be administered *individually* (i.e., given to one individual at a time) by a very active, very knowledgeable test examiner or administered to a *group* of individuals at the same time. Tests can also be *self-administered*, in which case the examinee reads the instructions alone and takes the test. Other forms of test administration include computer-administered tests, video or audio administration, and nonverbal administration. The complexity of the test will dictate the level of training required to become competent in administration.

Tests may differ in the procedures for scoring and interpretation. Tests may be hand scored, computer scored, sent to the publisher for scoring, or self-scored by the client. Some test scores are based on the number of items answered correctly, whereas others simply elicit information about one's opinions, preferences, and so forth. Tests that are scored on the basis of correctness are usually used to measure some aspect of a person's knowledge, skills, or abilities. Tests that are not evaluative are usually grouped under the rubric of personality tests (Urbina, 2014).

After tests are scored, the process of *interpretation* involves making sense out of test scores by converting test data into meaningful information. For example, raw scores can be converted to other types of scores (such as percentiles or standard scores), which are used to help describe and interpret an examinee's performance. Although published tests often have available software for computer-generated interpretations, the examiner is ultimately responsible for scoring, interpreting, and explaining test results to examinees.

The cost of tests varies widely. Most standardized tests must be purchased from test publishers, and tests prices can range from under $100 to thousands of dollars. The cost of a test is often broken down by components. For example, many publishers charge separately for the test manual, test booklets, scoring sheets, computer software, and other items. Some test publishers offer a starter kit that includes all of the test materials for one set price. Also, some test booklets are reusable, requiring examiners to purchase only answer sheets for another testing. Some tests are offered through computer software and can have single-use or subscription costs. Some tests are available free of charge in published research journals or textbooks.

Categories of Tests

Because there are thousands of tests, it is useful to have a way to classify tests into categories. However, because tests differ from each other in a variety of ways, there is no uniformly accepted system of classification (Domino & Domino, 2006). Instead, tests can be categorized based on a variety of aspects, such as the area of assessment, whether or not the test is standardized, how scores are interpreted, how the test is administered, and item type. As with most practices in assessment, professionals use different terminology to categorize tests, depending on their particular training, experience, and the settings in which they work. We will review some of the common approaches to classifying tests.

AREA OF ASSESSMENT Tests can be classified according to the area of assessment, such as the following:

- *Intellectual Ability Tests* Assess variables related to intelligence and cognitive abilities, such as verbal ability, numeric ability, reasoning, memory, and processing speed.

- *Aptitude Tests* Estimate a person's potential to succeed in an activity requiring certain skills.
- *Achievement Tests* Measure an individual's level of knowledge in a particular area.
- *Career or Employment Inventories* Assess an individual's interests and help classify those interests in terms of jobs and careers.
- *Personality Inventories* Measure a wide range of stable and unique personality traits, states, and attitudes, as well as emotional problems or psychological disorders.

STANDARDIZED AND NONSTANDARDIZED TESTS Tests may be broadly categorized as standardized (formal) or nonstandardized (informal). Standardization implies uniformity of procedures in administering and scoring the test; thus, *standardized tests* are those that have structured test materials, specific instructions for administration, and specific scoring methods. Test users are expected to follow carefully the standardized procedures for administering, scoring, and interpreting tests, as described in the test manual. The scores on standardized tests have generally proven reliability (i.e., consistency) and validity (i.e., the inferences based on test scores are sound and appropriate). Standardized tests are also presumed to have relevancy to the population for which they were intended. This means that they were typically developed using a large, representative norm group. Because of their validity, reliability, and norming data, standardized tests are frequently of higher quality than nonstandardized tests.

In contrast to standardized tests, *nonstandardized tests* are informally constructed tests without proven reliability or validity and have limited use and application. Examples of nonstandardized tests include teacher-made tests, projective drawings, checklists, and questionnaires.

INDIVIDUAL AND GROUP TESTS Tests can be categorized based on how they are administered. For example, individual tests are designed for administration to only a single examinee at a time. Group tests are administered to multiple individuals simultaneously. Individual tests are typically used for diagnostic decision making and generally require examiners to meet and establish rapport with examinees. They allow examiners to observe verbal and nonverbal behaviors during the test administration, enabling examiners to gain more insight about the source of the examinee's problems. Usually, administering individual tests requires competency. This means that a counselor should have special training, expertise, familiarity with materials, and practice with timing procedures. A competent test user, according to the International Test Commission (intestcom.org/ Guidelines/Test+Use.php), must have full understanding of the tests to use them appropriately; users must also respect all involved in the testing process by acting professionally and appropriately.

Group tests are typically more efficient than individual tests. They are usually less expensive than individually administered tests, they minimize the time needed for administration and scoring, and they require less examiner skill and training. Group tests usually contain items that can be scored objectively, usually by a computer, which reduces or eliminates the scoring errors commonly found in individual tests.

MAXIMUM-PERFORMANCE AND TYPICAL-PERFORMANCE TESTS In assessment, some tests evaluate test-taker responses on the basis of correctness (i.e., right/wrong, pass/fail). These types of tests, called *maximum-performance tests*, are usually used to appraise some aspect of a person's knowledge, skills, or abilities. For example, an achievement test generally measures maximum performance. However, many instruments used in psychological assessment are not evaluative and do not have items with correct or incorrect answers. These types of instruments, called *typical-performance tests*, simply elicit information about one's opinions and preferences and are used to appraise an individual's motivations, attitudes, interests, and opinions. For example, when a counselor is helping someone to identify career choices, he or she might administer a career interest inventory. This type of assessment instrument simply helps an individual to determine areas of the work world that are more interesting than others. There are no right or wrong responses to these types of assessment instruments.

VERBAL AND NONVERBAL TESTS Tests can be classified as either verbal or nonverbal. *Verbal tests* rely heavily on language usage, particularly oral or written responses. These tests may involve grammar, vocabulary, sentence completion, analogies, and following verbal instructions. Because verbal tests require examinees to understand the meaning of words and the structure and logic of language, they discriminate very heavily toward native speakers of the language in which the test was developed. In contrast to verbal tests, *nonverbal tests* reduce or completely eliminate the need for examinees to use language when taking the test. Nonverbal tests provide opportunities for examinees to comprehend directions with little or no language, have limited linguistic content, and allow examinees to respond to items nonverbally. For example, a nonverbal test may require a test taker to respond to pictorial materials rather than verbal items. An example of a nonverbal test is the Peabody Picture Vocabulary Test (4th edition; Dunn & Dunn, 2007) or the PPVT. The PPVT is a norm-referenced test that is individually administered. The normative sample for the test included national representation for cultural diversity and special education. Thus, the PPVT can be used to address some of the issues relative to English as a second language and special education issues specific to speech production.

OBJECTIVE AND SUBJECTIVE TESTS A common way to distinguish tests is based on the types of items on the test. An *objective test* (i.e., *structured test*) contains selected-response items (e.g., multiple choice, true/false), each of which contains a single correct or best answer. It is considered objective, because scoring consists of matching the test taker's item responses to previously determined correct answers; there are no subjective or judgmental decisions involved in the scoring process. In contrast, *subjective tests* consist of constructed-response items (e.g., essay questions, performance tasks, portfolios) that require the examiner to make judgmental decisions to score the test.

OTHER TERMINOLOGY Strictly speaking, the term *test* should be used only for those procedures in which test takers' responses are evaluated based on their correctness or quality (Urbina, 2014). Such instruments are usually maximum-performance tests that measure a person's knowledge, skills, or abilities. Tests that do not evaluate individuals on the basis of correct and incorrect item responses (i.e., typical-performance tests) may be referred to by several different names, such as *inventories, questionnaires, surveys, checklists, schedules,* or *projective techniques*. These instruments typically elicit information about an individual's motivations, preferences, attitudes, interests, opinions, and emotional makeup (Urbina, 2014).

The term *scale* is commonly used in connection with tests. Scales can refer to any of the following (Urbina, 2014): (a) a whole test made up of several parts (e.g., the Stanford–Binet

Intelligence Scale); (b) a whole test focusing on a single characteristic (e.g., the Internal–External Locus of Control Scale); (c) a subtest, which is a set of items within a test that measures specific characteristics (e.g., the depression scale of the MMPI-2); (d) a group of subtests that share some common characteristic (e.g., the verbal scales of the Wechsler intelligence tests); or (e) a numerical system used to rate or categorize some measured dimension (e.g., a rating scale).

Battery is another term that we often see in assessment. A battery is a group of tests or subtests administered to one person at one time (Urbina, 2014). For example, in assessing achievement, test batteries may be administered that consist of separate tests that measure such areas as reading, mathematics, and language.

PARTICIPANTS IN THE TESTING PROCESS There are many stakeholders involved in the test industry, and therefore the Standards for Educational and Psychological Testing were developed to provide guidelines for developing and evaluating tests, standards for conducting assessment, and methods of validating the interpretation of assessment data (American Educational Research Association (AERA), American Psychological Association (APA), & National Council on Measurement in Education (NCME), 2014). As such, it is important to clarify the various parties and their roles in the testing industry. For example, *test developers* are usually, but not always, academicians or investigators who are mainly interested in research. They are interested in developing a test that accurately measures the intended construct and will conduct research studies to support their claims. Test developers provide documentation (in the test manuals) for test users to make sound judgments about the nature and quality of the test (American Educational Research Association (AERA) et al., 2014). *Test publishers* are the organizations or corporations that publish, market, and sell tests. They also sometimes provide scoring services. *Test users* are the individuals or agencies that select tests for some purpose. They may also be involved in administering and scoring tests and using test results to make decisions. Test users are most interested in the appropriateness of the tests for their purposes, whereas test publishers are naturally more inclined toward profit margins (Urbina, 2014). *Test takers* are the individuals who take the test by choice, direction, or necessity. Table 2.4 summarizes the various parties and their roles.

TABLE 2.4 Participants Involved in the Testing Process

Test developers	The people or organizations that construct tests. They should provide information and supporting evidence that test users need to select appropriate tests.
Test publishers	The organizations or corporations that publish, market, and sell tests.
Test users	The people or agencies that select tests that meet their purposes and are appropriate for the intended test takers. Test users may also be involved in administering, scoring, and interpreting tests or making decisions based on test results.
Test takers	The individuals who take the tests.
Test reviewers	The individuals who conduct a scholarly review to critically evaluate a test based on its psychometric and practical qualities.

COMPUTER-BASED TESTS Computers were first introduced to the field of psychology in the 1950s. Since that time, and particularly in the last few decades, the use of computers in assessment has grown exponentially. Advancements in computer technology and the continued integration of this technology into educational, psychological, and counseling practice are changing the way professionals conduct assessment. *Computer-based testing* refers to using computers for test administration, scoring, and interpretation and for generating narratives and written reports (Butcher, 2003). Computer-based testing has dramatically changed the practice of assessment from an overwhelmingly complex process involving face-to-face administration, extensive preparation time, hand scoring using overlay templates and hand calculations, manual interpretation, and manual report writing (Cohen et al., 2012). Today, with the help of computers test takers can respond to test items on a computer monitor, and the computer program scores the test, analyzes the results, and even provides some form of interpretive report or narrative (Cohen & Swerdlik, 2012).

Needless to say, computer-based testing saves test users a great deal of time and has made the process of testing much more convenient. Computer-based tests offer other advantages over traditional paper-and-pencil tests through immediate scoring and reporting of test results, test administration efficiency, flexible test administration schedules, greater test security, and reduced costs. Computer-based testing also allows for the use of innovative item types that are not feasible in the paper-and-pencil format, such as audio- and video-based test items (Parshall, Spray, Kalohn, & Davey, 2002).

During the past 25 years, more than 400 studies have investigated whether results from computer-based tests could be used interchangeably with paper-and-pencil test results. Increasingly, tests are being adapted for computerized administration and have scores comparable to paper-and-pencil administration of the same tests (Boo & Visopel, 2012). It is important to note that some tests have not been adapted effectively for computer-based administration. Counselors should review the psychometric properties of the test in relation to the mode of administration prior to selecting a computerized version. Although some limits to computer-based testing still exist, the process continues to expand, and more tests are becoming available via computer administration. One test that is of interest to many counselors is the National Counselor Exam (NCE). This 200-item, multiple-choice test is available in both paper-and-pencil and computer-based administrations. The NCE is the exam required to become a National Certified Counselor and also the exam required for licensure in many states.

One type of computer-based test commonly used in achievement testing is computer-adaptive tests. A *computer-adaptive test* is a test that tailors (or adapts) test questions to the ability of each test taker. Each time a test taker answers a question, the computer adjusts to the individual's responses when determining what question to present next. For example, a computer-adaptive test will start with a question that is moderately difficult. If the question is answered correctly, then the next question will be more difficult. If it is answered incorrectly, then the next question will be easier. This process continues until all questions are answered, at which point the computer will determine the test taker's ability level. Because the computer scores each item before selecting the next one, only one question is presented at a time, and the test takers may not skip, return to, or change responses to previous questions. One example of a computer-adaptive test is the Graduate Management Admission Test (GMAT), which is used as part of the admission process for a graduate degree in business. The GMAT computer-adapted test begins with the assumption that the test taker has an average score and thus begins with an item of medium difficulty.

Based on performance on the first question, the difficulty level and points of the exam are adjusted by the computer.

OBSERVATION

So far, we have covered two methods of assessment: interviews and tests. The third method is observation, which is widely used in psychological and educational assessment. *Observation* is monitoring the actions of others or oneself in a particular context and making a record of what is observed (Aiken & Groth-Marnat, 2006). It is a way of seeing what a person actually *does* in situations, rather than simply making inferences about behavior based on information from interviews or test results. Behavioral observation can provide professionals with information about an individual's functioning, such as emotional responses, social interactions, motor skills (i.e., body movements), and job performance, to name just a few (Murphy & Davidshofer, 2005). It is particularly useful for identifying patterns of behavior—that is, identifying the immediate behavior, its antecedents (what happened just before the behavior), and its consequences (what happened afterward). The process of identifying behavior patterns is often employed in P–12 schools through an approach called *functional behavior assessment* (FBA), which seeks to identify the problem behavior of a student and determine the function or purpose of the behavior. Counselors can use the results of an FBA to develop interventions or teach acceptable alternatives to the behavior.

Understanding the function of behavior is not limited to the P–12 system. Counselors working with children and adolescents in any area should have an understanding of behavioral observation and FBA. In many cases, counselors can help parents, schools, residential facilities, or inpatient settings to develop behavioral interventions for children and adolescents. Understanding the elements of observation and behavioral function are critical for this task. For example, imagine a child who is disrupting an activity because he does not want to participate. The function (purpose) of his behavior in this case is probably to escape the activity. If you used time out as a consequence and removed the child from the activity, then the child would actually be removed from the activity, and get what he wanted. This would reinforce his behavior rather than change it. One of the more appropriate actions in this scenario would be to ignore the behavior or to find opportunities to reinforce the appropriate actions of others.

Counselors may use *formal* assessment instruments (e.g., standardized rating scales and computer-based observation software) or *informal* strategies (e.g., raw notes) to conduct observations. Observations can be a one-shot affair or consist of several samplings over a longer time span. Observers may center on specific behaviors that are objective and measurable or on general, overall behavior or adjustment. Depending on the context and the age of the client, observations can be made and recorded by professionals, significant others, any other person acquainted with the client, or the client himself or herself. Examples of observation include the following:

- A school counselor observes a child interacting with his classmates on the school playground to evaluate his social skills.
- A family therapist views a videotape of parents and children playing together to assess parenting skills.
- An adult who wants to change his eating patterns records his thoughts and feelings prior to feeling an urge to overeat.

• While administering a structured clinical interview, a counselor observes and notes the client's disposition, conversational skills, and overall mood.

There are a variety of strategies and approaches used for observation. We will present information about informal and formal observation, direct and indirect observation, the settings of observation, and unobtrusive and participant observation. Furthermore, we will discuss the various ways of recording data obtained through observation.

Formal and Informal Observation

Formal and informal methods of observation differ primarily in the degree of structure required. *Formal observation* is a highly structured process in which the observer decides ahead of time who will be observed, what behavior will be observed, when and where the observation will take place, and how the behavior will be recorded. The process requires the use of trained observers and sophisticated procedures for recording, analyzing, and interpreting data. Formal observation often relies on the use of standardized instruments for recording data, such as published rating scales. However, in recent years a large number of software applications have been developed to assist in the observation process. These observation applications have standard observation processes for various behavioral issues, timers, and observation schedules. The results of the observations can be presented in graph or table format. In addition to allowing for standard observations, the programs are also customizable.

In contrast, informal observation is much less structured and occurs whenever professionals make notes of a client's behavior. They may take rough notes of any behavior they observe, which is usually not predetermined, and write a more elaborate summary after the observation. For example, during an interview a counselor may notice that the client appears sluggish in movement, does not make eye contact, and has slowed speech. These behaviors are often indicative of an individual with depressive symptoms. By recording these observations and considering them with information obtained from the interview and other assessment data, the counselor can determine if the client is indeed depressed. It is important to note that although informal observation provides rich data for understanding an individual's problem, it is not sufficient by itself for diagnosing a problem or determining an effective intervention plan. As is the case with formal observations, there are also software applications for informal observations. Some software programs provide the opportunity to conduct both forms of observation in a single application.

Direct and Indirect Observation

Direct observation is a firsthand account of actual behavior as it occurs. As the term implies, observations of behavior are not filtered through the perceptions of some informant: The individual's behaviors are observed directly (Kamphaus, Barry, & Frick, 2005). In contrast, professionals using *indirect observation* rely on reported observations of behaviors by others who have direct contact with the individual. In direct observation, an observer may use a checklist or other instrument to record the presence and frequency of specific behaviors, or the observer can simply watch and record as much as possible of whatever appears to be useful or important. In addition to tracking target behaviors, direct observations can be used to identify a pattern of certain events or stimuli that consistently precede the behavior's occurrence.

Natural and Contrived Settings

Observations that take place in naturally occurring settings, such as an individual's work or school, are called *naturalistic observations*. For example, a school-based mental health counselor may use naturalistic observations to assess a child's behaviors (such as leaving his seat) in a classroom, or a child who fights during recess may be observed at school during recess. Observations may also occur in a laboratory or other *contrived setting* (also known as *analogue assessment*). This type of observation aims to evaluate behavior in a theoretical situation that is developed to mimic a real-life (natural) situation (Hersen, 2006). For example, a researcher may observe an individual performing a particular task in a simulated work environment.

Unobtrusive and Participant Observation

Observations are said to be *unobtrusive* when there is no interaction between the observer and those being observed and when the individual's behavior is not affected by the observation itself. Observers can monitor an individual unobtrusively through the use of a one-way mirror or video recording. For example, a clinical supervisor may use video recordings to observe a counselor trainee's counseling skills. In contrast, *participant observation* entails the observer both watching and interacting with the individual as part of the observational situation. Participant observation is commonly used in qualitative research studies and enables researchers to provide more detailed and accurate information about the people they are studying.

Methods of Recording Observations

Because the purpose of observation is to identify and record behaviors, many methods are available for documenting observations. The method of observation selected depends on whether the counselor uses formal or informal observation. In formal observation, structured methods of data recording are used, such as event recording, duration recording, time sampling, and rating scales. For informal observation, counselors may use anecdotal records or raw notes of clients' behaviors. Although there are affordable software applications available to record all types of observations, it is important to understand the basic principles of observation before using the software. In order to illustrate these principles, we discuss observation using paper-and-pencil procedures.

EVENT RECORDING *Event recording* (also called *frequency recording*) is the simplest of the observation data collection methods. It requires an observer to observe, count, and record the number of times a behavior has occurred. Event recording is best suited to recording occurrences of *low-rate behaviors*, which are behaviors that have a definite beginning and ending and do not often occur (e.g., a student leaving his or her seat; Shapiro, 1987). A tally sheet listing the behaviors to be observed and counted is useful: When the observer sees the behavior of interest, he or she simply makes a tick mark on the sheet (see Figure 2.2). After the observation, the tick marks can be totaled.

DURATION RECORDING *Duration recording* is used when it is more important to know for how long a behavior occurs rather than the frequency of the behavior. In duration recording, the length of time of a behavior from beginning to end is tracked. It is most applicable

Date(s) 2/1 to 2/5

Name ————————————————

Observer ————————————————

Description of Behavior: Leaving seat during science class

Days	Tallies	Total Count
Monday	/ / / / / / / /	8
Tuesday	/ / / / / / / / / /	10
Wednesday	/ / / / / / /	7
Thursday	/ / / / / / / / / / / /	12
Friday	/ / / / / / / / / / / / / / /	15
Average = 10.4		

FIGURE 2.2   Tally sheet used to record the frequency of behavior.

for recording sustained behaviors that have a clear beginning and a clear ending; it is not recommended for behaviors that occur at a very high rate. Crying, temper tantrums, and thumb sucking are examples of behaviors that can be documented using duration recording (see Figure 2.3; Shapiro, 1987). Duration recording usually requires a watch or clock so that a precise measurement of the behavior can be recorded.

TIME SAMPLING In both event and duration recording techniques, all occurrences of the behaviors are documented during the observational period. However, some behaviors occur too frequently to obtain accurate counts or have no clear beginning or ending, which prevents effective event and duration recording (Kamphaus, Barry, & Frick, 2005). In these cases, time sampling is a more appropriate data collection method. *Time sampling* (sometimes referred to as *interval recording, interval sampling,* or *interval time sampling*) divides observation periods into specific time intervals; then, behaviors are simply coded as being

Date(s) 10/5 to 10/8

Name ————————————————

Observer ————————————————

Description of Behavior: Crying

Date	Time episode started	Time episode ended	Duration of episode
10/5	9:15 a.m.	9:26 a.m.	11 minutes
10/5	9:45 a.m.	9:57 a.m.	12 minutes
10/6	9:05 a.m.	9:11 a.m.	6 minutes
10/7	9:03 a.m.	9:09 a.m.	6 minutes
10/8	9:15 a.m.	9:20 a.m.	5 minutes

FIGURE 2.3   Record of the duration of behavior.

Problem Behaviors	1' 30"	1' 30"	1' 30"	1' 30"	1' 30"	1' 30"	1' 30"	1' 30"	1' 30"	1' 30"	1' 30"	1' 30"	1' 30"	1' 30"	1' 30"	Total
Inappropriate Movement																
Inattention																
Inappropriate Vocalizations																
Repetitive Motor Movements																
Aggression																

FIGURE 2.4   Sample items from the BASC-2 student observation scale.

Note: Quotation marks (") refer to seconds. Apostrophes (') refer to minutes.

Source: Behavior Assessment System for Children, Second Edition (BASC-2). Copyright © 2004 by NCS Pearson, Inc. Reproduced with permission. All rights reserved.

either present or absent during each time interval. Interval length varies, depending on the frequency of the behavior, the amount of time allowed for the observation, and the skill of the observer in monitoring and recording child behavior (Nock & Kurtz, 2005). As an example, the Behavior Assessment System for Children (BASC-2; Reynolds & Kamphaus, 2001) is a published, comprehensive system that assesses children's behavior. It includes a time-sampling method for observing students in which observers code behaviors (such as responses to the teacher, peer interactions, or working on school subjects) repeatedly during 3-second intervals spaced 30 seconds apart for a total of 15 minutes. The percentage of intervals during which a given behavior occurred can be calculated to provide information about the frequency of adaptive and maladaptive behaviors. An example of the BASC-2 Student Observation Scale is shown in Figure 2.4.

RATING SCALES In observation, *rating scales* are used to describe and evaluate an individual's specific behaviors. Rating scales often appear as preprinted sheets on which the observer rates each behavior to indicate either its quality or how often the behavior occurred. Rating scales are an efficient means of collecting information about a variety of behaviors, from general functioning to such specific behaviors as social skills, aggressive behavior, anxiety, and hyperactivity, to name a few. They can be used repeatedly and across settings and can be completed by various sources (e.g., the client, teachers, parents, counselors).

Rating scales usually list the important dimensions of the behaviors being rated and quantify those dimensions in some way to convey meaning (Rutherford, Quinn, & Mathur, 2007). A few commonly used rating scale formats in observation include Likert scales, graphic scales, and semantic differential scales. The *Likert scale* (named after the psychologist who developed it) consists of a series of written statements to which respondents indicate how much they agree or disagree (i.e., *strongly disagree, disagree, neither agree nor disagree, agree, strongly agree*). The *graphic rating scale* is similar to the Likert scale, except that it presents respondents with a graphic 5- or 7-point continuum ranging from *never* to *always* or from *strongly disagree* to *strongly agree*. Verbal anchors are typically placed at

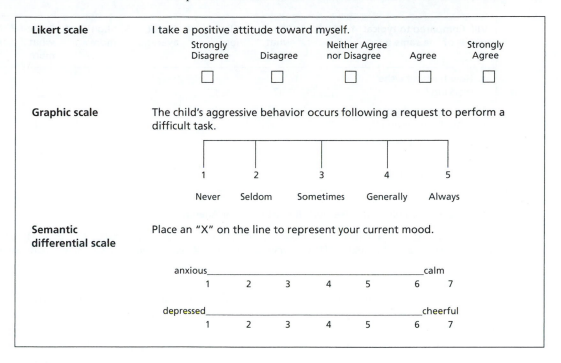

Likert scale

I take a positive attitude toward myself.

Strongly Disagree	Disagree	Neither Agree nor Disagree	Agree	Strongly Agree
☐	☐	☐	☐	☐

Graphic scale

The child's aggressive behavior occurs following a request to perform a difficult task.

1	2	3	4	5
Never	Seldom	Sometimes	Generally	Always

Semantic differential scale

Place an "X" on the line to represent your current mood.

anxious_____calm
1   2   3   4   5   6   7

depressed_____cheerful
1   2   3   4   5   6   7

FIGURE 2.5   Examples of rating scales.

various points along the scale. *Semantic differential rating scales* consist of bipolar adjectives separated by a 7-point scale on which respondents select one point to indicate their response. These rating scales are illustrated in Figure 2.5.

An important issue in using rating scales is the identity of the informant (i.e., source of information) who completes the scale. Typically, *informants* are teachers, parents, or others who know the individual being assessed or the individual himself or herself. Some informants are in a better position to rate certain behaviors; for example, parents are more likely to be knowledgeable about a child's sleep patterns, sibling interactions, eating behaviors, and so forth (Rutherford et al., 2007). Some published rating scales may be designed for only one informant (e.g., parents only, children only), and some have separate forms for multiple informants (e.g., teachers, parents, child). For example, the Achenbach System of Empirically Based Assessment (ASEBA) includes a series of rating scales designed to assess children's behavior problems and social competencies by using separate rating forms for parents, teachers, and children (see Figure 2.6 for a sample from the Teacher's Report Form [TRF] for Ages 6–18; Achenbach & Rescorla, 2001). The best practice in using rating scales is to employ multiple informants across situations and settings (Rutherford et al., 2007). This provides a more complete view of an individual's behavior across situations and settings.

The most significant criticism of rating scales involves rater (informant) bias, which can affect the validity of the instrument. Table 2.5 provides a list of common rating errors.

ANECDOTAL RECORDS   An *anecdotal record* is a brief, descriptive narrative of an individual's behavior that is recorded after the behavior occurs. An anecdotal record may be a running

VIII. Compared to typical pupils of the same age:	1. Much less	2. Somewhat less	3. Slightly less	4. About average	5. Slightly more	6. Somewhat more	7. Much more
1. How hard is he/she working?	☐	☐	☐	☐	☐	☐	☐
2. How appropriately is he/she behaving?	☐	☐	☐	☐	☐	☐	☐
3. How much is he/she learning?	☐	☐	☐	☐	☐	☐	☐
4. How happy is he/she?	☐	☐	☐	☐	☐	☐	☐

FIGURE 2.6 Sample of the Teacher's Report Form for Ages 6–18.

Source: Reprinted with permission from *Manual for the ASEBA School-Age Forms and Profiles,* by T. M. Achenbach & L. A. Rescorla, 2001, Burlington, VT: University of Vermont, Research Center for Children, Youth, & Families.

account of what an individual says and does during a particular period of time, or it may be a single record of a significant incident (e.g., critical incident report). As a method of informal observation, anecdotal records may consist of notes written on index cards or in a log, which are more fully elaborated upon and summarized after the observation. As a formal observation method, anecdotal records can be very detailed accounts written on formal record forms. They typically include the name of the individual observed; the name of observer; the date, time, and setting of the observation; the anecdote (i.e., the description

TABLE 2.5 Rating Scale Errors

Leniency or generosity	Ratings tend to always be at the top of the range.
Severity	Ratings tend to always be at the lower end of the range.
Central tendency	Ratings tend to fall consistently in the middle or average range.
Response acquiescence	Rater tends to agree with each item.
Response deviance	Rater tends to respond in a deviant, unfavorable, uncommon, or unusual way.
Social desirability	Test responses are interpreted to provide the most favorable view of the examinee.
Halo effect	Ratings tend to be influenced by good impressions of the examinee. High ratings on some traits are generalized to others.
Negative halo	Ratings tend to be influenced by bad impressions of the examinee.
Logical error	Ratings are similar on characteristics the rater feels are logically related.
Contrast error	Ratings on the current candidate are influenced by the previous candidate.
Proximity error	Ratings made on items that are printed close together tend to be rated the same.
Most recent performance error	Ratings are influenced by the person's most recent performance rather than his or her usual level of performance.

of the observation); and a reflection on or interpretation of the observation. The following are procedural suggestions for recording behavior anecdotes:

- Focus on a single specific incident.
- Be brief but complete.
- Objectively describe specific behaviors using examples.
- Use phrases rather than sentences.
- List the behaviors in the sequence in which they occurred.
- Include direct quotations whenever possible and significant.
- Record both positive and negative statements.
- Write the anecdote immediately after the observation occurs.

Self-Monitoring

Self-monitoring (also called self-assessment) is one of the most commonly used assessment approaches in research and practice (Hersen, 2006). *Self-monitoring* is a process by which an individual tracks and records their own specific behaviors and related (Cohen et al., 2012). It can be successfully employed to monitor and record the frequency, antecedents, and consequences of problematic behaviors (e.g., social anxieties, phobias, social skills problems, habits). For example, individuals with anger-management problems may use self-monitoring to record the date, time, and location of an anger episode and the events, thoughts, and feelings that preceded the episode.

Self-monitoring can be used for both assessment and intervention. Simply gaining awareness about one's patterns of behavior can affect the frequency with which behaviors occur. However, the usefulness of self-monitoring depends a great deal on the individual's compliance in recording his or her behavior. Self-monitoring requires individuals to be aware that they are engaging in the behavior and to have a timely and efficient means of logging behavior occurrences. Behaviors can be recorded using frequency marks, check-lists, or other means. To help with recording behaviors in a timely fashion, various devices are available, such as golf wrist score counters and digital timers or alarms.

Self-monitoring can also include the use of autobiographies, diaries, journals, letters, stories, and poems. These approaches help provide insight into an individual's behavior, attitudes, and personality dimensions.

COLLATERAL SOURCES

Typically, the primary source of information is the individual who is being evaluated—but not always. Sometimes, a wellspring of information can come from people who know the individual best. Any third party who provides information is considered a *collateral source* (Table 2.6 provides a list of potential collateral sources). Family members, spouses or partners, and others close to the individual being evaluated are useful personal sources of information. Information can also be obtained from professional sources involved with the individual, such as teachers, physicians, and mental health professionals. Collateral information is generally obtained from *interviews* with the third party, either face-to-face or by telephone (Heilbrun, Warren, & Picarello, 2003). Although family and friends often want to give opinions, information should focus primarily on behavior descriptions (i.e., what the informant has personally observed or witnessed). Rating scales completed by collateral sources are often an effective means for obtaining behavioral descriptions of the client.

TABLE 2.6 Sources of Collateral Information

Personal sources	Spouses or partners
	Family members
	Roommates
	Employers or coworkers
	Neighbors
Professional sources	Mental health professionals
	Teachers or other school personnel
	Medical professionals
	Social services workers
	Guardians ad litem
	Probation or parole officers
Records	Mental health records
	School records
	Medical records
	Department of Social Services records or reports
	Court records
	Military records
	Criminal history records

Another valuable source of collateral information can be found in *records* (Craig, 2009), which can include school grades or attendance, previous psychological or educational assessments, mental health treatment plans or summaries, court documents, and letters from medical providers, to name just a few. In general, information from collateral sources, especially from more neutral professional sources, can be considered more objective and reliable than information obtained directly from examinees (Austin, 2002).

The extent to which a counselor uses collateral information depends on the purpose of the evaluation, the complexity of the client's presentation, and the intervention goals. It is particularly important in cases involving individuals with impaired insight into their problems, such as those with substance-abuse problems or cognitive disabilities (American Psychiatric Association, 2006). For example, in a psychiatric crisis center, collateral information may be crucial to understanding a client's acute mental health problems. When assessing children, counselors regularly obtain information from parents about the child's behavior at home, or they may contact the child's teacher to obtain information about the child's functioning at school.

Collateral information is considered a necessary component in all *forensic evaluations*, which are evaluations that address a given legal issue (e.g., child custody evaluations; Cavagnaro, Shuster, & Colwell, 2013; Ertelt & Matson, 2013). Information from third parties may offset the potential bias of the examinee's self-report. For example, it can be expected that the parents in a child custody evaluation may intentionally or unintentionally distort, exaggerate, or minimize the information they present during an interview so that the examiner will view them favorably. In this case, collateral information from professional sources can help evaluators scrutinize the credibility of data obtained from parents (Patel & Choate, 2014).

An important issue in obtaining information from collateral sources is the confidentiality of the individual being evaluated. Permission must be obtained through consent forms signed by the client (or the client's parent) before professionals can request information or contact third parties.

Summary

In this chapter, we provided an overview of the three types of assessment. We will continue to integrate information about interviews, tests, and observations throughout the remainder of the textbook. It is important to note that counselors and other helping professionals need supervised training on each type of assessment in order to achieve competency. In addition to covering the types of assessment, we also introduced you to types of data and sources of information used to obtain a complete and accurate picture of the individual being evaluated.

Regardless of the type of assessment, counselors may choose from a wide array of formal or informal instruments and strategies. Although the client is usually the primary source of information, collateral information is often gathered from relatives, friends, teachers, health professionals, and other relevant parties. Information may also come from documents, such as medical records, school records, and written reports of earlier assessments. Counselors are required to integrate information from multiple data collection methods and multiple sources to form impressions and make recommendations about the individual being assessed.

Questions for Discussion

1. What is the difference between formal and informal methods of assessment?
2. Among the methods of assessment (i.e., interviews, tests, observation), which one do you think yields the most valuable information about a client?
3. How does the use of multiple assessment instruments and strategies (as opposed to using just one method) benefit the assessment process?
4. If you were engaged in the assessment process, which sources of assessment information would you use? What would your decision be based on?

Suggested Activities

1. Write a brief essay on the subject of assessment. Discuss your thoughts on assessment in general and your beliefs about its purpose in the helping professions.
2. Interview a school counselor, mental health counselor, or marriage and family therapist. Inquire about which assessment instruments and strategies he or she uses on a regular basis.
3. In triads, develop a semistructured interview. Use the general domains listed in Table 2.3, and brainstorm and construct as many questions as possible for each domain.
4. Using the semistructured interview developed in the previous activity, role-play an interview in which one student is the counselor, one is the client, and one is an observer. The counselor asks the client the questions that were developed for the semistructured interview. After the interview, all three may then discuss the following: How did the counselor feel asking questions? How much

did the client respond to questions? Were some questions harder to ask or answer than other questions? What counselor and client behaviors did the observer notice throughout the interview?

5. In a small group, develop a behavior rating scale that evaluates counseling skills. To do this, you must first determine the specific counseling skills to be evaluated and then decide on the type of scale (numerical scales, graphic scales, or semantic differential scales) used to measure the skills.

6. Search the Internet for behavior observation charts. Select three different charts to compare and contrast. In small groups, discuss the three charts and the types of observations for which they might be designed. Determine a behavior that the group would want to observe, and discuss which form might be the best choice. What modifications would the group have to make in order to conduct the observation?

References

Achenbach, T. M., & Rescorla, L. A. (2001). *Manual for the ASEBA School-Age Forms and Profiles.* Burlington, VT: University of Vermont, Research Center for Children, Youth, & Families.

Aiken, L. A., & Groth-Marnat, G. (2006). *Psychological testing and assessment* (12th ed.). Boston, MA: Pearson.

American Counseling Association. (2014). *ACA Code of Ethics.* Alexandria, VA: Author.

American Educational Research Association (AERA), American Psychological Association (APA), & National Council on Measurement in Education (NCME). (2014). *Standards for educational and psychological testing.* Washington, DC: Authors.

Hardwood, T. M., Beutler, L. E., & Groth-Marnat, G. (2011). *Integrative assessment of adult personality.* New York: Guilford Press.

American Psychiatric Association. (2006). *Practice guidelines for the psychiatric evaluation of adults* (2nd ed.). Arlington, VA: Author.

Austin, W. G. (2002). Guidelines for using collateral sources of information in child custody evaluations. *Family Court Review, 40*(2), 177–184.

Beck, A. T., Steer, R. A., & Brown, G. K. (1996). *Manual for the Beck Depression Inventory-II.* San Antonio, TX: Psychological Corporation.

Boo, J., & Vispoel, W. (2012). Computer versus paper-and-pencil assessment of educational development: A comparison of psychometric features and examinee preferences. *Psychological Reports, 111*(2), 443–460. doi:10.2466/10.03.11. PR0.111.5.443-460

Butcher, J. N. (2003). Computerized psychological assessment. In J. R. Graham, J. A. Naglieri, & I. B. Weiner (Eds.), *Handbook of psychology: Assessment psychology* (Vol. 10, pp. 141–163). New York, NY: John Wiley & Sons.

Cavagnaro, A. T., Shuster, S., & Colwell, K. (2013). Classification discrepancies in two intelligence tests: Forensic implications for persons with developmental disabilities. *Journal of Forensic Psychology Practice, 13*(1), 49–67. doi:10.1080/15228932.2013.750968

Cohen, R. J., & Swerdlik, M. E., & Struman, E. (2012). *Psychological testing and assessment: An introduction to tests and measurement* (8th ed.). Boston, MA: McGraw-Hill.

Craig, R. J. (2005). The clinical process of interviewing. In R. J. Craig (Ed.), *Clinical and diagnostic interviewing* (2nd ed., pp. 21–41). Lanham, MD: Jason Aronson.

Craig, R. J. (2009). The clinical interview. In J. N. Butcher (Ed.), *Oxford handbook of personality assessment* (pp. 201–225). New York, NY: Oxford University Press. doi:10.1093/oxfordhb/9780195366877.013.0012

Domino, G., & Domino, M. L. (2006). *Psychological testing: An introduction.* New York, NY: Cambridge University Press.

Dunn, L. M. & Dunn, D. M. (2007). *The Peabody Picture Vocabulary Test* (4th ed.). Bloomington, MN: NCS Pearson Inc.

Erford, B. T. (2006). *Counselor's guide to clinical, personality, and behavioral assessment.* Boston, MA: Lahaska.

Erford, B. T. (2013). *Assessment for counselors.* (2nd ed.). Boston, MA: Houghton Mifflin Company.

Ertelt, T., & Matson, K. (2013). Accurately presenting your forensic examination in a cohesive forensic report. *PsycCRITQUES, 58*(43). doi:10.1037/a0034697

Groth-Marnat, G. (2009). *Handbook of psychological assessment.* Hoboken, NJ: John Wiley & Sons.

Harwood, R. M., Beutler, L. E., & Groth-Marnat, G. (Eds.). *Integrative Assessment of Adult Personality* (3rd ed.). New York, NY: Guilford Press.

Heilbrun, K. (2001). *Principles of forensic mental health assessment* (Perspectives in law and psychology, Vol. 12). New York, NY: Kluwer.

Heilbrun, K., Warren, J., & Picarello, K. (2003). Third-party information in forensic assessment. In A. M. Goldstein & I. B. Weiner (Eds.), *Handbook of psychology: Forensic psychology* (Vol. 2, pp. 69–86). Hoboken, NJ: John Wiley & Sons.

Hersen, M. (2006). *Clinician's handbook of adult behavioral assessment*. Burlington, MA: Elsevier.

Hersen, M., & Turner, S. M. (2012). *Adult psychopathology and diagnosis* (6th ed.). Hoboken, NJ: Wiley & Sons.

International Test Commission. (2013, October 8). *ITC guidelines on test use*. Retrieved from http://www.intestcom.org/upload/sitefiles/41.pdf

Jones, K. (2010). The unstructured clinical interview. *Journal of Counseling & Development*, 88(2), 220–226. doi:10.1002/j.1556-6678.2010.tb00013.x

Kamphaus, R. W., Barry, C. T., & Frick, P. J. (2005). *Clinical assessment of child and adolescent personality and behavior* (3rd ed.). New York, NY: Springer.

Miller, C. (2009). Interviewing strategies. In M. Hersen & D. L. Segal (Eds.), *Diagnostic interviewing* (4th ed., pp. 47–66). New York, NY: Kluwer Academic/Plenum Publishers.

Morrison, J. (2008). *The first interview* (3rd ed.). New York, NY: Guilford.

Murphy, K. R., & Davidshofer, C. O. (2005). *Psychological testing: Principles and applications* (6th ed.). Upper Saddle River, NJ: Merrill/Prentice Hall.

Nock, M. K., & Kurtz, S. M. S. (2005). Direct behavioral observation in school settings: Bringing science to practice. *Cognitive and Behavioral Practice, 12,* 359–370.

Opie, C. (2004). *Doing educational research: A guide to first-time researchers*. London: Sage.

Parshall, C. G., Spray, J. A., Kalohn, J. C., & Davey, T. (2002). *Practical considerations in computer-based testing*. New York, NY: Springer.

Patel, S., & Choate L. (2014). Conducting child custody evaluations: Best practices for mental health counselors who are court-appointed as child custody evaluators. *Journal of Mental Health Counseling, 36*(1), 18–30.

Reynolds, C. R., & Kamphaus, R. W. (2001). *Behavior assessment system for children: Manual*. Circle Pines, MN: American Guidance Service.

Rutherford, R. B., Quinn, M. M., & Mathur, S. R. (2007). *Handbook of research in emotional and behavioral disorders*. New York, NY: Guilford.

Sacks, P. (2001). *Standardized minds: The high price of America's testing culture and what we can do to change it*. New York, NY: Da Capo Press.

Salkind, N. J. (2012). *Tests and measurement for people who (think they) hate tests and measurement* (2nd ed.). Thousand Oaks, CA: Sage.

Sattler, J. M., & Hoge, R. D. (2006). *Assessment of children: Behavioral, social, and clinical foundations* (5th ed.). San Diego, CA: Jerome M. Sattler Publisher Inc.

Shapiro, E. S. (1987). Academic problems. In M. Hersen & V. Van Hasselt (Eds.), *Behavior therapy with children and adolescents: A clinical approach* (pp. 362–384). New York, NY: John Wiley & Sons.

Sommers-Flanagan, J., & Sommers-Flanagan, R. (2008). *Clinical interviewing* (4th ed.). Hoboken, NJ: John Wiley & Sons.

Urbina, S. (2014). *Essentials of psychological testing* (2nd ed.). Hoboken, NJ: John Wiley & Sons.

Wang, S., Jiao, H., Young, M. J., Brooks, T., & Olson, J. (2008). Comparability of computer-based and paper-and-pencil testing in K–2 reading assessments: A meta-analysis of testing mode effects. *Educational & Psychological Measurement, 68,* 5–24.

Weiner, I. B. (2013). The assessment process. In J. R. Graham, J. A. Naglieri, & I. B. Weiner (Eds.), *Handbook of psychology: Assessment psychology* (2nd ed., Vol. 10, pp. 3–25). Hoboken, NJ: John Wiley & Sons.

Young, M. E. (2012). *Learning the art of helping: Building blocks and techniques* (5th ed.). Upper Saddle River, NJ: Merrill/Prentice Hall.

3

Statistical Concepts

In our experience, students preparing to be counselors and other helping professionals often cringe when they hear the word *statistics*. Although numbers can be scary for many, they play an important role throughout the counseling process. Counselors must be competent consumers of statistics in order to understand research as it applies to practice and to evaluate change in clients, measure outcomes, demonstrate accountability, and conduct assessment. In order to be competent in assessment, counselors need knowledge about statistical concepts in order to evaluate the appropriateness of assessment instruments and to understand, interpret, and communicate assessment results.

Statistics help counselors to understand assessment data in comparison to larger populations of people. Statistics also help counselors to evaluate the psychometric properties (e.g., reliability, validity, standardization) of tests, which is important for evaluating and selecting tests. Although statistics can be scary, our goal is to provide a framework for understanding how statistics are used in assessment. In this chapter, we present the basic statistical concepts required for counselors to be competent in selecting, scoring, and interpreting assessment results. By understanding some of these basic elements, counselors will be able to take an additional step toward competency in the assessment process.

After studying this chapter, you should be able to:
- Describe the use of statistics in assessment.
- Describe the scales of measurement, including nominal, ordinal, interval, and ratio scales.
- Explain how to construct frequency distributions, histograms, and frequency polygons.
- Describe measures of central tendency, including the mean, median, and mode.
- Describe measures of variability, including range, variance, and standard deviation.
- List and explain the properties of the normal curve.
- Describe the various measures of relationship.

STATISTICAL CONCEPTS FOR ASSESSMENT

The field of educational and psychological measurement is based on core statistical principles that allow us to summarize, describe, and interpret assessment data and to make decisions using data. For example, we may want to know the average of a group of test scores, how frequently certain scores can be obtained, or how spread out scores were among a group of test takers. Because counselors frequently are involved in the assessment process and in making decisions based on assessment results, they should be familiar and comfortable with some basic statistical concepts. A *statistic* is a numerical representation of information. Whenever we quantify or apply numbers to data in order to organize, summarize, or analyze information, we are using statistical methods. There are two general classes of statistical methods: descriptive and inferential. *Descriptive statistics* play an important role in interpreting instrument scores. They are used to describe and summarize large amounts of data in a clear and understandable way. In assessment, the simplest descriptive statistic used is *frequency*, or the count of the occurrences of a particular test score. Other descriptive statistics used in assessment include measures of central tendency (e.g., mean, median, mode), measures of variability (e.g., variance, standard deviation), and measures of relationship (i.e., correlation). *Inferential statistics* are used when we want to make inferences about a large group of people, called a *population*, by examining the characteristics of randomly selected subgroups from the population, called *samples*. Whereas descriptive statistics are used to describe the basic features of data, inferential statistics are used to reach conclusions that extend beyond the immediate data alone.

One of the most basic concepts frequently encountered when discussing statistics is associated with the term *variable*. A variable is simply anything that can take on more than one value. Variables can be visible (e.g., gender, hair color) or invisible (e.g., personality, intelligence, aptitude). Variables can be defined in terms of numerical values (e.g., the number of children in a family, the average income of individuals in a country) or by different categories (e.g., gender, relationship status; Urbina, 2014). In formal terms, variables may be classified as quantitative, qualitative, discrete, continuous, observable, or latent (see Table 3.1). In assessment, we are interested in measuring variables related to educational or psychological constructs, such as achievement, intellectual ability, interests, and personality traits.

TABLE 3.1 Types of Variables

Variable	Description
Quantitative	Have a numerical value (e.g., age, income, numerical test scores)
Qualitative	Nonnumeric in nature (e.g., gender, relationship status, political party affiliation)
Continuous	Quantitative variables that can take on any value and be subdivided infinitely; a measure of "how much" (e.g., height, weight, time spent completing a task, degree of anxiety)
Discrete	Quantitative variables that consist of a basic unit of measurement that cannot be subdivided; a measure of "how many" (e.g., the number of people in a household)
Observable	Can be observed and directly measured
Latent	Cannot be directly observed or measured, but are inferred from other variables that are observed and measured; also called *hidden variables*, *model parameters*, *hypothetical variables*, or *hypothetical constructs*

SCALES OF MEASUREMENT

Any discussion of statistics must begin with an understanding of measurement. *Measurement* is the process of assigning numbers or symbols to represent objects, traits, or behaviors (i.e., variables) according to a set of logical rules. For example, to complete a customer satisfaction survey, customers must use a specific set of rules to assign numbers that indicate their level of satisfaction. They might rate service on a 10-point scale, where 1 means *very dissatisfied* and 10 means *very satisfied*.

We use descriptive statistics to describe or summarize measurement data; however, the way that data can be summarized depends on the scale of measurement. *Scales of measurement* refers to ways in which variables are defined and categorized. There are four scales of measurement: *nominal, ordinal, interval,* and *ratio*. The type of scale is determined by the presence or absence of three qualities: (a) *magnitude*, meaning the inherent order of numbers from smaller to larger; (b) *equal intervals*, which means that there are equal distances between adjacent points on the scale; and (c) the presence of an *absolute* or *true zero*, which refers to the zero point representing the absence of the property being measured (e.g., no behavior, none correct; see Table 3.2).

Nominal Scale

The simplest scale of measurement is the *nominal scale*, which is used to describe qualitative variables that can be categorized based on one or more distinguishing characteristics. Because the nominal scale represents only names, it has none of the three qualities (i.e., magnitude, equal intervals, absolute zero). Nominal scale variables are considered *discrete* and can be placed into one (and only one) mutually exclusive and exhaustive category. The following are some examples:

Relationship status:

_____ Single

_____ Married

_____ Widowed

_____ Divorced

_____ Separated

TABLE 3.2 Scales of Measurement

Scales of Measurement	Scale Qualities	Examples
Nominal	None	Names, lists of words
Ordinal	Magnitude	Rank-ordered, Likert scales
Interval	Magnitude Equal intervals	Temperature
Ratio	Magnitude Equal intervals Absolute zero	Age, height, weight

Gender:

    _____ Male

    _____ Female

Highest educational level completed:

    _____ Some high school

    _____ High school diploma or GED

    _____ Vocational, business, or technical school

    _____ Associate's degree

    _____ Bachelor's degree

    _____ Graduate degree

Ordinal Scale

Similar to nominal scales, ordinal scales involve classification of discrete variables. However, in addition to classification, the scale includes the property of magnitude. This means that variables are rank-ordered from the greatest to the least or the best to the worst. For example, on an introversion–extroversion continuum, an extremely introverted individual might be assigned the lowest rank of 1, whereas an overly extroverted individual might receive the highest rank. On other scales, students could be placed in rank order on the basis of such attributes as height (arranged from tallest to shortest), examination results (arranged from best to worst), or grade point average (arranged from highest to lowest). Here is another example:

Please rate your degree of competence in the listed behaviors using the following key: 1 = *low*, 2 = *below average*, 3 = *average*, 4 = *above average*, 5 = *high*.

1. Oral communication skills	1	2	3	4	5
2. Written communication skills	1	2	3	4	5
3. Listening skills	1	2	3	4	5

Problems can arise with the ordinal scale, because the size of the intervals can be unequal. For example, an individual might be extremely strong in certain areas, with minute differences distinguishing those competencies, and extremely weak in others. Problems can also occur when comparing rankings across groups. Individuals with rankings of 1 in each group might vary tremendously on the variable being ranked. In addition, the numbers used for rankings do not reflect anything quantitative about the variable being ranked.

Interval Scale

The interval scale represents a higher level of measurement than the ordinal scale. Not only does the interval scale consist of ordered categories, but the categories form a series of equal intervals across the whole range of the scale. Thus, interval scales encompass qualities of both magnitude and equal intervals. An important characteristic of interval scales is that there is *no absolute zero point*; that is, there can be no absence of the variable being measured. For instance, the Fahrenheit scale is an interval scale, because each degree is equal but with no absolute zero point. This means that although we can add and subtract degrees (100 °F is 10 degrees warmer than 90 °F), we cannot multiply values or create ratios (100 °F is not twice as warm as 50 °F).

Ratio Scale

In addition to all the qualities of nominal, ordinal, and interval scales, the ratio scale consists of a true or absolute zero point. This means that it contains all three qualities: magnitude, equal intervals, and absolute zero. Thus, this scale permits all types of meaningful mathematical calculations. Age, height, weight, and scores on a 100-point test are examples of ratio scales.

DESCRIBING SCORES

As stated earlier in the chapter, descriptive statistics are used to describe the basic features of the data in a clear and understandable way. In this section, we will discuss the basic descriptive statistics that are used to describe and organize test scores to make them more manageable and understandable. Let's begin with a picture of what test scores look like.

Let's suppose we have administered three tests to 30 youthful offenders who have been assigned to our cottage in a correctional facility. The scores of the Nowicki–Strickland Locus of Control Scale, Slosson Intelligence Test (SIT-R3), and the Jesness Inventory are listed in Table 3.3.

Let's look first at the scores on the Nowicki–Strickland Locus of Control Scale, given in the LOC column, which measures children's locus of control (internal or external) as defined by Rotter (1966). Individuals with a strong *internal locus of control* tend to attribute outcomes of events to their own control, whereas individuals with a strong *external locus of control* tend to attribute outcomes of events to external circumstances. On the Nowicki–Strickland scale, low scores indicate internality and high scores indicate externality. With the way that the scores are listed on the table, it is hard to get a picture of the characteristics of this group of youths. To visualize the data better, we could arrange the scores from high to low:

15	9, 9, 9	6, 6	3, 3, 3, 3
14	8, 8, 8	5, 5, 5, 5	2, 2, 2
13	7, 7	4, 4, 4, 4, 4	1

We can determine at a glance the highest score and the lowest score, and we can find the approximate middle. However, when a large number of test scores has a greater range (the spread between the high and low scores), it is not as easy to organize and record the scores and see an overall picture. To organize and describe large numbers of scores, researchers and test developers use several different types of descriptive statistics:

- Frequency distributions
- Measures of central tendency
- Measures of variability
- Measures of relationship

Frequency Distributions

A *distribution* is simply a set of scores. These scores can represent any type of variable and any scale of measurement. One of the most common procedures for organizing and

TABLE 3.3 Scores on the Nowicki–Strickland Locus of Control Scale, Slosson Intelligence Test, and Jesness Inventory*

Youth	LOC	SIT-R3	AC	IS	CA	SO	CO	EN	RA	CM	IN	SC	CS	RE	FR	UN
1	1	110	12	27	24	17	23	18	22	20	13	12	28	37	18	26
2	3	120	18	27	28	23	27	16	20	24	15	18	29	33	19	34
3	5	99	15	30	20	21	28	23	19	21	12	16	31	34	18	27
4	3	95	12	22	23	16	22	18	19	21	19	15	26	33	19	33
5	8	93	12	28	18	17	25	18	22	19	12	15	30	36	18	26
6	3	112	15	24	24	20	20	17	22	22	20	12	24	35	19	29
7	9	108	13	26	16	15	23	15	19	17	19	16	18	34	15	31
8	8	82	9	21	19	16	22	16	14	16	18	11	22	30	11	24
9	2	115	11	30	21	17	23	18	19	24	20	18	25	41	21	26
10	14	70	19	20	19	22	21	18	21	14	14	15	30	40	17	30
11	9	99	20	28	22	25	27	13	25	21	13	16	23	37	21	35
12	5	83	8	24	23	15	18	22	18	18	10	9	24	34	15	17
13	5	88	17	29	19	22	26	20	23	18	16	18	24	29	16	31
14	15	75	12	21	15	15	20	15	17	18	17	11	19	34	18	26
15	6	102	15	25	21	21	29	16	19	16	16	14	28	32	16	32
16	7	76	13	28	16	17	19	13	14	19	17	16	22	32	16	27
17	3	85	16	28	15	21	25	17	16	19	17	17	32	41	19	30
18	2	112	14	29	21	19	24	20	18	21	20	18	25	40	20	32
19	13	79	13	17	20	14	27	17	12	18	15	12	25	18	16	25
20	2	117	16	24	22	22	23	17	15	15	15	15	25	32	16	28
21	4	113	15	27	16	20	23	18	22	17	15	15	29	33	22	27
22	9	91	9	27	17	11	18	14	21	16	15	12	26	32	14	18
23	6	107	9	20	18	15	29	16	18	13	18	15	22	28	14	29
24	5	105	18	28	25	23	24	16	20	20	17	15	25	35	19	26
25	4	109	15	27	22	22	22	19	15	20	17	15	26	39	15	23
26	4	107	18	25	25	22	30	17	17	18	18	19	29	38	18	33
27	7	83	17	27	23	22	21	16	23	21	18	15	27	33	17	28
28	4	111	16	16	16	20	25	8	16	13	11	18	21	34	20	32
29	4	109	9	20	13	13	20	18	14	14	16	12	23	28	13	19
30	8	101	17	27	19	21	26	13	21	10	16	16	28	33	20	27

*LOC = Nowicki–Strickland Locus of Control Scale. SIT-R3 = Slosson Intelligence Test. The Jesness scales are Anger Control (AC), Insight (IS), Calmness (CA), Sociability (SO), Conformity (CO), Enthusiasm (EN), Rapport (RA), Communication (CM), Independence (IN), Social Concern (SC), Consideration (CS), Responsibility (RE), Friendliness (FR), and Unobtrusiveness (UN).

visually presenting scores is by using a frequency distribution. A *frequency distribution* takes a disorganized set of scores and places them in order (usually in a table or graph), showing how many people obtained each of the scores. Scores are usually arranged in vertical columns from the highest to the lowest value, and each individual test score is tallied and the frequency recorded (see Table 3.4). Frequency distributions are useful in allowing examiners to see (a) the entire set of scores "at a glance," (b) whether scores are generally high or generally low, or (c) whether scores are concentrated in one area or spread out. Frequency distributions are also useful in comparing one person's test score to the scores of the entire group.

TABLE 3.4 Frequency Distribution Table of the Nowicki–Strickland Locus of Control Scale

Score	Tally	Frequency
15	/	1
14	/	1
13	/	1
12		0
11		0
10		0
9	///	3
8	///	3
7	//	2
6	//	2
5	////	4
4	/////	5
3	////	4
2	///	3
1	/	1

Sometimes there is a greater range of scores because there are more items on the test and greater variability of performance among the test takers. In such a situation, it is easier to make a frequency distribution by using a *group* or series of scores rather than using each individual score. That grouping is called a *class interval*. For example, looking at the Slosson Intelligence Test (SIT-R3) scores in Table 3.3, we notice that scores range from 70 to 120. To list each individual score on a frequency distribution table would be much too cumbersome with 51 different score values. Instead, let's group the scores into a more manageable size—say, 10 (the choice of grouping is arbitrary). To construct a table, we need to determine the size of each of the 10 class intervals—that is, the number of score values to be included in each class interval. To find the class interval size, use the following formula:

$$\text{Class interval size} = \frac{\text{highest score} - \text{lowest score}}{\text{desired number of class intervals}}$$

Putting this all together, the steps for determining the class intervals on the SIT-R3 include the following:

Step 1 Select the number of class intervals to be used.   10

Step 2 Find the highest score.   120

Step 3 Find the lowest score.   70

Step 4 Calculate the range (subtract the lowest from the highest score). $120 - 70 = 50$

Step 5 Divide the range by the size of the class interval selected to $50 \div 10 = 5$
determine the number of score points to be included
in each interval.

TABLE 3.5 Group Frequency Distribution on the Slosson Intelligence Test

Class Interval	Tally	Frequency
120–124	/	1
115–119	//	2
110–114	/////	5
105–109	//////	6
100–104	//	2
95–99	///	3
90–94	//	2
85–89	//	2
80–84	///	3
75–79	///	3
70–74	/	1

As we can see from Table 3.5, the frequency distribution table lists each class interval arranged from lowest to highest value followed by a tally of the scores that fall into each interval.

GRAPHIC PRESENTATIONS OF FREQUENCY DISTRIBUTIONS Frequency distributions of test scores can also be illustrated graphically. A *graph* is a diagram or chart composed of lines, points, bars, or other symbols that provides a pictorial representation of the distribution of test scores. Among the most common kinds of graphs are histograms, frequency polygons, and frequency curves.

A *histogram* is a type of graph that uses vertical lines and bars to portray the distribution of test scores. Figure 3.1 shows the histogram of the Slosson Intelligence Test scores

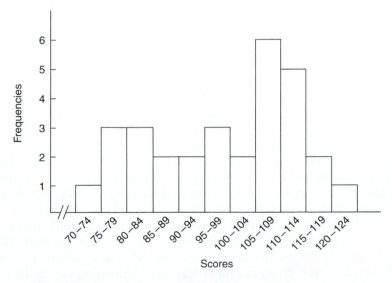

FIGURE 3.1   Histogram of Slosson Intelligence Test scores.

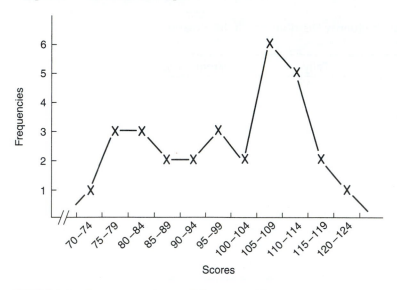

FIGURE 3.2   Frequency polygon of Slosson Intelligence Test scores.

using class intervals from Table 3.4. The graph's horizontal axis (also referred to as the *abscissa* or the *X axis*) represents the class intervals. The vertical axis (also referred to as the *ordinate* or the *Y axis*) represents the frequencies of scores appearing at each class interval. The intersection of the *X* and *Y* axes represents the zero point for each.

A *frequency polygon* is a variation of a histogram in which the bars are replaced by lines connecting the *midpoint* of each class interval. In the frequency distribution of scores on the Slosson Intelligence Test, a class interval of 5 was used; therefore, the midpoint of the class interval 70–74 is 72, the midpoint for 75–79 is 78, the midpoint for 80–84 is 82, and so on. If the class interval consists of an odd number of score points, then the midpoint is a whole number; if it contains an even number of points, then the midpoint is expressed as a decimal number, such as 1.5. A frequency polygon of the Slosson Intelligence Test scores is presented in Figure 3.2.

If there were many more individuals and a greater number of intervals, then the frequency polygon would reflect a smoother curve. A *smoothed frequency polygon* (or a *frequency curve*) gives a better idea of the shape of the distribution and the frequency of the scores. If we made the intervals progressively smaller and increased the number of individuals tested on the Nowicki–Strickland Locus of Control Scale, then the smoothed frequency polygon might look like that shown in Figure 3.3.

When we create smoothed frequency polygons, we will see that the distributions are sometimes symmetrical (bell-shaped or normal curve) or asymmetrical (*skewed*; see Figure 3.4). In a *symmetrical distribution*, each side of the curve is a mirror image of the other. This shows that most of the scores are situated around the mean, with the rest tailing off symmetrically away from the mean. A frequency curve that is not symmetrical is called a *skewed* curve. In everyday terms, *skewed* refers to something that is out of proportion or distorted on one side. In frequency distributions, *skewness* indicates a lack of symmetry of the distribution. A distribution with an asymmetrical "tail" extending out to the right is referred to as *positively skewed*; this means that the majority of scores fell near the lower end

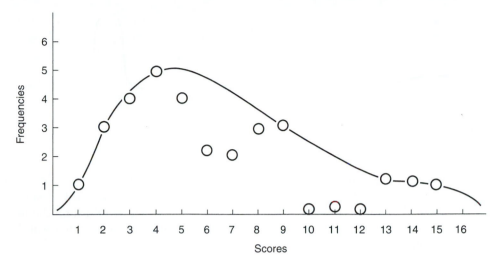

FIGURE 3.3   Smoothed frequency polygon of Nowicki–Strickland Locus of Control Scale.

of the scale. A distribution with an asymmetrical tail extending out to the left is *negatively skewed*. For example, if the majority of students scored poorly on a class midterm, then the result would be a positively skewed curve with most of the scores concentrated on the left end of the distribution. If most of the students performed well on the test, then the distribution would be negatively skewed. A skewed curve is *not* a normal distribution; normal distributions will be discussed later in the chapter.

   Kurtosis is a statistic that reflects the peakedness or flatness of a distribution relative to a normal distribution. A distribution could be mesokurtic, leptokurtic, or platykurtic (see Figure 3.5). Kurtosis with a zero value signifies a *mesokurtic distribution*, which is similar in height to a normal distribution. Positive values of kurtosis indicate a *leptokurtic distribution* that is more peaked than the normal curve, meaning that scores cluster in the middle of the distribution. Negative values indicate a *platykurtic distribution*, which is flatter than the normal curve. This means that test scores spread out rather evenly from the lowest to highest points.

Measures of Central Tendency

When summarizing a group of test scores, we often want to know about the typical or average performance of the group. *Measures of central tendency* are ways of describing a distribution based on the typical or average performance of test scores. Three common measures of central tendency are the mean, median, and mode.

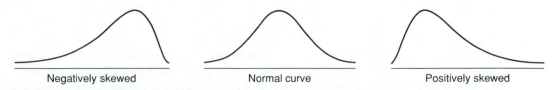

Negatively skewed   Normal curve   Positively skewed

FIGURE 3.4   Skewed and normal curves.

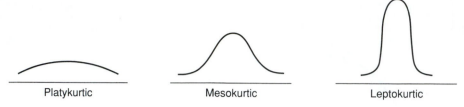

Platykurtic   Mesokurtic   Leptokurtic

FIGURE 3.5   Kurtosis.

MEAN The *mean*, the most frequently used measure of central tendency, is the arithmetic average score in a distribution. It is used with interval or ratio scales and whenever additional statistical analysis is needed. To calculate the mean, we would total the test scores and divide the sum by the number of individuals who took the test. The formula for the mean is as follows:

$$\overline{X} = \frac{\Sigma X}{N}$$

where

$\overline{X}$ = the mean

Σ = sigma, which means summation

X = a test score

N = the number of cases

If we add together the scores of the 30 individuals taking the Nowicki–Strickland, our total is 178. To compute the mean, we divide 178 by 30; therefore, the mean is 5.93.

MEDIAN The *median* is the middle score, or the score that divides a distribution in half; 50% of the scores will fall below the median, and 50% will fall above. When a set of scores consists of an odd number, the median is the middle score. For example, if the scores are 4, 6, and 8, then the median is 6. With an even number of scores—such as 4, 6, 8, and 10—the sum of the two middle scores is divided by 2; the median in this case is 7. As a measure of central tendency, the median can be used with ordinal, interval, or ratio scales or with highly skewed distributions.

MODE The *mode* is the score or numerical value that appears most frequently in a set of scores. Referring back to the test scores in Table 3.3, the mode of the scores on the Nowicki–Strickland Locus of Control Scale is 4. For the Anger Control scale on the Jesness Inventory, try to determine the mode yourself: Is the mode 9, 12, or 15? Sometimes, there is a *bimodal* or *multimodal* distribution; in other words, two or more scores may appear most frequently in the distribution. For example, the distribution of scores on the Jesness Friendliness scale is multimodal: The same number of individuals had scores of 16, 18, and 19. The mode is commonly used with variables that are measured at the nominal level, but it can also provide a quick and easy measure for ordinal, interval, and ratio variables.

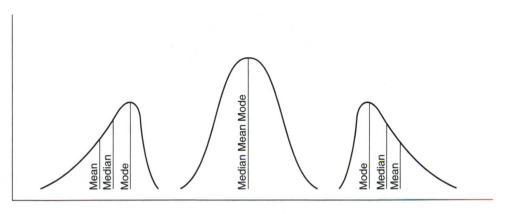

FIGURE 3.6   Measures of central tendency with skewed and normal curves.

COMPARING MEASURES OF CENTRAL TENDENCY For symmetrical distributions, the mean, median, and mode are equal. For the other types of distributions, no single best measure of central tendency exists. Although the mean is the most common measure of central tendency, extreme scores (known as *outliers*) can affect it (a few extremely low scores will move the mean down, and a few extremely high scores will move it up), making it ill-suited for skewed distributions. In contrast, the median works better with skewed distributions, because it is not impacted by outliers. The mode is the least stable statistic of central tendency: It can be erratic and not very accurate in smaller groups of scores, and it is not an accurate measure of central tendency in skewed distributions. Figure 3.6 shows measures of central tendency with different types of distributions.

Measures of Variability

Whereas measures of central tendency attempt to describe a distribution based on typical or average performance of scores, *variability* refers to the degree that scores are spread out and differ from one another. A distribution of test scores can have the same mean, but the scores may be scattered or dispersed either *widely* or *narrowly* around the mean. *Measures of variability* are statistics that describe the dispersion of scores—that is, the typical distances of scores from the mean. In general, when describing a distribution, we consider both the *central tendency* and the *variability* of the distribution. Figure 3.7 graphically displays these two important characteristics. Three commonly used measures of variability are the range, variance, and standard deviation. Of these, the standard deviation is perhaps the most informative and the most widely used.

RANGE A quick measure of the spread of scores can be obtained by computing the range. The *range* is computed by subtracting the lowest score from the highest score. In the following formula, r represents range, h is the highest score in the dataset, and 1 is the lowest score:

$$r = h - 1$$

For example, in the distribution of Nowicki–Strickland scores (Table 3.3), the high score is 15 and the low score is 1, making the range 14 ($15 - 1 = 14$). On the Slosson Intelligence

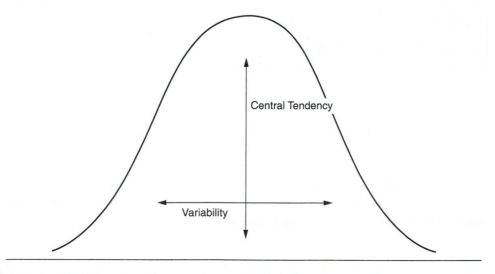

FIGURE 3.7   Graphical display of central tendency and variability.

Test score distribution, the high score is 120 and the low score is 70, making the range 50 ($120 - 70 = 50$).

The range is easy to compute. However, an extreme score in the distribution can make the range a misleading statistic. For example, a test might produce these scores:

$$1, 2, 2, 3, 3, 3, 4, 4, 5, 5, 6, 6, 40$$

The range here would be 39, even though all the scores except for the one score of 40 are grouped closely together.

VARIANCE The *variance* is the average amount of variability in a group of scores. It is computed as the average squared deviations of values from the mean. Variance is calculated using the following formula:

$$S^2 = \frac{\Sigma(X - \overline{X})^2}{N - 1}$$

where

S^2 = the variance

X = a test score

$\overline{X}$ = the mean of all the test scores

Σ = summation

N = the number of cases

Variance is rarely used as a standalone statistic. Rather, it is used as a step in the calculation of other statistics (e.g., analysis of variance) or, with a slight manipulation, transformed into the standard deviation.

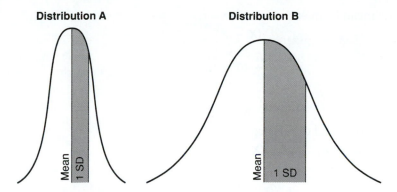

FIGURE 3.8   Relationship of size of standard deviation to the type of distribution.

STANDARD DEVIATION The *standard deviation* is the most frequently used measure of variability. In practical terms, it is the average distance of test scores from the mean. It is an important statistic for interpreting the relative position of an individual within a distribution of test scores. The wider the spread of scores from the mean, the larger the standard deviation. The smaller the standard deviation, the more scores will tend to cluster around the mean. To illustrate this, let's look back at the scores on the Nowicki–Strickland scale and the Slosson Intelligence Test. Because there is a small range of scores on the Nowicki–Strickland, just 15 points rather than the 50 points of the Slosson, the standard deviation on the Nowicki–Strickland will be smaller than the standard deviation on the Slosson. Figure 3.8 presents a hypothetical illustration.

As a statistic, standard deviation (*s*) is calculated by taking the square root of the variance, via the following formula:

$$s = \sqrt{\frac{\Sigma(X - \overline{X})^2}{N - 1}}$$

Let's use this formula for some hands-on experience calculating standard deviation. Begin with the following students' test scores:

Student	Test Score (*X*)
1	85
2	92
3	87
4	74
5	62

Using these five test scores, work through the following step-by-step example of how to compute standard deviation:

Step 1 Compute the mean ($\overline{X}$).

$$\overline{X} = \frac{\Sigma X}{N} = \frac{(85 + 92 + 87 + 74 + 62)}{5} = \frac{400}{5} = 80$$

Step 2 Subtract the mean from each test score.

Student	$(X - \bar{X})$
1	$85 - 80 = 5$
2	$92 - 80 = 12$
3	$87 - 80 = 7$
4	$74 - 80 = -6$
5	$62 - 80 = -18$

Step 3 Square each individual difference.

Student	$(X - \bar{X})$	$(X - \bar{X})^2$
1	5	25
2	12	144
3	7	49
4	−6	36
5	−18	324

Step 4 Sum the squared differences.

Student	$(X - \bar{X})^2$
1	25
2	144
3	49
4	36
5	324

$$\text{Sum} = \Sigma(X - X)^2 = 578$$

Step 5 Divide the sum of the squared differences by the number of test scores minus 1.

$$\frac{\Sigma(X - \bar{X})^2}{N - 1} = \frac{578}{4} = 144.5$$

Step 6 Compute the square root of 144.5.

$$\sqrt{144.5} = 12.02$$

Thus, the standard deviation is 12.02, indicating that the average variation of the test scores from the mean is 12.02. What does this mean? Because we know that the mean of test scores is 80, the standard deviation tells us that the majority of test scores that are within −1 or +1 standard deviation of the mean fall between 67.98 ($80 - 12.02$) and 92.02 ($80 + 12.02$).

The Normal Curve

Now that we have discussed various ways of describing distributions, including measures of central tendency and measures of variability, we need to introduce the concept of the normal curve. The *normal curve*, also known as the *normal distribution* or the *bell curve*, is a visual representation of an ideal or theoretical distribution consisting of an infinite number of scores (see Figure 3.9). The curve is based on the probability theory, which assumes that many chance events, if repeated a sufficient number of times, generate distributions that approximate a normal curve. Normal curve properties include the following:

• It is bell shaped.
• It is *bilaterally symmetrical,* which means that its two halves are identical.

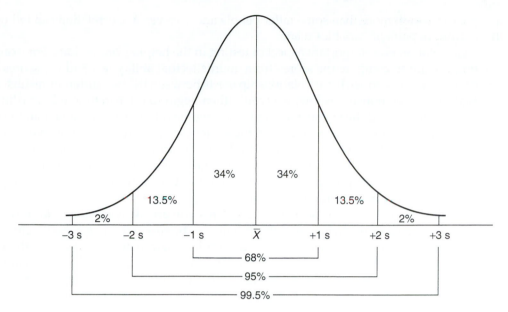

FIGURE 3.9   Normal curve.

- The mean, median, and mode are equal to one another.
- The tails are *asymptotic*, meaning that they approach but never touch the baseline.
- It is unimodal, which means that it has a single point of maximum frequency or maximum height.
- 100% of the scores fall between −3 and +3 standard deviations from the mean, with approximately 68% of the scores falling between −1 and +1 standard deviations, approximately 95% of the scores falling between −2 and +2 standard deviations, and approximately 99.5% of the scores falling between −3 and +3 standard deviations.

The normal curve is important because many of the measures researched in the social sciences (e.g., achievement, intelligence, aptitude) yield scores that correspond very closely to the normal curve. For each of these examples, test scores for most people would fall toward the middle of the curve, with fewer people at each extreme. However, normal distributions *cannot* be assumed for instruments measuring personality, behavior, or learning or emotional disorders. These instruments typically produce skewed distributions. An instrument measuring depression, for example, has a skewed distribution, because only about 6.9% of adult Americans experience depression within a given year (National Institute of Mental Health, 2014). This means that the majority of scores on a depression inventory in the U.S. population would be low, resulting in a positively skewed distribution.

Measures of Relationship

Measures of central tendency and measures of variability are not the only descriptive statistics that can be used to get a picture of what test scores look like. *Measures of relationship* can show the degree of relationship (or *correlation*) between two variables or scores. For example, height and weight are related: Taller people tend to weigh more than shorter people. However, the relationship between height and weight is not perfect: Some shorter people can weigh more than some taller people and vice versa. Correlation can tell us just how strongly pairs of variables relate.

Correlation is an important aspect of testing in the helping professions. For example, we might want to compare the scores from an intellectual ability test and the scores from an achievement test to see if any relationship exists between the two different results. If the strength of the relationship is low, we would then begin to interpret the relationship and attempt to understand the factors that are impacting the differences. Imagine that the intelligence test scores are above average and the achievement scores are below average. This might be an indication that a student is underperforming. However, we would need a great deal of additional information before we could arrive at that determination. Another possible reason could be poor instruction. We wouldn't know the cause of the discrepancy without a thorough investigation.

Another example of the use of correlation that you are likely familiar with is the relationship between admission tests and the potential to be successful in graduate school. The correlation between GRE scores and first-year grades in graduate school is .3 without correction for range restriction, which means that the basic correlation is quite low. However, the interpretation of this correlation is much more complex. Ahead, we provide a more in-depth discussion of correlation coefficients and how they relate to assessment.

CORRELATION COEFFICIENTS To measure the correlation, we use a statistic known as the *correlation coefficient*. There are two fundamental characteristics of correlation coefficients: direction and strength. In terms of *direction*, correlation coefficients can be either positive or negative. A *positive correlation* indicates that the two variables move in the same direction; that is, when scores on one variable go up, scores on the other variable go up as well. In contrast, a *negative correlation* means that the two variables move in the opposite, or inverse, direction—when scores on one variable go up, scores on the other variable go down.

In regard to *strength*, correlation coefficients describe the magnitude of the relationship between two variables. Correlation coefficients range in strength between -1.00 and $+1.00$. Thus, a correlation coefficient of $+1.00$ is considered a *perfect positive correlation*, meaning that higher values on one variable are directly related to higher values on the second variable. In contrast, a coefficient of -1.00 is a *perfect negative correlation*, indicating that higher values on one variable are associated with lower values on the second variable. The closer the coefficient is to either of the two extremes, the stronger the degree of relationship between the two variables. A coefficient of 0 would indicate the complete absence of a relationship. Most relationships will fall somewhere between a perfect association and no association. It is important to remember that correlation is not the same as cause. We cannot determine from an estimate of correlation that one variable causes the other; we can simply recognize that an association between the two variables exists.

Different methods of statistical analyses are used to calculate correlation coefficients, depending on the kinds of variables being studied. For this textbook, we will discuss the Pearson Product Moment Correlation, Spearman's rho, and the phi coefficient.

Pearson Product Moment Correlation. The Pearson Product Moment Correlation, represented by the small letter r, is used for measuring a linear relationship between two continuous variables—such as weight and intelligence in children. Continuous variables can take on any value over a range of values. The example of weight and intelligence in children is perfect to illustrate that correlation does not equal causation. Although a relationship might exist between the two, there is no evidence to suggest that weight causes intelligence or vice versa. Why might a relationship exist? There are a number of reasons that could be explored, but the most plausible would be that another variable exists that is related to both and that is impacting the relationship of weight and intelligence. Let's imagine that parental intelligence is the variable. The explanation might be that parents with high intelligence produce children with high intelligence. These parents also have better understanding of nutrition, and their children have healthy weight levels. Conversely, parents with less intelligence might produce children with less intelligence. These parents may also have less understanding of nutrition and subsequently have children who are overweight. Although these explanations might seem plausible, they are spurious. While you might be able to make a case for the connection between weight and intelligence, there are many other important variables that may impact either or both variables. For example, people with less intelligence may have lower income potential. As a result, these individuals have less money for food. Fast food and high fat foods are often cheaper than healthy food choices. As a result, the families end up with higher overall weight levels. There are numerous explanations for a relationship between weight and intelligence, none of which indicate a causative factor.

To demonstrate Pearson's r, let's say we want to compare how a group of students performed on a reading ability test (Test A) and a writing ability test (Test B). Let's look at the following student scores on Test A and Test B:

Student	Test A	Test B
1	1	3
2	2	2
3	3	4
4	4	6
5	5	5

The formula for the Pearson r is as follows:

$$r = \frac{N(\Sigma XY) - (\Sigma X)(\Sigma Y)}{\sqrt{[N(\Sigma X^2) - (\Sigma X)^2][N(\Sigma Y^2) - (\Sigma Y)^2]}}$$

where

  X = the individual's score on the X variable (in this case, X is assigned to Test A)

  Y = the individual's score on the Y variable (in this case, Y is assigned to Test B)

  Σ = summation

  N = the number of paired scores

To calculate Pearson's r, we take the following steps (Table 3.6 provides the data for steps 1 to 3):

Step 1 Find the sums of X (Test A) and Y (Test B).

Step 2 Square each of the X and Y scores, and find the sum of each column of squared scores.

Step 3 Multiply each individual X and Y score, and find the sum of all XY scores.

TABLE 3.6 Data for Calculating Pearson's r

Student	X	Y	X^2	Y^2	XY
1	1	3	1	9	3
2	2	2	4	4	4
3	3	4	9	16	12
4	4	6	16	36	24
5	5	5	25	25	25
Sums:	15	20	53	90	68

Step 4 We plug the numbers into the formula and complete the calculation. Because we have five sets of scores, $N = 5$.

$$r = \frac{5(68) - (15)(20)}{\sqrt{[5(55) - (15)^2][5(90) - (20)^2]}}$$

$$= \frac{340 - 300}{\sqrt{[275 - 225][450 - 400]}} = \frac{40}{50} = .80$$

The correlation of .80 indicates a positive degree of association between the two tests. This means that a relationship exists between reading and writing levels for the students who took these tests. Now that we know the correlation, we can have a general idea of the student's ability in one area if we have data from the other. For example, if a student only took the reading test and scored high, then we could estimate that they would also perform well on the writing test.

Spearman's Rho. *Spearman's rho* is a variant of Pearson's r that is used for finding the association between two ordinal (rank-ordered) variables. Denoted by the Greek letter ρ (rho), it is a nonparametric measure of correlation; that is, it does not require linear relationships between variables or variables that are measured on interval scales. For example, Spearman's rho is frequently used for correlating responses from Likert scales (i.e., rating scales running from *never* to *always* or *strongly disagree* to *strongly agree*). For example, imagine that you provided a couple with a marital satisfaction instrument that contained a Likert scale and asked both members of the couple to complete it. You would want to know the relationship between both of their instruments. In other words, you would want to know the level of agreement about their marital satisfaction. Because the instrument measured responses in a Likert format, a Spearman's rho would be the appropriate correlation. Fortunately, many scoring programs for assessment instruments calculate level of agreement for you.

Phi Coefficient. The *phi coefficient* (ϕ) is used to assess the degree of association between two nominal variables. For example, let's say that a researcher is interested in studying the relationship between gender and counseling group program completion. Gender is a nominal scale variable with two categories: male and female. If group completion is also measured on a nominal scale using *yes* or *no*, then a phi coefficient would be the appropriate statistic to assess the relationship between the two variables.

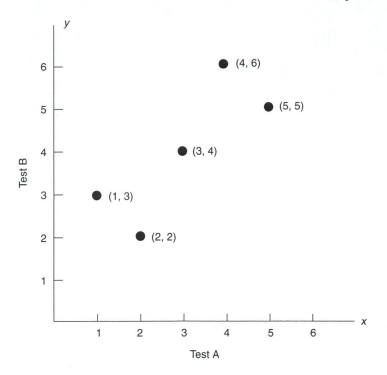

FIGURE 3.10   Scatterplot.

SCATTERPLOTS Calculating the correlation coefficient should be undertaken in conjunction with a scatterplot of the two variables. A *scatterplot* is a graphical display consisting of two axes—*X* (horizontal) and *Y* (vertical)—with one axis for each variable. Figure 3.10 shows a scatterplot of our earlier example, with each data point on the scatterplot representing the scores on Test A (*X* axis) and the scores on Test B (*Y* axis). Most scatterplots consist of large numbers of data points, and the more the points cluster toward a straight line, the stronger or more *linear* the relationship between the two variables. Figure 3.11 provides several scatterplots graphically displaying various correlation coefficients. As can be seen, a correlation coefficient (*r*) of +1.00 indicates a *perfect positive* relationship, and all of the data points fall on a straight, positive line. A correlation of −1.00 indicates an inverse (or *perfect negative*) relationship, and the points fall on a straight line slanted in the opposite direction. Correlations that are less than perfect, such as +.80, consist of data points that cluster around, but do not fall directly on, a straight line. A correlation of zero indicates no relationship, and the data points show no direction on the scatterplot.

REGRESSION Correlation is used to assess the size and direction of a relationship between variables. Regression is a statistical method related to correlation but is primarily used for prediction. *Regression* is the analysis of relationships among variables for the purpose of understanding how one variable may predict another. In the helping professions, we often use regression to determine whether changes in test scores are related to changes in performance. For example, do individuals who score better on the Graduate Records Exam (GRE) perform better in graduate school? Can certain personality tests predict job

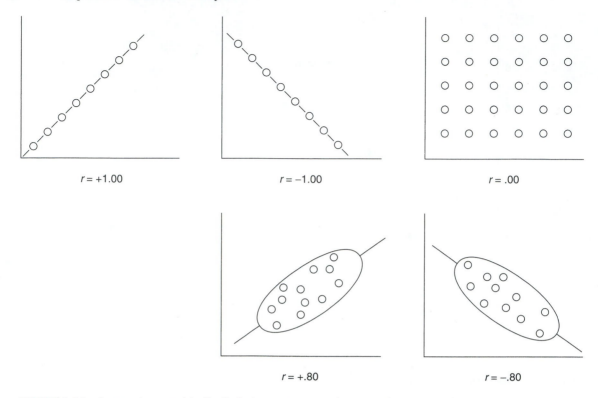

FIGURE 3.11   Scatterplots graphically displaying various correlation coefficients.

performance? Can IQ measured during high school predict success in later life? Regression is a common statistical analysis used in counseling research, and it is important for you to understand the basic principles of regression so that you can apply them to practice.

Simple linear regression is a form of regression analysis used to predict the value of one variable (the *dependent* or *outcome variable*) based on the value of another variable (the *independent* or *predictor variable*). It involves plotting a straight line through a set of points on a scatterplot with the minimal amount of deviations from the line (see Figure 3.12). This line, called the *regression line* or the *line of best fit*, best represents the association between the two variables and illustrates the linear relationship between the variables. The deviation of the points from the line is called *error*. Once the equation is determined, you can predict the *dependent* variable (on the X axis) based on the value of the *independent* variable (on the Y axis). The equation for regression is the same as the algebraic equation of a straight line: $Y = a + bX$, where a is the Y intercept and b is the slope of the line.

Multiple regression is the same as simple linear regression, except that it attempts to predict the *dependent variable* from *two or more independent variables*. For example, let's say that a researcher wants to predict outcomes in counseling from three variables: age, gender, and scores from the MMPI-2. The researcher would use multiple regression analysis to find the linear combination of the three variables that best predicts counseling success. The formula for multiple regression is an extension of the simple regression formula $Y = a + b_1X_1 + b_2X_2 + \cdots b_nX_n$.

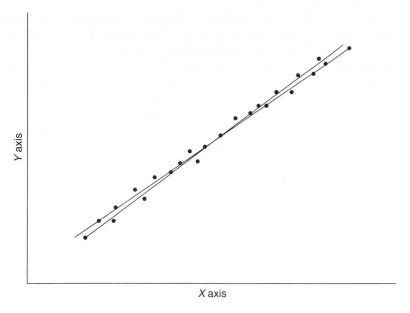

FIGURE 3.12   Regression line.

FACTOR ANALYSIS The objective of multiple regression is to analyze the relationship among variables to predict a single dependent variable by a set of independent variables. *Factor analysis* also analyzes the relationship among variables, but not for purposes of predicting a dependent variable. The principal objective of factor analysis is to simplify the description of data by reducing the number of necessary variables. Thus, it is considered a *data-reduction technique* used to analyze the relationships among large numbers of variables to explain the variables by their common underlying *dimensions* (i.e., *factors*). The dimensions that are generated from the process are much fewer in number and are thought to be representative of the original variables.

Factor analysis has been used to construct and refine personality tests by condensing numerous personality traits into fewer dimensions of personality that can then be measured and evaluated. For example, Cattell, Eber, and Tatsuoka (1988) developed the Sixteen Personality Factor Questionnaire (16PF), which consists of 16 primary factors of personality that were derived from 18,000 personality trait names using factor analysis. The factor analytic statistical process that resulted in 16 distinct personality factors from 18,000 traits is quite complex, but it is important to have a basic understanding of the process, because many assessment instruments are developed using this technique.

In order to illustrate the concept of factor analysis, think about coin-sorting machines that are available in grocery stores and other public venues. You can take a jar of coins to the machine, dump the coins in, and receive a cash payout in paper money. The machine is designed to weigh the coins and to count the iterations of each coin that weighs the same amount. For example, the machine determines that a quarter is a different weight from a dime. Once the machine weighs the coins, it provides a value based on each weight and produces a final amount. A very similar process is used for factor analysis. As you might guess, when examining 18,000 personality traits, there are many that are of the same weight statistically. In other words, the traits measured very similar (if not the same) concepts. Traits like *friendly* and *gregarious* might have overlapped extensively. As a result, the factor analysis process categorizes these as having the same weight. After all 18,000 traits were examined, the result was only 16 distinct personality factors.

Of course, factor analysis is more complex than the illustration provided. As a consumer of statistics, the preceding example can help you to understand how assessment instruments are developed. However, the example does not provide you with the knowledge of whether the statistic was used correctly or if the interpretation was appropriate. Statistical techniques like factor analysis require training beyond the scope of this textbook to use competently. If you are interested, there are books that discuss factor analysis in greater detail (see Aron, Aron, & Coups, 2012; Cudeck & MacCallum, 2007; Lomax, 2012).

Summary

To be competent in assessment, counselors need to understand the statistical concepts pertinent to understanding, interpreting, and communicating assessment results. Statistics provide test developers and users with a way to summarize, describe, and interpret assessment data. Statistics also help counselors to evaluate the psychometric properties (e.g., reliability, validity, standardization) of tests, which is important for evaluating and selecting tests. Any discussion of statistics begins with an understanding of the four scales of measure: nominal, ordinal, interval, and ratio. The type of scale of measurement and the size of the sample being tested influence what statistics are computed. Descriptive statistics are widely used in the assessment field to describe and summarize a set of data. There are several different types of descriptive statistics, such as frequency distributions, measures of central tendency, measures of variability, and measures of relationship. Inferential statistics are used to draw inferences on the population being studied.

Questions for Discussion

1. What are the four scales of measurement, and what are the advantages and disadvantages of each? Give examples of each type of scale.
2. How do the various measures of central tendency compare with each other?
3. Why is variability an important construct in testing? What are the measures of dispersion used in testing?
4. Why are measures of relationship important to measurement consumers?
5. What are the uses of inferential statistics in measurement contexts? Discuss the uses of multivariate statistical approaches, such as factor analysis.

Suggested Activities

1. Study a test manual, and identify the different types of statistics reported. Make an annotated set of cards with definitions and illustrations of the statistics identified.
2. Compute the mean, mode, and median of the Anger Control and Calmness scores that are included in Table 3.3.
3. Compute the standard deviations and range of the Anger Control and Calmness scores that are included in Table 3.3.
4. Compute a Pearson correlation between the Anger Control and Calmness scores that are included in Table 3.3.
5. Construct a frequency distribution of the Sociability or Conformity scale reported in Table 3.3. Then, make a histogram and frequency polygon of the scores.

References

Aron, A., Aron, E. N., & Coups, E. (2012). *Statistics for psychology* (6th ed.). Upper Saddle River, NJ: Merrill/Prentice Hall.

Cattell, R. B., Eber, H. W., & Tatsuoka, M. M. (1988). *Handbook for the Sixteen Personality Factor Questionnaire* (16PF). Champaign, IL: Institute for Personality and Ability Testing.

Cudeck, R., & MacCallum, R. C. (Eds.). (2007). *Factor analysis at 100: Historical developments and future directions*. Mahwah, NJ: Lawrence Erlbaum Associates.

Lomax, R. G. (2012). *Statistical concepts: A second course* (4th ed.). Mahwah, NJ: Lawrence Erlbaum Associates.

National Institute of Mental Health. (2014). *Major depression among adults*. Retrieved from http://www.nimh.nih.gov/statistics

Rotter, J. B. (1966). Generalized expectancies for internal versus external control of reinforcement. *Psychological Monographs, 80,* 609.

Urbina, S. (2014). *Essentials of psychological testing* (2nd ed.). Hoboken, NJ: John Wiley & Sons.

4   **Understanding Assessment Scores**

Because assessment is an integral part of the counseling process, counselors must be able to interpret the results of tests, rating scales, structured interviews, and various other instruments and then be able to relay the information from that interpretation in an understandable way. For example, a client might complete a depression inventory and obtain a score of 88. The counselor would have to understand that score in relationship to the norm group and then be able to explain the score in relation to depression. As another example, a counselor might need to explain the scores of a career interest inventory to a client and explain how the client can use the scores to make career decisions. In yet another example, a school counselor might interpret and explain the scores of an achievement test to students or parents. Scores can be expressed in different forms. Sometimes, the meaning of the various types of scores is confusing to clients, because they have little exposure to the terminology used in measurement. Therefore, it is crucial that counselors have knowledge about the different methods of scoring and ways of communicating those scores in a manner that clients can understand.

After studying this chapter, you should be able to:

▪ Describe raw scores and convey their limitations.

▪ Define *criterion-referenced* and *norm-referenced interpretations* and explain the distinctions between the two.

▪ Define *norm groups* and describe their importance in norm-referenced score interpretation.

▪ Describe and interpret percentile ranks.

▪ Describe the types of standard scores and their relationship to the normal curve.

▪ Describe grade and age equivalent scores and explain their limitations.

▪ Explain the purpose of qualitative descriptions of assessment scores.

ASSESSMENT SCORES

Because scores reflect the performance of the individual taking an assessment instrument, having a clear understanding of scores and their meaning is extremely important. Imagine that you receive a grade of 60 for a midterm exam in one of your university classes. What does the score mean, and how should you interpret it? By itself, the number has no meaning at all and cannot be interpreted: You cannot determine if it is a perfect score, a failing score, or anything in between. This would be considered a *raw score*, which is simply representing the number of correctly answered questions coded in some specific manner, such as correct/incorrect, true/false, and so on. By itself, a raw score does not convey any meaning. A score has meaning only when there is some standard with which to compare it; thus, part of the process of understanding scores is transforming a raw score into some meaningful form. These *transformed scores* are crucial in helping us interpret test scores. In most cases, scores can be divided into two general classes: norm-referenced scores and criterion-referenced scores. This classification provides us with a frame of reference to interpret the meaning of a given score. With *norm-referenced scores*, an individual's test score is compared to the scores of other people who took the same test (i.e., a norm group). With *criterion-referenced scores*, the individual's score is measured against a specified level of performance (i.e., a criterion). We will discuss these concepts further, beginning with criterion-referenced score interpretation.

CRITERION-REFERENCED SCORES

Many tests measure how well individuals master specific skills or meet instructional objectives, and in these situations, test results are interpreted using criterion-referenced scores. *Criterion-referenced score interpretation* emphasizes the use of some criterion or standard of performance (e.g., instructional objectives or competencies) to interpret an examinee's test results. For example, most tests and quizzes written by school teachers are criterion-referenced tests. The objective is simply to determine whether or not the student has learned the class material; thus, knowledge of class material becomes the standard of performance by which a student's test results are evaluated. Because the emphasis is on the test taker's achievement level or mastery, criterion-referenced test scores are interpreted in *absolute* terms, such as the percentages, scale scores, and performance categories. Typically, *percentages* are used to reflect the number of correct responses (e.g., the student correctly answered 80% of the items on a test). *Scale scores* are usually three-digit scores that have been converted from raw scores. The meaning of a scale score varies depending on the test; however, lower scores typically indicate the ability to do easier work, and higher scores typically indicate the ability to do more difficult work. *Performance categories* (also called *achievement levels* or *proficiency levels*) describe an individual's performance by sorting or classifying scores into categories based on the quality of performance, such as failing, basic, proficient, and advanced, or Level 1, Level 2, and so on. Performance categories are actually specified ranges of a particular score, such as scale scores. For example, the Florida state achievement test—which measures student performance in reading, math, science, and writing—has five clearly defined proficiency levels that represent a scale score ranging from 100 to 500. On the reading test, Level 1 consists of scale scores that range from 100 to 258, Level 2 scores range from 259 to 283, Level 3 from 284 to 331, Level 4 from 332 to 393, and Level 5 from 394 to 500.

Frequently, criterion-referenced scores involve the use of a *cutoff score* (i.e., the passing score), which represents the minimum number of items the examinee must answer correctly in order to demonstrate mastery. An example of the use of cutoff scores is the achievement testing of students as a result of the No Child Left Behind legislation. In this case, the federal government requires students to achieve a minimum proficiency level on statewide exams (e.g., 75% of items correct in reading) to prove that they have mastered certain basic skills. Criterion-referenced instruments are also commonly used for professional licensure or certification tests in which a cutoff score qualifies an individual for the job or for appropriate licensure or certification. In these situations, the cutoff score may be set by using the *Angoff method* (Angoff, 1971), which is a procedure that requires a panel of experts to judge each test item based on the probability or likelihood that a candidate with minimal competency of the material would answer the question correctly. Analysis of the probability input from the experts is used to generate a cutoff score for the test.

An important consideration with criterion-referenced scores involves the content domain (i.e., the criterion). Because a score is thought to reflect an individual's knowledge of a specific content domain, that domain must be clearly defined. In education, states and school districts have set standards or competencies for students to meet—for example, mastery of essential or basic skills. Criterion-referenced tests are commonly used to evaluate mastery of basic skills in classrooms, and the criteria reflect the educational content that is presented through various learning activities. An example of a well-defined content domain for second-grade math students is, "Students should understand the relative size of whole numbers between 0 and 1,000."

NORM-REFERENCED SCORES

With *norm-referenced interpretation*, we do not look at a test taker's mastery of a particular content area; rather, we compare an individual's test scores to the test scores of a group of people (Table 4.1 summarizes the differences between norm-referenced and criterion-referenced scores). Norm-referenced score interpretation is used when one wishes to make comparisons across large numbers of individuals on a particular domain being measured. For example, it might be reported that a high school student scored higher on an achievement test than 95% of a national sample of high school students who took the same test. Thus, with norm-referenced tests, individual performance is determined by relative ranking among the group of individuals who took the test. The group scores to which each individual is compared are referred to as *norms*, which provide the basis for interpreting test scores. As you recall from the previous section, there are only a few different types of criterion-referenced scores (e.g., percentages, scale scores, performance categories). Comparatively speaking, the various types of norm-referenced scores substantially outnumber the types of scores used with criterion-referenced. The numerous and diverse types of norm-referenced scores will be presented later in the chapter.

Probably the most important issue in norm-referenced score interpretation involves the relevance of the group of individuals against whom the test taker's score is weighed. This group, called the *norm group*, provides the standard against which a particular

TABLE 4.1 Differences Between Norm-Referenced and Criterion-Referenced Scores

	Interpretation	Important Considerations
Norm-referenced	How well the test taker does in comparison with other individuals (a norm group).	The norm group must be clearly defined.
Criterion-referenced	What the test taker knows or does not know with respect to a specified content domain.	The content domain (i.e., the criterion) must be clearly defined.

individual's performance can be compared; thus, the nature of the interpretation to be drawn from that comparison is influenced by the composition of the norm group. As such, the composition of the norm group is critical.

Norm Group

The *norm group* (also called the *normative group, normative sample, norming sample,* or *standardization sample*) refers to the large group of individuals who took the test and on whom the test was standardized. It is the norm group's performance to which the examinee's performance is compared and interpreted, and for interpretations to be meaningful, the norm group must be *relevant*. For example, on measures of intelligence, test results from 10-year-old children must be compared to results from other 10-year-old children, not to 6-year-old children or 13-year-old children. To determine if the norm group of a particular instrument is relevant, counselors evaluate whether the norm group is *representative, current,* and has *adequate sample size.*

Representativeness refers to the extent to which the characteristics of the norm group correspond to the individual being tested. Norm groups typically include individuals who represent the age and demographic characteristics of those for whom the test is intended. For example, if a test is used to assess the math skills of U.S. middle school students in grades 6 to 8, then the test's norm group should represent the national population of sixth-, seventh-, and eighth-grade students in all pertinent areas. To ensure that a norm group is representative, many test developers select groups from the general population using stratified sampling procedures. *Stratified sampling* involves choosing norm groups based on certain important variables; in the United States, many psychological and educational tests use *national norms* that are stratified in accordance with U.S. Census Bureau population statistics, which include such variables as gender, age, education, ethnicity, socioeconomic background, region of residence, and community size. For example, the Kaufman Brief Intelligence Test (KBIT-2) was standardized using a stratified normative sample comprised of 2,120 individuals (ages 4 to 25) that closely resembled the U.S. population based on the 2001 U.S. Census Bureau Survey (Kaufman & Kaufman, 2004). The sample matched such demographic variables as education level, parental education, race, ethnicity, and geographic region. Furthermore, in 2001, the Census Bureau reported that 15% of 11-year-old children in the United States were Hispanic; thus, 15% of the 11-year-old children within KBIT-2's norm group were Hispanic.

Another issue in determining the relevance of norm groups involves whether the sample is *current*. Over the last few decades, the demographic composition of the U.S. population has changed dramatically, such as the increasing numbers of minority populations. These newer demographics may impact test scores that are interpreted using older, outdated normative samples. For example, the U.S. population is now over 17% Hispanic (United States Census Bureau, 2014). Thus, the normative sample of the KBIT-2 is out-of-date. This does not mean that the instrument is no longer useful, but it does mean that the results should be interpreted with caution and that further research is needed to ensure that the scores are accurate reflections when testing Hispanic individuals.

Other norm group variables that fluctuate over time include language, attitudes, and values; even intelligence has been shown to change over time, as evidenced by the steady increase in intelligence test scores over the past century (read about the Flynn Effect in Chapter 8). Overall, it is generally preferable to use tests with the most up-to-date norm groups, because these test results will be the most representative of the performance of the test takers. Although no specific guidelines are available to determine whether a normative group is too old, it is reasonable to expect that instruments will be revised at least every 10 years and that new norms will accompany the revisions (Thorndike, 2011).

The *size* of the norm group can vary tremendously depending on the type of test and population that the norm group represents. For example, broadband achievement tests developed for use with K–12 students throughout the United States will have norm groups that number in the thousands. The Basic Achievement Skills Inventory (BASI; Bardos, 2004) was standardized on over 2,400 students (for Form A), the Wide Range Achievement Test (WRAT4; Wilkinson & Robertson, 2006) had a norm group of over 3,000 individuals, and the Stanford Achievement Test (Stanford 10; Pearson Inc., 2004) had a national normative sample of 275,000 students. Instruments with a more narrow focus that require samples from specialized populations (e.g., individuals from certain occupational groups, having specific psychiatric disorders, with learning disabilities) typically have smaller normative samples. For example, the normative sample of the Beck Depression Inventory (BDI-II; Beck, Steer, & Brown, 1996) consisted of 500 individuals who were diagnosed with various psychiatric disorders, and the Posttraumatic Stress Diagnostic Scale (PDS; Foa, 1995) had a normative sample of 248 individuals who were receiving treatment for Posttraumatic Stress Disorder. The size of a norm group holds importance for a couple of reasons: First, the larger the normative sample, the more likely it is to represent the population; second, a large norm group increases the stability and accuracy of statistical analysis.

Because the relevance of the norm group is essential when using norm-referenced tests, test publishers are responsible for providing detailed information about the norm group in the test manual. Counselors are also obligated to evaluate the norm group and determine whether it is suitable for comparison with their client's scores. Table 4.2 lists questions needed to evaluate a norm group.

TABLE 4.2 Questions to Evaluate a Norm Group

- Does the norm group include the type of person with whom the test taker should be compared?
- How were individuals identified and selected for the norm group?
- How large is the norm group?
- When (what year) was the sample gathered?
- What is the composition of the norm group in terms of:
  - Age?
  - Gender?
  - Ethnicity?
  - Race?
  - Language?
  - Education?
  - Socioeconomic status?
  - Geographic region?
  - Other relevant variables (e.g., mental health, disabilities, medical problems)?

Types of Norm-Referenced Scores

It is often useful to have a means for comparing an individual's performance to others. Making such a comparison allows for an understanding of the individual's performance in relative standing to a reference or norm group. The type of norm-references score selected is dependent upon the purpose of the test and the use of the results. Some norm-referenced scores have a stronger basis for interpretation than others (e.g., percentile ranks, standard scores), and users should have a clear understanding of each type before applying them in practice.

PERCENTILE RANKS *Percentile ranks* are the most common form of scores that expresses the examinee's relative position on a norm-referenced test. A percentile rank represents the percentage of a distribution of scores that falls below a particular test score. For example, if a test taker has a percentile score of 80, then he or she has performed equal to or better than 80% of the individuals who took the test. Percentile ranks range from the 1st percentile (lowest) to the 99th percentile (highest), and the 50th percentile normally signifies the average ranking or average performance. The formula for calculating the percentile rank for any raw score is as follows:

$$PR = \frac{B}{N} \times 100$$

where

PR = percentile rank
B = the number of cases with lower values
N = the total number of cases

To calculate a percentile rank, as an example, say that a math teacher had 10 raw scores on an exam ranging in value from 10 to 20 (see Table 4.3). From the table, you can see that Denzel achieved a raw score of 17 on the test. To calculate the percentile rank, sum the total

TABLE 4.3 Raw Scores Ranked in Descending Order

Student ID	Name	Raw Score
1	Michelle	20
2	Carlos	18
3	Denzel	17
4	Halle	16
5	Dante	16
6	Corrine	15
7	Maria	15
8	Grant	14
9	Monica	13
10	Joe	10

TABLE 4.4 Percentile Ranks and Percentages

Percentile Ranks

- Scores that reflect the rank or position of an individual's test performance on a continuum from 0 to 99 in comparison to others who took the test.
- Symbols for percentile rank: *PR* or *%ile*.
- Example: Shari scored in the 80th percentile on the test, meaning that Shari scored equal to or better than 80% of the other individuals who took the test.

Percentages

- A form of raw score that reflects the number of correct responses obtained out of the total possible number of correct responses on a test.
- Symbol for percentage score: %.
- Example: Shari scored 70% on her test. This means that she answered 70% of the test items correctly.

---

number of cases that fall below this score of 17; in this case, seven scores have lower values. Then, calculate the rest of the formula:

$$PR = \frac{7}{10} \times 100$$
$$= 70$$

Denzel's score is in the 70th percentile, meaning that he scored equal to or better than 70% of the students who took the math test.

Percentile ranks should not be confused with percentages. Although the two terms are similar, they are different concepts conveying different meanings. Table 4.4 describes the differences between these terms.

Quartiles are another term referred to in percentile measure. Quartiles are similar to percentile ranks, except that they divide the data set into four equal parts instead of 100 equal parts. The first quartile (also called the lower quartile) is the same as the 25th percentile, the second quartile (median quartile) is the 50th percentile, and the third quartile (upper quartile) is the 75th percentile. The distance between the first quartile and the third quartile is called the *interquartile range* and contains 50% of all values in the distribution.

Many standardized tests report a *percentile band* rather than a single percentile rank. A percentile band is the range of percentile values in which a test taker's "true" percentile rank would lie. Usually, the band extends one standard error of measurement above and below the obtained percentile rank. For example, if a test taker had a percentile rank of 35 and the standard error of measurement was 5, then the percentile band would range from the 30th percentile to the 40th percentile.

Although percentile ranks are the most common way to compare the relative ranking of an individual's test score, percentiles are *not* an equal-interval scale of measurement. This means that percentile ranks are not equally spaced across all parts of a distribution: They are compressed near the middle of the distribution (where the majority of scores fall) and spread out near the tails (where there are fewer scores; see Figure 4.1). This implies that small differences in percentile ranks near the middle of the distribution may be less important than differences at the extremes. In addition, without an equal-interval scale, they do not accurately reflect the differences between scores; for example, the difference

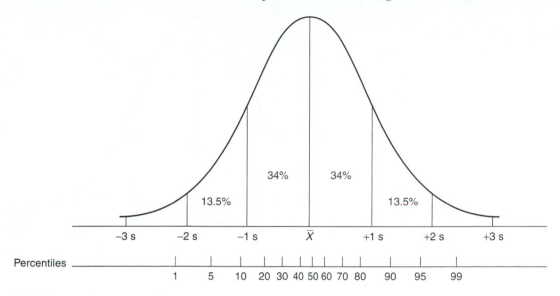

34%   **34%**

13.5%   **13.5%**

−3 s   −2 s   −1 s $\overline{X}$ +1 s   +2 s   +3 s

Percentiles

1   5   10   20 30 40 50 60 70 80   90   95   99

FIGURE 4.1   Percentiles and the normal curve.

between 20th and 30th percentiles is not the same as the difference between the 50th and 60th percentiles. Furthermore, because most meaningful mathematical calculations require measurement on equal-interval scales, percentiles cannot be added or averaged.

STANDARD SCORES *Standard scores* are a means of presenting the relative position of an individual's test score, assuming a normal distribution. Standard scores are *linear transformations* of raw scores. This means that raw scores are converted into a particular standard score using certain mathematical equations; as such, standard scores retain a direct relationship with the raw score. There are several types of standard scores: z scores, T scores, deviation IQs, stanines, sten scores, and other standard score scales. Each type of standard score has a set mean and standard deviation. By using standard deviation units, standard scores reflect the distance that an individual's test score falls above or below the mean of the distribution of scores. Thus, the standard deviation of the test becomes its yardstick. These scores are called "standard" because no matter what the distribution size or the scale of measurement, standard scores will always be the same, with a fixed mean and fixed standard deviation (Figure 4.2 shows the various standard scores and their relationship to the normal curve). Remember that standard scores assume a normal distribution of scores; however, many variables measured in assessment are not distributed normally. For example, measures of certain psychological symptoms (e.g., depression, anxiety) may deviate substantially from the normal distribution. In these situations, test developers may elect to use normalized standard scores. *Normalized standard scores* are not derived from the linear transformations of raw scores; rather, they are *nonlinearly* derived scores that are computed by (a) finding the percentile rank of each raw score, (b) transforming the percentiles into z scores using a conversion table, and (c) transforming the z score into any other standard score desired. In most situations, normalized standard scores will be interpreted similarly to other standard scores obtained by linear transformations (e.g., z scores, T scores, deviation IQs); they will have the same mean and standard deviation as their counterparts. However, they should be identified as *normalized standard scores* to alert the test user to the fact that they come from a distribution that was not normal.

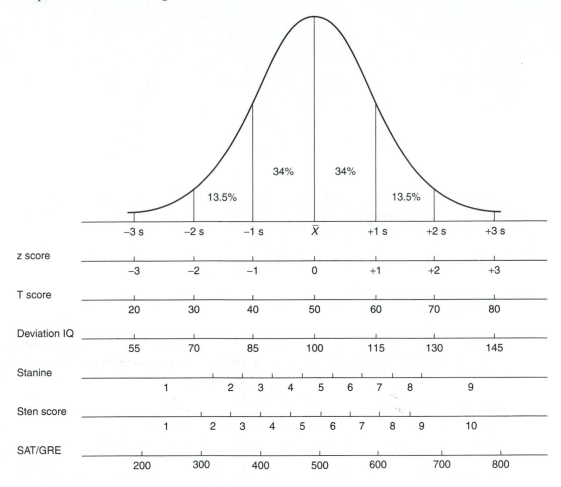

FIGURE 4.2 The normal curve and standard scores.

z Scores. *z scores* are the simplest form of standard scores. A z score conveys the value of a score in terms of how many standard deviations it is above or below the mean of the distribution. The mean for a distribution of z scores is 0, and the standard deviation is 1.0. The range of z scores is approximately from −3.0 to +3.0; thus, scores that fall below the mean will have negative z scores and those that fall above the mean will have positive z scores. The z score is computed using the following formula:

$$z = \frac{X - \overline{X}}{s}$$

where

z = the z score
X = the raw score of any individual taking the test
$\overline{X}$ = the mean of the raw scores
s = the standard deviation of the raw scores

TABLE 4.5 Raw Scores Transformed to z Scores

Test	Raw Score	Mean	Standard Deviation	z score
Reading	100	80	10	+2.00
Mathematics	50	50	15	0.00
Science	45	55	5	−2.00
History	98	82	16	+1.00

For example, if we know that the mean of a test's raw scores was 80 and the standard deviation was 10 and that an individual scored 100 on the test, then we have the data to compute the z score:

$$z = \frac{100 - 80}{10}$$
$$= \frac{20}{10}$$
$$= +2.00$$

z scores tell us instantly how large or small an individual score is relative to other scores in the distribution. Thus, the z score above tells us that the person scored 2 standard deviations above the mean on the exam. Table 4.5 provides more examples of transforming raw scores into z scores. Because standard scores are linear units, they can be transformed in a number of ways without having the properties of the original raw score distribution changed. For example, z scores can be converted into T scores, as described in the next section.

T **Scores.** A *T score* is another commonly used standard score that has a fixed mean of 50 and a fixed standard deviation of 10. Using a predetermined mean and standard deviation eliminates the need for decimals and negative values; thus, T scores will always be positive whole numbers. The formula is as follows:

$$T = 10z + 50$$

The fixed mean of 50 becomes a constant that is added to each score; the fixed standard deviation of 10 becomes a constant multiplied by each z score. Thus, if we know the z score, then we can calculate the T score. For example, if a test's raw score was converted into a z score, which came to +2.00, then the T score would be computed as follows:

$$T = 10(2.00) + 50$$
$$= 20 + 50$$
$$= 70$$

T scores are very popular in assessment and are often used to report personality test results (see Table 4.6 for examples of assessment instruments and resulting scores). An example is the MMPI-2, which uses uniform T scores. The average score on an MMPI-2 scale is 50. Scores on the MMPI-2 are not considered clinically significant until they are 1.5 standard deviations above the mean (i.e., 65 and above). When an individual obtains a

TABLE 4.6 Examples of Commonly Used Assessment Instruments in Counseling

Category	Instrument	Type of Score
Initial Assessment	Symptom Checklist-90-Revised	T scores
	Brief Symptoms Inventory	T scores
	Beck Scale for Suicide Ideation	Total score
	BDI-II	Total score
	SASSI-2	T scores
	CAGE	Total score
Ability	Wechsler Preschool and Primary Scale of Intelligence, Revised (WPPSI-IV)	IQ Scores, Percentile
	Wechsler Intelligence Scale for Children-Fourth Edition (WISC-IV)	IQ Scores, Percentile
	Wechsler Adult Intelligence Scale-Fourth Edition	IQ Scores
	Kaufman Assessment Battery For Children, Second Edition (K-ABC-II)	IQ Scores, Percentile
	Stanford–Binet, Fifth Edition (SB-5)	IQ Scores, Percentile
Achievement/Aptitude	Terra Nova, Third Edition	National Percentile Rank
	Wide Range Achievement Test 3 (WRAT3)	IQ Scores, Percentile, Stanine
	Kaufman Test of Educational Achievement, Second Edition (K-TEA-II)	IQ Scores, Percentile, Stanine
Career	Strong Interest Inventory (SII)	Transformed standard scores
	Self-Directed Search (SDS)	Three-letter Holland Code
	Campbell Interest and Skills Survey	T scores and three-letter Holland Code
	Kuder System	Various scores
	Differential Aptitude Tests, Fifth Edition (DAT-5)	Percentile, Stanine, and Scaled Scores
	SIGI-PLUS	Three-letter Holland Code
Personality	Minnesota Multiphasic Personality Inventory-2 (MMPI-2)	Uniform T scores
	Minnesota Multiphasic Personality Inventory-Adolescent Version (MMPI-A)	Uniform T scores
	Millon Clinical Multiaxial Inventory-III, (MCMI-III)	T scores
	NEO-PI-R	T scores
	California Psychological Inventory (CPI)	T scores
	Myers-Briggs Type Indicator (MBTI)	Four-letter code
	Sixteen Personality Factor Questionnaire (16PF)	STEN
	State-Trait Anxiety Inventory (STAI)	Total score
Marriage and Family	Marital Satisfaction Inventory-Revised (MSI-R)	T scores
	Family Environment Scale (FES)	Standard scores

Transforming Raw Scores to Any Type of Standard Score

In this chapter, we presented formulas for transforming raw scores into z scores. With this calculation, you can transform raw scores into any type of standard score. We have already shown how to convert z scores into T scores, but there are alternative standard score systems with different means and standard deviations to which one might want to convert a raw score.

There are two steps for transforming a raw score into any type of standard score:

Step 1. Convert the raw score to a z score as follows:

$$z = \frac{X - \bar{X}}{S}$$

where

z = the z score
X = the raw score of any individual taking the test
$\bar{X}$ = the mean of the raw scores
S = the standard deviation of the raw scores

Step 2. Convert the z score to any standard score as follows:

$$X' = S'(Z) + \bar{X}'$$

where

X' = the new standard score
S' = the standard deviation of the new standard score
z = the z score
$\bar{X}'$ = the mean of the new standard score

For example, say that you want to convert a raw score ($X = 95$) into a CEEB score (which has a mean of 500 and a standard deviation of 100, as described later in the chapter). You calculated the standard deviation and mean for the raw scores (see Table 4.5) and found the raw scores' mean to be 80 and the standard deviation to be 10. Using the preceding steps, the calculations would be as follows:

Step 1. $z = \dfrac{X - \bar{X}}{S}$

$= \dfrac{95 - 80}{10}$

$= \dfrac{15}{10}$

$= +15$

Step 2. $X' = S'(Z) + \bar{X}'$

$= 100(1.5) + 500$

$= 650$

T score of 65, this means that the score is equal to or higher than 91% of the population. When using this lens, the score is clearly different from the rest of the norm group. A T score of 70 is only five points higher than 65 but means that the score is actually equal to or higher than 98% of the population. Although a difference of 5 points might appear minimal upon initial inspection, it actually distinguishes the individual from the rest of the normative group.

Deviation IQs. The IQ, or intelligence quotient, was originally conceptualized as a ratio of mental age to chronological age. However, various problems with calculating IQ in this way were found. For example, it was assumed that mental age was directly correlated with chronological age over time (i.e., mental age increased as chronological age increased), but in fact mental age increases very slowly after an individual reaches the chronological age of 16 and then eventually begins to decline. Thus, most intelligence tests today no longer use the mental age/chronological age formula to compute intelligence; they use *deviation IQ* scores instead. *Deviation IQ* scores have a mean of 100 and a standard deviation of 15. However, the standard deviations may vary depending on the test; for example, the Cognitive Abilities Test (CogAT) uses a standard deviation of 16. In general, most of the major intelligence tests use 15 as the fixed standard deviation.

CEEB Scores (SAT/GRE). CEEB scores are standard scores that were developed by the College Entrance Examination Board (now called the Educational Testing Service [ETS]) and used with tests including the SAT and the GRE. CEEB scores range from 200 to 800 and have a mean of 500 and a standard deviation of 100.

Stanines. *Stanines* (short for *STAndard NINE*) are a type of standard score that convert raw scores into values ranging from 1 to 9, making it possible to translate various kinds of information into one-digit scores. Stanines have a mean of 5 and a standard deviation of 2, and they have a constant relationship to percentiles in that they represent a specific range of percentile scores in the normal curve; that is, a given percentile always falls within the same stanine. Because they categorize test performance into only nine broad units, stanines provide less detail about an examinee's performance than other derived scores. In general, stanines of 1 to 3 are considered below average, stanines of 4 to 6 represent average performance, and stanines of 7 to 9 are above average. A stanine-to-percentile-rank conversion table is presented in Table 4.6. Stanines are widely used in education.

Sten Scores. *Sten scores* (short for *Standard TEN*) are normalized standard scores similar to stanines, but stens range from 1 to 10, have a mean of 5.5, and have a standard deviation of 2. Sten scores of 4 to 7 are considered average, stens of 1 to 3 fall in the low range, and stens of 8 to 10 fall in the high range. A sten-to-percentile-rank conversion table is presented in Table 4.7.

TABLE 4.7 Stanine-to-Percentile-Rank Conversion Table

Stanine	Percentile Rank
1	1–4
2	5–11
3	12–23
4	24–40
5	41–59
6	60–76
7	77–88
8	89–95
9	96–99

TABLE 4.8 Sten-to-Percentile-Rank Conversion Table

Sten	Percentile Rank
1	1–2
2	3–7
3	8–16
4	17–31
5	32–50
6	51–69
7	70–84
8	85–93
9	94–98
10	99–100

Normal Curve Equivalent. The normal curve equivalent (NCE) is a normalized standard score that ranges from 1 to 99, with a mean of 50 and a standard deviation of 21.06. Used primarily in education, an NCE score of 50 represents the national average of any grade level at the time of year the test was normed. NCE scores can be used to compute group statistics, compare the performance of students who take different levels of the same test, compare student performance across subject matter, and evaluate gains over time. To interpret NCEs, it is necessary to relate them to other standard scores, such as percentile ranks or stanines. NCEs may be thought of as roughly equivalent to stanines to one decimal place; for example, an NCE of 73 may be interpreted as a stanine of 7.3. To evaluate a student's gains over time, NCE scores should be interpreted as follows: a zero gain indicates that a student made one year of academic progress after one year of instruction, a positive gain indicates the student made more than one year's progress, and a negative gain indicates less than one year's progress. The main advantage of NCEs is that they are derived through the use of comparable procedures by the publishers of the various tests used in federal (i.e., U.S. Department of Education) research projects.

GRADE AND AGE EQUIVALENTS In addition to percentiles and standard scores, other norm-referenced scores are used for interpreting test performance. We will discuss two scales that implicitly compare the test taker's raw score to the average raw score of people at various developmental levels: age equivalents and grade equivalents. Although we present these forms of test scores in this text, both types have many limitations that make them subject to misinterpretation. Thus, we do not recommend their use as primary scores. If you are required to use age or grade equivalents, never base interpretations on them alone: Always include standard scores and percentile ranks when interpreting test scores.

Grade Equivalents. *Grade equivalents* are norm-referenced, developmental scores that represent the average score for children at various grade levels. They are most frequently used for achievement tests. Grade equivalents are divided into 10 units that correspond to the September-to-June school year. Thus, 5.0 would represent September of the fifth grade, and 5.9 would represent May of fifth grade. A grade-equivalent score is intended to represent a student's test performance in terms of the grade level at which the "average" student's performance matches that of the examinee. For example, a grade-equivalent score of 4.9 indicates that a student's performance is similar to the average performance of students in May of fourth grade. A student who scores above his grade level has performed above the average for students in his grade; likewise, a student who scores below his grade level has scored below the average for students in his grade. Because grade equivalent scores are based on a mean, in a typical grade about half of the students would score below grade level and half above grade level.

Although grade equivalents appear easy to understand, teachers, parents, and professionals must be cautious when interpreting these scores. For example, say that Katy, a fifth-grade student, receives a grade equivalent score of 7.4 on a fifth-grade math test. Katy's parents might assume that this means that she is ready for seventh-grade math instruction. In reality, the score simply means that Katy knows fifth-grade math better than most students at her grade level. Specifically, it means that a typical seventh grader in the fourth month would have received the same score if seventh graders had taken the fifth-grade math test. Thus, the grade equivalent score doesn't indicate how well Katy would perform in seventh-grade math, because she was tested only on fifth-grade math. Grade equivalent scores are not equal units of measurement; thus, they are not as well-suited as standard scores for comparing different scores on the same test or for comparing scores on different tests.

Counselors should consider the following points about grade equivalent scores:

1. Grade equivalent scores are not an estimate of the grade at which the student should be placed.
2. The grade equivalent score of one student cannot be compared to the grade equivalent score of another student.
3. Grade equivalent scores cannot be compared with the scores on other tests.
4. Grade equivalent scores on different subtests of the same test cannot be compared. For example, grade equivalent scores of 4.0 on the reading and math subtests of the same achievement test do not indicate that the student has equal proficiency in the two areas.

Age Equivalents. *Age equivalent* scores represent an examinee's test performance in terms of the age at which the "average" individual's performance matches that of the examinee. For example, an age equivalent score of 9-3 indicates that a person's performance is similar to the average performance of children 9 years and 3 months old. Although age equivalents can be used to describe an examinee's performance in comparison to the typical performance of test takers of various ages, they have the same limitations as grade equivalents. In addition, although age equivalents have meaning when the behaviors being measured have a direct, linear relationship with age, the rate of growth for most behaviors varies from year to year. Thus, an even progression is not always expressed; there may be rapid growth during some periods and a plateau or no growth during others.

QUALITATIVE ASSESSMENT

So far, we have presented information about standard scores, focusing primarily on *quantitative* test scores. However, counselors often collect assessment data that does not lend itself to quantitative evaluation. *Qualitative* assessment methods involve interpretive criteria and descriptions of data. Although our focus in this chapter is on assessment scores, it is important to lend attention to alternate types of data produced during the assessment process. There are many types of qualitative assessment data that can be collected during the assessment process. According to Losardo and Syverson (2011), there are at least nine categories of qualitative assessment, including naturalistic, ecological, focused, performance, portfolio, dynamic, authentic, Functional Behavior Analysis (FBA), and informed clinical opinion.

In order to assess the performance of students in a counselor education program, it is important to examine both quantitative and qualitative data. From a quantitative perspective, test scores and grades can provide a great deal of insight into learning outcome attainment. However, examination of student portfolios that include key projects, resumes, field experience forms, and other materials helps to provide a richer understanding of student performance. Qualitative data has some limitations on its own, but it can be very useful in combination with qualitative data. We will discuss qualitative assessment processes in more detail in Chapter 14.

Although quantitative and qualitative assessment can be separate processes, test developers often provide *qualitative descriptors* in addition to the assignment of numbers to test scores. Qualitative descriptors help professionals communicate test results verbally or in written reports by providing easy-to-understand classifications based on particular score ranges (Reynolds, Livingston, & Willson, 2008). Qualitative descriptors are widely used in intelligence and achievement tests. For example, the Wechsler intelligence tests, a series of standardized assessments used to evaluate cognitive and intellectual abilities in children and adults, provide the following descriptive classifications:

IQ	Classification
130 and above	Very Superior
120–129	Superior
110–119	High Average
90–109	Average
80–89	Low Average
70–79	Borderline
69 and below	Extremely Low

A similar approach is used with many of the typical-performance tests (i.e., personality inventories). Many of these instruments use descriptors such as nonclinical (or normal), borderline clinical range, and clinical range. In general, scores in the clinical range fall well above the mean scores, thus indicating the presence of severe psychological symptoms. Other classification systems divide qualitative descriptors into severe, moderate, and mild categories. An example of this is the BDI-II (Beck, Steer, & Brown, 1996):

Score	Level of Depression
29–63	Severe
20–28	Moderate
14–19	Mild
0–13	No or minimal depression

TABLES AND PROFILES

Often, an instrument will provide results in terms of several different score types. *Tables* are often provided to aid in score interpretation. For example, Figure 4.3 shows a summary report for the BASI, which presents standard scores (with a mean of 100 and a standard

Composite or Subtest	SS	Confidence Interval	%ile	GE	AE
Reading Total	88	83–94	21		
Vocabulary	87	80–96	19	<3.0	8–0
Reading Comprehension	92	85–100	30	<3.0	8–9
Written Language Total	91	85–97	27		
Spelling	99	99–107	47	4.6	9–8
Language Mechanics	87	79–97	19	3.6	<8–0
Math Total	126	116–132	96		
Math Computation	126	116–132	96	9.1	14–6
Math Application	126	111–130	94	12.8	17–11

SS = Standard Score (mean = 100, SD = 15), %ile =Percentile Rank, GE =Grade Equivalent, AE =Age Equivalent

FIGURE 4.3   Sample scores for the BASI.

Exercise 4.1
Interpreting Test Scores: Marisol

Marisol, age 11, is in the fifth grade. The following table contains her scores on the BASI, an achievement test battery that measures math, reading, and language skills for children and adults. It provides scores on three composites and six subtests. The composites are Reading Total, Written Language Total, and Math Total. The subtests are Vocabulary, Reading Comprehension, Spelling, Language Mechanics, Math Computation, and Math Application.

Composite or Subtest	SS	Confidence Interval	%ile	GE	AE
Reading Total	88	83–94	21		
Vocabulary	87	80–96	19	<3.0	8–0
Reading Comprehension	92	85–100	30	<3.0	8–9
Written Language Total	91	85–97	27		
Spelling	99	91–107	47	4.6	9–8
Language Mechanics	87	79–97	19	3.6	<8–0
Math Total	126	116–132	96		
Math Computation	126	116–132	96	9.1	14–6
Math Application	123	111–130	94	12.8	17–11

SS = Standard Score (mean = 100, SD = 15), %ile = Percentile Rank, GE = Grade Equivalent, AE = Age Equivalent

1. Interpret the standard scores on the Reading Total, Written Language Total, and Math Total.
2. Interpret the percentile ranks on the Reading Total, Written Language Total, and Math Total.
3. Interpret the stanine scores on the Reading Total, Written Language Total, and Math Total.
4. Interpret the grade equivalent scores on the Vocabulary and Math Computation subtests.
5. Interpret the age equivalent score on the Reading comprehension test and the Math Application subtests.
6. Explain the meaning of the confidence intervals for Reading Total, Written Language Total, and Math Total.

deviation of 15), percentile ranks, growth scale values, grade equivalents, and age equivalents. Results may also include confidence intervals, which indicate the range of standard scores that likely includes the test taker's true score (see Chapter 5).

Profiles also help in interpreting results by providing a visual representation of scores. Guidelines for interpreting charts and profiles include the following:

1. Small differences should not be over interpreted.
2. The normal curve can be used as a frame of reference to interpret standard scores.
3. The standard error of measurement should be used in interpretation.
4. Patterns in the shape of a profile are important (are the scores all high or low?).

Professional

Business Communication

Clerical ## Service

Consumer
Outdoor ## Science ## Arts

Skilled

Economics ## Technology

FIGURE 4.4   Word Cloud Representation of California Occupational Profile Scales.

NORM REFERENCED, CRITERION REFERENCED, OR BOTH?

In this chapter, we presented the two major approaches for interpreting test scores: criterion-referenced and norm-referenced interpretation. Can a test be interpreted using both approaches? The quick answer is "yes," but there are some reasons that it is usually best for tests to be explained using either norm-referenced *or* criterion-referenced interpretation—not both. To understand these reasons, we must first recognize that tests can be broadly categorized as either maximum-performance tests or as typical-performance tests. *Maximum-performance tests* generally measure one's *best* performance. The test items have correct or incorrect answers, and test takers are directed, at least implicitly, to achieve the best or highest score possible. Examples of maximum-performance tests include aptitude, intelligence, and achievement tests. *Typical-performance tests* are designed to measure one's usual or normal performance; in other words, what a test taker is really like, rather than his or her ability. Test items do not have right or wrong answers, and examples of typical-performance tests are personality, attitude, and interest tests. Norm-referenced interpretation can be applied to both types. However, because criterion-referenced scores specifically reflect an examinee's achievement or knowledge about a particular content area, it makes sense that they be used only with maximum-performance tests (Reynolds et al., 2008). Let's use the BDI–II—a type of personality test that measures an individual's level of depression—as an example. The test includes cutoff scores that distinguish various levels of depression; if an individual scores above 29, this would indicate that he or she is severely depressed. A criterion-referenced interpretation of this test score would mean that a person has mastered the knowledge and skills to be depressed. As you can see, it is just not logical to interpret the score in this way. Criterion-referenced interpretation lends itself better to educational achievement tests or other tests designed to measure one's skills or abilities.

Another reason for choosing *either* norm-referenced *or* criterion-referenced interpretation involves the comprehensiveness or breadth of the construct being measured. Some constructs that assess a broad range of variables, such as intelligence or personality, lend themselves best to norm-referenced interpretations (Reynolds et al., 2008). In contrast, criterion-referenced interpretation is often applied to more narrowly defined constructs, such as educational tests that assess mastery of a single subject area, like math or spelling. Even the construct of achievement, which is commonly interpreted with criterion-referenced scores, is often better suited for norm-referenced interpretations when achievement tests cover more extensive knowledge and skill domains.

A comparison of the various types of scores is presented in Table 4.9.

TABLE 4.9 Comparison of Different Types of Scores

Type of Score	Advantages	Disadvantages
Raw	Gives precise number of points scored on a test easy to compute.	Cannot be interpreted or compared.
Percentile rank	Shows how the test taker's score ranks in relation to the national or local norm. Easily understood by most test takers.	Not an equal-interval scale; uses ordinal units of measurement. Cannot be added or averaged. Can be confused with percentages.
Standard	Show the relative performance of a test taker within a group. Derived from properties of the normal curve. Equal-interval scale of measurement. Can be averaged and correlated. Comparable from test to test if reference groups are equivalent.	Inappropriate if data are markedly skewed. Hard to explain to test takers.
Stanine	One-digit scores. Can be averaged. Used for simplicity and utility.	May not provide enough scoring units to differentiate among scores. Insensitive to sizable differences within a stanine. Misleadingly sensitive to small differences on either side of the point separating adjacent stanines.
Grade and age equivalents	Good if area measured is systematically related with age or grade level. Compares an individual's performance with the average for that age or grade.	Uses unequal units of measurement. Leads to score interpretation that is too literal. Can mislead in the case of scores that do not signify an ability to perform or understand at the higher grade level. Has little practical meaning beyond sixth grade or age 12.

Summary

This chapter presented information about understanding test scores. For counselors to understand and interpret assessment results, raw scores need to be transformed using some frame of reference to give meaning to test results. In general, scores can be divided into two broad classifications: criterion-referenced scores and norm-referenced scores. Interpreting test scores can involve relating the score to a performance level (criterion referenced) or comparing it to the scores of a norm group (norm referenced). Standard scores provide a basis to interpret scores by describing how many standard deviations an individual's score is from the mean. There are numerous types of standard scores, including z scores, T scores, deviation IQs, stanines, sten scores, and other standard score scales.

Questions for Discussion

1. What are the differences in interpreting norm-referenced and criterion-referenced scores?
2. What are the different types of standard scores used in norm-referenced testing? Discuss when you would use each type of score, and analyze the strengths and limitations of each type of score.
3. If you were developing a new achievement test for college students, how would you select your norming group? If you were developing a new inventory measuring personality types, how would you select an appropriate norming group?

Suggested Activities

1. Write a position paper on one of the following topics: bias in test scoring, use of grade equivalents, norm-referenced versus criterion-referenced interpretation, or selecting appropriate norms.
2. Explain the differences among raw scores, standard scores, and normalized standard scores.
3. Select any five students from the distribution of test scores in Table 4.3, and convert their raw scores into percentiles.
4. Jeffrey, a college senior, earned a raw score of 52 on a chemical engineering midterm exam. Assuming that the mean of scores was 40 and the standard deviation was 12, convert Jeffrey's raw score into a T score.
5. A parent has brought you the following Stanford Achievement Test results for her child, who is in fourth grade:

Subtests	Scaled Score	Percentile	NCE	Stanine	Grade Equivalent
Reading	639	59	54.8	5	5.4
Mathematics	633	57	57.5	5	5.5
Language	610	39	44.1	4	3.5
Spelling	647	73	62.9	6	6.4
Science	643	69	60.4	6	6.3
Social Science	607	40	44.7	4	3.5
Listening	608	35	41.9	4	3.4
Thinking Skills	623	56	53.2	5	5.1

The parent doesn't understand the types of scores and the results and wants you to help her interpret them. What would you tell her?

References

Angoff, W. H. (1971). Scales, norms, and equivalent scores. In R. L. Thorndike (Ed.), *Educational measurement* (2nd ed., pp. 508–600). Washington, DC: American Council on Education.

Bardos, A. N. (2004). *Basic Achievement Skills Inventory (BASI)–comprehensive*. Minneapolis, MN: Pearson Assessments.

Beck, A. T., Steer, R. A., & Brown, G. K. (1996). *BDI-II manual.* San Antonio, TX: Psychological Corporation.

Foa, E. B. (1995). *The Posttraumatic Diagnostic Scale manual.* Minneapolis, MN: Pearson Assessments.

Kaufman, A. S., & Kaufman, N. L. (2004). *KBIT-2: Kaufman Brief Intelligence Test* (2nd ed.). Circle Pines, MN: AGS.

Losardo, A., & Syverson, A. N. (2011). *Alternative approaches to assessing young children.* Baltimore, MD: Brookes Publishing.

Pearson Inc. (2004). *Stanford Achievement Test series, tenth edition technical data report.* San Antonio, TX: Author.

Reynolds, C. R., Livingston, R. B., & Willson, V. (2008) *Measurement and assessment in education* (2nd ed.). Boston, MA: Pearson.

Thorndike, R. M. (2011). *Measurement and evaluation in psychology and education* (8th ed.). Upper Saddle River, NJ: Pearson Education.

United States Census Bureau. (2014). USA quick facts. Retrieved from http://quickfacts.census.gov/qfd/states/00000.html

Wilkinson, G. S., & Robertson, G. J. (2006). *Wide Range Achievement Test 4 professional manual.* Lutz, FL: Psychological Assessment Resources.

5   Reliability/Precision

Reliability/precision is the psychometric property concerned with the consistency, dependability, and reproducibility of test scores (American Educational Research Association (AERA), American Psychological Association (APA), & National Council on Measurement in Education (NCME), 2014). For example, if you weighed yourself on the same bathroom scale five times in succession, would you weigh the same amount each time? If the scale reads the same weight each time, then the results are said to be reliable and precise, because the measurement is consistent. However, if the scale fluctuates and produces different results on each weighing, then the scores are said to be *unreliable*, which means that your weight scores were affected by sources of error (i.e., measurement error) that were irrelevant to how much you actually weighed. As you might guess, consistency and precision are very important aspects of assessment. As counselors, we want to be sure that an assessment instrument designed to help with the diagnostic process would produce the same results if, for example, we tested the same person five times in succession. Thus, it is important to be knowledgeable about the concept of reliability and how it applies to assessment.

In order to understand reliability/precision, we review a number of formulas and will likely activate any math phobia that you may have. Although the information may require additional time for review, the formulas are important for understanding the complexity of reliability. However, as you select assessment instruments or review journal articles related to assessment, reliability will likely be reported for you. It will be your job to interpret the reported reliability and determine the acceptable degree of reliability for the assessment you are performing. If you conduct research on assessment instruments or develop assessment instruments, then the calculation of reliability becomes more salient.

A variety of statistical methods may be used to evaluate the impact of measurement error on test score reliability. Reliability of test scores can be estimated across time (test-retest), across different forms of the same instrument (alternate forms), or across items within a single instrument (internal consistency). All instruments have some degree of inconsistency, meaning that there are measurement errors that can reduce the reliability of test scores.

After studying this chapter, you should be able to:
- Define and explain the importance of *reliability* in assessment.
- Define and explain the concept of *measurement error*.

- Describe and provide examples of the major sources of measurement error.
- Identify the major methods of estimating reliability and describe their relationship to the various sources of measurement error.
- Describe the factors that should be considered when selecting a reliability coefficient.
- Describe the factors that should be considered when evaluating the magnitude of reliability coefficients.
- Define *standard error of measurement* and explain its relationship to reliability.
- Explain how confidence intervals are calculated and what they mean in psychological and educational assessment.
- Describe the various ways of increasing the reliability of instrument scores.

RELIABILITY

Reliability/precision is one of the most important characteristics of assessment results. Because many important decisions about individuals are based, wholly or in part, on the basis of instrument scores, we need to make sure that the scores are reliable. In the context of measurement, *reliability/precision* refers to the degree to which test scores are dependable, consistent, and stable across items of a test, across different forms of the test, or across repeat administrations of the test. For example, if we administered a test to an individual on two separate occasions, how consistent would the two scores be? Say that a counselor administered the Wide Range Achievement Test (WRAT4) to a client on Monday morning and discovered that the scores indicated average achievement. If the counselor administered the WRAT4 to the same client on Monday afternoon, would the client score the same way the second time as he did the first time? If the client felt more fatigued in the afternoon rather than the morning, might that affect his score? What if the client remembered some of the test questions from the first testing? Would that affect how he performed on the test the second time? Instead of administering the test twice, what if the counselor used two separate forms of the test—that is, form A and form B? Would the client perform better on one test form than the other? What if the counselor asked another counselor to help score the WRAT4? Would the client receive the same score no matter which counselor scored the instrument?

As you can see from these examples, numerous factors can affect reliability/precision and whether a test produces consistent scores. To correctly interpret the results of a test, we need to have evidence that the scores from the test would be stable and consistent if the test were repeated on the same individual. In other words, we need to know the degree to which test scores are reliable.

When referring to reliability/precision in relation to assessment, consider the following points:

1. Reliability/precision refers to the *results* obtained with an assessment instrument, not the instrument itself (Miller, Linn, & Gronlund, 2012).
2. An estimate of reliability/precision always refers to a *specific type of reliability/precision*. The reliability/precision of instrument scores may be based on certain intervals of time, the items on the instrument, different raters, and so on. Instrument developers provide estimates of the specific types of reliability/precision, depending on the use of test results.

3. Scores on assessment instruments are rarely totally consistent or error free. In fact, *all instruments are subject to some degree of error and fluctuation* (Urbina, 2014). Therefore, counselors must evaluate the evidence to determine whether an instrument's results have an adequate degree of reliability/precision.

Measurement Error

A critical issue in assessment is the amount of measurement error in any instrument. We know that the same individual tested on different occasions would score differently, even on the same test. This difference is equated with measurement error. In testing, *measurement error* may be defined as any fluctuation in scores that results from factors related to the measurement process that are irrelevant to what is being measured (Urbina, 2014). These fluctuations could result from factors unique to the test taker, flaws in testing procedures, or simply from random chance. For example, the test taker may guess better during one test administration than during another, know more of the content on one test form than another, or be less fatigued or less anxious during one time than another. Alternately, the items on a test may not adequately represent the content domain being tested, or test takers may get different test results depending on the person grading the test. These are all factors that can cause measurement errors—that is, changes in an individual's scores from one occasion to the next. The greater the amount of measurement error on test scores, the lower the reliability/precision.

Measurement error may also be understood as the difference between an individual's observed (or obtained) score and his or her true score. The *true score* is considered the true, 100% accurate reflection of one's ability, skills, or knowledge (i.e., the score that would be obtained if there were no errors; Boyd, Lankford, Loeb, & Wyckoff, 2013). The *observed score* is the actual score a test taker received on a test. If a person could be tested repeatedly (without carryover or practice effects), the average of the obtained scores would approximate the true score. The observed score is made up of two components: the true score and measurement error. This can be represented in a very simple equation:

$$\text{Observed Score} = \text{True Score} + \text{Measurement Error}$$

This formula demonstrates that measurement error may raise or lower the observed score. As stated earlier, error represents any other factor that randomly affects the measurement process; therefore, the less error, the more reliable the observed score.

The concept of true scores is completely theoretical; we can only hypothesize what a true score might be. However, we can estimate the score range, or at least the boundaries, within which a true score may fall. We do this by calculating the *standard error of measurement* (SEM), which is a simple measure of how much an individual's test score varies from the true score. SEM will be discussed later in the chapter.

Sources of Measurement Error

As mentioned earlier, some degree of error is inherent in all instrument scores, and there are various sources of measurement error. In identifying sources of error, we are trying to answer this question: What causes the difference between an individual's true score and his or her actual observed score? The most common forms of measurement error are time-sampling error and content-sampling error. These forms, along with other common sources of measurement error, are presented in this section.

TIME-SAMPLING ERROR *Time-sampling error* is associated with the fluctuation in test scores obtained from repeated testing of the same individual. With time-sampling error, it is assumed that whatever construct being measured may vacillate over time. In other words, how an individual performs on an intelligence test today will most likely have a degree of difference from how he or she performs next time on the same test. How large the difference is between the intelligence test scores is important. Because of time-sampling error, we might expect that the scores will differ (either positively or negatively) by only a couple of points. If an individual scored 100 (50th percentile) one week and then 115 (84th percentile) the next week, we would be quite suspicious of the score differential. Intelligence is not a construct that changes dramatically.

Constructs differ in their susceptibility to time-sampling error; for example, most constructs related to personality traits (e.g., introvert/extrovert) and abilities (e.g., verbal comprehension, spatial reasoning) are usually less prone to fluctuation over time (Urbina, 2014). In contrast, some constructs associated with emotional states (e.g., depression, anxiety) and achievement are more susceptible to the influence of transient conditions and can vary widely over time. As a rule, we assume that time-sampling error enters into the scores on tests that are given repeatedly; however, one should expect less time-sampling error in tests that measure relatively stable traits (Urbina, 2014).

Several specific issues associated with time-sampling error are related to the length of the time interval between test administrations. If the time interval is too short (e.g., a day or two), then there is an increased risk of a *carryover effect*, which occurs when the first testing session influences the scores on the second session (Kaplan & Saccuzzo, 2013). For example, test takers may remember their answers from the first test administration, thus inflating their scores on the second test administration. Similar to this is *practice effect*. Because some skills improve with practice, when an instrument is given a second time, test takers' scores may increase because they have sharpened their skills by having taken the test the first time. If the length of time between tests is too long, then we may be faced with test results confounded with *learning*, *maturation* (i.e., changes in the test takers themselves that occur over time), or other *intervening experiences* (i.e., treatment).

CONTENT-SAMPLING ERROR Assessment instruments typically cannot include every possible item or question relevant to the specific content area, dimension, or construct being measured. For example, a spelling test cannot include every word in the dictionary, and a personality inventory cannot include every one of the thousands of traits or characteristics that make up the construct of personality. However, each of these instruments can select items that adequately represent the content domain being measured. Thus, test items can be thought of as a random sample taken from an infinitely large number of possible items relevant to a particular content domain.

An instrument that does not include items that adequately represent the content domain has an increased risk of content-sampling error. *Content-sampling error* (also called *domain sampling* or *item sampling*) is the term used to label the error that results from selecting test items that inadequately cover the content area that the test is supposed to evaluate. Test items that poorly represent the domain or universe of knowledge on a particular construct increase content-sampling error and decrease reliability/precision. Content-sampling error is considered the largest source of error in instrument scores. Estimating content sampling errors involves evaluating the extent to which an instrument's items or components measure the same construct or content domain. This is achieved by analyzing the interrelationships among test items and components (e.g., scales, subtests). Methods for estimating content-sampling error will be discussed later in this chapter.

INTERRATER DIFFERENCES Instruments involving observation require the use of raters (i.e., observers, scorers, judges) to record and score the behaviors of others. When instrument results rely heavily on the subjective judgment of the individual scoring the test, it is important to consider differences in scorers as a potential source of error. For example, say that two raters are recording the number of times a third-grade student is out of seat in class. Without a definition of *out of seat*, it is difficult to accurately observe the behavior. For example, one rater might classify out of seat as having no contact with the seat and thus record every occurrence when the student leaves full contact with his seat; another observer might classify out of seat as any time the student's bottom is out of contact with the desk. The difference in definitions could lead to differences in agreement about the out-of-seat behavior. This lack of agreement results in discrepancies between the student's true score and his observed score as recorded by the raters. It is assumed that different raters will not always assign the same scores or ratings to a given test performance, even if the scoring directions specified in the test manual are explicit and the raters are conscientious in applying those directions (Urbina, 2014). To assess interrater differences, we need to estimate the reliability/precision of the raters, which is usually referred to as *interrater reliability* (also called *interscorer reliability*). This will be discussed later in the chapter.

OTHER SOURCES OF ERROR Content-sampling error and time-sampling error account for the major proportion of measurement error in all types of instruments, and interrater differences are associated with error in instruments involving behavior observations. In addition to these, other sources may contribute to the random error in test scores, including the following:

- *Quality of Test Items* Quality of test items refers to how well test items are constructed. If items are clear and focused, then they will provide reliable information about the construct being measured. If items are vague and ambiguous, then they are open to many interpretations, which may confuse test takers and result in unreliable test scores.
- *Test Length* In general, as the number of items on any test increases, the test represents the content domain being measured more accurately. Thus, the greater the number of items, the greater the reliability/precision.
- *Test-Taker Variables* Certain test-taker variables can affect reliability/precision by influencing the individual's performance on a test. Motivation, fatigue, illness, physical discomfort, and mood can all be sources of error variance.
- *Test Administration* Sources of measurement error that occur during test administration may interfere with an individual's test results, such as the examiner not following specified administration instructions, room temperature, lighting, noise, and critical incidents occurring during test administration.

METHODS OF ESTIMATING RELIABILITY/PRECISION

Now that we have described the various sources of measurement error, we will present several methods of estimating reliability/precision applicable to those sources of error. Although the psychometric properties (including reliability/precision) of most assessment instruments are available for review (e.g., Mental Measurements Database, test publishers, Association for Assessment and Research in Counseling [AARC] test reviews) when you are selecting an instrument, it is important to understand the manner in which reliability/precision is calculated so that you can evaluate the reported reliability coefficients. In many cases, test developers and researchers estimate reliability/precision using more than one method. The format and nature of the test will dictate the methods of reliability/precision that are applicable.

As stated earlier, reliability/precision reflects the consistency, dependability, and reproducibility of scores upon additional test administrations—and those additional test administrations can take place at different times, involve the use of different forms of the same test, or some combination of the former and latter. The methods most often used to estimate reliability/precision involve correlating two sets of test scores to obtain a *reliability coefficient*, which is the same as any correlation coefficient, except that it specifically represents the reliability/precision of test scores. Conceptually, reliability/precision can be interpreted as the amount of the variability of the observed scores that is explained by the variability of the true scores; thus, the reliability/precision coefficient is the ratio of the true score variance to the observed score variance:

$$r = \frac{s_T^2}{s_X^2}$$

where

r = the reliability coefficient

s_T^2 = the variance of the true scores

s_X^2 = the variance of the observed scores

In this formula, the *variance* of true scores and observed scores is used because we are looking at the score variability of a group of examinees. Thus, reliability coefficients always relate to a *group* of test scores, not to an *individual* score. The closer the reliability coefficient is to 1.00, the more the observed score approximates the true score, and the better the reliability/precision. In other words, the higher the reliability coefficient, the more that variation in test scores is due to actual differences among the test takers in whatever characteristic or trait is being measured. The closer reliability coefficients are to 0, the more that test scores represent random error, not actual test-taker performance.

The reliability coefficient can also be thought of as a percentage. If we subtract the reliability coefficient from 1.00, we have the percentage of the observed variation that is attributable to random chance or error:

$$\text{Error} = 1 - r$$

For example, suppose that college students must take an admissions test to be eligible to enroll in a particular academic program, and the reliability coefficient of the test is .35. This means that 35% of the variation in scores is explained by real differences, and 65% of the differences must be attributed to random chance or error, because $1 - .35 = .65$. How likely would you be to accept an admission decision based on this test score? If a test of this nature was the only criteria for admission, then you would want to have a high degree of certainty that differences in scores of applicants are due to different ability rather than error.

TABLE 5.1 Methods of Estimating Reliability

Method	Procedure	Coefficient	Sources of Error
Test-Retest	Same test given twice with a time interval between testings	Stability	Time sampling
Alternate Forms			
Simultaneous Administration	Equivalent tests given at the same time	Equivalence	Content sampling
Delayed Administration	Equivalent tests given with a time interval between testings	Stability and equivalence	Time sampling and content sampling
Internal Consistency			
Split-Half	One test is divided into two comparable halves, and both halves are given during one testing session	Equivalence and internal consistency	Content sampling
Kuder–Richardson Formulas (KR) and Coefficient Alpha	One test given at one time (items compared to other items or to the whole test)	Internal consistency	Content sampling
Interrater	One test given, and two individuals independently score the test	Interrater agreement	Interrater differences

Reliability/precision is usually estimated using one of four methods: test-retest, alternate forms, internal consistency, and interrater reliability. Each of these methods provides a reliability coefficient that reflects its particular source(s) of error (e.g., time sampling, content sampling, interrater differences). No method of estimating reliability/precision is perfect; each method has strengths and weaknesses that we will review. Table 5.1 describes the major methods of estimating reliability.

Test-Retest

The *test-retest* method is one of the oldest and perhaps one of the most commonly used methods of estimating the reliability/precision of test scores. Reliability/precision is concerned with the consistency of test scores, and the test-retest method directly assesses the consistency of test takers' scores from one test administration to the next (Murphy & Davidshofer, 2005). An estimate of test-retest reliability is relatively easy to calculate: simply administer the same instrument on two separate occasions and then correlate the first set of scores with the second. This correlation is called a *coefficient of stability*, because it reflects the stability of test scores over time.

Because test-retest reliability estimates error related to time sampling, the time interval between the two test administrations must be specified, because it will affect the stability of the scores. Although there is no fixed time interval that can be recommended for all tests, we know that if the interval is very short, then such factors as carryover effect and practice effect could influence scores on the second test administration. On the other hand, if the interval is very long, then learning, maturation, or intervening experiences may affect the scores on the second occasion (Resch et al., 2013).

The test-retest method is most useful when measuring traits, abilities, or characteristics that are stable and do not change over time. For example, one would *not* expect adult intelligence test scores to change between two separate test administrations, because intellectual ability typically remains stable through adulthood (assuming that no unusual circumstances, such as brain injury, affect it). As such, we would expect test-retest reliability for intelligence test scores to be high; specifically, there would be a strong correlation between the results of the first test administration and the results of the second test administration. Instruments that measure variables that are transient and constantly changing are not appropriate for test-retest evaluation. For example, a mood state (e.g., an individual's level of mood at an exact moment in time) can fluctuate from day to day, hour to hour, and even moment to moment (Furr & Bacharach, 2013). In this case, the scores on a particular mood-state inventory would not be stable during any significant time interval. Thus, test-retest reliability on the inventory scores would be low. This could be mistakenly interpreted as the inventory's scores not being reliable when, in reality, the reliability coefficient is reflecting the individual's change in mood across the two testing occasions.

Thus, when reviewing test-retest reliability in an instrument manual, it is important to consider two things: (1) the length of the time interval between test administrations and (2) the type of construct being tested. Examples of test-retest reliability as reported in test manuals include the following:

- On the Multidimensional Self-Esteem Inventory (MSEI), the test-retest coefficient on the Global Self-Esteem scale was .87 over a 1-month interval.
- The subset of 208 college students in a 3-month retest on the five domains of the NEO Personality Inventory-Revised (NEO PI-R) resulted in coefficients of .79, .79, .80, .75, and .83 for neuroticism, extraversion, openness, agreeableness, and conscientiousness, respectively.
- The test-retest coefficients on the Vocational Preference Inventory (VPI) for a group of 100 females on the Realistic scale were .79 over 2 weeks, .57 over 2 months, .86 over 1 year, and .58 over 4 years.

Alternate Form

Alternate form reliability, also called *parallel forms* reliability, helps us determine whether two equivalent forms of the same test are really equivalent. The two forms use different items, but the items come from the same content domain. In addition, the forms have the same number of items, use the same type of format, have almost equal difficulty, and include the same directions for administering, scoring, and interpreting the test. There are two procedures for establishing alternate forms reliability: simultaneous administration and delayed administration (Reynolds, Livingston, & Willson, 2009). *Simultaneous administration* involves giving the two forms of the test *simultaneously*—that is, to the same group of people on the same day. This procedure eliminates the problem of memory and practice, which affects test-retest reliability. *Delayed administration* involves giving the two forms on two different occasions. Alternate form reliability based on simultaneous administration is sensitive to sources of error related to content sampling. The resulting correlation, called a *coefficient of equivalence*, tells us how closely the two forms measure the same construct. Alternate form reliability based on delayed administration reflects both content-sampling and time-sampling errors; it provides both a *coefficient of stability* (because an individual's behavior is measured at two different times) and a coefficient of equivalence. The following are examples of alternate forms reliability as reported in test manuals:

- On the Peabody Picture Vocabulary Test (PPVT-4), correlations between Form A and Form B standard scores for five age groups were reported. The alternate form reliabilities are very high, falling between .87 and .93.
- With regard to alternate form reliability for the two forms of the WRAT4, correlations between each form's raw scores for the Reading, Spelling, and Arithmetic subtests are .98, .98, and .98, respectively.

A limitation to the alternate forms approach to estimating reliability/precision is that relatively few tests, standardized or teacher made, have alternate forms (Reynolds, Livingston, & Willson, 2009). Some of the comprehensive achievement tests and aptitude batteries may have two or more forms, but most do not. The process of developing an equivalent test form is time-consuming and requires considerable planning and effort, because the forms must truly be parallel in terms of content, difficulty, and other factors; thus, most test developers do not pursue this option.

Internal Consistency Reliability

Internal consistency reliability, as the name implies, is concerned with the interrelatedness of items within an instrument. It is another method of estimating reliability/precision that reflects errors associated with content sampling; that is, it evaluates the extent to which the items on a test measure the same ability or trait. This method bases reliability/precision on the relationship among items within a test; in other words, internal consistency tells us how well each item relates independently to other items on a test and how well the items relate to the overall test score. High internal consistency reliability means that test items are *homogeneous*, which increases confidence that items assess a single construct. The concept of internal consistency can be confusing. In order to illustrate the concept, consider a test of depression that uses a Likert scale. The questions on the instrument all relate to symptoms of depression and level of depression. Because the items are all related to depression, you can expect that the items all correlate with each other or are consistent. If the items all correlate strongly, then there is a high degree of internal consistency.

Internal consistency estimates have practical appeal, because they require only a single test and a single test administration to gather the initial psychometric property, in contrast to other reliability/precision methods that require two or more testings or two forms of the same test. Typical ways of computing internal consistency reliability coefficients include the split-half method, the Kuder–Richardson (KR) formulas, and the coefficient alpha. As is the case with most assessment instruments, test publishers typically provide an estimate of internal consistency in their technical manuals.

SPLIT-HALF RELIABILITY In estimating *split-half reliability*, a test is divided into two comparable halves, and both halves are given during one testing session. The results on one half of the test are then correlated with the results on the other half of the test, resulting in a coefficient of equivalence that demonstrates similarity between the two halves. Once again, this process is often used when test developers and researchers are attempting to evaluate the psychometric properties of an instrument. The split-half reliability estimate is often reported in a technical manual for a test.

For example, when Ayeni (2012) developed the Social Anxiety Scale, she administered it to 464 participants and then evaluated the psychometric properties of the instrument based on the data collected. Based on her research, she was able to estimate that the total split-half reliability was .87, indicating an acceptable degree of relationship between halves of the test. What does the split-half coefficient mean in this case? The result indicates consistency in the test: It tells us that one half of the test is consistent with the other and that the items consistently measure the construct of social anxiety.

There are various ways of dividing tests in half: separate the first half of the test from the second half, assign test items randomly to one half or the other, or assign odd-numbered items to one half and even-numbered items to the other half. The calculation of reliability/precision is based on the full length of a test. Because we are comparing the relationship between two halves rather than full-length tests, we use an adjusted formula commonly referred to as the *Spearman–Brown prophecy formula* to calculate the coefficient. This formula provides an estimate of what the coefficient would be if each half had been the length of the whole test. The formula is as follows:

$$\text{Reliability of Full Test} = \frac{2r}{1 + r}$$

In this formula, r represents the correlation between the two halves of the test. If the correlation is .60, we can substitute the coefficient in the formula and calculate a reliability/precision estimate for the full test:

$$\text{Reliability of Full Test} = \frac{2(.60)}{1 + (.60)} = \frac{1.20}{1.60} = .75$$

The reliability coefficient of .75 estimates the reliability/precision of the full test when the two halves are correlated at .60. When you see a reliability coefficient reported as a Spearman–Brown coefficient, you automatically know that reliability/precision has been assessed using the split-half method.

An advantage of the split-half method of estimating reliability/precision is that it involves administering a test on a single occasion (Beckstead, 2013). However, because only one testing is involved, this approach reflects errors due only to content sampling; it is not sensitive to time-sampling errors.

THE KUDER–RICHARDSON FORMULAS The *Kuder–Richardson formulas* (known as the KR 20 and KR 21) are widely used alternatives to the split-half method of estimating internal consistency. Like other estimates, these are often reported in the professional literature when discussing psychometric properties of assessment instruments. The KR 20 and KR 21 are special-case calculations for tests that have dichotomous items. In other words, the KR 20 and KR 21 are used for items that are answered as simply right or wrong, with 0 indicating an incorrect answer and 1 a correct answer. The formulas were developed by Kuder and Richardson in 1937 to calculate the reliability/precision of a test by using a single form and a single test administration, without arbitrarily dividing the test into halves (Kuder & Richardson, 1937). Using the formulas is tantamount to doing a split-half reliability on all combinations of items resulting from different splits of the test. The KR 20 formula is as follows:

$$r = \frac{N}{N-1}\left(1 - \frac{\Sigma pq}{s^2}\right)$$

where

r = reliability

N = number of items on the test

Σ = summation

p = percentage of examinees that get each item correct

q = percentage of examinees get each item incorrect

s^2 = the variance of the test

To apply this formula, say that you wish to see how well the items on a five-item test are related to each other. You could begin by calculating the percentage of examinees that got each item correct and the percentage that got each item incorrect. This could be displayed as follows:

Item	1	2	3	4	5
p	.5	.4	.8	.6	.7
q	.5	.6	.2	.4	.3
pq	.25	.24	.16	.24	.21

This shows that 50% of the examinees answered item 1 correctly, and 50% answered it incorrectly; 40% of examinees answered item 2 correctly, and 60% answered it incorrectly; and so on. If we calculate the variance of the test ($s^2 = 2.00$), then we can plug the remaining numbers into the KR 20 formula:

$$r = \frac{5}{5-1}\left(1 - \frac{.25 + .24 + .16 + .24 + .21}{2.00}\right)$$

$$= \frac{5}{4}\left(1 - \frac{1.10}{2.00}\right)$$

$$= 1.25(.45)$$

$$= .56$$

The KR 21 formula is very similar to the KR 20. The KR 21 is used to calculate the reliability/precision of dichotomous items that are homogeneous or about the same level of difficulty. The only difference between the KR 20 and KR 21 equations is that instead of calculating the p's and q's for every item and summing the results, we simply use the mean test score ($\overline{X}$). The KR 21 formula is as follows:

$$r = \frac{N}{N-1}\left[1 - \frac{\overline{X}\left(1 - \frac{\overline{X}}{N}\right)}{s^2}\right]$$

Suppose we gave an 80-item test, and the mean score ($\overline{X}$) was 50, and the variance (S^2) was 100. The KR 21 reliability is computed as follows:

$$r = \frac{80}{80 - 1}\left[1 - \frac{50\left(1 - \dfrac{50}{80}\right)}{100}\right]$$

$$= \frac{80}{79}\left[1 - \frac{50(.375)}{100}\right]$$

$$= 1.013\left[1 - \frac{18.75}{100}\right]$$

$$= 1.013[1 - .1875]$$

$$= 1.013[0.8125]$$

$$= .82$$

COEFFICIENT ALPHA Another internal consistency method of estimating reliability/precision is called the *coefficient alpha* (also called *Cronbach's Alpha*; Cronbach, 1951). This method is used when the items on a test are *not* scored dichotomously; that is, there are no "right" or "wrong" answers. An example of this is a rating scale that requires test takers to indicate whether they *strongly disagree, disagree,* are *neutral, agree,* or *strongly agree* with test items.

The formula for the coefficient alpha is as follows:

$$\alpha = \frac{N}{N - 1}\left(\frac{s^2 - \Sigma s_i^2}{s^2}\right)$$

The coefficient alpha formula is similar to the KR 20 formula, except Σpq has been replaced by Σs_i^2. This new term, s_i^2, stands for the variance of the individual items (i). This means that instead of summing the proportion of correct and incorrect answers we sum the individual item variance. This subtle change in the formula allows us to describe the variance in test items that have multiple possible responses, not just items with a right/wrong format.

The formula for Cronbach's Alpha is equal to and produces the same result as KR 20 but is not limited to dichotomous items. As a result, Cronbach's Alpha has been increasingly used in place of KR 20 as a reliability estimate (Suter, 2012). Although different issues must be considered when selecting a reliability/precision calculation, coefficient alpha has become the primary measure. As you begin the process of evaluating instruments for use in counseling practice, it will be important to have a thorough understanding of Cronbach's Alpha.

Interrater Reliability

As described earlier, tests that require direct observation of behavior rely on use of raters (i.e., observers, scorers, judges) to record and score the behaviors. A potential source of error with observations is a lack of agreement (i.e., lack of reliability/precision) among individuals who score the test. *Interrater reliability* is the extent to which two or more raters agree. Say that two raters use a 4-point scale (1 means least effective and 4 means most effective) to rate an individual's communication skills. Interrater reliability assesses how consistently the raters implement the rating scale. For example, if one rater scores a 1 for the individual's response and another scores a 4 for the same response, then this would mean that the two raters do not agree on the score and that there is low interrater reliability.

There are various ways to estimate interrater reliability, but the basic method for assessing the level of agreement among observers is by correlating the scores obtained independently by two or more raters. Very high and positive correlations, in the order of .90 or higher, suggest that the proportion of error that is accounted for by interrater differences is 10% or less, because $1 - (.90) = .10$ (Urbina, 2014). It is important to remember that interrater reliability does *not* reflect content-sampling or time-sampling error; rather, it reflects *interrater agreement* and is sensitive only to differences due to the lack of agreement between the raters scoring the test.

Selecting a Reliability Coefficient

As we have discussed throughout this chapter, sources of measurement error can dictate the type of reliability/precision we need to estimate. For example, if a test is designed to be given more than one time, one would choose test-retest or alternate form reliability with delayed administration, because both are sensitive to time-sampling errors. Alternately, if a test involves the use of two or more raters, then interrater reliability would be chosen. Other conditions beyond error sources should be considered when selecting an estimate of reliability/precision. For example, one difficulty with internal consistency methods involves the assumption that test items represent a single trait, construct, domain, or subject area (i.e., homogeneous items). Measures of internal consistency evaluate the extent to which the different items on a test measure the same content domain; therefore, if test items are heterogeneous and designed to measure several constructs, then reliability/precision estimates will be low. For example, a test that measures depressed mood assesses a single content domain and thus contains homogeneous test items. In this case, the KR 20 or the coefficient alpha would be appropriate, because both assess internal consistency by correlating test items with each other. However, if an instrument measured two separate constructs (such as depressed mood and anxiety), then the heterogeneity of the test items would cause the KR 20 and coefficient alpha to underestimate internal consistency reliability. In other words, both reliability/precision estimates would assume that the lack of uniformity of test items was an indicator of content-sampling error, not that the test items actually measured different constructs. To compute internal consistency reliability for a test with heterogeneous content, the split-half method would be appropriate, which would involve dividing the test into two equivalent halves, each one consisting of both depressed mood items and anxiety items, and correlating the halves. Alternately, the homogeneous items within the test may be placed into separate groupings in order to compute separate measures of internal consistency among groups of similar items. For example, the items on a test measuring both depressed mood and anxiety could be subdivided into two groups (one measuring depressed mood and one measuring anxiety), and the KR 20 or coefficient alpha reliability estimates could be calculated for each group.

Evaluating Reliability Coefficients

When selecting a test to be used in individual assessment, the importance of critically examining the test's reliability/precision information cannot be overemphasized. The question becomes, "How large do reliability coefficients need to be?" In general, we want reliability coefficients to be as large as possible (between +.00 and +1.00). We know that a coefficient of 1.00 means that an observed score is equal to the true score, meaning there is no error variance. Thus, the closer a reliability coefficient approaches 1.00, the more reliable it is. For example, a reliability coefficient (r) of .95 would indicate that 95% of the variation in test scores is explained by real differences, and only 5% (i.e., $1 - .95$) of the variation is attributed to error; the test scores would be considered very reliable. This is infinitely better than an r of .20, which means that 80% of the score variations are due to error.

Unfortunately, there is no minimum threshold for a reliability coefficient to be considered appropriate for all tests. What constitutes an acceptable reliability coefficient can depend on several factors, such as the construct being measured, the way the test scores will be used, and the method used for estimating reliability (Reynolds, Livingston, & Willson, 2009). Because this textbook is concerned with evaluating assessment methods, we will suggest what level of reliability/precision is sufficient; however, readers must remember that there is no absolute standard on values that constitute adequate reliability coefficients. We generally consider that for most assessment instruments reliability coefficients of .70 or higher are acceptable, reliability/precision estimates below .70 are marginally reliable, and those below .60 are unreliable (Sattler & Hoge, 2006; Strauss, Sherman, & Spreen, 2006). If a test is being used to make important decisions that significantly impact an individual (i.e., a high-stakes test), then reliability coefficients should be at least .90 (Reynolds, Livingston, & Willson, 2009; Wasserman & Bracken, 2013). For interrater reliability, coefficients should also be no less than .90 (Smith, Vannest, & Davis, 2011). Table 5.2 provides some general guidelines for evaluating the magnitude of reliability coefficients.

Standard Error of Measurement

Thus far, we've presented information about the various methods of estimating reliability/precision, which are estimates of the amount of variation due to measurement error. Recall that reliability coefficients do not represent the score for an individual; they always relate to a group of scores. How do we get an estimate of the reliability/precision for a single individual's observed score? Although it is impractical to administer the same test many times to the same test takers, it is possible to estimate the amount of variation in test scores for a single test taker. We use the standard error of measurement.

SEM is a simple measure of an individual's test score fluctuations (due to error) if he or she took the same test repeatedly (McManus, 2012). It is an estimation of the accuracy of an individual's *observed scores* as related to the *true score* had the individual been tested infinite times. In other words, SEM is like a standard deviation of observed scores about one's true score. Although we never know what an individual's true score is, we assume that numerous observed scores would cluster about the individual's true score. We call

TABLE 5.2 Evaluating Reliability Coefficients

Very High	>.90
High	.80–.89
Acceptable	.70–.79
Moderate/Acceptable	.60–.69
Low/Unacceptable	<.59

this group of observed scores the *error distribution*, which is assumed to be normal, with a mean of zero and a standard deviation equal to SEM. Furthermore, we consider the mean of the error distribution to be the true score. If test scores are very reliable, then the observed scores are close to the true score (the mean of the error distribution); if test scores are not reliable, then they fall away from the true score.

It is important to understand the differences between SEM and standard deviation. Unlike standard deviation, which is the measure of the spread of scores obtained by a *group of test takers* on a *single test*, SEM is the measure of the spread of scores obtained by a *single individual* if the individual was tested *multiple* times. SEM is a function of both the reliability/precision and standard deviation of a test and is calculated using the following formula:

$$SEM = s\sqrt{1 - r}$$

where

SEM = the standard error of measurement

s = the standard deviation

r = the reliability coefficient of the test

Say that we want to calculate SEM for the Verbal Comprehension Index (VCI) of the Wechsler Intelligence Scale for Children (WISC-IV). The reliability coefficient for the VCI is .94, the mean is 100, and the standard deviation is 15 (which is the same mean and standard deviation for all index scores on the WISC-IV). SEM is computed as follows:

$$SEM = 15\sqrt{1 - .94}$$
$$= 15\sqrt{.06}$$
$$= 15(.245)$$
$$= 3.67$$

Now, let's calculate SEM for the Processing Speed Index (PSI) of the WISC-IV, which has a reliability coefficient of .88 and a standard deviation of 15:

$$SEM = 15\sqrt{1 - .88}$$
$$= 15\sqrt{.12}$$
$$= 15(.346)$$
$$= 5.19$$

Note that in these examples both tests have the same standard deviation ($S = 15$); thus, SEM becomes a function solely of the reliability coefficient. Because the PSI has a lower reliability coefficient ($r = .88$) than the VCI ($r = .94$), the PSI SEM is higher than the SEM for the VCI.

Because SEM depends on both the standard deviation and the reliability coefficient of a test, and because different tests have different standard deviations, the SEM cannot be used by itself as an index of reliability/precision (Urbina, 2014). You must be able to evaluate SEM in context. For example, tests that have greater score range and larger standard deviations, such as the SAT (standard deviation = 100), will have much larger SEM numbers than tests with small standard deviations, such as the WISC-IV (standard deviation = 3; Urbina, 2014). Although the standard deviation and SEM may be different, the reliability coefficients can still be similar. Although we do not use SEM alone to interpret reliability/precision, we use SEM in creating confidence intervals around specific observed scores, which can guide score interpretations.

Confidence Intervals

Once we have computed the SEM for a given test score, we can build a confidence interval around an individual's *observed* score so that we can estimate (with a certain level of confidence) his or her *true* score. Although we will never know what an individual's true score is, forming intervals around the individual's observed score allows us to estimate the probability that the true score falls within a certain interval. Thus, *confidence intervals* tell us the upper limit and lower limit within which a person's true score will fall. In assessment, we are interested in confidence intervals at the 68% (within ±1 standard deviations from the mean), 95% (within ±2 standard deviations), and 99.5% (within ±3 standard deviations) probability levels. The z scores associated with the 68%, 95%, and 99.5% probability levels are 1.00, 1.96, and 2.58, respectively. We choose the appropriate level or probability depending on how confident we want to be in our estimate of the test taker's true score. We calculate the ranges of the confidence intervals (CI) at the 68%, 95%, and 99.5% levels as follows:

$$\text{CI } 68\% = X \pm 1.00 \text{ SEM}$$
$$\text{CI } 95\% = X \pm 1.96 \text{ SEM}$$
$$\text{CI } 99.5\% = X \pm 2.58 \text{ SEM}$$

To illustrate this, say that Leticia received a score of 110 on the VCI of the WISC-IV. We previously calculated the SEM on the VCI as 3.67. Using this information, we would first compute the ranges of the confidence intervals as follows:

$$\text{CI } 68\% = X \pm 1.00(3.67) = 3.67 \text{ (round to the nearest whole number, } \pm 4)$$
$$\text{CI } 95\% = X \pm 1.96(3.67) = 7.19 \text{ (round to the nearest whole number, } \pm 7)$$
$$\text{CI } 99.5\% = X \pm 2.58(3.67) = 9.47 \text{ (round to the nearest whole number, } \pm 9)$$

Using these score ranges, we could calculate the confidence intervals for Leticia's VCI score as follows:

$$\text{CI } 68\% = 110 \pm 4 = 106 - 114$$
$$\text{CI } 95\% = 110 \pm 7 = 103 - 117$$
$$\text{CI } 99.5\% = 110 \pm 9 = 101 - 119$$

These confidence intervals reflect the range in which an individual's *true* test score lies at various probability levels. Thus, based on the information provided previously, we can conclude that at the 99.5% confidence interval we are 99.5% confident that Leticia's true score falls in the range of 101 to 119.

Sidebar 5.1 Increasing Reliability by Increasing Test Length

How much does test length impact reliability/precision? If we already know the reliability/precision of an existing test, we can use the Spearman–Brown formula to predict what the new reliability/precision would be if we increased the number of items:

$$r_{new} = \frac{n \times r_{xx}}{1 + (n - 1)r_{xx}}$$

where

r_{new} = the new reliability/precision estimate after lengthening (or shortening) the test

r_{xx} = the reliability/precision estimate of the original test

n = the multiplier by which test length is to be increased or decreased (the new test length divided by the old test length)

For example, let's assume that the r_{xx} for a 10-item test is 0.30. We decide to increase the test to 50 items. To determine the reliability coefficient for the longer test, we first calculate the n:

$$n = \frac{\text{new test length}}{\text{old test length}}$$

$$= \frac{50}{10} = 5$$

Next, we apply this to the Spearman–Brown formula:

$$r_{new} = \frac{5.30}{1 + (5 - 1).30}$$

$$= \frac{15}{1 + (4).30}$$

$$= \frac{1.5}{1 + 1.20}$$

$$= \frac{1.5}{2.20}$$

$$= .68$$

We can see that by increasing the number of items from 30 to 80, we increased the total test score reliability/precision from .30 to .68. To further illustrate this, the following list of tests begins with a 10-item test that has a reliability/precision of .30. You can see how reliability/precision increases as the number of test items increases:

Number of Items	Reliability/precision
10	.30
20	.46
50	.68
100	.81
200	.90
500	.96

Increasing Reliability/Precision

Although measurement error exists in all tests, test developers can take steps to reduce error and increase the reliability/precision of test scores. Probably the most obvious approach is simply to increase the number of items on a test (Reynolds, Livingston, & Willson, 2009). This is based on the assumption that a larger number of test items can more accurately represent the content domain being measured, thereby reducing content-sampling error. Sidebar 5.1 illustrates how the reliability/precision of a 10-item test with a reliability coefficient of .30 can be increased by adding items. Other ways of improving reliability/precision include writing understandable, unambiguous test items; using selected-response items (e.g., multiple choice) rather than constructed-response items (e.g., essay); making sure that items are not too difficult or too easy; having clearly stated administration and scoring procedures; and requiring training before individuals can administer, grade, or interpret a test.

Summary

In this chapter, we presented information about the reliability/precision of test scores, which is the degree to which test scores are dependable, consistent, and stable upon additional test administrations. An important concept in reliability/precision is measurement error. In testing, we try to determine how much measurement error may impact an individual's true score. Measurement error results from factors that are irrelevant to the construct being measured, such as time-sampling error, content-sampling error, interrater differences, test-taker characteristics, flaws in testing procedures, and even random chance.

We estimate the reliability/precision of test scores by calculating a reliability coefficient. The type of reliability coefficient that we use depends on several factors, such as test content, testing procedures, testing conditions, and the use of raters. Although no minimum level for reliability coefficients exists, we know that the higher the coefficient, the more reliable the test scores. Calculating the standard error of measurement can be helpful in interpreting reliability/precision by using the statistic to create confidence intervals, which tell us the upper and lower limits within which a person's true score will fall.

Questions for Discussion

1. Define *reliability/precision* and describe its importance in assessment.
2. Identify and describe the various sources of measurement error and their related reliability/precision estimates. What are the advantages and disadvantages of each method?
3. Which method of estimating reliability/precision provides the most useful information in the following situations? Why?
   a. Selecting an aptitude test for predicting success in a vocational program
   b. Determining whether the items on a test are homogeneous
   c. Determining the degree to which scores obtained from different raters are consistent
4. If a teacher were developing a midterm exam for a psychological testing class, what type of measurement error would be of most concern? Why?
5. In what way would the following factors effect reliability/precision?
   a. Having heterogeneous test items
   b. Increasing the number of items on a test
   c. Having a very short time interval between testings on a math test

Suggested Activities

1. Review several standardized tests and identify the types of reliability/precision presented in the test manuals.
2. Write a paper or prepare a class report on one of the following topics: factors that affect test score reliability/precision, increasing reliability/precision, or reliability/precision of teacher-made tests.
3. Read the critical reviews of some of the tests that you have taken and see how the reviewers rate the reliability/precision of the tests' scores.
4. A teacher wrote a test consisting of five dichotomous items and wants to know if the items adequately cover the content domain being tested. He decides to use the KR 20 formula to determine the internal consistency of the test. Using the following information, calculate the internal consistency using the KR 20 formula. Are the test scores reliable in terms of internal consistency?

Item	1	2	3	4	5
p	.3	.4	.6	.5	.4
q	.7	.6	.4	.5	.3
pq	.21	.24	.24	.25	.12

5. Construct an achievement test based on the concepts introduced in this chapter and administer it to a number of students in your class. Then, compute the reliability/precision of the test's scores using split-half and KR 20 or KR 21.

6. Sara scored a 98 on the Working Memory Index (WMI) of the WISC-IV. We know that the reliability coefficient for WMI scores is .92, the mean is 100, and the standard deviation is 15. Calculate the standard error of measurement, and then create confidence intervals for Sara at ± 1 SEM and ± 2 SEM.

References

American Educational Research Association (AERA), American Psychological Association (APA), & National Council on Measurement in Education (NCME). (2014). *Standards for educational and psychological testing*. Washington, DC: Authors.

Ayeni, E. (2012). Development, standardization, and validation of Social Anxiety Scale. *IFE Psychologia, 20*(1), 263–274.

Beckstead, J. W. (2013). On measurements and their quality. Paper 1: Reliability–History, issues and procedures. *International Journal of Nursing Studies, 50*(7), 968–973. doi:10.1016/j.ijnurstu.2013.04.005

Boyd, D., Lankford, H., Loeb, S., & Wyckoff, J. (2013). Measuring test measurement error: A general approach. *Journal of Educational and Behavioral Statistics, 38*(6), 629–663. doi:10.3102/1076998613508584

Cronbach, L. J. (1951). Coefficient alpha and the internal structure of tests. *Psychometrika, 16,* 297–334.

Furr, R. M., & Bacharach, V. R. (2013). *Psychometrics: An introduction* (2nd ed.). Thousand Oaks, CA: Sage Publications.

Kaplan, R. M., & Saccuzzo, D. P. (2013). *Psychological testing: Principles, applications, and issues* (8th ed.). Belmont, CA: Wadsworth.

Kuder, G. F., & Richardson, M. W. (1937). The theory of estimation of test reliability. *Psychometrika, 2,* 151–160.

McManus, I. C. (2012). The misinterpretation of the standard error of measurement in medical education: A primer on the problems, pitfalls, and peculiarities of the three different standard errors of measurement. *Medical Teacher, 34*(7), 569–576. doi: 10.3109/0142159X.2012.670318

Miller, M. D., Linn, R. L., & Gronlund, N. E. (2012). *Measurement and assessment in teaching* (11th ed.). Upper Saddle River, NJ: Pearson.

Murphy, K. R., & Davidshofer, C. O. (2005). *Psychological testing: Principles and applications* (6th ed.). Upper Saddle River, NJ: Prentice Hall.

Resch, J., Driscoll, A., McCaffrey, N., Brown, C., Ferrara, M. S., Macciocchi, S., & Walpert, K. (2013). ImPact test-retest reliability: Reliably unreliable? *Journal of Athletic Training, 48*(4), 506–511. doi:10.4085/1062-6050-48.3.09

Reynolds, C. R., Livingston, R. B., & Willson, V. (2009). *Measurement and assessment in education* (2nd ed.). Boston, MA: Pearson.

Sattler, J. M., & Hoge, R. D. (2006). *Assessment of children: Behavioral, social, and clinical foundations* (5th ed.). San Diego, CA: Jerome M. Sattler Publisher Inc.

Smith, S. L., Vannest, K. J., & Davis, J. L. (2011). Seven reliability indices for high-stakes decision making: Description, selection, and simple calculation. *Psychology in the Schools, 48*(10), 1064–1075. doi:10.1002/pits.20610

Strauss, E., Sherman, E. M. S., & Spreen, O. (2006). *A compendium of neuropsychological tests: Administration, norms, and commentary* (3rd ed.). New York, NY: Oxford University Press.

Suter, W. N. (2012). *Introduction to educational research: A critical thinking approach*. Thousand Oaks, CA: Sage Publications.

Urbina, S. (2014). *Essentials of psychological testing* (2nd ed.). Hoboken, NJ: John Wiley & Sons.

Wasserman, J. D., & Bracken, B. A. (2013). Fundamental psychometric considerations in assessment. In J. R. Graham & J. A. Naglieri (Eds.), *Handbook of psychology* (Vol. 10: Assessment psychology, 2nd ed., pp. 50–81). Hoboken, NJ: John Wiley & Sons.

6

Validity

In everyday terms, when we refer to something as valid, we are saying that it is sound, meaningful, or accurate. Similarly, when applied to measurement, *validity* refers to whether the claims and decisions made on the basis of assessment results are sound, meaningful, and useful for the intended purpose of the results. Traditionally, the definition of validity centered on simply whether a test or questionnaire (i.e., assessment instrument) "measured what it was supposed to measure." Today, the concept of validity refers to evidence that supports the use of an assessment instrument for specific purposes. An argument for the validity of an instrument can be made using five sources of information: test content, response process, internal structure, relations to other variables, and testing consequences (American Educational Research Association (AERA), American Psychological Association (APA), & National Council on Measurement in Education (NCME), 2014). This new perspective on creating a validity argument is particularly relevant in recent years due to the accountability movement affecting both educational and psychological assessment. Therefore, assessment results are often used for making important and sometimes life-changing decisions about an individual, which further emphasizes the importance of evaluating the appropriateness of the interpretations made from assessment results (i.e., validity).

After studying this chapter, you should be able to:

- Define *validity* and explain its importance in the context of assessment.
- Define *construct* and provide examples of constructs examined in psychological and educational assessment.
- Describe the major threats to validity.
- Explain the relationship between validity and reliability/precision.
- Describe the major sources of validity evidence and provide examples of the procedures used for assessing each source.
- Explain how to evaluate a criterion.
- Explain how validity coefficients are interpreted.
- Explain the importance of considering the consequences of testing in the validation process.

THE NATURE OF VALIDITY

According to *Standards for Educational and Psychological Testing* (American Educational Research Association (AERA) et al., 2014), validity is defined as "the degree to which evidence and theory support the interpretations of test scores for proposed uses of the test" (p. 11). In other words, if test scores are used to make decisions about a person, how valid are those scores for making those decisions?

Gorin (2007) more concisely defined validity as "the extent to which test scores provide answers to targeted questions" (p. 456). For example, if our targeted question is, "What is the client's level of anxiety?", then we would expect that the questions on a test would be designed to measure anxiety and that the resulting scores from that test would be indicators of anxiety level. Although evaluating the test for this purpose may appear easy at face value, the process is inherently more complex. For example, the test may have questions about the clients' sleep patterns. Do they have difficulty falling asleep? Do they wake up early and cannot get back to sleep? These questions can be related to anxiety, but they can also be related to depression and other issues. Thus, we need a standard process for determining the degree to which the items on a test and the resulting scores of a test measure the construct we are examining.

The ability to evaluate our targeted question is only one facet of validity. Validity also refers to the adequacy and appropriateness of the uses of assessment results. For example, an assessment instrument that leads to unfair treatment of women, individuals of different cultures, or English-language learners would not be considered either adequate or appropriate (Miller, Linn, & Gronlund, 2012) nor would instruments that discriminate against a certain group based on gender, race, ethnicity, socioeconomic status, or disability. In both cases, the lack of fairness would indicate a lack of validity for the use of assessment results.

When using the term *validity* in relation to tests and measurement, consider the following points:

1. Validity refers to the appropriateness of the use and interpretation of *test results*, not of the test itself. Although we often speak of the "validity of a test" for the sake of convenience, this is actually incorrect, because no test is valid for all purposes in all situations. Statements about validity should always refer to particular interpretations and uses. As Kane (2013) more recently reiterated, "To validate an interpretation or use of test scores is to evaluate the plausibility of the claims based on the scores." (p. 1). In other words, because the purpose of tests is to make some inference or decision about an individual based on his or her test results, we want to know that the argument behind the inferences and assumptions is valid.

2. Validity is a *matter of degree*; it does not exist on an all-or-none basis (Oren, Kennet-Cohen, Turvall, & Allalouf, 2014). Although validity was sectioned into various components prior to the development of the current edition of the *Standards for Educational and Psychological Testing* (American Educational Research Association (AERA) et al., 2014), it is now thought of as a unitary concept (see point 3 ahead). The argument for validity must incorporate all of the accumulated evidence to support the interpretation of test scores for specific purposes (Oren et al., 2014). As a counselor using assessment, you must be able to evaluate the argument for validity made by a test developer or researcher and determine if it is sound.

3. Validity is a *unitary concept*. This means that validity is a single, unified concept that centers on construct validity, which is supported by sources of validity evidence.

Historically, validity was subdivided into three distinct types: content validity, criterion validity, and construct validity (known as the *tripartite view* of validity). The most recent edition of the *Standards* (American Educational Research Association (AERA) et al., 2014) makes no reference to distinct types of validity; rather, it emphasizes the unitary concept by referring to five sources of validity evidence. Despite this current unitary view of validity, the tripartite language remains entrenched in testing; you will see references to it (i.e., content validity, criterion-related validity, construct validity) in many of the test manuals and test reviews today. Furthermore, some current educational researchers are questioning the unitary concept (centering on construct validity) and are reemphasizing the importance of content validity (Sireci & Faulkner-Bond, 2014). Thus, many textbooks continue to include the traditional terminology when describing types and sources of validity evidence.

4. Validity is *specific to some particular group, use, or purpose of the test score interpretations*; no test is valid for all purposes or all groups. For example, the validity evidence might support the interpretation of results from a reading test for current reading comprehension levels of test takers but have little evidence for predicting future levels. Alternately, a math test might have strong evidence for using the results to interpret arithmetic skills for fifth-grade students, but have little support for the interpretation of skills for third graders. Thus, when evaluating or describing validity evidence, it is important to consider how test scores are intended to be interpreted and used and the appropriateness of the population for which the test is employed (American Educational Research Association (AERA) et al., 2014).

Revisiting Construct

Because we use the term *construct* so frequently in this chapter, we will revisit the meaning of the term before discussing validity evidence. Constructs (also called *latent variables*) are scientifically developed concepts, ideas, or hypotheses that are used to describe or explain behavior (Cohen & Swerdlik, 2012). As such, constructs cannot be measured directly or observed. Instead, a construct is defined or inferred by a group of interrelated variables or dimensions that can be directly measured or observed (known as *manifest*, or *observed*, *variables*). For example, although we cannot measure or observe the construct *aggression*, it can be inferred from the interrelationships among the measurable variables that make up aggression, such as physical violence, verbal attacks, poor social skills, and so on.

Constructs can be very comprehensive and complex (e.g., personality) or narrowly defined (e.g., depressed mood). In psychology, the term *construct* may be applied to traits, characteristics, or behaviors, such as personality, mood, anxiety, aptitude, adjustment, attention, and self-esteem, to name just a few. In education, examples of constructs include intelligence, achievement, emotionally disturbed, and learning disabled. Examples of employment- or career-related constructs include job performance, motivation, clerical aptitude, interests, or work values. These examples represent only a few of the potential constructs. In terms of validity, *construct* is an important concept, because if we have evidence that the interpretations of assessment results are valid based on the purpose of the test, then the results are considered to accurately reflect the construct being measured.

Threats to Validity

Numerous factors can make test results invalid for their intended use. Two main threats include construct underrepresentation and construct-irrelevant variance (American

Educational Research Association (AERA) et al., 2014). These terms simply refer to a test measuring less (construct underrepresentation) or more (construct irrelevant) of the construct than it is supposed to be measuring (Reynolds, Livingston, & Willson, 2008). *Construct underrepresentation* implies that a test is too narrow and fails to include important dimensions or aspects of the identified construct. An example of this is a test that is supposed to measure writing skills. If the test only contains spelling questions and leaves out other aspects of writing (such as grammar and punctuation), then it is an inaccurate representation of writing skills.

In contrast, *construct-irrelevant variance* means that the instrument is too broad and contains too many variables, many of which are irrelevant to the construct. For example, if a test on a particular subject area requires undue reading comprehension (e.g., extensive and complex instructions on a math test), then test scores might be invalidly low, reflecting the test taker's difficulty with reading (Messick, 1995; Reynolds et al., 2008). Alternately, if the items on a test contain clues that permit the test taker to respond correctly, then the resulting score may be invalidly high. An example of this is a reading comprehension test that includes a passage that is well known to some test takers; their performance may be a result of their familiarity with the passage, not with their reading comprehension ability. Thus, construct-irrelevant variance is viewed as a contaminant to accurate test score interpretation.

In addition to construct underrepresentation and construct-irrelevant variance, other factors can impact the validity of the interpretation of test results, including the following (Miller et al., 2012):

- *Factors within the Test* Ambiguous, inappropriate, or poorly constructed test items; too few test items; improper arrangement of items; identifiable patterns of answers
- *Administration and Scoring Procedures* Failure to follow standard directions and time limits, giving test takers unfair aid, scoring errors
- *Test-Taker Characteristics* Test takers with emotional disturbances, test anxiety, lack of motivation
- *Inappropriate Test Group* Giving the test to individuals who differ from the validation group

Validity and Reliability/Precision

In the preceding chapter, we discussed the concept of the reliability/precision of measurement, and it is important to understand the relationship between reliability/precision and validity. Reliability/precision refers to the stability or consistency of test scores and is a necessary but insufficient condition for validity. A measure that produces totally inconsistent results cannot possibly provide valid score interpretations. However, no matter how reliable assessment results are, it is not a guarantee of validity. In other words, assessment results may be highly reliable but may be measuring the wrong thing or may be used in inappropriate ways. For example, we might construct an "intelligence" test that measures an individual's ability to answer trivia questions related to 1990's pop songs. Scores on this test might be perfectly consistent across items (the individual may be a 90's music virtuoso) and across time. This perfect reliability/precision, however, would not confirm that we had a valid measurement of intelligence (assuming that the ability to correctly identify 90's pop songs is not an accurate measure of intelligence). Although a test with low reliability/precision always indicates a low degree of validity, a highly reliable test does not ensure validity.

SOURCES OF VALIDITY EVIDENCE

The *Standards* (American Educational Research Association (AERA) et al., 2014) assert that validity is "the most fundamental consideration in developing and evaluating tests" (p. 11). Validity centers on the relationship between the purpose of a test and the interpretations or decisions made about individuals based on their test scores. Thus, the process of *test validation* involves gathering and evaluating multiple sources of validity evidence that support the interpretations and inferences made from test scores. Assessing sources of validity evidence may involve scrutinizing a test's content, relating test scores to some external criterion, or relating test scores to the scores on other tests or measures (Cohen & Swerdlik, 2012).

Traditionally, validity evidence was organized into three categories: content, criterion related, and construct validity evidence. However, the most recent edition of the *Standards* (American Educational Research Association (AERA) et al., 2014) abandoned the traditional nomenclature and identified five *sources* of validity evidence based on (a) test content, (b) response processes, (c) internal structure, (d) relations to other variables, and (e) consequences of testing. The common denominator of these sources of validity evidence is that they emphasize evidence of relationships between assessment scores and other variables (Urbina, 2014). Despite the introduction of the five sources of validity evidence, the old classification is still widely used by test developers, researchers, authors, educators, and counselors. Furthermore, four of the traditional methods of accumulating validity evidence include the first four sources of evidence cited in the *Standards* (mostly under the umbrella of construct validity; Miller et al., 2012). Although there may be a need for counselors to recognize the outdated concept of validity, we believe it is important to focus our discussion on validity evidence based on the current standards: test content, response processes, internal structure, relations to other variables, and consequences of testing. We want to caution readers against mistaking the sources of validity evidence as separate categories of validity; they should always be regarded as parts of the unitary concept of validity. All sources of validity evidence relate to the construct being measured.

The process of test validation is ongoing and rigorous, similar to amassing support for a complex scientific theory. After compiling validity evidence, judgment is then made about whether a given interpretation or inference from assessment results is valid. The greater the significance or impact of assessment results to the test taker, the more convincing the evidence needs to be. In general, the more types of validity evidence established, the better. Although it is the responsibility of test developers to report validation data in the test manual, it is the responsibility of test users to carefully read the validity information and evaluate the suitability of the test for their specific purposes.

Test Content Validity Evidence

Test content validity evidence refers to evidence of the relationship between a test's content and the construct it is intended to measure. In other words, the content of an instrument (which includes items, tasks, and/or questions, as well as administration and scoring procedures) must clearly represent the content domain that the instrument is designed to assess. For example, a college student would probably be most concerned with the content validity of a final exam; the student would want to be assured that the test questions represent the content that was covered in the classroom and in the class materials. See Figure 6.1 for a representation of various forms of validity evidence.

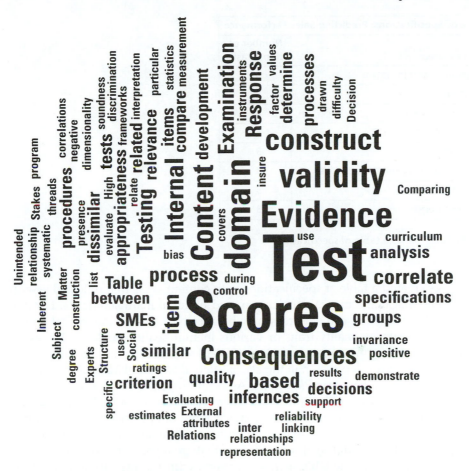

FIGURE 6.1   Word cloud of validity evidence vocabulary.

The content validation process begins at the outset of instrument construction and follows a rational approach to ensure that the content matches the test specifications. The first step in the process is clearly delineating the construct or the content domain to be measured. The definition of the construct determines the subject matter and the items to be included on the instrument.

Once the construct or content domain has been defined, the second step is to develop a table of specifications. A *table of specifications*, or a *test blueprint*, is a two-dimensional chart that guides instrument development by listing the content areas that will be covered on a test, as well as the number (proportion) of tasks or items to be allocated to each content area. The content areas reflect essential knowledge, behaviors, or skills that represent the construct of interest. Test developers decide on relevant content areas from a variety of sources, such as the research literature, professional standards, or even other tests that measure the same construct. The content areas of instruments measuring achievement or academic abilities often come from educational or accreditation standards, school curricula, course syllabi, textbooks, and other relevant materials. For example, in constructing the KeyMath 3, a norm-referenced achievement test measuring essential math skills in K–12 students, test

Table of Specifications: Predicting Sales Performance	
Content areas	Number of items/tasks
Motivation and initiative	5
Persistence	5
Competitiveness	4
Communication skills	4
Extroversion	3
Planning and organizational skills	3
Cooperativeness	3
Self-confidence	3

FIGURE 6.2 Sample table of specifications.

developers created a table of specifications with content areas that reflected essential math content, national mathematical curriculum, and national math standards. For personality and clinical inventories, content areas may be derived from the theoretical and empirical knowledge about personality traits or various mental health problems. For example, the content on the Beck Depression Inventory (BDI-II) was designed to be consistent with the diagnostic criteria for depression in the *Diagnostic and Statistical Manual of Mental Disorders, Fifth Edition* (DSM-5; American Psychiatric Association (APA), 2013). In employment assessment, content areas may reflect the elements, activities, tasks, and duties related to a particular job; for example, Figure 6.2 displays a table of specifications for an instrument designed to predict sales performance. Instrument manuals should always provide clear statements about the source(s) of content areas that are represented on the test.

After developing the table of specifications with the identified content areas, test developers write the actual test items. Thus, the next step in the content validation process involves recruiting multiple outside consultants (i.e., *subject matter experts* [SMEs]); these consultants review the test items to determine if they do in fact represent the content domain. The SMEs can consist of both content experts in the field and lay experts. For example, to evaluate the content validity of an instrument assessing depression, two groups of experts should participate: (1) people who have published in the field or who have worked with depressed individuals and (2) people who are depressed (Rubio, 2005). There are a number of methods that can be used to report the data provided by the SMEs. Although a test developer can report SME ratings as evidence, it is more useful to represent the degree of agreement among SMEs through a variety of statistics (e.g., Aiken's Validity Index). In addition, SMEs can perform an analysis of alignment between the test and content standards of external bodies (e.g., state department of education). The SME analysis of alignment can be conducted by using a variety of methods (e.g., Webb Method and Achieve Method) and can be presented in a matrix format.

Evidence Based on Internal Structure

Evidence of validity should be gathered based on the internal structure of the test (i.e., dimensionality, measurement invariance, reliability/precision). When examining dimensionality, it is important to note that some instruments are designed to measure a general construct, but other instruments are designed to measure several components or dimensions of a construct. For example, the Piers–Harris Children's Self-Concept Scale (Piers–Harris 2; Piers & Herzberg, 2002) has six subscales designed to measure the construct of global self-concept. For instruments that assess multiple dimensions, part of assessing construct validity is checking the *internal structure* of the test to ensure that the test components (e.g., scales, subscales, subtests) measure a single underlying construct. A useful technique for this process is factor analysis. *Factor analysis* is a statistical procedure that analyzes the relationships among test components to determine whether a test is unidimensional (i.e., all of the components measure a single construct). There are two basic ways to conduct factor analysis. If we are uncertain of the possible dimensions underlying our scale, we can use *exploratory factor analysis*. If we have strong theoretical expectations about dimensions that already exist in the scale, we can use *confirmatory factor analysis* (CFA).

A form of structural equation modeling, CFA is the preferred method for demonstrating validity evidence for the internal structure of an instrument (Rios & Wells, 2014). The reason that CFA is a preferred method is that the test developer must specify the factor models before starting the research. In other words, the test developer is not simply fishing for emerging factors in the test data. The factor models that are set prior to beginning the research are based on theory and often have an empirical rationale. Aside from the theoretical basis of CFA, the analytic procedure also is more robust than other procedures for factor analysis.

Exploratory factor analysis is frequently used in test construction if a test developer wants to identify the characteristics or attributes associated with a particular factor or dimension (Kline, 2000). For example, say that test developers designed a test to identify characteristics associated with the single dimension of extraversion. They wrote test items they believed assessed these characteristics and, after obtaining scores from a large sample of individuals, submitted the items to factor analyses. Based on the results, the developers chose to keep only those items on the test that were related to the single dimension of extraversion.

In addition to dimensionality, it is important to evaluate evidence in relation to *measurement invariance*. When developing tests, researchers must ensure that fairness is addressed for all aspects of the test. According to the 2014 *Standards for Educational and Psychological Testing* (AERA et al., 2014), test developers should collect validity evidence that demonstrates the applicability of results to the examinee population and each relevant subgroup. A form of factor analysis, Multiple Group Confirmatory Factor Analysis (MGCFA) can be used to provide evidence of measurement invariance or fairness for distinct groups of people (Rios & Wells, 2014). The process of calculating MGCFA is beyond the scope of this chapter. However, as counselors selecting instruments, information provided from an MGCFA analysis can indicate that the test developer attended to issues of systematic bias.

The final component of validity related to internal structure of a test is reliability/ precision. We discussed reliability/precision in detail in the previous chapter, but it is important to note that internal consistency data can serve as important evidence of the quality of the internal structure of a test. To reiterate our discussion from Chapter 5, internal consistency reliability is a measure of the degree to which scores on a test are reproduceable when the test is administered on additional occasions (Rios & Wells, 2014).

Relations to Other Variables Evidence

Relations to other variables evidence involves examining the relationships between test results and external variables that are thought to be a direct measure of the construct. It focuses on the effectiveness of test results in predicting a particular performance or behavior. For this purpose, test results (known as the predictor variable) are checked against a *criterion*, which is a direct and independent measure that the test is designed to predict or be correlated with. For example, test users might want evidence that a particular aptitude test can predict job performance. The aptitude test is the predictor variable, and job performance is the criterion to which test results are compared; if test results can accurately predict job performance, then the test has evidence of relations to other variables. The modern conceptualization from the 2014 *Standards* that corresponds to this category is Evidence Based on Relations to Other Variables (American Educational Research Association (AERA) et al., 2014).

There are two forms of relations to other variables evidence. Concurrent evidence is based on the degree to which a predictor variable is related to some criterion at the same time (concurrently). For example, a test that measures depressed mood should have a strong relationship with a current diagnosis of depression. Predictive evidence is based on the degree to which a test score estimates some future level of performance. For example, the SAT, which is used to forecast how well a high school student will perform in college, should predict college success. Whereas validity in general focuses on whether a test is valid or not, evidence of relations to other variables demonstrates what a test measures (Shultz, Whitney, & Jickar, 2014). Thus, test scores may be valid in predicting one criterion, but not another. For example, an intelligence test may be a good predictor of academic performance, but may be a poor predictor of morality (p. 101). Therefore, the chosen criterion must be appropriate to the intended purpose of the test.

Evidence of relations to other variables is provided when there are high correlations between test results and a well-defined criterion. We are interested in comparing test scores to a particular criterion because we assume that the criterion better reflects or is a more accurate representation of the construct we are measuring. Criteria are represented by *criterion measures*, which are indexes designed to assess or measure the particular criterion (Urbina, 2014). For example, a criterion of job performance may correspond to such criterion measures as supervisor ratings, productivity records, employee self-reports, and so forth. Therefore, an aptitude test (the predictor variable) could be designed to predict job performance (the criterion) as measured by supervisor ratings (the criterion measure). There is an almost infinite number of criterion measures that can be used in validating test scores, including academic achievement and certification, professional aptitude, and behavioral characteristics. Furthermore, in most validation studies more than one criterion measure is used to represent a single criterion (Urbina, 2014).

Because of the many possible criterion measures available, instrument manuals should always provide a rationale for the criterion measures selected in the validation process. In general, criterion measures should be *relevant*, *reliable*, and *uncontaminated*. To determine if a criterion measure is relevant to the intended purpose of the test, one must ascertain whether it is a valid representation of the behavior or outcome in question. For example, grade point average (GPA) is considered a relevant measure of success in college; therefore, it is often chosen as the criterion measure for validating admissions tests, such as the SAT.

Because an instrument is judged based on its relationship to a criterion, the criterion itself needs to be measured accurately; it must be *reliable*. Say that a test is related to job performance, as determined by a productivity scale and supervisor ratings. If an employee's job productivity is ranked as *high* one week and then *low* the next week or if the employee receives a high performance rating from one supervisor and a low rating from another, then the test will be unable to predict job performance, because the criterion measures used to assess job performance (the productivity scale and the supervisor ratings) are unreliable.

A criterion measure should be *uncontaminated*, meaning that the measure should not be influenced by any external factors that are unrelated or irrelevant to the criterion. Criterion contamination is present when a criterion measure includes aspects unrelated to the construct we are trying to measure. For example, if a vocabulary test for a child is affected by the child's expressive language disorder (which impacts a child's ability to retain new words), then we would consider the criterion (i.e., vocabulary) contaminated. If a test assessing depression is given to individuals suffering from chronic pain, then the chronic pain symptoms—which can include symptoms similar to depression, such as sleep disturbance, low energy, slow motor behavior, and change in appetite and weight—may contaminate the criterion (i.e., depression). If a criterion measure is contaminated by some irrelevant external variable(s), the scores on the test can be inflated or deflated as a result of the external variable.

VALIDITY COEFFICIENTS Evidence of relations to other variables is evaluated using *validity coefficients*, which indicate the relationship between test results and a criterion measure. Validity coefficients can range from −1.0 to 1.0. A validity coefficient of 0 means that there is no relationship between the instrument scores and the criterion, and a coefficient of 1.00 indicates a perfect, positive relationship; thus, the higher the validity coefficient, the stronger the validity evidence. Exactly how large should coefficients be in order to be considered strong evidence of relations to other variables? As with any correlation coefficient, there are no hard and fast rules of interpretation. The size of a validity coefficient depends on several factors, such as the nature and complexity of the criterion, a statistically significant validity coefficient, the composition and size of the validation sample, and the interactions among all of these (Anastasi, 1988; Urbina, 2014). In general, validity coefficients tend to be lower (than reliability coefficients), because we are comparing our test to different or other tests or criteria (even when they are measuring or represent the same construct). In contrast, reliability coefficients provide a measure of relationships among items or components of the test itself, so we would expect reliability coefficients to be larger. In general, it is rare to see validity coefficients larger than .50, and coefficients less than .30 are not uncommon. Textbooks on testing (e.g., Anastasi, 1988; Anastasi & Urbina, 1997; Cronbach, 1990) have traditionally given .20 as a guideline for a minimum validity coefficient value. Cohen (1992) established the standard for effect size of a validity coefficient: less than .20 is *weak*, .21 to .40 is *moderate*, and greater than .50 is *strong*. The U.S. Department of Labor (DOL; 2000) also provided guidelines for interpreting validity coefficients: below .11 is *unlikely to be useful*, .11 to .20 *depends on circumstances*, .21 to .35 is *likely to be useful*, and above .35 is *very beneficial*. So many different perspectives about the meaning of validity coefficients can be overwhelming; thus, we integrated these various perspectives to develop a general set of guidelines for interpreting validity coefficients (see Table 6.1).

PREDICTION ERRORS Ultimately, the purpose of relations to other variables evidence is to show that test scores accurately predict the criterion performance of interest. However, in making predictions we might commit two types of *prediction errors*: false positive errors and false negative errors. To explain prediction errors, say that a company requires job

TABLE 6.1 General Guidelines for Interpreting Validity Coefficients

Very high	>.50
High	.40–.49
Moderate/Acceptable	.21–.40
Low/Unacceptable	<.20

applicants to complete an aptitude test as part of the application process. Because the company believes that the scores on the aptitude test (the predictor variable) will predict job success (the criterion), the company will only hire individuals who score equal to or greater than a designated cutoff score. In this situation, two types of errors might occur: a *false positive error*, which means predicting that a positive outcome will occur and it does not; or a *false negative error*, which means predicting that a negative outcome will occur and it does not. Figure 6.3 presents a graph of the two types of error in our example. From the graph, four quadrants are evident. A person who is predicted to succeed in a job and subsequently

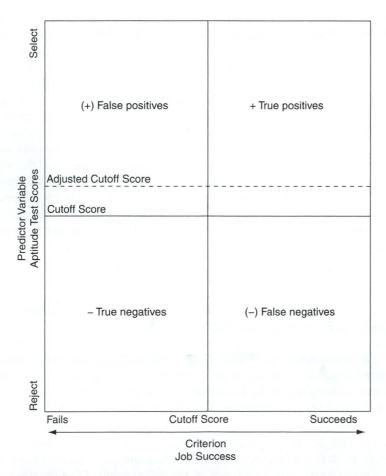

FIGURE 6.3 Prediction errors.

does succeed would fall into the *true positive* quadrant. Someone who is predicted to succeed but fails would be rated as a *false positive*. The person who is predicted to fail and does so would be tallied as a *true negative*. Anyone who is predicted to fail but actually succeeds would be a *false negative*. Prediction errors can be analyzed, and adjustments to the predictor variable can be made if needed. In our example, if too many false positive errors were occurring and too many individuals were being hired who did not have job success, then the cutoff score on the aptitude test could be raised. This would mean that almost everyone hired would be an above-average performer, and the number of false positives for job success would be reduced.

Evidence of relationships between test scores and other variables can be gathered from several sources. It is important to remember that the accumulation of evidence across the different types of validity lends credence to an argument for validity. In order to further demonstrate the process of gathering evidence of relations to other variables, we provide a discussion of the following sources:

- Evidence of homogeneity
- Convergent and discriminant evidence
- Group differentiation studies
- Age differentiation studies
- Experimental results
- Factor analysis

Evidence of Homogeneity

Test homogeneity refers to how uniform the items and components (i.e., subtests, scales) of a test are in measuring a single concept (Cohen & Swerdlik, 2012). In reference to the 2014 *Standards for Educational and Psychological Testing* (American Educational Research Association (AERA) et al., 2014), test homogeneity is one means of providing *evidence of the internal structure* of a test. One way test developers can provide evidence of homogeneity is by showing high internal consistency coefficients. As you will recall from the previous chapter on reliability/precision, an estimate of internal consistency reliability, such as the coefficient alpha, evaluates the extent to which items on a test measure the same construct by examining the intercorrelations among test items. High internal consistency reliability means that test items are homogeneous, which increases confidence that items assess a single construct.

In addition to intercorrelations of items, evidence of homogeneity can also be obtained by correlating the scores on each test item with the scores on the total test (i.e., the item-to-total correlation). For example, if you want to obtain evidence of homogeneity on a test of student motivation, then you could give the test to a group of students and then correlate the scores on each item with the scores on the total test. If all the items correlated highly with the total test score, then there is evidence that the items measured the construct of student motivation. The same procedure can be used for the scales or subtests on a test. High correlations between scales or subtests on the same test provide evidence that these components measure the construct that the test is intended to measure.

Convergent and Discriminant Evidence

Test developers frequently use convergent and discriminant evidence to prove that a particular instrument measures the construct it purports to measure. Convergent evidence is obtained by correlating instrument results with the results of other instruments that assess the same construct. Unlike relations to other variables evidence, which makes score comparisons with criterion measures that are considered a *better representation* of the construct of interest, convergent validity evidence compares instrument scores to scores from other instruments assumed to be *equivalent representations* of the construct. High positive correlations between the two tests help demonstrate evidence of overall construct validity. Test developers show convergent evidence typically by correlating their test's scores with the scores of comparable, well-established tests (i.e., a *gold standard*). For example, researchers have suggested that the Stanford–Binet Intelligence Scale (SB-5) global composite score is often higher than scores produced on other measures of intelligence (Minton & Pratt, 2006). Garred and Gilmore (2009) investigated the relationship between the SB-5 and the Wechsler Preschool and Primary Scales of Intelligence, Third Edition (WPPSI-III). After testing a sample of 32 four-year-olds with the SB-5 and WPPSI-III, the researchers calculated a correlation of .79. Although this is a statistically significant result, the relationship clearly has some error. What does this mean in practice? The decision to use one test over another may produce different results. In their research, Garred and Gilmore found that some students' IQ scores differed by as much as 16 points. If you consider the implications of IQ scores for school placement, then a difference of 16 points is incredibly large and quite problematic. This example provokes thought about relations to other variables, but it also has meaning for the discussion of consequences of testing. Keep this example in mind as you review the information later in this chapter.

Another common procedure for establishing convergent evidence occurs when tests are revised (Urbina, 2014). In this case, test developers report high correlations between the new test and previous editions as evidence that both are measuring the same construct. For example, the BDI-II test manual cites a correlation (r) of .94 between the BDI-I (Beck, Ward, & Mendelson, 1961) and the BDI-II (Beck, Steer, & Brown, 1996) as evidence that both editions measure the construct of depression. Evidence of convergent validity can also be obtained from correlations across the scores of *subtests*, or *subscales*, of different scales. For example, BDI-II has correlations with the Symptom Checklist-90-R Depression subscale ($r = .89$; Beck et al., 1996) and with the Millon Clinical Multiaxial Inventory Major Depression scale ($r = .71$; Millon, Millon, & Davis, 1994).

Another similar method used to substantiate validity involves discriminant evidence. In contrast to convergent evidence, *discriminant evidence* is based on consistently low correlations between the test and other tests that are supposed to measure different constructs. For example, we would assume that SAT scores would be unrelated to scores on a social skills measure or that scores from a measure of physical aggression would have low correlation with the scores on a measure assessing withdrawal.

The Multitrait-Multimethod Matrix. Campbell and Fiske (1959) proposed a design they called the *multitrait-multimethod matrix* (MTMM), which provides convergent and discriminant evidence of validity of a test. This approach involves measuring *two or more distinct traits* (i.e., constructs) with *two or more distinct measurement methods*. For example, we might measure the constructs of anxiety and depression using two methods: a self-report inventory and a clinical interview. Data is then collected and assembled into a matrix (also called a table of correlations) that displays correlations between

- the *same trait* assessed by the *same method* (i.e., reliability coefficients),
- the *same trait* assessed by *different methods* (i.e., convergent evidence),

TABLE 6.2 Sample of a Multitrait-Multimethod Matrix

Method	Traits	Self-Report			Observation			Teacher Ratings		
		AB	ATT	WD	AB	ATT	WD	AB	ATT	WD
Self-Report	AB	(.90)								
	ATT	.47	(.88)							
	WD	.35	.45	(.93)						
Observation	AB	**.61**	.25	.10	(.90)					
	ATT	.29	**.61**	.20	.46	(.93)				
	WD	.20	.28	**.59**	.32	.43	(.86)			
Teacher Ratings	AB	**.60**	.28	.15	**.58**	.25	.13	(.94)		
	ATT	.21	**.59**	.20	.20	**.62**	.21	.47	(.89)	
	WD	.12	.19	**.58**	.14	.20	**.63**	.37	.43	(.86)

Note: AB = Aggressive Behavior; ATT = Attention Problems; WD = Withdrawal.

- *different traits* measured by the *same methods*, and
- *different traits* measured by *different methods* (i.e., discriminant evidence).

The MTMM emphasizes the use of truly different multiple methods (e.g., self-report tests, observations, rating scales, projective measures, clinical interviews), and ideally each trait should be measured by each method. Table 6.2 is a hypothetical MTMM composed of three traits (i.e., aggressive behavior, attention problems, withdrawal) measured by three methods (i.e., self-rating, observation, teacher ratings).

The matrix shows the following:

- The highest coefficients (appearing in parentheses) are the reliability coefficients, which represent correlations between the *same method* measuring the *same trait*. These coefficients are highest because a trait should be more highly correlated with itself than anything else.
- The next highest coefficients (appearing in **bold** print) are validity coefficients that represent *different methods* measuring the *same trait*, which are evidence of convergent validity. For example, aggressive behavior as measured by observations and teacher ratings has a strong validity coefficient (r) of .60, showing that the two methods measure the same trait.
- The moderate coefficients (in *italics*) represent the *same methods* measuring *different traits*. We would expect these coefficients to be moderate, because they have the same method in common. For example, aggressive behavior and attention problems as measured by self-report resulted in a coefficient (r) of .47.
- The smallest coefficients (in plain type) represent *different methods* measuring *different traits*, indicating evidence of discriminant validity. We would expect these to be very low, because they share nothing in common: no traits or method similarities. For example, the correlation (r) between aggressive behavior as measured by self-report and withdrawal as measured by teacher ratings is .12.

The MTMM provides a great deal of data and a rigorous framework for assessing both convergent and discriminant validity evidence. Because it requires the use of multiple distinct methods that measure each trait, it is sometimes not feasible in educational and psychological assessment to meet the stringent requirements needed to use the process. For example, it may be difficult to find three distinct methods to measure one particular trait. However, variations of the MTMM are increasingly being used in validation studies that involve using only tests or subtests (instead of distinct methods) that measure both similar and dissimilar constructs.

GROUP DIFFERENTIATION STUDIES Another way to provide evidence of construct validity is to demonstrate that an instrument's scores can correctly and significantly differentiate between two groups of people known to or thought to differ on a particular trait. *Group differentiation* (or *contrasted group*) studies are used to analyze whether an instrument differentiates between different groups of individuals in ways predicted by theory. If two groups' test scores are found to be significantly different in a predicted way, then the test has evidence of construct validity. For example, the Kaufman Assessment Battery for Children (KABC-II; Kaufman & Kaufman, 2014) is an individually administered measure of processing and cognitive abilities in children and adolescents aged 3 to 18. As part of its validation process, it analyzed test scores among several different groups that represented such diagnostic or special education categories as learning disabilities, mental retardation, Attention Deficit/Hyperactivity Disorder (ADHD), gifted, and others. Each group's average scores were significantly different in expected ways from the *nonclinical group* (i.e., children who were not classified in diagnostic or special education categories) based on the standardization sample (i.e., the norm group). For example, it was expected that children with ADHD would score lower than the children in the norm group, and analysis indicated that there was a significant difference in scores on the KABC-II scales between children with ADHD and children in the standardization sample (Kaufman & Kaufman, 2014), with scores for the ADHD group being significantly lower than scores for the nonclinical group.

AGE DIFFERENTIATION STUDIES Related to group differentiation studies are age differentiation studies (also called *developmental studies*). *Age differentiation studies* focus on demonstrating validity by showing the degree to which test scores increase or decrease with age. We will look at intelligence as an example. According to intelligence theorists Horn and Cattell (1966, 1967), intelligence encompasses two general types: fluid intelligence and crystallized intelligence. *Fluid intelligence* is the ability to solve problems and adapt to new situations. *Crystallized intelligence* refers to acquired knowledge and ability obtained through education and personal experience. According to Horn and Cattell, fluid intelligence improves through childhood and adolescence and then begins to decline as early as late adolescence and into adulthood. In contrast, crystallized intelligence continues to increase through middle age and maintains during old age. In the development of the Kaufman Adolescent and Adult Intelligence Test (KAIT; Kaufman & Kaufman, 1993), which is a measure of general intelligence composed of separate scales for fluid and crystallized intelligence, the authors conducted age differentiation studies on several groups of individuals between 11 years and 85+ years. They found that crystallized intelligence scores increased until the mid-20s and then plateaued until age 54. After age 54, scores dropped steadily but not dramatically. By ages 75 to 85+, crystallized intelligence scores are similar to the scores for preadolescents and adolescents. Kaufman and Kaufman also found that fluid intelligence scores increase until around the early 20s. Fluid intelligence scores drop a bit but then remain the same until after age 54, when scores drop dramatically. By ages 75 to 85+, fluid intelligence scores are well below the mean for age 11. The results of the KAIT's age differentiation studies somewhat follow the pattern of age-related changes in intelligence predicted by Horn and Cattell.

EXPERIMENTAL RESULTS Another source of construct validity evidence is provided when a test is used to measure the effects of experimental interventions. For example, say that a researcher is interested in studying whether teaching children to use verbal rehearsal (i.e., verbally reciting information) helps them on a short-term memory task. After the intervention, the researcher compares the children's pretest and posttest scores on a short-term memory test to determine if the intervention was effective in improving short-term memory performance. If the scores increased significantly for children exposed to the intervention—versus no change for a matched group that did not participate—then the change in scores could be viewed as evidence of the test's validity, as well as evidence of the efficacy of the intervention.

Evidence Based on Consequences of Testing

Evidence based on consequences of testing is a type of validity evidence identified in the *Standards* (American Educational Research Association (AERA) et al., 2014) that refers to examining the *intended* and *unintended consequences* of the use of test results. Tests are commonly administered with the expectation that some benefit will come from the interpretation of test scores. Consequential evidence involves appraising the actual and potential consequences of test use, as well as the social impact of interpretations (Messick, 1989). Social consequences of testing may be either positive (such as improved educational policies) or negative (such as test score bias or unfair test use). It is important to gather evidence that the positive consequences of testing outweigh the adverse consequences. For example, consequential test validity of an academic admissions test would involve investigating whether the test unfairly selects or rejects members of different demographic groups for access to desirable or undesirable educational opportunities.

Lane (2014) discussed testing consequences from the framework of state-level performance assessment. Student performance in U.S. schools has received critical attention in recent decades. In response to emerging performance issues, states have implemented mandated testing programs. When mandated programs are implemented, there should be evidence that the programs are suitable for the intended outcomes (Lane, 2014). In order to construct a suitable validity argument for mandated programs, evidence should be reviewed that examines intended and unintended consequences. For example, in some cases curriculum might be narrowed in order to align strongly with the standards being measured and to improve the overall test scores of a school. By narrowing the curriculum, broader aspects of the standards might be ignored, and students are not exposed to material that might be important. As another example, imagine that a school district has a poor performance record on state tests. Because of the poor record, state funding is impacted, and the school district may be subject to state control. In this case, a superintendent and school principals might make changes in teacher or student assignments as an effort to improve performance of the district. The principals in the district might provide struggling teachers with materials that relate closely to test content. These efforts would not be related to the well-being of the students and could be problematic.

Evidence Based on Response Processes

The term *response processes* refers to the actions, thought processes, and emotional traits that the test taker invokes in responding to a test. Evidence based on response processes, sometimes viewed as part of content validity, provides validity support that examinees used intended cognitive and psychological processes during test taking. Differences in response processes may reveal sources of variance that are irrelevant to the construct being measured. For example, if a test is designed to measure an individual's ability to solve mathematical problems, then the individual's mental processes should reflect problem solving rather than remembering an answer he or she had already memorized. Understanding how test content affects test-taker response processes is very important for creating tests that assess the intended content domain and for avoiding unnecessary cognitive or emotional demands on student performance. Methods of examining response processes include think-aloud protocols (i.e., test takers think their responses out loud during the performance of a test item or task), posttest interviews (i.e., test takers explain reasons for their responses after taking the test), measurements of brain activity, and eye movement studies.

The superficial appearance of what a test measures from the perspective of the test taker or other untrained observer is part of the cognitive process that should be considered when investigating evidence of validity (Urbina, 2014). In other words, does a test *appear* to be measuring what it claims to be measuring? Does the test look legitimate to examinees who take it, to those who administer the test, and to other technically untrained observers? Anastasi and Urbina (1997) described how a test designed for children and extended for adult use was initially met with resistance and criticism because of its lack of surface legitimacy. To the adult test takers, the test appeared silly, childish, and inappropriate, thus impacting their cognitive process as they completed the test. As a result, the adults cooperated poorly with the testing procedure, thereby affecting the outcome of the test.

Summary

In this chapter, we introduced the concept of validity. Validity refers to whether the inferences and decisions made on the basis of test results are sound or appropriate. Threats to validity include construct underrepresentation (i.e., the test fails to include important dimensions or aspects of the identified construct) and construct-irrelevant variance (i.e., the test is too broad and contains too many variables, many of which are irrelevant to the construct), in addition to factors within the test, administration and scoring procedures, test-taker characteristics, and inappropriate test groups.

The process of test validation involves evaluating various sources of validity evidence. Evidence may focus on the content of the test (i.e., content evidence), the relationship between test results and external variables (i.e., relations to other variables), the internal structure of the test, test consequences, or the response process. Methods to evaluate construct validity evidence include evaluating evidence of the internal structure, convergent and discriminant validity evidence, group differentiation studies, age differentiation studies, experimental results, and factor analysis. Multiple methods are used to provide overall evidence of validity and to support the use of a test for different applications. It is the responsibility of test users to carefully read the validity information in the test manual and to evaluate the suitability of the test for their specific purposes.

Questions for Discussion

1. What is the meaning of the unitary concept of validity?
2. What types of validity evidence might be useful in the validation of each of the following? Explain.
   a. A reading test
   b. A depression symptom checklist
   c. A job performance test
3. What type of validity evidence is represented by each of these questions:
   a. Do the test items match the objectives of our school?
   b. How do the test results of the Pryor's Work Aspect Preference Scale compare with results from Super's Work Values Inventory?
   c. How well does the Orleans–Hanna Algebra Prognosis Test predict success or failure in Algebra I?

d. Is there a relationship between the score on the Minnesota Rate of Manipulation Test and workers' rate of assembly of a product?
e. Is there a relationship between the Mechanical Ability Test and performance of individuals in a 6-week training program in mechanics?
f. Is creativity a distinct factor measured by the test?
4. For each of the following criteria, identify at least two criterion measures that might be useful in validation studies:
   a. Success in a master's degree program in school counseling
   b. A medical student's "bedside manner" as a doctor
   c. Success in a retail sales position
5. If you wanted to construct a new instrument that assesses counseling skills in counselor trainees, describe the steps you would take to provide evidence of content validity.

Suggested Activities

1. We have provided a list of words and phrases (i.e., constructs) that describe various aspects of personality. Select one of the constructs and address the questions that follow.
   List of Possible Constructs:
   - Empathy
   - Genuineness
   - Selfishness
   - Patience
   - Intolerance
   a. Develop a clear definition of the construct.
   b. Brainstorm and identify several content areas that reflect the traits or behaviors of your construct.
   c. Construct a table of specifications based on the content areas.
2. Review several standardized tests and identify the types of validity evidence presented in the test manuals.
3. Review the manuals of two instruments that measure intelligence. Describe how the instruments define the construct of intelligence. In what ways are their definitions similar or different? What types of content evidence do the manuals provide? Based on this, which one do you think is a better measure of intelligence?

4. Study the validity sections of a test manual for an achievement test and personality test. How does information differ for these two types of tests? Explain.
5. Read critical reviews of some of the tests that you have taken and see what the reviewers say about the validity of the tests.
6. Read the test manual or a critical review of the Kaufman Brief Intelligence Instrument (KBIT-2). Identify two other cognitive ability tests that were used in the KBIT-2 validation process that provided convergent evidence.
7. Study the following descriptions of two tests and answer the questions that follow the descriptions:

Test A: 40 items
Description: Measure of self-esteem
Scales: Total Score, General Self-Esteem, Social Self-Esteem, Personal Self-Esteem
Reliability: Test-retest $r = .81$; coefficient alphas for the Total Score, General Self-Esteem, Social Self-Esteem, Personal Self-Esteem scales are .75, .78, .57, and .72, respectively.
Validity: Content—developed construct definitions for self-esteem, developed table of specifications,

wrote items covering all content areas, used experts to evaluate items. Convergent—correlated with Coopersmith's Self-Esteem Inventory $r = .41$. Discriminant—correlated with Beck Depression Inventory $r = .05$. Factor analysis revealed that the three subscales (General Self-Esteem, Social Self-Esteem, Personal Self-Esteem) are dimensions of self-esteem. Homogeneity—correlations between the scales indicate that the General scale correlated with the Social scale at .67, the Personal scale at .79, and the Total scale at .89.

Test B: 117 items

Scales: Global self-esteem, competence, lovability, likability, self-control, personal power, moral self-approval, body appearance, body functioning, identity integration, and defensive self-enhancement.

Reliability: Test-retest for each scale ranges from .65 to .71. Coefficient alphas range on each scale from .71 to .77.

Validity: Content—based on a three-level hierarchical model of self-esteem. Convergent—correlated with the Self-Concept and Motivation Inventory $r = .25$ and with the Eysenck Personality Inventory $r = .45$. Discriminant—correlated with Hamilton Depression Inventory $r = .19$.

a. Given the technical information provided, which of the preceding instruments would you select?

b. What additional information would you want to have to make your decision?

References

American Educational Research Association (AERA), American Psychological Association (APA), & National Council on Measurement in Education (NCME). (2014). *Standards for educational and psychological testing*. Washington, DC: Authors.

American Psychiatric Association (APA). (2013). *Diagnostic and statistical manual of mental disorders* (5th ed.). Washington, DC: Author.

Anastasi, A. (1988). *Psychological testing* (6th ed.). New York, NY: Macmillan.

Anastasi, A., & Urbina, S. (1997). *Psychological testing* (7th ed.). Upper Saddle River, NJ: Prentice Hall.

Beck, A. T., Steer, R. A., & Brown, G. K. (1996). *Manual for the Beck Depression Inventory-II*. San Antonio, TX: Psychological Corporation.

Beck, A. T., Ward, C., & Mendelson, M. (1961). Beck Depression Inventory (BDI). *Archives of General Psychiatry, 4*, 561–571.

Campbell, D.T., & Fiske, D.W. (1959). Convergent and discriminant validation by the multitrait-multimethod matrix. *Psychological Bulletin, 56*, 81–105.

Cohen, J. (1992). A power primer. *Psychological Bulletin, 112*, 155–159.

Cohen, R. J., & Swerdlik, M. E. (2012). *Psychological testing and assessment: An introduction to tests and measurement* (8th ed.). Boston, MA: McGraw-Hill.

Cronbach, L. J. (1990). *Essentials of psychological testing*. New York, NY: Harper & Row.

Garred, M., & Gilmore, L. (2009). To WPPSI or to Binet, that is the question: A comparison of the WPPSI-III and SB-5 with typically developing preschoolers. *Australian Journal of Guidance and Counselling, 19*(2), 104–115. doi:10.1375/ajgc.19.2.104

Gorin, J. S. (2007). Test construction and diagnostic testing. In J. P. Leighton & M. J. Gierl (Eds.), *Cognitive diagnostic assessment in education: Theory and practice* (pp. 173–201). Cambridge: Cambridge University Press.

Horn, J. L., & Cattell, R. B. (1966). Age differences in primary mental ability factors. *Journal of Gerontology, 21*, 210–220.

Horn, J. L., & Cattell, R. B. (1967). Age differences in fluid and crystallized intelligence. *Acta Psychologica, 26*, 107–129.

Kane, M. T. (2013). Validating the interpretations and uses of test scores. *Journal of Educational Measurement, 50*(1), 1–73.

Kane, M. T. (2006). Validation. In R. Brennan (Ed.), *Educational measurement* (4th ed., pp. 17–64). Westport, CT: Praeger.

Kaufman, A. S., & Kaufman, N. L. (1993). *Manual for Kaufman Adolescent and Adult Intelligence Test (KAIT)*. Circle Pines, MN: American Guidance Service.

Kaufman, A. S., & Kaufman, N. L. (2014). *Kaufman Assessment Battery for Children, second edition manual (KABC-II)*. Circle Pines, MN: American Guidance Service.

Kline, P. (2000). *The new psychometrics: Science, psychology, and measurement*. London: Routledge.

Lane, S. (2014). Validity evidence based on testing consequences. *Psicothema, 26*(1), 127–135.

Messick, S. (1989). Validity. In R. L. Linn (Ed.), *Educational measurement* (3rd ed., pp. 13–103). New York, NY: American Council on Education/Macmillan.

Messick, S. (1995). Validity of psychological assessment: Validation of inferences from persons' responses and performances as scientific inquiry into score meaning. *American Psychologist, 50,* 741–749.

Miller, M. D., Linn, R. L., & Gronlund, N. E. (2012). *Measurement and assessment in teaching* (11th ed.). Boston, MA: Allyn Bacon/Merrill Education.

Miller, S. A. (2012). *Developmental research methods* (4th ed.). Thousand Oaks, CA: Sage Publications.

Millon, T., Millon, C., & Davis, R. (1994). *MCMI-III manual: Millon Clinical Multiaxial Inventory–III.* Minneapolis, MN: National Computer Systems.

Minton, B. A., & Pratt, S. (2006). Gifted and highly gifted students: How do they score on the SB-5? *Roeper Review, 28,* 232–236.

Oren, C., Kennet-Cohen, T., Turvall, E., & Allalouf, A. (2014). Demonstrating the validity of three general scores of PET in predicting higher education achievement in Israel. *Psicothema, 26*(1), 117–126.

Padilla, J., & Benítez, I. (2014). Validity evidence based on response processes. *Psicothema, 26*(1), 136–144.

Piers, E. V., & Herzberg, D. S. (2002). *Piers–Harris Children's Self-Concept Scale manual* (2nd ed.). Los Angeles, CA: Western Psychological Services.

Psychological Corporation. (1997). *WAIS-III/WMS-III technical manual.* San Antonio, TX: Author.

Reynolds, C. R., Livingston, R. B., & Willson, V. (2008). *Measurement and assessment in education* (2nd ed.). Boston, MA: Pearson.

Rios, J., & Wells, C. (2014). Validity evidence based on internal structure. *Psicothema, 26*(1), 108–116.

Rubio, D. M. (2005). Content validity. *Encyclopedia of Social Measurement, 1,* 495–498.

Shultz, K. S., Whitney, D. A., & Jickar, M. J. (2014). *Measurement theory in action: Case studies and exercises* (2nd ed.). Thousand Oaks, CA: Sage Publications.

Sireci, S. G. (1998). The construct of content validity. *Social Indicators Research, 45,* 83–117.

Sireci, S., & Faulkner-Bond, M. (2014). Validity evidence based on test content. *Psicothema, 26*(1), 100–107.

Sireci, S., & Padilla, J. (2014). Validating assessments: Introduction to the special section. *Psicothema, 26*(1), 97–99

Urbina, S. (2014). *Essentials of psychological testing* (Vol. 4, 2nd ed.). Hoboken, NJ: John Wiley & Sons.

7 Selecting, Administering, Scoring, and Interpreting Assessment Results

In the previous chapters, we described the methods and sources of assessment data and discussed important information about statistical and measurement concepts. It will be important for you to keep the previous chapters in mind as you move into the next area of assessment training. Remember that everything we have covered thus far relates to the practice of assessment and that you should be working to integrate the information into a comprehensive framework of counseling assessment. In order to illustrate the primary concepts in this chapter, we will reiterate some information from previous chapters. We believe that repetition will help reinforce your learning of difficult concepts. Before we proceed to the next section of the textbook, which focuses on specific areas of assessment (e.g., intelligence, achievement, aptitude, career, personality), we need to address the process of selecting, administering, and scoring assessment instruments and interpreting assessment results.

After studying this chapter, you should be able to:

- Identify and describe the steps involved in selecting assessment instruments and strategies.
- List and describe the various resources that provide information about assessment instruments.
- Describe the process of evaluating assessment instruments or strategies.
- Describe the various procedures for administering assessment instruments.
- Describe the methods for scoring instruments and discuss their strengths and limitations.
- Describe the counselor's responsibilities in interpreting assessment results.

SELECTING ASSESSMENT INSTRUMENTS AND STRATEGIES

Selecting the most appropriate assessment instrument or strategy is a critical decision. The choice of instruments or strategies for a specific assessment will depend on several factors, such as the type of information needed, the needs of the client, resource constraints, the time frame available for the assessment, the quality of the assessment instrument, and the qualifications of the counselor. Therefore, the selection of assessment methods involves careful consideration and evaluation of instruments and strategies. The following steps (discussed in more detail ahead) may be helpful in selecting assessment instruments and strategies:

1. Identify the type of information needed.
2. Identify available information.
3. Determine the methods for obtaining information.
4. Search assessment resources.
5. Evaluate and select an assessment instrument or strategy.

Identify the Type of Information Needed

The first step in the process of selecting assessment methods is to identify the type of information needed. Any assessment instrument or strategy is useful only if it provides the information required for the assessment. Counselors determine what information to collect based on the purpose of assessment. As we stated in Chapter 1, there are several general purposes for assessment: screening, identification and diagnosis, intervention planning, and progress and outcome evaluation. As an example, say that a career counselor is trying to determine an intervention plan for a client dealing with a midcareer crisis. The counselor might be interested in obtaining such information as the client's employment history, current and future job desires, educational background, aptitudes, values, and interests. Alternately, a mental health counselor assessing a client for depression would want to know if the client is experiencing specific symptoms of depression, how the client is functioning at work, or if the client has ever had previous treatment for depression.

Identify Available Information

The next step is to identify and review existing assessment information. In clinical settings, intake questionnaires, biographical data, and preliminary diagnoses by clinicians and physicians are often available. School settings provide access to cumulative folders containing family information, educational history, grades, assessment and test results, anecdotal records, and attendance and health information. This existing information often provides useful, relevant information about a client that may be used in the current assessment process. Unfortunately, overtesting may sometimes occur; that is, a client may be asked to repeat a recent test or take a similar one. For example, one school district gave all of its students in grades 9 and 10 the Otis–Lennon School Ability Test, the Differential Aptitude Test, the School and College Ability Tests, and the California Test of Mental Maturity. These tests repeatedly assessed the same factors, and the results of multiple tests did not provide enough additional information to warrant such testing practices (recall the discussion of testing consequences in Chapter 6). On an individual basis, it is sometimes valuable to have more than one measure of scholastic aptitude or ability. However, when clients are asked to repeat the same test in a short time frame, they may lose motivation or even become hostile. It may be helpful to develop a checklist of information typically available on clients in a particular context. Figure 7.1 presents a sample checklist for a counselor in a school setting.

Determine the Methods for Obtaining Information

After identifying the type of information needed and reviewing any existing data, counselors need to determine the methods for obtaining assessment information. Recall that counselors have both formal and informal assessment instruments and strategies available for selection. Counselors can use interviews, tests, and observations when they have

	Needed?	
Cumulative folder of student	Yes	No
Birth date	_____	_____
Family information	_____	_____
Record of attendance	_____	_____
Permanent report card	_____	_____
Academic records from other schools	_____	_____
Attendance records	_____	_____
State achievement test results	_____	_____
Other achievement test results	_____	_____
College entrance exam results	_____	_____
Health data and records	_____	_____
Disciplinary actions	_____	_____
Functional behavior assessment	_____	_____
Behavioral intervention plans	_____	_____
Individualized Education Program	_____	_____
Class records		
Grades on tests and assignments	_____	_____
Progress in reading	_____	_____
Reading level	_____	_____
Competencies mastered	_____	_____
Samples of work	_____	_____
Anecdotal observations	_____	_____
Notes from parent conferences	_____	_____
School counselor's records		
Interest data	_____	_____
Behavior problems	_____	_____
Career and educational goals	_____	_____
Participation in school activities	_____	_____
Cooperative work experience data	_____	_____
Parent or guardian's records		
Nonschool activities and achievements	_____	_____
Health records	_____	_____
Transcripts or report cards	_____	_____
Papers or assignments	_____	_____

FIGURE 7.1   Sample checklist of client information available in school settings.

established appropriate competency. For example, if the goal of assessment is to evaluate a student for the potential of an existing learning disability, then the counselor might use a range of strategies and tests including a functional behavior assessment (FBA), rating scales, and an individual battery of ability tests. If a client is being assessed for career exploration, then an interest inventory may be administered. If an individual is being evaluated to determine eligibility for a counseling group for individuals with depression, then a counselor could use an unstructured interview to evaluate the client's depressive symptoms. Using a combination of formal and informal interviews, tests, and observations is recommended to obtain an in-depth evaluation of the client. The right combination of formal and informal assessment methods will vary from assessment to assessment.

Counselors should also consider assessment methods that are best suited to the client (e.g., paper-and-pencil test, computer assessment) and to the setting (Whiston, 2009). In addition, counselors need to choose assessment methods that they are qualified to administer and interpret.

Search Assessment Resources

With literally thousands of formal and informal instruments and strategies available to assess a multitude of abilities, character traits, attitudes, and more, counselors need to know how to locate and access information about assessment instruments. There is no single source available that catalogs every possible formal and informal assessment instrument. Sources vary with respect to detail; some provide comprehensive information, whereas others merely provide descriptions of tests. A list of the types of sources and their advantages and disadvantages is given in Table 7.1. We will review some of the most common sources of information, including reference sources, publishers' websites and catalogs, instrument manuals, research literature, Internet resources, professional organizations, and directories of unpublished instruments.

REFERENCE SOURCES   Probably the best source of information about commercial tests is the *Mental Measurements Yearbook* (*MMY*) series. Now in its 19th edition, the yearbook was founded in 1938 by Oscar K. Buros to provide evaluative information needed for informed test selection. Published at the Buros Institute of Mental Measurement at the University of Nebraska–Lincoln, the yearbooks provide descriptive information for over 2,800 tests,

TABLE 7.1 Sources of Assessment Instrument Information

Type	Advantages	Disadvantages
Reference Sources (*Mental Measurements Yearbook, Tests in Print, Test Critiques*)	Contain critical reviews of the test by experts Contain bibliography of studies done using the test, such as those to assess the validity and reliability of the test	May present dated information, because some volumes are published infrequently Can present a spotty or biased review, because reviewers do not follow a common format Do not discuss thoroughly the purposes and possible applications of the test
Publisher's Website or Catalog	Can get current information on the cost of the test and scoring services available Can get information on new tests and services available	Sometimes presents biased picture of the test Sometimes does not have necessary technical and practical information, such as time required, age or grade levels appropriate, sources from which to get complete test package, and basic information to screen quickly for appropriateness (such as a description of scales or subtests)
Specimen Sets	Can see test and test format; read and evaluate technical information; and judge validity, reliability, and interpretability of the test	Do not always include all pertinent information, such as technical manual or manual for interpretation or scoring keys

(continued)

TABLE 7.1 Sources of Assessment Instrument Information   (*Continued*)

Type	Advantages	Disadvantages
Manuals	Provide in-depth information on the nature of the instrument Describe the processes involved in test development Provide technical information Describe norm groups Provide guidelines for administration and interpretation	May present dated and biased material Can be highly technical or oversimplified May require background in measurement theory
Research Literature	Contains validity and reliability studies Contains reviews of certain instruments Contains research on issues in assessment	Contains spotty reviews without a common format and reviews only a few tests May take 2 to 3 years to get information into print because of publication backlog
Internet Resources	Present information that is retrievable through computerized searches Identify from a variety of sources the major tests and instruments developed May be updated systematically and published regularly	Identify sources that are not always readily available May use unfamiliar tests Involve a time lag between article publication and inclusion in the abstract
Professional Organizations	Keep abreast of new tests, texts, reference books in field, and issues related to test construction, administration, and interpretation Sometimes offer up-to-date bibliographies of articles and research reports using or evaluating a given test or test procedure	Can present biased information Can require a subscription cost Do not index sources, so information may be hard to retrieve
Directories of Unpublished Instruments	Provide information on instruments not commercially available	May include dated and sometimes incomplete sources May not present information on many of the technical and practical issues, such as cost and time

including the publisher, prices, population for whom the test is appropriate, and psychometric information (i.e., reliability, validity, norming data). As a distinctive feature, the *MMY* also includes critical reviews by test experts as well as a list of reviewer's references. The *MMY* may be found in hardcopy at academic libraries, electronically through the EBSCO and OVID/SilverPlatter databases, and at the Buros website (buros.org; for a fee, test reviews are available online exactly as they appear in the *MMY* series).

   Tests in Print (*TIP*) is another Buros Institute publication. Now in its eighth edition, it is a comprehensive listing of all commercially available tests written in the English language. It includes the same basic information about a test that is included in the *MMY*, but it does *not* contain reviews or psychometric information. The *TIP* guides readers to the *MMY* for more detailed information about tests. The *TIP* can be found in hardcopy in academic libraries and electronically through the EBSCO database.

Other widely used reference sources include *Test Critiques* and *Tests*, both published by Pro-Ed, Inc. *Tests* provides a comprehensive listing of all tests available in the English language. It provides descriptions of tests, but does not contain critical reviews or psychometric information; this information can be found for selected instruments in *Test Critiques*. *Test Critiques,* designed to be a companion to *Tests*, contains a three-part description of each test: Introduction, Practical Application/Uses, and Technical Aspects. It also provides psychometric information and a critical review of each test.

PUBLISHERS AND WEBSITE CATALOGS All of the major test publishers have websites that include online catalogs of their products. These online catalogs can be a good source of descriptive information about the most recent editions of tests. The information may include the cost of materials and scoring, types of scoring services, and ancillary materials available through the publisher. It is important to remember that publishers' websites are marketing tools aimed at selling products; they do not provide all the information needed to fully evaluate a test. Counselors can also order a *specimen set* of the test from the publisher, which includes the manual, test booklet, answer sheet, and scoring key. Table 7.2 provides a list of some of the major U.S. test publishers and their website addresses. Many publishers also provide hardcopy versions of their catalogs.

MANUALS Test manuals, available from test publishers, provide administrative and technical information about a test. Indeed, because most of the information one would want about a particular psychological or educational test can be found in test manuals, they are

TABLE 7.2 Some Major U.S. Test Publishers

Academic Therapy Publications *academictherapy.com*	Harcourt Assessment (see Pearson Education)	The Psychological Corporation (see Pearson Education)
	Institute for Personality and Ability Testing (IPAT) *ipat.com*	
The American College Testing Program (ACT) *act.org*	Pearson Education *pearsonassessments.com*	Riverside Publishing Company *riverpub.com*
CTB/McGraw-Hill *ctb.com*	Pearson Instructional Resources *pearsonschool.com*	Scholastic Testing Service, Inc. *ststesting.com*
	Pearson Education *pearsonassessments.com*	
CPP and Davies-Black Publishing *cpp.com*	Pro-Ed *proedinc.com*	Slosson Educational Publications *slosson.com*
Educational Testing Service *ets.org*	Psychological Assessment Resources *parinc.com*	Stoelting Company *stoeltingco.com*

	Yes	No
1. Test manual available at time of publication of test	_____	_____
2. Test manual is complete, accurate, and clearly written	_____	_____
3. Rationale and uses of test discussed	_____	_____
4. User cautioned about possible misuses	_____	_____
5. Norming population described	_____	_____
6. Reliability evidence provided	_____	_____
7. Validity evidence provided	_____	_____
8. Special qualifications of users stated	_____	_____
9. Bibliography of research and studies on test presented	_____	_____
10. Test manual updated and revised when new edition of test was published	_____	_____
11. Test administration conditions and modes explained	_____	_____
12. Interpretive aids provided for test takers	_____	_____
13. Test interpretation easy to understand	_____	_____
14. Evidence supporting the accuracy of computer-generated interpretations	_____	_____
15. Automated test interpretation service available	_____	_____
16. Rationale presented and conceptualized if cutoff scores are given	_____	_____
17. Technical information is presented about appropriateness of the instrument for diverse groups, e.g., age, grade level, language, cultural background, gender	_____	_____
18. Method of recommended linguistic modification described in detail	_____	_____

FIGURE 7.2   Checklist for evaluating a test manual.

the primary source to consult in the test selection process. Tests manuals should be complete, accurate, current, and clear. The manual should provide information about test specifications (i.e., purpose of the test, definition of constructs measured, description of the population for which the test is intended, information about interpretation) and general standards for the preparation and publication of test documentation: manuals and user guides (American Educational Research Association (AERA), American Psychological Association (APA), & National Council on Measurement in Education (NCME), 2014). Figure 7.2 shows a checklist summary of those standards.

RESEARCH LITERATURE Published research is an excellent source of information about tests. *Academic journals* are available that focus specifically on assessment and testing used in education, psychology, and other fields (see Table 7.3). In addition, specific *journal articles* on test reviews or about research studies using specific tests can provide professionals with information about widely used assessment instruments.

INTERNET RESOURCES The Internet provides a number of ways to search for test information. A test locator or test collection allows users to search for information about instruments from a variety of sources. Access to test locators is available through several sponsored websites, including the Buros Institute (buros.unl.edu/buros/jsp/search.jsp), the Educational Testing Service (ETS; ets.org/testcoll), and the ERIC Clearinghouse on

TABLE 7.3 Journals Related to Assessment

Applied Measurement in Education

Applied Psychological Measurement

Assessment

Assessment and Evaluation in Higher Education

Assessment in Education

Educational and Psychological Measurement

Educational Assessment

Educational Measurement: Issues and Practices

Journal of Psychoeducational Assessment

Journal of Career Assessment

Journal of Educational Measurement

Journal of Personality Assessment

Measurement and Evaluation in Counseling and Development

Psychological Assessment

Assessment and Evaluation (ericae.net). In addition, as previously stated, test reviews from the MMY are available online for a fee (marketplace.unl.edu/buros/).

Information about instruments can also be found through an online search of *PsycINFO*, which is an abstract database that indexes all published research in psychology from the 1800s to the present. *Psychological Abstracts* is the print counterpart to *PsycINFO*, and *PsycLIT* is the CD-ROM version of *PsycINFO*.

PROFESSIONAL ORGANIZATIONS A number of *professional organizations* exist that provide information on assessment. Most have websites or publish journals, newsletters, or other publications about general assessment issues or about assessment in a specific context (e.g., assessment in the schools, employment testing). Table 7.4 presents a list of some professional associations.

DIRECTORIES OF UNPUBLISHED INSTRUMENTS Assessment instruments are not limited to published tests. There is a vast quantity of unpublished or noncommercial inventories, checklists, projective techniques, and other instruments that exists in the social sciences research literature. The *Directory of Unpublished Experimental Measures* (2008) is one of the most popular printed directories of unpublished instruments. This directory provides access to recently developed tests that are not commercially available. These instruments have been used by other researchers on a variety of topics in education and psychology. The directory groups tests according to function and content and provides information about tests' purpose, format, psychometric information, and related research.

Evaluate and Select an Assessment Instrument or Strategy

When selecting which assessment instruments and strategies to use, counselors must evaluate instruments on the basis of several factors (e.g., purpose, test scores, reliability,

TABLE 7.4 Professional Associations Related to Assessment	
American Counseling Association (ACA) *counseling.org*	International Personnel Management Association Assessment Center (IPMAAC) *ipmaac.org*
American Educational Research Association (AERA) *aera.net*	National Academy of Science's Board on Testing and Assessment (BOTA) *nationalacademies.org/cbsse/bota.nsf*
American Psychological Association (APA) *apa.org*	National Association of Test Directors (NATD) *natd.org*
American Speech-Language-Hearing Association (ASHA) *asha.org*	National Association of School Psychologists (NASP) *naspweb.org*
The Association for Assessment and Research in Counseling (AARC) *aarc-counseling.org*	The National Center for Fair and Open Testing *fairtest.org*
Association of Test Publishers *testpublishers.org*	The National Center for Research on Evaluation, Standards, and Student Testing (CRESST) *cse.ucla.edu*
The Division of Evaluation, Measurement, and Statistics *apa.org/divisions/div5*	National Council on Measurement in Education (NCME) *assessment.iupui.edu/ncme*
Educational Testing Service (ETS) *ets.org*	
ERIC Clearinghouse on Assessment and Evaluation *ericae.net*	

validity). For most published formal assessment instruments, the test manual is the primary source of evaluative information. However, prior to selecting an assessment instrument for close evaluation, you may elect to read published test reviews as a primary evaluation. This section presents several questions to guide professionals in evaluating and selecting a formal assessment instrument or strategy. As you read, you should recall information from previous chapters and attempt to apply that information to the information here. By going through these questions and applying the information you have already learned, you will improve your ability to successfully evaluate an assessment instrument.

What is the purpose of the instrument? Who is the intended population? The first question to ask when investigating an instrument is whether the purpose of the instrument is appropriate for the counselor's needs. If an instrument does not measure the behavior or construct of interest, then there is no need to further evaluate the instrument. Another factor is the extent to which an instrument is appropriate for the individual(s) being assessed. The manual should clearly state the instrument's recommended uses as well as describe the population for which it was intended.

What is the makeup of the norm group? This question addresses whether the sample of individuals (i.e., norm group) used during instrument development represents the population of potential examinees. The norm group must reflect the population from which it is drawn. This is particularly important with norm-referenced instruments, because it is the norm group's performance to which an examinee's performance is compared and by which it is interpreted. Counselors should evaluate the suitability of the norm group in terms of representativeness, the year that the sample was gathered, and the size of the norm group (see Chapter 4).

Are the results of the instrument reliable? Reliability addresses the degree to which scores are consistent, dependable, and stable. Any fluctuation in scores that results from factors irrelevant to what is being measured is called measurement error. There are several methods of estimating the reliability applicable to the various sources of measurement error, including test-retest, alternate forms, internal consistency, and interrater reliability (see Chapter 5).

Do the instrument's results have evidence of validity? Validity refers to whether the claims and decisions that are made on the basis of assessment results are sound or appropriate. Evidence of validity can be obtained by systematically examining the content of the instrument, by considering how the instrument's scores relate to other similar instruments, or by considering the association between scores and other variables related to the construct being measured. The manual or published research studies are sources of validity information (see Chapter 6).

Does the instrument's manual provide clear and detailed instructions about administration procedures? All administration specifications should be fully described in the manual, including instructions and time limits. Depending on the type of instrument, other administration issues may be presented, including the use of reference materials and calculators, lighting, equipment, seating, monitoring, room requirements, testing sequence, and time of day.

Does the manual provide sufficient information about scoring, interpreting, and reporting results? The instrument's manual should present information about the materials and resources available to aid in scoring the instrument, such as scoring software, mail-in scoring services, or scoring keys and templates. Information should also be provided about the methods used to interpret and report results. Many instrument developers provide computer-generated profiles and narrative reports based on test results. Counselors need to determine whether profiles are clear and easy to understand and whether narrative reports provide accurate and comprehensive information.

Is the instrument biased? An instrument is considered biased if differences in results are attributable to demographic variables (e.g., gender, race, ethnicity, culture, age, language, geographic region) rather than to the construct being measured. Instrument developers are expected to exhibit sensitivity to the demographic characteristics of examinees and to document appropriate steps taken to minimize bias (see Chapter 6).

What level of competency is needed to use the instrument? In the past few decades, increasing concerns about the possibility of test misuse have led professional organizations to disseminate information about test user competencies and qualifications. To use certain assessment instruments, counselors need education, training, and supervised experience particular to the instrument. In general, qualified test users should have knowledge and skills in psychometric principles and statistics; instrument selection; and procedures for administering, scoring, interpreting, communicating, and securing test results (Association for Assessment and Research in Counseling, 2003). The purchase of assessment instruments is generally restricted to persons who meet certain minimum qualifications of education and training. Most publishers rely on a three-level system for classifying test user qualifications that was first developed by the APA in 1950. The APA dropped the classification system in 1974, but many publishers continue to use it or a similar system. The classification includes the following levels:

A-Level: These instruments do *not* require users to have advanced training in administration and interpretation. To purchase an A-level instrument, an individual may have a bachelor's degree in psychology, human services, education, or related disciplines; training or certification relevant to assessment; or practical experience in the use of assessment instruments. Examples of A-level tests include some aptitude and career exploration tests.

B-Level: To use B-level instruments, practitioners typically have a graduate degree in psychology, counseling, education, or related disciplines; have completed specialized training or coursework in assessment; or have licensure or certification documenting training and experience in assessment. In addition, being a member of a professional organization such as the American Speech-Language-Hearing Association (ASHA) or the American Occupational Therapy Association (AOTA) may make one eligible to purchase B-level products. Examples of B-level tests include general intelligence tests and interest inventories.

C-Level: C-level instruments require users to have B-level qualifications plus a doctorate degree in psychology or a related discipline (that provides appropriate training in the administration and interpretation of assessment instruments) or licensure/certification or to be under direct supervision of a qualified professional in psychology or a related field. Examples of C-level instruments include intelligence tests, personality tests, and projective measures (e.g., the Wechsler Intelligence Scale for Children [WISC-IV], the Minnesota Multiphasic Personality Inventory [MMPI-II], the Rorschach Inkblot Test).

What practical issues should be considered for this instrument? When evaluating a particular assessment instrument, counselors should consider issues of practicality. These include the time required for administration, cost of the instrument, format, readability, administration procedures, scoring procedures, and interpretation.

Time Required to Administer the Instrument: The time it takes to give a test may be a factor. In a school setting, can the test be administered during the regular class period, or does the examiner need more time? In an outpatient mental health counseling center, can an instrument be completed by the client within the traditional 50-minute time period for individual counseling? How many individually administered tests can an examiner reasonably schedule during a day? We know that the longer the test, the more reliable the results, but how much reliability is necessary for a particular purpose might be a concern if it significantly extends the time of testing.

Ease of Administration: Administration of tests is discussed in more detail later in the chapter, but it should be noted here that there are different procedures for test administration. Some require extensive training to administer and score; others do not. Some tests are more difficult to administer because they have a number of individually timed subtests and elaborate instructions for the test taker. The test users should read through the test manual and evaluate the difficulty of test administration.

Ease of Scoring: How an instrument is scored is an important issue, because it is possible for scoring to take more time than administering a test. Tests may be hand scored, computer scored, or sent to the publisher for scoring. In most cases, hand-scored instruments are more time-consuming; if the instrument's publishers provide scoring templates or answer keys, then hand-scoring may be somewhat quicker. Some instruments also require considerable training and experience on the part of the examiner.

Ease of Interpretation: Results are not useful unless they are interpretable, and both test developers and examiners are expected to provide explanation. Many instruments provide computer-based interpretations based on test results. Instruments may also provide detailed sections in the manual, or separate manuals, that focus specifically on interpretation. The better tests have sample or illustrative case studies. Test users should also check to see whether an instrument provides computer-generated narratives, profile or summary sheets, or other materials to guide the test takers in understanding the results.

Format: Just as in the evaluation of other printed material, test users should consider factors such as size of print, attractiveness of format, and clarity of illustrations. Some tests are attractively designed and utilize a variety of colors and print sizes. Some, however, have print that is too small or dark paper that is hard to read. Some tests may use double columns to cut down on necessary eye movements; others spread the items across the whole page. The test user should think of the test taker when evaluating such characteristics. An attractive format may provide more valid results.

Readability: The readability of the test is an important factor. In general, unless the intent is to test the reading level or verbal facility of the test taker, the reading level should be kept simple so that the desired construct is measured rather than a reading comprehension factor. Even a test presented in audio format should have an appropriate reading level and vocabulary to ensure comprehension.

Cost of the Instrument: Cost is an important feature when considering a particular instrument, because most schools and agencies have limited budgets. Purchasing a commercially available instrument can become quite expensive and may require buying the manual, test booklets, answer sheets, scoring templates, computer software, or ancillary materials. Some test publishers now lease tests, especially achievement test batteries, rather than requiring the user to purchase them. Also, some test booklets are reusable, requiring the examiner to purchase only answer sheets for another testing. Computer software might increase the initial outlay for an instrument, but may become more cost effective per test administration if the instrument is used frequently. There are also scoring services to which most of the major tests and test batteries can be sent for scoring and interpretation—at an additional cost, of course.

USING AN INSTRUMENT EVALUATION FORM One way to make the process of evaluating and selecting assessment instruments easier is to use an *instrument evaluation form* (see Figure 7.3). Such a form provides a convenient way to document important aspects of an

Instrument Evaluation Form

Instrument title _____   Author(s) _____

Publisher _____   Publication date _____

Examiner qualifications _____

Brief Description of the Instrument
General type (group achievement test,
  multiple aptitude battery, interest
  inventory, personality inventory, etc.)
Population (age, gender, culture, etc.)
Purpose of the instrument
Scores provided
Types of items

Technical Evaluation
Reliability evidence (test-retest, split-half,
  alternate-form, internal consistency,
  interrater, standard error of measurement)
Validity evidence (content, criterion-related,
  construct)
Norm group (composition, size, appropriate
  to potential test taker)

Practical Features
Administration procedures/time
Scoring and interpretation procedures
Adequacy of test manual cost

Previous Reviews
Mental Measurements Yearbook
Other sources

Evaluation of Instrument
Summary of strengths
Summary of weaknesses
Final recommendation

FIGURE 7.3   Instrument evaluation form.

instrument and increases the likelihood that important facts will not be overlooked. When utilizing an instrument review form, counselors are encouraged to obtain information from both the instrument manual and a reference source, preferably one that provides reviews (such as the *MMY*). An important aspect of using an instrument evaluation form is identifying the instrument's strengths and weaknesses. This aids in the final process of integrating information and making a selection decision. It is imperative that counselors have the requisite skills to evaluate a test before using it in practice. Exercises 7.1 and 7.2 provide an opportunity to practice the test review process and to test your knowledge.

Exercise 7.1
Conducting a Test Review: Beck Depression Inventory-II

You are a mental health counselor currently working in an outpatient counseling clinic with adult clients. You are considering whether or not to adopt the Beck Depression Inventory-II (BDI-II; Beck, Steer, & Brown, 1996) in your practice. Many of your clients seem to suffer from depression, and you think that using an instrument that specifically assesses depressive symptoms would help you in making an accurate diagnosis. You currently work 40 hours each week at the clinic and see about 20 clients each week for hour-long individual counseling sessions. The rest of your time is devoted to treatment planning, writing progress notes, staff meetings, and supervision.

Information about the BDI-II is located in Chapter 13. After reviewing the information about the BDI-II, answer exercise questions 1–7.

Norm Group

Conduct a search of the Mental Measurements Yearbook (MMY) for reviews of the Beck Depression Inventory II. As you read the reviews, make note of the following pieces of information related to the instrument.

1. A clinical sample was used in the development of the BDI-II, In the reviews, note the number of participants, geographic locations of the sample, demographic data (e.g., number of men vs. women, average age, racial/ethnic distributions, and any other relevant data about the participants.

2. A nonclinical sample was also used in the development of the BDI-II, In the reviews, note the number of participants, geographic locations of the sample, demographic data (e.g., number of men vs. women, average age, racial/ethnic distributions, and any other relevant data about the participants.

Reliability

3. *Internal consistency* was one of the methods used to establish reliability of the BDI-II. Make note in the reviews of the data related to internal consistency.

4. *Test-retest reliability:* Test-retest reliability was the other method of establishing reliability for the BDI-II. Make note in the reviews of the data related test-retest reliability.

Validity

5. *Content validity:* Examine the test reviews to determine the criteria that the BDI-II item content was validated against.

6. *Convergent validity:* Correlations were examined between the BDI-II and other instruments. Consider the various other tests that were used to validate the BDI-II

7. *Discriminant validity:* Several tests were performed to determine expected differences between the BDI-II and certain scales on other instruments. Search the MMY reviews for information related to discriminant validity.

After reviewing all of the information in items 1–7, answer the exercise questions that follow.

Exercise Questions:

1. Describe and evaluate the norm group. Do you think it is representative? Do you think the norm group is current? Do you believe the size of the norm group was large enough? Are the samples related to the population you intend to use the test with? Explain.

2. Describe and evaluate each method used to estimate reliability. Does the reliability evidence support a decision to use the instrument? Explain.

3. Describe and evaluate each type of validity evidence.

4. Does the validity evidence support a decision to use the instrument? Explain.

5. Describe the practical aspects of the instrument, focusing on issues related to time required for administration, ease of administration, and ease of scoring.

6. Summarize the strengths and weaknesses of the inventory. Based on your review of the BDI-II, would you adopt this instrument? Explain your answer.

Exercise 7.2
Conducting a Test Review: Coopersmith Self-Esteem Inventory

You are a middle school counselor starting a new group aimed at enhancing self-concept in students. You work at a large urban school with a culturally and linguistically diverse population of students. You have heard about the Coopersmith Self-Esteem Inventory (SEI), but you're not sure if it's the appropriate instrument to use.

After reviewing the information ahead about the Coopersmith SEI, answer the questions that follow.

Description:

The Coopersmith SEI (Coopersmith, 1981) measures evaluative attitudes toward the self in social, academic, family, and personal areas of experience. Coopersmith defined self-esteem as a judgment of worthiness that is expressed by the attitudes an individual holds toward his or her self. Coopersmith believes that self-esteem is significantly associated with effective functioning, such as school performance.

Each questionnaire presents respondents with generally favorable or generally unfavorable statements about the self, which they indicate as *Like Me* or *Unlike Me*. The School Form is a 50-item inventory designed for 8- to 15-year-old children. It provides a Total Self Score as well as scores on four subscales: General Self (Gen), Social Self/Peers (Soc), Home/Parents (H), and School/Academic (Sch). The School Form is accompanied by an eight-item Lie Scale to assess defensiveness. The School Short Form is comprised of 25 items from the School Form. The Adult Form is an adaptation of the School Short Form for individuals over 15 years of age.

Administration time rarely exceeds 10 minutes. The instrument can be hand scored in a few minutes via scoring keys.

For interpretation, high scores correspond to high self-esteem. A high Lie Scale score suggests defensiveness (indicates that the test taker attempted to respond positively to all items).

Technical Information

Norm group: The SEI was administered to 643 public school children in grades 3 through 8. The sample consisted primarily of students from the lower and middle upper socioeconomic ranges. The test manual stated that "a considerable number of Spanish surnamed and Black children were included in the sample." The manual strongly recommends that users develop local norm groups.

Reliability

Test-retest: The test-retest reliability coefficient after a 5-week interval (with a sample of 30 fifth graders) was .88. Test-retest reliability after a three-year interval (with a sample of 56 public school children) was .70.

Internal consistency: Studies reported KR20 coefficients ranging from .87 to .92 on scores for school children in grades 4 to 8.

Alternate forms: A study comparing the SEI to a Canadian version of the test (using a sample of 198 children in third through sixth grades) found correlation coefficients ranging from .71 to .80.

Validity

Content validity evidence: Most of the items on the SEI School Form were adapted from scale items used by Rogers and Dymond (1954) in their classic study of nondirective psychotherapy; several original items were also included. All of the statements were worded for use with children aged 8 to 10. Five psychologists sorted the items into two groups: those indicative of high self-esteem and those indicative of low self-esteem. Items that seemed repetitive or ambiguous or about which there was disagreement were eliminated.

Exercise Questions:

1. Describe and evaluate the norm group. Do you think it is representative? Do you think the norm group is current? Do you believe the size of the norm group was large enough? Are the samples related to the population you intend to use the test with? Explain.

2. Describe and evaluate each method used to estimate reliability. Does the reliability evidence support a decision to use the instrument? Explain.

3. Describe and evaluate each type of validity evidence.

4. Does the validity evidence support a decision to use the instrument? Explain.

5. Describe the practical aspects of the instrument, focusing on issues related to time required for administration, ease of administration, and ease of scoring.

6. Summarize the strengths and weaknesses of the inventory.

7. Based on your review of the Coopersmith SEI, would you adopt this instrument? Explain your answer.

ADMINISTERING ASSESSMENT INSTRUMENTS

Many counselors are responsible for administering assessment instruments, whether it be a standardized test, an informal questionnaire, or a behavioral observation checklist. The process of administering assessment instruments is an important task, because assessment results can be invalidated by careless administration (Whiston, 2009). There are numerous ways that assessment instruments can be administered to a client, each having distinct advantages and disadvantages (see Table 7.5). Regardless of which mode or format is

TABLE 7.5 Modes of Administering Assessment Instruments

Mode	Description	Advantages	Disadvantages
Self-Administered	Examinees read the instructions themselves and take the test. The examiner does not need to be present.	The examiner does not need to be present.	The motivation or attitudes of test takers are not known. They may be confused or unclear about tasks.
Individually Administered	The examiner administers the test to one individual at a time.	The examiner can assess the motivation and attitudes of the test taker as well as thought processes and cognitive level. The examiner can probe to gain more information.	This method is expensive, and only a few individuals can be tested each day. The examiner needs special training and experience in administering individual tests.

(continued)

TABLE 7.5 Modes of Administering Assessment Instruments   (*Continued*)

Mode	Description	Advantages	Disadvantages
Group Administered	The test is administered simultaneously to many examinees.	This is the most cost-effective method involving an examiner.	The motivation and attitude of the test takers are unknown.
Computer Administered	The directions for taking the test and the test itself are presented on the computer screen.	The test taker often can get immediate feedback. The examiner does not necessarily have to be present. This method allows for flexibility in scheduling. The computer can score, analyze, and interpret the tests of a large group of individuals. Computer-adaptive tests usually take less time to complete.	Some individuals may not perform well because of certain disabilities or because of their attitude toward computers. This method may not be practical if many individuals are to be tested.
Video Administration	Test directions and/or actual test items are presented using video recordings.	This method allows for both audio and visual stimuli to be combined. Simulated or real situations can be presented. A wider variety of behaviors can be assessed.	The method may be inappropriate for individuals with certain disabilities.
Audio Administration	The test is presented using audio recordings.	The examiner can circulate to see whether there are any problems. Testing time can be controlled. The quality of the recording and the type of voice can be uniformly controlled. This method is good to use with individuals who have reading problems.	This method is inappropriate for individuals with hearing, listening, or attention deficits.
American Sign Language	The examiner gives directions and presents the test items using sign language.	American Sign Language is the first language of many individuals with hearing impairments.	The examiner needs to be experienced in signing and working with individuals with hearing impairments. Some of these individuals might have learned a different system.
Nonverbal	The examiner avoids oral or written directions and relies on universal hand and body gestures to explain tasks to the examinee.	This method is appropriate for certain individuals with disabilities, such as those with speech disabilities.	The examiner must be trained in administering such tests and experienced in working with the various special populations.

Pretesting Procedures
_____ Review manuals and materials.
_____ Read and practice the directions for administering the test.
_____ Schedule room and facilities.
_____ Orient client(s) about the purpose of testing.
_____ Send out notice to remind client(s) of testing time.
_____ Get informed consent if needed.
_____ Identify any special materials or tools needed.
_____ Have testing materials on hand.
_____ Highlight directions in the manual.
_____ Decide on order of administration of tests.
_____ Decide on procedures for collection of test materials.
_____ Prepare answers for specific questions clients might ask.

Immediately Before Administration
_____ Organize test materials.
_____ Make and check seating arrangements.
_____ Check lighting and ventilation.
_____ Arrange clear and adequate work space.
_____ Organize materials and arrange for distribution.

During the Administration
_____ Distribute assessment instrument and materials in the specified manner.
_____ Administer instrument using specified instructions.
_____ Check time limits for the test.
_____ Record any critical incidents.
_____ Note any irregularities in test behavior.

After the Administration
_____ Collect materials in the specified manner.
_____ Follow directions for storing materials.

FIGURE 7.4   Checklist for administering assessment instruments.

used, counselors are responsible for following specified administration procedures. Procedures for administering instruments include activities that take place before, during, and after administration. A counselor might benefit from a checklist of administration activities like the one illustrated in Figure 7.4.

Before Administration

The first major responsibility of the counselor prior to administering the instrument is to know all about the instrument. Counselors should review the manual, forms, answer sheets, and other materials. They should also be familiar with the content of the instrument, the type of items, and the directions for administering the test. One of the best ways to become familiar with an assessment instrument is to follow the procedures and actually take the test.

For many instruments, there are management tasks that must be accomplished prior to the day of administration. For example, when administering a group achievement test, it is necessary to secure the appropriate number of tests as well as answer sheets and other test materials. Other pretesting procedures may include scheduling the date for administering the test; scheduling rooms or facilities; ensuring accurate numbers of book-lets, answer sheets, pencils, and any other needed materials; arranging materials for distri-bution; and so on.

Examiners must also obtain and document *informed consent* from examinees orally or in writing prior to the assessment (American Counseling Association (ACA), 2014). Clients must be informed about the nature and purpose of the evaluation and of information con-cerning confidentiality limits and how the security of test results will be maintained (Urbina, 2014). If the client is a minor, then it is necessary to get parental consent before the assess-ment process begins. Furthermore, the Code of Ethics of the National Board for Certified Counselors (NBCC, 2013) states that prior to administering assessment instruments or tech-niques counselors must provide specific information to examinees so that the results may be put in the proper perspective with other relevant factors. Explaining why an instrument is being administered, who will have access to the results, and why it is in the test taker's best interest to participate in the assessment process can help ensure cooperation (Graham, 2011). Examiners can provide orientation sessions that can cover the following topics:

1. Purpose of the assessment instrument
2. Criteria used for selecting the assessment instrument
3. Conditions under which the instrument is to be taken
4. Range of skills or domains to be measured
5. Administrative procedures and concerns (e.g., group or individual administration, time involved, cost)
6. Types of questions on the instrument and an overview
7. Type of scoring, method, and schedule for reporting results to the test taker

Many standardized tests provide sample items and an overview of the test. The examiner should be sure that all who are going to take a given test have had specific practice with sample problems or have worked on test-taking skills prior to the test. This requirement is especially appropriate for aptitude, achievement, and ability testing.

When administering an instrument to a large number of clients or students, the coun-selor will need help from other individuals, such as teachers, administrators, or counse-lors. These assistants must be trained on the instrument; this includes a general overview of the instrument and preferably some practice giving and taking it. Hands-on experience helps in identifying some of the types of problems that might arise—for example, what to do with clients or students who finish early. All administrators need to know the guide-lines for answering questions about the test and the importance of following standardized procedures in administering the test. In order to make determinations about the test and its appropriateness for certain clients, counselors should have a comprehensive under-standing of validity and reliability. Exercise 7.3 provides an opportunity to practice an evaluation of validity and reliability for a pair of instruments. Review the information and then complete the exercise questions.

During Administration

When it's time to administer an assessment instrument, the counselor may begin with a final check to see that all is in order. For group tests, examiners need to check on materials, lighting, ventilation, seating arrangements, clear work space for examinees, sharpened pencils, a "Do Not Disturb" sign, and so on. Individual tests should be administered in a

Exercise 7.3
Examining Instrument Validity and Reliability

Concurrent validity evidence: SEI scores correlated with the SRA Achievement Series and the Lorge Thorndike Intelligence Test at .33 and .30, respectively.

Predictive validity evidence: Reading Gifted Evaluation Scale (a measure of reading achievement) scores correlated with the SEI General Self subscale and the Lie Scale scores at .35 and .39, respectively.

Convergent validity Evidence: Correlation between SEI scores and the California Psychological Inventory Self-Acceptance Scale was .45.

Subscale intercorrelations (internal structure):

	General Self	Social Self-Peers	Home-Parents	School-Academic	Lie Scale*
General Self	—	.49	.52	.42	−.02
Social Self-Peers		—	.28	.29	−.09
Home-Parents			—	.45	−.04
School-Academic				—	−.12

Exercise Questions:

1. Describe and evaluate the norm group. Do you think it is representative? Do you think the norm group is current? Do you believe the size of the norm group was large enough? Is the sample related to the population you intend to use the test with? Explain.

2. Describe and evaluate each method used to estimate reliability. Does the reliability evidence support a decision to use the instrument? Explain.

3. Describe and evaluate each type of validity evidence. Does the validity evidence support a decision to use the instrument? Explain.

4. Describe the practical aspects of the instrument.

5. Summarize the strengths and weaknesses of the inventory.

6. Based on your review of the SII, would you adopt this instrument? Explain your answer.

quiet, comfortable place. One of the most important tasks on standardized instruments is to deliver verbatim instructions given in the test manual and to follow the stated sequence and timing. Any deviation may change the nature of the tasks on the instrument and may negate any comparison of results with those of the norming group. There are numerous ways that assessment instruments can be administered to a client, each with distinct advantages and disadvantages. Regardless of which mode or format is used, counselors are responsible for following specified administration procedures.

The counselor also needs to establish rapport with the examinees. For some, the assessment process may be a new and frightening experience; they may feel fear, frustration, hostility, or anxiety. When individually administering an instrument, the counselor can assess these emotional and motivational factors and positively support the test taker. In group administration, it is harder to establish rapport, but the examiner can be warm, friendly, and enthusiastic. The goal is for the results to give a valid picture of the attributes measured, so the examiner should encourage the examinees to do their best on each task. Examiners should also recognize the need to be genuine and to understand and recognize personal biases in order to be both positive and objective. One way this is done is by listening carefully and observing nonverbal cues. Impartial treatment of all those being assessed is essential.

Throughout the course of administration, the counselor must be alert to the unique problems of special populations. Young children and individuals with disabilities may need shorter test periods and perhaps smaller numbers in the testing group. The examiner may have to administer tests individually or make special provisions for visual, auditory, or perceptual-motor impairments, being sure to record any deviation from standardized administrative procedures. Many assessment instruments are designed to test people with disabilities or give suggested procedures to accommodate various disabilities. The test administrator must also carefully observe what is going on during the process of administering the instrument. The examiner should record any test behavior or other critical incidents that may increase or reduce an individual's opportunity to perform to capacity. Some instruments have observation forms or rating sales on which an examiner can record an individual's test behavior (see Figure 7.5). Problems in test administration are often the result of inadequate preparation for test taking. The awareness or orientation phase is an important element in helping to alleviate response-set problems, anxiety, and tension. However, certain problems present themselves only during the testing situation. Some of these, with possible solutions, are detailed in Table 7.6.

Attention	1 2 3 4 5
	Low ⟶ High
Response time	1 2 3 4 5
	Slow ⟶ Quick
Activity level	1 2 3 4 5
	Passive ⟶ Active
Security	1 2 3 4 5
	Ill at ease ⟶ Calm and collected
Anxiety	1 2 3 4 5
	Low ⟶ High
Relationship to examiner	1 2 3 4 5
	Poor ⟶ Good
Need for reinforcement	1 2 3 4 5
	Low ⟶ High
Task orientation	1 2 3 4 5
	Gives up ⟶ Sticks to task
Reaction to failure	1 2 3 4 5
	Poor ⟶ Good
Interest in test	1 2 3 4 5
	Low ⟶ High

FIGURE 7.5 Sample observational scale for test administration.

TABLE 7.6 Problems Encountered in Test Administration

Problem	Possible Solution
Cheating	Create an environment in which cheating is impossible because of spacing of desks, work areas, and so on.
Client Asks a Question that Is Not Addressed in the Manual	Respond with good judgment based on experience with similar tests.
Guessing	Encourage examinees to work on known items first, leaving unknown items until the latter part of the testing time. Advise clients to guess if they wish, if the test does not penalize guessing.
Lack of Effort	Be positive and businesslike in explaining the purpose and importance of the test and exhorting the test taker to do well.
Questions during Testing	Explain in the beginning that questions will not be answered during the test session. While circulating around the test room, quietly answer only questions resulting from confusion.
Distractions	Eliminate the distraction if possible. Apologize to test takers and explain as much as possible. Allow extra time.
Refusal to Answer	In individual testing, repeat the question and ask whether the test taker understands it. After testing, inquire further if the test taker should have been able to answer.
Examiner Indecision in the Use of Praise and Encouragement	Positive reinforcement may help in establishing rapport and reducing anxiety. It should not be artificial and should not be overused.
Examiner Effects	Recognize personal biases and be positive but objective. Listen carefully and observe nonverbal cues.

After Administration

Once the administration is completed, the counselor may have several more tasks to attend to. For example, when administering a group achievement test, the counselor may need to collect materials according to a predetermined order, counting the test booklets and answer sheets and arranging them all face up. In addition, everything should be put back in the testing kit in the proper way so that it is ready for future use. The counselor should also take time immediately to record any incident that might invalidate scores.

SCORING ASSESSMENT INSTRUMENTS

As we learned from Chapter 4, counselors must have a clear understanding of assessment scores and their meaning and interpretation. Recall that there are several different types of scores that relay an individual's performance on an assessment, such as percentiles, T scores, deviation IQ scores, age/grade equivalents, stanines, and more. Assessment instruments may differ in the method of scoring. Assessment instruments may be hand scored, computer scored, sent to the publisher for scoring, or self-scored by the client. *Hand scoring* an instrument typically entails the use of scoring keys or templates to aid in the scoring process and instructions and conversion charts for transforming raw scores into standard scores. Hand scoring is neither efficient nor cost-effective given the time it takes to score the instrument, the need for qualified scorers, and the propensity for errors. *Computer scoring* involves inputting test results or scanning an answer sheet into a software program, which then automatically generates test results. Compared to hand scoring, computer scoring is typically easier to perform, less time-consuming, requires scorers with less training, and produces fewer scoring errors. However, we recommend that you understand the process of scoring and the information related to standard scores in order to develop competency in the interpretation of computer-scored assessment instruments.

Some hand-scored instruments demand that the scorer judge the degree of correctness of the response or compare the responses to standards provided. For example, essay questions on many college placement examinations are scored using a holistic scoring procedure. The raters have model answers that have been given certain weights, and they compare the examinee's essays to these. Such raters are asked to assess answers on a 4-point scale and to make an overall rating, or holistic judgment, rather than assign a certain number of points to each possible component of the answer.

Scoring Performance Assessment

As opposed to most traditional forms of assessment instruments that may yield scores in percentiles or standard scores, performance assessments (e.g., projects, portfolios, performance tasks, and open-ended exercises) do not have clear-cut right or wrong answers. Therefore, scoring a performance assessment typically involves the use of a *scoring rubric*, which is a set of predetermined criteria or guidelines used to evaluate the test taker's work. Scoring rubrics typically include the following components:

1. *One or More Dimensions or Attributes on Which Performance Is Rated* These dimensions are clearly stated verbal descriptions of performance that need to be displayed in an individual's work to demonstrate proficient performance. For example, a written essay may be rated on such dimensions as content, organization and format, and grammar and vocabulary.
2. *Descriptors or Examples that Illustrate Each Dimension or Attribute Being Measured* For each dimension, there are usually three to five descriptors (each of which corresponds to a particular rating of performance). For example, the descriptors on the grammar and vocabulary dimension on a rubric for a written essay may include the following:
   • *Poor:* lacks fluency; poor sentence construction; many grammar and spelling errors
   • *Fair:* some fluency; some mistakes in sentence construction; frequent grammar and spelling errors
   • *Good:* adequate fluency; sentence constructions used effectively; some grammar and spelling errors
   • *Excellent:* fluent expression; effective use of complex sentence structures; very few grammatical errors
3. *A Rating Scale for Each Dimension* Rating scales used to assess dimensions are expressed using rank-ordered categories, such as unsatisfactory, *below satisfactory*, *satisfactory*, and *exemplary* or *novice, apprentice, proficient*, and *excellent*. These categories may also be assigned numerical values, with more points awarded to higher levels of proficiency.

Because rubrics rely heavily on the subjective judgment of the individual scoring the assessment, it is important to consider differences in scorers as a potential source of scoring errors. Interrater reliability should be estimated to determine how consistently scorers implement the scoring rubric. One way to improve the reliability of a scoring rubric is to have at least two individuals score the instrument; if there are discrepancies, then the results are checked by a third reviewer. Workshops for scoring and frequent consistency checks often improve reliability of the scoring, and renewal sessions for readers allow them to review responses from earlier tests. Advance placement tests and many state assessment tests use procedures similar to these to maintain scoring consistency.

Scoring Errors

A key issue in scoring assessment instruments is *scoring errors*, which can affect significantly how test results are interpreted. Scoring errors occur frequently, regardless of who is scoring the instrument or the scorer's level of experience with testing. Allard and Faust (2000) found that 20 (13.3%) out of 150 administrations of the Beck Depression Inventory, 56 (28.7%) of 300 administrations of the State-Trait Anxiety Inventory, and 22 (14.7%) of 150 administrations of the MMPI-II had scoring errors of some kind. Even test takers make scoring errors: Simons, Goddard, and Patton (2002) found that scoring errors by test takers ranged from approximately 20% to 66%. Typical scoring errors include assignment of incorrect score values to individual responses, incorrectly recording responses, incorrectly converting raw scores to derived scores, and making calculation errors. Instrument developers have certain responsibilities in making clear to the examiner how the instrument is to be scored. In addition, the examiner has specific responsibilities to ensure that the test is scored correctly.

Computer scoring helps reduce scoring errors, but errors still occur if data is inputted incorrectly. If optical scanners are used to input data, then answer sheets must be carefully examined for incomplete erasures or other such problems prior to the scanning. When hand scoring instruments, errors can be reduced if scorers understand the absolute importance of accuracy and if procedures are instituted to regularly monitor the required calculations and score transformations (Urbina, 2014).

Standards for Scoring Assessment Instruments

The 2000 Guidelines of the International Test Commission (ITC) state that test users should apply quality control procedures to the scoring, analysis, and reporting (SAR) process and that test users should maintain high standards. Scoring of assessments should be conducted properly and efficiently so that the results are reported accurately and in a timely manner. We strongly recommend that you review the ITC standards thoroughly (see intestcom.org/guidelines). Although we have focused primarily on the Standards for Educational and Psychological Testing (AERA et al., 2014), which guide assessment in the United States, the ITC standards are used to guide assessment processes throughout the world. Although we are not able to fully review all of the standards in this book, some of the outlined responsibilities for persons who score and prepare reports of assessments follow:

1. Provide complete and accurate information to users about how the assessment is scored, such as the reporting schedule, scoring process to be used, rationale for the scoring approach, technical characteristics, quality control procedures, reporting formats, and the fees, if any, for these services.

2. Ensure the accuracy of the assessment results by conducting reasonable quality control procedures before, during, and after scoring.
3. When using a new test, perform trial or practice runs to establish competency prior to administering to a client.
4. Create test-specific standards.
5. Minimize the effect on scoring of factors irrelevant to the purposes of the assessment.
6. Inform users promptly of any deviation in the planned scoring and reporting service, or schedule and negotiate a solution with users.
7. Provide corrected score results to the examinee or the client as quickly as practicable should errors be found that may affect the inferences made on the basis of the scores.
8. Protect the confidentiality of information that identifies individuals as prescribed by state and federal laws.
9. Release summary results of the assessment only to those persons entitled to such information by state or federal law or to those who are designated by the party contracting for the scoring services.
10. Establish, where feasible, a fair and reasonable process for appeal and rescoring the assessment.

INTERPRETING ASSESSMENT RESULTS

Once an assessment instrument is scored, counselors often have the responsibility of interpreting results for clients, parents, teachers, and other professionals. To interpret a score on any type of assessment instrument, counselors must first determine whether the score reflects norm-referenced or criterion-referenced interpretation. As we discussed in Chapter 4, *norm-referenced score interpretation* involves comparing an individual's test score to the scores of other people (i.e., a norm group) who have taken the same instrument. When using *criterion-referenced score interpretation*, an individual's score is measured against a specified standard or criterion. With a criterion-referenced instrument, the focus is *not* on how the individual's performance compares with others, but rather on how the individual performs with respect to a particular standard of performance.

Another approach to interpreting assessment instruments is based on the interindividual (normative) and intraindividual (ipsative) models. Using an *interindividual* approach, we examine differences on the same construct across test takers. In other words, we look at score variations among the different individuals who took the test. Using an *intraindividual* approach, we compare a test taker's scores on various scales within the same test. We are looking for score discrepancies within the individual. Whenever an instrument provides a profile of an examinee's scores on various scales and subtests, an intraindividual approach is being used.

Responsible interpretation of assessment instruments requires counselors to have knowledge of the different methods of scoring and the ways of communicating those results in a manner that clients can understand. Counselors should be well informed about the various types of scores, such as percentiles, standard scores, and age and grade equivalents.

When interpreting scores, counselors should consider any major differences between the norm group and the actual test takers. They should also consider the impact any modifications of administration procedures may have had on test results. The counselor should be able to explain how any passing scores were set, demonstrate what the results reveal, and provide evidence that the instrument satisfies its intended purposes. The *Code of Fair*

Testing Practices in Education (2004) states that test users should avoid using a single test score as the sole determinant of decisions about test takers. Test scores should be interpreted in conjunction with other information about individuals.

Computer-based assessment instruments often provide computer-generated reports or narratives. These reports are canned interpretations that the computer generates when certain test scores are obtained (Butcher, 2012). The reports may contain very complex and detailed statements or paragraphs that are to be printed out. It's important that counselors not view computer-generated reports or narratives as standalone interpretations. Computers are unable to take into account the uniqueness of the test taker and incorporate important contextual elements, such as a client's personal history, life events, or current stressors. Therefore, computer-generated reports or narratives are considered broad, general descriptions that should not be used without the evaluation of a skilled counselor. If a counselor chooses to use computer-generated reports, it is the counselor who is ultimately accountable for the accuracy of interpretations.

Interpreting assessment instruments requires knowledge of and experience with the instrument, the scores, and the decisions to be made. The *Responsibilities of Users of Standardized Tests* document (Association for Assessment in Counseling, 2003) identifies several factors that can impact the validity of score interpretations. These include the following:

- *Psychometric Factors* Factors such as the reliability, norms, standard error of measurement, and validity of the instrument can impact an individual's scores and the interpretation of test results.
- *Test-Taker Factors* The test taker's group membership (e.g., gender, age, ethnicity, race, socioeconomic status, relationship status) is a critical factor in the interpretation of test results. Test users should evaluate how the test taker's group membership can affect his or her test results.
- *Contextual Factors* When interpreting results, test users should consider the relationship of the test to the instructional program, opportunity to learn, quality of the educational program, work and home environment, and other factors. For example, if the test does not align to curriculum standards and how those standards are taught in the classroom, then the test results may not provide useful information.

Summary

This chapter presented information relevant to selecting, administering, scoring, and interpreting assessment results. Counselors need to be aware of the steps involved in selecting appropriate assessment instruments, which include identifying the type of information needed, identifying available information, determining the methods for obtaining information, searching assessment resources, and evaluating and selecting an assessment instrument or strategy.

How an instrument is administered can affect the accuracy and validity of the results. Counselors must have important competencies,

such as knowledge of and training in the instrument being administered. The counselor must be aware of the many tasks that occur before, during, and after the administration process.

Studies have shown that examiners make numerous errors in scoring assessment instruments. Consequently, a number of guidelines and standards address scoring procedures. The scoring of assessments should be conducted properly and efficiently so that the results are reported accurately and in a timely manner.

To accurately interpret instrument results, counselors need to be well informed about the various types of scores, such as percentiles, standard scores, and age and grade equivalents. When interpreting scores, counselors should also consider any major differences between the norm group and the test takers.

Questions for Discussion

1. What are the sources of information about assessment instruments? What are the advantages and disadvantages of each source in terms of the type of information provided?
2. What practical issues need to be considered in selecting an assessment instrument?
3. Why is it important to follow the directions strictly when administering a standardized test?
4. How would you handle the situation if certain test results did not appear to be accurate or did not agree with the results of previous tests you had taken? If you were the examiner and found out that you had made some errors in scoring a client's test, what would you do? What steps and procedures should be taken to ensure the accuracy of test scores?
5. Do you agree that counselors should be extremely careful about interpreting test results for individuals from diverse backgrounds? Why or why not?

Suggested Activities

1. Devise a checklist to use to evaluate assessment instruments.
2. Critically review an assessment instrument in your field. Use the guidelines for evaluating and selecting instruments presented in this chapter to organize your review.
3. Find a test review in the *MMY* and summarize the review. What strengths and weaknesses do the reviewers emphasize?
4. Read the manual for administration for a widely used test, such as the SAT or the Graduate Record Examination. Interview an individual who is responsible for administering the test. What kinds of problems has the person encountered in administering the test? How adequate were the directions in the manual for handling those problem situations?
5. Discuss the following four scenarios:

Scenario 1
You are scheduled to administer a diagnostic achievement test to a 6-year-old child. You usually have no problem establishing rapport, but when you get into the testing room, the child says to you, "I don't like you. I am not going to take any tests for you!" The child puts her hands over her ears.

Scenario 2
You are administering a state achievement test to a large group of students, and you see evidence of a student cheating.

Scenario 3
You are administering a symptom inventory to a client in an outpatient counseling center. After reading the instructions, you leave the client alone to complete the inventory. After the client has completed the instrument and left the counseling center, you look over his results and notice that he has left a large number of items unanswered.

Scenario 4
You are administering a test to a group and have read the instructions to the individuals and gotten them started on the test. Five minutes into the test, one of the test takers raises his hand, asks a question loudly, and disrupts others who are taking the test.

6. Read the case study and answer the questions that follow:

   A company administered a basic skills test to aid in selecting new employees. The assistant to the division supervisor administered the test. Because the assistant administering the test was often interrupted by telephone calls and minor crises, he paid little attention to the applicants taking the test. He estimated the time limit allowed for taking the test.
   a. What steps could be taken to ensure that the test is administered properly and fairly to all applicants?
   b. What other procedures would you implement?

References

Allard, G., & Faust, D. (2000). Errors in scoring objective personality tests. *Assessment, 7*(2), 119–131.

American Counseling Association (ACA). (2014). *ACA Code of Ethics.* Alexandria, VA: Author.

American Educational Research Association (AERA), American Psychological Association (APA), & National Council on Measurement in Education (NCME). (2014). *Standards for educational and psychological testing.* Washington, DC: Authors.

American Psychological Association (APA). (2010). *Ethical principles of psychologists and code of conduct* (Rev. ed.).Washington, DC: Author.

Association for Assessment and Research in Counseling. (2003). *Responsibilities of users of standardized tests (RUST).* Alexandria, VA: Author.

Beck, A. T., Steer, R. A., & Brown, G. K. (1996). *Manual for the Beck Depression Inventory-II.* San Antonio, TX: Psychological Corporation.

Butcher, J. N. (2012). Computerized psychological assessment. In I. B. Weiner, D. K. Freedheim, J. A. Schinka, & W. F. Velicer (Eds.), *Handbook of psychology* (pp. 165–191). Hoboken, NJ: John Wiley & Sons.

Coopersmith, S. (1981). *Coopersmith Self-Esteem Inventories: Manual.* Menlo Park, CA: Mind Garden, Inc.

Graham, J. R. (2011). *MMPI-2: Assessing personality and psychopathology* (5th ed.). New York, NY: Oxford University Press.

International Test Commission (ITC). (2000). *International guidelines for test use.* Retrieved from http://www.intestcom.org/itc_projects.htm

National Board for Certified Counselors (NBCC). (2013). *Code of ethics.* Greensboro, NC: Author.

Simons, R., Goddard, R., & Patton, W. (2002). Hand-scoring error rates in psychological testing. *Assessment, 9,* 292–300.

Urbina, S. (2014). *Essentials of psychological testing.* Hoboken, NJ: John Wiley & Sons.

Whiston, S. C. (2009). *Assessment in counseling* (3rd ed.). Belmont, CA: Brooks/Cole.

8 Assessment of Intelligence and General Ability

The study of intelligence dates back more than a century; over the decades, it has been characterized by scholarly debates, research breakthroughs, and paradigm shifts about what constitutes the nature of intelligence. It also brought about the birth of a commercial industry that generates hundreds of millions of dollars of annual revenue (Wasserman, 2003). Assessing intelligence typically encompasses measuring one's ability to understand complex ideas, adapt effectively to the environment, think abstractly, learn from experience, learn quickly, and engage in various forms of reasoning.

After studying this chapter, you should be able to:

- Describe the various definitions of intelligence.
- Explain the major theories of intelligence and describe their differences.
- Define the *g* factor of intelligence.
- Articulate Terman's study and its relevance in the study of human intelligence.
- Describe the various cognitive abilities measured in intelligence tests.
- Describe individual intelligence tests and group intelligence tests and explain the distinctions between the two.
- Describe specialized tests of intelligence.
- Identify and describe the major tests of intelligence, such as the Wechsler scales and the Stanford–Binet Intelligence Scale.
- Explain special issues in intelligence testing, such as heredity, test bias, stability of test scores, and the Flynn Effect.

DEFINING INTELLIGENCE

What is intelligence? Despite the history behind the study of intelligence, there is still a lack of agreement on the definition of intelligence. In the book *Intelligence 101*, Plucker and Esping (2014) dedicated five pages of text to 19 different definitions proffered by psychologists over the years. The reason for so many differing definitions is that intelligence is a complex construct that involves both genetic and social learning components. As long as theorists and researchers have been studying intelligence, there have been various definitions of the concept and how to measure it. Theorists and researchers have argued over the traits and dimensions that comprise the construct of intelligence, and literally thousands of books, research articles, and popular essays on intelligence have been published over the last 100 years. And yet, there remains no clearly articulated definition of the construct of intelligence. As such, we will not tender our own definition, but will discuss the concept from a broad perspective. There is even divergence among professionals about the term itself: Some professionals prefer using the term *general ability* rather than intelligence due to the negative connotations associated with intelligence testing (Whiston, 2012).

Part of the reason scholars have disagreed on how to define intelligence involves the ongoing debate of whether intelligence is a single, monolithic ability. In other words, is intelligence a general, unitary concept that governs performance on all tasks and abilities? This notion, referred to as the *general intelligence factor* (i.e., *g factor*), was supported by some early psychometric research, but it failed to stand the test of scrutiny in educational settings (Mayer, 2000). Although *g* as a total representation of intelligence is no longer in vogue, it is often considered part of the broader construct of intelligence along with smaller component abilities (e.g., memory, knowledge, processing speed; Ackerman & Beier, 2012).

Abilities are enduring characteristics of individuals, sometimes called *ability traits*, because they are usually stable across time. Abilities can be seen in many domains of individual differences, including cognitive, physical (motor skills), visual, auditory, mechanical, and job related, to name a few. When related to intelligence, one refers to *cognitive abilities*, which generally constitutes one's ability to understand complex ideas, solve novel problems, think abstractly, and engage in various forms of reasoning. In this paradigm, intelligence is often referred to as *general intellectual ability*. Therefore, the next logical question is this: What specific cognitive abilities make up general intellectual ability? Unfortunately, there is little agreement among researchers as to what those abilities are and which ones are more important, although some researchers have suggested a common taxonomy of cognitive abilities (Flanagan & Harrison, 2012; Plucker & Esping, 2014).

New theories that emerged in the 1980s and 1990s took a completely different view of intelligence. Some theorists refuted the existence of one or several intellectual abilities altogether and instead favored the notion of *multiple* separate intelligences. Other theorists, instead of conceptualizing intelligence in terms of abilities, focused on *information processing*, which encompasses the cognitive processes required for people to perform intellectual tasks, such as taking in information (attention, perception) and holding that information (memory, recall) for further information processing (reasoning, problem solving, decision making, communication).

As you can see, the construct of intelligence and its meaning have been extensively discussed, but a multitude of definitions remain. To explore the commonalities among researchers' definitions of intelligence, Sternberg and Berg (1986) published a well-known study that compared definitions from experts in the field of intelligence who met in two symposia held in 1921 and 1986. The authors reported that common features of definitions included such attributes as adaptation to the environment, basic mental processes, and higher-order thinking (e.g., reasoning, problem solving, decision making). In addition, they found that in 1986 more emphasis was placed on metacognition (i.e., awareness and control of one's cognitive processes), information processing, and cultural context. Table 8.1 provides several well-known definitions of intelligence from theorists and researchers over the last century.

Despite the numerous definitions, the nature of intelligence continues to be elusive. However, the idea that some individuals are brighter or smarter than others is accepted in

TABLE 8.1 Some Definitions of Intelligence

Author	Year	Definition
Spearman	1904	Intelligent behavior is generated by a single, unitary quality within the human mind or brain.
Stern	1912	A general capacity of an individual consciously to adjust his thinking to new requirements . . . a general mental adaptability to new problems and conditions of life.
Binet & Simon	1916	Good judgment and the ability to adapt to the environment.
Terman	1921	The ability to carry on abstract thinking.
Boring	1923	Intelligence is what is measured by intelligence tests.
Henmon	1921	The capacity for knowledge along with knowledge possessed.
Pinter	1921	The ability to adapt oneself adequately to relatively new situations in life.
Thorndike	1921	The power of good responses from the point of view of truth or facts.
Thurstone	1924	The capacity for abstraction, which is an inhibitory process.
Wechsler	1953	The aggregate or global ability of the individual to act purposefully, to think rationally, and to deal effectively with his environment.
Vernon	1979	The product of the interplay between genetic potentiality and environmental stimulation.
Piaget	1963	Intelligence is assimilation and adaptation.
Gardner	1983	Being able to either solve problems or create new products that benefit at least a portion of society.
Anastasi	1992	Intelligence is not a single, unitary ability, but rather a composite of several functions. The term denotes that combination of abilities required for survival and advancement within a particular culture.
Sternberg	2004	Your skill in achieving whatever it is you want to attain in your life within your sociocultural context by capitalizing on your strengths and compensating for, or correcting, your weaknesses.

human society and reflected in language descriptors of ability (Chamorro-Premuzic, 2011). *Roget's Thesaurus*, for example, provides the following synonyms for intelligence: acumen, aptitude, brainpower, brilliance, discernment, information, insight, knowledge, learning, news, notice, report, sense, smarts, understanding, and wisdom. In the field of intellectual assessment, Wechsler's definition of intelligence as comprising both aggregate and global abilities is perhaps the most widely referenced and enduring definition (Wasserman & Tulsky, 2012); it persists in guiding and influencing the present-day practice of intelligence testing (Flanagan & Harrison, 2012).

THEORIES OF INTELLIGENCE

Just as there are many definitions of intelligence, there are many theories of intelligence. The first and most widely accepted approach is based on *psychometrics*, which reveals the structure or dimensions of intelligence through statistical procedures (such as factor analysis) that analyze the interrelationships of scores on mental ability tests. This approach was used to develop and support the concept of one overall general (*g*) factor of intelligence. However, this view was by no means universally accepted among intelligence theorists. Some theorists endorse the notion of a *g* factor along with *specific abilities* that comprise general intelligence; some view intellectual ability as a *hierarchy* of general and specific abilities; and some theorists diverge completely from individual intellectual abilities and focus on *information processing* (i.e., the mental operations or processes associated with performing a cognitive task), *cognitive development*, or *multiple intelligences*. Although we are unable to present all of the many theorists' views of intelligence, we will present an overview of a few of the more prominent theories (Table 8.2 provides a comparison of the theories of intelligence).

Spearman's Two-Factor Theory

Charles E. Spearman is credited as having developed the concept of the *g* factor of intelligence. He pioneered the statistical technique called factor analysis and used it to offer a

TABLE 8.2 Comparison of the Theories of Intelligence

	g Factor	Psychometric	Specific Abilities	Hierarchical	Cognitive Development	Multiple Intelligences	Information Processing
Spearman's Two-Factor Theory	X	X	X				
Thurstone's Multifactor Theory		X	X				
Vernon's Hierarchical Model	X	X	X	X			
Cattell–Horn Gf-Gc Theory		X	X	X			
Guilford's Structure-of-Intellect Model		X	X				
Piaget's Theory of Cognitive Development					X		
Sternberg's Triarchic Theory of Intelligence			X	X			X
Gardner's Theory of Multiple Intelligences						X	
Carroll's Three-Stratum Theory	X	X	X	X			
Das, Naglieri, and Kirby's PASS Theory of Cognitive Processing							X
Cattell–Horn–Carroll Theory of Cognitive Abilities	?	X	X	X			

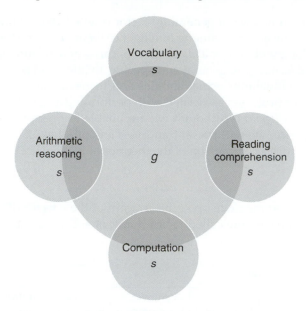

FIGURE 8.1   Diagram of Spearman's *g* and *s* factors.

viable psychometric definition of intelligence. As a graduate student in 1904, Spearman published a paper on a *two-factor theory* of intelligence that emphasized (1) a *general intelligence* factor (*g*), which is general intellectual ability, and (2) *specific factors* (*s*) that vary according to an individual's specific abilities. He derived the notion of *g* through factor analysis and demonstrated that scores on all mental tests were positively correlated, offering compelling evidence that all intelligent behavior is derived from one general fund of mental ability (Plucker, 2003). Spearman's paper was almost instantly controversial and generated ongoing scholarly debates related to the *g* factor and the dissection of intelligence (Wasserman & Tulsky, 2012).

To explain Spearman's theory, say that we have four cognitive tests measuring vocabulary, reading comprehension, computation, and arithmetic reasoning. According to Spearman, each of these tests measures both the *g* factor and the particular *s* factor. As Figure 8.1 illustrates, he believed that *s* factors overlap the *g* factor, but the *g* is the most important estimate or measurement of someone's intellectual ability. Although Spearman's theory was developed over 100 years ago, the issue of *g* versus multiple factors of intelligence is an issue still hotly debated today (Flanagan & Harrison, 2012).

Thurstone's Multifactor Theory

Louis L. Thurstone (1938) challenged Spearman's theory, particularly the notion of a general factor of intelligence, and was in the forefront of psychometric research identifying multiple ability factors underlying measures of intelligence. By analyzing scores on 56 different tests taken by children of different age groups and university students, he identified seven fairly distinctive factors (rather than a single *g* factor) that he called *primary mental abilities*:

1. *Numerical Ability* Ability to perform basic mathematic processes accurately and rapidly.

2. *Verbal Comprehension* Ability to understand ideas expressed in word form.
3. *Word Fluency* Ability to speak and write fluently.
4. *Memory* Ability to recognize and recall information such as numbers, letters, and words.
5. *Reasoning* Ability to derive rules and solve problems inductively.
6. *Spatial Ability* Ability to visualize and form relationships in three dimensions.
7. *Perceptual Speed* Ability to perceive things quickly, such as visual details and similarities and differences among pictured objects.

In his research, Thurstone did not find evidence of an overall *g* factor:

> As far as we can determine at present, the tests that have been supposed to be saturated with the general common factor divide their variance among primary factors that are not present in all tests. We cannot report any general common factor in the battery of fifty-six tests that have been analyzed in the present study. (Thurstone, 1938, p. ix)

Thurstone recommended that individuals be described in terms of a profile of cognitive abilities rather than a single index of intelligence. In later years, however, he became more accepting of *g* if it was conceived to be divisible into primary factors (Thurstone, 1947).

Vernon's Hierarchical Model

Philip E. Vernon (1950) proposed a *hierarchical model of intelligence* that organized abilities at four different levels (see Figure 8.2). The first level of the hierarchy was Spearman's

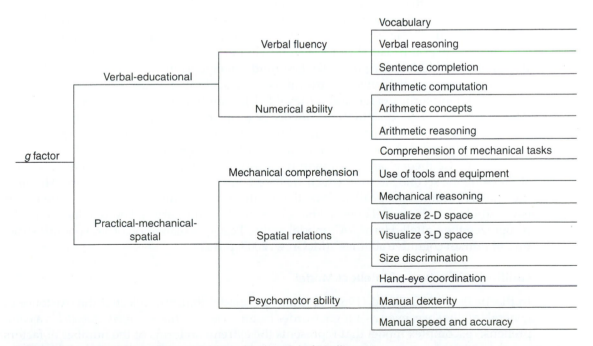

FIGURE 8.2 Adaptation of Vernon's hierarchical model of intelligence.

general factor of intelligence. The second level included two broad abilities: verbal-educational ability and practical-mechanical-spatial ability. Each broad ability was further subdivided into specific abilities shown on the third level: verbal-educational comprises verbal fluency and numerical ability, and practical-mechanical-spatial includes mechanical ability, psychomotor ability, and spatial relations. The fourth level consists of even more special and specific factors particular to the abilities in each of the domains above it. Because Vernon's model accounted for a g factor as a higher-order factor as well as other specific factors, it was viewed as a way to reconcile Spearman's two-factor theory (which emphasized the g factor) and Thurstone's multiple-factor theory (which did not have a g element; Plucker & Esping, 2014).

Cattell–Horn *Gf-Gc* Theory

Like Thurstone, Raymond B. Cattell disagreed with Spearman's concept of g and believed that one general factor of intelligence was not enough. Instead, he maintained that general intelligence has two major parts: fluid intelligence and crystallized intelligence (Cattell, 1941, 1950, 1971). *Fluid intelligence* (designated by Gf) has been described by Cattell as the ability to solve problems and adapt to new situations. It is considered to be more genetically determined and based on physiological aspects of an individual. Because fluid abilities are considered relatively culture free, they are often reflected in memory span and spatial thinking tests. *Crystallized intelligence* (designated by Gc), on the other hand, refers to acquired knowledge and ability obtained through education and personal experience. Tests of verbal comprehension and knowledge draw on crystallized abilities. Both types of intelligence increase throughout childhood and adolescence; however, fluid intelligence tends to peak in adolescence and begins to decline around age 30 or 40. Crystallized intelligence continues to grow throughout adulthood.

John Horn, a student of Raymond Cattell, worked on a series of studies to enrich and validate Gf and Gc. However, Horn believed that the available research supported the presence of several broad abilities beyond Gf and Gc. He extended Cattell's model to include nine to 10 *broad cognitive abilities*: fluid intelligence (Gf), crystallized intelligence (Gc), short-term acquisition and retrieval (Gsm), visual intelligence (Gv), auditory intelligence (Ga), long-term storage and retrieval (Glr), cognitive processing speed (Gs), correct decision speed (CDS), quantitative knowledge (Gq), and reading and writing skills (Grw; Horn & Cattell, 1966a, 1966b, 1967). In addition, he found that over 80 abilities (also called *primary mental abilities*) constituted the nine to 10 broad cognitive abilities.

The Gf-Gc theory can be thought of as a two-stratum model. The broad cognitive abilities are the second stratum, which are based on over 80 first-stratum factors. Although the model continued to be called Gf-Gc theory, the broad cognitive abilities were treated as equals (note that the model does not have a g factor). By the early 1990s, scholars generally recognized the Cattell–Horn Gf-Gc model as the "best approximation of a taxonomic structure of human cognitive abilities" (McGrew, 2005, p. 143).

Guilford's Structure-of-Intellect Model

In the 1960s, J. P. Guilford (1967) developed a model that also rejected the existence of general intelligence, even as a higher-order factor. The *structure-of-intellect model* is a comprehensive, complex model that represents the extreme in terms of the number of factors

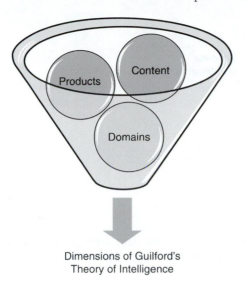

Dimensions of Guilford's
Theory of Intelligence

FIGURE 8.3 Dimensions of Guilford's Theory of Intelligence.

associated with intellectual ability. The model includes 180 unique intellectual factors organized around three dimensions: operations, contents, and products (see Figure 8.3). *Operations* are rules of logic or mental procedures that solve problems. *Contents* refers to a particular kind of information. *Products* are items of information from the same content category. According to his model, intellectual functioning involves the application of *operations* to *contents*, which results in *products*. There are six types of operations: cognition, memory retention, memory recording, divergent thinking, convergent thinking, and evaluation. Each of these operations could be applied to one of five types of contents: visual, auditory, symbolic, semantic, or behavioral. The application of operations to these contents results in one of six products: units, classes, relations, systems, transformations, or implications.

Piaget's Theory of Cognitive Development

In contrast to the psychometric theories of intelligence, Piaget (1970) conceptualized a *theory of cognitive development*. From his work on the French standardization of Burt's intelligence tests in 1920, he noticed that children of the same age tended to make exactly the same type of mistakes. He became interested in understanding how individuals develop intellectual abilities rather than individual differences in intelligence test performance. He suggested that intelligence develops through the interaction of biological maturation and experience and progresses through four stages: *sensorimotor, preoperational, concrete operational,* and *formal operational* periods (see Figure 8.4). Children move through these stages through the use of two intellectual functions: assimilation and accommodation. *Assimilation* is the process by which a child relates new objects and ideas to familiar objects and ideas. *Accommodation* is the process by which a child changes behavior and psychological structures in response to environmental events. Piaget's theories have been the basis of the

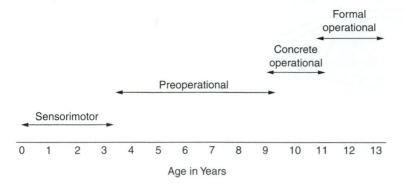

FIGURE 8.4 Piaget's stages of cognitive development.

design of curriculum materials and educational programs, and a number of scales have been published to assess an individual's stage of intellectual development.

Luria's Model

A. R. Luria (1970) was a Russian neuropsychologist who is best known for his seminal work on structures of the brain and the behavioral and cognitive deficits associated with various brain lesions (i.e., areas of brain tissue that appear abnormal). Luria's research has had considerable influence on intelligence testing; for example, the Kaufman Assessment Battery for Children (KABC-II) focuses on mental processes based on Luria's theory. Luria's work involved mapping the brain's systems and functions responsible for human cognitive processes, especially the high-level processes associated with the intake and integration of information and with problem-solving abilities (Kaufman & Kaufman, 2004a; Luria, 1970). He identified three main blocks in the brain that represented the brain's functional systems: Block 1 is responsible for arousal, concentration, and attention. Block 2 involves the use of one's senses to analyze, code, and store information. Block 3 applies executive functions for formulating plans and programming behavior; it represents the output or response center of the brain. Although Luria distinguished the three blocks of brain functions and their separate cognitive processes, his main emphasis was on the integration of these blocks in order to support all cognitive activity (Kaufman & Kaufman, 2004b).

Sternberg's Triarchic Theory of Successful Intelligence

Sternberg's Triarchic Theory of Successful Intelligence (1985, 1988, 1997, 1999, 2007) is also based on the information processing model of intelligence. He believed that intelligence is comprised of three separate (but interrelated) abilities: analytical (componential), creative (experiential), and practical (contextual). *Analytical intelligence* refers to the ability to perform academic, problem-solving tasks. *Creative intelligence* involves the ability to react effectively to novel situations and to find new solutions to problems. *Practical intelligence* refers to the ability to solve real-life problems as they arise (also known as common sense). Sternberg contended that intelligent behavior arises from a balance between analytical, creative, and practical abilities, which function collectively to allow individuals to achieve success within particular sociocultural contexts. In addition, he believed that intelligent individuals are those who can figure out their strengths and weaknesses and find ways to optimize their strengths and minimize their weaknesses so they succeed in their environment.

Gardner's Theory of Multiple Intelligences

Howard Gardner's theory of multiple intelligences (1993, 2006, 2011) rejected the traditional views of intelligence and contended that human intelligence was neither a single complex entity nor a set of specific abilities. Instead, Gardner suggested that there are several relatively autonomous intelligences and that an individual's intelligence reflects a unique configuration of these intellectual capacities. He stated that "intelligences work together to solve problems to yield various kinds of end states—vocations, avocations, and the like" (1993, p. 9). To date, Gardner has identified eight intelligences:

1. *Linguistic Intelligence* Describes the ability to perceive and generate spoken or written language.
2. *Logical/Mathematical Intelligence* Involves the ability to understand and utilize numerical, abstract, and logical reasoning to solve problems.
3. *Spatial Intelligence* Entails the ability to perceive, modify, transform, and create visual or spatial images.
4. *Bodily/Kinesthetic Intelligence* The ability to use all or part of one's body to express ideas and feelings or to produce or transform things.
5. *Musical/Rhythmic Intelligence* Involves the ability to perceive, reproduce, or create musical forms.
6. *Interpersonal Intelligence* Describes the ability to perceive, appreciate, and contend with the moods, intentions, motivations, and feelings of other people.
7. *Intrapersonal Intelligence* The ability to understand one's own feelings and to use such knowledge in regulating one's own life.
8. *Naturalistic Intelligence* Involves the ability to recognize and classify living and nonliving forms in one's environment.

Although not every researcher or theorist accepts Gardner's theory, his framework has been applied successfully in many educational settings. Based on the theory of multiple intelligences, many teachers and administrators have tailored educational practices toward a broader view of intelligence and have sought other ways to assess the various intellectual abilities of their students.

Carroll's Three-Stratum Model of Human Abilities

John B. Carroll was an educational psychologist who, over the course of his more than 50-year career, rigorously pursued "the field's need for a thoroughgoing survey and critique of the voluminous results in the factor-analytic literature on cognitive abilities" (Carroll, 1993, p. vii). Using an empirical approach, he developed the *three-stratum model*, which was an extension of previous theories (particularly the Cattell–Horn *Gf-Gc* model) that specified what kinds of individual differences in cognitive abilities exist and how those kinds of individual differences are related to one another (Carroll, 1993). Carroll's model was a hierarchical theory composed of three layers, or *strata*, of cognitive abilities:

- Stratum III: *general ability*, similar to *g*.
- Stratum II: *broad cognitive abilities*, which include fluid intelligence, crystallized intelligence, general memory and learning, broad visual perception, broad auditory perception, broad retrieval ability, broad cognitive speediness, and processing speed.
- Stratum I: *narrow cognitive abilities*, which are specific factors grouped under the Stratum II abilities.

The three-stratum taxonomy suggests that at the highest level cognitive abilities converge to form a general common factor (*g*; Jensen, 1998); the inclusion of the *g* is distinct from the Cattell–Horn *Gf-Gc* model. As a psychometric approach, Carroll's theory was based on a factor analytic study involving over 480 datasets of cognitive ability variables from psychological tests, school grades, and competence ratings.

Planning-Attention-Simultaneous-Successive Theory of Cognitive Processing

J. P. Das, Jack Naglieri, and John R. Kirby (1994) developed a modern theory of cognitive ability that is linked to the work of Luria (1966). Das, Naglieri, and Kirby's (1994) theory centers on the concept of *information processing*. They suggested that four cognitive processes are the basic building blocks of human intellectual functioning:

1. *Planning*   A mental activity that involves setting goals, problem solving, knowledge, intentionality, and self-regulation to achieve a desired goal.
2. *Attention*   The process involving focused cognitive activity (while ignoring other distractions).
3. *Simultaneous Processing*   Involves the ability to synthesize information from a whole (e.g., spatially) to solve problems.
4. *Successive (Sequential) Processing*   Involves the ability to solve problems by mentally arranging input in a sequential or serial order.

The Planning-Attention-Simultaneous-Successive (PASS) theory offers an innovative approach in the field of intellectual assessment. The theory rejected the traditional *g* factor of intelligence and adopted the term *cognitive processes* to replace the term *intelligence*. The authors maintain that intelligence tests should rely as little as possible on achievement-like content, such as vocabulary or arithmetic; rather, tests should emphasize the cognitive processes associated with performance (Naglieri, 2005).

Cattell–Horn–Carroll Hierarchical Three-Stratum Model

The *Cattell–Horn–Carroll* (CHC) Hierarchical Three-Stratum Model is an integration of the Cattell–Horn *Gf-Gc* theory and Carroll's three-stratum theory (Flanagan, McGrew, & Ortiz, 2000; McGrew & Woodcock, 2001). The CHC model was formed in the fall of 1985 through a meeting of professionals working on the latest revision of the Woodcock–Johnson-Revised (WJ-R). Attendees included Richard W. Woodcock, John Horn, John B. Carroll, and many others. At the time, Carroll was conducting extensive factor analytic studies that provided support for a wide variety of cognitive abilities, but he did not view his work as a "theory" of intelligence. Nevertheless, both Carroll's work and the Cattell–Horn model essentially started from the same point as Spearman's (1904) *g* factor theory and ended up with very consistent conclusions about the spectrum of broad cognitive abilities (Kaufman & Kaufman, 2004a). Thus, the convergence of the leading test developer (Woodcock), the leading proponent of the Cattell–Horn *Gf-Gc* model (Horn), and a preeminent scholar of factor analysis of cognitive abilities (Carroll) resulted in the birth of the CHC theory.

The CHC model has been described as a hierarchical, multiple-stratum model with *general intelligence* (*g*) at the apex (or Stratum III), nine *broad cognitive abilities* (*G*; Stratum II), and at least 69 narrow *cognitive abilities* (Stratum I). The distinguishing feature between the CHC model and the Cattell–Horn *Gf-Gc* model is that the CHC model supports the

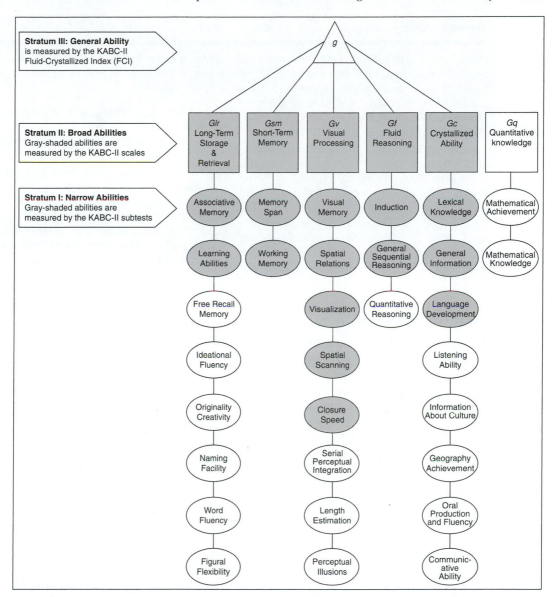

FIGURE 8.5   Cattell–Horn–Carroll (CHC) model applied to the Kaufman Assessment Battery for Children (KABC-III).

Source: Kaufman, A. S., & Kaufman, N. L. (2004). *Kaufman Assessment Battery for Children—Second Edition (K-ABC-II).* Circle Pines, MN: American Guidance Service. Copyright © 2004 by NCS Pearson, Inc. Reproduced with permission. All rights reserved. "KABC" is a trademark, in the U.S. and/or other countries, of Pearson Education, Inc. or its affiliates(s).

existence of a *g* factor (Floyd, Bergeron, Hamilton, & Parra, 2010). The Kaufman Assessment Battery for Children, Second Edition (KABC-II), an intelligence test for children ages 3 to 18, is founded on the CHC model (as well as Luria's processing theory). Figure 8.5 depicts the CHC model as it applies to the KABC-II.

Terman's Study

Lewis Terman (1877–1956) is well known for his research on intelligence in children. In 1922, he began a longitudinal study that sought to answer the following question: What kind of adults do children with high IQs become (Terman & Oden, 1959)? He followed the lives of 1,528 "gifted" (i.e., having IQ scores of 135 or higher) children, who have been tracked for over 80 years (50 years after Terman's death). The study is the longest-running survey ever carried out with regard to intelligence and ability. Contrary to the stereotypes, Terman found that the gifted children were taller, healthier, physically better developed, and superior in leadership and social adaptability. They also excelled in school and often moved ahead in the curriculum. As adults, those in Terman's sample had the following characteristics:

- More likely to earn graduate degrees and doctorates
- Earned incomes well above population averages
- More satisfied with their life and life's work
- Low criminality
- Achieved greater marital success
- Physically healthier than the average adult
- Lower incidence of psychological problems (e.g., substance abuse, suicide)

INTELLIGENCE TESTS

Intelligence tests measure a broad spectrum of cognitive abilities, such as reasoning, comprehension, judgment, memory, and spatial ability. They help us gain an understanding of an examinee's cognitive strengths and weaknesses and are considered excellent predictors of academic achievement and academic success (Sattler, 2008) as well as success in training and job performance (Muchinsky, 2008). Most intelligence tests include items that require verbal and nonverbal reasoning and a variety of other cognitive abilities. The terminology used on tests to delineate abilities is numerous and varied and may be based on a particular theory of intelligence or factor analytic evidence. Table 8.3 presents just a few of the common types of cognitive abilities assessed in intelligence testing. As with other types of assessment instruments, measures of intellectual ability can be used for a number of purposes. They may be used for *screening*; for *identification* of intellectual disabilities, learning disabilities, or giftedness; to *place* individuals into specialized academic or vocational programs; or as a *cognitive adjunct* to a comprehensive clinical evaluation, in which the main focus is on personality or neuropsychological assessment (Kaufman, 2000, p. 453).

Intelligence tests typically yield an overall measure of global intelligence as well as scores on subtests or groups of subtests that represent different cognitive abilities. Historically, the most famous index of intelligence is the *IQ*, or intelligence quotient. This term came about when Lewis Terman (1916) adopted German psychologist William Stern's concept of a mental quotient, renaming it *intelligence quotient*. (Stern defined *mental quotient* as the ratio of mental age [MA] to chronological age [CA] multiplied by 100: IQ = MA/CA × 100.) Thus, if a child's MA of 5 equals his or her CA of 5, then the IQ is 100 (5/5 × 100), or average intelligence. Although the formula worked fairly well for children who have a somewhat steady pace of intellectual growth, it did not work for adolescents and adults, because intellectual development does not steadily increase throughout the life span; thus, CA would continue growing while MA stayed the same,

TABLE 8.3 Cognitive Abilities	
Abstract reasoning	Ability to use concepts and symbols to solve problems
Knowledge	The accumulated fund of general information
Memory	Ability to recognize and recall information such as numbers, letters, and words
Nonverbal reasoning	Ability to solve tasks using spatial ability and visualization
Numerical reasoning	Ability to solve problems with numbers or numerical concepts
Perceptual ability	Ability to perceive, understand, and recall patterns of information
Processing speed	The speed of performing basic cognitive operations
Reasoning	Ability to derive rules and solve problems inductively
Spatial ability	Ability to visualize and manipulate visual images, geographic shapes, or objects in three dimensions
Verbal comprehension	Ability to understand words, sentences, and paragraphs

resulting in unreliably low IQ scores. Today, the term *intelligence quotient* and its original formula are no longer used. Instead, overall test scores are usually converted to a *standard score* with a mean of 100 and a standard deviation of 15 or 16, depending on the test. Tests that still refer to IQ scores (such as the Wechsler scales and the Stanford–Binet Intelligence Scales) are alluding to standard scores, not to actual quotients. Tests may also provide descriptive classifications in addition to standard scores. It's important to remember that hypotheses or recommendations generated solely on IQ scores are not valid without the inclusion of contextual information gathered from multiple sources, such as interviews with the client; behavior observations; collateral information from parents, teachers, and therapists; or other appropriate sources (e.g., information from records or previous test data).

Intelligence tests can also be categorized based on whether they are administered to individuals or groups. *Individual intelligence tests* are administered to a single individual by a highly qualified examiner. Examiners must be specially trained to administer and score the varied item types on individual intelligence tests; for example, many tests have items requiring oral responses from the examinee, have set time limits for certain tasks, and require examiners to observe qualitative aspects of a test taker's performance. Individual tests are considered clinical instruments and are used when intensive psychological evaluation of an individual client is needed—for example, for the identification and classification of intellectual disabilities (i.e., mental retardation), learning disabilities, or other cognitive disorders (Flanagan & Harrison, 2012). In contrast to individual tests, *group intelligence tests* can be administered to large groups of people either simultaneously or within a limited time frame by a minimally trained examiner. Less training is required for administration, because most group tests only require the examiner to read simple instructions and accurately keep time. The typical group test employs multiple-choice, true/false, or other selected-response items to ensure uniformity and objectivity of scoring (Flanagan & Harrison, 2012). Group tests are useful for screening to determine the need for an in-depth evaluation, estimating intelligence scores for academic or vocational purposes, and estimating intelligence scores for research studies. Because group tests offer the advantage of being able to assess many individuals quickly and inexpensively, they are principally applied in education, business, government, and military settings for screening and placement purposes.

Intelligence tests can also be classified as verbal or nonverbal, or they may contain items of both types. *Verbal intelligence tests* presume that examinees have a certain standard of language ability; they are able to understand language and use it to reason or respond (Plucker & Esping, 2014). *Nonverbal measures of intelligence* reduce language in directions, items, or responses. They may use oral directions, allow examinees to respond to test items nonverbally, or use puzzles or other manipulatives. Nonverbal tests are appropriate for special populations, such as individuals who are non-English speaking, who are deaf or hearing impaired, or who have other types of language or physical disabilities or reading problems.

Ability, Intelligence, Achievement, and Aptitude

Intelligence can be referred to using a number of different terms, such as *ability*, *intellectual ability*, *general ability*, and *cognitive ability*. Similarly, *intelligence tests* are often called *cognitive ability tests*, *general ability measures*, or simply *ability tests*. Although this terminology is generally accurate, in the context of assessment, intelligence, achievement, and aptitude are all aspects of an individual's overall ability, and there are separate tests that measure each area:

- *Intelligence Tests* Measure an individual's current intellectual ability level
- *Achievement Tests* Measure what an individual knows or can do right now, *in the present*
- *Aptitude Tests* Are *future oriented*, predicting what an individual is capable of doing with further training and education

To obtain an overall picture of an individual's abilities, examiners analyze information from all three areas (achievement and aptitude assessment will be discussed further in Chapters 9 and 10 of this text). Table 8.4 provides a description of the general features and distinguishing characteristics of intelligence, achievement, and aptitude tests.

In the next section, we will describe a few of the more prominent individual, group, and specialized tests of intelligence. We do not attempt to provide a comprehensive description of each test, which would be outside the scope of this textbook. We recommend that readers examine test manuals for more information about specific intelligence tests.

Individual Intelligence Tests

Individual intelligence tests are used widely and for various purposes. Each individual test has been normed on a specific population and population subsets. It is important to be familiar with a number of individual tests and to select the appropriate one based on the person being assessed.

THE WECHSLER SCALES Despite the number of intelligence tests available, the Wechsler scales continue to dominate the field; their popularity is unrivaled in the history of intellectual assessment. In 1939, David Wechsler, a psychologist at Bellevue Hospital in New

TABLE 8.4 **Distinguishing Characteristics of Intelligence, Achievement, and Aptitude Tests**

	Purpose	Orientation	Use
Intelligence tests	Measure a broad spectrum of cognitive abilities	Present and future	• To determine need for more in-depth evaluation • To identify intellectual disabilities, learning disabilities, or giftedness • For placement/selection into specialized academic or vocational programs • As part of a comprehensive clinical evaluation
Achievement tests	Measure knowledge and skills learned as a result of instruction	Present	• To identify academic strengths and weaknesses • For placement/selection into specialized academic or vocational programs • To track achievement over time • To evaluate instructional objectives and programs • To identify learning disabilities • As part of a comprehensive clinical evaluation
Aptitude tests	Measure talents or performance abilities prior to instruction	Future	• To predict future performance • For placement/selection into specialized academic or vocational programs • For job placement decisions • As part of a comprehensive clinical evaluation

York, first published an individual intelligence test (i.e., the Wechsler–Bellevue Intelligence Scale). Since that time, he developed a series of three intelligence scales designed for different age groups. The *Wechsler Adult Intelligence Scale* (WAIS-IV) is designed to assess the cognitive abilities of individuals aged 16 to 89 years. The *Wechsler Intelligence Scale for Children* (WISC-V) is for children of ages 6 years through 17 years. As is the case when new assessment instruments are released, there is an overlap of time between the use of the previous version and the adoption of the new version. In preparing to become professional counselors, you should become familiar with the information related to the WISC-IV because it is still currently used and also explore the information related to the WISC-V because it will be widely adopted in the coming years.

The *Wechsler Preschool and Primary Scale of Intelligence* (WPPSI-IV) is designed for very young children of ages 2 years through 6 years. The Wechsler scales continue to be the most widely used measure of intelligence the world over. A study by Camara, Nathan, and Puente (2000) found that among intelligence tests the WAIS-II and the WISC-III were the most frequently used by psychologists. In this section, we will discuss the WAIS-IV, the WISC-IV, and the WPPSI-IV.

TABLE 8.5 Indexes and Subtests for the Wechsler Intelligence Scales (WAIS-IV, WISC-IV, WPSSI-III)	
Wisc IV	• Verbal Comprehension Index - two subtests - two supplemental
	• Visual Spatial/Fluid Reasoning Index - four subtests - two supplemental
	• Working memory Index - two subtests - one supplemental
	• Processing Speed Index - two subtests - one supplemental
WAIS-V	• Verbal Comprehension Index - three subtests - one supplemental
	• Perceptual Reasoning Index - three subtests - two supplemental
	• Working Memory Index - two subtests - one supplemental
	• Processing Speed Index - one subtests - two supplemental
	• General Ability Index - optional
WPPSI-IV	• Verbal IQ - five subtests
	• Performance IQ - six subtests
	• Working Memory - two subtests
	• Processing Speed - two subtests

Each of the three Wechsler scales yields a Full-Scale IQ (FSIQ), index composite scores, and subtest scaled scores (Table 8.5 lists the indexes and subtests for the Wechsler scales). The *FSIQ* is considered the most representative estimate of global intellectual functioning and is derived from a combination of the subtest scores. The *index composite scores* measure more narrowly defined cognitive domains and are composed of the sum of various subtest scores. *Subtest scores* are measures of specific abilities. The FSIQ and index composite scores have a mean of 100 and a standard deviation of 15. The subtest scaled scores have a mean of 10 and a standard deviation of 3.

Earlier versions of the Wechsler scales did not use index scores, but utilized a *dual IQ structure* that included two IQ scores: *verbal IQ* (VIQ) and *performance IQ* (PIQ). The VIQ score summarized an individual's performance on subtests designed to measure vocabulary, general knowledge, verbal comprehension, and working memory. The PIQ score measured visual-motor skills, alertness to details, nonverbal reasoning, processing speed, and planning ability. The use of the dual IQ structure appears to be changing, as the latest edition of the WISC completely eliminated the VIQ and PIQ scores in favor of the four index scores (see Table 8.6 for a description of the WISC-IV indexes and subtests). The WPPSI-IV now has five index scores: Verbal Comprehension Index (VCI), Visual Spatial Index (VSI), Working Memory Index (WMI), Fluid Reasoning Index (FRI), and Processing Speed Index (PSI).

Interpreting scores on the Wechsler scales is very complicated and requires considerable education and training. Interpretation strategies, described fully in the test manuals (The Psychological Corporation, 1997, 2002, 2003), are beyond the scope of this textbook; however, we will review a few basic interpretive steps. The first step is reporting and describing the examinee's FSIQ score (i.e., the examinee's overall level of intellectual

TABLE 8.6 Description of Full-Scale IQ, Indexes, and Subtests on the WISC-IV	
Full-Scale IQ (FSIQ)	Global and aggregate measure of intelligence.
Verbal Comprehension Index (VCI)	This index measures verbal knowledge/understanding obtained through both informal and formal education. It reflects application of verbal skills to new situations. One of the best predictors of overall intelligence.
Similarities	This subtest measures verbal reasoning and concept formation. The individual must identify the similarity between two dissimilar words and describe how they are similar.
Vocabulary	Measures word knowledge and verbal concept formation. The individual is required to name the pictures displayed in the stimulus book and give definitions for words the examiner reads aloud.
Comprehension	Measures verbal reasoning and conceptualization, verbal comprehension, and verbal expression. The individual must answer questions based on his or her understanding of general principles and social situations.
Information*	Measures the individual's ability to acquire, retain, and retrieve general factual knowledge. The test requires the child to answer questions that address a broad range of general knowledge topics.
Word Reasoning*	Measures verbal comprehension, word reasoning, verbal abstraction, domain knowledge, the ability to integrate and synthesize different types of information, and the ability to generate alternative concepts. This test requires the individual to identify the common concept being described in a series of clues.
Perceptual Reasoning Index (PRI)	This index measures one's ability to interpret and organize visual information and to solve problems.
Block Design	This subtest measures the ability to analyze and synthesize abstract visual stimuli. The individual views a constructed model or a picture in the stimulus book. Within a specified time limit, the examinee recreates the design using nine identical blocks; each block has two sides that are all red, two sides that are all white, and two sides that are half red/half white.
Matrix Reasoning	Measures fluid intelligence, attention to detail, concentration, and reasoning ability; overall, a reliable estimate of general nonverbal intelligence. In this exercise, a child examines a matrix (filled with pictures of certain objects) that is missing a section. The child then selects the missing portion from a group of picture options.
Picture Concepts	Measures abstract, categorical reasoning ability. The individual sees rows with pictures of various objects and selects those objects that are similar and should be grouped together. For example, the similar items might be trees or animals.
Picture Completion*	Measures visual perception and organization, concentration, and visual recognition of essential details of objects. This test requires the individual to view a picture and then point to or name the important part missing within a specified time limit.

(continued)

TABLE 8.6 Description of Full-Scale IQ, Indexes, and Subtests on the WISC-IV   *(Continued)*

Working Memory Index (WMI)	This index measures one's ability to temporarily retain information in memory, perform some operation or manipulation with it, and produce a result. Involves attention, concentration, and mental control.
Digit Span	This subtest is composed of two parts. The Digit Span Forward task requires the individual to repeat numbers in the same order as read aloud by the examiner. Digit Span Backward requires the individual to repeat the numbers in the reverse order of that presented by the examiner. This subtest measures auditory short-term memory, sequencing skills, attention, and concentration.
Letter-Number Sequencing	Measures attention, short-term memory, concentration, numerical ability, and processing speed. The individual is asked to read a sequence of numbers and letters and recall the numbers in ascending order and the letters in alphabetical order.
Arithmetic*	Measures mental manipulation, concentration, attention, short- and long-term memory, numerical reasoning ability, and mental alertness. It requires the individual to mentally solve a series of orally presented arithmetic problems within a specified time limit.
Processing Speed Index (PSI)	This index measures one's ability to quickly and correctly scan, sequence, or discriminate simple visual information. Involves concentration and rapid eye-hand coordination.
Coding	This subtest measures the individual's short-term memory, learning ability, visual perception, visual-motor coordination, visual scanning ability, cognitive flexibility, attention, and motivation. The individual copies symbols that are paired with simple geometric shapes or numbers.
Symbol Search	Measures processing speed, short-term visual memory, visual-motor coordination, cognitive flexibility, visual discrimination, and concentration. The individual is presented with a series of paired groups of symbols, with each pair containing a *target* group and a *search* group. The individual scans the search group and indicates whether the target symbol(s) matches any of the symbols in the search group within a specified time limit.
Cancellation*	Measures processing speed, visual selective attention, vigilance, and visual neglect. The individual scans both a random and a structured arrangement of pictures and marks target pictures within a specified time limit.

*Supplemental subtest

ability). Examiners compare the examinee's FSIQ to those of the general population (as identified by the performance of the norm group, from which all scores are derived). The population of the United States has an average intelligence score of 100. Table 8.7 identifies the descriptive classifications for FSIQ and index composite score ranges on the Wechsler scales. Using this table, we see that a person who has an FSIQ score of 100 is functioning within the average range of intellectual ability. Examiners should report the FSIQ score

TABLE 8.7 Descriptive Classifications for FSIQ and Index Composite Scores

Composite Score	Classification	Percentile Range %	Percent Included in Normal Curve
130 and above	Very Superior	98–99	2.2
120–129	Superior	91–97	6.7
110–119	High Average	75–90	16.1
90–109	Average	25–74	50.0
80–89	Low Average	9–24	16.1
70–79	Borderline	3–8	6.7
69 and below	Extremely Low	1–2	2.2

along with the appropriate percentile rank and descriptive classification in relation to the level of performance (e.g., average, high average).

Another step in interpretation involves interpreting the index scores. Examiners may begin by reporting each index score, including the qualitative description and the percentile rank. Examiners can also analyze an examinee's strengths and weaknesses on the index scores by identifying *significant statistical differences* between the index scores (based on the normal curve). For example, an examinee may have a good verbal ability (high VCI) but a weakness in working memory (a relatively lower score on WMI). In order to determine if differences between index scores are significant, examiners refer to tables located in the test manual that identify critical index score values by age group. For example, according to the WISC-IV manual, a 13-year-old child whose VCI score is 15 points higher than his WMI score is considered *statistically significant* (at the .05 level). Examiners can also identify differences between an examinee's index scores and *base rate* data, which are scores observed within the general population. Interestingly, it is possible for index scores to be statistically different from each other and yet, because the difference occurs so often within the population (base rate), have difference between the two scores be meaningless. Therefore, it is very important to consider both significant differences and base rates between an individual's index scores when making clinical and educational planning decisions.

Interpretation can also involve describing and analyzing subtest scores within an individual's profile. Using a three-category descriptive classification, subtest scores may be described as follows (understanding that subtests have a mean of 10 and a standard deviation of 3; Sattler & Dumont, 2004):

- Subtest scaled scores of 1 to 7 indicate a *relative weakness* (one to three standard deviations below the mean).
- Subtest scores of 8 to 12 indicate *average* ability (within one standard deviation from the mean).
- Subtest scores of 13 to 19 indicate a *relative strength* (one to three standard deviations above the mean).

Significant differences between the highest and lowest subtest scores are called *subtest scatter*, which can be useful in specifying particular strengths and weaknesses of an individual's performance. Examiners can also analyze subtest scores using a base-rate approach to compare an examinee's subtest scores with the scores of the general population.

Because of the complexity of interpretation, it is very important for the skilled examiner to not only be trained in the administration of the Wechsler scales but also receive advanced graduate training in the interpretation of examinees' performance. Furthermore, it's essential to remember that test scores are only one method of assessment. Interpretations for test results are always made in conjunction with an individual's background information, direct behavioral observation, and other assessment results. Table 8.8 shows sample WISC-IV test results.

TABLE 8.8 WISC-IV Sample Test Results

	Composite Score	Percentile	Descriptive Classification
Verbal Comprehension (VCI)	116	86	High Average
Perceptual Reasoning Index (PRI)	92	30	Average
Working Memory Index (WMI)	110	75	High Average
Processing Speed Index (PSI)	97	42	Average
Full-Scale IQ (FSIQ)	106	66	Average

	Scaled Score	Percentile
Verbal Comprehension Subtests		
Similarities	16	98
Vocabulary	10	50
Comprehension	13	84
Information	11	63
Word Reasoning	12	75
Perceptual Reasoning Subtests		
Block Design	8	25
Picture Concepts	10	50
Matrix Reasoning	8	25
Picture Completion	6	9
Working Memory Subtests		
Digit Span	11	63
Letter-Number Sequencing	13	84
Arithmetic	13	84
Processing Speed Subtests		
Coding	9	37
Symbol Search	10	50
Cancellation	10	50

Source: Wechsler Intelligence Scale for Children–Fourth Edition (WISC-IV). Copyright © 2003 by NCS Pearson, Inc. Reproduced with permission. All rights reserved. "Wechsler Intelligence Scale for Children" and "WISC" are trademarks, in the United States and/or other countries, of Pearson Education, Inc. or its affiliates(s).

In terms of psychometric properties, the Wechsler scales were standardized on large samples of individuals that were selected to match U.S. Census Bureau data on the variables of age, gender, geographic region, race/ethnicity, and parental education/education level. The sizes of the normative samples are 2,200 and 1,700 for the WAIS-IV and WISC-IV, respectively. The latest Wechsler scales have considerable evidence that supports construct validity; that is, the scales measure overall general intellectual abilities as well as verbal comprehension, perceptual organization/perceptual reasoning, working memory, and processing speed (Wechsler, 1997, 2002, 2003, 2012), and many studies indicate that the Wechsler scales correlate highly with other measures of intelligence. In terms of reliability, the internal consistency reliability coefficients of the Full-Scale IQ scores and index scores are in the .90s (except for PSI, which ranges from .87 to .89), and test-retest reliabilities range from .86 to .96 (The Psychological Corporation, 1997, 2002, 2003). Exercise 8.1 provides an opportunity to apply the information you are learning about intelligence assessment to a case study. Consider the information provided, and complete the three exercise questions.

Exercise 8.1
Understanding Intelligence Assessment: Jackie

Jackie is a 10-year-old Caucasian female who was referred for an evaluation because of academic problems. She is currently in the fifth grade. According to her mother, Jackie has attended the same school since initial enrollment in school, including pre-kindergarten. She has an excellent attendance record, is extremely well-behaved in school, and has an exemplary conduct record in the past. Regarding her academic performance, Jackie is currently experiencing many academic difficulties and has had many academic difficulties in the past. Most recent standardized achievement test results show that she scored below average in reading, math, and language.

Jackie arrived on time for the assessment and was accompanied by her mother. Jackie appeared alert and highly motivated and appeared to put her best effort into the testing process.

1. Identify the descriptive classifications of the FSIQ, index scores, and subtest scaled scores.

2. Interpret Jackie's index composite scores, and describe what each index measures. Use the following interpretation of the FSIQ as the format for your answers:

The Full Scale IQ (FSIQ) is an estimate of global intellectual functioning. Jackie's FSIQ is 97, which is within the average range of intellectual functioning. She scored at the 42nd percentile, which means that her score is equal to or exceeds approximately 42% of the national comparison group.

- Verbal Comprehension Index
- Perceptual Reasoning Index
- Working Memory Index
- Processing Speed Index

3. Based on her subtest scores, how would you describe any relative subtest strengths and weaknesses Jackie may have?

Exercise 8.1
(*Continued*)

FSIQ and Index Scores	Composite Score	Percentile	Descriptive Classification
Verbal Comprehension (VCI)	104	61	
Perceptual Reasoning Index (PRI)	102	55	
Working Memory Index (WMI)	86	18	
Processing Speed Index (PSI)	91	27	
Full-Scale IQ (FSIQ)	97	42	

Subtest Scores	Scaled Score	Percentile	Descriptive Classification
Verbal Comprehension Subtests			
Similarities	11	63	
Vocabulary	11	63	
Comprehension	11	63	
Information	10	50	
Word Reasoning	10	50	
Perceptual Reasoning Subtests			
Block Design	9	37	
Picture Concepts	10	50	
Matrix Reasoning	13	84	
Picture Completion	10	50	
Working Memory Subtests			
Digit Span	8	25	
Letter–Number Sequencing	7	16	
Arithmetic	10	50	
Processing Speed Subtests			
Coding	8	25	
Symbol Search	9	37	
Cancellation	8	25	

STANFORD–BINET INTELLIGENCE SCALE, FIFTH EDITION One of the oldest and most widely used intelligence tests is the *Stanford–Binet Intelligence Scale*, now in its fifth edition. The Stanford–Binet, which originated from the Binet–Simon scale in 1905, was first published in 1916 by Lewis Terman at Stanford University (Becker, 2003). The latest edition of the Stanford–Binet was published in 2003 and is appropriate for use with individuals between the ages of 2 and 85-plus years. It normally takes 45 to 75 minutes to administer the test.

The fifth edition of the Stanford–Binet was constructed on a five-factor hierarchical cognitive model that includes the following scales:

- *Full-Scale IQ* Measures the ability to reason with both words and visual material, the ability to store and later retrieve and apply important knowledge, broad span of memory for both words and visual details, spatial-visualization ability, and the ability to solve novel problems with numbers and number concepts.
- *Nonverbal IQ (NVIQ)* Measures reasoning skills in solving picture-oriented, abstract problems; remembering facts and figures presented in visual displays; solving numerical problems shown in picture form; assembling visual puzzles; and remembering information presented in visual space.
- *Verbal IQ (VIQ)* Measures general verbal reasoning ability—solving problems presented in printed or spoken words, sentences, or stories.

The FSIQ, VIQ, and NVIQ have composite scores with a mean of 100 and a standard deviation of 15, and the VIQ and NVIQ each include five subtests, each having a mean of 10 and a standard deviation of 3. The subtests are organized into five *cognitive factors* in both the verbal and nonverbal domains:

1. *Fluid Reasoning* The ability to solve novel problems, whether presented verbally or nonverbally
2. *Knowledge* The accumulated fund of general information acquired at home, school, work, and in daily life
3. *Quantitative Reasoning* The ability to solve problems with numbers or numerical concepts
4. *Visual Spatial Processing* The ability to see patterns and manipulate visual images, geographic shapes, or 3-D objects
5. *Working Memory* The ability to store information in short-term memory and then sort or transform that information

Interpreting the Stanford–Binet involves identifying and evaluating any significant discrepancies between the NVIQ and VIQ and among the subtest scores. Extensive tables for evaluating score differences are available in the Stanford–Binet Technical Manual. The FSIQ is interpreted using the descriptive categories shown in Figure 8.6 (Roid, 2003).

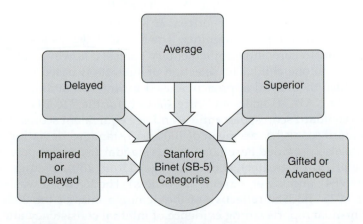

FIGURE 8.6 Descriptive Categories for the Stanford–Binet Full-Scale IQ

Extensive reliability and validity studies were conducted as part of the standardization of the fifth edition of the Stanford–Binet. The test norms were based on 4,800 individuals and were stratified according to a 2001 U.S. Census Bureau report on age, gender, race/ethnicity, geographic region, and socioeconomic level. Internal consistency reliability ranged from .95 to .98 for IQ scores, from .90 to .92 for the five Factor Index scores, and from .84 to .89 for the 10 subtests. Correlations between the Stanford–Binet and other intelligence tests yielded .90, .84, .82, and .83 for the Stanford–Binet fourth edition, WISC-III, WAIS-III, and WPPSI-R, respectively. Test-retest and interrater reliability studies were also conducted and showed the stability and consistency of scoring of the Stanford–Binet.

THE KAUFMAN INSTRUMENTS Another important name in the area of intelligence testing is Kaufman. In the 1970s and early 1980s, husband-and-wife team Alan and Nadeen Kaufman created a series of intelligence tests (based on their extensive clinical and research experience and their great knowledge in the assessment field), which included the Kaufman Assessment Battery for Children (KABC-II; Kaufman & Kaufman, 2004a), the Kaufman Adolescent and Adult Intelligence Test (KAIT; Kaufman & Kaufman, 1993), the Kaufman Brief Intelligence Test (KBIT-2; Kaufman & Kaufman, 2004b), and many other instruments. The first edition of the KABC was the first intelligence test to be founded on two theoretical models: Luria's processing model and the CHC model. We will present further information about the KABC-II and the KAIT.

The *Kaufman Assessment Battery for Children, Second Edition* (KABC-II; Kaufman & Kaufman, 2004a) was designed to measure a range of cognitive abilities in children aged 3 to 18. The instrument is grounded in two modern theoretical models: Luria's neuropsychological theory of processing and the CHC model of broad and narrow abilities. Because of its dual theoretical foundation, the KABC-II may be interpreted based on either interpretive approach (i.e., the Luria model or the CHC approach), depending on which approach the examiner chooses to take. The KABC-II yields a separate global score for each of the two theoretical models: the Mental Processing Index (MPI), which measures mental processing ability from the Luria perspective, and the Fluid-Crystallized Index (FCI), which measures general cognitive ability from the CHC model. The primary difference between these two global scores is that the MPI (Luria's model) *excludes* measures of acquired knowledge, whereas the FCI (CHC theory) *includes* measures of acquired knowledge (Kaufman, Lichtenberger, Fletcher-Janzen, & Kaufman, 2005). Only one of these two global scores is computed for any examinee. The KABC-II also yields scores on five broad abilities scales and 18 core and supplementary subtests; however, an examiner would not use all 18 with one child. The selection of subtests is based on the age range of the child and which theoretical approach is used for interpretation. Table 8.9 provides a description of the KABC-II scales and core subtests for the 7 to 18 age range. The instrument provides standard scores, percentiles, and age equivalent scores. For the broad ability scales, standard scores have a mean of 100 and a standard deviation of 15. Descriptive categories are also provided based on various standard score ranges: upper extreme (standard score of 131 or greater), above average (116 to 130), average (85 to 115), below average (70 to 84), and lower extreme (79 or less). The KABC-II was standardized on a sample of 3,025 children reflective of the demographics of the 2001 U.S. Census report. The test manual reports strong evidence of internal consistency and test-retest reliabilities as well as evidence of construct validity. Global scores of the KABC-II

TABLE 8.9 KABC-II Scales and Core Subtests

Scales and Subtests	Description
Sequential/*Gsm*	Measures the ability to arrange input into a sequential or serial order to solve a problem.
Number Recall	Measures sequential processing and short-term memory; the examiner speaks a series of numbers, and the child repeats them.
Word Order	Measures sequential processing and short-term memory; the examiner speaks a series of words, and the child points to pictures of those words in the same sequence.
Simultaneous/*Gv*	Measures ability to integrate and synthesize input simultaneously, usually spatially, to solve a problem.
Rover	Measures visual processing; the child moves a toy dog to a bone on a checkerboard-like grid that contains obstacles (rocks and weeds) and tries to find the "quickest" path (e.g., the one that takes the fewest moves).
Triangles (7–12)	Measures visual ability and spatial relationships; the child arranges shapes to match a model or picture.
Block Counting (13–18)	Measures visualization of objects in three dimensions; the child counts how many blocks are present in a picture.
Planning/*Gf*	Measures high-level, decision-making, executive processes including analysis, planning, and organization.
Pattern Reasoning	Nonverbal measure of reasoning skills and hypothesis testing necessary for problem solving; the examinee is presented with set of images and must select an image that completes the pattern (most images are abstract, geometric shapes).
Story Completion	Nonverbal measure of planning and reasoning skills; the child is shown an incomplete series of pictures and has to choose picture cards to complete the story.
Learning/*Glr*	Measures ability to integrate cognitive processes associated with learning, retaining, and efficiently retrieving information.
Atlantis	Measures ability to learn new information through association between pictures and nonsense names; the child is taught names for fanciful pictures of fish, plants, and shells; the child then demonstrates learning by pointing to and naming each picture.
Rebus Learning	Measures ability to learn new information; the examiner teaches the child the word or concept associated with each particular rebus (drawing), and the child then "reads" aloud phrases and sentences composed of these rebuses.
Knowledge/*Gc*	Measures verbal knowledge, verbal comprehension, and verbal reasoning.
Riddles	Measures verbal comprehension, verbal reasoning, and word retrieval; the examiner reads a riddle, and the child answers the riddle by either pointing to a picture of a concrete or abstract concept or naming it.
Verbal Knowledge	Measures vocabulary and general information; the child selects a picture that corresponds to a vocabulary word or answers a general information question.

correlated strongly with the WISC-III, WISC-IV, and WPPSI-III FSIQs. Raiford and Coalson (2014) found that the correlation remained strong between the KABC-II and the WPPSI-IV.

The *Kaufman Adolescent and Adult Intelligence Test* (KAIT; Kaufman & Kaufman, 1993) is designed for individuals of ages 11 to 85 years. The core battery consists of three intelligence scales (i.e., Fluid, Crystallized, and Composite Intelligence) and six subtests—three that assess fluid intelligence and three that assess crystallized intelligence. The *Fluid* scale measures the ability to solve novel problems by using reasoning, which is considered a function of biological and neurological factors. The *Crystallized* scale measures ability to solve problems and make decisions based on acquired knowledge, verbal conceptualization, formal and informal education, life experience, and acculturation. The *Composite* score provides a measure of overall intellectual functioning. The instrument was standardized on a national sample of 2,000 individuals. The manual reports validity and reliability information, including information on correlational studies with the WISC-IV, the WAIS-III, and the KABC-II, as well as internal consistency reliability coefficients in the .90s. Additional studies have shown similar relationships with the WAIS-IV (Lichtenberger & Kaufman, 2012)

WOODCOCK–JOHNSON III TESTS OF COGNITIVE ABILITIES The *Woodcock–Johnson III Tests of Cognitive Abilities* (WJ III COG; Woodcock, McGrew, & Mather, 2007) is one of the most widely used instruments for assessing cognitive abilities in individuals aged 2 to 90-plus years. The *WJ III COG* is based on the CHC theory of cognitive abilities. On the WJ III COG, scores represent cognitive ability at four different levels:

- *First Level* Consists of 31 cognitive tests that measure broad and narrow cognitive abilities. Rarely do examiners use all 31 tests; rather, they select appropriate tests based on the purpose of assessment.
- *Second Level* Several clusters of broad cognitive abilities derived from the 31 cognitive tests.
- *Third Level* Three categories of broad cognitive abilities, including *verbal ability* (acquired knowledge and language comprehension), *thinking ability* (intentional cognitive processing), and *cognitive efficiency* (automatic cognitive process).
- *Fourth Level* Consists of a *general intellectual ability* (GIA) score.

The WJ III ACH provides a variety of scores, including age and grade equivalents, raw score/number correct, percentile ranks, and standard score (mean = 100; SD = 15). It also provides the following average standard score descriptors: standard scores of 131 and above are *very superior*, 121–130 are *superior*, 111–120 are *high average*, 90–110 are *average*, 80–89 are *low average*, 70–79 are *low*, and 69 and below are *very low*.

The WJ III COG was developed with the *Woodcock–Johnson III Tests of Achievement* (WJ III ACH), and together these instruments provide a comprehensive assessment for measuring intellectual abilities and academic achievement. Using the WJ III COG and the WJ III ACH together, professionals can make accurate comparisons of an individual's cognitive abilities, oral language ability, and achievement scores (Schrank, Flanagan, Woodcock, & Mascolo, 2010).

ADDITIONAL INDIVIDUAL INTELLIGENCE TESTS The *Differential Ability Scales, Second Edition* (DAS–II; Elliot, 2007) is a comprehensive, individually administered instrument for assessing cognitive abilities of children aged 2 years through 17 years. The DAS was initially developed to provide professionals assessing children with learning disabilities and developmental disabilities with information at a finer level of detail than an IQ score; thus, its main focus is on specific abilities rather than on general "intelligence." In addition to learning disabilities, the DAS-II is also appropriate for children with a variety of special classifications, including ADHD, language impairment, limited English proficiency, mild to moderate intellectual impairment, and gifted/talented children. The DAS-II consists of 20 core and diagnostic subtests that are grouped into three batteries: *Early Years Battery (Lower Level)* for ages 2 years, 6 months to 3 years, 5 months; *Early Years Battery (Upper Level)* for ages 3 years, 6 months to 6 years, 11 months; and *School Age Battery* for ages 7 years to 17 years, 11 months. These batteries provide the *General Conceptual Ability* score (*GCA*), which is a composite score that focuses on reasoning and conceptual abilities.

The *Slosson Intelligence Test-Revised for Children and Adults* (SIT-R3) is a 187-item oral screening instrument that was designed to provide a quick estimate of general verbal cognitive abilities of individuals aged 4 to 65. It measures the following cognitive areas: vocabulary, general information, similarities and differences, comprehension, quantitative, and auditory memory. As a screening instrument, it can be used to provide tentative diagnoses or to determine if further in-depth evaluation is needed.

The *Das–Naglieri Cognitive Assessment System* (CAS; Naglieri & Das, 1997) was built on the PASS theory of cognitive processes, which emphasizes cognitive processes that are related to performance rather than to a general intelligence model. The CAS assesses cognitive processes in children aged 5 through 17 and yields scores for the Planning, Attention, Simultaneous, and Successive subscales as well as a full-scale score. The test may be used for identifying ADHD, learning disabilities, intellectual disabilities, and giftedness as well as for evaluating children with traumatic brain injury.

Group Intelligence Tests

As stated earlier, group intelligence tests are useful when large numbers of examinees must be evaluated either simultaneously or within a limited time frame. The World War I *Army Alpha* and *Army Beta* tests were the first major group intelligence tests developed and were used to screen millions of recruits. Since then, many more have been produced, and group tests are used far more extensively than individual intelligence tests, particularly for screening purposes. We will describe some of the more well-known group intelligence tests.

COGNITIVE ABILITIES TEST The *Cognitive Abilities Test* (CogAT; Lohman & Hagen, 2001) measures K–12 students' learned reasoning and problem-solving skills. It was designed to help educators make important student placement decisions, such as selecting students for gifted and talented programs. The CogAT can be administered in whole or in part, and 30 to 60 minutes of time is allowed per session, depending on the child's grade level. It provides scores for three batteries as well as an overall composite score:

1. *Verbal Battery* Measures a child's ability to remember and transform sequences of English words, to understand them, and to make inferences and judgments about them. It includes subtests on Verbal Classification, Sentence Completion, and Verbal Analogies.

2. *Quantitative Battery* Measures a child's understanding of basic quantitative concepts and relationships that are essential for learning mathematics. It includes subtests on Quantitative Relations, Number Series, and Equation Building.
3. *Nonverbal Battery* Measures reasoning through the manipulation and classification of geometric shapes and figures.
4. *Composite Score* Derived from the results of the three batteries, the composite score is a general statement of a student's overall reasoning ability.

Raw scores are converted to stanines, percentile ranks, and standard age scores. *Standard age scores* (SAS) have a mean of 100 and a standard deviation of 16 and are used to allow comparisons between a student's scores and the scores of other students in the same age group. SAS range from 50 to 150; scores from 128 to 152 are considered *very high*, scores from 112 to 127 are *above average*, from 89 to 111 are *average*, from 73 to 88 are *below average*, and from 50 to 72 are *very low*. An interesting feature of the CogAT is that its website (riverpub.com/products/CogAT) contains an *Interactive Profile Interpretation System* that enables teachers, counselors, and parents to interpret test scores by inputting the child's test profile. The interactive system also provides intellectual characteristics and instructional suggestions for children based on their CogAT profiles.

OTIS–LENNON SCHOOL ABILITY TEST, EIGHTH EDITION The *Otis–Lennon School Ability Test, Eighth Edition* (OLSAT-8; Otis & Lennon, 2003) is a widely used group intelligence test sold only to accredited schools and school districts, often used for screening children for gifted and talented programs. First published in 1918, the OLSAT-8 yields an overall *school ability index* and consists of five subtests designed to measure abstract thinking and reasoning abilities of children. The subtests are Verbal Comprehension, Verbal Reasoning, Pictorial Reasoning, Figural Reasoning, and Quantitative Reasoning. The test has seven levels extending from grade K through grade 12.

RAVEN'S PROGRESSIVE MATRICES The *Raven's Progressive Matrices* (RPM; Raven, Raven, & Court, 2003) are multiple-choice tests that measure fluid intelligence, which is the ability to make sense out of complex data, to perceive new patterns and relationships, and to forge constructs (largely nonverbal). The tests consist of a series of visual matrices (i.e., a 2 × 2 or 3 × 3 grid), each of which has a piece missing. The examinee studies the pattern on the grid and selects the missing piece from a group of options. The RPM is available in three formats: the *Standard Progressive Matrices* (SPM), which is used with the general population; the *Colored Progressive Matrices* (CPM), which is designed for younger children, the elderly, and people with moderate or severe learning difficulties; and the *Advanced Progressive Matrices* (APM), appropriate for adults and adolescents of above-average intelligence. The tests are called *progressive* because each test consists of "sets" of items, and each item and each set are progressively more difficult.

Other commonly used group intelligence tests include the *California Test of Mental Maturity*, the *Kuhlmann–Anderson Intelligence Tests*, and the *Henmon–Nelson Tests of Mental Ability*.

Specialized Tests

So far, we've provided information about a number of well-known individual and group intelligence tests. For the most part, these tests can be used for multiple purposes for

TABLE 8.10 Specialized Intelligence Tests

Population	Test
Culturally and linguistically diverse populations	Comprehensive Test of Nonverbal Intelligence
	Culture Fair Intelligence Test
	Leiter International Performance Scale
	Naglieri Nonverbal Ability Test, Third Edition
	Test of Nonverbal Intelligence, Third Edition
	Universal Nonverbal Intelligence Test
Giftedness	Screening Assessment for Gifted Elementary and Middle School Students, Second Edition
	Structure of Intellect Learning Abilities Test, Gifted Screening Form
Learning disabilities, deafness or hearing impaired, speech problems, or other disabilities	Comprehensive Test of Nonverbal Intelligence
	Leiter International Performance Scale, Third Edition
	Naglieri Nonverbal Ability Test, Second Edition
	Test of Nonverbal Intelligence, Third Edition
	Universal Nonverbal Intelligence Test
Preschoolers	Bayley Scales of Infant Development, Third Edition
	Extended Merrill–Palmer Scale
	McCarthy Scales of Children's Abilities
	Mullen Scales of Early Learning

assessing diverse populations. However, some tests are more specialized, meaning they were developed specifically for use with certain populations, such as preschool children, individuals with learning disabilities or other disabilities, children with gifted abilities, or individuals from diverse cultural or linguistic backgrounds. Examples of intellectual ability tests designed for special populations include the Test of Nonverbal Intelligence (TONI-4), the Leiter Performance Scale, Third Edition (Leiter-3), and the Universal Nonverbal Intelligence Test (UNIT). A more complete (though not exhaustive) list is available in Table 8.10.

TEST OF NONVERBAL INTELLIGENCE, THIRD EDITION A well-known specialized test is the *Test of Nonverbal Intelligence, Third Edition* (TONI3). This 45-item instrument is a language-free measure of intelligence, aptitude, abstract reasoning, and problem solving in individuals aged 6 through 89 years. It is completely nonverbal, requiring no reading, writing, speaking, or listening on the part of the test taker. Examiners administer the test by pantomiming instructions, and the test takers indicate their response choices by pointing, nodding, or using a symbolic gesture. The test is well suited for use with individuals who have severe spoken language disorders (i.e., aphasia), individuals who are deaf or hearing impaired, non-English speakers or English-language learners, and individuals with cognitive, language, or motor impairments due to intellectual disabilities, deafness, developmental disabilities, autism, cerebral palsy, stroke, disease, head injury, or other neurological impairment. The TONI3 requires approximately 15 to 20 minutes to administer and score. The test provides raw scores, deviation IQ scores, percentile ranks, and age equivalent scores. It is sound psychometrically, with strong validity and reliability evidence, and was normed on a demographically representative and stratified sample of 3,451 people.

LEITER INTERNATIONAL PERFORMANCE SCALE, THIRD EDITION The Leiter International Performance Scale, Third Edition (Leiter-3) has four subtests to calculate nonverbal IQ, two subtests to calculate nonverbal memory, two subtests to calculate processing speed, and one nonverbal neuropsychological screener. The Leiter-3 was normed on a range of children who range from cognitive impairment to intellectual superiority. The normative sample also included children with hearing issues; deafness; cognitive impairment; developmental delays; autism; ESL; and speech and language deficits. The authors have included a complete profile of cognitive strengths and weaknesses. Scores are presented for each subtest and skill area. The Leiter was found to correlate with the WISC-IV ($r = .88$), the WJ-III ($r = .77 - .92$), and the SB-5 ($r = .85$). The Leiter-3 has been used to test a wide variety of individuals, including those with hearing and language disabilities, mental disabilities, cultural disadvantages, or non-English-speaking backgrounds. The Leiter-3 measures dimensions of perceptual and conceptual abilities. In the third edition of the Leiter, the number of subtests was reduced from 20 to 10 (i.e., Figure-Ground, Form Completion, Classification and Analogies, Sequential Order, Visual Patterns, Attention Sustained, Forward Memory, Attention Divided, Reverse Memory, and Nonverbal Stroop). The Leiter-3 is a valuable tool in the assessment of the cognitive abilities of children with hearing impairments, children with severe expressive or receptive language disabilities, and adults with severe or profound intellectual disability. The Leiter-3 is also considered an appropriate instrument for those who have motor and manipulative difficulties in addition to impaired communication skills.

UNIVERSAL NONVERBAL INTELLIGENCE TEST The Universal Nonverbal Intelligence Test (UNIT) is a language-free test that requires no receptive or expressive language from the examiner or examinee. The UNIT measures a number of types of intelligence and cognitive abilities. The test is made up of six subtests designed to measure the functioning of the client according to a two-tier model of intelligence: memory and reasoning. The memory subtests are Object Memory, Spatial Memory, and Symbolic Memory. The reasoning subtests are Analogic Reasoning, Cube Design, and Mazes. Although five of the subtests require motoric manipulation, they can be adapted for a pointing response. On the Spatial Memory subtest, the examinee must remember and recreate the placement of colored chips. On the Object Memory scale, the examinee is shown a visual array of common objects (such as a pan, computer, and rose) for 5 seconds and then has to identify the objects shown from a larger array of objects in pictures. The internal consistency coefficient for 5- to 7-year-olds ranged from .83 in analogic reasoning to .89 in design.

Interviews and Observations

Adequate assessment of intellectual ability requires more than test results. It will also include *interviews* with the test taker and relevant collateral sources, such as parents and teachers (if the test taker is a child). Through the interview, examiners can gather important background information about the examinee and establish the basis for a good working relationship.

Observations of examinees can provide counselors with information relevant to intelligence assessment. For example, an examiner can observe a test taker's appearance, emotional responses, social interactions, communication skills, and thought processes, which can give the examiner insight into the test taker's functioning. The following is an example of an observation from a report of an evaluation that included the use of the WISC-IV:

> James, a 12-year-old white male, was assessed using the WISC-IV. All testing was conducted using standard procedures. Due to good lighting, a comfortable room temperature and appropriate sized furniture, conditions for all testing sessions were considered to be adequate. The assessment process was performed in a private room with minimal distractions. James did not wear glasses or hearing aids during testing.
>
> Rapport was established with James through informal conversation and maintained adequately for all testing. James provided open and clear responses to all questions while maintaining adequate eye contact. When asked about his friends, James was eager to discuss his baseball team and his recent placement on the all-star team. Overall, James appeared to be a cooperative, happy, and developmentally appropriate child.
>
> With regard to testing, James indicated verbally that he understood the reasons for the assessment process and that he understood the directions. His behavior during testing (e.g., immediately beginning tasks when directed) also supported his understanding. Overall, the examiner believed that the results of all tests were a valid estimate of current functioning abilities in all areas assessed.

ISSUES IN ASSESSING INTELLIGENCE

Intelligence testing is still an issue of controversy. Many definitions of the construct of intelligence have led to the development of many different models, theories, and tests. There is no shared agreement as to what intelligence is and how it should be measured. Is it just one general (g) ability? Or many abilities? In addition, there is no consensus on the terminology to describe the construct: Is it ability, aptitude, cognitive abilities, intelligence, or potential?

The issue of heredity and intelligence has been debated for decades. The influence of heredity on IQ has been misinterpreted to imply that there is little point in trying to educate or be educated or that IQ is somehow impervious to change. This is a fallacy; many environmental factors—including family environment, parenting, socioeconomic status, nutrition, and schooling—influence the course of intellectual development (Toga & Thompson, 2005). The best estimate of the heritability of intelligence is .50, which suggests that genetic variation accounts for about 50% of the individual difference in intelligence test scores, with the other 50% attributable to environmental factors (Plomin, DeFries, Knopils, & Neiderhiser, 2012). From this information, it could be suggested that enriched environments would help everyone achieve their potential; however, the complex relationships among genes, the environment, and the brain make conclusions about the extent of specific influences on intelligence difficult to determine.

Much concern is still focused on the *biased* nature of intelligence tests. Many assessment instruments were originally developed by European and American psychologists who did not consider how cultural and ethnic factors affected their tests (Sattler, 2008), and sometimes their notions about intelligence are not shared by other cultures (Sternberg, 2003). For example, European Americans emphasize verbal ability, problem solving, and mental processing speed as important intellectual abilities, whereas other cultures or ethnic groups may emphasize social skills, cooperativeness, or obedience (see Sternberg, 2003 for review). Only in the latter half of the 20th century did test developers begin to consider cultural and ethnic factors and focus on constructing or revising tests to minimize cultural bias. For example, verbal intelligence tests, especially those dealing with vocabulary and general information, are highly *culturally loaded*, which means they have items specific to a particular culture. In contrast, nonverbal tests are *culturally reduced*, because they are less dependent on items with specific language symbols.

Another issue often debated involves the *stability* of intelligence over time. An intelligence test score is not viewed as a fixed attribute. IQs change over the course of development, especially from birth through 5 years of age (research has indicated that intelligence test scores are very unstable in early childhood and are poor predictors of later intelligence). Scores obtained on intelligence tests administered during school years show a more substantial relationship with scores obtained in adult years (Sattler, 2008). Later, scores may decline with age on some types of test items and increase on others.

A final issue is the Flynn Effect. The *Flynn Effect* refers to the general trend in increased IQs over time with each subsequent generation. This was first discovered by James Flynn (1998, 1999, 2000, 2009), who investigated IQ scores over the past 100 years. He found that on average IQ scores have continuously improved to a gain of about two standard deviations across the 20th century. Even if gains are now beginning to tail off, as Flynn believes, the change is massive. It translates into 30 IQ points, which, if taken literally, would mean that 50% of the population 100 years ago would have had intellectual capabilities consistent with intellectual disability as defined by current intelligence test score classifications. Many view this proposition as absurd, because there is "no evidence that people 100 years ago were less intelligent than people now" (Nettelbeck & Wilson, 2005, p. 614). It seems unlikely that there is a single factor that accounts for the increase; however, some suggested reasons for rising IQ include the following (Dickens & Flynn, 2001; Flynn, 2000, 2007):

- Widespread public education
- Reduced family size
- More leisure time
- More intellectually demanding work
- Greater use of technology
- Better prenatal care
- Improved nutrition
- Changes in child-rearing practices
- Increased familiarity with tests and testing

Summary

Early interest in measuring intelligence dates back to the late 19th century. Different scientists had differing ideas about the nature of intelligence and how to measure it, but all of these ideas contributed to our current understanding of the concept of intelligence. Numerous theories of intelligence have been presented over the decades, with varied perspectives about (a) the existence of a *g* factor, (b) broad and specific abilities that constitute intelligence, (c) intelligence as a hierarchy of abilities, (d) multiple intelligences, and (e) information processing.

Intelligence tests measure a broad spectrum of cognitive abilities, such as reasoning, comprehension, judgment, memory, and spatial ability. Tests can be used for screening, identification, and placement purposes, as well as a cognitive adjunct to in-depth psychological evaluation. The most prominent individual intelligence tests are the Wechsler scales and the Stanford–Binet, although numerous tests are available for multiple purposes for assessing diverse populations.

There are several controversial aspects of intelligence assessment. Scholars still discuss the existence of a *g* factor, debate the issue of heredity and intelligence, are concerned with test bias, and question the stability of intelligence over time. Despite these issues, the variety of published intelligence tests has proliferated in the last 100 years.

Questions for Discussion

1. Develop your own definition of intelligence. How does it compare to some of the existing definitions?
2. Compare the different theories of intelligence. Which theory do you find most acceptable, and why?
3. What are the advantages and disadvantages of group intelligence tests? Of individual tests? When would you use each?
4. Which environmental factors do you think influence an individual's performance on an intelligence test? Explain.

Suggested Activities

1. Critique an intelligence test discussed in this chapter.
2. Interview a psychologist or counselor who uses intelligence tests. Find out which tests he or she uses, and why. Report your results to the class.
3. Write a review of the literature or a position paper on one of the following topics: bias in intelligence testing, history of intelligence testing, or genetic studies of intelligence.
4. Take a group IQ test, score it, and write a report of the results.
5. Read *The Bell Curve: Intelligence and Class Structure in American Life* by Richard Herrnstein and Charles Murray (Free Press, 1994) and be prepared to discuss the book in class. The book is available for download at https://lesacreduprintemps19.files.wordpress.com/2012/11/the-bell-curve.pdf.
6. Review the WISC-IV scores presented in Table 8.8. How would you describe the test taker's overall level of intelligence? How would you describe any relative strengths the test taker might have? How would you describe any relative weaknesses?

References

Ackerman, P. L., & Beier, M. E. (2012). The problem is in the definition: G and intelligence in I-O psychology. *Industrial and Organizational Psychology: Perspectives on Science and Practice, 5*(2), 149–153.

Anastasi, A., & Urbina, S. (1997). *Psychological testing* (7th ed.). Upper Saddle River, NJ: Prentice Hall.

Becker, K. A. (2003). *History of the Stanford–Binet Intelligence Scales: Content and psychometrics*. Itasca, IL: Riverside Publishing.

Braden, J. P., & Athanasiou, M. S. (2005). A comparative review of nonverbal measures of intelligence. In D. P. Flanagan & P. L. Harrison (Eds.), *Contemporary intellectual assessment* (2nd ed., pp. 557–578). New York, NY: Guilford.

Camara, W. J., Nathan, J. S., & Puente, A. E. (2000). Psychological test usage: Implications in professional psychology. *Professional Psychology: Research and Practice, 31*, 141–154.

Carroll, J. B. (1993). *Human cognitive abilities: A survey of factor-analytical studies*. New York, NY: Cambridge University Press.

Carroll, J. B. (2012). The three-stratum theory of cognitive abilities. In D. P. Flanagan & P. L. Harrison (Eds.), *Contemporary intellectual assessment* (2nd ed., pp. 69–76). New York, NY: Guilford.

Cattell, R. B. (1941). Some theoretical issues in adult intelligence testing. *Psychological Bulletin, 38,* 592.

Cattell, R. B. (1950). *Personality*. New York, NY: McGraw-Hill.

Cattell, R. B. (1971). *Abilities: Their structure, growth, and action*. Boston, MA: Houghton-Mifflin.

Chamorro-Premuzic, T. (2011). *Personality and individual differences*. Malden, MA: Blackwell.

Das, J. P., Naglieri, J. A., & Kirby, R. J. (1994). *Assessment of cognitive processes*. New York, NY: Allyn & Bacon.

Dickens, W. T., & Flynn, J. R. (2001). Heritability estimates versus large environmental effects: The IQ paradox resolved. *Psychological Review, 108*, 346–369.

Elliott, C. (2007). *Differential ability scales: Administration and scoring manual* (2nd ed.). San Antonio, CA: PsychCorp.

Flanagan, D. P., & Harrison, P. L. (2012). *Contemporary intellectual assessment: Theories, tests, and issues* (3rd ed.). New York, NY: Guilford Press.

Flanagan, D. P., McGrew, K. S., & Ortiz, S. (2000). *The Wechsler Intelligence Scales and Gf-Gc Theory: A contemporary approach to interpretation*. Needham Heights, MA: Allyn & Bacon.

Floyd, R. G., Bergeron, R., Hamilton, G., & Parra, G. R. (2010). How do executive functions fit with the Cattell–Horn–Carroll model? Some evidence from a joint factor analysis of the Delis–Kaplan executive function system and the Woodcock–Johnson III Tests of Cognitive Abilities. *Psychology in the Schools, 47*(7), 721–738.

Flynn, J. R. (1998). IQ gains over time: Toward finding the causes. In U. Neisser (Ed.), *The rising curve: Long-term gains in IQ and related measures* (pp. 25–66). Washington, DC: American Psychological Association.

Flynn, J. R. (1999). Searching for justice: The discovery of IQ gains over time. *American Psychologist, 54*, 5–20.

Flynn, J. R. (2000). IQ gains, WISC subtests, and fluid g: G theory and the relevance of Spearman's hypothesis to race. In Novartis Foundation Symposium 233 (Ed.), *The nature of intelligence* (pp. 202–227). Chichester, UK: Wiley.

Flynn, J. R. (2009). *What is intelligence? Beyond the Flynn Effect*. Cambridge, UK: Cambridge University Press.

Gardner, H. (2011). The theory of multiple intelligences. In M. Gernsbacher, R. W. Pew, L. M. Hough, & J. R. Pomerantz (Eds.), *Psychology and the real world: Essays illustrating fundamental contributions to society* (pp. 122–130). New York, NY: Worth Publishers.

Gardner, H. (1993). *Multiple intelligences: The theory in practice*. New York, NY: Basic Books.

Gardner, H. (2006). *Changing minds: The art and science of changing our own and other people's minds*. Boston, MA: Harvard Business School Publishing.

Guilford, J. P. (1967). *The nature of human intelligence*. New York, NY: McGraw-Hill.

Horn, J. L., & Cattell, R. B. (1966a). Refinement and test of the theory of fluid and crystallized general intelligences. *Journal of Educational Psychology, 57*, 253–270.

Horn, J. L., & Cattell, R. B. (1966b). Age differences in primary mental ability factors. *Journal of Gerontology, 21*, 210–220.

Horn, J. L., & Cattell, R. B. (1967). Age differences in fluid and crystallized intelligence. *Acta Psychologica, 26*, 107–129.

Horn, J. L., & Noll, J. (1997). Human cognitive capabilities: Gf-Gc theory. In D. P. Flanagan, J. L. Genshaft, & P. L. Harrison (Eds.), *Contemporary intellectual assessment: Theories, tests, and issues* (pp. 53–91). New York, NY: Guilford.

Jensen, A. R. (1998). *The g factor: The science of mental ability*. Westport, CT: Praeger.

Kaufman, A. S. (2000). Tests of intelligence. In R. J. Sternberg (Ed.), *Handbook of intelligence* (pp. 445–476). New York, NY: Cambridge University Press.

Kaufman, A. S., & Kaufman, N. L. (1993). *Manual for Kaufman Adolescent and Adult Intelligence Test (KAIT)*. Circle Pines, MN: American Guidance Service.

Kaufman, A. S., & Kaufman, N. L. (2004a). *Kaufman Assessment Battery for Children, second edition manual (KABC-II)*. Circle Pines, MN: American Guidance Service.

Kaufman, A. S., & Kaufman, N. L. (2004b). *Kaufman Brief Intelligence Test, second edition manual (KBIT-2)*. Circle Pines, MN: American Guidance Service.

Kaufman, A. S., Lichtenberger, E. O., Fletcher-Janzen, E., & Kaufman, N. L. (2005). *Essentials of KABC-II assessment*. Hoboken, NJ: John Wiley & Sons.

Lichtenberger, E. O., & Kaufman, A. S. (2012). *Essentials of WAIS-IV assessment*. Hoboken, NJ: Wiley.

Lohman, D. F., & Hagen, E. (2001). *Cognitive Abilities Test (Form 6)*. Itasca, IL: Riverside Publishing.

Luria, A. R. (1980). *Higher cortical functions in man*. New York, NY: Basic Books.

Luria, A. R. (1970). The functional organization of the brain. *Scientific American, 222*, 66–78.

Luria, A. R. (1966). *Higher cortical functions in man*. New York: Basic Books.

Mayer, R. E. (2000). Intelligence and education. In R. J. Sternberg (Ed.), *Handbook of intelligence* (pp. 519–533). Cambridge, UK: Cambridge University Press.

McGrew, K. S. (2005). The Cattell–Horn–Carroll theory of cognitive abilities: Past, present, and future. In D. P. Flanagan & P. L. Harrison (Eds.), *Contemporary intellectual assessment* (2nd ed., pp. 136–181). New York, NY: Guilford.

McGrew, K. S., & Woodcock, R. W. (2001). *Technical manual: Woodcock–Johnson III*. Itasca, IL: Riverside Publishing.

Muchinsky, P. M. (2008). *Psychology applied to work: An introduction to industrial and organizational psychology*. (9th ed.). Belmont, CA: Wadsworth.

Naglieri, J. A. (2005). The Cognitive Assessment System. In D. P. Flanagan & P. L. Harrison (Eds.), *Contemporary intellectual assessment* (2nd ed., pp. 441–460). New York, NY: Guilford.

Naglieri, J. A., & Das, J. P. (1997). The PASS cognitive processing theory. In R.F. Dillon (Ed.), *Handbook on testing* (pp.138–163). London, UK: Greenwood Press.

Neisser, U., Boodoo, G., Bouchard, T. J., Jr., Boykin, A. W., Brody, N., Ceci, S. J. . . . Urbina, S. (1996). Intelligence: Knowns and unknowns. *American Psychologist, 51*(2), 77–101.

Nettelbeck, T., & Wilson, C. (2005). Intelligence and IQ: What teachers should know. *Educational Psychology, 25*, 609–630.

Otis, A., & Lennon, R. (2003). *Otis–Lennon School Ability Test (OLSAT8)* (8th ed.). Marrickville, Australia: Harcourt Assessment.

Pearson Assessment. (2004). *WISC-IV integrated perceptual domain case study*. San Antonio, TX: Author.

Piaget, J. (1970). *The science of education and the psychology of the child*. New York, NY: Orion.

Plomin, R., DeFries, J. C., Knopils, V. S., & Neiderhiser, J. M. (2012). *Behavioral genetics* (6th ed.). New York, NY: Worth.

Plucker, J. A. (Ed.). (2003). *Human intelligence: Historical influences, current controversies, teaching resources*. Retrieved from http://www.intelltheory.com

Plucker, J. A., & Esping, A. (2014). *Intelligence 101*. New York, NY: Springer Publishing Co.

Raiford, S. E., & Coalson, D. L. (2014). *Essentials of WPPSI-IV assessment*. Hoboken, NJ: Wiley.

Raven, J., Raven, J. C., & Court, J. H. (2003). *Manual for the Raven's Progressive Matrices and Vocabulary Scales. Section 1: General overview*. Oxford, UK: Oxford Psychologists Press.

Roid, G. H. (2003). *Stanford–Binet Intelligence Scales, interpretive manual: Expanded guide to the interpretation of SB5 test results* (5th ed.). Itasca, IL: Riverside Publishing.

Sattler, J. M. (2008). *Assessment of children: Cognitive foundations* (5th ed.). San Diego, CA: Jerome M. Sattler Publisher, Inc.

Sattler, J. M., & Dumont, R. (2004). *Assessment of children: WISC-IV and WPPSI-III supplement*. San Diego, CA: Jerome M. Sattler Publisher, Inc.

Schrank, F. A., Flanagan, D. P., Woodcock, R. W., & Mascolo, J. T. (2010). *Essentials of the WJ III cognitive abilities assessment*. Hoboken, NJ: Wiley.

Sternberg, R. J. (1985). *Beyond IQ: A triarchic theory of human intelligence*. New York, NY: Cambridge University Press.

Sternberg, R. J. (1988). *The triarchic mind: A new theory of human intelligence.* New York, NY: Viking.

Sternberg, R. J. (1997). *Successful intelligence.* New York, NY: Plume.

Sternberg, R. J. (1999). The theory of successful intelligence. *Review of General Psychology, 3,* 292–316.

Sternberg, R. J. (2003). *Wisdom, intelligence, and creativity synthesized.* Cambridge, UK: Cambridge University Press.

Sternberg, R. J., & Berg, C. A. (1986). Definitions of intelligence: A quantitative comparison of the 1921 and 1986 symposia. In R. J. Sternberg & D. K. Detterman (Eds.), *What is intelligence? Contemporary viewpoints on its nature and definition* (pp. 155–162). Norwood, NJ: Ablex.

Terman, L. M., & Oden, M. H. (1959). *Genetic studies of genius: The gifted group at mid-life: Thirty-five years of follow-up of the superior child* (Vol. 5). Stanford, CA: Stanford University Press.

Terman, L. M. (1916). *The Measurement of Intelligence.* Boston: Houghton Mifflin.

The Psychological Corporation. (1997). *WAIS-III—WMS-III technical manual.* San Antonio, TX: Author.

The Psychological Corporation. (2002). *WPPSI-III technical and interpretive manual.* San Antonio, TX: Author.

The Psychological Corporation. (2003). *WISC-IV administration and scoring manual.* San Antonio, TX: Author.

Thurstone, L. L. (1938). *Primary mental abilities.* Chicago, IL: University of Chicago Press.

Toga, A. W., & Thompson, P. M. (2005). Genetics of brain structure and intelligence. *Annual Review of Neuroscience, 28,* 1–23.

Vernon, P. E. (1950). *The structure of human abilities.* London, UK: Methuen.

Wasserman, J. D. (2003). Assessment of intellectual functioning. In J. R. Graham, J. A. Naglieri, & I. B. Weiner (Eds.), *Handbook of psychology: Assessment psychology* (Vol. 10, pp. 417–442). Hoboken, NJ: John Wiley & Sons.

Wasserman, J. D., & Tulsky, D. S. (2012). A history of intelligence assessment. In D. P. Flanagan & P. L. Harrison (Eds.), *Contemporary intellectual assessment* (2nd ed., pp. 3–22). New York, NY: Guilford.

Wechsler, D. (1997). *Wechsler Adult Intelligence Scale: Technical manual* (3rd ed.). San Antonio, TX: The Psychological Corporation.

Wechsler, D. (2002). *Manual for the Wechsler Preschool and Primary Scale of Intelligence* (3rd ed.). San Antonio, TX: Psychological Corporation.

Wechsler, D. (2003). *Wechsler Intelligence Scale for Children* (4th ed.). San Antonio, TX: Harcourt Assessment.

Whiston, S. C. (2012). *Principles and applications of assessment in counseling* (2nd ed.). Belmont, CA: Brooks/Cole.

Woodcock, R. W., McGrew, K. S., & Mather, N. (2007). *Woodcock–Johnson III.* Itasca, IL: Riverside Publishing.

Assessment of Achievement

Assessment of achievement involves the use of instruments and procedures to measure an individual's current knowledge and skills. Achievement by nature is retrospective, meaning that one's current level of knowledge is based on prior educational experiences. As such, achievement tests are usually constructed to reflect national, state, or local educational standards and curriculum.

Achievement tests are widely used in education, but they are also used in business, industry, and the military. The number of achievement tests administered each year exceeds that of all other types of psychological and educational instruments. In U.S. schools, achievement tests are used for a number of purposes, such as monitoring students' achievement over time, making placement or selection decisions, evaluating instructional objectives and programs, and assisting with diagnosing learning disabilities. Professional counselors use achievement testing and/or the results of achievement testing for a variety of purposes, including individualized educational planning, consultation with school systems, determination of accommodations in college settings, and awarding professional credentials, such as certification or licensure.

After studying this chapter, you should be able to:
- Define *achievement*.
- Describe the main characteristics of achievement tests.
- Describe the primary uses of standardized achievement tests in schools.
- Describe the characteristics of achievement test batteries, diagnostic achievement tests, individual achievement tests, and subject-area tests and explain their strengths and weaknesses.
- Describe the other types of achievement assessment (i.e., criterion-referenced tests, minimum-level skills tests, state achievement tests, the National Assessment of Educational Progress, curriculum-based assessment or measurement, performance assessment, portfolio assessment).

ASSESSING ACHIEVEMENT

Achievement can be defined as an individual's knowledge or skills in a particular content area in which he or she has received instruction (American Educational Research Association (AERA), American Psychological Association (APA), & National Council on

Measurement in Education (NCME), 2014). A diverse array of tests and procedures can be used to assess achievement, including achievement test batteries, individual and diagnostic tests, subject-area tests, curriculum-based assessment and measurement, statewide assessment programs, observations, and more. Instruments that assess achievement are comprised of items that require test takers to demonstrate some level of knowledge or skill. The results of achievement testing inform individuals and relevant parties (i.e., parents, teachers, school administrators, and other helping professionals) about an individual's academic strengths and weaknesses or any learning difficulties. In addition, achievement tests may be used to monitor individual achievement and to evaluate the effectiveness of educational and social programs. In schools, they provide teachers and administrators with information for planning or modifying the curriculum to better serve a particular student or group of students.

Scores on achievement tests are often related to scores on other ability measures, such as intelligence tests and aptitude tests. As stated in Chapter 8, all three (achievement, intelligence, and aptitude tests) may have some overlap in content, but they are distinct in terms of their focus. *Achievement tests* focus more on the present—that is, what an individual knows or can do right now. However, achievement tests are also considered an excellent predictor of academic performance and are frequently used to predict future performance in educational programs (e.g., college) or vocational programs.

It is highly unlikely that an individual can graduate high school without participating in some form of achievement testing. In the schools, many informal *teacher-made tests* constructed to reflect the learning objectives specific to a particular teacher, course, or unit of instruction are considered informal achievement tests. In contrast, *standardized achievement tests* are commercially developed tests designed to reflect learning outcomes and content common to the majority of U.S. schools. Each year, schools throughout the world administer standardized achievement tests to large groups of students to determine student performance levels and overall school performance. Some standardized tests (particularly diagnostic tests and individual achievement tests) are designed specifically to identify students' strengths and weaknesses or the presence of a learning problem. Teacher-made tests differ from standardized tests in terms of the quality of test items, the reliability of test scores, administration and scoring procedures, and interpretation of test scores (Miller, Linn, & Gronlund, 2012). Because of their differences, teacher-made tests and standardized tests are complementary rather than opposing methods of evaluating achievement, and both types can be employed to assess student achievement (Aiken & Groth-Marnat, 2006). In fact, Phelps (2012) examined studies from 1910 to 2010 and discovered that testing with feedback had a significant impact on overall achievement.

In this chapter, we will continue our discussion of achievement testing, focusing primarily on standardized achievement tests. Although achievement testing is performed in various settings (e.g., schools, business, industry, military), much of our discussion will center on standardized achievement testing in the schools.

STANDARDIZED ACHIEVEMENT TESTS

Standardized achievement tests are commercially developed instruments that are sold to public schools or to other institutions, agencies, or qualified professionals. They are developed to cover broad content areas common to most U.S. schools. In education, standardized achievement tests are used for the following purposes:

- Establishing a student's present achievement level
- Monitoring student achievement over time
- Identifying a student's academic strengths and weaknesses
- Screening students for placement or selection decisions
- Evaluating instructional objectives and programs
- Assisting with diagnosis of learning disabilities
- Evaluating individuals for certification and licensure

Standardized achievement tests as a whole have several universal features, such as uniform administration and scoring procedures, sound psychometric qualities, and nationally representative norm groups. Most use standard scores, but some may also provide percentiles, age or grade equivalent scores, normal curve equivalents (NCEs), and performance categories. Standardized tests may be norm referenced, criterion referenced, or both. With *norm-referenced score interpretation*, an individual's test score is compared to the scores of the normative sample, which enables test users to estimate an individual's position relative to other test takers. With *criterion-referenced interpretation*, an individual's test score is measured against a specific level of achievement. This usually involves a *cutoff score* that the individual must achieve in order to demonstrate mastery of the content area.

Standardized achievement tests vary somewhat from each other in terms of administration procedures, content coverage, and use of test results. For example, although most achievement tests are group administered, some are designed to be individually administered. Some may consist of a battery of tests covering a broad range of academic skills and content areas, whereas others focus on a single subject area. Some provide a measure of general learning outcomes, while others provide diagnostic information. Understanding the various categories used to differentiate standardized achievement tests can be challenging, because professionals may use different terminology to describe tests, and tests often fall into more than one category. We will present information about standardized achievement tests using the following categories:

- Achievement test batteries
- Diagnostic achievement tests
- Individual achievement tests
- Subject-area tests

To help elucidate the differences among the categories of achievement tests, Table 9.1 provides a chart of the characteristics of the four categories of achievement tests. It is important to note that some achievement tests fall into more than one category.

Achievement Test Batteries

The most popular standardized achievement tests are those that measure multiple achievements, called *achievement test batteries* (also called *survey achievement batteries*). These are comprehensive tests that provide a general, overall measure of learning in several broad areas of the academic curriculum. They are comprised of a series of tests that assess major content areas, such as reading, language, mathematics, and, at the appropriate grade level, study skills, social studies, and science. Within the major content areas are various subtests. Because achievement test batteries assess knowledge in broad content areas, each subtest in a battery contains a fairly limited number of items, which restricts their value for identifying students with serious learning problems. Thus, the primary

TABLE 9.1 Characteristics of Standardized Achievements Tests

	Assess Current Achievement Level	Individually Administered	Group Administered	Track Achievement
Achievement test batteries	X		X	X
Diagnostic achievement tests	X	X	X	
Individual achievement tests	X	X		X
Subject-area tests	X		X	

purpose for administering an achievement test battery is to determine an individual's general standing in various subjects. For example, using an achievement battery, it is possible to determine that a student has strengths in language skills and reading skills but is weak in mathematics skills.

Most achievement test batteries are *group administered* and can be administered to more than one examinee at a time. They can be used with large numbers of individuals, enabling them to be administered to thousands of students throughout the nation each year. Group tests usually contain items that can be scored objectively, usually by a computer, which reduces or eliminates scoring errors commonly found in individually administered tests. The main advantage of group tests is their cost-effectiveness: (a) they are usually less expensive than individually administered achievement tests, (b) they minimize the time needed for administration and scoring, and (c) they require less examiner skill and training.

Table 9.2 provides a list of widely used achievement batteries. Descriptions of these tests can be found in the various editions of the *Mental Measurements Yearbook*, *Tests in Print*, *Tests*, and *Test Critiques* and from the tests' publishers. To provide an example of an achievement test battery, information about the Stanford Achievement Test, 10th Edition will be presented in the next section.

STANFORD ACHIEVEMENT TEST, 10TH EDITION The Stanford Achievement Test Series (Stanford 10) is one of the leading test batteries utilized by school districts in the United States. The original Stanford Achievement Test was first published over 80 years ago. The Stanford 10 test series, sold only to school districts, is a norm-referenced, standardized battery of tests designed to measure school achievement from kindergarten through

TABLE 9.2 Achievement Test Batteries

Basic Achievement Skills Inventory—Comprehensive Version (BASI)

TerraNova, Third Edition

TerraNova Comprehensive Test of Basic Skills (CTBS)

Iowa Tests of Basic Skills (ITBS)

Metropolitan Achievement Test, 8th Edition (MAT 8)

Stanford Achievement Test, 10th Edition (Stanford 10)

Identify Strengths and Weaknesses	Evaluate Instructional Objectives and Programs	Screen for Placement/ Selection Decisions	Assist with Diagnosis of Learning Disabilities	Certification and Licensure
	X	X		
X		X	X	
X		X	X	
		X		X

grade 12. These 13 test levels are divided into three groups: the *Stanford Early School Achievement Test* (SESAT) for students in kindergarten and the first half of first grade, the *Stanford Achievement Test* for students in the second half of first grade through ninth grade, and the *Stanford Test of Academic Skills* (TASK) for grades 9 through 12 and for beginning college students. The Stanford 10 consists of several composites and subtests assessing major academic content areas. The content areas vary somewhat depending on the level (K–12) and the group (SESAT, Stanford Achievement Test, Stanford Test of Academic Skills). The following are some content areas assessed in the series:

- *Total Reading* Measures reading skills, such as word sounds and spellings, determining word meanings and synonyms, and reading comprehension. This section includes subtests in Reading Vocabulary and Reading Comprehension and Word Study Skills.
- *Total Mathematics* Measures problem-solving skills involving number sense, arithmetic operations, patterns and algebra, data and probability, geometry, and measurement concepts. Two subtests comprise Total Mathematics: Mathematics Problem Solving and Mathematics Procedures.
- *Science* Measures students' understanding of life science, Earth science, physical science, and the nature of science.
- *Language* Measures students' application of language principles in writing, including capitalization, punctuation, word usage, sentence structure, organization, and composing and editing.
- *Spelling* Measures students' ability to recognize the correct spelling of words.
- *Social Science* Measures achievement in history, geography, political science, and economics.
- *Listening* Measures recognition of spoken words and the ability to construct meaning from dictated material.

The Stanford 10 can be administered as either the full-length battery or the abbreviated battery. It offers a variety of item formats, including multiple-choice, short-answer, and extended-response questions. Besides requiring a written answer of five or six sentences, the extended response may also require the student to graph, illustrate, or show work. An interesting feature of the Stanford 10 is the arrangement of test items. Rather than the typical "easy to hard" arrangement found in most achievement tests, the Stanford 10 mixes easy items with difficult items. The rationale is that in the traditional arrangement,

Stanford 10
INDIVIDUAL STUDENT RESULTS

Jennifer R Dillard
Grade 01, Primary 1, Form D

Teacher: Poche
School: Newtown Elementary - 00010001
District: Newtown

Grade: 01
Test Date: 04/03

Age: 07 Yrs 02 Mos
Student No.: 8

Test Name	Number Possible	Number Correct	Scaled Score	National NCE	National PR	Grade Equivalent	AAC Range	National Grade Percentile Bands 1 10 30 50 70 90 99
Total Reading	130	82	589	64.9	76	2.6	MIDDLE	
Word Study Skills	30	17	610	65.6	77	3.1	HIGH	
Word Reading	30	20	592	69.3	82	3	HIGH	
Sentence Reading	30	18	566	48.4	47	1.7	MIDDLE	
Reading Comp	40	27	588	64.2	76	2.6	MIDDLE	
Total Math	72	31	523	45.2	41	1.6	MIDDLE	
Math Prob Solv	42	22	546	51.6	53	1.9	MIDDLE	
Math Procedures	30	9	491	39	30	1.5	MIDDLE	
Language	40	22	579	59.8	68	2.5	MIDDLE	
Spelling	36	30	622	84.6	95	4.8	HIGH	
Environment	40	26	607	68.5	81	2.8	HIGH	
Partial Battery	0	165	0	60.3	69	2.6	MIDDLE	
Total Battery	0	191	0	61.2	70	2.6	MIDDLE	

Back

FIGURE 9.1   Stanford 10 sample report.

students tend to get frustrated as they encounter consistently harder items and "give up," but with the "easy-hard-easy" format, difficult questions are surrounded by easy questions to encourage students to complete the test. The test is also purported to be the only achievement test battery to provide realistic, full-color illustrations, which is thought to improve student motivation.

The Stanford 10 provides several types of scores, including scaled scores, percentile ranks, stanines, grade equivalents, and NCEs (see Figure 9.1). Stanines of 1, 2, and 3 are considered *below average*; 4, 5, and 6 are *average*; and 7, 8, and 9 are *above average*. Because the Otis–Lennon Scholastic Ability Test (OLSAT 8) is often administered in conjunction with the Stanford 10, the Stanford 10 score summary provides an Achievement/Ability Comparison (AAC) Range, which describes a student's scores on the Stanford 10 in relation to the scores of other students of similar ability as measured by the OLSAT 8. Compared to other students, a student's AAC score is considered *high* if it falls in the top 23%, *middle* if in the middle 54%, and *low* if in the bottom 23%. Scores categorized as *middle* indicate that the student's ability (i.e., intelligence) and achievement are about the same; the student is working up to his or her level of ability. *High* range scores indicate that the student's achievement is actually above what would be expected. *Low* scores indicate that the student's achievement is not as high as may be expected.

The psychometric properties of the Stanford 10 are generally strong, with internal consistency reliability coefficients ranging from the mid-.80s to .90s and alternate forms coefficients in the .80s. Evidence of content validity was based on a well-defined test blue-print and a test-development process that involved extensive review of several national and state educational standards. For example, the mathematics subtests were developed with careful consideration of the National Council of Teachers of Mathematics (NCTM) publication *Principles and Standards for School Mathematics* (2000), which emphasizes the necessity of problem solving as the focus of school mathematics. Even with the strong content validity, test users are recommended to review the test to determine if the test content matches the curriculum and goals of the particular school. Evidence of convergent validity is provided through numerous correlations between the various subtests and totals of the Stanford 10 with the Stanford 9 subtests. Construct validity evidence is shown through strong correlations between the Stanford 10 and the OLSAT. In order to increase your understanding of the Stanford 10 and the principles of achievement testing, complete Exercise 9.1.

Exercise 9.1
Achievement Testing: Marcus

Marcus, age 9 years 8 months, is in the fourth grade and is having some academic difficulties in school. He was administered the Stanford 10 (see summary report below). After reviewing Marcus's summary report, answer the exercise questions.

Stanford 10 Student Summary Report

Subtests and Total	Number Possible	Number Correct	Scaled Score	National PR-S*	National NCE	Grade Equivalent	AAC Range	National Grade Percentile Bands
								1 10 30 50 70 90 99
Total Reading	114	82	639	59-5	54.8	5.4	Middle	
Total Mathematics	80	29	629	22-3	33.7	3.3	Low	
Language	48	28	610	39-4	44.1	3.5	Middle	
Spelling	40	30	647	73-6	62.9	6.4	High	
Science	40	12	619	18-3	30.7	2.8	Low	
Social Science	40	22	607	40-5	44.7	3.5	Middle	
Listening	40	22	608	35-4	41.9	3.4	Middle	
Complete Battery	402	270	NA	56-5	53.4	5.0	Middle	

*PR-S: Percentile Rank and Stanine

Exercise Questions

1. Interpret the percentile ranks (PR) for each of the subtests and total score.
2. Interpret the stanine scores (S) for each subtest and total score.
3. Across subtest and total scores, identify Marcus's relative strengths and weaknesses based on his stanine scores.
4. The percentile bands provide a graphic display of measurement error. The wider the bands, the more error on the subtests.
   a. Which subtest score(s) appear to have the greatest error?
   b. Which subtest score(s) appear to have the least error?
5. Marcus's grade equivalent score on spelling is 6.4. Based on this score, Marcus's parents believe he is ready for instruction in spelling at the sixth-grade level. Do you agree with this? Why or why not?

Individual Achievement Tests

Because most achievement tests are group administered, tests that are individually administered are regarded as a separate category of tests called *individual achievement tests*. Similar to
achievement test batteries, individual achievement tests cover several broad academic areas,
such as reading, mathematics, and written language; no one content area is assessed in
depth. The broad content coverage is useful for identifying general weak subject areas of
relative weakness for individuals; once a weakness is identified, a diagnostic test (discussed
in the next section) may be used to identify or diagnose the specific skill deficit or learning
problem. Individual achievement tests are typically designed for a wide age span (often
preschool through high school) and cover a broad range of skill levels. Individual achievement tests may be used in conjunction with intelligence tests to diagnose learning disabilities. As such, some individual tests are concurrently normed with intelligence tests; for
example, the Wechsler Individual Achievement Test (WIAT-III) and the Wechsler Intelligence Scale for Children (WISC-IV) were co-normed on the same national sample so that
intelligence and achievement test scores can be compared. Because the tests are administered
individually, they contain a wider variety of item formats than group tests (which contain
primarily multiple-choice items); for example, an individual achievement test may contain
items requiring oral responses or fairly lengthy essays from the test taker. The advantage of
individual administration is that examiners are able to meet and establish rapport with
examinees and observe them more closely, which may enable examiners to gain more insight
into the source of learning problems (Reynolds, Livingston, & Willson, 2008). Although
many individual achievement tests exist, we present an overview of the Wide Range Achievement Test, Fourth Edition and the Woodcock–Johnson III Tests of Achievement.

WIDE RANGE ACHIEVEMENT TEST, FOURTH EDITION A widely used individual achievement
test is the *Wide Range Achievement Test, Fourth Edition* (WRAT4). The WRAT4 is a test of basic
academic skills for individuals aged 5 years to 74 years, 11 months. It takes approximately
30 minutes to complete and is often administered as a screening test to determine if a more
comprehensive achievement test is needed. As with most individual achievement tests, the
results of the WRAT4 by themselves are not intended to provide formal identification of
learning or cognitive disorders. The WRAT4 includes four subtests and one composite:

1. *Word Reading* Measures letter and word decoding through letter identification and
   word recognition.
2. *Sentence Comprehension* Measures an individual's ability to gain meaning from
   words and to comprehend ideas and information contained in sentences through the
   use of a modified cloze technique.
3. *Spelling* Measures an individual's ability to encode sounds into written form through
   the use of a dictated spelling format containing both letters and words.
4. *Math Computation* Measures an individual's ability to perform basic mathematics
   computations through counting, identifying numbers, solving simple oral problems,
   and calculating written mathematics problems.
5. *Reading Composite* A composite raw score calculated from the Word Reading and
   Sentence Comprehension subtests.

The WRAT4 has two alternate forms (Blue and Green) that can be used interchangeably as pretest and posttest measures or can be combined for a more comprehensive

evaluation. Standard scores, percentile ranks, stanines, NCEs, and grade equivalents are provided. The WRAT4 was standardized on a representative national sample of over 3,000 individuals selected according to a stratified national sample based on age, gender, ethnicity, geographic region, and parental education. In order to help further your understanding of the WRAT4, complete Exercise 9.2. Review the case study of Maria, her grades, and her WRAT4 scores. After considering all of the information, respond to the exercise questions.

WOODCOCK–JOHNSON III TESTS OF ACHIEVEMENT The *Woodcock–Johnson III Tests of Achievement* (WJ III ACH; Woodcock, McGrew, & Mather, 2001, 2007) were designed to measure achievement in individuals aged 2 to 95-plus years. The WJ III ACH was developed as a companion instrument to the *Woodcock–Johnson III Tests of Cognitive Abilities* (WJ III COG), and together these instruments provide a comprehensive assessment for measuring intellectual abilities and academic achievement. The WJ III ACH has a total of 22 different tests. The Standard Battery is comprised of 12 tests, and the Extended Battery includes an additional 10 tests. We will describe the Standard Battery tests, which are organized into four cluster areas:

Reading Tests

- *Letter-Word Identification* Identify and pronounce letters, and read words from a list.
- *Reading Fluency* Rapidly read and comprehend simple sentences.
- *Passage Comprehension* Read a short passage and supply a key missing word (e.g., "The boy ____ off his bike").

Oral Language Tests

- *Story Recall* Listen to a story passage and then orally recall story elements.
- *Understanding Directions* Follow oral directions to point to different parts of pictures.

Written Language Tests

- *Spelling* Write spellings of words presented orally.
- *Writing Fluency* Quickly formulate and write simple sentences when given three words and a picture.
- *Writing Samples* Write sentences according to directions.

Mathematics Tests

- *Calculation* Perform mathematical computations, from simple addition to complex equations.
- *Math Fluency* Calculated speed of performing simple calculations for 3 minutes.
- *Applied Problems* Oral, math "word problems," solved with paper and pencil.

The WJ III ACH provides a variety of scores, including age and grade equivalents, raw score or number correct, percentile ranks, and standard scores (mean = 100; SD = 15). It also provides verbal labels for standard score ranges: standard scores of 151 and above are *exceptionally superior*, 131 to 150 are *very superior*, 121 to 130 are *superior*, 111 to 120 are *high average*, 90 to 110 are *average*, 80 to 89 are *low average*, 70 to 79 are *low*, 50 to 69 and below are *very low*, and 49 and below are *exceptionally low*.

Exercise 9.2
Wide Range Achievement Test: Maria

Maria is a 10th-grade student who was referred to the school counselor because of her unacceptable behavior in the classroom and her poor peer relationships.

School personnel are concerned about Maria's inability to function well in a school setting. Although she exhibits problematic behavior, it is not severe enough for suspension. Maria has an excellent vocabulary and a good sense of humor. However, she does not know how to respond to teasing or correction and seems to enjoy telling stories about how she gets back at people who offend her. In the classroom, Maria is frequently off task, asks inappropriate questions, comes unprepared, wanders about the classroom, and seeks to make herself the center of attention. Outside of the classroom, she keeps to herself, but she stands out in the crowd. Her mannerisms and dress set her apart. She appears to be preoccupied and also seems to fear her parents, not wanting them to know what happens in school.

To obtain more information about Maria, the school counselor looked at her current grades as well as her scores on the WRAT4.

Current Grades (10th Grade)

English II	C
Geometry	C
Biology	D
World History	C
Physical Education	B
Spanish I	C

Wide Range Achievement Test Scores

Subtest	Standard Score	Confidence Interval 95%	Percentile Rank	Stanine
Word Reading	127	116–138	95	8
Sentence Comprehension	125	115–135	94	8
Spelling	139	127–151	99	9
Math Computation	124	111–137	93	8

Exercise Questions

1. Describe and interpret each of Maria's subtest standard scores, percentile ranks, and stanine scores.
2. What does the confidence interval for the Word Reading subtest score mean?
3. Overall, what does Maria's WRAT4 results tell you about her academic ability?
4. Are Maria's WRAT4 subtest scores consistent with her grades? Explain.
5. What additional information would you like to have about Maria?

ADDITIONAL INDIVIDUAL ACHIEVEMENT TESTS The *Basic Achievement Skills Individual Screener* (BASIS) is designed for students from grades 1 through 9. It includes three subtests—reading, spelling, and mathematics—and an optional writing exercise. Both criterion referenced and norm referenced, the test provides beginning-of-the-grade and end-of-the-grade norms as well as age and adult norms. It takes about 1 hour to administer and is designed to help examiners formulate individual educational plans for exceptional and special populations.

The *Peabody Individual Achievement Test-Revised/Normative Update* (PIAT-R/NU) was designed for individuals aged 5 to adulthood. The PIAT-R/NU takes about 60 minutes to administer and assesses achievement in six content areas: General Information, Reading Recognition, Reading Comprehension, Mathematics, Spelling, and Written Expression. The test yields age and grade equivalents, percentile ranks, NCEs, and stanines.

The *Wechsler Individual Achievement Test, Second Edition* was developed for use in conjunction with the Wechsler Intelligence Scale for Children-IV (WISC-IV). The WIAT-II has four composites, each comprised of specific subtests: (1) Reading (Word Reading, Reading Comprehension, and Pseudoword Decoding subtests), (2) Mathematics (Numerical Operations and Math Reasoning subtests), (3) Written Language (Spelling and Written Expression subtests), and (4) Oral Language (Listening Comprehension and Oral Expression subtests). The test can be given to individuals aged 4 through 85. It yields standard scores, percentile ranks, stanines, NCEs, and age and grade equivalents. In order to further your understanding of achievement assessment, complete Exercise 9.3. This exercise provides an opportunity to examine the relationship among intelligence, achievement, and academic functioning. After reading the case material and considering it in the context of what you have learned thus far, complete the exercise questions.

Diagnostic Tests

The primary purpose for using *diagnostic tests* is to identify an individual's academic strengths or weaknesses and then to design an educational program or intervention to meet this person's needs. As compared to achievement batteries and individual achievement tests, diagnostic tests usually have a narrower focus (on one skill or knowledge area), contain a larger number and variety of test items, and usually take longer to administer. The majority of diagnostic tests are in reading, but tests in math and language are widely used as well.

Diagnostic tests are also used for identifying and diagnosing learning disabilities. *Learning disability* is defined by the Individuals with Disabilities Education Improvement Act of 2004 (IDEA) as "a disorder in one or more of the basic psychological processes involved in understanding or in using language, spoken or written, which disorder may manifest itself in the imperfect ability to listen, think, speak, read, write, spell, or do mathematical calculations" (US Department of Education, 2004, para. c.10). In education, diagnosing learning disabilities in students who show signs of difficulties involves a process of monitoring their progress through a series of increasingly intensive, individualized instructional or behavioral interventions. In addition, assessment instruments (such as diagnostic achievement tests) are administered as part of the evaluation process. IDEA mandates that achievement tests must measure eight areas of achievement (e.g., oral language, basic language, total reading, reading comprehension and fluency, written expression, mathematics, math fluency, total achievement).

Exercise 9.3
Achievement and Intelligence Assessment: Danny

Danny, age 9, is a third grader at Highland Elementary School. He has been referred to the school counselor due to concerns expressed by his teacher about academic and behavioral issues.

Background Information

Danny's parents are divorced, and he currently lives with his grandparents. Danny's father graduated from high school and works as a heating and air-conditioning technician; his mother earned her GED after dropping out of high school and works as a waitress. Danny has lived with his grandparents since he was age 4. Last year, the Department of Social Services investigated his living situation with his grandparents due to allegations of neglect. His grandparents lack interest in how he is doing at school. Over the last couple of years, his grandparents have moved three times; as a result, Danny has changed schools three times.

Danny currently belongs to no organizations or clubs, and he does not have any close friends. He frequently starts arguments in class and on the playground. He is very outspoken. In terms of academics, Danny is not meeting basic educational standards. He fails to do his homework most of the time. He was retained in third grade.

Danny has interest in making things; this is evident in his art class. He has special skills in making things with his hands. He enjoys reading, but he reportedly watches TV for several hours every day. Danny's teacher commented on his family environment and said that his frequent moves have deprived Danny of companions. The teacher also commented on Danny's constant battle with fellow classmates in class and that he doesn't seem to have any friends. The teachers believe that Danny acts out to gain attention.

The school counselor decides to review Danny's academic records. She reviews his report cards from first grade to the present and his test records.

Danny's Elementary School Record Card

Performance Score Key:
  4: Advanced—applying standard at complex levels
  3: Proficient—meeting standard
  2: Basic—making progress toward standard
  1: Not meeting standard

First Grade		Second Grade		Third Grade		Third Grade (This Year)	
Reading	3	Reading	2	Reading	1	Reading	2
Writing	2	Writing	1	Writing	1	Writing	2
Math	2	Math	2	Math	1	Math	1
Social Studies	2	Social Studies	1	Social Studies	1	Social Studies	2
Science	1	Science	2	Science	1	Science	1
Physical Ed.	2	Physical Ed.	2	Physical Ed.	1	Physical Ed.	2
Art	3	Art	2	Art	2	Art	3

Test Records

Wechsler Intelligence Scale for Children (Administered in Third Grade—This Year)

Index Scores	Standard Score	Percentile Rank	Descriptive Category
Verbal Comprehension (VCI)	112	79	
Perceptual Reasoning Index (PRI)	108	70	
Working Memory Index (WMI)	108	70	
Processing Speed Index (PSI)	110	75	

Wechsler Individual Achievement Test (Administered in Third Grade—This Year)

Composites	Standard Score	Percentile Rank	Descriptive Category
Reading	85	16	
Mathematics	89	23	
Written Language	79	8	
Oral Language	87	19	

Exercise Questions

1. Interpret each of Danny's scores (standard score, percentile rank) on the WISC-IV indexes. Determine the descriptive category for each index. How would you describe his overall level of intelligence? How would you describe any relative intellectual strengths or weaknesses that Danny might have?

2. Interpret each of Danny's scores (standard score, percentile rank) on the WIAT-II composites. Determine the descriptive category for each composite. How would you describe his overall level of achievement? How would you describe any relative strengths or weaknesses that he might have?

3. Compare Danny's scores on the WISC-IV to his scores on the WIAT-II. Are the scores on these two tests consistent? Explain.

4. Are Danny's test results consistent with his grades? Explain.

5. What factors could account for any discrepancies between his test results and his academic performance (i.e., grades)?

6. What additional information about Danny would you like to have?

7. What would you recommend for Danny?

Table 9.3 provides a list of just a few of the many available diagnostic tests. Note that some individual achievement tests (e.g., the Kaufman Test of Educational Achievement, the Peabody Individual Achievement Test-Revised, the Woodcock–Johnson III Tests of Achievement) can also be used for diagnostic purposes. We will provide further information about two well-known diagnostic tests: the KeyMath-3 Diagnostic Assessment and the Peabody Picture Vocabulary Test.

TABLE 9.3 Diagnostic Achievement Tests	
Math	KeyMath-3 Diagnostic Assessment (KeyMath-3 DA)
	Test of Mathematical Abilities, Third Edition (TOMA-3)
Language	Clinical Evaluation of Language Fundamentals, Fourth Edition (CELF-4)
	OWLS Series
	Peabody Picture Vocabulary Test, Fourth Edition (PPVC-4)
	Test of Written Language, 4 (TOWL-4)
	Test of Written Spelling, 5 (TWS-5)
	Writing Process Test (WPT)
Reading	Diagnostic Assessments of Reading, Second Edition (DAR)
	Early Reading Diagnostic Assessment, Second Edition (ERDA)
	Gates–MacGinitie Reading Tests, Fourth Edition (GMRT)
	Group Reading Assessment and Diagnostic Evaluation (GRADE)
	Gray Diagnostic Reading Test, Second Edition (GDRT-2)
	Slosson Oral Reading Test, Revised (SORT-R3)
	Test of Early Reading Ability, Third Edition (TERA3)
	Woodcock Reading Mastery Tests, Third Edition (WRMT-III)

KEYMATH-3 DIAGNOSTIC ASSESSMENT The *KeyMath-3 Diagnostic Assessment* (KeyMath-3 DA) is a widely used, comprehensive measure of mathematical concepts and skills. The test is an untimed, individually administered test designed to be used with individuals aged 4 years, 6 months through 21 years. The content reflects the standards described in the *Principles and Standards for School Mathematics* of the National Council of Teachers of Mathematics (National Council of Teachers of Mathematics (NCTM), 2000). The test has three content areas, each comprised of several subtests:

1. *Basic Concepts* Numeration, Algebra, Geometry, Measurement, and Data Analysis and Probability
2. *Operations* Mental Computation and Estimation, Addition and Subtraction, and Multiplication and Division
3. *Applications* Foundations of Problem Solving and Applied Problem Solving

The KeyMath-3 DA score summary includes scale scores, standard scores, confidence intervals, percentile ranks, grade and age equivalents, and descriptive categories (see Figure 9.2 to examine strategies for addressing deficits identified by the KeyMath3). It was normed on a sample of 3,630 individuals aged 4 years, 6 months through 21 years, 11 months that reflected the demographic characteristics (i.e., gender, race or ethnicity, parent's education, geographic region) of the U.S. Census Bureau population report.

PEABODY PICTURE VOCABULARY TEST, FOURTH EDITION Another well-known diagnostic test is the Peabody Picture Vocabulary Test, Fourth Edition (PPVC-4; Dunn & Dunn, 2007). The PPVC-4 has been widely used to measure oral vocabulary knowledge in

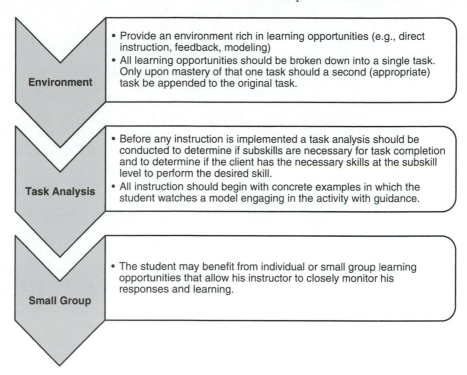

Environment
- Provide an environment rich in learning opportunities (e.g., direct instruction, feedback, modeling)
- All learning opportunities should be broken down into a single task. Only upon mastery of that one task should a second (appropriate) task be appended to the original task.

Task Analysis
- Before any instruction is implemented a task analysis should be conducted to determine if subskills are necessary for task completion and to determine if the client has the necessary skills at the subskill level to perform the desired skill.
- All instruction should begin with concrete examples in which the student watches a model engaging in the activity with guidance.

Small Group
- The student may benefit from individual or small group learning opportunities that allow his instructor to closely monitor his responses and learning.

FIGURE 9.2   Strategies for addressing deficits identified by the KeyMath3.

children and adults for many years. It was first published in 1959, and its most recent edition was published in 2007. The PPVT-4 is an individually administered, norm-referenced test designed for people aged 2 years 6 months through 90 years and older. It assesses the ability to comprehend spoken words in Standard American English and is often used for screening individuals from diverse linguistic backgrounds or those who have language or communication disorders. The instrument can also be used with individuals who have autism, cerebral palsy, or other physical disabilities. The PPVT has 228 items that cover a broad range of receptive vocabulary levels, from preschool through adult. Items consist of words representing 20 content areas (e.g., actions, vegetables, tools) and parts of speech (e.g., nouns, verbs, adjectives). The test is available in two parallel forms: Form A and Form B.

The 228 items consist of four full-color pictures arranged on one page. A nonthreatening approach is used to assess vocabulary knowledge: while showing the examinee a set of four pictures, the examiner says, "I will say something; then I want you to put your finger on the picture of what I have said. Let's try one." Then, the examiner uses a prompt that precedes the stimulus word: "Put your finger on the *star*." The test taker indicates which picture best represents the word spoken by the examiner. Test administration takes approximately 10 to 15 minutes, and scoring is rapid and objective, usually occurring during test administration.

The PPVT-4 provides standard scores (with a mean of 100 and a standard deviation of 15), confidence intervals, growth scale values (GSV), percentiles, NCEs, stanines, and

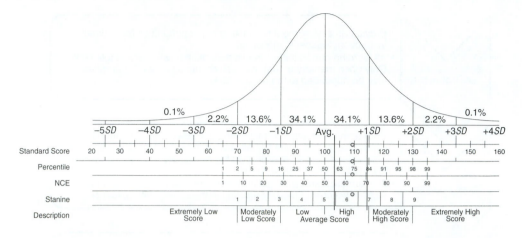

Score Summary

Raw Score	Standard Score	90% Conf. Interval	GSV	Percentile	NCE	Stanine	Age Equivalent	Description
159	109	102–115	181	73	63	6	10.7	Average Range

FIGURE 9.3   Graphical profile of the Peabody Picture Vocabulary Test (PPVC-4).

Source: Peabody Picture Vocabulary Test, Fourth Edition (PPVT-4). Copyright © 2007 by NCS Pearson, Inc. Reproduced with permission. All rights reserved. "PPVT" is a trademark, in the U.S. and/or other countries, of Pearson Education, Inc. or its affiliates(s).

age equivalents (see Figure 9.3). In addition, it provides a descriptive classification of scores, including *extremely low, moderately low, low average, high average, moderately high*, and *extremely high*.

Subject-Area Tests

The term *subject-area tests* generally refers to standardized achievement tests that measure content-area knowledge in specific academic or vocational subject areas. They usually have more items than an achievement battery's subtests, providing a better sample of performance and more reliable scores on specific subject areas (Miller et al., 2012). Like other types of achievement tests, subject-area tests measure an individual's knowledge and skills in a particular area; however, they are also used to predict how well an individual will perform in the future (i.e., aptitude).

Subject-area tests are part of major national testing programs used by colleges and universities to determine advanced placement or credit or as part of the requirements for admission. For example, some colleges and universities require students to take a particular subject-area test offered by the SAT for admission into competitive programs. The SAT offers subject tests in such areas as English, history, mathematics, science, and language. The College-Level Examination Program (CLEP) from the College Board also offers subject-area tests in 34 areas, including composition, literature, foreign languages, history, science, math, and business, to name just a few. Students can take a CLEP subject-area test and, by obtaining a passing score, earn college credit.

Subject-area tests can also be used as part of certification requirements. For example, teachers often have to earn a qualifying score on a subject-area exam to become certified to teach; the particular subject-area test corresponds to the academic subject area in which they are seeking certification.

ADULT ACHIEVEMENT TESTS

Although most achievement test batteries are developed for use with children, some are designed for adults. Adult achievement tests are often used in adult basic education programs and literacy settings. Probably the most well-known example of an adult achievement test is the General Educational Development Tests (GED). The GED is sometimes referred to as a *General Equivalency Diploma* or *General Education Diploma*, although these names are not recognized by the American Council on Education, which developed the test. The testing program is available internationally, with more than 3,400 official GED testing centers accessible around the world. In 2010, nearly 760,000 adults worldwide took some portion of the GED test battery, and 474,000 earned a passing score. The GED is comprised of five tests: Mathematics, Language Arts, Reading, Writing, and Social Science. Examinees who pass the GED are certified as having American or Canadian high-school-level academic skills. Examples of other adult achievement tests include the Adult Basic Learning Examination, Second Edition (ABLE-2), the Comprehensive Adult Student Assessment System (CASAS), the Scholastic Abilities Test for Adults (SATA), and the Test of Adult Basic Education (TABE).

OTHER TYPES OF ACHIEVEMENT ASSESSMENT INSTRUMENTS

Achievement is a broad area of assessment, and the resulting scores can have a significant impact on the future of those who are assessed. For example, some tests (e.g., minimum-level skills tests) can determine a person's ability to move to the next grade level or to graduate from high school. State achievement tests can impact a school district's funding and, subsequently, the job security of school district employees. National achievement test scores gauge the overall performance of the nation's educational system in comparison to other countries. Regardless of the type, there can be high stakes related to achievement testing. As such, it is critical that counselors have a thorough understanding of the many types of achievement tests.

Criterion-Referenced Tests and Minimum-Level Skills Tests

Criterion-referenced tests and minimum-level skills tests are often used to determine if an individual or group of individuals have attained a specific level of performance. In many cases, the level of performance is necessary for advancement. For example, as a counselor in training, you will eventually be required to take a comprehensive exam, a certification exam, and/or a licensure exam. Each of these types of exams has a specific criterion that must be reached in order to graduate, have a specific credential, or be able to practice independently. We review the various types of these measures and their role in achievement assessment.

Criterion-referenced tests, sometimes called *domain-referenced tests*, are designed with specific objectives and skills to determine if a certain academic standard is met. They differ from norm-referenced tests in that they focus on mastery of a given objective or skill. Norm-referenced tests usually include only one or two items to measure a given objective, whereas criterion-referenced tests include many items on a specific objective. The criterion-referenced test is scored to an absolute standard, usually the percentage of correct answers. Students may be required to meet a certain score on a criterion-referenced achievement test, say 70%, as evidence of mastery. In systems requiring mastery of objectives, the test taker is not allowed to go on to the next unit until he or she passes the one being studied. Criterion-referenced tests can be used for other purposes:

1. To evaluate the curriculum
2. To identify topics that should be remediated or enriched
3. To provide information for the counselor to use in educational and vocational planning with students
4. To help students select courses
5. To document student mastery of objectives
6. To provide systematic evidence of student attainment of objectives across levels and fields over time
7. To help the counselor mark the progress of the individual over time

An example of a criterion-referenced test is the *College Basic Academic Subjects Examination* (College BASE), which assesses the degree to which college students have mastered particular skills and competencies consistent with the completion of general education coursework. The instrument measures achievement in four subject areas: English, mathematics, science, and social studies. As of 2001, the exam was used by approximately 150 institutions nationwide. The users included both community colleges and 4-year institutions whose Carnegie designations ranged from baccalaureate college to research university. Some universities use the College BASE for admission into a particular program. For example, Missouri requires all institutions to use the College BASE as a screening tool for admission into educator preparation programs.

Another example of a criterion-referenced achievement test is the *Criterion Test of Basic Skills* (CTOBS-2), which was designed to measure reading and arithmetic skills in students from grades 6 through 11. The Reading subtest assesses basic word-attack skills in the following areas: letter recognition, letter sounds, blending, sequencing, decoding of common spelling patterns and multisyllable words, and sight-word recognition. The Arithmetic subtest assesses skills in these areas: counting, number concepts and numerical recognition, addition, subtraction, multiplication, division, measurement concepts, fractions, decimals, percents, geometric concepts, prealgebra, and rounding and estimation.

Criterion-referenced tests are often referred to as *minimum-level skills tests*, particularly in education, where students must earn a minimum score on a test to be promoted to the next grade level, graduate, or be admitted into a desired educational program. For example, satisfactory performance on the State of Texas Assessments of Academic Readiness (STAAR) is required to receive a high school diploma in Texas. Although the STAAR tests are minimum-level tests, they are still high-stakes tests. Failure on a single test in the STAAR battery could prevent graduation. Tests like the STAAR are controversial because of the impact on school funding and the identified disparities in achievement scores by race. For example, the results of the 2013 STAAR testing showed a large disparity when comparing White and Asian students with Black and Hispanic students (Texas Education Agency, 2014). Over 25% of Black and Hispanic students in Texas did not attain passing scores on the STAAR in 2013.

Because of issues like the ones with STAAR, states have been retiring assessment instruments and implementing new ones. Achievement testing is mandated by legislatures in many states, because federal funding for schools is tied to the No Child Left Behind Act (NCLB) of 2002, and each state has its own process for achievement testing. Because the approaches vary from state to state, the issues are varied. We discuss state achievement tests in detail in the next section.

State Achievement Tests

State achievement tests are state-developed standardized tests used in statewide assessment programs to measure academic achievement across multiple grade levels in elementary, middle, and high school. They are criterion-referenced tests, which are used to determine if a student meets minimum standards for promotion from grade to grade and for high school graduation (see the section on Factors Affecting Student Achievement later in this chapter). As part of the No Child Left Behind Act of 2002 states are required to develop achievement tests in order to receive federal funding for schools. Because educational standards are set by each individual state, NCLB does not require schools to use a specific national achievement test; rather, schools develop their own standardized tests that closely match their state's educational curriculum. For example, Florida developed the Florida Comprehensive Assessment Test (FCAT-2.0) to assess the standards and curriculum specified in the Sunshine State Standards (see fldoe.org). The FCAT-2.0 is administered to students in grades 3 through 11 and consists of criterion-referenced tests in mathematics, reading, science, and writing, which measure student progress toward meeting the state's curriculum standards. Students in third grade must pass the FCAT-2.0 Reading test to be promoted to the fourth grade, and ninth graders must pass the FCAT-2.0 Reading, Mathematics, and Writing tests to be promoted. Seniors must pass both the Reading and Mathematics sections to graduate from high school.

Although an advantage of state-developed achievement tests is their alignment with a state's educational standards and curriculum, a disadvantage is that student performance cannot be compared to that of students in other states across the nation. To address this limitation, some states and school districts administer commercially published norm-referenced achievement batteries in addition to their state achievement tests. For example, Alabama uses the Stanford Achievement Test, 10th Edition in addition to the Alabama Reading and Mathematics Test in its statewide assessment program. Commercially published tests are also widely used among private, parochial, and home schools, because these schools are not required by NCLB to administer state-developed tests.

National Assessment of Educational Progress

The National Assessment of Educational Progress (NAEP), also known as the *Nation's Report Card*, is the only measure of student achievement in the United States that allows for comparison of student performance across states. Since 1969, the NAEP has periodically administered achievement tests to students, covering such content areas as reading, mathematics, science, writing, U.S. history, civics, geography, and the arts. Tests are administered to representative samples of students drawn at grades 4, 8, and 12 for the main assessments, or samples of students at ages 9, 13, or 17 years for long-term trend assessments. Test results are widely reported by the national and local media and are often used to support legislative action involving public education.

The goal of the NAEP program is to compare student achievement among states and to track changes in the achievement of fourth, eighth, and 12th graders. The NAEP does not provide scores for individual students or schools, because its original purpose was to report on the achievement of the nation, to examine performance of demographic subgroups, and to track trends in educational progress over time. Starting in 1990, the NAEP began providing feedback to participating states. In 2001, after the passage of NCLB, states that received Title I funding (i.e., financial assistance for high-poverty schools) were required to participate in NAEP in reading and mathematics at grades 4 and 8 every 2 years.

Curriculum-Based Assessment and Curriculum-Based Measurement

Curriculum-based assessment (CBA) is an alternative approach to student assessment that emphasizes repeated measures, the linking of instruction and assessment, and the use of material from local curriculum. It is designed to assess regular education students in a regular education curriculum by using direct observation and recording of student performance on materials presented in a class. An example of CBA is asking a child to read from a reading passage in a classroom textbook for 1 minute. Information about the child's reading ability can then be obtained and compared with the abilities of other students in the class, school, or district. CBA can be an important tool for educators in (a) evaluating a student's learning environment, (b) assessing the effectiveness of various task-approach activities, (c) evaluating student products, and (d) determining a student's instructional needs (Ysseldyke & Algozzine, 2006).

Curriculum-based measurement (CBM) is a type of curriculum-based assessment often associated with special education. It also emphasizes monitoring of student performance through repeated measures of student achievement. Brief measures of specific subject areas are administered to a student weekly or monthly to measure progress toward long-term instructional goals.

Performance Assessment

Performance assessment (also called *authentic assessment* or *alternative assessment*) is a form of assessment in which students are asked to perform real-world tasks that demonstrate meaningful application of essential knowledge and skills. The tasks are either replicas of or analogous to the kinds of problems faced in the real world. Tasks are chosen that would allow students to demonstrate mastery of a given educational standard.

Mueller (2006) distinguished performance assessment from traditional assessment in several ways. The most obvious is the type of items on the test. Traditional assessments typically consist of multiple-choice, true/false, matching, and other similar items, whereas performance assessments can include essays, projects, portfolios, performance tasks, and open-ended exercises. Mueller also stated that traditional approaches to assessment are typically *curriculum driven*. The curriculum (which delivers a predetermined body of knowledge and skills) is developed first, then assessments are administered to determine if students have acquired the intended knowledge and skills. In contrast, with performance assessment, the *assessment drives the curriculum*. That is, teachers first determine the tasks that students will perform to demonstrate their mastery, and then a curriculum is developed that will enable students to perform those tasks well, which would include the acquisition of essential knowledge and skills.

Teachers often use a mix of traditional and performance assessments to serve different purposes (Mueller, 2006). For example, traditional assessment may be used to assess whether a student has acquired specific knowledge and skills, and performance assessment may be used to measure the student's ability to apply the knowledge or skills in a real-world situation. In other cases, both traditional assessment and performance assessment are used to gather a more comprehensive picture of performance. For example, achievement in STEM areas can be difficult to measure accurately. In order to have a complete picture, it may be necessary to measure both macro- and microunderstanding of concepts (Kim, VanTassel-Baska, Bracken, Feng, & Stambaugh, 2014). In order to do this in a comprehensive manner, both traditional standardized assessments and performance assessments may prove useful.

Portfolio Assessment

Portfolio assessment is a type of performance assessment widely used in educational settings as a means of examining and measuring students' progress by reviewing a collection of work in one or more curriculum areas (McDonald, 2012). Portfolios can vary in style and format. In some cases, portfolios can be viewed as a kind of scrapbook or photo album that documents the progress and activities of a student through his or her educational program. In other cases, portfolios are more comprehensive pictures of students' academic activities. At Lamar University, all graduate students in counseling complete portfolios as part of their graduate training. In their portfolios, students are required to include key artifacts (major course projects) from each course that tie to primary learning outcomes. Students can also add field experience documents, resumes, disclosure statements, and other materials. These portfolios are reviewed and graded by a team of at least three professors as the capstone project for the degree program.

As can be seen from our examples, the contents of portfolios can include a variety of items (sometimes called *artifacts* or *evidence*), such as writing or other work samples, drawings, photos, video or audio recordings, computer disks, or copies of other tests or assessment instruments. Portfolio artifacts are not selected haphazardly; rather, they are chosen through a dynamic process of planning, reflecting, collecting, and evaluating that occurs throughout an individual's entire instructional program (McDonald, 2012). Artifacts can come from the student, teachers, parents, education staff, and other relevant community members. Furthermore, self-reflections from students are also a common component of portfolios.

FACTORS AFFECTING STUDENT ACHIEVEMENT

It is important that counselors have knowledge of the broader social and economic factors that surround the lives of students and how these factors can affect students' performance on measures of achievement. Factors that affect academic achievement can be categorized as either in-school factors or out-of-school factors (Barton, 2003). Examples of in-school factors include the following:

- *Rigor of the Curriculum* The extent to which students take challenging, higher-level academic courses affects achievement test scores.
- *Teacher Knowledge and Skills* Students perform better on achievement tests when taught by teachers with appropriate training and education for the subject they are teaching.
- *Teacher Experience and Attendance* Research indicates that students learn more from teachers with experience than they do from novice teachers.
- *Class Size* Smaller class sizes (20 students or less) are associated with greater academic achievement in students, especially for elementary school students and for students from low-income or diverse backgrounds.
- *Technology* Access to technology-assisted instruction increases academic achievement.
- *School Safety* Students perform better academically when they feel safe at school.

Examples of out-of-school factors include the following:

- *Low Birth Weight* Birth weight affects development and can cause learning disabilities.
- *Lead Poisoning* Studies show that lead poisoning is related to learning disabilities, delayed development, and behavior problems.
- *Hunger and Poor Nutrition* Healthier students who eat a balanced diet tend to perform better academically than those who do not.
- *Reading to Young Children* Children with parents who read to them at home tend to achieve at a higher level.
- *Amount of TV Watching* Watching 6 or more hours of television per day may contribute to poorer achievement test scores in children.
- *Parental Involvement* Parental involvement with children is linked to higher academic achievement.
- *Home Learning Activities* The extent to which parents manage time spent on learning is linked to academic achievement.
- *Positive Social Skills* Parental focus on the development of positive social skills is also linked to academic achievement.
- *Student Mobility* Mobility—that is, changing schools frequently—is associated with lower academic achievement.

It's important to remember that an achievement test is only one instrument that may be used to collect achievement information. Because of the many in-school factors and out-of-school factors that affect academic achievement, decisions made about students should encompass information obtained from a variety of assessment instruments and strategies, such as the following:

- *Achievement Data* Results from achievement test batteries, diagnostic tests, individual tests, and state achievement tests; teacher observational notes of students' performance in class; samples of students' class work, student portfolios; informal classroom assessment; and classroom grades (i.e., report cards)
- *Ability Data* The results of intellectual ability assessment instruments or aptitude assessment instruments

- *Other Relevant Student Data* Attendance data, disciplinary records, grade retention, and homework completion
- *Contextual Data* Factors such as the student's cultural background, linguistic background, gender, out-of-school experiences, health and nutrition, self-concept, and socioeconomic level

ANALYSIS OF CLASS PROFILE

Up to this point, we have reviewed large-scale achievement testing and individual achievement testing. It is important to note that teachers are often interested in the achievement test results of the students in their class. They might want to know how the class is performing in particular subject areas or if there are certain students who need help or who are having problems in one or more achievement areas. To answer these questions, school personnel often have access to summary charts that display the test results of groups of students in a class, a school, or even a district. Although we reviewed the results of achievement testing earlier in the chapter, we do so again to demonstrate the importance of results at various levels. Table 9.4 provides an example of a sixth-grade results chart that shows grade equivalent scores for the several subtests on the Stanford 10 as well as the OLSAT 8 School Ability Index, which is a measure of total ability (with mean of 100 and a standard deviation of 16). The scores listed permit comparison of achievement and ability for the sixth-grade class. If we assume that the Stanford 10 is a valid instrument to measure achievement in this school district, then students with average ability should score around grade level, and students with below-average ability should score below grade level. Care should be taken not to over-interpret minor differences in individual scores. Student 19, for example, is technically below grade placement in seven achievement areas, but the 5.8 in Mathematics Concepts is not significantly lower than grade placement when the standard error of measurement is considered. As you review Table 9.4, consider the purposes of achievement testing and the ways in which the information can be used by teachers, counselors, and other helping professionals.

One of the first tasks required to understand the results and be able to make them useful is to organize them in a useful manner. To begin evaluating the test scores, the teacher might graph the scores or compute some measures of central tendency. Remember that the computation of central tendency measures is a way to understand one score in comparison to the group. For example, on the Stanford 10, the means for the Science and Spelling subtests are 7.00 and 6.21, respectively. The median of the Complete Battery is 6.15, and the median on the Spelling subtest is 6.1. Having an understanding of mean and standard deviation could help the teacher to classify students as *below average*, *average*, or *above average* in terms of achievement. Of course, the teacher can take a more informal approach and simply count how many students are at or above grade level and how many are below. For the sixth-grade class in this example, there are 11 at or above grade placement in Spelling and 13 below; 14 at or above grade placement in Total Mathematics and 10 below; and 15 at or above in Science and 9 below. This type of analysis is fast, but the ability levels of the group must be kept in mind. The teacher might also be interested in looking at item information, perhaps the specific items that presented problems to the class. In this example, there are a number of students below grade level in each category. What does that mean for the teacher? There are of course numerous reasons why performance may be below level. Having the scores is just one piece of the puzzle. Based on the results, the teachers would have to begin to examine the test, the curriculum, teaching

TABLE 9.4 Test Results for a Sixth-Grade Class

Student	Gender	OLSAT 8 SAI	CB	TR	TM	LG	SP	SC	SS	LI
						Stanford 10 Subtests				
1	F	127	8.3	8.7	6.6	8.0	10.5	9.2	6.8	8.3
2	F	116	8.3	8.7	7.3	9.0	7.0	10.0	8.3	8.3
3	F	130	8.0	8.0	8.0	10.7	7.8	7.2	9.0	8.0
4	F	132	7.8	7.8	7.6	10.5	8.8	7.8	7.9	7.8
5	F	121	7.3	9.6	6.3	8.8	7.0	6.0	8.5	7.3
6	M	122	7.0	7.0	6.8	8.5	5.4	10.0	11.4	7.0
7	F	116	6.9	7.0	6.8	10.0	8.2	5.8	7.0	6.9
8	M	118	6.8	7.0	6.3	6.7	5.6	6.9	7.4	6.8
9	F	110	6.7	7.2	5.4	6.7	6.3	8.1	7.2	6.7
10	F	114	6.6	6.9	6.6	9.3	8.0	6.0	5.6	6.6
11	M	115	6.5	6.5	5.9	7.2	6.0	9.2	8.1	6.5
12	M	104	6.2	6.2	6.3	6.0	5.7	6.4	6.3	6.2
13	M	117	6.1	6.1	7.3	6.2	4.1	9.2	6.4	6.1
14	F	115	6.0	6.7	5.9	5.7	6.6	9.0	6.0	6.0
15	M	115	5.8	6.1	5.4	7.0	4.7	5.8	6.6	5.8
16	M	109	5.8	6.6	4.8	7.1	4.7	6.7	5.9	5.8
17	M	108	5.6	5.6	6.3	5.8	4.3	6.7	5.6	5.6
18	M	103	5.6	4.9	5.9	5.6	3.0	5.8	6.8	5.6
19	F	102	5.6	5.6	6.5	5.3	3.6	4.1	6.3	5.6
20	F	93	5.5	5.9	5.4	6.6	4.7	6.6	6.3	5.5
21	F	112	5.4	6.4	4.8	5.4	5.1	5.8	5.3	5.4
22	F	112	5.3	6.1	5.4	4.6	6.9	4.2	5.3	5.3
23	M	89	5.1	4.7	6.1	4.3	3.4	4.3	5.2	5.1
24	M	96	4.9	6.1	4.5	5.5	4.3	6.4	4.9	4.9

OLSAT 8: SAI = School Ability Index.

Stanford 10: CB = Complete Battery, TR = Total Reading, TM = Total Mathematics, LG = Language, SP = Spelling, SC = Science, SS = Social Science, LI = Listening.

methods, factors impacting achievement, and other issues. As a counselor, you might consult with the teacher and help to uncover the issues impacting achievement.

Although there may be a number of causes, the first step in an investigation is to examine the purpose of the test. The scores in this example might be low in some areas because the test was given early in the year, before the students had been exposed to many of the concepts and objectives taught in the sixth grade. Some school districts intentionally give this test at the beginning of the year to obtain an overall estimate of the entry level of the students. If you didn't understand the purpose of the test in this example and tried to interpret the scores, you could develop some poor perceptions of student performance. In order to further your understanding of score interpretation, complete Exercise 9.4. Consider the case of James, the background information, and data. Relate the information to the material you have read in this chapter as well as others and then respond to the exercise questions.

Exercise 9.4
Interpreting Achievement: James

The case study of James illustrates the process involved in interpreting achievement data. James is in fifth grade and is having some academic difficulties in school. He is 10.3 years old, weighs 80 pounds, and is 4 feet 9 inches tall. A graph of his scores on the Stanford Achievement Test is shown in Figure 9.4. The derived scores plotted on the graph are percentile bands and represent how James performed in relation to students in the national sample. The median is the 50th percentile and represents typical or average performance. Some tests use different systems to classify superior or poor performance. In this case, the Stanford 10 uses a classification of *below average*, *average*, and *above average*. Counselors need to be familiar not only with what scores mean, but also with what is measured by each subtest and which scores are combined to give total scores. The Total Reading score, comprised of the Reading Vocabulary and Reading Comprehension subtests, helps identify students who might

have deficiencies in reading comprehension as well as overall scholastic achievement. The Total Mathematics score includes Mathematics Problem Solving and Mathematics Procedures subtests. The Listening score is based on the combination of the Vocabulary and Listening Comprehension scores, which provide data on the learner's ability to understand and remember information presented orally.

The scores on the Stanford 10 graph show that James scored high in relation to other fifth graders in Total Mathematics; clearly, his strongest area of achievement is mathematics. His score on the Listening test is below average as compared to his peers. He is also below average in Total Reading, Language, Spelling, and Science. His score in Social Science is average.

Additional Information

One of the first questions to consider is how James's current test performance compares with other achievement data,

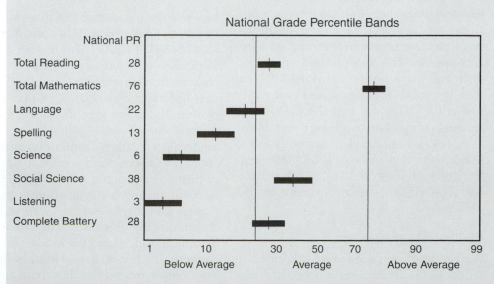

FIGURE 9.4   Profile of James's scores on the Stanford Achievement Test.

Exercise 9.4
(Continued)

such as his performance in class, other achievement test results, and report cards. In terms of his class performance, James's teacher reports that he is an average student in mathematics but has problems in reading comprehension and following directions. He does not seem to listen at times and cannot remember what he is supposed to do. His problems in reading comprehension also create problems in understanding his science and social studies materials.

James's results on the Stanford 10 can also be compared with the results of other achievement tests. For example, James recently completed a local minimum-skills-level test (a criterion-referenced test) that was based specifically on the educational objectives taught in James's class (in contrast to the Stanford 10, which is based on a wide sampling of objectives and textbooks from schools across the nation). On the minimum-skills-level test, James failed the following areas (i.e., he had fewer than 75% of the items correct): vocabulary, listening comprehension, synonyms, antonyms, sequencing, facts and opinions, recalling details, main ideas, and sentence completion. This information combined with his score on the Stanford 10 Total Reading subtest (James scored at the 28th percentile) indicates that the problem of reading comprehension is very real. However, his reading problem did not seem to affect his performance in Total Mathematics, in which he scored at the 76th percentile. Test results are inconsistent in this dimension.

Ability Data

We can also compare James's Stanford 10 scores to his ability. In the schools, *ability* typically refers to intellectual ability. If a student has been previously referred for assessment, then school counselors may have access to the results of such instruments as the Slosson Intelligence Test, the Otis–Lennon School Ability Test, the Stanford–Binet Intelligence Scale, or the WISC-IV. Ability testing would help in developing an individually prescribed educational program for James, but no intelligence data were available in his cumulative folder.

Other Relevant Data

Other relevant student data may include James's attendance record, disciplinary records, grade retention, and homework completion. James has progressed normally in school; he was never retained at a grade level and has been at the same school since the beginning of the third grade. He did attend two schools in other states prior to that time. James has not missed many days of school.

Contextual Data

James is the oldest child of three siblings; he has an 8-year-old brother and a 3-year-old sister. He lives with his mother and his stepfather, who works as a carpenter for a construction company. His mother works part-time as a checkout clerk in a supermarket. His father is in the Navy, and his parents were divorced when James was in kindergarten. James's mother is concerned about his progress and is open to any suggestions the teacher or counselor may have to improve his academic performance. James relates fairly well with his classmates, but gets easily frustrated when he cannot understand his lessons or recite correctly for the teacher. He likes to perform duties around the classroom and has become strongly attached to his teacher.

Postscript

James was referred to an Individualized Education Program (IEP) meeting and was observed and tested by the school psychologist. On the basis of the information collected, he was assigned to work in a specific learning disabilities resource room.

Exercise Questions

1. Given the amount of information available, what other options could have been considered for James?

2. What other information might you collect in order to arrive at a decision?

3. What types of intervention should be tried before being assigned to a learning disabilities classroom?

4. What positive behavior supports might be necessary?

5. Are there any other interpretation points to consider from the data provided?

Summary

Achievement tests are used to assess an individual's knowledge or skills in a particular content area. Standardized achievement tests can be divided into four broad categories: achievement test batteries, diagnostic achievement tests, individual achievement tests, and subject-area tests. Each type of achievement test has distinct characteristics and is used for various purposes, such as monitoring achievement over time, making placement or selection decisions, evaluating educational programs and curriculum, diagnosing learning disabilities, and providing endorsement for certification and licensure.

Standardized achievement tests play a large role in the U.S. education system. Students are administered tests that can directly affect their educational opportunities or choices, such as being promoted or retained at a grade level, graduating high school, or being admitted into a desired educational program.

Used properly and interpreted wisely, standardized achievement tests can provide valuable information about a student's achievement level and can be useful for making decisions or inferences based on test scores. Misused, they can be a source of inestimable harm, not only to students, but to the teachers, schools, and the community as well. As with any type of test, any decisions (such as promotion of students) should never be made solely on the basis of test scores alone. Other relevant information should be taken into account to enhance the overall validity of such decisions.

Questions for Discussion

1. Describe the major categories of standardized achievement tests, and explain their differences.

2. What are the advantages of a teacher-made test as opposed to a standardized achievement test?

3. How would you go about developing a standardized achievement test that covers the content of your current assessment class? Include several sample items.

4. In what circumstances would norm-referenced or criterion-referenced interpretation be appropriate in achievement testing?

5. What are the distinctions between intelligence tests and achievement tests?

6. Do you think the No Child Left Behind Act is working? Why or why not?

Suggested Activities

1. Select one of the major achievement tests, and write a critique of it.
2. Interview counselors who use achievement tests in their work. Find out what tests they use and why and how they use the results. Report your findings to the class.
3. Administer an individual achievement test or diagnostic test and write a report of the results.

4. Go to the library and find a research article that uses a standardized test, and then answer the following questions:
   a. What is the name of the test?
   b. For what purpose(s) was the test used in the research study?
   c. Was the test reliable and valid? How do you know?

References

Aiken, L. A., & Groth-Marnat, G. (2006). *Psychological testing and assessment* (12th ed.). Boston, MA: Pearson.

American Educational Research Association (AERA), American Psychological Association (APA), & National Council on Measurement in Education (NCME). (2014). *Standards for educational and psychological testing*. Washington, DC: Authors.

Barton, P. E. (2003). *Parsing the achievement gap: Baselines for tracking progress*. Princeton, NJ: ETS Policy Information Center.

Dunn, L. M., & Dunn, D. M. (2007). *The Peabody Picture Vocabulary Test* (4th ed.). Bloomington, MN: NCS Pearson, Inc.

Johnson, R. S., Mims, J. S., & Doyle-Nichols, A. (2009). *Developing portfolios in education: A guide to reflection, inquiry, and assessment*. Thousand Oaks, CA: Sage.

Kim, K. H., VanTassel-Baska, J., Bracken, B. A., Feng, A., & Stambaugh, T. (2014). Assessing science reasoning and conceptual understanding in the primary grades using standardized and performance-based assessments. *Journal of Advanced Academics, 25*(1), 47–66.

McDonald, B. (2012). Portfolio assessment: Direct from the classroom. *Assessment & Evaluation in Higher Education, 37*(3), 335–347.

Miller, M. D., Linn, R. L., & Gronlund, N. E. (2012). *Measurement and assessment in teaching* (11th ed.). Upper Saddle River, NJ: Pearson.

Mueller, J. (2006). *Authentic assessment toolbox*. Retrieved from http://jonathan.mueller.faculty.noctrl.edu/toolbox

National Council of Teachers of Mathematics (NCTM). (2000). *Principles and standards for school mathematics*. Reston, VA: Author.

Phelps, R. P. (2012). The effect of testing on student achievement, 1910–2010. *International Journal of Testing, 12*(1), 21–43.

Reynolds, C. R., Livingston, R. B., & Willson, V. (2008). *Measurement and assessment in education*. Boston, MA: Pearson.

Schrank, F. A., Mather, N., & McGrew, K. S. (2014). *Woodcock–Johnson IV*. Itasca, IL: Riverside Publishing.

Sewell, M., Marczak, M., & Horn, M. (2001). *The use of portfolio assessment in evaluation*. Retrieved from http://ag.arizona.edu/fcs/cyfernet/cyfar/Portfo~3.htm

Texas Education Agency. (2014). STAAR Statewide Summary Reports 2013–2104. Retrieved from http://www.tea.state.tx.us/index2.aspx?id=25769809035

US Department of Education. (2004). *Building the Legacy: IDEA. Section 300.8 child with a disability*. Retrieved from http://idea.ed.gov/explore/view/p/,root,regs,300,A,300%252E8

Woodcock, R. W., McGrew, K. S., & Mather, N. (2001, 2007). *Woodcock Johnson III Tests of Achievement*. Rolling Meadows, IL: Riverside.

Ysseldyke, J. E., & Algozzine, B. (2006). *Effective assessment for students with special needs: A practical guide for every teacher*. Thousand Oaks, CA: Corwin Press.

10 Assessment of Aptitude

Aptitude can be defined as an innate or acquired ability to be good at something. Aptitude tests measure an individual's capacity, or potential, for performing a given skill or task and are used to predict behavior: Will the individual be successful in a given educational program, vocational program, or occupational situation? Thus, rather than focusing on one's current level of performance (i.e., achievement), aptitude tests are used to predict what an individual is capable of doing in the future.

After studying this chapter, you should be able to:

- Describe the purpose of aptitude tests.
- Explain the differences between achievement tests and aptitude tests.
- Describe multiple-aptitude test batteries, specialized aptitude tests, admissions tests, and readiness tests.
- Explain some key areas assessed with specialized aptitude tests, such as clerical ability, mechanical ability, and artistic ability.
- Describe admission tests and explain their purpose.
- Describe the use of readiness tests.

APTITUDE TESTS

Aptitude can be defined as an innate or acquired ability to be good at something. Aptitude should not be confused with ability, although the two terms are often interchanged. *Abilities* typically refer to one's "present-day" capabilities or the power to perform a specified task, either physical or cognitive; whereas *aptitudes* are about one's "potential" capabilities. One of the best predictors of an individual's potential to do well is whether they have a high aptitude for a certain type of activity. Some people have strong mechanical abilities and thus would do well working as engineers, technicians, or auto mechanics. Other individuals might have high artistic abilities and be best suited to working as interior designers or in the performing arts. Thus, understanding an individual's aptitudes can be very helpful in advising him or her about appropriate training programs or career paths.

Aptitude tests (also referred to as *prognostic tests*) measure a person's performance on selected tasks to predict how that person will perform sometime in the future or in a different situation. The aptitude could be related to school performance, job performance, or some other task or situation. Aptitude tests measure one's (a) *acquired knowledge* (from instruction) and (b) *innate ability* in order to determine one's potential.

Aptitude tests were originally designed to augment intelligence tests. It was found that the results of intelligence tests did not have strong correlations with future success; instead, certain abilities were identified as the largest contributors to success (Sparkman, Maulding, & Roberts, 2012). This led to the construction of aptitude tests that targeted more concrete or practical abilities. These tests were developed particularly for use in career counseling and in the selection and placement of industrial and military personnel. Some tests were designed to assess multiple aptitudes at one time, whereas others focus on a single area. There are a vast number of aptitudes that tests may assess, either singly or in multiples; the most commonly tested are mechanical, clerical, musical, and artistic aptitude. Because these measures attempt to determine how someone will do in the future on the basis of current test results, there must be research that demonstrates the relationship between identified abilities and future success.

The content of aptitude, intelligence, and achievement tests overlaps. For example, vocabulary items are often part of all three types, as are numerical computations and reasoning items. One of the primary differences among these tests is how the tests are used. Aptitude tests and intelligence tests are often used for predictive purposes, whereas achievement tests measure what has been learned and are most often used for descriptive purposes and assessment of growth and change. There is often confusion about the difference between aptitude and achievement tests.

Because of their future orientation, counselors use aptitude tests to help people plan their educational and vocational futures on the basis of what appear to be their abilities and interests. Although aptitude tests are more used by career, rehabilitation, and school counselors, they are applicable to all areas of professional counseling. These measures are frequently used in the selection of entry-level workers and for admissions into educational and vocational programs. The aptitude tests we will discuss in this chapter are standardized, norm-referenced tests that are either group or individually administered. Like achievement tests, some aptitude tests are *batteries* that cover a number of aptitudes, whereas others focus on a *specialized* area. We will present information about aptitude tests using the following categories:

- Multiple-aptitude test batteries
- Specialized aptitude tests
- Admissions tests
- Readiness tests

Multiple-Aptitude Test Batteries

Multiple-aptitude test batteries consist of a series of subtests that assess several aptitudes at one time. The use of multiple-aptitude batteries has a long history in business, industry, and the military. Aptitude batteries do not provide a single score; rather, they yield a profile of subtest scores, one subtest for each aptitude. Thus, they are suitable for comparing an individual's scores across subtests (i.e., intraindividual analysis) to determine his or her high or low aptitudes. Multiple-aptitude batteries measure such abilities as numerical aptitude, mechanical reasoning, and spatial reasoning. Such tests are used primarily for educational and vocational counseling. They permit intraindividual score comparisons, showing the highs and lows of an individual's performance on the various subtests. The

TABLE 10.1 Comparison of Subtests on Multiple-Aptitude Batteries

ASVAB	DAT	GATB	CAPS
Arithmetic reasoning	Abstract reasoning	Clerical perception	Language usage
Auto and shop information	Clerical speed and accuracy	Finger dexterity	Manual speed and dexterity
Electronics information	Language usage	Form perception	Mechanical reasoning
General science	Mechanical reasoning	General learning ability	Numerical ability
Mathematics knowledge	Numerical ability	Manual dexterity	Perceptual speed and accuracy
Mechanical comprehension	Space relations	Motor coordination	Spatial relations
Paragraph comprehension	Spelling	Numerical aptitude	Verbal reasoning
Word knowledge	Verbal reasoning	Spatial aptitude	Word knowledge
		Verbal aptitude	

most well-known multiple-aptitude batteries are the Armed Services Vocational Aptitude Battery (ASVAB); the Differential Aptitude Test, Fifth Edition (DAT); the General Aptitude Test Battery (GATB); and the Career Ability Placement Survey (CAPS). Table 10.1 shows a comparison of the subtests on the ASVAB, DAT, GATB, and CAPS.

ARMED SERVICES VOCATIONAL APTITUDE BATTERY Offered at more than 13,000 schools and taken by more than 900,000 students per year, The ASVAB is the most widely used multiple-aptitude test battery in the world (Powers, 2014). Originally developed in 1968 by the U.S. Department of Defense, it is a norm-referenced test that measures aptitudes for general academic areas and career areas that encompass most civilian and military work. The U.S. military uses the ASVAB as an entrance examination as well as to determine specific job assignments and enlistment bonuses. There are three versions of the ASVAB: the CAT-ASVAB (computer adaptive test), the MET-site ASVAB (mobile examination test site), and the Student ASVAB (also referred to as the ASVAB Career Exploration Program [ASVAB CEP]).

Although the ASVAB was originally developed for use by the military, the ASVAB Career Exploration Program (ASVAB CEP) is used primarily with the civilian population (United States Military Entrance Processing Command (USMEPC), Testing Division, 2005). It is designed specifically to assist high school and postsecondary students with career planning, whether students plan to enter the workforce, military, or other college or vocational programs. The ASVAB CEP provides both web-based and printed materials to help students explore possible career choices. Program materials include (1) the original aptitude battery (the ASVAB), (2) an interest inventory (Find Your Interests [FYI]), and (3) other career planning tools. The main aptitude battery, the ASVAB, consists of eight tests, contains a total of 200 items, and requires 3 hours to complete. The eight tests include General Science, Mathematics, Word Knowledge, Paragraph Comprehension, Electronics Information, Auto and Shop Information, and Mechanical Comprehension. The ASVAB yields standard scores (with a mean of 50 and a standard deviation of 10) and percentiles for the eight tests as well as for three *Career Exploration Scores*: Verbal Skills, Math Skills, and Science and Technical Skills (see the ASVAB summary results sheet in Figure 10.1).

The Military Entrance Score (also known as the Air Force Qualifying Test [AFQT]) is presented on the summary results sheet as a single percentile rank, which is the score that determines a test taker's eligibility for enlistment into the military. Each branch of the military has minimum AFQT score requirements to quality for enlistment: Air Force recruits must score at least 36 points on the AFQT, the Army requires a minimum score of 31, Marine Corp recruits must score at least 32, Navy recruits must score at least 35, and the Coast Guard requires a minimum score of 36. Although there are minimum scores listed, the majority of armed services enlistees score 50 or above (Powers, 2014). Because of ongoing military efforts in various countries, the Army has issued waivers for those individuals who score as low as 26 on the ASVAB (Powers, 2014).

The *FYI* is a 90-item interest inventory developed for the ASVAB program. Based on John Holland's widely accepted theory of career choice, it assesses students' occupational interests in terms of six interest types: realistic, investigative, artistic, social, enterprising, and conventional (i.e., *RIASEC*). Once test takers receive their ASVAB and FYI scores, they can look up potential occupations in the *OCCU-Find*, an online resource from which students can view descriptions of careers and learn how their skills compare with the skills profiles of the occupations they are exploring. OCCU-Find contains information on almost 500 occupations sorted by Holland's RIASEC codes.

A unique feature of the ASVAB is that counselors are able to compare an individual's results on the ASVAB tests and the Career Exploration Scores with the results of other groups of test takers. To do this, the ASVAB summary results sheet provides separate percentile scores for three different groups: same grade/same sex, same grade/opposite sex, and same grade/combined sex. For example, according to the summary results sheet shown in Figure 10.1, the test taker earned a standard score of 55 on Verbal Skills. Results indicate that this score corresponds to the 62nd percentile of performance for 11th-grade females, the 64th percentile for 11th-grade males, and the 63rd percentile for all 11th-grade students (males and females).

Information about the ASVAB's psychometric properties is reported in the counselor manual (United States Military Entrance Processing Command (USMEPC), Testing Division, 2005). The ASVAB CEP has nationally representative norms of approximately 4,700 students in the 10th, 11th, and 12th grades and about 6,000 postsecondary students. The norming sample was poststratification weighted by grade, gender, and the three broad race/ethnic groupings of Black, Hispanic, and Other. (Note that poststratification weights are used when there is an oversample of individuals with certain characteristics, such as age, education, race, etc. With the ASVAB CEP, the unweighted norming sample was oversampled by gender and race/ethnic groups.) The ASVAB appears to have evidence of criterion-related validity in predicting success in educational and training programs and in various civilian and military occupations. It also has strong convergent validity evidence with the ACT, the Differential Aptitude Tests, and the General Aptitude Test Battery. Internal consistency reliability coefficients of the ASVAB composites and subtests range from .88 to .91 and from .69 to .88, respectively. In order to further your understanding of the ASVAB, complete Exercise 10.1, and respond to the exercise questions. Consider all of the information provided within the context of your learning experience related to assessment.

DIFFERENTIAL APTITUDE TESTS FOR PERSONNEL AND CAREER ASSESSMENT The Differential Aptitude Tests for Personnel and Career Assessment (DAT for PCA) are a series of tests

Exercise 10.1
ASVAB: Halle

You are a school counselor working in at a local high school. Halle, an 11th-grade student, recently received her ASVAB summary results sheet. She is confused by her scores, particularly the three separate sets of percentile scores. She asks you to help her understand her test scores.

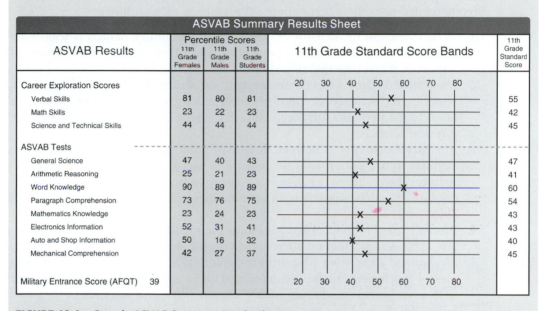

ASVAB Summary Results Sheet						
ASVAB Results	**Percentile Scores**			**11th Grade Standard Score Bands**		11th Grade Standard Score
	11th Grade Females	11th Grade Males	11th Grade Students			
Career Exploration Scores						
Verbal Skills	81	80	81			55
Math Skills	23	22	23			42
Science and Technical Skills	44	44	44			45
ASVAB Tests						
General Science	47	40	43			47
Arithmetic Reasoning	25	21	23			41
Word Knowledge	90	89	89			60
Paragraph Comprehension	73	76	75			54
Mathematics Knowledge	23	24	23			43
Electronics Information	52	31	41			43
Auto and Shop Information	50	16	32			40
Mechanical Comprehension	42	27	37			45
Military Entrance Score (AFQT)	39					

FIGURE 10.1 Sample ASVAB Summary Results sheet.

Source: ASVAB Career Exploration Program: Counselor Manual (United States Military Entrance Processing Command (USMEPC), Testing Division, 2005).

1. Interpret Halle's Career Exploration percentile ranks based on the three norm groups: 11th-grade females, 11th-grade males, and 11th-grade students.
2. Interpret her standard scores on the ASVAB tests.
3. From your interpretation of Halle's test results, how would you describe any relative strengths or weaknesses she may have?
4. Halle's standard score on the ASVAB Auto and Shop Information test was 40.

a. According to the Summary Results Sheet, what is the percentile rank for this score for 11th-grade females?
b. What is the percentile rank for this score for 11th-grade males?
c. Why do you think there is such a large difference in percentile scores between these two groups on this test?

designed to measure an individual's ability to learn or to succeed in a number of areas. The test is suitable for group administration and is used primarily for educational and career counseling as well as for employee selection. Organizations from various types of industries and occupations use the DAT for PCA to evaluate a job applicant's strengths and weaknesses and to improve the accuracy and efficiency of their hiring decisions. The DAT for PCA can be used with students in grades 7 through 12 and adults, takes about 2.5 hours to administer, and can be hand or computer scored. Test results are reported in percentile ranks, stanines, and scaled scores. The DAT yields scores in eight subtests, which are directly related to various occupations. The subtests are as follows:

1. *Verbal Reasoning* Measures general cognitive ability, which is useful for placing employees in professional, managerial, and other positions of responsibility that require higher-order thinking skills.
2. *Numerical Ability* Tests the understanding of numerical relationships and facility in handling numerical concepts. This subtest is a good predictor of job success in such fields as mathematics, physics, chemistry, engineering, and other fields related to the physical sciences.
3. *Abstract Reasoning* A nonverbal measure of the ability to perceive relationships in abstract figure patterns. This measure is useful for job selection when a position requires the ability to perceive relationships among things rather than among words or numbers, such as positions in mathematics, computer programming, drafting, and automobile repair.
4. *Clerical Speed and Accuracy* Measures the speed of response in a simple perceptual task. This is important for such clerical duties as filing and coding.
5. *Mechanical Reasoning* Measures the ability to understand basic mechanical principles of machinery, tools, and motion. This is useful in selection decisions for jobs such as carpenter, mechanic, maintenance worker, and assembler.
6. *Space Relations* Measures the ability to visualize a three-dimensional object from a two-dimensional pattern. This ability is important in fields such as drafting, clothing design, architecture, art, die making, decorating, carpentry, and dentistry.
7. *Spelling* Measures an applicant's ability to spell common English words.
8. *Language Usage* Measures the ability to detect errors in grammar, punctuation, and capitalization.

Both the Language Usage and Spelling subtests provide a good estimate of the ability to distinguish correct from incorrect English usage. The Verbal Reasoning and Numerical Ability subtest scores are combined to create a composite index of scholastic aptitude.

Overall, the DAT for PCA is useful in exploring an individual's academic and vocational possibilities. The test may also be used for the early identification of students with superior intellectual promise. Test limitations relate to the lack of independence of some of the scales and the separate gender norms. Both computerized-scoring services and hand-scoring stencils are available for the test. Figure 10.2 presents an example of a profile from the DAT. A Career Interest Inventory had been available with the DAT for PCA but was discontinued as of September 2014.

General Aptitude Test Battery (GATB). The General Aptitude Test Battery (GATB) is one of the oldest general aptitude tests still used today. Developed by the U.S. Employment Service (USES; Dvorak, 1947), the GATB was originally designed for use by employment

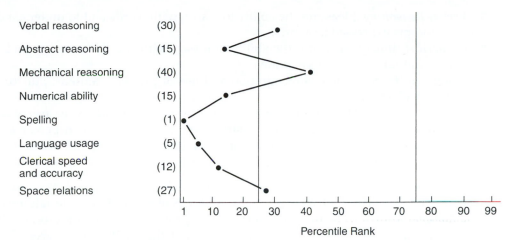

FIGURE 10.2   Profile from the Differential Aptitude Tests.

counselors in state employment services offices to match job applicants with potential employers in the private and public sectors. Although it is still used in employment offices, the instrument has become popular in both government and private organizations as a method to screen large numbers of job applicants, as well as in high schools for career counseling. The GATB is a paper-and-pencil test, can be administered to students from grades 9 through 12 and adults, and takes approximately 2.5 hours to complete. The battery consists of 12 separately timed subtests, which make up nine aptitude scores:

1. *Verbal Aptitude* Vocabulary
2. *Numerical Aptitude* Computation, Arithmetic Reasoning
3. *Spatial Aptitude* Three-Dimensional Space
4. *Form Perception* Tool Matching, Form Matching
5. *Clerical Perception* Name Comparison
6. *Motor Coordination* Mark Making
7. *Finger Dexterity* Assemble, Disassemble
8. *Manual Dexterity* Place, Turn
9. *General Learning Ability* Vocabulary, Arithmetic Reasoning, Three-Dimensional Space

CAREER ABILITY PLACEMENT SURVEY The CAPS is a multiple-aptitude test battery designed to measure vocationally relevant abilities. It is part of the COPSystem Career Measurement Package, which is a comprehensive system that assesses an individual's interests, abilities, and values related to career choice (see Chapter 11). The CAPS is the ability measure that can be used for matching students' ability with occupational requirements, educational or training program selection, curriculum evaluation, career assessment, or employee evaluation. The battery takes 50 minutes to complete and can be used with middle through high school students, college students, and adults. The CAPS measures eight ability dimensions:

1. *Mechanical Reasoning* Measures understanding of mechanical principals and devices and the laws of physics.
2. *Spatial Relations* Measures the ability to think and visualize in three dimensions.

3. *Verbal Reasoning* Measures the ability to reason with words and to understand and use concepts expressed in words.
4. *Numerical Ability* Measures the ability to reason with and use numbers and work with quantitative materials and ideas.
5. *Language Usage* Measures recognition and use of proper grammar, punctuation, and capitalization.
6. *Word Knowledge* Measures understanding of the meaning and precise use of words.
7. *Perceptual Speed and Accuracy* Measures how well a person can perceive small details rapidly and accurately within a mass of letters, numbers, and symbols.
8. *Manual Speed and Dexterity* Measures rapid and accurate hand movements.

There are self-scoring and machine-scoring forms for the test, as well as a computerized scoring and reporting software program. All types of supportive materials are available for the counselor and client: a self-interpretation profile sheet and guide, occupational cluster charts, the COPSystem Career Briefs Kit, and the COPSystem Career Cluster Booklet Kits, in addition to an examiner's manual, tapes for administration, and visuals for orientation.

Specialized Aptitude Tests

Unlike the multiple-aptitude batteries, specialized aptitude tests typically measure a single aptitude. Certain aptitudes (such as clerical abilities, motor dexterity, and artistic talents) are considered to be too specialized to justify inclusion in multiple-aptitude batteries, yet they are often considered vital to a certain job or task (Fletcher-Janzen & Reynolds, 2014). In response to this limitation, *specialized aptitude tests* were designed to measure these specific abilities. In contrast to aptitude test batteries that assess several aptitudes, specialized aptitude tests typically measure a single ability. See Figure 10.3 for a depiction of specialized ability test areas. The following is a description of some common specialized aptitude test categories.

CLERICAL ABILITY Clerical ability refers to the skills needed for office and clerical duties. Individuals with high clerical aptitude can process information quickly, are detail oriented, and may be successful as bank tellers, administrative assistants, data processors, or cashiers. Abilities related to clerical aptitude include the following:

- *Calculation* Ability to perform a series of simple arithmetic calculations.
- *Checking* Ability to quickly and accurately check verbal and numerical information (e.g., names, addresses, code numbers, telephone numbers) against a target.
- *Coding* Ability to copy letter- and number-like symbols according to a specified pattern.
- *Filing* Ability to identify the correct location for a set of named files.
- *Keyboarding* Ability to quickly and accurately type on a computer keyboard.
- *Numerical Ability* Ability to use numbers efficiently in clerical and administrative contexts.
- *Verbal Reasoning* Includes spelling, grammar, understanding analogies, and following instructions.

There are several instruments commercially available to assess clerical ability. The descriptions of these tests reveal that they are similar to some of the subtests of the group intelligence tests and the multiple-aptitude test batteries. Although the tests have been around for decades, they remain valid measures for predicting performance (Whetzel et al., 2011). The following are examples of several well-known clerical ability tests.

General Clerical Test-Revised. The *General Clerical Test-Revised* (GTC-R) was developed to assess one's ability to succeed in a position requiring clerical skills. It can be either group or individually administered and takes approximately 1 hour. The instrument consists of three subtests: Clerical, Numerical, and Verbal. The Clerical subtest assesses speed and accuracy in performing perceptual tasks (checking and alphabetizing) that involve attention to detail. The Numerical subtest assesses math computation, numerical error location, and math reasoning. The Verbal subtest evaluates spelling, reading comprehension, vocabulary, and grammar.

Minnesota Clerical Test. The *Minnesota Clerical Test* (MCT) was developed to assist employers in selecting individuals to fill detail-oriented jobs, especially positions that require attention to number and letter details (such as bank tellers, receptionists, cashiers, and administrative assistants). The instrument consists of two parts: number comparison and name comparison. There are 200 pairs of numbers and 200 pairs of names, and in a specified amount of time the examinee must correctly select the pairs with elements that are identical.

Clerical Abilities Battery. The *Clerical Abilities Battery* (CAB) was developed in cooperation with General Motors Corporation and assesses skills most commonly needed for administrative tasks. The battery is comprised of seven tests: Filing, Copying Information, Comparing Information, Using Tables, Proofreading, Basic Math Skills, and Numerical Reasoning. The tests can be administered in any combination to reflect the skills needed for a particular position or task.

MECHANICAL ABILITY Mechanical ability is the capacity to learn about mechanical objects. It is reflected in familiarity with everyday physical objects, tools, devices, and home repairs, as well as spatial reasoning (i.e., the ability to visualize a three-dimensional object from a two-dimensional pattern). Individuals with strong mechanical aptitude may be successful working as engineers, mechanics, millwrights, machine operators, tool setters, and tradespersons, to name a few. The following are examples of mechanical ability tests.

Bennett Mechanical Comprehension Test. A well-known mechanic aptitude test is the Bennett Mechanical Comprehension Test (BMCT; Bennett, 1980). This test has been used for over 60 years to select individuals for a wide variety of civilian and military occupations as well as training programs requiring mechanical aptitude. It focuses on spatial perception and tool knowledge and is well suited for assessing individuals for jobs requiring the operation and repair of mechanical devices. It has 68 multiple-choice items focusing on the application of physical and mechanical principles in practical situations. Each item portrays a drawing illustrating an object that reflects the concepts of force, energy, density, velocity, and so on. The test is one of the most widely used mechanical aptitude tests, and a considerable amount of research has supported the technical quality of this instrument. However, the test is not without its concerns. For example, some items portray mechanical concepts involving objects that females may be less familiar with than males. Another concern involves the norm group. Although the test was renormed in 2005 and included groups based on the industries and occupations in which the test is most frequently used (i.e., auto mechanic, engineer, installation/maintenance/repair, industrial/technical, skilled tradesperson, transportation/equipment operator), separate norming data for males, females, and minorities was not reported.

FIGURE 10.3   Various Specialized Ability Test Areas.

Mechanical Aptitude Test. The *Mechanical Aptitude Test* (MAT 3-C) is a quick evaluation of a person's ability to learn production and maintenance job activities. The test was designed specifically to measure an individual's potential to be successful in apprenticeship or trainee programs for maintenance mechanics, industrial machinery mechanics, millwrights, machine operators, and tool setters. The test contains 36 multiple-choice items and takes approximately 20 minutes to complete.

Wiesen Test of Mechanical Aptitude. The *Wiesen Test of Mechanical Aptitude* (WTMA) is designed for selecting entry-level personnel for jobs involving the operation, maintenance, and repair of mechanical equipment of various types. The WTMA measures basic ability rather than formal schooling or job experience. It is a 60-item paper-and-pencil test that takes approximately 30 minutes to complete. Each test item uses a simple drawing of everyday objects to illustrate a mechanical principle or fact (e.g., basic machines, movement, gravity or center of gravity, basic electricity or electronics, transfer of heat, basic physical properties). Test items are brief and involve the function and/or use, size, weight, shape, and appearance of common physical objects, tools, and devices. The WTMA is appropriate for individuals aged 18 and older.

PSYCHOMOTOR ABILITY Psychomotor ability refers to one's capacity to perform body motor movements (e.g., movement of fingers, hands, legs, body) with precision, coordination, or strength. Psychomotor tests were among the first measures of special abilities to be constructed, and many psychomotor tests were developed during the 1920s and 1930s to predict performance in certain jobs or trades. Psychomotor abilities are important to occupations that involve working with things and objects (e.g., building, repairing, assembling, organizing, writing). Examples of psychomotor abilities include the following:

- *Arm-Hand Steadiness* Ability to keep your hand and arm steady while moving your arm or holding your arm in one position.

- *Finger Dexterity* Ability to make precisely coordinated movements of the fingers to grasp, manipulate, or assemble very small objects.
- *Manual Dexterity* Ability to make precisely coordinated movements with your hand, with your hand and arm, or with two hands to grasp, manipulate, or assemble objects.
- *Multilimb Coordination* Ability to coordinate two or more limbs while standing, sitting, or lying down.
- *Static Strength* Ability to exert muscular force to move, push, lift, or pull a heavy or immobile object.
- *Visual-Motor Skills (Eye-Hand Coordination)* Ability to coordinate vision with the movements of the body.

Psychomotor tests may require test takers to engage in various tasks, such as moving arms and legs in coordination, pulling a lever, placing pins into holes, or using a screwdriver, to name just a few. The following are a few examples of psychomotor tests.

Bennett Hand Tool Dexterity Test. This test assesses whether an individual has the basic skills necessary for any job requiring hand tools, such as aircraft or automobile mechanics, machine adjusters, maintenance mechanics, and assembly line workers. The test requires examinees to use wrenches and screwdrivers to take apart 12 assemblies of nuts, bolts, and washers from a wooden frame and then reassemble them (see Figure 10.4). The test is recommended for industrial applicants and employees, students in training programs, and adults in vocational training.

Purdue Pegboard Test. The Purdue Pegboard Test is a dexterity test designed to aid in the selection of employees for industrial jobs that require fine and gross motor dexterity and coordination, such as assembly, packing, operation of certain machines, and other manual jobs. It measures gross movements of hands, fingers, and arms, as well as fingertip dexterity. The first part of the test requires test takers to put pins into holes first with the

FIGURE 10.4 The Bennett Hand Tool Dexterity Test.

right hand, then with the left hand, and finally with both hands. Five separate scores can be obtained with the Purdue Pegboard Test: (1) right hand, (2) left hand, (3) both hands, (4) right plus left plus both hands (R + L + B), and (5) assembly. The test takes about 10 minutes to administer.

The Purdue Pegboard Test is also used to assess and identify issues related to functional impairment in fine and gross motor dexterity. For example, the Purdue Pegboard Test has been shown to be a valid tool for identifying functional impairment due to carpal tunnel syndrome (Amirjani, Ashworth, Olson, Morhart, & Chan, 2011). As another example, the Pegboard has been used to evaluate treatment effects on individuals diagnosed with Parkinson's disease (Eggers, Fink, & Nowak, 2010).

Bruininks–Oseretsky Test of Motor Proficiency, Second Edition. The *Bruininks–Oseretsky Test of Motor Proficiency, Second Edition* (BOT-2) measures motor skills in individuals ranging from 4 to 21 years of age. The test assesses fine motor skills, manual dexterity, coordination, balance, and strength and agility. The test can be used for making decisions about educational or vocational placement, developing and evaluating motor training programs, screening as part of in-depth psychological evaluations, and assessing neurological development. The BOT-2 consists of eight subtests that require examinees to do a variety of tasks:

1. *Fine Motor Precision* Cutting out a circle, connecting dots
2. *Fine Motor Integration* Copying a star, copying a square
3. *Manual Dexterity* Transferring pennies, sorting cards, stringing blocks
4. *Bilateral Coordination* Tapping feet alternately while making circles with index fingers; jumping jacks
5. *Balance* Standing on one leg and holding position for 10 seconds, walking forward on a line
6. *Running Speed Agility* Running from a start line to an end line and returning
7. *Upper-Limb Coordination* Throwing a ball at a target, catching a tossed ball
8. *Strength* Standing long jump, sit-ups

In some cases, the BOT-2 is used to determine the severity of movement disorders. For example, the BOT-2 is one of the primary tools used to identify developmental coordination disorder. This disorder is associated with difficulty in learning and performing motor activities (Cermak, Gubbay, & Larkin, 2002). However, the BOT-2 has not correlated well with other measures of motor skills functioning (Spironello, Hay, Missiuna, Faught, & Cairney, 2010). Thus, counselors are cautioned to use multiple measures across multiple settings to more accurately identify motor issues.

ARTISTIC ABILITY The concept of artistic ability often suggests an ability to draw and paint or appreciate great art. However, because what is considered great art varies from person to person and from culture to culture, the criteria for measuring artistic ability is difficult to determine (Aiken & Groth-Marnat, 2006). A number of tests have been published that measure artistic ability; however, most are old and are no longer commercially available. Some artistic tests measure art appreciation (i.e., judgment, perception), whereas others assess artistic performance or knowledge of art. One of the most popular tests of art appreciation is the *Meier–Seashore Art Judgment Test* (Meier, 1940), which measures one's ability to discern between better and worse artistic works. The test consists of pairs of pictures that differ in one feature. One of the pictures is "real" (i.e., corresponds to an original work of art), and the other represents a simple variation of the original. Test takers are asked to identify the better (original) picture. A related artistic ability test is the *Meier Art Test of Aesthetic Perception*. This test presents four versions of the same work—each differing in terms of proportion, unity, form, or design—and test takers are asked to rank each set in order of merit. The *Graves Design Judgment Test* measures artistic ability by presenting test takers with 90 sets of two- or three-dimensional designs that vary in unity, balance, symmetry, or other aspects of aesthetic order. Test takers are then asked to select the best in each set.

MUSICAL ABILITY Most musical ability tests assess the skills that musicians should possess, such as the capacity to discriminate pitch, loudness, tempo, timbre, and rhythm. Tests are available that purport to measure musical abilities, but all suffer from poor validity and reliability. Probably the oldest and most famous musical ability test is the *Seashore Measures of Musical Talents*. The test takes about 1 hour of testing time and can be administered to students from grade 4 through grade 12 and adults. The test presents on tape six subtests measuring dimensions of auditory discrimination: pitch, loudness, time, timbre, rhythm, and tonal memory. Other tests that purport to measure musical aptitude include the *Kwalwasser Music Talent Test*, which is used with fourth-grade to college-age students. The 50-item test presents test takers with three-tone patterns that are repeated with variations in pitch, tone, rhythm, or loudness. Another instrument is the *Musical Aptitude Profile* (MAP), which consists of seven components: tonal imagery (melody and harmony), rhythm imagery (tempo and meter), and musical sensitivity (phrasing, balance, and style). The test takes about 3.5 hours to administer. Unfortunately, research has been limited on the value of these tests, and many tests of musical aptitude have been criticized for a lack of ecological validity. In other words, the tests do not approximate a realistic experience by which musical aptitude could be accurately measured (Karma, 2007). Music teachers tend to rely more on their own clinical judgment and look for individual performance of music as it is written.

OTHER ABILITIES The categories of abilities that we discussed in this section (e.g., clerical, mechanical, artistic, psychomotor, musical aptitude) represent only a few of the many specialized aptitude tests. Tests are available to assess numerous other specific areas, such as food services, industrial skills, legal skills, medical office, retail sales, transcription, and many, many more. Furthermore, businesses can have aptitude tests custom made to identify qualified applicants for specialized jobs.

Admissions Tests

predict performance

Most academic programs use aptitude test scores as part of their admissions requirements. Admissions tests (sometimes referred to as *entrance exams* or *academic ability tests*) are designed to predict performance in a particular educational program. Used in combination with other relevant information (e.g., high school grade point average, teacher recommendations), they are a general indicator of future academic success. Thus, students who score high on admissions tests would most likely perform better in college than those who do not score high.

Most admissions tests assess some combination of verbal, quantitative, writing, and analytical reasoning skills or discipline-specific knowledge. The tests aim to measure the most relevant skills and knowledge for mastering a particular discipline. A key psychometric aspect of admissions tests is predictive validity, which is typically evaluated by correlating test scores with a measure of academic performance, such as first-year grade point average (GPA), graduate GPA, degree attainment, qualifying or comprehensive examination scores, research productivity, research citation counts, licensing examination performance, or faculty evaluations of students. Although the general verbal and quantitative scales are effective predictors of academic success, the strongest predictor of success is high school GPA (Fu, 2012).

One concern in admissions tests concerns bias against certain groups, including racial, ethnic, and gender groups. Overall and across tests, research has found that average test scores do not differ by race or ethnic group but do tend to underpredict the performance of women in college settings (Kuncel & Hezlett, 2007). Fu (2012) conducted research on a sample of approximately 33,000 undergraduate and graduate students from the United States and abroad. Overall, Fu confirmed that traditional admission tests were good predictors of success for all students. In fact, Fu found that scores on the SAT had a high correlation with first-year GPA for international undergraduate students.

We will present information about some prominent admissions tests, including the SAT, ACT, and others.

SAT Nearly every college in America accepts the SAT (formerly called the Scholastic Aptitude Test and the Scholastic Achievement Test) as a part of its admissions process. Published by the College Board, millions of college- and university-bound high school students take the SAT each year. The SAT consists of two tests: the Reasoning Test and Subject Tests. The *SAT Reasoning Test* assesses the critical thinking skills needed for college and has three sections: mathematics, critical reading, and writing (see Table 10.2). The test takes 3 hours and 45 minutes to complete, including an unscored 25-minute experimental section (used for development of future test questions). It includes several different item types, including multiple-choice questions, student-produced responses (grid-ins), and a student-produced essay. The *SAT Subject Tests* are optional tests designed to measure knowledge in specific subject areas, such as biology, chemistry, literature, various languages, and history. Many colleges use the subject tests for admission and course placement or to advise students about course selection. Some colleges specify the subject tests required for admission, whereas others allow applicants to choose which

TABLE 10.2 SAT Reasoning Tests

Section	Content	Item Types	Time
Critical Reading	Reading comprehension, sentence completion, paragraph-length critical reading	Multiple choice	70 minutes
Mathematics	Number and operations; algebra and functions; geometry; statistics, probability, and data analysis	Multiple choice, grid-ins	70 minutes
Writing	Grammar, usage, and word choice	Multiple choice, essay	60 minutes
Experimental	Critical reading, mathematics, or writing	Any	25 minutes

tests to take. Scores on the SAT Reasoning Test and SAT Subject Tests range from 200 to 800, with a mean of 500 and a standard deviation of 100. Percentiles are also given to provide comparisons among test takers' scores.

Research studies have looked at the SAT's ability to predict college success (i.e., predictive validity) by examining the relationship between test scores and first-year college GPA (FYGPA). A study sanctioned by the College Board (Kobrin, Patterson, Shaw, Mattern, & Barbuti, 2008) found correlation coefficients of .26, .29, and .33 between FYGPA and the scores on the three SAT Reasoning Test sections—Mathematics, Critical Reading, and Writing, respectively. They also found a correlation of .46 between FYGPA and combined SAT score and high school GPA (HSGPA), indicating that colleges should use both HSGPA and SAT scores to make the best predictions of student success. Fu (2012) confirmed these findings and demonstrated the utility of the SAT in predicting success for international students. However, because there is a degree of error in the correlation between FYPGA and SAT scores, it is important to consider a combination of information sources when making admission decisions.

PRELIMINARY SAT/NATIONAL MERIT SCHOLARSHIP QUALIFYING TEST The *Preliminary SAT/ National Merit Scholarship Qualifying Test* (PSAT/NMSQT) is a standardized test that provides high school students firsthand practice for the SAT Reasoning Test. It also gives students a chance to enter National Merit Scholarship Corporation (NMSC) scholarship programs. The PSAT/NMSQT measures critical reading skills, math problem-solving skills, and writing skills. It provides students with feedback on their strengths and weaknesses in skills necessary for college study, helps students prepare for the SAT, and enables students to enter the competition for scholarships from the National Merit Scholarship Corporation.

THE ACT INFORMATION SYSTEM The ACT program is a comprehensive system for collecting and reporting information about students planning to enter college or university. It consists of four major components: the Tests of Educational Development, the Student Profile section, the Course/Grade Information section, and the UNIACT Interest Inventory. A description of each component follows.

- The *Tests of Educational Development* are multiple-choice tests designed to assess students' general educational development and their ability to complete college-level work. Like the SAT, the ACT Tests of Educational Development can be taken by students in the 11th or 12th grades. The tests cover four skill areas: English, mathematics, reading, and science. The optional Writing Test is a 30-minute essay test that measures students' writing skills in English. The tests emphasize reasoning, analysis, problem solving, and the integration of learning from various sources, as well as the application of these proficiencies to the kinds of tasks that college students are expected to perform.
- The *Course/Grade Information* section provides 30 self-reported high school grades in the areas of English, mathematics, natural sciences, social studies, language, and the arts. The courses include those that usually form a college's core preparatory curriculum and are frequently required for admission to college.
- The *Student Profile* section contains information reported by students when they register for the ACT. This information includes the following categories: admissions or

enrollment information; educational plans, interests, and needs; special educational needs, interests, and goals; college extracurricular plans; financial aid; demographic background information; factors influencing college choice; characteristics of high school; high school extracurricular activities; and out-of-class accomplishments.

- The *UNIACT Interest Inventory* is a 72-item survey that provides six scores that parallel John Holland's six interest and occupational types. The main purpose of the interest inventory is to help students identify majors congruent with their interests.

THE PLAN PROGRAM The PLAN assessment is part of the ACT program. It is considered a "pre-ACT" test, similar to the PSAT, and is a predictor of success on the ACT. Designed to be taken by 10th graders, the PLAN consists of four academic achievement tests in English, mathematics, reading, and science. Other components of the PLAN program include (a) students' needs assessment, (b) high school course and grade information, (c) the *UNIACT Interest Inventory*, and (d) the *Educational Opportunity Services* (EOS), which links students with college and scholarship information based on their PLAN results.

GRADUATE RECORD EXAMINATIONS The GRE is taken by individuals applying to graduate schools. Graduate program admissions are usually based on the GRE score, undergraduate grade point average, and other requirements specific to that graduate program. The GRE consists of two tests: the General Test and Subject Tests. The GRE General Test measures verbal reasoning, quantitative reasoning, critical thinking, and analytical writing skills that are not related to any specific field of study. The Subject Tests gauge undergraduate achievement in specific fields of study (e.g., biochemistry, biology, and chemistry).

The GRE General Test has both computer-based and paper-based formats; the Subject Tests only offer a paper-based format. The computer version is an *adaptive test*. This means that the questions given to the test taker are dependent partially on the answers the test taker has provided to previous questions. The test begins with questions of middle difficulty. As the individual answers each question, the computer scores that question and uses that information to determine which question is presented next. If the test taker answers an item correctly, then an item with increased difficulty will be presented next. If the test taker responds incorrectly, then a less difficult item will be presented next.

Reliability coefficients, as measured by the KR 20 formula, are in the high .80s to .90s for both the GRE General Test and the Subject Tests. In terms of predictive validity evidence, the GRE General Test was positively correlated with FYGPA (r = low .40s; Kuncel & Hezlett, 2007). The Subject Tests tend to be better predictors of first-year GPA for specific departments than either the verbal or quantitative scales of the General Test. Again, because the correlations between GRE and FYGPA contain a degree of error, many graduate schools have developed an array of admission criteria that includes the GRE rather than making decisions based on GRE alone.

MILLER ANALOGIES TEST The *Miller Analogies Test (MAT)* is another admissions exam taken by individuals applying to graduate schools. The MAT is a 50-item, group-administered test consisting of 100 multiple-choice analogy items. The content for the analogies comes from literature, social sciences, chemistry, physics, mathematics, and general information. In each MAT analogy item, one term is missing and has been replaced with four answer options, only one of which correctly completes the analogy. The terms in most of the MAT analogy items are words, but in some cases they may be numbers, symbols, or word parts. For example:

PLANE : AIR :: CAR : (a. submarine, b. fish, c. land, d. pilot)

The first step in solving a MAT analogy is to decide which two of the three given terms form a complete pair. In the example, this could either be "PLANE is related to AIR" (the first term is related to the second term) or "PLANE is related to CAR" (the first term is related to the third term). On the MAT, it will never be "PLANE is related to (a. submarine, b. fish, c. water, d. pilot)"; the first term is never related to the fourth term.

OTHER ADMISSIONS TESTS Other widely used admission tests in higher education include the *Medical College Admissions Test* (MCAT), *Law School Admissions Test* (LSAT), and the *Graduate Management Admissions Test* (GMAT). The most important consideration in the use of these tests is whether the validity of the test for a particular program has been established, especially through studies at a local college or university.

Readiness Tests

The term *readiness test* is applied to aptitude tests used to predict success when a child enters school. School readiness has historically been defined as readiness to learn specific material and be successful in a typical school context (Bracken & Nagle, 2007). Schools frequently use readiness tests to judge whether children are "ready" for kindergarten or the first grade. These tests are similar to admissions tests, because they measure current knowledge and skills in order to forecast future academic performance; the distinction is that the term *readiness test* is used specifically in reference to tests for young children.

In most states, eligibility to enroll in kindergarten begins at age 5.1. Although children may meet this specific age requirement, they vary widely in how well prepared they are for kindergarten. For example, some children have considerable prekindergarten education experiences and are able to recognize letters, numbers, and shapes, whereas other children may have fewer abilities related to kindergarten success. Readiness tests are used to determine the extent to which children have mastered the underlying skills deemed necessary for school learning. Most readiness tests assess facets of the following five domains (Boan, Aydlett, & Multunas, 2007, p. 52):

- *Physical* Focuses on impairments in sensory functions, motor skills, illnesses or medical conditions, growth, and overall well-being
- *Social and Emotional* Involves age-appropriate social skills, psychological well-being, self-perceptions, and interpersonal interactions
- *Learning* Includes attention, curiosity, and enthusiasm for learning
- *Language* Involves verbal communication skills, nonverbal communication skills, and early literacy skills
- *Cognition and General Knowledge* Emphasizes problem-solving skills, abstract reasoning, early mathematical skills, and overall fund of knowledge

The majority of schools in the United States administer readiness tests (Csapó, Molnár, & Nagy, 2014). Children who are deemed "not ready" often wait another year before starting school. Readiness tests can be used to develop curricula and to establish individualized instruction. Most readiness tests are designed to assess areas related to school tasks, such as general knowledge, language, and health and physical functioning. Research finds the predictive validity of these tests to be extremely limited; thus, their use in making decisions about kindergarten enrollment is highly questionable. Often, the concept of readiness is impacted more by parental factors than academic readiness. For example, socioeconomic adversity, parental demoralization, and support for learning have been shown to impact readiness (Okado, Bierman, & Welsh, 2014). Thus, there is a potential for cultural bias when assessing school readiness. We caution counselors and other helping professionals in the use of such assessments without a range of other substantial information to support the findings. Examples of school readiness tests include the Kaufman Survey of Early Academic and Language Skills (K-SEALS), the Kindergarten Readiness Test (KRT), the School Readiness Test (SRT), the Metropolitan Readiness Tests, and the Bracken School Readiness Assessment (BSRA-3).

There have been several concerns cited about using readiness tests for making important decisions about children's lives. Although most researchers, educators, and policymakers agree on the dimensions essential to school readiness (e.g., physical development; emotional and social development; learning, language, and cognition; general knowledge), there is some debate as to whether these dimensions are accurate or complete (Meisels, 1999). Also, assessing preschool-age children is challenging because of their rapid and uneven development, which can be greatly impacted by environmental factors (Saluja, Scott-Little, & Clifford, 2000). Furthermore, typical standardized paper-and-pencil tests suitable for older children are not appropriate for children entering school (Shepard, Kagan, & Wurtz, 1998).

Summary

Aptitude tests measure an individual's performance on selected tasks to predict how that person will perform sometime in the future or in a different situation. The aptitude could involve school performance, job performance, or some other task or situation. Aptitude tests measure both acquired knowledge and innate ability in order to determine one's potential. Multiple-aptitude batteries are used in educational and business contexts, as well as with career guidance systems. The most widely used batteries are the Armed Services Vocational Aptitude Battery, the General Aptitude Test Battery, and the Differential Aptitude Test battery.

Specialized aptitude tests are designed to measure the ability to acquire proficiency in a specific area of activity, such as art or music. Mechanical and clerical aptitude tests have been used by vocational education and business and industry personnel to counsel, evaluate, classify, and place test takers. Both multifactor and special aptitude tests are designed to help the test takers gain a better understanding of their own special abilities.

Questions for Discussion

1. What are the major multiple-aptitude test batteries? When should they be used, and why? What are the advantages and disadvantages of this type of test?
2. When would you use specialized aptitude tests, and why? What are the advantages and disadvantages of such tests?
3. Some school districts require that all students be given an aptitude battery at some time during their 4 years of high school. Do you agree or disagree with this requirement? Why?
4. Do you feel that there can be pencil-and-paper aptitude tests to measure aptitudes in art, music, and mechanics? Why or why not?

Suggested Activities

1. Write a critique of a widely used multiple-aptitude test battery or specialized aptitude test.
2. Interview counselors who use aptitude tests—employment counselors, career counselors, and school counselors—and find out what tests they use and why. Report your findings to the class.
3. Take a multiple-aptitude test battery or specialized aptitude test, and write a report detailing the results and your reaction to the test.
4. Make an annotated bibliography of aptitude tests you would use in your field.
5. Albert is a 23-year-old male who dropped out of school in the 10th grade. He is enrolled in a high school equivalency program at a local community college sponsored by the Private Industry Council. He has had numerous jobs in the food services industry but has not been able to hold on to them. He has a wife and three children and now realizes he needs further training and education to support his family. He participated in

vocational assessment and was administered the DAT, with the following results:

Scale	Percentile
Verbal Reasoning	40%
Numerical Reasoning	55%
Abstract Reasoning	20%
Mechanical Reasoning	55%
Space Relations	30%
Spelling	3%
Language Usage	5%
Perceptual Speed and Accuracy	45%

a. How would you characterize Albert's aptitudes?
b. What additional information about Albert would you like to have?
c. If you were a counselor, what educational and vocational directions would you encourage Albert to explore?

References

Ackerman, D., & Barnett, W. S. (2005). *Prepared for kindergarten: What does "readiness" mean?* New Brunswick, NJ: National Institute for Early Education Research, Rutgers University.

Aiken, L. A., & Groth-Marnat, G. (2006). *Psychological testing and assessment* (12th ed.). Boston, MA: Pearson.

Amirjani, N., Ashworth, N. L., Olson, J. L., Morhart, M., & Chan, K. M. (2011). Validity and reliability of the Purdue Pegboard Test in carpal tunnel syndrome. *Muscle & Nerve, 43*(2), 171–177. doi: 10.1002/mus.21856

Bennett, G. K. (1980). *Test of mechanical comprehension.* New York, NY: The Psychological Corporation.

Boan, C., Aydlett, L. A., & Multunas, N. (2007). Early childhood screening and readiness assessment. In B. A. Bracken & R. J. Nagle (Eds.), *Psychoeducational assessment of preschool children* (4th ed., pp. 49–67). Mahwah, NJ: Lawrence Erlbaum Associates.

Bracken, B. A., & Nagle, R. J. (Eds.). (2007). *Psychoeducational assessment of preschool children* (4th ed.). Mahwah, NJ: Lawrence Erlbaum Associates.

Cermak, S. A., Gubbay, S. S., & Larkin, D. (2002). What is developmental coordination disorder? In S. A.

Cermak & D. Larkin (Eds.), *Developmental coordination disorder* (pp. 1–22). Albany, NY: Delmar.

Csapó, B., Molnár, G., & Nagy, J. (2014). Computer-based assessment of school readiness and early reasoning. *Journal of Educational Psychology, 106*(3), 639–650.

Dvorak, B. J. (1947). New United States employment service general aptitude test battery. *Journal of Applied Psychology, 31*, 372–376.

Eggers, C., Fink, G., & Nowak, D. (2010). Theta burst stimulation over the primary motor cortex does not induce cortical plasticity in Parkinson's disease. *Journal of Neurology, 257*(10), 1669–1674. doi: 10.1007/s00415-010-5597-1

Fletcher-Janzen, C. R., & Reynolds, E. (2014). *Encyclopedia of special education: A reference for the education of children, adolescents, and adults with disabilities and other exceptional individuals* (Vol. 1). Hoboken, NJ: John Wiley & Sons.

Fu, Y. (2012). The effectiveness of traditional admissions criteria in predicting college and graduate success for American and international students. *Dissertation Abstracts International Section A, 73*, 1383.

Karma, K. (2007). Musical aptitude definition and measure validation: Ecological validity can endanger the construct validity of musical aptitude tests. *Psychomusicology: A Journal of Research in Music Cognition, 19*(2), 79–90.

Kobrin, J. L., Patterson, B. F., Shaw, E. J., Mattern, K. D. & Barbuti, S. M. (2008). *Validity of the SAT for predicting first-year college grade point average* (College Board Research Report No. 2008-5). New York, NY: College Board Publications.

Kuncel, N. R., & Hezlett, S. A. (2007). Standardized tests predict graduate students' success. *Science, 315,* 1080–1081.

Meier, N. C. (1940). *Meier Art Tests: Part I. Art judgment.* Iowa City, IA: Bureau of Educational Research and Service, University of Iowa.

Meisels, S. (1999). Assessing readiness. In R. C. Pianta & M. Cox (Eds.), *The transition to kindergarten: Research, policy, training, and practice* (pp. 39–66). Baltimore, MD: Paul Brookes.

Okado, Y., Bierman, K. L., & Welsh, J. A. (2014). Promoting school readiness in the context of socioeconomic adversity: Associations with parental demoralization and support for learning. *Child & Youth Care Forum, 43*(3), 353–371.

Powers, R. A. (2014). *Types of ASVAB tests.* Retrieved from http://usmilitary.about.com/od/joiningthemilitary/a/asvabtype.htm

Saluja, G., Scott-Little, C., & Clifford, R. (2000). Readiness for school: A survey of state policies and definitions. *ECRP Early Childhood Research & Practice.* Retrieved from http://ecrp.uiuc.edu/v2n2/saluja.html

Saluja, G., Scott-Little, C., Clifford, R. M. (2000). Readiness for School: A Survey of State Policies and Definitions. *Early Childhood Research & Practice, 2*(2). Retrieved from http://ecrp.uiuc.edu/vsns/saluja.html

Shepard, L. A., Kagan, S. L., & Wurtz, E. (Eds.). (1998). *Principles and recommendations for early childhood assessments.* Washington, DC: National Education Goals Panel.

Sparkman, L. A., Maulding, W. S., & Roberts, J. G. (2012). Noncognitive predictors of student success in college. *College Student Journal, 46*(3), 642–652.

Spironello, C., Hay, J., Missiuna, C., Faught, B. E., & Cairney, J. (2010). Concurrent and construct validation of the short form of the Bruininks–Oseretsky Test of Motor Proficiency and the Movement-ABC when administered under field conditions: Implications for screening. *Child: Care, Health, and Development, 36*(4), 499–507. doi: 10.1111/j.1365-2214.2009.01066.x

United States Military Entrance Processing Command (USMEPC), Testing Division. (2005). *ASVAB career exploration program: Counselor manual.* North Chicago, IL: Author.

Whetzel, D. L., McCloy, R. A., Hooper, A., Russell, T. L., Waters, S. D., Campbell, W. J., & Ramos, R. A. (2011). Meta-analysis of clerical performance predictors: Still stable after all these years. *International Journal of Selection and Assessment, 19*(1), 41–50. doi: 10.1111/j.1468-2389.2010.00533.x

11 Career and Employment Assessment

Career development is one of the foundational areas of practice in professional counseling. Whether you specialize in career development or provide career assistance as part of your generalized practice, it is essential that you have a strong background in career counseling. As is the case in all areas of counseling, assessment is a key component. Career assessment is a systematic process undertaken for the purpose of helping individuals with career exploration, career development, or decision making. Professionals who provide career counseling use a variety of formal and informal instruments and procedures to assess an individual's interests, skills, values, personality, needs, and other factors associated with career choice. In the context of employment, various assessment strategies may be used by businesses and organizations to assist in staffing and other personnel-related decisions. This chapter will acquaint you with the instruments and procedures used in career and employment assessment.

After studying this chapter, you should be able to:

- Describe career assessment.
- Explain the use of the initial interview in career assessment.
- Explain the use of interest inventories in career assessment and describe several key inventories, including the Self-Directed Search (SDS), the Strong Interest Inventory (SII), and the Campbell Interest and Skill Survey (CISS).
- Describe work values and explain how they influence the process of career decision making.
- Describe the use of personality inventories in career assessment.
- Discuss combined assessment programs, such as the COPSystem, the Kuder Career Planning System, and DISCOVER.
- Describe the various instruments and strategies used in employment assessment.

CAREER ASSESSMENT

Career assessment is the foundation of career planning. It is used to help individuals understand themselves better and to find career options to their liking. People may need help with career decisions at many points in their lives, such as when entering the world of work after high school or college graduation, during midlife career change, after losing a job, or after moving to a new town. Career assessment is a process that helps individuals make informed decisions about future career prospects. It can help individuals to identify and clarify their interests, values, and personality and to begin exploring career options. Career assessment involves gathering information using several assessment instruments and strategies. We will describe these methods, focusing on interest inventories, values inventories, personality inventories, abilities assessment, career development instruments, combined assessment programs, and interviews.

Interest Inventories

Interest inventories are among the most popular tools selected by career counselors. *Interests* are likes or preferences, or, stated another way, things that people enjoy (Harrington & Long, 2013). In psychological theory, some theorists hold to the doctrine that learning cannot take place without a feeling of interest. Sometimes, interest is synonymous with motivation. Career development theorists have pointed out the importance of interest. Strong (1927) postulated that interest is in the domain of motivation and that there are clusters of attitudes, interests, and personality factors related to choice of and satisfaction with an occupation.

Most people want a career that is tied to their interests, and evaluating interest is a common component of career assessment. Various techniques that measure interest are available, such as inventories, checklists, structured and unstructured interviews, and questionnaires. Interest inventories have been used in the helping professions for over half a century. E. K. Strong published his first version of the *Strong Interest Blank* in 1927. A current version of the test, the *Strong Interest Inventory*, is widely used in the field today. It provides a profile of how an individual's interests compare with those of successful people in certain occupational fields. Another interest inventory, the *Kuder Preference Record—Vocational*, was first published in 1932. Kuder's test initially measured interest in 10 general areas, such as outdoor, literary, musical, artistic, and scientific. Today, Kuder, Inc. provides a wide range of Internet-based tools and resources that help individuals identify their interests, explore their options, and plan for career success.

In career assessment, interest inventories are used specifically for evaluating how closely an individual's interests match those of various occupations or with education or training requirements that correspond to occupations. Some interest inventories are part of a comprehensive career assessment package that includes measures of ability, work values, and personality. We will provide information about a few of the more prominent interest inventories.

SELF-DIRECTED SEARCH, FIFTH EDITION The SDS (Holland, 1994) is one of the most widely used career interest inventories. It was first developed by Dr. John Holland in 1971 and has been revised several times. The SDS guides examinees through an evaluation of their abilities and interests. This inventory is a tool for high school and college students or adults returning to the workforce to find occupations that best fit their interests and abilities. It can be used by anyone between the ages of 15 and 70 in need of career guidance. The SDS is easy and uncomplicated to administer and score and is available to take online. The website for the fifth edition of the SDS has been redesigned to allow greater access to the general public (see self-directed-search.com). The SDS is based on

Holland's theory (i.e., the RIASEC model) that people can be classified into six different groups:

Realistic (R) These people are usually practical, physical, hands-on, tool-oriented individuals. They like realistic careers, such as auto mechanic, aircraft controller, surveyor, electrician, and farmer.

Investigative (I) These people are analytical, intellectual, scientific, and explorative. They prefer investigative careers, such as biologist, chemist, physicist, geologist, anthropologist, laboratory assistant, and medical technician.

Artistic (A) These people are typically creative, original, and independent. They like artistic careers, such as composer, musician, stage director, dancer, interior decorator, actor, and writer.

Social (S) These people are cooperative, supportive, helping, and healing/nurturing. They like social careers, such as teacher, counselor, psychologist, speech therapist, religious worker, and nurse.

Enterprising (E) These people like competitive environments, have strong leadership qualities, and like to influence people. They prefer enterprising careers, such as buyer, sports promoter, business executive, salesperson, supervisor, and manager.

Conventional (C) These people are detailed oriented and have strong organizational skills. They prefer conventional careers, such as bookkeeper, financial analyst, banker, tax expert, secretary, and radio dispatcher.

On the inventory, individuals evaluate and record their interests and abilities; specifically, they are asked to identify their daydreams, activities, likes or dislikes, competencies, occupations of interest, and self-appraisals in mechanical, scientific, teaching, sales, and clerical fields. After taking the inventory, the SDS provides an individual with his or her *three-letter summary code*. This code is based on the RIASEC categories and reflects a combination of the test taker's interests. For example, say that an examinee's three-letter summary code is IEA (i.e., Investigative, Enterprising, and Artistic). The first letter of the code shows the type the individual most closely resembles, the second letter shows the type he or she next most closely resembles, and the third letter shows the third closest type he or she resembles.

The SDS has several forms for use with specific populations:

- *Form R, Career Development* Helps individuals not yet in the workforce gain insight into the world of work and match occupations with their interests and skills
- *Form E, Vocational Guidance* Assists individuals with limited reading skills as they explore vocational options
- *Form CP, Career Path Management* Focuses on the needs of individuals who have or aspire to have high levels of responsibility

SDS Form R also has an Internet version (Holland et al., 2001) that provides a printable *Interpretive Report*. The report identifies the examinee's three-letter summary code and lists the occupations, fields of study, and leisure activities that correspond to the summary code. To describe potential occupations, the report provides information in four columns (see Table 11.1). Column one is the SDS code. Column two (Occupation) lists the occupations that are determined from the test taker's three-letter summary code. The

TABLE 11.1 Sample List of Occupations from the Self-Directed Search Interpretive Report

SDS Code	Occupation	O*NET Code	ED
ISC	Computer network specialist	15-1152.00	3
	Dialysis Technician	29-2099.00	3
	Linguist	19-3099.00	5
	Market Research Analyst	11-2011.01	4
	Microbiologist	19-1022.00	5
	Physician, Occupational	29-1062.00	5

Source: Reproduced by special permission of the Publisher, Psychological Assessment Resources, Inc., 16204 North Florida Avenue, Lutz, Florida 33549, from the Self-Directed Search Software Portfolio (SDS-SP) by Robert C. Reardon, Ph.D. and PAR Staff, Copyright 1985, 1987, 1989, 1994, 1996, 1997, 2000, 2001, 2005, 2008, 2013. Further reproduction is prohibited without permission from PAR, Inc.

occupations are taken from the Occupational Information Network (O*NET), which has a taxonomy of nearly 1,000 occupations. Column three is the O*NET code that provides the corresponding number for each occupation. Column three (*ED*) shows the level of education required for each occupation. The numbers under ED have the following meanings:

1. means that elementary school training or no special training is required;
2. means that high school or GED is usually needed;
3. means that community college or technical education is usually needed;
4. means that college is required; and
5. means that an advanced degree is required.

STRONG INTEREST INVENTORY The SII (or the Strong) is one of the most respected measures of vocational interests in the United States. The inventory has been widely used in educational settings, public institutions, and private organizations for over 80 years. The first version of the SII instrument (then called the *Strong Vocational Interest Blank*) was published by E. K. Strong in 1927, and its most recent revision was in 2012 (Donnay, Thompson, Morris, & Schaubhut, 2012). The SII instrument was designed for evaluating career-related interests with adults, college students, and high school students aged 14 and up (Harmon, Hansen, Borgen, & Hammer, 1994). It assesses a client's interests among a broad range of occupations, work and leisure activities, and educational subjects and yields results for several themes and scales:

- *Six General Occupational Themes* Interest patterns based on Holland's RIASEC categories (i.e., realistic, investigative, artistic, social, enterprising, and conventional)
- *30 Basic Interest Scales* Specific interest areas within the six General Occupational Themes
- *244 Occupational Scales* The individual's interests related to satisfied workers within various occupations
- *Five Personal Style Scales* The individual's preferences related to work style, learning environment, leadership style, risk taking, and team orientation

Results are provided on the SII® *Profile and Interpretive Report*, which is several pages long and consists of a comprehensive presentation of an individual's scores. A *Profile Summary*

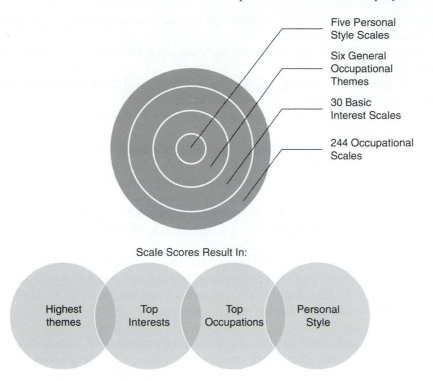

Scale Scores Result In:

Highest themes | Top Interests | Top Occupations | Personal Style

FIGURE 11.1   Overview of the Strong Interest Inventory.

is also provided that gives a graphic snapshot of the test taker's results for immediate easy reference. This includes the individual's (a) three highest General Occupational Themes, (b) top five interest areas, (c) areas of least interest, (d) top 10 Strong occupations, (e) occupations of dissimilar interest, and (f) personal style scales preferences. Figure 11.1 shows an example of an SII® Profile Summary.

CAMPBELL INTEREST AND SKILL SURVEY   The CISS (Campbell, Hyne, & Nilson, 1992) is another instrument that measures interests as well as self-estimates of skills. Its major purpose is to help individuals understand how their interests and skills map into the occupational world, thus helping them make better career choices. It focuses on careers that require postsecondary education and is most appropriate for use with individuals who are college bound or college educated. The CISS contains 200 interest items, and test takers are asked to rate their level of interest on each item using a 6-point scale ranging from *Strongly Like* to *Strongly Dislike*. The CISS also contains 120 skill items, which ask respondents to rate their skill level on a 6-point scale from *Expert: Widely recognized as excellent in this area* to *None: Having no skills in this area*. The CISS yields scores on the three scales: Orientation Scales, Basic Interest and Skills Scales, and Occupational Scales.

I. *Orientation Scales*   These scales cover seven broad themes of occupational interests and skills. Each Orientation Scale corresponds to Holland's RIASEC themes (the comparable Holland dimensions are noted in parentheses):
    1. Influencing (Enterprising)—influencing others through leadership, politics, public speaking, sales, and marketing

2. Organizing (Conventional)—organizing the work of others, managing, and monitoring financial performance
3. Helping (Social)—helping others through teaching, medicine, counseling, and religious activities
4. Creating (Artistic)—creating artistic, literary, or musical productions and designing products or environments
5. Analyzing (Investigative)—analyzing data, using mathematics, and carrying out scientific experiments
6. Producing (Realistic)—producing products, using "hands-on" skills in farming, construction, and mechanical crafts
7. Adventuring (Realistic)—adventuring, competing, and risk taking through athletic, police, and military activities

II. *Basic Interest and Skill Scales*   There are 29 Basic Interest and Skill Scales, which are essentially subscales of the Orientation Scales. Scores on the Basic Scales are usually closely related to occupational membership.

III. *Occupational Scales*   There are 59 Occupational Scales that provide scores comparing an individual's interest and skill patterns with those of workers in a wide range of occupations. Each Occupational Scale represents a specific occupation, such as commercial artist, physician, or human resource director.

For each CISS scale (Orientation Scales, Basic Interest and Skill Scales, and Occupational Scales), two scores are calculated, one based on the test taker's interests and the other based on skills. The *interest score* shows how much the respondent likes the specified activities; the *skill score* shows how confident the respondent feels about performing these activities. The CISS uses T scores (with a mean of 50 and a standard deviation of 10), and the combination of interest and skill score results in four patterns:

- *Pursue* When interest and skill scores are both high (≥ 55), the respondent has reported both attraction to these activities and confidence in his or her ability to perform them well. This is an area for the respondent to *Pursue*.
- *Develop* When the interest score is high (≥ 55) and the skill score is lower (< 55), this is a possible area for the respondent to *Develop*. The respondent may enjoy these activities but feels uncertain about his or her ability to perform them. Further education, training, or experience with these skills might lead to better performance and greater confidence, or these skills may simply be enjoyed as hobbies.
- *Explore* When the skill score is high (≥ 55) and the interest score is lower (< 55), this is a possible area for the respondent to *Explore*. The respondent is confident of his or her ability to perform these activities but does not enjoy them. With some exploration, the respondent may find a way to use these skills in other areas that hold more interest.
- *Avoid* When interest and skill scores are both low (≤ 45), this is an area for the respondent to *Avoid* in career planning. The respondent has reported not enjoying these activities and not feeling confident in his or her ability to perform them.

OTHER INTEREST INVENTORIES *The Career Assessment Inventory-Vocational Version* (CAI-VV) compares an individual's vocational interests to those of individuals in 91 specific careers that reflect a range of positions in today's workforce—including skilled trades and technical and service professions—requiring 2 years or less of postsecondary training. The Career Assessment Inventory-Enhanced Version compares an individual's occupational interests to those of individuals in 111 specific careers that reflect a broad range of technical and professional positions in today's workforce.

The *Harrington–O'Shea Career Decision-Making System—Revised* (CDM-R) is appropriate for individuals ages 12 and older. The CDM-R provides scale scores in six interest areas (e.g., crafts, arts, scientific, social). It assesses abilities, interests, and work values in one instrument. The CDM Level 1 is for middle school students. The CDM Level 2 is for high school and college students and adults.

The *Interest Determination, Exploration, and Assessment System* (IDEAS) provides scores on such scales as mechanical, electronics, nature/outdoor, science, numbers, writing, arts/crafts, social service, child care, medical service, business, sales, office practice, and food service. The instrument is designed for use in grades 6 through 12.

The *Jackson Vocational Interest Survey* (JVIS) is used with high school students, college students, and adults and has 34 basic interest scales, such as creative arts, performing arts, mathematics, skilled trades, dominant leadership, business, sales, law, human relations, management, and professional advising. It also has 10 occupational themes, such as assertive, enterprising, helping, and logical.

Counselors need to be aware of a number of problem areas when using interest inventories. First, interest does not equate to aptitude. Although someone may be interested in pursuing a career as an attorney, they may not have the potential for academic success in that area. Also, because interest inventories are completed based on an individual's own perception of him- or herself (self-report), there may be some issues with reliability of the results. Counselors should check the validity of test results by asking examinees about their interests and activities, inquiring about their preferences, and finding out why areas are liked and disliked. For example, individuals may have had no experience or opportunity in certain interest areas and may not have been able to identify some potential career options. Also, some of the reported likes and dislikes by a client may be influenced by parent, spouse, or family attitudes and not be true indicators of the individual's preferences. As you work with clients on career assessment, it is important that you stress that interests should not be determined by how clients spend their time. Time may be spent doing things under pressures from parents, spouse, family, or peers. Or individuals simply may not have time to do the things they most enjoy. Other problems with interest inventories include the following:

1. Even though there is much evidence of the stability of interests, especially from the late teens on, some clients change their interests dramatically in their adult years.
2. Instruments given before grade 10 or 11 may not be accurate measures of interests. Students may not have had the necessary background of experiences, real or vicarious.
3. Job success is usually correlated more to abilities than interests.
4. Many interest inventories are susceptible to faking, either intentional or unintentional.
5. Response set may affect the validity of an individual's profile. Clients may choose options they consider more socially desirable or acquiescence may prevail.
6. High scores are not the only valuable scores on an interest inventory. Low scores, showing what people dislike or want to avoid, are often more predictive than high scores.

7. Societal expectations and traditions may prove more important than interest in determining vocational selection. Gender bias was a major concern in interest measurement during the past several decades and needs to be considered when selecting instruments and interpreting profiles.

8. Socioeconomic class may affect the pattern of scores on an interest inventory.

9. The inventories may be geared to the professions rather than to skilled and semi-skilled areas. Many inventories were criticized because they were geared exclusively to college-bound students.

10. A profile may be flat and hard to interpret. In such a situation, a counselor should use other instruments and techniques to determine interests.

11. Tests use different types of psychometric scoring procedures. Some interest inventories use forced-choice items, in which individuals are asked to choose from a set of options. Examinees may like or dislike all of the choices but still must choose. Scoring procedures will have an impact on interpretation of results.

Work Values Inventories

The most widely accepted definition of *values* comes from the seminal work of Rokeach (1973), who defined *values* as "enduring beliefs that a specific mode of conduct or end-state of existence is personally or socially preferable to an opposite or converse mode of conduct or end-state of existence" (p. 5). In this definition, Rokeach regards values as stable beliefs that can refer to oneself or to others (i.e., society). Values may be enduring, yet Rokeach also believed that values can change as people learn to make decisions favoring one value over another.

Aspects of a job or occupation that are important to a person's satisfaction are called *work values*. Work values are an important determinant in career decision making and account for a significant part of job satisfaction and tenure (Sinha & Srivastava, 2014). Super (1970) believed that understanding an individual's value structure is important in clarifying goals and determining the psychological appropriateness of a given type of training or employment. Work values can include such dimensions as prestige and recognition, independence, social interaction, compensation, and working conditions.

Work values inventories are used to identify an individual's work-related values in order to match that individual with a suitable job choice. Examples of work values inventories include the *Super's Work Values Inventory-Revised* (SWVI-R); the *Rokeach Values Survey* (RVS); the *Salience Inventory* (SI); the *Hall Occupational Orientation Inventory, Fourth Edition*; and the *Minnesota Importance Questionnaire* (MIQ).

SUPER'S WORK VALUES INVENTORY-REVISED The SWVI-R (Zytowski, 2006) is an instrument that measures the relative importance of a number of work values considered most important in career decision making. It is one of the instruments used in the *Kuder Career Planning System*, which is a comprehensive, Internet-based system that provides a variety of resources and instruments for career planning. The SWVI-R measures several values thought to be important in career choice and development. It can be given to middle and high school students, college students, and adults who are planning to enter, continue, or leave a given educational program, occupation, or job. The test is administered online and provides instantaneous scoring and reporting of results. Examinees rate test items using descriptive statements that correspond to levels of importance (1 = not important at all; 2 = somewhat important; 3 = important; 4 = very important; 5 = crucial). The inventory yields results on 12 work-related values scales. A score report provides percentile scores for each work value, which are presented in a rank-ordered bar graph to depict high (75 to 100), medium (25 to 74), and low (0 to 24) scores. The length of the bar above the titles (see Figure 11.2) indicates how an individual ranks his or her work values. Examinees are recommended to consider their top three or four work values when exploring career options.

ROKEACH VALUES SURVEY The RVS is a rank-order instrument in which the test taker is presented with 18 instrumental values and 18 terminal values and asked to rank them. *Terminal values* are the end state we hope to achieve in life, such as freedom, a world of peace, family, security, pleasure, health, excitement, or a comfortable economic life. *Instrumental values* are the means by which we achieve terminal values, such as being polite, ambitious, caring, self-controlled, obedient, or helpful.

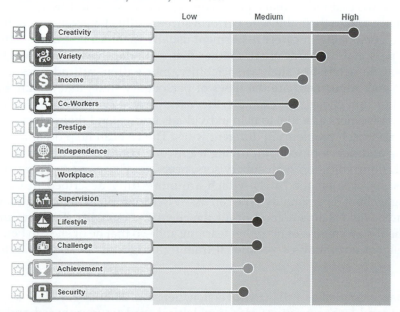

FIGURE 11.2 Super's Work Values Inventory sample score report.

SALIENCE INVENTORY The SI measures the value and preference that an individual places on his or her career roles in comparison to other life roles. The SI measures the importance of five major life roles: student, worker, homemaker, leisurite, and citizen. The inventory consists of 170 items, resulting in 15 scales that examine the relative importance of the five major life roles in participation, commitment, and value expectations. The inventory can be administered to adults and high school students.

HALL OCCUPATIONAL ORIENTATION INVENTORY, FOURTH EDITION The *Hall Occupational Orientation Inventory* is based on the humanistic theory of personality of Abraham Maslow and emphasizes the dynamic, changing, developing nature of one's work motivation and behavior. The inventory is designed to help individuals understand their values, needs, interests, and preferred lifestyles, and how these relate to career goals and future educational plans. Three forms are available: Intermediate (grades 3–7), Young Adult/College, and Adult Basic (used for adults with GED and below).

MINNESOTA IMPORTANCE QUESTIONNAIRE The MIQ measures 20 vocational needs and six underlying values related to those needs. The values assessed are achievement, altruism, autonomy, comfort, safety, and status. The instrument is for individuals ages 15 and up and takes about 20 to 35 minutes to complete.

Personality Inventories

When we think of *personality*, we think of the thoughts, behaviors, and emotions that are enduring and distinguish one person from another. The career development theories of John Holland (1996) and Donald Super (1990) identify personality as a key factor in career choice. They believe that individuals' personality characteristics and traits are related to their career choice and to their ability to perform successfully at a given occupation.

Assessing personality in career assessment usually involves instruments that measure "normal" personality characteristics rather than maladaptive or "pathological" personality traits. Characteristics such as sociability, motivation, attitude, responsibility, independence, and adjustment are the types of personality traits that are important for career exploration and choice. For example, the *Myers–Briggs Type Indicator* (MBTI) can be used in career assessment as a tool to help individuals understand themselves and others, and how they approach problems in different ways. The test can help organizations with career planning and development, improving teamwork, conflict resolution, and improving individual communication with supervisors, peers, and employers. There are 16 personality types possible on the MBTI, which are more fully described in Chapter 12. Understanding a client's personality type can assist in career planning by helping the client select a career field that is a good fit for the client's personality. Furthermore, it can increase the client's awareness of his or her learning style so that he or she can benefit more from career-related education or vocational training programs. Consider the following example:

> Individuals classified as ESTJ (Extroversion, Sensing, Thinking, Judgment) by the MBTI tend to be analytical, decisive, logical, and tough-minded and are adept at planning and organization. Such people have an ability to see flaws in

advance, to critique problems logically, and to organize people, processes, and products. In the work environment, ESTJs are take-charge leaders who are able to use past experiences to solve problems. They tend to make decisions quickly. They like to work in environments that are task oriented, organized, and structured and where the achievement of goals is rewarded. They like their associates to be hard-working people who want to get the job done correctly. However, these individuals do have potential problem areas. They tend to decide too quickly and may lack diplomacy in working with others to get the job done. Sometimes they may not see the need for change. ESTJs may need to consider all sides before deciding on strategies and the benefits of change. They need to make sure they show appreciation of others and also take time to reflect on their feelings and values.

Other personality inventories commonly used in career assessment include the *Sixteen Personality Factor Questionnaire, Fifth Edition* (16PF); the *NEO Personality Inventory* (NEO PI-R); and the *Eysenck Personality Inventory*.

Abilities and Skills Assessment

Every occupation requires a different mix of knowledge, skills, and abilities. Therefore, an important function of career assessment is helping an individual identify current and potential abilities and skills and the career options that capitalize on them (Harrington & Long, 2013). The term *ability* refers to one's *present-day* skills or capabilities to perform a specific task, whether physical or cognitive. Abilities are considered to be innate, neurologically based, fairly stable characteristics of the individual. In contrast, *skills* may come from educational experiences, work experiences, and personal life experiences. Related to abilities, the term *aptitude* refers to one's *potential* capabilities, which can include the potential ability to learn or succeed in future endeavors.

In career assessment, instruments that appraise skills and abilities are used to help individuals identify job possibilities that their skills and abilities suggest. This involves assessing abilities that can be immediately transferred into job-related skills. To help clients choose jobs or careers that offer them a high likelihood of success, counselors need to be familiar with the duties and abilities required of various occupations. By having knowledge of a client's abilities and the abilities required of a wide variety of occupations, counselors can help propose career options that capitalize on a client's current and potential strengths (Arulmani, 2014).

Many resources are available to provide counselors with information about the skills and abilities required by various occupations. Websites from government agencies—particularly the U.S. Department of Labor—and private companies are the major sources of this information. Educational institutions, professional associations, and commercial companies also provide online information about technical schools, colleges, and continuing education. In addition, national and state websites provide information on trends in the labor market, including projections of future job openings. *O*NET OnLine* (located at onetonline.org) is the nation's primary source of occupational information. The O*NET database, an online version of the *Dictionary of Occupational Titles*, contains information on thousands of occupations with descriptions about several distinguishing characteristics of each occupation, such as the tasks, knowledge, skills, abilities, work activities, interests, work values, and wages. The database is continually updated by surveying a broad range of workers from each occupation. See Figure 11.3 for a description of the skills and abilities required for educational, vocational, and school counselors from the O*NET summary report (U.S. Department of Labor National Center for O*NET Development, 2007). Another resource is the *Occupational Outlook Handbook* (OOH) from the U.S. Department of Labor (dol.gov), which is a classic reference

---

Skills:

- *Active Listening*: Giving full attention to what other people are saying, taking time to understand the points being made, asking questions as appropriate, and not interrupting at inappropriate times.

- *Social Perceptiveness*: Being aware of and understanding others' reactions.

- *Reading Comprehension*: Understanding written sentences and paragraphs in work related documents.

- *Service Orientation*: Actively looking for ways to help people.

- *Speaking*: Talking to others to convey information effectively.

- *Critical Thinking*: Using logic and reasoning to identify the strengths and weaknesses of alternative solutions, conclusions or approaches to problems.

- *Time Management*: Managing one's own time and the time of others.

- *Writing*: Communicating effectively in writing as appropriate for the needs of the audience.

- *Active Learning*: Understanding the implications of new information for both current and future problem-solving and decision-making.

- *Coordination*: Adjusting actions in relation to others' actions.

Abilities

- *Oral Expression*: The ability to communicate information and ideas in speaking so others will understand.

- *Oral Comprehension*: The ability to listen to and understand information and ideas presented through spoken words and sentences.

- *Problem Sensitivity*: The ability to tell when something is wrong or is likely to go wrong. It does not involve solving the problem, only recognizing there is a problem.

- *Speech Clarity*: The ability to speak clearly so others can understand you.

- *Inductive Reasoning*: The ability to combine pieces of information to form general rules or conclusions (includes finding a relationship among seemingly unrelated events).

- *Written Expression*: The ability to communicate information and ideas in writing so others will understand.

- *Deductive Reasoning*: The ability to apply general rules to specific problems to produce answers that make sense.

- *Speech Recognition*: The ability to identify and understand the speech of another person.

- *Written Comprehension*: The ability to read and understand information and ideas presented in writing.

- *Near Vision*: The ability to see details at close range (within a few feet of the observer).

FIGURE 11.3   O*NET Description of skills and abilities required for educational, vocational, and school counselors.

Source: U.S. Department of Labor National Center for O*NET Development (2007). O*NET Online Summary Report for: 21-1012.00—Educational, Vocational, and School Counselors. Retrieved August 1, 2007 from http://online.onetcenter.org/link/summary/21-1012.00

about occupations, organized from A to Z. This national source of career information is designed to provide assistance to individuals making decisions about their future work lives. Revised every 2 years, the OOH describes occupations in detail, including educational and experience prerequisites, places of employment, employment outlook, earnings, working conditions, chances for advancement, and lists of government resources that provide additional information.

There are several assessment instruments that evaluate an individual's skills and abilities as they relate to career performance. Many of the instruments used are the same as those we discussed in Chapter 10. For example, the *Armed Services Vocational Aptitude Battery* (ASVAB) is a multiple-aptitude test battery that measures aptitudes for both civilian and military career areas. The ASVAB is often used with high school and postsecondary students as part of the ASVAB Career Exploration program. It assesses such abilities as general science, arithmetic reasoning, word knowledge, paragraph comprehension, mathematics knowledge, electronics information, auto and shop information, and mechanical comprehension. Another instrument is the *Career Ability Placement Survey* (CAPS), a multiple-aptitude battery designed to measure such vocationally relevant abilities as mechanical reasoning, spatial relations, verbal reasoning, numerical ability, language usage, word knowledge, and perceptual speed and accuracy. The instrument was designed for middle through high school students, college students, and adults. See Chapter 10 for more information about these multiple-aptitude tests. Other skills and abilities assessment instruments include the Kuder Skills Assessments (KSA) and the Ability Explorer.

KUDER SKILLS ASSESSMENT The KSA is part of the comprehensive online *Kuder Career Planning System*, which includes two partner assessments, the *Kuder Career Search with Person Match* and the revised *Super's Work Values Inventory*. The instruments measure various skills that are aligned with specific occupational clusters, such as finance, manufacturing, health science, information technology, and education and training. There are two levels, one for middle and high school students (the KSA) and one designed for college students and adults (the KSA-CA). The KSA has 90 items that require students to rate their current skill level for various tasks using a 4-point scale: 1 (I don't think I could ever learn to do this task), 2 (I could probably learn to do this task, but it would be hard), 3 (I could easily learn to do this task), and 4 (I can already do this task). The KSA-CA is a 160-item instrument that requires adult test takers to rate their degree of certainty in performing a wide variety of activities using a 5-point scale from 1 (Cannot do at all) to 5 (Completely certain can do).

ABILITY EXPLORER The Ability Explorer (Harrington, Harrington, & Wall, 2012) measures strengths in the 14 abilities important in today's workplace. This 140-question assessment enables individuals to learn their strongest abilities, plus related courses, activities, and careers for developing and using these abilities. Designed for individuals from high school to adult, the instrument is written at an eighth-grade reading level and takes about 30 minutes to complete. Test takers are asked to read each statement and then indicate how good they are or would be at doing an activity. The Ability Explorer measures 14 abilities: artistic, clerical, interpersonal, language, leadership, manual, musical/dramatic, numerical/mathematical, organizational, scientific, persuasive, spatial, social, and technical/mechanical.

Career Development Inventories

The concept of *career development* has been used to describe both the process by which individuals make career choices appropriate to their age and stage of development and their ability to successfully transition through the specific developmental tasks of each of these stages. Also known as *career maturity*, career development takes into account both attitudinal and cognitive dimensions (Brown & Lent, 2013). Attitudinal dimensions include individuals' attitudes and feelings about making an effective career choice. Cognitive dimensions involve their awareness of the need to make a career decision and their understanding about their vocational preferences.

Career development is particularly important in career assessment with adolescents. At this stage in life, teenagers often have to make important educational and career decisions that they are not developmentally ready to make. Many adolescents are unable to integrate their interests, skills, and abilities into focusing on a particular career goal, which is the main objective of career assessment. Therefore, helping adolescents evaluate their skills and interests and engage in career exploration is an important goal of career counseling with individuals at this age.

Many career development instruments can be utilized to help counselors assess a client's attitudes and career awareness and knowledge. These instruments can provide counselors with valuable information about the career development and educational needs of clients and can provide survey information to help in planning career guidance programs. Career development is a continuous process, and at various points throughout life, most people have to make a variety of decisions concerning their career. Examples of career development instruments include the Career Maturity Inventory (CMI), the Career Development Inventory (CDI), and the Career Factors Inventory (CFI).

CAREER MATURITY INVENTORY, REVISED The CMI was developed for students from grades 6 through 12 to measure attitudes and competencies related to variables in the career-choice process. The inventory has two parts: an attitude inventory and a competence inventory. The attitude inventory measures attitudes toward the decisiveness, involvement, independence, orientation, and compromise dimensions of career maturity. The competence inventory has five subscales: Self-Appraisal, Occupational Information, Goal Selection, Planning, and Problem Solving.

CAREER DEVELOPMENT INVENTORY The CDI (Super, Zelkowitz, & Thompson, 1981) was developed for K–12 and college and university students. The inventory contains five scales: Career Planning, Career Exploration, Decision Making, World-of-Work Information, and Knowledge of Preferred Occupational Group. The scales are combined to give scores in Career Development Attitudes, Career Development Knowledge and Skills, and Career Orientation.

CAREER FACTORS INVENTORY The CFI is designed to help people determine whether they are ready to engage in the career decision-making process. The CFI can be used for individuals age 13 and above; its 21-item, self-scoreable booklet takes 10 minutes to complete. It explores an individual's perceived issues of lack of self-awareness, lack of career information, career anxiety, and generalized indecisiveness.

Combined Assessment Programs

The trend in career assessment is to include interests, values, and other dimensions, such as aptitude, career development, and maturity.

COPSYSTEM The Career Occupational Preference System (COPS) is a comprehensive career assessment program that combines interests, abilities, and values inventories. The instruments can be used alone or in combination to provide comprehensive career-related information that can assist individuals with their career decision-making process. The program includes the following inventories:

- *Career Occupational Preference System (COPS) Interest Inventory* Designed to measure interests related to 14 *career clusters*. It is targeted for use with students from seventh grade through college as well as adults.
- *Career Ability Placement Survey (CAPS)* Designed to measure vocationally relevant abilities, such as mechanical reasoning, spatial relations, verbal reasoning, numerical ability, language usage, word knowledge, perceptual speed and accuracy, and manual speed and dexterity.
- *Career Orientation Placement and Evaluation Survey (COPES)* A values inventory that matches an individual's personal values with occupational areas.

KUDER CAREER PLANNING SYSTEM The *Kuder Career Planning System* is an Internet-based system that was developed based on the work of Dr. Frederick Kuder, a pioneer in the career development industry. The Kuder system provides several customizable career development tools to help individuals identify their interests, explore their career options, and plan for career success. It can be used by middle school, high school, and college students, as well as adults. The Kuder system includes an interest inventory, a skills assessment, and a values inventory, all available online:

- *Kuder Galaxy* is designed for students in pre-K through grade five. The online system allows for an interactive process that involves games, activities, and video to help identify areas for career exploration.
- *Kuder Skills Assessment* is designed for grades 6 through 12 and provides an interactive online system to help identify college and career paths. The assessment can be completed in under 20 minutes and helps students to develop multi-year career plans.
- *Kuder Journey* is an online interactive system designed to aid in career planning for college students and adults. This research-based system provides the user with an analysis of interests, skills, and work values.

Interviews

As is the case in all areas of counseling, the initial *interview* is an important aspect of career assessment. During the interview, counselors gather general background information common to any unstructured interview (see Chapter 2). In addition, they may ask the client questions relevant to career assessment, such as the client's work experience, education and training, interests, and leisure activities (Barclay & Wolff, 2012). Counselors may also ask clients to describe their typical day, including (a) how much they like routine or spontaneity and (b) how much they rely on others or are independent. An important aspect of career planning is the client's readiness to make career decisions as well as his or her knowledge about the world of work and personal abilities and skills. Barclay and Wolff suggested that counselors may use a structured career interview (e.g., Career Construction Interview) to analyze life themes, patterns, self-concept, and salient interests. Further, Barclay and Wolff determined that raters of the Career Construction Interview could identify RIASEC themes from the content of the interview. Although further research is needed to validate these results, the idea that interviews can result in the same coding as standardized assessments is promising.

McMahon and Watson (2012) argued that a narrative approach to career assessment can provide a rich qualitative analysis of career interests and potential career paths. Gibson and Mitchell (2006, p. 112) provided sample questions that may be asked of clients who have expressed an interest in changing careers:

1. Would you give me a brief review of your employment experiences?
2. What is your educational background?
3. Do you have any unique experience or interest that might be related to the choice of career, such as hobbies or special interests?
4. Why have you decided, at this time, to change careers?
5. Tell me about your ideas about a new or different career.

EMPLOYMENT ASSESSMENT

In the context of employment, businesses and organizations use various assessment strategies to make recommendations or decisions about employees or job applicants. For example, various personnel assessment procedures can be used to select individuals for entry-level positions, make differential job assignments, select individuals for advanced and specialized positions, decide who will be promoted within an organization, decide who is eligible for training, and provide diagnostic and career development information for individuals. Effective personnel assessment involves a systematic approach to gathering information about applicants' job qualifications. Not all assessment instruments are appropriate for every job and organizational setting; agencies must determine the most appropriate assessment strategy for their particular needs. The effective use of assessment tools will reduce the degree of error in making hiring decisions (U.S. Office of Personnel Management, 2009). In this section, we will discuss common procedures specific to employment assessment, including selection interviews, biographical information, and tests. We will also present information about job analysis and assessment centers.

Selection Interviews

The selection interview is one of the most widely used methods of assessing job applicants. The purpose of the interview is to gain information about candidates' qualifications and experiences relevant to the available job. Although there is limited evidence that interviews are valid procedures for personnel selection, they continue to be widely used (Hebl, Madera, & Martinez, 2014). According to Hebl, Madera, and Martinez, there are numerous issues with interview processes, and they can be highly impacted by cultural or racial bias. Although interviews are widely used as a primary selection process, little research attention has been paid to multicultural issues, bias, and prejudice in the interview (Manroop, Boekhorst, & Harrison, 2013).

Although interviews can be impacted greatly by the lens of the interviewer, they remain a viable approach to assessment of suitability for personnel selection. In lieu of unstructured approaches, Hebl, Madera, and Martinez (2014) suggested that interviewers take a more systematic, structured, job-related interview approach. These structured approaches tend to have higher validity. However, the interviewer should be trained in personnel selection and understand the relationship of traits to job performance.

As an example of structured interviewing, the situational interview, with specific questions based on job-related critical incidents, has also proven to be a valid assessment tool (Seijts & Kyei-Poku, 2010). Although the use of structured approaches tends to mitigate some of the bias issues in interviewing, it is important to identify some of the ongoing concerns. Studies of the interview show that interviewers tend to make decisions about candidates early in the interview. Negative information tends to be weighed more heavily than positive information, and visual cues tend to be more important than verbal cues (Levashina, Hartwell, Morgeson, & Campion, 2014). In addition, ratings are affected by how many others are being rated at the same time; clients who share similarities with the interviewer (the same race, gender, and so on) tend to be more favorably rated. Often, applicants are rated the same in evaluations, either superior (leniency error), average (central tendency error), or poor (stringency error). Sometimes, one or two either good or bad characteristics of an applicant tend to influence the ratings of all the other characteristics (halo error). Sometimes, the interviewer allows the quality of the applicants who preceded the present applicant to influence the ratings of the present applicant (contrast effect). Interviewers are overconfident at times in their ability to evaluate applicants; as a result, they make hasty decisions. Interviewers need training and instruction in the following skills (Gatewood, Feild, & Barnick, 2010):

1. Setting the stage for open communication
2. Consistency in the questioning/interview process
3. Keeping the interview on target
4. Using appropriate speech
5. Mastering listening skills
6. Using notes to keep track of information
7. Using good interviewing skills to maintain the flow of communication and maintaining a collaborative process
8. Managing nonverbal aspects of the interview process

The selection interview can be valuable if the interviewers are trained in the process, panels are used whenever possible, job-related questions are used, and multiple questions are designed for the requirements of the job.

Biographical Information

Almost all employers require prospective employees to complete an application blank, a biographical information blank, or a life history. Employers believe that these forms provide information on what the candidate has done in the past and can be used to predict future behavior. Biographical data has received a great deal of attention in the world of career development. Overall, there are some assumptions that individuals use when evaluating biographical data from a rational perspective. Chernyshenko, Stark, and Drasgow (2011) identified three assumptions for the use of biographical data: (1) The best predictor of applicants' future behavior is what they have done in the past. (2) Applicants' life experiences provide an indirect measure of their motivational characteristics. (3) Applicants are less defensive in describing their previous behaviors on the form than discussing their motivations for these behaviors. Biographical data has been shown to be one of the best predictors of employee retention and career success (Breaugh, 2014). Biographical data also has been valuable in assessing individuals and classifying them into subgroups for purposes of better placement and utilization. Personnel directors sometimes divide large groups of current and former employees into categories of successful and unsuccessful workers and determine which items differentiate the two groups. According to Breaugh, biodata instruments are less expensive than other custom-made tests and can predict employee turnover and subsequent employee ratings.

Tests

Many employers use tests as part of the assessment process to develop work-related information and recommendations or decisions about people who work for them or are seeking employment with them. To be effective, instruments must be valid for the intended purpose and should be the least discriminating tool for the decisions that need to be made. Tests can help ensure fair treatment of workers in an employment context.

TESTS USED IN THE PRIVATE SECTOR Employees in the private sector work primarily in manufacturing, retail trades, and service occupations. Tests used in these settings measure such attributes as general aptitude, cognitive ability, clerical achievement, spatial and mechanical abilities, perceptual accuracy, and motor ability. Other factors, such as attitudes, motivation, organizational commitment, and work environment, can also be assessed to diagnose strengths and weaknesses in an organization and to monitor changes in the workforce. Job satisfaction instruments are used to measure dimensions such as attitude toward supervision, the company, coworkers, salary, working conditions, promotion, security, subordinates, autonomy, and esteem needs. Personality inventories are also used in some employment contexts. In general, the most widely used personality inventories in these settings include the Myers–Briggs Type Indicator, the California Psychological Inventory, the Edwards Personal Preference Inventory, and the Guilford–Zimmerman Temperament Scale.

Examples of standardized instruments used in the private sector include the following:

- The Career Attitudes and Strategies Inventory (CASI) helps to identify career problems requiring further discussion and exploration. It includes a career checkup; a self-assessment of the client's career or situation; and a survey of the beliefs, events, and forces that affect the client's career.
- The Comprehensive Ability Battery (CAB) contains 20 pencil-and-paper subtests that measure a single primary-ability factor related to performance in an industrial setting. The subtests are Verbal Ability, Numerical Ability, Spatial Ability, Perceptual Completion, Clerical Speed and Accuracy, Reasoning, Hidden Shapes, Rote Memory, Mechanical Ability, Meaningful Memory, Memory Span, Spelling, Auditory Ability, Esthetics Judgment, Organizing Ideas, Production of Ideas, Verbal Fluency, Originality, Tracking, and Drawing.

- The Wonderlic Comprehensive Personality Profile (CPP) is a personality inventory for positions requiring significant client interaction, such as customer service, telemarketing, and sales. The primary traits assessed are emotional intensity, intuition, recognition, motivation, sensitivity, assertiveness, trust, and good impression.
- The Employee Aptitude Survey Test Series (EAS) consists of 10 tests that measure cognitive, perceptual, and psychomotor abilities required for successful job performance in a wide variety of occupations. Tests include verbal comprehension, visual pursuit, visual speed and accuracy, space utilization, numerical reasoning, verbal reasoning, word fluency, mechanical speed and accuracy, and symbolic reasoning.
- The Employee Reliability Inventory is an 81-item, preinterview questionnaire designed to help employers identify reliable and productive individuals prior to making a hiring decision. It measures emotional maturity, conscientiousness, trustworthiness, long-term commitment, safe job performance, and courteous behavior with customers.
- The Job Effectiveness Prediction System is a selection system for entry-level employees in clerical positions (e.g., administrative assistant, customer service representative) and technical/professional positions (e.g., underwriter, annuity analyst). It includes tests such as Coding and Converting, Comparing and Checking, Filing, Language Usage, Mathematical Skill, Numerical Ability, Reading Comprehension, Spelling, and Verbal Comprehension.
- The Personnel Selection Inventory (PSI) is a popular system designed to identify high-caliber employees who can contribute positively to an organization. The system is based on extensive research and is designed to comply with federal Equal Employment Opportunity Commission (EEOC) guidelines on fair employment practices and the Americans with Disabilities Act. The PSI also provides scores on an overall Employability Index (applicant's suitability for hire) and Significant Behavioral Indicators (areas of concern that might need further investigation). It also has 18 other scales that assess the attitudes of potential employees, such as honesty, drug avoidance, nonviolence, stress tolerance, and supervision attitudes, to name just a few.
- The Wesman Personnel Classification Test assesses general verbal and numerical abilities and is used for selection of employees for clerical, sales, supervisory, and managerial positions.
- The Wonderlic Personnel Test measures general verbal, spatial, and numerical reasoning and is used for selection and placement purposes. It measures a candidate's ability to learn a specific job, solve problems, understand instructions, apply knowledge to new situations, benefit from specific job training, and be satisfied with a particular job. It can be administered using a paper-and-pencil or computer/Internet format.

TESTS USED IN GOVERNMENT The federal government became involved in employment assessment in 1883, when Congress created the U.S. Civil Service Commission. In 1979, the U.S. Office of Personnel Management (OPM) became involved in the assessment process and established standards for job classification and competitive examinations for more than 1,000 types of jobs. The OPM has responsibility for two-thirds of the federal civilian workforce, and a large percentage of these workers are selected by one of the assessment programs.

Other government agencies develop and administer their own tests. The U.S. Department of State, for example, uses its own tests to select Foreign Service officers. The U.S. Employment Service (USES) has developed instruments for use in the local and state employment offices. The General Aptitude Test Battery (GATB) is widely used; it compares examinee scores with workers in more than 600 jobs. The USES has also developed interest inventories and tests of proficiency in dictation, typing, and spelling.

State and local government agencies often require tests for selection purposes. Tests are frequently required of police officers and firefighters, as well as clerical workers. Local governmental agencies tend to use tests less than state agencies. However, both state and local agencies use oral and performance examinations more than federal agencies do (Friedman & Williams, 1982). Skilled workers tend to be given tests more than unskilled workers, and tests are not used as a sole criterion. Education, experience, character, and residence requirements are other important factors considered in hiring.

States often mandate *occupational and professional licensing* for which some type of examination is required. This is true even in education in many states, with teachers and principals required to pass licensing examinations. States often establish a licensing board for a specific occupation. Occupations requiring licensing examinations include the following: architects, acupuncturists, audiologists, chiropractors, dentists, dental hygienists, engineers, funeral directors, landscape architects, land surveyors, occupational therapists, psychologists, speech pathologists, hearing aid counselors, optometrists, registered nurses, practical nurses, pharmacists, physical therapists, physicians, physician's assistants, podiatrists, and social workers.

TESTS USED IN THE MILITARY The military makes extensive use of tests for selection and classification purposes. For example, the ASVAB is a comprehensive aptitude test that helps identify the proper technical training or education needed for various types of occupational areas in the armed forces. In addition, specific tests are used to select candidates for admission to the service academies, reserve officer training programs, officer candidate schools, and specialized programs (such as flight training). The Cadet Evaluation Battery (CEB), the Air Force Officer Qualifying Test (AFOQT), the Alternate Flight Aptitude Selection Test (AFAST), and the Defense Language Aptitude Battery (DLAB) are examples.

Job Analysis

One of the key elements in effective personnel assessment is job analysis. *Job analysis* is a purposeful, systematic process for documenting the particular duties and requirements of a job and the relative importance of these duties. It is used to analyze information about the duties and tasks of a given job; environment and working conditions; tools and equipment; relationships among supervisors and employees; and the knowledge, skills, and abilities requirement for the job. Job analysis is conducted to (a) help determine the training requirements of a given job, (b) make decisions about compensation, (c) aid in selecting job applicants, and (d) review job performance.

The interview is an excellent method for obtaining information for job analysis and can be conducted with employees, supervisors, and other individuals knowledgeable about the job. An example of a job analysis interview for employees is shown in Table 11.2.

TABLE 11.2 Job Analysis Interview

What is your job title?

Where do you work?

Of what department or division are you a member?

Job Tasks

What do you do? How do you do it? Do you use special equipment?

What are the major tasks you perform on your job? What percentage of time do you spend on each task?

Knowledge Requirements

For each task you perform, what type of knowledge is necessary?

What types of formal and informal knowledge do you need to perform these tasks?

Do you need formal coursework, on-the-job training, or other forms of training?

What level of knowledge is required?

Skill Requirements

What types of manual, mechanical, or intellectual skills are necessary to perform your job?

What types of tasks require these skills?

Ability Requirements

What types of communication skills, oral or written, are required for your job?

Do you have to prepare reports or complete records as part of your job?

What types of thinking, reasoning, or problem-solving skills are required?

What types of quantitative and mathematical abilities are required for your job?

What types of interpersonal abilities are required?

Are you responsible for the supervision of other employees?

What types of physical abilities are required?

Physical Activities

What types of physical activities are required to perform your job?

How often are you engaged in physical activities?

Environmental Conditions

What types of environmental conditions do you encounter on your job?

Other

Describe a typical day.

Are there any other facets of your job that need to be described?

Job analysis can also take place in focus groups or multiperson interviews, which are conducted by one person with several interviewees. A multiperson job analysis should follow these steps:

1. Read and review existing materials and data on the job to be analyzed.
2. Have supervisors and experienced workers in the field meet together in a group and discuss the job requirements, producing a list of tasks and roles that are performed.
3. Display the tasks and job characteristics identified so that the group can react to what you have written.

4. List outputs, knowledge, skills, and abilities (including use of machines, tools, equipment, and work aids) needed to get the job done. Get agreement from the group on the tasks performed.
5. Have the workers determine the percentage of time spent on each task or skill.
6. Combine common tasks together.
7. Have the workers explain how they know or recognize excellent, satisfactory, or poor performance of the tasks and the job.
8. Construct an instrument to assess job performance, and have supervisors and workers react to the tasks and performance standards identified.

Several standardized instruments are available for use with job analysis. They usually contain three major sections: background information on the respondents, job tasks, and other miscellaneous information. Examples include the Position Analysis Questionnaire (PAQ) and the WorkKeys.

THE POSITION ANALYSIS QUESTIONNAIRE The PAQ is a structured job analysis questionnaire that measures the human attributes needed to perform a job. It consists of 195 items divided into six major categories:

1. *Information Input* Where and how does the worker get the information that is used in performing the job?
2. *Mental Processes* What reasoning, decision-making, planning, and information-processing activities are involved in performing the job?
3. *Work Output* What physical activities are required to perform the job, and what tools or devices are used?
4. *Relationships with Other Persons* What relationships with other people are required in performing the job?
5. *Job Context* In what physical and social contexts is the work performed?
6. *Other Job Characteristics* What activities, conditions, or characteristics other than those described previously are relevant to the job?

Using rating scales, items may be evaluated on the (a) extent of use in the given job, (b) amount of time, (c) importance to the job, (d) possibility of occurrence, or (e) applicability to the job in question.

WORKKEYS WorkKeys is a system developed by the ACT that gives students and workers reliable, relevant information about their workplace skill levels. It includes eight tests, six of which correspond to basic academic skills and two of which assess other, nonacademic workplace skills, such as applied technology and teamwork. WorkKeys also includes a job-analysis system that helps employers identify the skills employees need to be successful on the job. Three different job-analysis options are available:

1. *Job Profiling* Used with focus groups to identify the tasks most critical to a job and the skill levels required to enter the job and perform effectively
2. *SkillMap* Given to job administrators or job experts, who identify and rate the tasks and skills requirements needed for a particular job
3. *WorkKeys Estimator* Provides quick estimates of the skill levels needed for a given job

Assessment Centers

In terms of employment assessment, the term *assessment center* is considered a technique or approach to assessment (it does *not* refer to a place where assessment occurs). Assessment centers are group-oriented, standardized series of activities that provide a basis for judgments or predictions of human behaviors considered relevant to work performance in a particular organizational setting (Muchinsky, 2008). These activities can occur in some physical location in an organization or at some location away from the workplace. Assessment centers are used in human resource management to (a) decide whom to select or promote, (b) diagnose strengths and weakness in work-related skills, and (c) develop job-relevant skills (Thornton & Rupp, 2006). Because assessment centers are expensive, they have been used mainly by large organizations—but consulting firms may also provide assessment center services to smaller companies.

Muchinsky (2008, p. 120) lists four characteristics of the assessment center approach:

1. People who attend the center (assessees) are usually management-level personnel that the company wants to evaluate for possible selection, promotion, or training.
2. Assessees are evaluated in groups of 10 to 20, although subgroups may be formed for specific exercises. The group format provides opportunity for peer evaluation.
3. Several raters (the assessors) do the evaluation. They work in teams and collectively or individually make recommendations about selection and promotion.
4. The assessment program can take from one to several days to complete, and multiple assessment methods are employed. Many are group exercises, but inventories, personal history forms, and interviews are also used.

The assessment center approach often uses situational judgment tests and work sample tests. A *situational judgment test* is usually a paper-and-pencil test that presents the examinee with a written scenario and a list of possible solutions to the problem. The individual has to make judgments about how to deal with the situation. *Work sample tests* measure job skills by having the examinee perform a simulated work task. An example of this is the *In-Basket Test* (Frederiksen, Saunders, & Wand, 1957), a test that presents job applicants with materials in an "in-basket" related to tasks, problems, or situations that routinely occur in the position for which they have applied. The in-basket typically consists of memos, appointments, email messages, phone messages, correspondence, reports, forms, and other materials that reflect real-world, job-related tasks. The candidate's task is to review the in-basket items and then take action, recording any notes, comments, and responses on special forms. A number of versions of this approach have been developed for different groups, such as school administrators and military officers. Candidates demonstrate how they would handle each problem and are evaluated not only on their solutions but on other work-related skills, such as time-management, decision-making, and organizational skills.

Thornton and Byham (1982) identified nine dimensions frequently measured in assessment centers: communication skills, planning, organizational strategies, delegating of responsibilities, decisiveness, initiative, stress tolerance, adaptability, and tenacity. The administrator of an assessment center should keep in mind the following guidelines:

1. Assessment should be based on clearly defined dimensions of the position or behavior in question.
2. Multiple assessment techniques should be used.
3. A variety of job-sampling techniques should be used.

4. Familiarity with the job and the organization is needed; experience in the job or role is desirable.
5. Thorough training in assessment center procedures is necessary for all observers and raters.
6. All pertinent behavior should be observed, recorded, and communicated to other raters and observers.
7. Group discussion and decision-making procedures are used to integrate observations, rate dimensions, and make predictions.
8. Clients should be assessed against clearly understood external norms, not against each other.
9. Observers should guard against first impressions and other errors commonly made in rating and observation.

Guidelines for Employee Selection

As a professional counselor with an expertise in career development, you may be invited to consult with various companies on career selection processes. For example, a company may be experiencing retention issues with their employees. Because turnover is an expensive issue, the company has asked you to help them identify better procedures for employee selection. One of the primary directions you might provide is to collect assessment data. More specifically, you could offer your consultees some guidelines to follow based on research in the employee selection process:

1. Know the legal and ethical considerations thoroughly.
2. Know basic measurement concepts.
3. Know the steps in collecting evidence of criterion-referenced validity.
4. Be able to analyze the skills, competencies, and personal qualities that relate to successful performance on the job.
5. Consider practical factors, such as cost, number of employees involved, and time.
6. Locate tests that purport to measure the characteristics identified for the job.
7. Administer the tests to workers on the job and to new applicants.
8. Observe the workers tested, and have supervisors report on the performance of these workers.
9. Analyze how the test scores and ratings relate to success on the job.
10. If evidence is favorable, then formulate an operational plan to utilize the data for selection purposes. If evidence is not favorable, then select other instruments and get additional ratings.
11. Systematically monitor and evaluate the system.

Trends in Employment Assessment

The greatest trend in employment assessment has been the continued development and evolution of technology. The Internet has changed the process of assessment and made it more accessible to the general public. Web-based testing offers 24-7 access, ease-of-use, immediate scoring, and a more limited need for test administrators, leading to convenient, cost-effective, and efficient test use (Osborn, Dikel, & Sampson, 2011).

Jobseekers and hiring companies have been brought together by "virtual career centers" (Osborn et al., 2011). The centers offer a variety of services, including areas to post résumés, standardized résumé-building templates, job boards, background information on companies, and personnel assessments. Researchers need to investigate the impact of these career centers and the assessments they administer on employers and employees.

It is fair to say that Internet-based assessments have become the norm. Companies can use the Internet to administer prescreening questionnaires, job application blanks, structured behavioral interviews, and brief selection tests (Dozier, Sampson, Lenz, Peterson, & Reardon, 2014). Internet assessment companies can offer employers a seamless platform from which to administer skill assessment, employee evaluations, preemployment screenings, and postemployment evaluations. Along with the benefits of web-based assessment come such issues as verifying a test taker's identity, security measures to protect test item security, and the protection of test-taker test results.

Another ongoing issue is that of discrimination in employment tests. Employers need to be sensitive in how they use tests for hiring purposes; they do not want to engage in discrimination and unfair practices. Because employers must go through elaborate validation and documentation procedures when they employ tests for selection purposes, the use of tests for those purposes has declined. However, the use of tests for certification purposes has increased.

Because so many businesses are concerned about the cost of employee theft, many administer honesty tests in their hiring procedures and evaluations of current staff members. Honesty tests are standardized, commercially available written examinations that provide psychological evaluations of a candidate's ethical dispositions and attitudes toward work. These tests can purportedly identify problem employees who have either stolen in the past or who will be unproductive workers. Honesty tests have been hailed by some for helping to eliminate pilfering, reduce employee turnover, and increase productivity. They have also been criticized and challenged by those who feel the tests are either inaccurate or a violation of rights to privacy and other civil rights.

Summary

There are many approaches to career and employment assessment. Career and employment tests have had a long history, beginning with Strong's interest inventory in the 1920s. These tests have proven to be good measures of vocational success, but many factors need to be considered. The maturity, socioeconomic class, and educational level of the client all play important roles in assessing interests and career satisfaction. Environment and heredity issues are also involved. A client may not have had the opportunities and experiences necessary to make valid judgments. Family, societal, and peer expectations may influence an individual's pattern of behavior, and temperament may influence an individual's preferences. Career counselors need to have a comprehensive knowledge of the world of work as well as extensive knowledge of assessment techniques and counseling procedures.

Employment tests are more widely used in federal and state agencies than in business and industry. In addition, many skilled and professional workers must take certification or licensing examinations, such as those for certification as a school counselor or a mental health counselor, which then become the prerequisite for hiring. Tests in business and industry are primarily used for selection purposes. The decline in test use has led to a movement away from objective selection procedures. Analysis of research has indicated that research-based testing does not discriminate against minority groups and women and saves the organization money. Nevertheless, currently there is more reliance on clinical judgment and consideration of the applicant's experience and education. Career counselors need to be guided by the nine specific standards for the use of tests in employment contexts.

Questions for Discussion

1. What do you think is the best way to find out someone's interests: (a) using an interest inventory or (b) asking the person, "What are you interested in, or what would you like to do or be?" Explain your position.
2. What career assessment tests have you taken? When did you take these tests? How were the results presented to you? Did you agree with the results? What impact have these tests had on your career development? If you were displaced from a current job, would you seek career assessment to help you identify other possible jobs or career fields?
3. Imagine you are head of a human resources department in a large, privately owned children's hospital. You are asked to hire personnel to provide counseling to children who are patients at the hospital, but you must identify individuals who could be described as "natural-born counselors" for the jobs. Describe the assessment methods you would choose, including (a) a list of interview questions, and (b) the types of tests you would use. In your opinion, what results from these methods would you need to obtain from an individual to determine whether he or she were a "natural-born counselor"? What ethical issues would be relevant in this scenario?
4. How would you go about the task of setting up a licensing examination for workers in your field? What things would you do to ensure that you met all of the legal guidelines of that profession?

Suggested Activities

1. Evaluate an instrument listed or discussed in this chapter and write a critical review of it. Be sure to read the evaluations of the test in the *Mental Measurement Yearbooks*.
2. Administer several career assessment instruments and write an interpretation. Tape or role-play the results for the client.
3. Write a position paper on one of the following topics: the role of assessment in career counseling, gender and cultural bias in interest inventories, Internet-based career assessment, or the history of career assessment.
4. Design some nontest techniques to assess individual interests and values. Try out your assessment techniques on a sample of individuals and write a report of your findings.
5. Study the following hypothetical case and answer the questions that follow it.

Case of Erica

Erica is a 35-year-old mother of one and has been working in same job since graduating college. Erica was the first person in her family to go to college. Erica's family emigrated from Mexico and began working in trade jobs for several generations. Erica's family members take pride in working with their hands and have had some opposition to her pursuit of education. Today, Erica believes that she has advanced as far as possible in her current position and has gotten tired of working at the same job. She has experienced some job burnout and has decided to see what other types of careers she might be able to pursue. After discussing her career concerns with a career counselor, Erica agreed that an interest inventory might be a good starting point for discussion. The counselor administered the COPS and the CAPS. Erica had the following scores:

	Raw Scores	Percentiles
COPS Career Clusters		
1. Science, Professional	26	91
2. Science, Skilled	11	50
3. Technology, Professional	9	45
4. Technology, Skilled	4	30
5. Consumer Economics	11	50
6. Outdoor	18	70
7. Business, Professional	26	85
8. Business, Skilled	14	55
9. Clerical	1	2
10. Communication	15	45
11. Arts, Professional	17	35
12. Arts, Skilled	21	48
13. Service, Professional	30	87
14. Service, Skilled	17	50

CAPS Ability Dimensions

	Raw Scores	Percentiles
1. Mechanical Reasoning	13	83
2. Spatial Relations	15	92
3. Verbal Reasoning	24	98
4. Numerical Ability	18	92
5. Language Usage	22	83
6. Word Knowledge	41	68
7. Perceptual Speed and Accuracy	116	83
8. Manual Speed and Dexterity	230	32

a. How would you describe Erica's pattern of interests?

b. How would you describe Erica's pattern of aptitudes?

c. What further information would you want to have about Erica?

d. What further information would you want to have about the tests?

6. Interview an individual who is working in the personnel field in business and industry. Find out what types of assessment procedures that person's company uses to hire workers and to promote workers. Report your findings to the class.

7. Conduct a task or job analysis of your current job. Get the reactions of others—that is, your coworkers and your supervisors. See if they agree. Then, design assessment instruments to rate individuals in your field. Identify standardized instruments and procedures that might already be available.

8. Design an assessment program to hire workers in your field, to identify professional development needs, and to identify those who should be promoted to managerial levels.

9. Write a critical review of the literature on one of the following topics: assessment centers, job analysis, legal aspects of employment tests, or Internet-based employment tests. Critically analyze one of the widely used tests listed in this chapter.

References

Arulmani, G. (2014). Assessment of interest and aptitude: A methodologically integrated approach. In G. Arulmani, A. J. Bakshi, F. T. L. Leong, & A. G. Watts (Eds.), *Handbook of career development: International perspectives* (pp. 609–629). New York, NY: Springer Science & Business Media.

Barclay, S. R., & Wolff, L. A. (2012). Exploring the career construction interview for vocational personality assessment. *Journal of Vocational Behavior, 81*(3), 370–377. doi: http://dx.doi.org/10.1016/j.jvb.2012.09.004

Breaugh, J. A. (2014). Predicting voluntary turnover from job applicant biodata and other applicant information. *International Journal of Selection and Assessment, 22*(3), 321–332. doi: 10.1111/ijsa.12080

Brown, S. D., & Lent, R. W. (2013). *Career development and counseling.* Hoboken, NJ: John Wiley and Sons.

Chernyshenko, O. S., Stark, S., & Drasgow, F. (2011). Individual differences: Their measurement and validity. In S. Zedeck (Ed.), *APA handbook of industrial and organizational psychology* (Vol. 2: Selecting and developing members for the organization; pp. 117–151). Washington, DC: American Psychological Association.

Campbell, D. P., Hyne, S. A., & Nilsen, D. L. (1992). *Manual for the Campbell Interest and Skills Survey.* Minneapolis, MN: National Computer Systems.

Donnay, D. A. C., Thompson, R. C., Morris, M. L., & Schaubhut, N. A. (2012). *Technical brief for the newly revised Strong Interest Inventory assessment: Content, reliability, and validity.* Retrieved from https://www.cpp.com/Pdfs/StrongTechnicalBrief.pdf

Dozier, V. C., Sampson, J. P., Lenz, J. G., Peterson, G. W., & Reardon, R. C. (2014). The impact of the Self-Directed Search Form R Internet Version on counselor-free career exploration. *Journal of Career Assessment.* doi: 10.1177/1069072714535020

Frederiksen, N., Saunders, D. R., & Wand, B. (1957). The in-basket test. *Psychological Monograph, 71*(9), 1–28.

Friedman, T., & Williams, E. B. (1982). Current uses of tests for employment. In A. K. Wigdon & W. R. Garner (Eds.), *Ability testing: Uses, consequences, and controversies* (Pt. 2). Washington, DC: National Academy Press.

Gatewood, R. D., Feild, H. S., & Barnick, M. J. (2010). *Human resource selection.* Chicago, IL: Dryden.

Gibson, R. L., & Mitchell, M. H. (2006). *Introduction to career counseling for the 21st century.* Columbus, OH: Pearson.

Harmon, L. W., Hansen, J. I. C., Borgen, F. H., & Hammer, A. L. (1994). *Strong Interest Inventory applications and technical guide.* Palo Alto, CA: CPP.

Harrington, T. F., Harrington, J. C., & Wall, J. E. (2012). *Ability Explorer.* Indianapolis, IN: JIST Works.

Harrington, T., & Long, J. (2013). The history of interest inventories and career assessments in career counseling. *Career Development Quarterly, 61*(1), 83–92. doi: 10,1002/j.2161-0045.2013.00039.x

Hebl, M. R., Madera, J. M., & Martinez, L. R. (2014). Personnel selection. In F. T. L. Leong, L. Comas-Díaz, G. C. Nagayama Hall, V. C. McLoyd, & J. E. Trimble (Eds.), *APA handbook of multicultural psychology* (Vol. 2: Applications and training; pp. 253–264). Washington, DC: American Psychological Association.

Holland, J. L. (1994). *Self-Directed Search.* Odessa, FL: Psychological Assessment Resources.

Holland, J. L. (1996). Exploring careers with a typology. *American Psychologist, 51*, 397–406.

Holland, J. L., Reardon, R. C., Latshaw, R. J., Rarick, S. R., Schneider, S., Shortridge, M. A., & St. James, S. A. (2001). *Self-Directed Search Form R Internet Version 2.0. [Online].* Retrieved from http://www.self-directed-search.com

Levashina, J., Hartwell, C. J., Morgeson, F. P., & Campion, M. A. (2014). The structured employment interview: Narrative and quantitative review of the research literature. *Personnel Psychology, 67*(1), 241–293.

Manroop, L., Boekhorst, J. A., & Harrison, J. A. (2013). The influence of cross-cultural differences on job interview selection decisions. *The International Journal of Human Resource Management, 24*(18), 3512–3533.

McMahon, M., & Watson, M. (2012). Telling stories of career assessment. *Journal of Career Assessment, 20*(4), 440–451.

Muchinsky, P. M. (2008). *Psychology applied to work: An introduction to industrial and organization psychology* (9th ed.). Kansas City, KS: Hypergraphic Press.

Osborn, D. S., Dikel, M. F., & Sampson, J. P. (2011). *The Internet: A tool for career planning.* Broken Arrow, OK: National Career Development Association.

Rokeach, M. (1973). *The nature of human values.* New York, NY: Free Press.

Seijts, G. H., & Kyei-Poku, I. (2010). The role of situational interviews in fostering positive reactions to selection decisions. *Applied Psychology: An International Review, 59*(3), 431–453.

Sinha, N., & Srivastava, K. B. L. (2014). Examining the relationship between personality and work values across career stages. *Psychological Studies, 59*(1), 44–51.

Strong, E. R. (1927). Vocational Interest Test. *Educational Record, 8*, 107–121.

Super, D. E. (1970). *Manual, Work Values Inventory.* Chicago, IL: Riverside Publishing.

Super, D. E. (1990). A life-span, life-space approach to career development. In D. Brown, L. Brooks, & Associates (Eds.), *Career choice and development* (2nd ed., pp. 196–261). San Francisco, CA: Jossey-Bass.

Super, D. E., Zelkowitz, R. S., & Thompson, A. S. (1981). *Career Development Inventory: Adult Form I.* New York, NY: Teachers' College, Columbia University.

Thornton, G. C., & Byham, W. C. (1982). *Assessment centers and managerial performance.* New York, NY: Academic Press.

Thornton, G. C., & Rupp, D. E. (2006). *Assessment centers in human resource management.* Mahwah, NJ: Erlbaum.

U.S. Office of Personnel Management. (2009). *Assessment decision guide.* Retrieved from https://apps.opm.gov/ADT/Content.aspx? page=TOC

U.S. Department of Labor National Center for O*NET Development. (2007). *O*NET Online Summary Report for: 21-1012.00—Educational, Vocational, and School Counselors.* Retrieved from http://online.onetcenter.org/link/summary/21-1012.00

12 Personality Assessment

Personality includes all the special qualities people have that make them different from each other (e.g., charm, energy, disposition, attitude, temperament, cleverness) and the feelings and behaviors they exhibit. Personality assessments assist counselors in understanding the behavior of a particular individual, with the aim of making some decision about a future course of action or making a prediction about the person's unique future behavior. They give us a picture of the individual's enduring personality traits and transient personality states. Personality inventories are used in employment settings to aid in personnel selection, in forensic settings to aid in identification of problematic behavioral patterns, in clinical settings to identify personal problems and diagnose psychopathologies, and in clinical settings to evaluate growth or change in behavior after counseling. In recent years, personality assessment has become a popular approach for identifying the potential for relationship success or failure (Solomon & Jackson, 2014). Numerous instruments and techniques are used in personality assessment (such as structured personality inventories and projective techniques) to evaluate pathological aspects of personality. There are also instruments that focus primarily on assessing positive personality traits.

After studying this chapter, you should be able to:

- Provide a general definition of *personality*.
- Define the terms *state*, *trait*, and *type* as they relate to personality.
- Explain the various approaches (e.g., rational, theory, criterion group, factor analysis) by which personality instruments are constructed.
- Describe the characteristics of structured personality inventories and provide examples of inventories that fall in this category.
- Describe and provide examples of projective techniques and explain how they are distinct from structured personality inventories.
- Describe personality inventories that assess positive aspects of personality.

DEFINING PERSONALITY

The term *personality* has many meanings. Over the years, scientists and researchers have attempted to find a comprehensive definition of personality—their efforts resulting in dozens of diverse definitions appearing in the literature. For example, Gordon Allport

(1897–1967), considered by some to be the father of personality theory, alone described and classified over 50 meanings of personality. Some researchers regarded personality as synonymous with temperament—that is, the natural predisposition of an individual's thoughts, feelings, and behaviors. Some defined personality in terms of outward, observable behaviors; for example, John B. Watson (1878–1958) characterized personality as a by-product of habits. In contrast, some theorists focused on underlying inner, subjective qualities. In this vein, Allport viewed personality as a combination of psychosocial systems working to adapt to an environment. Consistency is probably at the heart of defining personality. Personality is generally considered to encompass *stable* and *enduring* behaviors. How you define personality will have a direct impact on the work you perform as a professional counselor. For example, if you view personality as a stable and unchanging collection of behaviors tied only to genetic predispositions, then you are likely to see some clients as hopeless. On the other hand, if you see personality as a combination of genetics and environmental (social) learning, then you might see opportunities for clients to manage behaviors that have been ingrained or even change long-standing behavior patterns.

Regardless of how you define personality, you have to admit that it is a complex construct. Because personality is complex, there are thousands of assessment instruments that measure all aspects of personality. For this textbook, we define personality as the reasonably stable patterns of thoughts, emotions, and behaviors derived from both genetic predisposition and social learning that distinguish one person from another and crystallize over time. Before presenting information about personality assessment, we will provide some background information on three fundamental terms related to personality: traits, states, and types.

Traits, States, and Types

Although theorists have debated the definition of personality, most would agree that it involves a system of thoughts, feelings, and behaviors. Some of the elements of this system are short acting (states), whereas others are longer lasting (traits). States and traits often combine to create different types of personalities. Much has been written about personality traits, states, and types, and whole courses can be dedicated to these concepts. We provide an overview of each in order to help to develop a foundational understanding of these concepts.

TRAITS Personality traits can be viewed as the distinguishing characteristics or qualities possessed by an individual. *Traits* can be defined as "dimensions of individual differences in tendencies to show consistent patterns of thoughts, feelings, and actions" (McCrae & Costa, 2003, p. 25). Traits are assumed to be relatively stable over time, differ among individuals, and influence behavior. Words such as "outgoing," "passive," "extrovert," "perfectionist," and "motivated" reflect specific personality traits related to an individual's behavior, whereas traits associated with emotional qualities include "happy," "anxious," and "moody." The collection of traits forms a profile of general social personality strengths and weaknesses that can be used to distinguish one person from another (Beutler, Groth-Marnat, & Hardwood, 2012). As professional counselors, we often become more concerned with those traits that are maladaptive. The *Diagnostic and Statistical Manual of Mental Disorders* (DSM-5) Personality and Personality Disorder workgroup proposed the identification of personality disorders using 25 pathological traits (Krueger, Derringer, Markon, Watson, & Skodol, 2012). Thomas et al. (2013) determined that these pathological traits fit within the framework of the Five Factor Model (FFM) of personality (discussed later in this chapter). More simply stated, there is some evidence that patho-logical and normative personality traits can be explained via a single model. However, more research needs to be conducted before a single model of explaining personality traits emerges.

The difficulty in researching personality traits is the sheer number of adjectives that people use to describe each other. Allport (1937), an American psychologist who pioneered the study of personality traits, was the first theorist to identify the thousands of words that discriminate human personality characteristics. After searching dictionaries, he found over 18,000 trait-like words. He whittled that list down to about 3,000 words and catego-rized them into three levels: cardinal traits (dominate and shape a person's behavior), central traits (general characteristics found in all persons within particular cultures), and secondary traits (characteristics seen in only certain circumstances). Despite his efforts, theorists disagree on which and how many traits explain human personality, and today hundreds of inventories are available that purport to measure one or more personality traits. Consider some popular dating sites that claim to be able to match clients on distinct aspects of personality. These sites claim to have success in creating lasting relationships using personality trait theory. However, the number of traits being matched differs across the board. The same is true for various standardized personality assessment instruments. Whereas some measure five factors, others measure 16 or more. The end result is that there are innumerable ways to measure personality traits.

STATES In reference to personality, the word *state* refers to the transitory exhibition of some trait (Kalimeri, 2013). Whereas *trait* refers to an enduring personality characteristic, *state* usually refers to a temporary behavioral tendency. For example, a person may be described as being in an anxious state after experiencing a traumatic event, but may not be consid-ered an anxious person (trait) in general. Although few personality inventories distinguish traits from states, Spielberger (1970, 1983) designed the State-Trait Anxiety Scale to iden-tify the anxiety an individual feels at a particular moment (state) versus the way he or she feels generally (trait).

TYPES Some researchers expanded on the trait approach of understanding personality by sorting traits into various clusters or *types*. If traits can be considered specific characteris-tics of an individual, then types can be regarded as a general description of a person. The first focuses on individual attributes, whereas the latter represents an enumeration of essential qualities or features that have more far-reaching implications (Kroeger & Thuesen, 2013). For example, extroversion can be considered a personality type that is associated with traits such as sociability, talkativeness, assertiveness, adventurousness, and high lev-els of energy. Personality typologies have existed at least since Hippocrates's classification of people into four types (i.e., melancholic, phlegmatic, choleric, sanguine), and many more typologies have been created over the years. Most notable is the personality typology developed by Carl Jung (1921) that became the basis for the Myers–Briggs Type Indicator (MBTI; Myers, McCaulley, Quenk, & Hammer, 1998), probably the best known instrument that assesses personality type.

PERSONALITY INVENTORIES

Personality inventories are commonly used to identify and measure the structure and features of one's personality or one's characteristic way of thinking, feeling, and behaving (Weiner & Greene, 2011). Some personality inventories measure specific traits (such as introversion) or states (such as anxiety), whereas others evaluate broad dimensions of personality that encompass a broad range of characteristics and attributes. In addition to measurement and evaluation, personality inventories can be used for other purposes, such as increasing self-knowledge and self-understanding (Urbina, 2014). Most personality inventories are self-report, meaning that the test taker supplies information about him- or herself; other instruments can be designed to elicit information from individuals other than the person being evaluated (e.g., parent, spouse, teacher). The following are examples of how professionals from various disciplines may use personality inventories:

- A career counselor administers a personality inventory in order to help a person choose a career.
- A clinical mental health counselor administers a personality inventory to narrow down a varied set of symptoms and determine the diagnosis of a particular psychological disorder.
- A school counselor looks at a high school student's personality inventory results to determine if any difficulties are related to the student's academic problems.
- An employment counselor uses a personality inventory to identify a client's personality attributes (e.g., conscientiousness, emotional stability, agreeableness) that contribute to effective work performance.
- A neuropsychologist administers a personality inventory to determine the extent to which an individual's brain injury has affected cognition and behavior.

Approaches to Personality Inventory Development

Personality inventories may differ in the approach by which they are constructed. Four common approaches to personality inventory development are rational, theory, criterion group, and factor analysis; combinations of these approaches are also employed.

RATIONAL APPROACH One of the oldest methods of personality test construction is the *rational approach*, which involves the use of reason and deductive logic to construct test items. In other words, items are developed based on the degree to which they are logically assumed to be related to a given construct. An example is the *Woodworth Personal Data Sheet* (Woodworth, 1920), considered to be the first structured (i.e., objective) personality inventory. The 116-item self-report inventory was assembled in response to needs for psychiatric screening during the U.S. entry into World War I. Test items consisted of statements that Woodworth believed were indicators of psychological maladjustment. Items were simply listed on paper (e.g., *Are you happy most of the time?*), and the respondent answered *yes* or *no*. Instrument development using the rational approach means that the measure is entirely dependent upon the test author's assumptions about the construct (i.e., personality) being measured, and these assumptions may or may not have been well-founded.

THEORY-BASED APPROACH Unlike the rational approach, personality inventories constructed using a *theory-based* approach are founded on an established theory of personality. For example, instruments that use *projective techniques* are based on the psychodynamic theory of personality, which emphasizes the importance of the *unconscious* (i.e., hidden emotions, internal conflicts). Thus, projective instruments are thought to reveal examinees' unconscious by allowing them to respond to some type of unstructured stimuli (e.g., an inkblot, a picture, an incomplete sentence), resulting in the examinee projecting or expressing unconscious fears, conflicts, or needs.

Similarly, the MBTI (Myers et al., 1998) was constructed based on Carl Jung's (1921) theory of psychological type. Jung identified two dimensions that combined to create personality types: attitudes (extraversion and introversion) and functions (sensation, intuition, thinking, and feeling). Based on Jung's original concepts, the MBTI sorts an individual's preferences into four separate categories: (a) extraversion or introversion, (b) sensing or intuitive, (c) thinking or feeling, and (d) judging or perceiving. Combinations of these four preferences result in 16 separate personality types that are used to describe the examinee.

CRITERION GROUP APPROACH The *criterion group approach* is an empirical method of personality test construction that involves selecting items that can discriminate between relevant criterion groups and control groups. The approach begins with a population sample with known personality characteristics, such as a group of individuals diagnosed with schizophrenia (i.e., the *criterion group*). An instrument based upon this population sample is administered to both the schizophrenic group and a *control group* (usually a "normal" population) to identify the items that distinguish the two groups. The items that distinguish the schizophrenic group from the control group are then placed in a separate scale. The scale is then *cross-validated* to see how well it distinguishes the schizophrenic group from other groups. Using the criterion group method, the emphasis is on the discriminating power of the instrument; what is important is the fact that the test discriminates, not the reason it does so. This method of instrument construction is exemplified by the creation of the Minnesota Multiphasic Personality Inventory (MMPI-2) and MMPI-2-RF, which were developed based on the ability of tests' items to detect symptoms of psychopathology in adults.

FACTOR ANALYSIS *Factor analysis* is another empirical approach that uses statistical procedures to (a) analyze interrelationships among a large number of variables (e.g., personality traits) and (b) explain these variables in terms of their common underlying dimensions (factors). For constructing personality inventories, factor analysis helps in condensing numerous personality traits into fewer dimensions of personality that can then be measured and evaluated. For example, Cattell, Eber, and Tatsuoka (1970) developed the Sixteen Personality Factor, Fifth Edition (16PF) by reducing 18,000 personality descriptors (originally identified by Allport) into 181 personality clusters, from which 12 factors were generated using factor analysis. These factors laid the foundation for the first 16PF published in 1949. More than half a century and several revisions later, the 16PF continues to be a widely used instrument for measuring normal adult personality. Another example is the NEO Personality Inventory (NEO PI-R), a 240-item inventory that is based on five dimensions of personality (known as the *Five Factor Model*): neuroticism, extraversion, openness, agreeableness, and conscientiousness. These broad factor-analytically derived categories have been shown to represent the underlying structure of Allport's 18,000 personality adjectives (Costa & McCrae, 2013) and have received much support from theorists and researchers

(Detrick & Chibnall, 2013; Furnham, Guenole, Levine, & Chamorro-Premuzic, 2013; Gorostiaga, Balluerka, Alonso-Arbiol, & Haranburu, 2011; Källmen, Wennberg, & Bergman, 2011; Van den Broeck, Rossi, Dierckx, & De Clercq, 2012; Vassend & Skrondal, 2011).

COMBINED APPROACHES   Many personality inventories are constructed using a combination of rational, theory-based, criterion groups, and factor analytic approaches. For example, the items of the Millon Clinical Multiaxial Inventory (MCMI-III) were initially theory-based items and derived from Millon's (1969) theories of personality and psychopathology. Then, criterion group procedures were employed to refine test items in terms of their ability to discriminate among groups with certain personality disorders or clinical syndromes.

CATEGORIES OF PERSONALITY INVENTORIES

In this section, we will present information about several personality assessment instruments and strategies grouped into three categories: structured personality inventories, projective techniques, and instruments that assess *positive aspects* of personality.

Structured Personality Inventories

Structured (also called *objective*) personality inventories are usually standardized, self-report instruments made up of items that are presented to a person who indicates how accurately the items describe his or her personality using a limited set of response options (Kamphaus & Frick, 2010). For example, many structured personality inventories use *selected-response items* (e.g., true/false, matching, multiple choice) or *rating scales*. Responses on personality inventories are not scored in terms of correctness (right or wrong), but are scored in reference to the personality characteristic being measured. For example, a *true* response on a personality test item may indicate the presence of a particular trait, not that the question was answered correctly. Because of the selected-response format, items on structured personality inventories can typically be answered rapidly, allowing for the use of numerous items covering many aspects of personality without lengthy administration times (Cohen & Swerdlik, 2010). In addition, items can be scored quickly and reliably using various means (e.g., hand scoring, computer scoring) as well as interpreted accurately and efficiently, particularly with the use of computer software programs.

Structured personality inventories can have a broad or narrow scope. An instrument with a *broad scope* measures and provides scores on a wide array of personality variables. Broadly focused personality inventories can be very comprehensive and time-consuming (taking 1 to 2 hours to complete), may contain hundreds of test items, and may provide several scores on scales or subscales. The MMPI-2 is the best example of a personality inventory with a broad scope; it contains 566 true/false items, resulting in scores on several separate scales. A version of the MMPI (MMPI-2-RF) was developed by Ben-Porath and Tellegen (2008) to be aligned with the MMPI-2's restructured clinical scales. This new version is 338 true/false and can be used for a wide range of assessment purposes.

In contrast, structured inventories with a *narrow scope* focus on targeted aspects of personality, such as specific symptoms (e.g., depression, anxiety) or behaviors. They are typically briefer than broad personality inventories, often taking no longer than 15 or

20 minutes to complete. Frequently used in *clinical assessment*, hundreds if not thousands of narrowly focused inventories are available that aid in (a) screening and diagnosing mental disorders (such as an eating disorder or a mood disorder), (b) developing treatment plans, (c) monitoring treatment progress, and (d) evaluating treatment outcome. For example, the Beck Depression Inventory (BDI-II) is a widely used inventory with items that focus specifically on symptoms of depression. Chapter 13 will provide more information about narrowly focused personality inventories.

Structured personality inventories can focus on *pathological* or *nonpathological* aspects of personality. *Pathology* refers to anything that deviates from a healthy, normal condition. In terms of personality, *pathological* is used to indicate symptoms or other manifestations of mental or behavioral disorders (i.e., *psychopathology*). Examples of psychopathology include such symptoms as depressed mood, anxiety, hallucinations, and delusions, to name just a few. The MMPI-2 and the MCMI-III are examples of personality inventories with a pathological focus; their general intent is to identify the presence or absence of symptoms or behaviors that relate to specific psychopathological categories. Both of these tests are discussed at length in Chapter 10.

Nonpathological inventories de-emphasize pathology as a defining characteristic of personality and focus on "normal" personality characteristics. They are developed for use with a normal population and assess the presence or absence of such nonpathological personality characteristics as sociability, responsibility, and flexibility. Personality inventories with a nonpathological focus include the California Psychological Inventory (CPI), the MBTI, the NEO PI-R, the 16PF, and the Riso–Hudson Enneagram Type Indicator (RHETI).

In this section, we will review several prominent structured personality inventories.

THE MINNESOTA MULTIPHASIC PERSONALITY INVENTORY The MMPI-2 (Butcher et al., 2001), one of the most widely used personality inventories, is a comprehensive, structured instrument that assesses major symptoms of adult psychopathology. It is often used by clinicians to assist with the diagnosis of mental disorders and the selection of appropriate treatment methods. The original MMPI was developed in the late 1930s and early 1940s by psychologist Starke R. Hathaway and psychiatrist and neurologist J. C. McKinley at the University of Minnesota. Because of concerns about the adequacy of the original standardization norm, the MMPI-2, released in 1989, implemented norms that were much more representative of the U.S. population. The MMPI-2 can be administered to individuals aged 18 years and older who can read at a minimum sixth-grade level. It has 567 true/false questions; takes 60 to 90 minutes to complete; can be administered by hand, audiocassette, and computer; and is available in English, Spanish, Hmong, and French (Canada). Use of the MMPI-2 is restricted to qualified professionals who are licensed or credentialed and have adequate training in assessment, personality theory, psychopathology, and diagnosis.

The MMPI-2 contains 10 *clinical scales* that assess dimensions of personality and psychopathology. The clinical scales were developed using an empirical approach: items were selected for each scale on the basis of their ability to discriminate between clinical and normal groups. It also has nine *validity scales* used to detect *response styles*, which refers to a test taker's pattern of responding to items. A test taker may respond to items in a variety of ways that can compromise the validity of the test (Butcher et al., 2001). For example, an examinee may leave a large number of items unanswered, distort his or her self-descriptions by underreporting or overreporting symptoms, choose answers randomly, or pick all true or all false answers. The MMPI-2 validity scales were designed to help detect sources of test invalidity and to evaluate the impact of such distortions on the test results. Table 12.1 provides a description of the clinical and validity scales.

TABLE 12.1 MMPI-2 Validity and Clinical Scales

Name	Abbr.	Description
Validity Scales		
1. Cannot Say	CNS	The total number of unanswered questions. If 30 or more items are omitted, then the test results are highly suspect or invalid.
2. Variable Response Inconsistency	VRIN	Detects random or inconsistent responding. A T score at or above 80 invalidates the test.
3. True Response Inconsistency	TRIN	Picking all true or all false answers. A T score at or above 80 invalidates the test. (*Note:* On the MMPI-2 profile, a letter "T" following the TRIN T score indicates more true responses, and the letter "F" following the TRIN T score indicates more false responses.)
4. Infrequency	F	Identifies overreporting of symptoms (faking bad). A T score at or above 90 might invalidate the test. T scores between 70 and 89 suggest exaggerated symptoms, perhaps a cry for help.
5. Back Infrequency	$F_{(B)}$	Detects overreporting in the second half of the test. If the T score on the $F_{(B)}$ is at least 30 points greater than the T score on the F, then scales with items in the latter part of the test may be invalid.
6. Infrequency-Psychopathology	$F_{(P)}$	Detects intentional overreporting of symptoms. A T score at or above 70 suggests exaggerated symptoms (perhaps a cry for help); a T score at or above 100 invalidates the profile.
7. Lie	L	Detects intentional underreporting (purposefully making self look favorable). A T score at or above 80 may indicate dishonest answers and invalidates the test.
8. Correction	K	Detects unintentional underreporting (due to denial, lack of insight, or a defensive approach to taking the test). A T score at or above 65 may invalidate the test.
9. Superlative Presentation	S	Assesses the tendency to present self as highly virtuous and responsible, with no psychological problems and few or no moral flaws. A T score at or above 70 may invalidate the test.

Clinical Scales

Note: In general, all clinical scale T scores at or above 65 are considered to be high scores and in the "clinical" range.

1. Hypochondriasis	Hs	Preoccupied with health problems; medical complaints with little or no organic basis; health problems may be associated with stress.

TABLE 12.1 MMPI-2 Validity and Clinical Scales (*Continued*)

Name	Abbr.	Description
2. Depression	D	Clinical depression; feels pessimistic, hopeless, guilty, suicidal, unworthy.
3. Hysteria	Hy	Difficulty dealing with stress; physical symptoms may worsen under stressful conditions.
4. Psychopathic Deviate	Pd	Antisocial behavior; trouble with the law; stealing, lying; rebellious, angry, and/or impulsive behavior; substance abuse.
5. Masculinity-Femininity	Mf	Nontraditional sex roles. High scores for men indicate lack of traditional masculine interests; high scores for women indicate a rejection of traditional feminine roles.
6. Paranoia	Pa	Paranoid symptoms, such as ideas of reference, delusions of persecution, suspiciousness, excessive sensitivity, rigid opinions.
7. Psychasthenia	Pt	Anxiety, extreme fear, tension, obsessive-compulsive.
8. Schizophrenia	Sc	Disturbances of thinking, mood, and behavior; hallucinations; delusions.
9. Hypomania	Ma	Hypomanic or manic symptoms, such as elevated mood, irritability, flight of ideas, grandiosity, excitability.
10. Social Introversion	Si	Tendency to withdraw from social contacts and responsibility; insecure, indecisive, introverted.

Since the original MMPI was published, a number of additional scales and subscales (e.g., Content Scales, Supplementary Scales) have been developed that measure numerous pathological or nonpathological aspects of personality. In addition, the MMPI-2-RF was published in 2008 as a shorter form of the MMPI. Although the MMPI-2-RF is a more recent form, the MMPI-2 continues to be the more widely used version because of the substantial research base to support it.

Scores for the MMPI-2 are reported as T scores. There are several steps involved in interpreting scores. First, clinicians examine the validity scale scores to determine whether the profile contains valid, useful, and relevant information about the client's personality and clinical problems. If the test taker scores at or above particular T score values on validity scales, then the results of the clinical scales may be invalid. For example, a T score of 80 or higher on the Lie (L) validity scale may indicate that the individual answered questions dishonestly, thus invalidating the test. Only after evaluating the validity scales and determining that the results are valid does the clinician proceed to examine the clinical scales scores. In general, T scores above 65 on the clinical scales are elevated and considered within the "clinical" range, which refers to the range of scores obtained by the sample of individuals experiencing the particular symptom measured by the scale. Inferences should not be based solely on a high score on one clinical scale; rather, inferences should be made on the basis of all elevated scale scores as well as the individual's background and presenting problem. Figure 12.1 provides a sample profile of the MMPI-2.

Level	Uniform T-Scores	Percentile Rank
• Extremely High	• 85–90	• > 99.8
• Very High	• 75–80	• 98–99
• High	• 65–70	• 92–96
• Moderately High	• 55–60	• 73–85
• Average	• 45–50	• 34–55
• Moderately Low	• 35–40	• 4–15
• Very Low	• 30	• < 1

FIGURE 12.1   Overview of MMPI-2 Scores.

The MMPI-2-RF is a shorter and newer version of the MMPI. The RF contains 338 true/false items, and the results can be used for a wide range of purposes—much like the longer form of the MMPI-2. The MMPI-2-RF has 51 empirically validated scores and a number of validity indicators. Many of the same scales from the long form are included in the MMPI-2-RF. The shorter form is based on the restructured clinical scales, which have been reported in the long form as well. The restructured clinical scales include the following:

RCd-(dem)—Demoralization

RC1-(som)—Somatic Complaints

RC2-(lpe)—Low Positive Emotions

RC3-(cyn)—Cynicism

RC4-(asb)—Antisocial Behavior

RC6-(per)—Ideas of Persecution

RC7-(dne)—Dysfunctional Negative Emotions

RC8-(abx)—Aberrant Experiences

RC9-(hpm)—Hypomanic Activation

Like the long form of the MMPI-2, interpretation of the scales requires specific training. The MMPI-2-RF is restricted to use by professionals who have a doctoral degree in a helping profession, licensure in an area of professional practice, or certification by a professional organization. Although licensed counselors are qualified users, we caution you to review state licensure laws to ensure state-specific privleges.

MILLON CLINICAL MULTIAXIAL INVENTORY The MCMI-III (Millon, Millon, Davis, & Grossman, 2009) is a 175-item self-report, true/false instrument designed for adults (18 years and older) and takes approximately 30 minutes to complete. It is one of the few inventories that focus on personality disorders along with symptoms that are frequently associated with these disorders. The inventory consists of 28 scales that are divided into

Exercise 12.1
Assessment Using the MMPI-2

Nicholas, age 35, was referred for evaluation by his psychiatrist. Nicholas was diagnosed with bipolar disorder (also known as manic-depressive illness), which is a brain disorder that causes dramatic mood swings—from overly "high" and/or irritable to sad and hopeless and then back again, often with periods of normal mood in between. The psychiatrist was treating Nicholas with medica- tions commonly prescribed in the treatment of bipolar disorder. Nicholas informed his psychiatrist that he is feeling much better and wants to stop taking the medications and terminate treatment. The psychiatrist wants to know if Nicholas is doing as well as he claims he is doing.

Review Nicholas' MMPI-2 profile report and answer the questions that follow.

MMPI-2 Profile

Validity Scales	Description
Cannot Say	The Cannot Say score was 4, indicating that David omitted three items on the inventory. This does not invalidate test results.
Variable Response Inconsistency—VRIN	The T score on the VRIN scale was 46, which indicates that David's responses were not random or inconsistent.
True Response Inconsistency—TRIN	
Infrequency—F	
Back Infrequency—F(B)	
Infrequency-Psychopathology—F(P)	
Lie—L	
Correction—K	
Superlative Presentation—S	

Exercise Questions:

1. Interpret the scores on each validity scale. Use the answers provided on the first two validity scales as a format for your answers.
2. Based on the validity scale scores, do you believe Nicholas's MMPI-2 results are valid? Explain.
3. Identify the clinical scale score(s) that are in the "clinical range" and interpret the scores.
4. How would you respond to the psychiatrist's question (is Nicholas is doing as well as he claims he is doing)?
5. What would you recommend to Nicholas and his psychiatrist?

TABLE 12.2 The MCMI-III Scales

Clinical Personality Pattern Scales		Clinical Syndrome Scales	
1	Schizoid	A	Anxiety
H	Somatoform	2A	Avoidant
N	Bipolar: Manic	2B	Depressive
D	Dysthymia	3	Dependent
B	Alcohol Dependence	4	Histrionic
5	Narcissistic	T	Drug Dependence
6A	Antisocial	R	Posttraumatic Stress Disorder
6B	Sadistic (Aggressive)	**Severe Syndrome Scales**	
7	Compulsive	SS	Thought Disorder
8A	Negativistic (Passive-Aggressive)	CC	Major Depression
8B	Masochistic (Self-Defeating)	PP	Delusional Disorder
Severe Personality Pathology Scales		**Modifying Indices**	
S	Schizotypal	C	Borderline
X	Disclosure	P	Paranoid
Y	Desirability	Z	Debasement
		V	Validity

the following categories: Modifying Indices, Clinical Personality Patterns, Severe Personality Pathology, Clinical Syndromes, and Severe Syndromes (see Table 12.2). The scales, along with the items that comprise the scales, are closely aligned to both Theodore Millon's (1969) theory of personality and the classification system of the DSM-5 (American Psychiatric Association (APA), 2013). The MCMI-III is often considered an alternative to the MMPI-2, because both instruments cover a broad range of adult psychopathology. However, the MMPI-2 focuses primarily on clinical symptoms, whereas the MCMI was specifically designed to assist in diagnosing personality disorders. An important advantage of the MCMI-III is that it is considerably shorter than the MMPI-2 (175 items vs. 567 items) and yet provides a wide range of information.

THE CALIFORNIA PSYCHOLOGICAL INVENTORY First published in 1957, the CPI is a self-administered personality inventory composed of 434 true/false statements that assess personality dimensions in "normal" people between the ages of 12 and 70 (Gough, 2000). Except for the MMPI-2, the CPI is the most thoroughly researched and frequently used personality inventory. Test items focus on typical behavior patterns, feelings and opinions, and attitudes relating to social, ethical, and family matters (e.g., "I enjoy social gatherings just to be with people"). The results are plotted on 20 scales (representing personality traits) that are clustered into four general domains (see Table 12.3). The inventory was normed on a standardization sample of 6,000 men and 7,000 women of varying age and socioeconomic status and included high school and college students, teachers, business executives, prison executives, psychiatric patients, and prison inmates.

THE MYERS–BRIGGS TYPE INDICATOR Another nonpathological personality inventory is the well-known and widely used MBTI (Myers et al., 1998). Developed in the 1940s by

TABLE 12.3 General Domains and Scales of the California Personality Inventory

General Domains	Scales
I. *Observable, interpersonal style, and orientation*	1. Dominance (leadership ability)
	2. Capacity for status (ambitious vs. unsure)
	3. Sociability (outgoing vs. shy)
	4. Social presence (self-assured vs. reserved)
	5. Self-acceptance (positive self vs. self-doubting)
	6. Independence (self-sufficient vs. seeks support)
	7. Empathy (empathetic vs. unempathetic)
II. *Normative orientation and values*	8. Responsibility (responsible vs. undisciplined)
	9. Socialization (conforms vs. rebellious)
	10. Self-control (overcontrol vs. undercontrol)
	11. Good impression (pleases others vs. complains about others)
	12. Communality (fits in vs. sees self differently)
	13. Well-being (optimistic vs. pessimistic)
	14. Tolerance (fair minded vs. fault finding)
III. *Cognitive and intellectual functioning*	15. Achievement via conformance (efficient and well organized vs. distracted)
	16. Achievement via independence (clear thinking vs. uninterested)
	17. Intellectual efficiency (keeps on task vs. hard time getting started)
IV. *Measures of role and personal style*	18. Psychological mindedness (insightful and perceptive vs. apathetic and unmotivated)
	19. Flexibility (likes change vs. not changeable)
	20. Femininity/masculinity (sensitive vs. unsentimental)

Katharine Cook Briggs and Isabel Briggs Myers, the MBTI was designed for measuring an individual's preference according to the typological theories of Carl Jung (Myers & Myers, 1995). The instrument sorts an individual's preferences into four separate categories, each composed of two opposite poles:

- *Extraversion (E) or Introversion (I)* Where an individual prefers to focus his or her energy. People who prefer *extroversion* direct their energy to the outside world of people, things, and situations. Those who prefer *introversion* focus their energy on the inner world of ideas, emotion, information, or beliefs.
- *Sensing (S) or Intuitive (I)* How an individual prefers to process or acquire information. *The sensing* type prefers to deal with facts, be objective, or use the five senses to notice what is real. The *intuitive* type prefers to look beyond the five senses to acquire information, to generate new possibilities and ways of doing things, or to anticipate what isn't obvious.
- *Thinking (T) or Feeling (F)* How an individual prefers to makes decisions. *Thinking* indicates a preference to make decisions based on logic and objective analysis of the evidence. *Feeling* types prefer to make decisions based on their values and subjective evaluation.

- *Judging (J) or Perceiving (P)* How an individual prefers to organize his or her life. The term *judging* does not mean "judgmental." It simply indicates a preference for living in a planned, stable, and organized way. *Perceiving* indicates a preference for more spontaneity and flexibility, responding to things as they arise.

These four categories are combined to form 16 possible personality types (or combinations of preferences) that best describe the examinee. Each type tends to be characterized by its own interests, values, and unique gifts. Types are often referred to by an abbreviation of four letters, indicating the four type preferences—for example:

ESTJ: Extraversion, Sensing, Thinking, Judging

INFP: Introversion, Intuition, Feeling, Perceiving

The results of the MBTI provide a detailed description of an individual's type. For example, an individual reported as an ENFP (Extraversion, Intuition, Feeling, and Perceiving) would be described as the following (Myers & Myers, 2004, p. 2):

- Curious, creative, and imaginative
- Energetic, enthusiastic, and spontaneous
- Keenly perceptive of people and of the outside world
- Appreciative of affirmation from others; readily expresses appreciation and gives support to others
- Likely to value harmony and goodwill
- Likely to make decisions based on personal values and empathy with others
- Usually seen by others as personable, perceptive, persuasive, and versatile

NEO PERSONALITY INVENTORY-REVISED The NEO PI-R is a well-known, highly regarded personality inventory based on the Five Factor Model of personality, which suggests that the basic dimensions of personality contain the following components: Neuroticism, Extraversion, Openness to Experience, Agreeableness, and Conscientiousness. The NEO PI-R includes scales for each of the five personality factors as well as six facet (trait) scales for each domain:

1. *Neuroticism* Tendency to experience negative emotions (anxiety, angry hostility, depression, self-consciousness, impulsiveness, vulnerability)
2. *Extraversion* Amount of energy directed outward into the social world (warmth, gregariousness, assertiveness, activity, excitement seeking, positive emotions)
3. *Openness to Experience* Level of openness to new ideas and new experiences (fantasy, aesthetics, feelings, actions, ideas, values)
4. *Agreeableness* Tendency toward friendly, considerable, and modest behavior (trust, straightforwardness, altruism, compliance, modesty, tender-mindedness)
5. *Conscientiousness* Associated with responsibility and persistence (competence, order, dutifulness, achievement striving, self-discipline, deliberation)

The NEO PI-R consists of 240 statements for which respondents are asked to rate their level of agreement on a 5-point scale. Scores are reported in terms of qualitative descriptors: *very low*, *low*, *average*, *high*, and *very high*. The test has two forms: Form S is for self-reports; form R is for observer reports. There is also a shorter version, the NEO Five-Factor Inventory (NEO-FFI), which has 60 items and yields just the five domain scores.

THE SIXTEEN PERSONALITY FACTOR QUESTIONNAIRE, FIFTH EDITION The 16PF (Cattell et al., 1970) is a comprehensive measure of adult personality traits. It has been widely used for a variety of applications, including treatment planning, couples' counseling, vocational guidance, and hiring and promotion recommendations. The questionnaire consists of 187 items and takes 35 to 50 minutes to complete. There are 16 personality factors, which are also grouped into five global factors. The 16 personality factors and five global factors are derived from client responses. The 16 personality factors are Warmth, Reasoning, Emotional Stability, Dominance, Liveliness, Rule-Consciousness, Social Boldness, Sensitivity, Vigilance, Abstractedness, Privateness, Apprehension, Openness to Change, Self-Reliance, Perfectionism, and Tension. The five global factors are Extraversion, Anxiety, Tough-Mindedness, Independence, and Self-Control. Raw scores on all personality and global factors are converted to sten scores: scores from 1 to 3 are classified as *low*, scores from 4 to 7 are *average*, and scores from 8 to 10 are classified as *high*. High and low scores designate opposite poles of the same personality factor. For example, an individual's score on the Warmth factor may fall from reserved (low) to warm (high). Figure 12.2 shows a score profile for the 16PF.

RISO–HUDSON ENNEAGRAM TYPE INDICATOR The RHETI is a 144-item personality type instrument that produces a personality profile across nine personality types. Riso and Hudson (1999) postulated that this ancient system will help individuals unlock their hidden aspects so that they can become freer and better-functioning individuals. He believes that the study of one's profile leads to self-understanding and then to the understanding of others. The nine Enneagram types include the following:

1. *Reformers* Idealistic, purposeful, orderly, self-controlled, perfectionistic
2. *Helpers* Generous, concerned, demonstrative, people-pleasing, possessive
3. *Achievers* Self-assured, adaptable, ambitious, driven, image-conscious
4. *Individualists* Creative, expressive, dramatic, introverted, temperamental
5. *Investigators* Perceptive, analytical, secretive, isolated
6. *Loyalists* Likable, dependable, anxious, suspicious
7. *Enthusiasts* Accomplished, extroverted, spontaneous, acquisitive, scattered
8. *Challengers* Powerful, self-confident, decisive, willful, autocratic
9. *Peacemakers* Peaceful, receptive, passive, agreeable, complacent

The nine Enneagram types can be further divided into three ranges of functioning: healthy, average, and unhealthy (see Table 12.4). The test authors believe that assessing the level of functioning is important, because people with the same personality type will differ significantly if they are healthy or unhealthy. The internal consistency for the RHETI has been shown to be adequate (Newgent, Parr, Newman, & Higgins, 2004). Although there have been mixed results with regard to evaluation of validity for the instrument, Newgent et al. suggested that the instrument has heuristic value.

Projective Instruments and Techniques

In contrast to structured personality inventories, *projective instruments and techniques* require examinees to answer questions related to ambiguous stimuli (e.g., inkblots, pictures, phrases) using open-ended responses. What is projective about these instruments is the requirement for clients to generate a response in the face of ambiguity; in so doing,

Personality Factors

Sten	Factor	Left Meaning	Low 1 2 3	Average 4 5 | 6 7	High 8 9	10	Right Meaning
6	Warmth (A)	Reserved					Warm
8	Reasoning (B)	Concrete					Abstract
6	Emotional Stability (C)	Reactive					Emotionally Stable
6	Dominance (E)	Deferential					Dominant
4	Liveliness (F)	Serious					Lively
6	Rule-Consciousness (G)	Expedient					Rule-Conscious
8	Social Boldness (H)	Shy					Socially Bold
6	Sensitivity (I)	Utilitarian					Sensitive
4	Vigilance (L)	Trusting					Vigilant
7	Abstractedness (M)	Grounded					Abstracted
4	Privateness (N)	Forthright					Private
6	Apprehension (O)	Self-Assured					Apprehensive
9	Openness to Change (Q1)	Traditional					Open to Change
4	Self-Reliance (Q2)	Group-Oriented					Self-Reliant
4	Perfectionism (Q3)	Tolerates Disorder					Perfectionistic
6	Tension (Q4)	Relaxed					Tense

Global Factors

Sten	Factor	Left Meaning	Low 1 2 3	Average 4 5 | 6 7	High 8 9	10	Right Meaning
7	Extraversion	Introverted					Extraverted
5	Anxiety	Low Anxiety					High Anxiety
3	Tough-Mindedness	Receptive					Tough-Minded
7	Independence	Accommodating					Independent
5	Self-Control	Unrestrained					Self-Controlled

FIGURE 12.2   16PF Profile.

Source: 16PF Fifth Edition. Copyright © 2002 by Institute for Personality & Ability Testing, Inc. (employer for hire). Reproduced with permission of the publisher NCS Pearson, Inc. All rights reserved. "16PF" is a trademark, in the U.S. and/or other countries, of Pearson Education, Inc. or its affiliates(s).

the person interprets instrument stimuli in a way that reveals or projects elements of his or her personal characteristics (e.g., concerns, needs, conflicts, desires, feelings). Although projective techniques are reviewed in the majority of counselor-preparation assessment courses, the time spent on review does not typically prepare counselors to use these instruments in practice (Neukrug, Peterson, Bonner, & Lomas, 2013). Counselors interested in projective techniques require additional coursework or training to be competent in this area. Of course, before using these techniques or any assessment techniques, you should consult your state laws to ensure that you have appropriate privileges under your certification or licensure.

TABLE 12.4 Types Included on the Riso–Hudson Enneagram Type Indicator

Type	Range of Functioning	
	Healthy	Unhealthy
1. Reformer	Idealistic, orderly	Perfectionist, intolerant
2. Helper	Concerned, helpful	Possessive, manipulative
3. Achiever	Self-assured, ambitious	Narcissistic, psychopathic
4. Individualistic	Creative, individualistic	Introverted, depressive
5. Investigator	Perceptive, analytical	Eccentric, paranoid
6. Loyalist	Likable, dependable	Masochistic, plagued by doubt
7. Enthusiast	Accomplished, extroverted	Excessive, manic
8. Challenger	Powerful, self-confident	Dictatorial, destructive
9. Peacemaker	Peaceful, reassuring	Passive, repressed

Although counselor licensure laws vary with regard to the use of projective assessment, it is still important to understand the principles related to this method. Various methods of interpretation are used with projective instruments to make inferences about the individual's underlying personality processes and social-emotional functioning (Smith, 2011). Projective instruments are strongly associated with the psychodynamic theory of personality, which emphasizes the importance of the *unconscious* (i.e., hidden emotions, internal conflicts). Thus, by responding to some type of unstructured stimuli (e.g., inkblot, picture, incomplete sentence), individuals are thought to reveal their unconscious fears, conflicts, or needs. Some well-known projective instruments and techniques are the Rorschach Inkblot Test, the Thematic Apperception Test (TAT), verbal projective techniques, and projective drawings.

THE RORSCHACH INKBLOT TEST The Rorschach Inkblot Test, developed by Herman Rorschach (1921), is a test that measures an individual's view or perception of his or her world or environment. It consists of a series of irregular but symmetrical inkblots (see Figure 12.3); subjects are asked to look at the inkblots and verbally describe what they see. By analyzing what someone sees on the inkblot, examiners can make various hypotheses about the individual's emotions, cognition, coping skills, perception of others and relationships, and self-perception. The test consists of 10 bilaterally symmetrical inkblots printed on separate cards. Five cards are black and white; two are black, white, and red; and three are multicolored.

The test has two phases. In the first free-association phase, the examiner presents the inkblots to the test taker one at a time and instructs him or her to tell what is on each card by asking questions such as "What might this be?" The examiner records all relevant information, including the test taker's verbatim responses, nonverbal gestures, length of time before the first response to each card, and so on. The second phase, referred to as the inquiry phase, involves the examiner attempting to determine what features on the inkblot played a role in the test taker's perception of the image. Questions such as "What makes it look like (whatever)?" and "Where on the inkblot did you see (whatever the examinee saw)?" are asked to gain information useful for interpreting the responses.

Examiners must be thoroughly trained in the use of the Rorschach. Clinicians can make numerous errors during administration, scoring, and interpretation. However, with

FIGURE 12.3   A Rorschach-like inkblot.

supervised training the number of errors can be significantly reduced (Callahan, 2014). The original test came with no test manual and no administration, scoring, or interpretation instructions. Over the years, a number of manuals and handbooks by various authors have become available; the most widely used is a "comprehensive system" devised by Exner and Exner (2013).

THEMATIC APPERCEPTION TEST The TAT (Murray, 1943) originally was based on Henry Murray's (1938) theory of personality. The TAT includes a series of black-and-white picture cards that contain a variety of characters, situations, and objects (see Figure 12.4 for an example of typical administration of a personality test.). Examinees are asked to look at and make up stories about each picture. After each TAT card story, an inquiry process begins, and the examiner asks a series of questions to better understand the examinee's story, such as what led up to the event shown, what is happening at the moment, what the characters are thinking and feeling, and what the outcome of the story was. Questions may involve further clarification of the characters' thoughts and feelings and how the story was generated. There are numerous approaches to interpreting the TAT. Some interpretations involve examiners identifying a hero or main character within the story, the belief being that the examinee will identify with the character and project his or her unconscious motives, feelings, and needs onto the character (Aronow, Weiss, & Reznikoff, 2013). Furthermore, common themes among the stories should be identified, and how the client relates the story should be noted.

FIGURE 12.4   Example of personality assessment with a client.

VERBAL EXPRESSIVE PROJECTIVE TECHNIQUES Verbal expressive projective techniques allow a counselor to understand elements of personality through the presentation of verbal stimuli and elicited verbal responses. The stimuli and responses can be transmitted orally or in writing. These types of projective techniques allow a counselor to evaluate personality information when an individual has difficulty with self-evaluation (Panek, Jenkins, Hayslip, & Moske, 2013). To use verbal projective techniques, the client needs good language skills and should be able to hear or read words and express himself or herself orally or in writing. An example of a verbal projective technique is *projective questions*. Examples of questions include the following:

If you could be anything you wanted to be, what would you be?

If you had three wishes, what would you wish for?

If you had a magic wand, what would you change about your life?

These types of questions allow individuals to reflect some degree of their personality traits and states in their responses (Weiner & Greene, 2011). Counselors can interpret an individual's view of him- or herself and the world through the use of these types of techniques.

Sentence-completion tasks are another verbal projective technique in which examinees are presented a list of sentence stems (the beginning of a potential sentence) with a blank space after each stem. The task of the examinee is to complete the sentence. The typical way to conduct sentence-completion tasks is for the examinee to read the stems and then provide a written response, but oral administration and response also is an option (Hodges, 2011). Sentence-completion instruments may range from only a small number of items (10 to 15) to 50 or more items. The basis of all sentence-completion forms is that the examinee's

---

TABLE 12.5 Sample Sentence Stems from the Rotter Incomplete Sentence Blank

1. I wish …	6. Sometimes …
2. I secretly …	7. The happiest time …
3. I feel …	8. The only trouble …
4. I regret …	9. What annoys …
5. I can't …	10. Other kids …

Source: Rotter Incomplete Sentences Blank, Second Edition. Copyright © 1950, renewed 1977 by NCS Pearson, Inc. Reproduced with permission. All rights reserved. "Rotter Incomplete Sentences Blank, Second Edition" and "*RISB*" are trademarks, in the U.S. and/or other countries, of Pearson Education, Inc. or its affiliates(s).

responses may provide insight into his or her self-image, developmental characteristics, interpersonal reactions, needs, and perceived threats. Although published sentence-completion instruments yield an overall score, most examiners simply read over the completed sentences and form impressions about what examinees' responses might signify about their personality characteristics. The Rotter Incomplete Sentence Blank, Second Edition (RISB) is probably the best known sentence-completion instrument. Table 12.5 provides 10 sample sentence stems from the RISB.

Similar to sentence completion is *story completion*. There are different versions of the story completion technique (Koppitz, 1982; Thomas, 1937), but in general, it involves developing stories about a hypothetical child of the same age and gender as the child being assessed. Koppitz (1982) gives an example of a story: "A boy is at the table with his parents. Father suddenly gets angry. Why?" (p. 278). The stories are designed to investigate a child's dreams, fantasies, attitudes, and defense mechanisms, and they can be analyzed for major themes.

PROJECTIVE DRAWINGS *Projective drawings* are perhaps the oldest category of projective assessment procedures and are often used with children and adolescents (Weiner & Greene, 2011). As with other projective approaches, drawings are thought to contain nonverbal clues and symbolic messages about a child's self-concept, motivations, concerns, attitudes, and desires (Cummings, 1986). One of the most common drawing techniques is the *Draw-a-Person* test (DAP; Machover, 1949; see Figure 12.5). In this technique, a child is simply given a paper and a pencil and asked to draw a picture of a whole person. The drawing must be created in the presence of the counselor. After the child completes his or her drawing, an inquiry process ensues in which counselors ask questions about the drawing, such as "Tell me a story about this person," "What is the person doing?" or "How is the person feeling?" Answers to the questions as well as the drawings themselves are used to form various hypotheses and interpretations about the child's personality and functioning. Although many methods are available to score human figure drawings, Koppitz's (1968) scoring system is one of the most frequently cited. Koppitz's scoring system focuses on 30 *emotional indicators* in children's drawings. *Emotional indicators* are specific details in drawings (e.g., tiny or large figures, transparent [X-ray] bodies, crossed eyes, showing teeth, hands cut off, no eyes) that distinguish between normally adjusted children and emotionally disturbed children. The presence or absence of three or more emotional indicators may indicate underlying problems or maladjustment in the child. For example, poor achievement might be reflected in poorly integrated body parts, a monster or grotesque

FIGURE 12.5   Example of the Draw-a-Person technique.

figure, omission of body, omission of arms, or omission of mouth (Koppitz, 1982, p. 285). The drawing of a hostile, aggressive child might show a big figure, transparency, crossed eyes, teeth, long arms, big hands, or genitals. Depressed, withdrawn children characteristically include tiny figures and short arms but no eyes. Some general guidelines for interpreting drawings are included in Table 12.6.

Another drawing technique is the House-Tree-Person Technique (HTP; Buck, 1948). In this technique, children are asked to draw a house, a tree, and a person on separate sheets of paper (see Figure 12.6). The picture of the house is supposed to arouse children's

FIGURE 12.6   Example of the House-Tree-Person drawing.

TABLE 12.6 General Guidelines for Interpreting Human Figure Drawings

Dimensions	Interpretation
The figure's location or placement on the page:	
Central	Normal, reasonable, secure person
Upper right	Intellectualizing tendencies, possible inhibition of expression of feeling
Upper left	Impulsive behavior, drive toward immediate emotional satisfaction of needs, orientation toward past
High on page	High level of aspiration, extreme optimism
Low on page	Feelings of insecurity, low levels of self-esteem, depressive tendencies, defeatist attitudes
Lower edge as base	Need for support, lack of self-confidence
Size of the figure:	
Unusually large	Aggressive, expansive, or grandiose tendencies, acting out potential
Unusually small	Feelings of inferiority, timidness, insecurity, ineffectiveness, inhibition, depressive behavior under stress
Pencil pressure; stroke or line quality:	
Heavy strokes	Sign of tension, high energy level, forcefulness, and possible acting-out tendencies
Light, sketchy strokes	Hesitant, indecisive, timid, insecure person; inhibited personality, low energy level
Shaded strokes	Anxiety
Long strokes	Controlled behavior, inhibition
Short strokes	Impulsive behavior
Straight, uninterrupted lines	Assertive and decisive behavior
Variable strokes	Flexible, adaptive person
Organization and symmetry of the figure:	
Bizarre	Schizoid tendencies
Boxed off	Indication of difficulty in controlling life; reliance on external structure or organizations
Element encapsulated	Desire to remove an area of conflict from life
Extremely symmetrical	Obsessive-compulsive, defensive, cold, distant, hypertensive, and perfectionist tendencies
Lacking symmetry	Insecurity, poor impulse control, unbalanced self-concept
Erasures:	
Excessive	Uncertainty, indecisiveness, and restlessness, obsessive-compulsive personality
Occasional or to improve	Flexibility, satisfactory adjustment
Localized	Conflict or concern about what that area represents

TABLE 12.6 General Guidelines for Interpreting Human Figure Drawings (*Continued*)

Dimensions	Interpretation
Detail:	
Absent	Psychosomatic, hypertensive conditions or depressive and withdrawing
Excessive	Obsessive-compulsive tendencies, rigidity and/or anxiety, highly emotional
Bizarre	Indicative of psychosis
Transparency/X-ray drawings	Schizophrenic or manic conditions, poor judgment, sexual disturbance indicated by sexual organs
Outer clothing	Voyeuristic or exhibitionist tendencies
Distortions and omissions:	
Distortions	Confused, psychotic or schizophrenic condition
Omissions	Conflict, denial
Perspective:	
From below	Rejection, unhappiness or inferiority, withdrawal tendencies
From above	Sense of superiority, compensation for underlying feelings of inadequacy
Distant	Inaccessibility, desire to withdraw
Close	Interpersonal warmth, psychological accessibility
Shading:	
Shaded area	Anxiety
Complete absence	Character disorder
Color:	
Red	Problem or danger, anger or violent reaction, need for warmth and affection
Orange	Extroversion, emotional responsiveness to outer world, life-or-death struggle, ambivalence
Yellow	Cheerfulness, intellectualizing tendencies, lack of inhibition, expansiveness, anxiety
Green	Regulation of affective tendencies, healthy ego, peacefulness, security
Blue	Quiet, calm, well-controlled, cold, distant, fading away or withdrawing
Purple	Inner emotional and affective stimulation, internalization of affect, bold exterior, need to control or possess
Brown	Sensuousness, security, fixations, rigidity, in touch with nature
Gray	Noninvolvement, repressions, denial, emotional neutralization
White	Passivity, emptiness, depersonalization, loss of contact with reality

feelings about their home life and family relationships. Drawing a tree is expected to elicit feelings about inner strengths or weaknesses. The picture of the person is believed to reveal children's view of themselves (i.e., self-concept).

Family drawings are a projective drawing technique that provide a nonthreatening way to assess a child's perception of his or her family. For example, the Kinetic Family Drawing (KFD) asks the child to "Draw a picture of everyone in your family, including you, doing something" (Burns & Kaufman, 1970, p. 5). The instructions emphasize the family engaging in some activity—hence the term *kinetic*. After the image is completed, an inquiry phase begins in which the child is asked to (a) explain who each figure is (e.g., name, age, relationship to the child); (b) describe all the figures, what they are doing in the picture, how they are feeling, and what they are thinking about; and (c) tell a story, including what happened immediately before the actions in the drawing and what happens next. Family drawings can be analyzed and interpreted in terms of actions, styles, and symbols (Burns & Kaufman, 1970, 1972), in addition to figures' positions, distance in relation to one another, and barriers between figures (Knoff & Prout, 1985).

ISSUES WITH STRUCTURED AND PROJECTIVE INSTRUMENTS Although most textbooks on assessment divide personality inventories into the dichotomy of structured (i.e., objective) and projective, some theorists and researchers argue that both terms are misleading (Ortner & Schmitt, 2014). For example, as a word, *objectivity* implies neutrality and impartiality, yet objective instruments are only objective from the vantage point of the scorer; test takers complete the test based on their own opinions and are certainly not objective in that regard. In truth, *objective* refers to the type of item response (e.g., multiple choice, true/false) that does not require the examiner administering the test to rely on his or her judgment to classify or interpret the test taker's response. On the other hand, the term *projective* typically refers to instruments in which the stimulus is a task or activity that is presented to a person who is required to generate a response with minimal external guidance or constraints imposed on the nature of that response. Nonetheless, what is projective is "the requirement for test takers to generalize a response in the face of ambiguity; thus, they project or put forward elements of their personal characteristics" (Meyer & Kurtz, 2006, p. 223).

Another issue is the question of whether projective instruments have adequate reliability and validity to justify their use. The Rorschach has mixed reviews in terms of its psychometric properties, and the TAT and projective drawings have generally failed to provide research support for their reliability and validity. Although many psychologists, counselors, and other helping professionals still believe that the instruments help them develop a better understanding of the test taker, the use of projective instruments has drastically decreased. In some cases, like the assessment of children, researchers have called for the elimination of projective techniques (Duvoe & Styck, 2014).

Personality Inventories with a Positive Focus

Some personality inventories are based on *positive psychology* (i.e., the study of the conditions and processes that contribute to the optional functioning of people) and assess *positive aspects* of personality (Spielberger & Butcher, 2013). Some researchers agree that an individual's happiness or satisfaction with life is an essential criterion for mental health and successful outcomes in counseling. Thus, positive personality variables include those quality-of-life variables associated with happiness or satisfaction, such as self-efficacy, resiliency, coping skills, life satisfaction, and well-being. The Quality of Life Inventory (QOLI) and the Satisfaction with Life Scale (SWLS) are examples of positively focused personality inventories.

Many positively focused inventories specifically assess self-esteem. We define *self-esteem* as the manner in which people evaluate themselves and the ensuing judgments about themselves based on those evaluations. Rosenberg (1965) defined self-esteem more broadly as a favorable or unfavorable attitude toward the self (p. 15). Self-esteem is a popular construct in counseling and psychology and is related to specific personality traits (e.g., shyness), behavior, academic achievement, anxiety, and depression. Examples of inventories that assess self-esteem are the Coopersmith Self-Esteem Inventory (SEI), the Piers–Harris Children's Self-Concept Scale, Second Edition (Piers–Harris 2), the Culture-Free Self-Esteem Inventory, Third Edition (CFSEI-3), Rosenberg's Self-Esteem Scale, the Multidimensional Self-Esteem Inventory (MSEI), and the Tennessee Self-Concept Scale, Second Edition (TSCS:2).

THE QUALITY OF LIFE INVENTORY The QOLI (Frisch, 1994) is a brief but comprehensive measure of a person's overall satisfaction with life. People's life satisfaction is based on how well their needs, goals, and wishes are being met in important areas of life. The inventory consists of 32 items that ask test takers to describe how important certain aspects of their lives (such as work or health) are and how satisfied they are with them. The QOLI yields an Overall Quality of Life score (reported as a T score and percentile) that is classified as *very low*, *low*, *average*, or *high*. The inventory also yields Weighted Satisfaction Ratings for 16 areas of life (such as health, self-esteem, love, work, etc.). The satisfaction ratings are summarized on a profile report with a ratings range from –6 (extreme dissatisfaction) to 6 (extreme satisfaction). Negative weighted satisfaction ratings denote an area of life in which the individual may benefit from treatment; ratings of –6 and –4 are considered of greatest concern and urgency.

COOPERSMITH SELF-ESTEEM INVENTORY The SEI (Coopersmith, 1981) assesses attitudes toward the self in general and in specific contexts: social, academic, and personal contexts. It was originally designed for use with children, drawing on items from scales that were previously used by Carl Rogers. The SEI consists of a school form for ages 8 to 15 years and an adult form for ages 16 and above. It has five scales for self-esteem in relation to general self, social self/peers, home/parents, and school/academic, and a lie scale. Respondents answer items by choosing *like me* or *unlike me*. Table 12.7 presents samples of items that are typical for instruments like the Coopersmith Self-Esteem Inventory, School Form.

PIERS–HARRIS CHILDREN'S SELF-CONCEPT SCALE, SECOND EDITION The Piers–Harris 2 instrument is a 60-item self-report questionnaire that assesses self-concept in children aged 7 to 18 (Piers & Herzberg, 2002). It can be administered in paper-and-pencil or computer format, and children usually complete the scale in 10 to 15 minutes. The scale yields a general measure of overall self-concept (Total [TOT]) as well as six subscales: Behavioral Adjustment (BEH), Intellectual and School Status (INT), Physical Appearance and Attributes (PHY), Freedom from Anxiety (FRE), Popularity (POP), and Happiness and Satisfaction (HAP).

TABLE 12.7 Sample Self Esteem Assessment Questions

Question	Strongly Disagree	Disagree	Agree	Strongly Agree
• People like to spend time with me				
• I am good at most things				
• I have trouble believing in myself				
• I feel useless most of the time				

Source: The table above represents typical types of questions posed in self-esteem assessment instruments. The items are not from published instruments..

1. *Behavioral Adjustment*   Measures admission or denial of problematic behaviors at home or school.
2. *Intellectual and School Status*   Measures the child's evaluation of his or her own intellectual abilities and academic performance.
3. *Physical Appearance and Attributes*   Measures a child's appraisal of his or her physical appearance, as well as attributes such as leadership and the ability to express ideas.
4. *Freedom from Anxiety*   Measures feelings of anxiety and negative mood.
5. *Popularity*   Measures the child's evaluation of his or her own social functioning.
6. *Happiness and Satisfaction*   Measures a child's feelings of happiness and satisfaction with life.

Test items are simple descriptive statements (e.g., "I am well behaved at school") written at a second-grade reading level. Children indicate whether each item applies to them by selecting a *yes* or *no* response. Scores are reported as T scores and percentiles, and higher scores indicate favorable self-concept (i.e., high degree of self-esteem or self-regard), whereas lower scores are associated with more negative self-concept. On the six subscales, scores can classified as *very low* (T score less than 29), *low* (T score of 30 to 39), *low average* (T score of 40 to 44), *average* (T score of 45 to 55), and *above average* (T score greater than 56). The TOT scale score uses the same classification for *very low*, *low*, and *above-average* rankings. From there it changes, adding *high average* (T score of 56 to 59), *high* (T score of 60 to 69), and *very high* (T score greater than 70).

OTHER SELF-ESTEEM INVENTORIES A number of other self-esteem inventories are available to counselors. The CFSEI-3 are a set of self-report inventories that measure self-esteem in children and adolescents aged 6 years and 0 months to 18 years and 11 months. They consist of different forms for three age categories: children of ages 6 to 8 years are administered the Primary form, youth of ages 9 to 12 are administered the Intermediate form, and adolescents of ages 13 to 18 are administered the Adolescent form. All three forms of the inventory provide a Global Self-Esteem Quotient (GSEQ). The Intermediate and Adolescent Forms provide scores in four areas: Academic Self-Esteem, General Self-Esteem,

Parental/Home Self-Esteem, and Social Self-Esteem. The Adolescent form provides an additional self-esteem score: Personal Self-Esteem. Raw scores can be converted into standard scores, percentiles, and descriptive ratings.

The TSCS:2 (Fitts & Warren, 1996) measures self-concept in individuals aged 7 to 90 years and is available in Adult and Child forms. The Adult form is designed for individuals 13 years of age and older, and the Child form can be used with 7- through 14-year-olds. Each form can be group or individually administered in 10 to 20 minutes. The scale is subdivided into 15 scores, including self-concept scores (physical, moral, personal, family, social, and academic/work), supplementary scores (identity, satisfaction, and behavior), summary scores (total self-concept and conflict), and validity scores (inconsistent responding, self-criticism, faking good, and response distribution). The TSCS:2 can be hand scored, computer scored, or scored through a mail-in service.

The MSEI (O'Brien & Epstein, 2012) is a 116-item Likert-type scale that measures self-esteem. The MSEI yields scores on (a) Global Self-Esteem, (b) eight components of self-esteem (Competence, Lovability, Likability, Personal Power, Self-Control, Moral Self-Approval, Body Appearance, and Body Functioning), (c) Identity Integration (sense of identity), and (d) Defensive Self-Enhancement (a validity scale measuring the tendency to embellish one's self-esteem).

Response Styles

The concept of the *response style* (also called *response bias*) in personality assessment refers to the ways in which a test taker responds to an item in some characteristic manner that distorts the test results. Response style is an important aspect of personality assessment. Because most personality assessment instruments are self-report, there is a possibility that individuals can either distort their responses to impress or distort their responses to imply that they are functioning poorly, depending on the purpose of the assessment (Ray et al., 2013). For example, an individual who is being evaluated to determine his or her fitness as parent may have a tendency to provide socially desirable answers to items. In this situation, the individual may be "faking good" because of defensiveness about his or her behavior and the desire to reunite with his or her children. Sometimes, the choice is unconsciously expressed. Some individuals purposely answer questions in way that results in a pathological or undesirable profile. In this case, they may have some motivation for appearing more symptomatic than they really. For example, imagine that you are a counselor evaluating an individual for the court system to determine if they are fit to stand trial for murder. If the individual can claim that their mental health issues impaired their ability to determine right from wrong, then they may be able to avoid prosecution. In this case, "faking bad" becomes a real possibility.

Some test takers may be more apt to respond *yes* or *true* on items than *no* or *false*, and others may answer questions with random responses. The problem with response bias is that the test taker is not providing honest, accurate answers to questions, which can render the results suspect or even invalid. For example, imagine you are conducting an assessment on an adolescent who is mandated to counseling services. That individual might be less than willing to fully participate in the assessment process. Instead of giving full effort in completing an assessment instrument, that person might simply answer yes to all of the items. Of course, there are more response styles that can emerge than just answering yes to all items. Common response styles are as follows (Cohen, Swerdlik, & Sturman, 2012):

- *Social Desirability* Choosing the response that bests presents self in a favorable light
- *Acquiescent* Tendency of the test taker to accept or agree with statements regardless of the item content (i.e., answering all items as *true* or *yes*)
- *Nonacquiescence* Disagreeing with whatever item is presented (i.e., answering all items as *false* or *no*)
- *Deviance* Making unusual or uncommon responses
- *Extreme* Choosing extreme, rather than middle, ratings on a rating scale
- *Gambling/Cautiousness* Guessing, or not guessing, when in doubt about the answer

All self-report inventories are subject to response biases; therefore, instrument developers use various means to try to control response bias. For example, the MMPI-2 and MMPI-2-RF have validity scales that are used to identify test-taker response styles that might affect or invalidate the test results. The Edwards Personal Preference Inventory (EPPI) attempts to control the social desirability response style by using forced-choice item matching on the basis of social desirability. In other words, items include paired phrases that may be both desirable and undesirable.

Summary

Personality inventories are a method of identifying and measuring the structure and features of one's personality, or one's characteristic way of thinking, feeling, and behaving (Cohen et al., 2012). Personality inventories assist professionals in understanding an individual's behavior with the aim of making some decision about a future course of action or to make a prediction about the person's unique future behavior. Counselors can choose from a wide array of personality instruments and techniques, which can be grouped into three categories: structured personality inventories, projective techniques, and instruments that assess positive aspects of personality.

Structured personality inventories are standardized, self-report instruments that ask respondents to describe their personality using a limited set of response options. Inventories such as the MMPI-2 and MMPI-2-RF, the MCMI-III, and the CPI are examples of structured personality inventories. Projective instruments and techniques require examinees to answer questions related to ambiguous stimuli using open-ended responses. Examples include the Rorschach Inkblot Test, the TAT, verbal projective techniques, and projective drawings. Some personality inventories, such as self-concept scales, are designed specifically to measure positive personality traits.

Questions for Discussion

1. How important are the various approaches to developing personality tests? Does one approach have advantages over others? Explain your answer.
2. Response sets are major problems on personality tests. How would you structure a testing situation to minimize faking? Do you believe that everybody fakes on personality inventories? Explain your answer.
3. A wide variety of item content measures dimensions of personality, from food choices to occupations to musical preferences. How important do you think the content of the items is in assessing personality?

Suggested Activities

1. Operationally define a personality construct and devise a method for measuring the construct. Develop some preliminary items and give them to your classmates. What was the reaction of the test takers to the form of the test?
2. Identify a personality test of interest to you. Critically analyze the test. Read the reviews of the test in the *Mental Measurement Yearbooks* and *Test Critiques*.
3. Interview workers in the helping professions who use tests and find out which personality tests they use and why. Report your findings to the class.

4. Review the research on one of the current issues in personality assessment and write a critical analysis of your findings.
5. Make an annotated bibliography of the personality tests that are appropriate for your current or future field.
6. **Enneagram activity:** In this Enneagram exercise, the following table shows the nine Enneagram types and four groups of adjectives that describe each type.

Enneagram Type	Group 1	Rank	Group 2	Rank	Group 3	Rank	Group 4	Total Score
1.	Principled		Orderly		Perfectionist		Idealistic	
2.	Caring		Generous		Possessive		Nurturing	
3.	Adaptable		Ambitious		Image-Conscious		Pragmatic	
4.	Intuitive		Individualistic		Self-Absorbed		Withdrawn	
5.	Perceptive		Original		Provocative		Cerebral	
6.	Engaging		Responsible		Defensive		Security-Oriented	
7.	Enthusiastic		Accomplished		Excessive		Busy	
8.	Self-Confident		Optimistic		Assertive		Decisive	
9.	Easy-Going		Stable		Accepting		Trusting	

a. Rank *each* adjective within each group in order from 1 (Least Like Me) to 9 (Most Like Me). No ties are allowed (each rank must be used only once for each adjective in each group).
b. Reading across each of the nine rows, add the total points for the four groups. Look at your high scores and low scores. Then turn back to Table 12.4 showing Enneagram types, and look at the description of the nine types. Row 1 gives a score for type 1 Reformer, row 2 for type 2 Helper, and so on. Identify the Enneagram type that you scored highest in.
c. Discuss your results in small groups. Do you agree that your Enneagram type matches your personality type? Explain.

7. Review the scores ahead of the NEO PI-R and answer the following questions:
   a. How would you describe the dimensions of this individual's personality?
   b. How does the absence of validity and lie scales on the NEO PI-R influence your ability to interpret the results of this instrument?

NEO PI-R Domain	Score Range
Neuroticism	Low
Extraversion	Very High
Openness to Experience	High
Conscientiousness	High
Agreeableness	High

References

Allport, G. W. (1937) *Personality*. New York: Holt, 1937.

Allport, G. W. (1951). *Personality: A psychological interpretation*. New York, NY: Henry Holt.

American Psychiatric Association (APA). (2013). *Diagnostic and statistical manual of mental disorders* (5th ed.). Washington, DC: Author.

Aronow, E., Weiss, K. A., & Reznikoff, M. (2013). *A practical guide to the Thematic Apperception Test: The TAT in clinical practice*. London, UK: Routledge.

Beutler, L. E., Groth-Marnat, G., & Hardwood, T. M. (2012). *Integrative assessment of adult personality* (3rd ed.). New York, NY: Guilford.

Buck, J. N. (1948). The H-T-P test. *Journal of Clinical Psychology, 4*, 151–159.

Burns, R. C., & Kaufman, S. H. (1970). *Kinetic family drawings (K-F-D)*. New York, NY: Brunner-Mazel.

Burns, R. C., & Kaufman, S. H. (1972). *Actions, styles, and symbols in kinetic family drawings (K-F-D)*. New York, NY: Brunner-Mazel.

Butcher, J. N., Graham, J. R., Ben-Porath, Y. S., Tellegen, A., Dahlstrom, W. G., & Kaemmer, B. (2001). *Minnesota Multiphasic Personality Inventory-2 (MMPI-2) manual for administration and scoring, second revision*. Minneapolis, MN: University of Minnesota Press.

Callahan, J. L. (2014). Evidence-based technical skills training in prepracticum psychological assessment. *Training and Education in Professional Psychology, 9*(1), 21–27.

Cattell, R. B., Eber, H. W., & Tatsuoka, M. M. (1970). *Handbook for the Sixteen Personality Factor Questionnaire (16PF)*. Champaign, IL: Institute for Personality and Ability Testing.

Cohen, R., & Swerdlik, M. (2010). *Test development: Psychological testing and assessment*. New York, NY: McGraw-Hill Higher Education.

Cohen, R. J., Swerdlik, M. E., & Sturman, E. D. (2012). *Psychological testing and assessment: An introduction to tests and measurement* (8th ed.). Boston, MA: McGraw-Hill.

Coopersmith, S. (1981). *Antecedents of self-esteem*. Palo Alto, CA: Consulting Psychologists Press. (Original work published 1967)

Costa, P. T., Jr., & McCrae, R. (2013). The Five-Factor Model of personality and its relevance. *Personality and Personality Disorders: The Science of Mental Health, 6*(4), 17.

Cummings, J. A. (1986). Projective drawings. In H. M. Knoff (Ed.), *The assessment of child and adolescent personality* (pp. 199–244). New York, NY: Guilford.

Detrick, P., & Chibnall, J. T. (2013). Revised NEO Personality Inventory normative data for police officer selection. *Psychological Services, 10*(4), 372–377.

Duvoe, K. R., & Styck, K. M. (2014). Book review: Oxford Handbook of Child Psychological Assessment. *Journal of Psychoeducational Assessment, 32*(5), 477–480.

Exner, J. E., Jr. (Ed.). (2013). *Issues and methods in Rorschach research*. London, UK: Routledge.

Fitts, W. H., & Warren, W. L. (1996). *Tennessee Self-Concept Scale: Manual* (2nd ed.). Los Angeles, CA: Western Psychological Services.

Frisch, M. B. (1994). *Manual and treatment guide for the Quality of Life Inventory*. Minneapolis, MN: Pearson.

Furnham, A., Guenole, N., Levine, S. Z., & Chamorro-Premuzic, T. (2013). The NEO Personality Inventory–Revised: Factor structure and gender invariance from exploratory structural equation modeling analyses in a high-stakes setting. *Assessment, 20*(1), 14–23.

Gorostiaga, A., Balluerka, N., Alonso-Arbiol, I., & Haranburu, M. (2011). Validation of the Basque Revised NEO Personality Inventory (NEO PI-R). *European Journal of Psychological Assessment, 27*(3), 193–205.

Gough, H. G. (2000). The California Psychological Inventory. In C. E. Watkins & V. L. Campbell (Eds.), *Testing and assessment in counseling practice* (2nd ed., pp. 45–71). Mahwah, NJ: Erlbaum.

Groth-Marnat, G. (2009). *Handbook of psychological assessment* (5th ed.). Hoboken, NJ: John Wiley & Sons.

Hodges, S. (2011). The sentence stem technique: An innovative interaction between counselor and client. *Journal of Creativity in Mental Health, 6*(3), 234–243.

Jung, C. G. (1971). *Psychological types* (H. G. Baynes, Trans.). Princeton, NJ: Princeton University Press. (Original work published 1921)

Kalimeri, K. (2013). *Towards a dynamic view of personality: Multimodal classification of personality states in everyday situations*. Paper presented at the Proceedings of the 15th ACM International Conference on Multimodal Interaction.

Källmen, H., Wennberg, P., & Bergman, H. (2011). Psychometric properties and norm data of the Swedish version of the NEO-PI-R. *Nordic Journal of Psychiatry, 65*(5), 311–314.

Kamphaus, R. W., & Frick, P. J. (2010). *Clinical assessment of child and adolescent personality and behavior* (3rd ed.). New York, NY: Springer.

Knoff, H. M., & Prout, H. T. (1985). The Kinetic Drawing System: A review and integration of the kinetic family and school drawing techniques. *Psychology in the Schools, 22*(1), 50–59.

Koppitz, E. M. (1968). *Psychological evaluation of children's human figure drawings.* New York, NY: Grune & Stratton.

Koppitz, E. M. (1982). Personality assessment in the schools. In C. R. Reynolds & T. B. Gutkin (Eds.), *Handbook of school psychology* (pp. 273–295). New York, NY: Wiley.

Kroeger, O., & Thuesen, J. M. (2013). *Type talk: The 16 personality types that determine how we live, love, and work.* New York, NY: Random House LLC.

Krueger, R. F., Derringer, J., Markon, K. E., Watson, D., & Skodol, A. E. (2012). Initial construction of a maladaptive personality trait model and inventory for DSM-5. *Psychological Medicine, 42*(9), 1879–1890.

Machover, K. (1949). *Personality projection in the drawing of the human figure.* Springfield, IL: Thomas.

McCrae, R. R., & Costa, P. T. (2003). *Personality in adulthood: A Five-Factor Theory perspective* (2nd ed.). New York, NY: Guilford.

Meyer, G. J., & Kurtz, J. E. (2006). Advancing personality assessment terminology: Time to retire "objective" and "projective" as personality test descriptors. *Journal of Personality Assessment, 87,* 223–225.

Miller, M. D., Linn, R. L., & Gronlund, N. E. (2012). *Measurement and assessment in teaching* (11th ed.). Upper Saddle River, NJ: Pearson.

Millon, T. (1969). *Modern psychopathology: A biosocial approach to maladaptive learning and functioning.* Philadelphia, PA: Saunders.

Millon, T., Millon, C., Davis, R. D., & Grossman, S. (2009). *Millon clinical multiaxial inventory-III (MCMI-III): Manual.* Upper Saddle River, NJ: Pearson/PsychCorp.

Murray, H. A. (1943). *Thematic Apperception Test manual.* Cambridge, MA: Harvard University Press.

Murray, H. A. (2007). *Explorations in personality.* New York, NY: Oxford University Press.

Myers, I. B., McCaulley, M. H., Quenk, N. L., & Hammer, A. L. (1998). *MBTI manual: A guide to the development and use of the Myers–Briggs Type Indicator* (3rd ed.). Palo Alto, CA: Consulting Psychologists Press.

Myers, I. B., & Myers, P. B. (1995). *Gifts differing: Understanding personality type.* Palo Alto, CA: Davis-Black.

Myers, P. B., & Myers, K. D. (2004). *Myers–Briggs Type Indicator Profile.* Retrieved from cpp.com /images/reports/smp261001.pdf

Neukrug, E., Peterson, C. H., Bonner, M., & Lomas, G. I. (2013). A national survey of assessment instruments taught by counselor educators. *Counselor Education & Supervision, 52*(3), 207–221. doi: 10.1002/j.1556-6978.2013.00038.x

Newgent, R. A., Parr, P. E., Newman, I., & Higgins, K. K. (2004). The Riso–Hudson Enneagram Type Indicator: Estimates of reliability and validity. *Measurement and Evaluation in Counseling and Development, 36*(4), 226–237.

O'Brien, E. J., & Epstein, S. (2012). *MSEI: The Multidimensional Self-Esteem Inventory.* Odessa, FL: Consulting Psychologists Press.

Ortner, T. M., & Schmitt, M. (2014). Advances and continuing challenges in objective personality testing. *European Journal of Psychological Assessment, 30*(3), 163–168.

Panek, P. E., Jenkins, S. R., Hayslip, B., Jr., & Moske, A. K. (2013). Verbal expressive personality testing with older adults: 25+ years later. *Journal of Personality Assessment, 95*(4), 366–376.

Piers, E. V., & Herzberg, D. S. (2002). *Piers–Harris Children's Self-Concept Scale—second edition manual.* Los Angeles, CA: Western Psychological Services.

Ray, J. V., Hall, J., Rivera-Hudson, N., Poythress, N. G., Lilienfeld, S. O., & Morano, M. (2013). The relation between self-reported psychopathic traits and distorted response styles: A meta-analytic review. *Personality Disorders: Theory, Research, and Treatment, 4*(1), 1.

Riso, D. R., & Hudson, R. (1999). *The wisdom of the Enneagram: The complete guide to psychological and spiritual growth for the nine personality types.* New York, NY: Bantam.

Rorschach, H. (1992). *Psychodiagnostik.* Bern, Switzerland: Bircher.

Rosenberg, M. (1965). *Society and the adolescent self-image.* Princeton, NJ: Princeton University Press.

Smith, S. R. (2011). Projective Assessment Techniques. *Encyclopedia of Child Behavior and Development,* 1163–1164.

Solomon, B. C., & Jackson, J. J. (2014). Why do personality traits predict divorce? Multiple pathways through satisfaction. *Journal of Personality and Social Psychology, 106*(6), 978–996. doi: 10.1037/a0036190.supp (Suppl.)

Spielberger, C. D. (1970). *Manual for the State-Trait Anxiety Inventory (Form Y)*. Palo Alto, CA: Consulting Psychologists Press, Inc.

Spielberger, C. D. (1983). *Manual for the State-Trait Anxiety Inventory (STAI)*. Palo Alto, CA: Consulting Psychologists Press.

Spielberger, C. D., & Butcher, J. N. (2013). *Advances in personality assessment* (Vol. 7). London, UK: Routledge.

Thomas, M. (1937). Méthode des histoires à completer pour le dépiste des complexes et des conflits affectifs enfantins. *Archives Psychologie, 26*, 209–284.

Thomas, K. M., Yalch, M. M., Krueger, R. F., Wright, A. G. C., Markon, K. E., & Hopwood, C. J. (2013). The convergent structure of DSM-5 personality trait facets and Five-Factor Model trait domains. *Assessment, 20*(3), 308–311.

Urbina, S. (2014). *Essentials of psychological testing* (Vol. 4, 2nd ed.). Hoboken, NJ: John Wiley & Sons.

Van den Broeck, J., Rossi, G., Dierckx, E., & De Clercq, B. (2012). Age-neutrality of the NEO-PI-R: Potential differential item functioning in older versus younger adults. *Journal of Psychopathology and Behavioral Assessment, 34*(3), 361–369.

Vassend, O., & Skrondal, A. (2011). The NEO personality inventory revised (NEO-PI-R): Exploring the measurement structure and variants of the Five-Factor Model. *Personality and Individual Differences, 50*(8), 1300–1304.

Weiner, I. B., & Greene, R. L. (2011). *Handbook of personality assessment*. Malden, MA: John Wiley & Sons.

Woodworth, R. S. (1920). *Personal data sheet.* Chicago, IL: Stoelting.

13 Clinical Assessment

The term *clinical assessment* generally refers to applying assessment procedures to (a) diagnose a mental disorder, (b) develop a plan of intervention, (c) monitor progress in counseling, and (d) evaluate counseling outcome. Traditionally employed in mental health settings, clinical assessment involves the counselor collecting relevant information about a client, organizing and integrating the data, and using his or her clinical judgment in forming an opinion about a client's diagnosis. In addition, counselors conduct clinical assessment to develop a plan of intervention, monitor a client's progress in counseling, and evaluate counseling outcomes. Although clinical assessment is typical for mental health settings, it is imperative that all counselors understand the process and are able to interpret the information from a clinical assessment. The results of clinical assessment inform counseling in all settings. As with all assessment, clinical assessment encompasses multiple data collection instruments and strategies as well as multiple sources of information.

After studying this chapter, you should be able to:

- Describe and explain the purpose of clinical assessment.
- Define *mental disorder*.
- Describe the *Diagnostic and Statistical Manual of Mental Disorders, Fifth Edition* (DSM-5) and explain its use in clinical assessment.
- Explain the use of dimensional assessment.
- Describe the use of structured, semistructured, and unstructured interviews in clinical assessment.
- Describe the mental status exam.
- List and describe instruments commonly used in clinical assessment.
- List the risk factors and warning signs of suicide and explain how suicide risk is assessed.
- Describe the value of observation in clinical assessment.
- Describe neuropsychological assessment.
- Discuss cultural considerations in clinical assessment.

FUNDAMENTALS OF CLINICAL ASSESSMENT

"Does this client have a mental disorder?" and "If so, what is the diagnosis?" are typical questions that can be answered through clinical assessment (Cohen, Swerdlik, & Sturman, 2012). A key function of *clinical assessment* is diagnosing mental disorders.

Mental disorders are common in the United States and internationally. In the United States, an estimated 26.4% of Americans of ages 18 and older suffer from a diagnosable mental disorder in a given year (Demyttenaere et al., 2013), and about 20% of children and adolescents are estimated to have mental disorders. Four of the 10 leading causes of disability are mental disorders: major depression, bipolar disorder, schizophrenia, and obsessive-compulsive disorder. The severity of mental disorders is often increased in developing countries because of a lack of appropriate services (Demyttenaere et al., 2013).

Political Issues in Diagnosis

Diagnosing mental disorders has become an integral part of the job for many counselors. Although counselors are trained to diagnose, state laws vary with regard to the privilege to diagnose. For example, in Texas, counselors are able to perform assessment and diagnose mental health disorders. However, in Louisiana (an adjourning state), a professional counselor is not able to diagnose a serious mental disorder unless supervised by a professional licensed by the State Board of Medical Examiners (*Louisiana Mental Health Counselor Licensing Act*, 1987). In one state, a counselor can diagnose independently; in another, the same counselor must be supervised. These differences are typically due to political issues rather than competency. Because the purpose of this book is to provide you with a foundation in assessment, our discussion of practice privileges is limited. As you prepare to become professional counselors, it will be important for you to review your state laws with regard to practice privileges. It will also be important for you to be active in advocating for counselor parity at state and national levels. Joining state counseling associations, being credentialed appropriately, and joining counseling advocacy efforts can help to create a more unified scope of practice for counselors.

Determining a Diagnosis

Although counselors have different privileges with regard to diagnosis from state to state, it is still essential to understand the process of determining a diagnosis. To determine a client's diagnosis, counselors may use various formal and informal instruments and strategies in the process of clinical assessment. Usually, the counselor conducts an interview first, and the background information gathered from the interview helps the counselor decide which additional assessment instruments or strategies should be employed. For example, a client who complains of being depressed during the interview may be asked to complete an inventory that assesses depressive symptoms. The information gathered from both the interview and the inventory can aid in deciding whether the client should be diagnosed with depression.

In addition to diagnosis, the clinical assessment can help guide decisions related to treatment. From the assessment, counselors can determine the client's diagnosis, and, based on this information, they can select a treatment plan that is effective for that particular diagnosis. For example, a client who is depressed may be treated with cognitive-behavioral therapy, which is a treatment approach shown to be effective in treating depression. Cognitive-behavioral therapy involves identifying and correcting the client's inaccurate thoughts associated with depressed feelings, helping the client increase social competence, and enhancing the client's problem-solving skills.

Researchers and clinicians may also use clinical assessment for monitoring treatment progress and evaluating treatment outcomes. They may analyze which treatment approach was most effective for a client with a particular disorder, or they may determine which population would most benefit from a certain treatment modality. They can monitor the client's progress throughout treatment to note improvements or worsening of symptoms and to evaluate the final outcome of treatment.

In this chapter, we will discuss the process of clinical assessment. We will begin by describing the diagnosis of mental disorders and then will present information about the use of interviews, formal instruments, and observations in clinical assessment.

DSM-5

A key function of clinical assessment is the diagnosis of mental disorders. Clinicians diagnose disorders using criteria from the DSM-5 (American Psychiatric Association (APA), 2013). The DSM-5 is the official classification system of mental disorders used by counselors, psychologists, social workers, psychiatrists, and other mental health professionals in the United States. It is used across settings (inpatient, outpatient, partial hospital, private practice, and primary care) and with community populations. Substantial training is needed in the use of the DSM-5, which is beyond the scope of this textbook. Those of you who are preparing to become clinical mental health counselors will receive coursework in abnormal human behavior, psychopathology, and diagnosis. For those of you in other counselor preparation specializations, it will be necessary to complete elective courses or continuing education to become competent in the diagnostic process. For all counselors, we recommend clinical supervision from an Approved Clinical Supervisor (ACS) or state board–qualified supervising counselor when developing skills in clinical assessment and diagnosis. Although we are unable to provide an in-depth exploration of clinical assessment, we will provide you with an introduction to diagnosis and a brief overview of the DSM-5 disorders.

To begin to understand the DSM-5, counselors need to understand the meaning of the term *mental disorder*. In general, a mental disorder is a complex construct comprised of various symptoms that impact mental health and a broad array of biological, social, occupational, and relational functioning. Mental disorders are classified using the DSM-5 based on the clinician's assessment of certain criteria. The DSM-5 contains over 300 separate disorders divided into 22 categories. For an example of how the various types of personality disorder fall under a category, see Table 13.1.

TABLE 13.1 DSM-5 Personality Disorders

Cluster A	Paranoid Personality Disorder
	Schizoid Personality Disorder
	Schizotypal Personality Disorder
Cluster B	Antisocial Personality Disorder
	Borderline Personality Disorder
	Histrionic Personality Disorder
	Narcissistic Personality Disorder
Cluster C	Avoidant Personality Disorder
	Dependent Personality Disorder
	Obsessive-Compulsive Personality Disorder

Each mental disorder has a list of *diagnostic criteria* (i.e., symptoms, emotions, cognitions, behaviors) that need to be met in order for a diagnosis to be made. For example, code 296.21 for Major Depressive Disorder can be marked by a variety of symptoms, such as almost daily insomnia and fatigue, unintended changes in weight, depressed mood, and lack of interest or pleasure in daily activities. This diagnosis may also be specified with applicable features, such as anxious distress, catatonia, seasonal patterns, or mood-congruent psychotic features (American Psychiatric Association (APA), 2013). Each disorder also includes a description of its features, including specific age, cultural, and gender-related features; prevalence, incidence, and risk; course (e.g., typical lifetime patterns); complications; predisposing factors; familial pattern; and differential diagnosis (e.g., how to differentiate this disorder from other similar disorders). The DSM-5 also provides code numbers for each disorder, which is helpful for medical record keeping, statistical analysis, and reporting to third parties.

In contrast to the multiaxial diagnostic system used in the *Diagnostic and Statistical Manual of Mental Disorders*, *Fourth Edition*, *Text Revision* (DSM-IV-TR), the DSM-5 moved to a nonaxial documentation of diagnosis that combines the information from Axes I, II, and III of the previous edition (Axis I: Clinical Disorders; Axis II: Personality Disorders and Mental Retardation; Axis III: General Medical Conditions). Counselors diagnose a client's current condition and rate the severity of the disorder using a new dimensional approach. Using this new dimensional assessment process, counselors provide the diagnostic information needed to ensure that clients receive the appropriate treatment for their current symptoms and disorders. Please see Table 13.2 for an overview of the DSM-5 classification system.

In order to illustrate the new dimensional assessment process, consider the case of Julio, a 3-year-old male whose parents are concerned about his progress on developmental

---

TABLE 13.2 DSM-5 General Classification of Disorders

- Neurodevelopmental Disorders
- Schizophrenia Spectrum and Other Psychotic Disorders
- Bipolar and Related Disorders
- Depressive Disorders
- Anxiety Disorders
- Obsessive Compulsive and Related Disorders
- Trauma and Stressor-Related Disorders
- Dissociative Disorders
- Somatic Symptom and Related Disorders
- Feeding and Eating Disorders
- Sleep-Wake Disorders
- Sexual Dysfunctions
- Gender Dysphoria
- Disruptive, Impulse-Control, and Conduct Disorders
- Substance-Related and Addictive Disorders
- Neurocognitive Disorders
- Paraphilic Disorders

milestones. Julio's mother reports that he was late on sitting up, crawling, walking, and other areas. Julio has difficulty with verbal communication but seems to understand what is being said to him. Julio's mother did not report any pregnancy or delivery complications. Julio's mother indicated that Julio has had some difficulty with maintaining weight and that he is a picky eater. Julio tends to only eat items that are of a certain texture. Also, Julio is highly sensitive to changes in routine. For example, he displays a tantrum if they take a different route to preschool than usual. When Julio plays with his toys, he does so in an atypical manner. For example, instead of rolling a car, he turns it over and only spins the wheels. Julio becomes very upset if his play is disrupted.

Julio's preschool teacher reports that he does not engage with other children and that he does not attempt verbal communication while in preschool. His teacher reports that Julio often seems to stare off in the distance and does not seem to attend to what is occurring in the classroom. She noted that he does make some verbalizations but that they seem to be just repeating what she has said.

Based on the information provided, Julio's DSM-5 diagnosis would be 299.0 Level 2 with accompanying language impairment. According to the DSM-5, individuals at Level 2 require substantial support for their disorder. In this case, Julio has marked deficits in verbal communication, clear social impairments, reduced responses to social overtures from others, inflexibility of behavior, and other symptoms. He is able to participate in preschool but is not being successful. He requires significant levels of intervention and support to manage his current behavior and to make progress on developmental milestones.

The new edition of the *Diagnostic and Statistical Manual* has launched with a degree of controversy that will not abate in a short time. The changes from the DSM-IV-TR to the DSM-5 were significant and have received numerous challenges. The critics of the DSM-5 have been adamant that the new edition lacks the science to drive the numerous changes (Whitbourne, 2013). Several groups, including the Center for Medicare and Medicaid Services have been so opposed to the changes that they are now requiring the use of the *International Classification of Disease Manual* (ICD) in lieu of the DSM-5 (APA, 2013). As a professional counselor, you will likely either use the DSM-5 to levy a diagnosis or need to understand the diagnosis that was given by another helping professional. Therefore, we will review some of the commonly cited advantages and disadvantages. One of the criticisms of the DSM-5 has been the inclusion of a *mild* category in the severity index. Many believe that such a classification will result in the pathologizing of common phenomena. For example, the diagnosis of mild neurological impairment may be difficult to differentiate from average cognitive changes in older adulthood (APA, 2013). In addition to the criticisms of the new edition, the overall DSM has been criticized because (a) it emphasizes pathological symptoms, (b) managed care organizations tend to use categories to deny authorization of client treatment for normal conflicts or for longer-term care, and (c) it has a strong medical orientation that runs counter to the wellness philosophy that counselors espouse (Remley & Herlihy, 2013). Further explanation of the DSM-5 is beyond the scope of this textbook. However, other sources of information are available that provide information about the DSM-5 and diagnosis (see Seligman & Reichenberg, 2014).

Of course, the changes in the DSM-5 have some positive attributes. As has been the case with all iterations of the manual, the DSM-5 has some distinct advantages for clinical practice: (a) it offers a universal system of diagnosis that permits dialogue among mental health professionals; (b) it includes attention to cultural, age, and gender features; and (c) the severity index requires that practitioners consider various physical, psychosocial, and environmental circumstances influencing the client's dysfunction. Regardless of how you see the changes to the new edition of the diagnostic manual, it will be imperative that you explore it in depth and develop a solid foundation in the diagnostic process.

Now that we have reviewed the manner in which disorders are classified, we will turn to the process involved in determining a diagnosis. As is the case with other areas reviewed in this book, assessment is the primary process used to arrive at a clinical answer. There are numerous forms of clinical assessment, and some are used more often than others. Throughout the remainder of this chapter, we will explore the various methods used to arrive at a diagnosis (e.g., interviews, mental status exams, standardized assessment instruments).

Interviews in Clinical Assessment

The initial client interview is a fundamental component in clinical assessment. Like any assessment instrument or strategy, the interview has the defined purpose of gathering data or information about an individual. In clinical assessment, the interview is often referred to as the *clinical interview* or the *diagnostic interview*, and it is used in conjunction with tests and observations to gather enough information about the client's background and presenting problem to formulate a diagnosis and treatment plan. As described in Chapter 2, interviews can vary in the degree of structure. Some interviews are flexible, allowing clients to discuss whatever topic they wish, whereas other interviews are highly structured and goal oriented. In terms of structure, interviews can be categorized as *structured, semistructured, or unstructured.* Each approach has benefits and drawbacks, but the primary purpose of all three types is to obtain relevant information about the client.

Structured interviews have proliferated since the publication of the DSM-IV. As we discussed earlier in the book, structured interviews consist of a specific set of questions used to determine whether or not a person meets the criteria for a particular mental disorder. Counselors must read all questions exactly as written and not deviate from the text. There are several structured interviews to assess children, adolescents, or adults for various mental disorders. Examples of structured interviews include following:

- Composite International Diagnostic Interview (CIDI)
- Diagnostic Interview Schedule (DIS)
- Diagnostic Interview Schedule for Children (DISC-IV)
- Structured Interview for PTSD (SIP)
- Substance Use Disorders Diagnostic Schedule (SUDDS-IV)

Semistructured interviews are less uniform than structured interviews and allow counselors more opportunity to probe and expand the client's responses. Although a predetermined set of questions is specified, counselors have some flexibility to rephrase questions or ask additional questions for clarification. An example of a well-known semistructured interview used for clinical assessment is the Structured Clinical Interview for DSM-IV Axis I Disorders (SCID-I; First, Spitzer, Gibbon, & Williams, 2012). Specifically used to help determine DSM-IV Axis I diagnoses, the SCID-I is divided into several modules, each containing interview questions that correspond directly to specific disorders. Although its title includes the term "structured," the SCID is considered a semistructured interview because counselors may tailor questions to fit the client's understanding, ask additional questions for clarification, and even use only specific portions of the interview. For example, if you have a client who has a history of clinical depression and is seeking help to manage the depression, then you may want to use only the Mood Disorder module to ask questions specifically about the symptoms of depression and to confirm the existing diagnosis. The SCID-I has two versions: the Clinician Version (SCID-CV) and the Research Version (SCID-I-RV). The Clinician Version is a streamlined, more user-friendly version of the Research Version that can be used in clinical settings. Administration time can range from 15 minutes to around 90 minutes, depending on how many modules are administered. The Biometrics Research Department at Columbia University is now in the process of revising the SCID to match the DSM-5. The new versions will be the SCID-CV and the SCID-5-RV. Because the diagnostic criteria for personality disorders did not change from the DSM-IV-TR to the DSM-5, the SCID II can still be used, although it is also under revision. The release of the new SCID versions is expected in 2015.

Examples of other semistructured interviews used for diagnosing include the following (note that one of the titles includes the word *structured*, but it is in fact a semistructured interview):

- Diagnostic Interview for Children and Adolescents-IV (DICA-IV)
- Schedule for Affective Disorders and Schizophrenia (SADS)
- Semistructured Clinical Interview for Children and Adolescents (SCICA)
- Structured Clinical Interview for DSM-IV Axis-II Disorders (SCID-II)

Unstructured interviews are the most frequently used type of interview in clinical assessment. They are considered unstructured because there is no standardization of questioning or recording of responses. It is the counselor who makes up the questions and determines how to document the responses (Jones, 2010). Although they are flexible, unstructured interviews are not without some direction or format. Counselors typically assess several general domains, including the presenting problem, family background, social and academic history, medical history, and substance use history. As you might guess, an unstructured interview requires a knowledgeable and skilled clinician to manage the various facets of the interview process and to chain together the pieces of information gathered within the context of a diagnostic decision tree. Table 2.2 in Chapter 2 provides a description of these general domains.

As part of clinical assessment, topics relevant to diagnosing mental disorders are addressed in the unstructured interview. For example, one of the domains involves gathering information about the client's "presenting problem," which is the client's primary problems or concerns. For clinical assessment, counselors may ask specifically about psychological symptoms (such as depression or anxiety) and about occupational/school functioning and social functioning to help determine a DSM-5 diagnosis. In addition, counselors will ask about the history of the client's presenting problem in three main areas (American Psychiatric Association (APA), 2013; Seligman & Reichenberg, 2014):

1. *Onset/Course* When did the problems begin? Was there a time when the client felt worse or better? Was there any particular pattern?
2. *Severity* Do the problems interfere with the client's life (e.g., work, relationships, and leisure pursuits) and/or lead to suffering or distress?
3. *Stressor* Does the client believe that some external event brought on the problems? Are any stressful life events associated with the problem?

Unstructured interviews in clinical assessment may also include questions about developmental history, focusing specifically on risk factors associated with the development of current or potential mental health problems from childhood through adulthood; questions about child abuse, domestic violence, and mental illness within the client's family; and questions focusing on substance use, including past and current alcohol or drug use (including prescription drugs), levels of consumption, and any consequences resulting from substance use (e.g., legal problems, job loss, financial difficulties).

Mental Status Exam

The mental status exam (MSE) is an important part of clinical assessment. It is a structured procedure for observing and describing a client's mental state, which includes appearance, speech, actions, mood, perception, and thoughts. The purpose of the MSE is to provide a broad description of a client's mental state, which, when combined with the background information obtained from the clinical interview, aids counselors in making an accurate diagnosis. The MSE was originally modeled after the physical medical exam; just as the physical medical exam is designed to review a patient's body and major organ systems, the mental status exam reviews the major systems of psychiatric functioning (Mitchell & Atri, 2014). In the clinical assessment, the MSE is performed when the clinician suspects that the client may have some level of intellectual disability. In hospital settings, it is not unusual for psychiatrists to request or administer daily MSEs for acutely disturbed patients (Sommers-Flanagan & Sommers-Flanagan, 2013). In fact, MSEs are a basic procedure in most medical settings. Anyone seeking employment in the medical mental health domain should be competent in their knowledge of MSE reports. The following is a description of several general categories of MSEs (Sadock & Sadock, 2007):

- *Appearance* How was the client dressed and groomed (e.g., neat, disheveled, unkempt)?
- *Behavior/Psychomotor Activity* Did the client exhibit slow movement, restlessness, or agitation? Did the client have any unusual behaviors, such as tics, mannerisms, or gestures?
- *Attitude toward Examiner* Was the client's attitude toward the examiner cooperative, friendly, attentive, defensive, hostile, evasive, guarded, or so forth?
- *Affect and Mood* Did the client have sad, angry, depressed, or anxious mood? Was the client emotionally responsive (affect)? Was affect congruent with mood?
- *Speech* How was the quantity, rate of production, and quality of the client's speech (e.g., minimal—mostly yes and no answers; talkative; rapid/pressured speech)?
- *Perceptual Disturbances* Did the client experience hallucinations or illusions? If so, what sensory system did they involve (e.g., auditory, visual, olfactory, tactile)?
- *Thought* Did the client have any disturbances in *thought process*, which involves the rate of thoughts and how they flow and are connected (e.g., racing thoughts, flight of ideas, tangential)? Were there any disturbances in *thought content*, such as delusions, obsessions, preoccupations, or suicidal or homicidal thoughts?
- *Orientation* Was the client aware of (a) the date and time, (b) where he or she was, and (c) who the people around him or her were (i.e., oriented to time, place, and person)?
- *Memory* How was the client's recent memory (e.g., remembering what he or she had for breakfast) and remote memory (e.g., memories from childhood)?
- *Concentration and Attention* Was the client's concentration or attention impaired? Was the client distractible?
- *Information and Intelligence* Can the client accomplish mental tasks that would be expected of a person of his or her educational level and background?

- *Judgment and Insight* Does the client have the capacity for social judgment? Does the client have insight into the nature of his or her illness?
- *Reliability* How accurately was the client able to report his or her situation?

A well-known screening test of mental status is called the *Mini Mental Status Examination* (MMSE; Folstein, Folstein, & McHugh, 1975). It is "mini" because it focuses only on the cognitive aspects of mental functions and excludes questions about mood, perceptual disturbances, and thought process or content. Thus, the exam is commonly used in the evaluation of Alzheimer's disease or other forms of dementia. The MMSE consists of 11 questions that measure five areas of cognitive function: orientation, registration, attention and calculation, recall, and language (see Table 13.3). It is important to gather information from each area, because neurocognitive issues may impact one aspect of brain functioning but not another. For example, clients may know their names and where they are but may not know the year. We stress that a screening tool such as the MMSE is not suitable alone for making a diagnosis but can be used as a brief general survey of a broad range of cognitive function and can screen for the need for more thorough neuropsychological evaluation. The maximum score of the MMSE is 30. A score of 23 or lower indicates significant cognitive impairment. The MMSE takes only 5 to 10 minutes to administer and is therefore practical to use repeatedly and routinely.

Instruments Used in Clinical Assessment

The primary types of formal instruments used in clinical assessment are inventories and checklists, both of which fall under the umbrella category of personality tests. The inventories and checklists used are those with a *pathological focus*; they detect clinical problems or psychological symptoms, such as depression, anxiety, hallucinations, delusions, and so on. In fact, many of these instruments are constructed to correspond directly with the DSM classification system. For example, the scales of the Millon Clinical Multiaxial Inventory (MCMI-III; see Chapter 11) are grouped into categories of personality and psychopathology that are consonant with the DSM nosology. As another example, the Beck Depression

---

TABLE 13.3 Sample Items from the Mini Mental Status Exam

Item	Instructions	Purpose
Orientation	"What is the date?"	To assess whether the client is oriented to the present.
Registration	"Listen carefully. I am going to say three words. You say them back after I stop. Ready? Here they are … APPLE [pause], PENNY [pause], TABLE [pause]. Now repeat those words back to me."	To assess the client's immediate recall and memory.
Naming	"What is this?" (Point to a pencil or pen.)	To assess the client's ability to name an object.
Reading	"Please read this and do what it says." (Show examinee a piece of paper with the words *CLOSE YOUR EYES* written on it.)	To assess the client's ability to read and follow a written command.

Source: Reproduced by special permission of the publisher, Psychological Assessment Resources, Inc., 16204 North Florida Avenue, Lutz, Florida 33549, from the Mini Mental State Examination, by Marshal Folstein and Susan Folstein, Copyright 1975, 1998, 2001, by Mini Mental LLC, Inc. Published 2001 by Psychological Assessment Resources, Inc. Further reproduction is prohibited without permission of PAR, Inc.

Inventory (BDI-II) was developed specifically to assess depression symptoms as listed in the DSM (Beck, Steer, & Brown, 1996). Many clinical tests indicate whether a respondent's score falls within the *clinical range*, which refers to the range of scores that align with a sample of individuals experiencing psychopathological symptoms. For example, a client scoring in the clinical range on the BDI-II indicates that he or she is experiencing symptoms similar to a normative sample of depressed individuals.

Clinical assessment instruments may have either a *broad scope* (i.e., evaluate a wide array of symptoms and problems) or a *narrow scope* (i.e., assess a particular set of related symptoms or problems). The Minnesota Multiphasic Personality Inventory (MMPI-2), the MCMI-III, and the Symptom Checklist 90–Revised (SCL-90-R) are examples of broadly focused tests that assess a range of adult psychopathological symptoms. In addition, there are literally hundreds if not thousands of narrowly focused tests available for assessing specific types of symptoms. Table 13.4 provides a very short list of the inventories and checklists commonly used in clinical assessment. We will provide more information on a few of the more well-known clinical tests.

TABLE 13.4 Sample of Inventories and Checklists Used in Clinical Assessment

Broad Focus

Brief Symptom Inventory (BSI)
Millon Clinical Multiaxial Inventory (MCMI-III)
Minnesota Multiphasic Personality Inventory (MMPI-2; MMPI-II-RF)
Outcome Questionnaire 45.2 (OQ 45.2)
Symptom Checklist 90–Revised (SCL-90-R)

Narrow Focus

Anxiety
Beck Anxiety Inventory (BAI)
Hamilton Anxiety Rating Scale (HARS)
Revised Children's Manifest Anxiety Scales: Second Edition (RCMAS-2)
State-Trait Anxiety Inventory (STAI)

Depression
Beck Depression Inventory (BDI-II)
Children's Depression Inventory, Second Edition (CDI-2)
Hamilton Depression Inventory (HDI)

Eating Disorders
Eating Attitudes Test (EAT-26)
Eating Disorder Inventory-3 (EDI-3)
Stirling Eating Disorders Scales (SEDS)

Relationship/Family
Conflict Tactics Scale (CTS)
Fundamental Interpersonal Relations Orientation-Behavior (FIRO-B)
Marital Satisfaction Inventory, Revised (MSI-R)

Substance Abuse
Alcohol Use Inventory (AUI)
Michigan Alcoholism Screening Test (MAST)
Substance Abuse Subtle Screening Inventory (SASSI-3)

Trauma
Detailed Assessment of Posttraumatic Stress (DAPS)
Multiscale Dissociation Inventory (MDI)
Posttraumatic Stress Diagnostic Scale (PDS)
Trauma Symptom Inventory-2 (TSI-2)
Trauma Symptom Checklist for Children (TSCC)

BECK DEPRESSION INVENTORY The BDI-II (Beck et al., 1996) is one of the most widely used instruments for measuring the severity of depression in persons 13 years of age and older. The 21-item self-report inventory takes approximately 5 to 10 minutes for clients to complete. The content of items reflects the diagnostic criteria for depression in the DSM-5 (American Psychiatric Association (APA), 2013) and includes sadness, pessimism, past failure, loss of pleasure, guilty feelings, punishment feelings, self-dislike, self-criticalness, suicidal thoughts or wishes, crying, agitation, loss of interest, indecisiveness, worthlessness, loss of energy, changes in sleeping pattern, irritability, changes in appetite, concentration difficulty, tiredness or fatigue, and loss of interest in sex. However, because there were some significant changes in the DSM-5 with regard to the diagnosis of depression, counselors are cautioned to use best practice and to conduct a multifaceted assessment process. For each item on the BDI-II, respondents are asked to choose from among a group of statements (rated on a 4-point scale from 0 to 3) those that best describe their feelings during the past 2 weeks. The simple rating-scale format of the inventory allows individuals to easily comprehend the questions and respond appropriately. To score the inventory, counselors simply sum the item scores. Total raw scores can range from 0 to 63; scores from 0 to 13 represent minimal depression, from 14 to 19 indicate mild depression, from 20 to 28 represent moderate depression, and from 29 to 63 indicate severe depression. The BDI-II is a fast, efficient way to assess depression in either a clinical or nonclinical setting. The publisher has recently lowered the classification of the BDI-II to a *B-Level* qualification, meaning that test users must have a master's degree in counseling or a related field or be licensed or certified to practice in their state. In terms of technical quality, the BDI-II has demonstrated strong evidence of internal consistency and test-retest reliability and evidence of convergent validity.

SYMPTOM CHECKLIST 90-REVISED The SCL-90-R is a 90-item self-report symptom inventory designed to measure psychological symptom patterns in individuals who are ages 13 years and older (Derogatis, 1994). It can be paper-and-pencil, audiocassette, or computer administered and requires about 12 to 15 minutes to complete. Each item represents a particular psychological symptom (e.g., feeling fearful, feeling low in energy, difficulty making decisions), which is rated on a 5-point scale of distress (0–4), ranging from *not at all* (0) to *extremely* (4). The SCL-90-R yields raw scores and T scores for three *global indices* and nine *primary symptom dimensions* (Derogatis, 1994). The three global indices provide measures of the level of an individual's distress and include the following:

1. *Global Severity Index (GSI)* This index is the average score of the raw scores of all 90 items of the questionnaire. It provides a single numeric indicator of the respondent's psychological status. In general, T scores at or above 63 suggest the presence of a clinically significant level of psychological difficulties.
2. *Positive Symptom Distress Index (PSDI)* This index is a measure of symptom intensity or severity. It is the average value of all items scored above zero (between 1 and 4). For example, if a client's raw score on the PSDI index was 2.5, then this means that the average of all items scored above zero was between 2 (Moderately) and 3 (Quite a Bit). Higher scores on the PSDI indicate increased symptom severity.
3. *Positive Symptom Total (PST)* This is the number of items scored above zero. Whereas PSDI is a measure of symptom severity, the PST index represents the number (or breadth) of symptoms. For example, if a client's raw score on the PST was 60, then this would mean that he or she answered 60 out of the 90 items with a rating from 1 to 4. A low PST would indicate relatively few symptoms, whereas a high PST would indicate a wide array of symptoms.

The nine *primary symptom dimensions* represent various psychological symptom patterns. T scores of 63 or more on two or more of the symptom dimensions suggest clinically significant levels of psychological distress. The primary symptoms are as follows:

1. *Somatization (SOM)* This dimension reflects distress from perceptions of bodily dysfunction. Complaints may focus on cardiovascular, gastrointestinal, respiratory, gross musculature, or other bodily areas (note responses to actual items). Pain and anxiety are both likely to be present as well.

2. *Obsessive-Compulsive (O-C)* This dimension focuses on obsessions and compulsions that cause distress. It focuses on impulses, thoughts, and actions that are unremitting, irresistible, and unwanted.

3. *Interpersonal Sensitivity (I-S)* This dimension reflects feelings of inadequacy and inferiority. Self-deprecation, self-doubt, and discomfort in interpersonal situations are evident among individuals who score high on this index. They have negative expectations regarding interpersonal behavior with others and are self-conscious.

4. *Depression (DEP)* Elevated scores on the DEP index reflect a range of depressive symptoms, such as withdrawal, lack of motivation, loss of energy, hopelessness, and suicidal thoughts.

5. *Anxiety (ANX)* This index focuses on general signs of anxiety, such as nervousness, tension, and trembling, as well as panic attacks and feelings of terror, apprehension, and dread.

6. *Hostility (HOS)* Elevated scores on the HOS dimension indicate thoughts, feelings, and behaviors that are characteristic of anger, such as aggression, irritability, rage, and resentment.

7. *Phobic Anxiety (PHOB)* This dimension focuses on the presence of persistent and irrational fear related to a specific person, place, object, or situation. Items in this dimension more closely reflect agoraphobia or panic attacks rather than merely phobias.

8. *Paranoid Ideation (PAR)* This dimension represents the key elements of paranoid thought, such as suspiciousness, hostility, grandiosity, fear of loss of autonomy, and delusions.

9. *Psychoticism (PSY)* Items on the PSY dimension are indicative of a withdrawn and isolated lifestyle as well as first-rank symptoms of schizophrenia, such as hallucinations and thought control. Scores reflect a range of psychoticism from minor levels of interpersonal alienation to severe psychotic symptoms.

To interpret SCL-90-R scores, counselors examine (1) the global indices, (2) the symptom dimensions, and (3) specific items. The SCL-90-R provides a clinical profile showing both raw scores and T scores for the global indices and the symptom dimensions. It also provides a list of items that were endorsed as *quite a bit* or *extremely* distressed. A sample clinical profile is presented in Figure 13.1. A unique feature of the SCL-90-R is that an individual's scores can be compared with and plotted based on four norm groups: psychiatric outpatients, nonpatients, psychiatric inpatients, and nonpatient adolescents. The SCL-90-R can be used as a one-time assessment of a client's clinical status, or it can be used repeatedly to document treatment outcome. In order to further your understanding of the SCL-90-R and how it can be used in the diagnostic process, complete Exercise 13.1. After reviewing the information, respond to the exercise questions.

Exercise 13.1
Clinical Assessment: Jada

Jada, age 25, worked part-time as a librarian. She was driving to work one day when she began to feel intensely anxious. Her heart started pounding, and she began sweating, had shortness of breath, felt dizzy and shaky, and felt like she was about to die. She pulled off to the side of the road and recovered after about 10 minutes. Jada drove on to work and was able to function that day but experienced similar incidents over the next couple of weeks. For the next few months, she was persistently worried about having more attacks and became increasingly anxious about having another attack while she was driving alone with no one to help her. She began avoiding driving, and she even began to fear leaving her house alone.

Jada sought counseling at an outpatient counseling center and was administered the SCL-90-R during her initial assessment. Review Jada's SCL-90-R Clinical Profile and answer the questions that follow.

SCL-90-R CLINICAL PROFILE

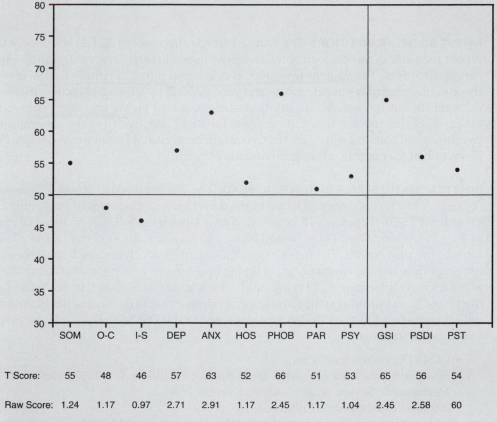

	SOM	O-C	I-S	DEP	ANX	HOS	PHOB	PAR	PSY	GSI	PSDI	PST
T Score:	55	48	46	57	63	52	66	51	53	65	56	54
Raw Score:	1.24	1.17	0.97	2.71	2.91	1.17	2.45	1.17	1.04	2.45	2.58	60

FIGURE 13.1 Symptom Checklist 90-Revised (SCL-90-R) clinical profile.

Symptoms of Note:

The following items were endorsed as Extremely distressed:

13. Feeling nervous when you are left alone.
25. Feeling afraid to go out of your house alone.

The following items were endorsed as Quite a Bit distressed:

39. Heart pounding or racing.
50. Having to avoid certain things, places, or activities because they frighten you.
72. Spells of terror or panic.

Exercise Questions

1. Interpret Jada's scores on the three global indices (e.g., GSI, PSDI, and PST).
2. Were any of Jada's scores on the primary symptom dimensions "clinically significant"? If yes, identify the dimension(s) and interpret the score(s).
3. Are Jada's scores on the SCL-90-R consistent with the information presented in the case study? Explain.
4. What inferences can you make about Jada based on the background information and her scores on the SCL-90-R?
5. What would you recommend for her?

EATING DISORDER INVENTORY The Eating Disorder Inventory (EDI-3) is a widely used self-report measure of psychological traits shown to be clinically relevant in individuals with eating disorders. The 91-item inventory is organized into 12 primary scales, consisting of three eating-disorder-specific scales and nine general psychological scales that are highly relevant to, but not specific to, eating disorders. It also yields six composites: one that is eating-disorder specific (i.e., Eating Disorder Risk) and five that are general integrative psychological constructs (i.e., Ineffectiveness, Interpersonal Problems, Affective Problems, Overcontrol, General Psychological Maladjustment).

POSTTRAUMATIC STRESS DIAGNOSTIC SCALE The Posttraumatic Stress Diagnostic Scale (PDS; Foa, 1995) was designed to aid in the detection and diagnosis of posttraumatic stress disorder (PTSD). It contains 17 items rated on a 4-point scale (i.e., 0 = *not at all or only once* to 3 = *five or more times a week/almost always*) to measure the severity of the PTSD symptoms in the past month. The items assess the extent to which respondents have symptoms of reexperiencing the trauma (e.g., "Having bad dreams or nightmares about the event"), avoidance symptoms (e.g., "Trying not to think about, talk about, or have feelings about the event"), and arousal symptoms (e.g., "Feeling irritable or having fits of anger"), all of which correspond to the PTSD symptoms listed in the DSM-IV. The scale provides results in the following areas:

- PTSD Diagnosis (yes or no)
- Symptom Severity Score and Rating (Mild = 1 − 10, Moderate = 11 − 20, Moderate to Severe = 21 − 35, and Severe > 36)
- Number of Symptoms Endorsed
- Level of Impairment of Functioning (No Impairment, Mild, Moderate, Severe)

Psychometrically, the PDS appears to meet its main objective of validly and reliably differentiating PTSD from non-PTSD subjects, although the instrument would benefit

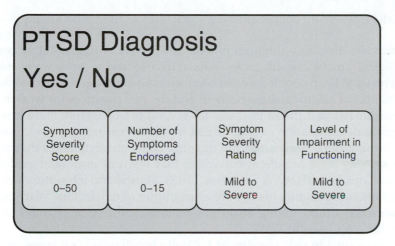

FIGURE 13.2   Overview of the PTSD Diagnostic Scale Elements.

from additional validation research utilizing larger and perhaps demographically more representative samples. Figure 13.2 shows a sample profile report.

SUBSTANCE ABUSE SUBTLE SCREENING INVENTORY   The Substance Abuse Subtle Screening Inventory (SASSI-3) is a brief, self-report, easily administered psychological screening measure that is available in separate versions for adults and adolescents. The instrument helps identify individuals who have a high probability of having a substance-dependence disorder. It is particularly useful in identifying persons who are experiencing difficulties with substance abuse but are unwilling or unable to acknowledge them. The SASSI-3 is now available for online assessment through sassionline.com. The SASSI-3 is comprised of 10 scales that measure the following dimensions:

1. Face Valid Alcohol (FVA)
2. Symptoms (SYM)
3. Subtle Attributes (SAT)
4. Supplemental Addiction Measure (SAM)
5. Correctional (COR)
6. Face Valid Other Drugs (FVOD)
7. Obvious Attributes (OAT)
8. Defensiveness (DEF)
9. Family vs. Control Measure (FAM)
10. Random Answering

Suicide Risk Assessment

Suicide is the 11th leading cause of death in the United States and the second leading cause of death among people between the ages of 15 and 24 years. It is almost impossible to have an exact account of the number of people who have experienced suicidal ideation or attempts, but in general we can estimate that for every person who completes suicide, there are an approximately 10 to 20 who have attempted suicide (Granello & Granello,

2006). Approximately 71% of all counselors will work with a client who attempts suicide (Granello, 2010).

These statistics are dire, and although no one can predict with absolutely certainty who will commit suicide, mental health professionals strive to find accurate ways of assessing suicide risk in order to keep people safe. As counselors-in-training, it is critical that you understand the nuances of suicide risk assessment and the best practices for working with suicidal clients. Suicide risk is difficult to assess for several reasons. First, there is no "one size fits all," meaning determination of suicide risk involves evaluating a combination of risk factors and warning signs. *Risk factors* are ongoing client characteristics that increase suicide risk, and *warning signs* are client behaviors that warn of imminent suicide risk (Hawton, Casañas i Comabella, Haw, & Saunders, 2013). Marital and job status, feelings of hopelessness or isolation, and family history are all examples of risk factors. Warning signs include settling personal affairs, giving away possessions, and drastic changes in mood and behavior (Granello & Granello, 2006).

A comprehensive suicide risk assessment typically involves several types of assessment methods and sources of information. The most common assessment method involves unstructured interviews in which mental health professionals assess suicide risk in several key areas, such as intent, a suicide plan with accessible means, a history of suicidal thoughts, and family history of suicidal thoughts and mental disorders (Granello & Granello, 2006).

It's important that questions about suicide risk be asked in clear and frank language (i.e., "Have you thought about suicide?" or "Are you considering killing yourself?"). Sometimes, clients will use euphemisms (e.g., "I just want to be with the angels" or "I won't be around for them to pick on anymore") that hint at suicide plans (Granello & Granello, 2006, p. 189). In these situations, it is vital that professionals ask the client in a direct manner about plans to commit suicide.

Many mental health professionals use suicide risk–assessment instruments in conjunction with the unstructured interviews, and there are hundreds of instruments available that assess suicide risk that are either commercially published or available in the research literature. Although these instruments were designed to directly measure suicide ideation and behavior, none have been universally supported as being effective in determining risk. Thus, a few of the more commonly used suicide risk–assessment instruments are listed in Table 13.5.

In addition to instruments assessing suicide ideation and behavior, there are instruments that measure variables that have been closely associated with suicide, such as

TABLE 13.5 List of Suicide Risk–Assessment Instruments

Adults	Children and Adolescents
Adult Suicidal Ideation Questionnaire (ASIQ)	Adolescent Suicide Inventory
Beck Scale for Suicidal Ideation (SSI)	Child Suicide Assessment (CSA)
Firestone Assessment of Self-Destructive Thoughts (FAST)	Harkavy Asnis Suicide Scale (HASS)
	Inventory of Suicide Orientation-30 (ISO-30)
Suicide Probability Scale (SPS)	Suicide Behaviors Questionnaire-Revised (SBQ-R)
Suicidal Ideation Scale (SIS)	Suicide Probability Scale (SPS)
Suicide Intent Scale (SIS)	Suicidal Ideation Questionnaire (SIQ)

hopelessness and reasons for living. For example, the Beck Hopelessness Scale (BHS; Beck & Steer, 1988) is a self-report instrument that is designed to measure the extent of positive and negative beliefs about the future. Another example is the Brief Reasons for Living Inventory (BRFL; Ivanoff, Jang, Smyth, & Linehan, 1994), which assesses the reasons for not killing oneself if the thought were to occur.

Many checklists and inventories that assess general psychological symptoms also have "critical items" assessing suicide risk. For example, the BDI-II has a suicide item that consists of four ratings: 1 ("I don't have any thoughts of killing myself"), 2 ("I have thoughts of killing myself, but I would not carry them out"), 3 ("I would like to kill myself"), and 4 ("I would kill myself if I had the chance"). Similarly, the Outcome Questionnaire 45 (OQ45; Lambert, Lunnen, Umphress, Hansen, & Burlingame, 1994) has a suicide potential screening item ("I have thoughts of ending my life") that respondents can rate on a 5-point scale from *never* to *almost always*. Although suicide risk cannot be adequately evaluated with one item alone, these types of items can be useful screening tools for indicating the need for more thorough assessment of suicide risk.

Although formal assessment instruments can be useful tools, they do not replace interviews and interactions with a client and are not a substitute for clinical judgment. Comprehensive suicide risk assessment involves examining information obtained from interviews, information from assessment instruments, and/or collateral information from individuals closest to the client.

OBSERVATION AND CLINICAL ASSESSMENT

As stated in Chapter 2, *observation* is an assessment method that involves monitoring the actions of others or oneself in a particular context and making a record of what is observed. In clinical assessment, observation is used to help determine a client's diagnosis, to target specific patterns of behavior, to provide behavioral baseline data, and to identify effective treatment approaches. In clinical assessment, observation is often *informal* and frequently begins with the initial handshake between the clinician and the client (O'Donohue, Cummings, & Cummings, 2006). In this situation, a client's damp palm may reveal something about his or her level of anxiety. Informal observation continues throughout the interactions with a client and involves the counselor taking note of a number of the client's characteristics or behaviors, such as body type and behaviors, eye movements, clothing, and facial features (Carlat, 2011). Some possible observations include the following:

- *General Appearance*–attractive, plain, flamboyant, meticulous
- *Eye Contact*–intermittent, averted, constant, absent
- *Dress*–appropriate to age and season, neat, disheveled, casual
- *Speech*–rapid, loud, soft
- *Gait*–walks with a limp, wheel-chair bound, no anomalies of gait, shuffle

Observations can also be *formal* and involve the use of structured instruments for recording data, such as event recording, duration recording, time sampling, and rating scales. There are several published *rating scales* commonly used in the clinical assessment of children. These rating scales can be completed by teachers, parents, or others who know the individual, as well as by the child himself or herself. An example of a widely used rating scale for assessing behavioral and emotional problems children is the Child Behavior

Checklist (CBCL/6-18). Other instruments measuring children's behavior include the Behavioral and Emotional Screening System (BASC-2), the Child Symptom Inventory (CSI-4), and the Conduct Disorder Scale (CDS).

CHILD BEHAVIOR CHECKLIST In clinical assessment, the CBCL/6-18 (Achenbach & Rescorla, 2001) is considered the gold standard for evaluating behavioral and emotional problems in children aged 6 to 18. The CBCL/6-18 is a rating scale completed by parents, guardians, and/or close relatives that assesses children's competencies and behavioral/emotional problems. It is part of the Achenbach System of Empirically Based Assessment (ASEBA), which includes an integrated set of rating forms that assess adaptive and maladaptive functioning in children and adults. For example, the CBCL/6-18 (completed by the parent/guardian) is designed to be administered in conjunction with the Youth Self-Report (YSR; completed by the child) and the Teacher's Report Form (TRF; completed by the child's teacher). All three instruments measure eight cross-informant syndrome constructs: Social Withdrawal, Somatic Complaints, Anxiety/Depression, Social Problems, Thought Problems, Attention Problems, Delinquent Behavior, and Aggressive Behavior.

On the CBCL/6-18, parents are asked to rate 118 items that describe their child's specific behavioral and emotional problems. Parents rate their child for how true each item is now or within the past 6 months using the following scale: 0 = *not true*; 1 = *somewhat or sometimes true*; 2 = *very true or often true*. Examples of items are "Acts too young for age," "Cries a lot," and "Gets in many fights." In addition, there are two open-ended items for parents to report additional problems. The CBCL/6-18 requires a fifth-grade reading ability, and most parents can complete the CBCL/6-18 in about 15 to 20 minutes. Results can be hand scored or computer scored.

The CBCL/6-18 provides several scales that measure parents' perceptions of their child's behavior and emotional problems: three competence scales and a Total Competence scale; eight syndrome scales; Externalizing, Internalizing, and Total Problems scales; and six DSM-oriented scales. The *competence scales* reflect the degree and quality of the child's participation in various activities (e.g., sports, hobbies, games), social relationships, and academic performance. The *syndrome scales* include empirically derived syndromes labeled as Anxious/Depressed, Withdrawn/Depressed, Somatic Complaints, Social Problems, Thought Problems, Attention Problems, Rule-Breaking Behavior, and Aggressive Behavior, as well as a list of Other Problems that consists of items that are not strongly associated with any of the syndrome scales. The first three syndrome scales (Anxious/Depressed, Withdrawn/Depressed, and Somatic Complaints) comprise the Internalizing scale, and the last two syndromes (Rule-Breaking Behavior and Aggressive Behavior) comprise the Externalizing scale. The Total Problems scale is the sum of all of the 120 items on the instrument. The *DSM-oriented scales* are comprised of items that experienced psychiatrists and psychologists rated as being very consistent with categories of diagnoses defined by the DSM-IV (American Psychiatric Association (APA), 1994). Table 13.6 provides a summary of each of the CBCL/6-18 scales.

The CBCL/6-18 provides separate scoring profiles for boys and girls of ages 6 to 11 and 12 to 18. Scoring profiles include raw scores, T scores, and percentile ranks for each scale (Figure 13.3 shows an example of a scoring profile for the syndrome scales). T scores are further categorized as being in the clinical range, borderline clinical range, or the normal range.

TABLE 13.6 CBCL/6-18 Scales

Scale	Description
Competence Scales	
Activities	Participation in sports, hobbies, clubs, teams, jobs, chores
Social	Number of friends; relations with peers, siblings, and parents; ability to work and play alone.
Academic Performance	Academic performance level, grade retention, special services, school problems.
Total Competence	Sum of the three competence scales.
Syndrome Scales	
Anxious/Depressed	Cries, fears school, phobias, perfectionist, feels unloved, feels worthless, nervous, fearful, feels guilty, self-conscious, suicidal thoughts, worries.
Withdrawn/Depressed	Enjoys little in life, prefers to be alone, won't talk, secretive, shy, lacks energy, unhappy and sad, withdrawn.
Somatic Complaints	Nightmares, dizzy, fatigued, aches or pains, headaches, nausea, eye problems, skin problems, stomach aches, vomiting.
Social Problems	Dependent on adults, feels lonely, doesn't get along with other kids, jealous, believes others are "out to get" him or her, accident-prone, teased, not like by other kids, clumsy, prefers to be with younger children, speech problems.
Thought Problems	Ruminates, harm to self, hears things, body twitches, skin picking, compulsions, sees things that aren't there, sleeps less, hoards things, strange behavior, strange ideas, sleepwalks, sleep problems.
Attention Problems	Acts too young for his or her age, fails to finish things, problems concentrating, trouble sitting still, daydreaming, impulsive, poor schoolwork, inattentive, stares.
Rule-Breaking Behavior	Drinks alcohol, no guilt after doing something wrong, breaks rules, socializing with "bad" kids, lies or cheats, prefers older kids, has run away from home, sets fires, often thinks about sex, uses tobacco, truant, uses drugs, vandalizes.
Aggressive Behavior	Argues, mean to others, demands attention, destroys own belongings, destroys others' belongings, disobeys parents, disobeys at school, fights, attacks, screams, stubborn, moody, sulks, suspicious, teases others, temper problems, threatens to hurt others, louder than other kids.
Internalizing, Externalizing, and Total Problems Scales	
Total Problems	The sum of the 0-1-2 scores on all 120 items.
Internalizing	The sum of scores for the Anxious/Depressed, Withdrawn/Depressed, and Somatic Complaints syndromes.
Externalizing	The sum of scores for the Rule-Breaking Behavior and Aggressive Behavior syndromes.

(continued)

TABLE 13.6 CBCL/6-18 Scales (*Continued*)

Scale	Description
DSM-Oriented Scales	
Affective Problems	Enjoys little in life, cries, harms self, feels worthless, feels guilty, fatigued, apathetic, suicidal thoughts, low energy, sad. This scale corresponds to the DSM-IV criteria for Major Depressive Disorder and Dysthymia.
Anxiety Problems	Dependent on adults, phobias, fears school, nervous, fearful, worries. Corresponds with the DSM-IV criteria for Generalized Anxiety Disorder, Social Anxiety Disorder, and Specific Phobia.
Somatic Problems	Aches or pains, headaches, nausea, eye problems, skin problems, stomach aches, vomiting. Corresponds with the DSM-IV criteria for Somatization and Somatoform Disorders.
Attention Deficit/ Hyperactivity Problems	Fails to finish things, problems concentrating, trouble sitting still, fidgets, difficulty following directions, disturbs others, impulsive, talks out, disruptive, inattentive, talks too much, louder than other kids. Corresponds with the criteria for ADHD, Hyperactive-Impulsive, and Inattentive types.
Oppositional Defiant Problems	Argues, defiant, disobeys at school, stubborn, temper problems. Corresponds with the criteria for Oppositional Defiant Disorder.
Conduct Problems	Mean, destroys others' belongings, no guilt after doing something wrong, breaks rules, fights, socializing with "bad" kids, lies or cheats, attacks, irresponsible, steals, swears, threatens, truant.

The value of T scores for each range varies depending on the scale. For example, on the competence scales, higher T scores are associated with normal functioning. On the syndrome scales, Internalizing, Externalizing, Total Problem, and DSM-oriented scales, lower T scores are associated with normal functioning. For a more thorough understanding of children's assessment using the CBCL, complete Exercise 13.2 and respond to the exercise questions.

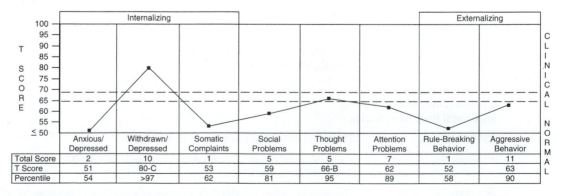

FIGURE 13.3   CBCL/6-18 sample profile of the syndrome scales.

Source: Reprinted with permission from Achenbach, T. M., & Rescorla, L. A. (2001). *Manual for the ASEBA School Age Forms & Profiles.* Burlington, VT: University of Vermont, Research Center for Children, Youth and Families.

Exercise 13.2
Child Clinical Assessment: CBCL

Name: Sabrina Robinson	Clinician: Darcy Young	Informant: Joanne Robinson
Gender: Female	Agency: Community Counseling Clinic	Relationship: Biological Mother
Age: 12	Date of Assessment: 05/28/2007	
Birth Date: 04/10/1995		

Sabrina, age 12, was brought to an outpatient counseling center by her biological mother, Joanne Robinson. Ms. Robinson reported concern about Sabrina's problems in school and her mood at home. Sabrina is in the sixth grade and is performing poorly academically; her most recent progress report showed D's in social studies, math, and science and a C in language arts. Ms. Robinson stated that Sabrina has difficulty concentrating on school and frequently does not finish her homework. She is often tired, taking a nap every day after school. Sabrina is well-behaved at home, has few if any behavior problems in

school, and has never been reprimanded or held after school for detention. Ms. Robinson reported that Sabrina has no friends at school but has two close friends who attend their church. Sabrina sees her friends less than once a week. At home, Ms. Robinson reported that Sabrina has a few chores (e.g., making her bed, putting away dishes). She reported that Sabrina enjoys playing games on her computer and reading.

Ms. Robinson completed the CBCL/6-18. The profile scores of Sabrina's CBCL/6-18 follow.

CBCL/6-18 Competence Scale for Girls 12–18

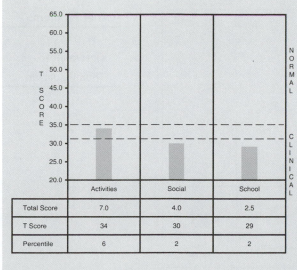

	Activities	Social	School
Total Score	7.0	4.0	2.5
T Score	34	30	29
Percentile	6	2	2

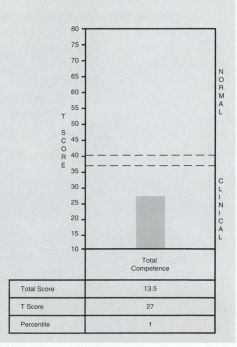

	Total Competence
Total Score	13.5
T Score	27
Percentile	1

• Three hobbies/activities (computer games, reading, dolls)	• No clubs or teams	• Below average to average school grades
• Two chores (making bed, cleaning room)	• Two friends	• Repeated third grade.
	• Contact with friends less than one time weekly	

CBCL/6-18 Syndrome Scales for Girls 12–18

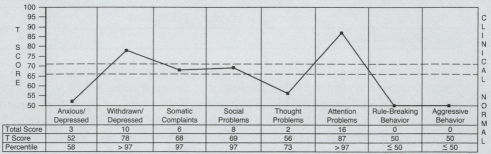

	Anxious/ Depressed	Withdrawn/ Depressed	Somatic Complaints	Social Problems	Thought Problems	Attention Problems	Rule-Breaking Behavior	Aggressive Behavior
Total Score	3	10	6	8	2	16	0	0
T Score	52	78	68	69	56	87	50	50
Percentile	58	> 97	97	97	73	> 97	≤ 50	≤ 50

• Perfectionist	• Prefers being alone	• Feels dizzy	• Lonely	• Hoarding	• Acts young for age
• Feels worthless	• Won't talk	• Tired	• Accident-prone	• Sleep problems	• Fails to finish things
• Self-conscious	• Secretive	• Aches or pains	• Gets teased		• Can't concentrate
	• Lacks energy	• Headaches	• Clumsy		• Confused
	• Sad	• Nausea	• Prefers younger kids		• Daydreams
	• Withdrawn	• Stomach aches			• Poor school work
					• Inattentive
					• Stares blankly

Note: The items that were endorsed as *somewhat or sometimes true* or *very true or often true* are listed under each scale.

CBCL/6-18 Internalizing, Externalizing, Total Problem, Other Problems for Girls 12–18

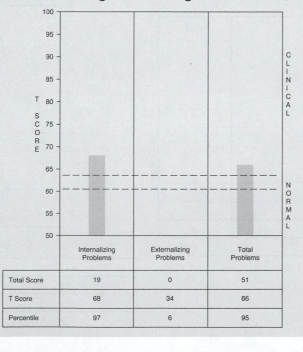

Other Problems

Overeats

Overweight

Thumb Sucking

	Internalizing Problems	Externalizing Problems	Total Problems
Total Score	19	0	51
T Score	68	34	66
Percentile	97	6	95

CBCL/6–18 DSM-Oriented Scales for Girls 12–18

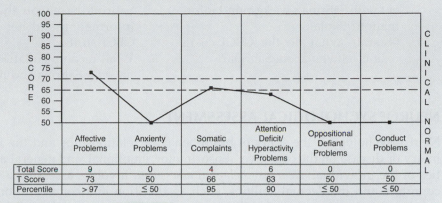

	Affective Problems	Anxiety Problems	Somatic Complaints	Attention Deficit/ Hyperactivity Problems	Oppositional Defiant Problems	Conduct Problems
Total Score	9	0	4	6	0	0
T Score	73	50	66	63	50	50
Percentile	> 97	≤ 50	95	90	≤ 50	≤ 50

- Worthless
- Underactive
- Sleep problems
- Tired
- Sad

- Aches
- Headaches
- Stomachaches

- Fails to finish things
- Can't concentrate
- Inattentive

Note: The items that were endorsed as *somewhat or sometimes true* or *very true or often true* are listed under each scale.

Exercise Questions

1. Identify and interpret the scores for each of the CBCL/6-18 scales that fall in the *clinical range* (the table ahead provides the cutoff scores for normal, borderline clinical, and clinical ranges). Use the following example as a format for your answers:

Withdrawn/Depressed scale: On the Withdrawn/Depressed scale, Sabrina obtained a standard score of 70 (which is greater than the 97th percentile). This indicates that she is functioning in the clinical range. This suggests that that she is experiencing significant psychological symptoms, such as lacking energy, sadness, and withdrawal. She prefers to be alone, won't open up and talk, and is secretive.

Table of Normal, Borderline, and Clinical Ranges

Scale	Normal Range	Borderline Clinical Range	Clinical Range
Activities, Social and Academic Performance Competence Scales	T scores > 35	T scores: 31–35	T scores < 31
Total Competence Scale	T scores > 40	T scores: 37–40	T scores < 37
Syndrome Scales	T scores < 65	T scores: 65–69	T scores > 69
Internalizing, Externalizing, and Total Problems Scales	T scores < 60	T scores: 60–63	T scores > 63
DSM-Oriented Scales	T scores < 65	T scores: 65–69	T scores > 69

2. Are the CBCL/6-18 results consistent with Sabrina's background information? Explain.

3. Overall, what do the CBCL/6-18 results tell you about Sabrina?

4. What inferences can you make about Sabrina based on the background information and her scores on the CBCL/6-18?

5. What recommendations would you have for Sabrina and her mother?

NEUROPSYCHOLOGICAL ASSESSMENT

Neuropsychology is the study of brain-behavior relationships and the impact of brain injury or disease on the cognitive, sensorimotor, emotional, and general adaptive capacities of the individual. *Neuropsychological assessment* involves assessing a wide variety of cognitive and intellectual abilities, such as attention and concentration, learning and memory, sensory-perceptual abilities, speech and language abilities, visuospatial skills (ability to perceive spatial relationships among objects), overall intelligence, and executive functions. In addition, psychomotor speed, strength, and coordination all would be addressed in some fashion. Three well-known neuropsychological instruments include the Halstead–Reitan Neuropsychological Test Battery, the Luria–Nebraska Neuropsychological Battery (LNNB), and the Bender Visual-Motor Gestalt Test, Second Edition (Bender-Gestalt II).

HALSTEAD–REITAN NEUROPSYCHOLOGICAL TEST BATTERY This test battery is designed to evaluate brain and nervous system functioning in individuals aged 15 years and older. The battery takes about 6 to 8 hours to administer and involves administering eight separate tests. It uses Wechsler Intelligence Scales but also includes a number of tests utilized originally by Halstead, some added by Reitan, and several added by others. Some tests within the battery call for tactual performance; for example, the Halstead Tactual Performance Test requires test takers to place 10 blocks of differing shapes into a matching 10-hole formboard while blindfolded, using only a sense of touch. On the Klove Roughness Discrimination Test, the test taker must order four blocks, each covered with a different grade of sandpaper. The blocks are presented behind a blind, and the test is scored on the time the client takes and the number of errors made with each hand. Also included in the Halstead-Reitan Battery are visual and psychomotor scales; for example, the Reitan Aphasia Screening Test contains both language and copying tasks. The copying tasks require the test taker to make a copy of a square, a Greek cross, a triangle, and a key. The language functions measured are naming, repetition, spelling, reading, writing, calculation, narrative speech, and left/right orientation. The language section is scored by listing the number of aphasic symptoms. The Klove Grooved Pegboard Test requires the test taker to place pegs shaped like keys into a board containing recesses oriented in randomly varying directions. The test taker performs first with one hand and then the other. Some of the other tests on the scale are the Halstead Category Test, the Speech Perception Test, the Seashore Rhythm Test, the Finger Tapping Test, the Trail-Making Test, the Perceptual Disorders Test, and the Visual Field Examination.

LURIA–NEBRASKA NEUROPSYCHOLOGICAL BATTERY The LNNB is another series of tests designed to assess neuropsychological function. It is designed for individuals ages 15 and older and can be administered in 1.5 to 2.5 hours. The LNNB assesses a wide range of cognitive functions on 11 clinical scales, two optional scales, three summary scales, and 11 factor scales. The following is a list and description of the clinical scales:

1. *Motor Functions* Measures a wide variety of motor skills
2. *Rhythm* Measures nonverbal auditory perception, such as pitch discrimination and rhythmic patterns
3. *Tactile Functions* Measures tactual discrimination and recognition
4. *Vision Functions* Measures visual-perceptual and visual-spatial skills
5. *Receptive Speech* Measures perception of sounds from simple to complex
6. *Expressive Speech* Measures ability to repeat sounds, words, and word groups and produce narrative speech
7. *Writing* Measures ability to analyze words into letters and to write under varying conditions
8. *Reading* Measures ability to make letter-to-sound transformations and read simple material
9. *Arithmetic* Measures knowledge of numbers, number concepts, and ability to perform simple calculations
10. *Memory* Measures short-term memory and paired-associate learning
11. *Intellectual Processes* Measures sequencing, problem-solving, and abstraction skills

BENDER VISUAL-MOTOR GESTALT TEST, SECOND EDITION The Bender-Gestalt II is widely used for screening neuropsychological impairment in both children and adults. Specifically, the Bender-Gestalt evaluates visual-motor ability and visual perception skills. *Visual-motor ability* is the ability of the eyes and hands to work together in smooth, efficient patterns. *Visual perception* refers to one's ability to receive, perceive, and make sense of visual stimulation. To assess these skills, the Bender-Gestalt uses nine stimulus cards, each displaying an abstract design (see Figure 13.4). The cards are presented to the examinee one at a time; then, the examinee is asked to reproduce the design on a blank sheet of paper.

Although several systems are available for scoring the Bender-Gestalt, the scoring process, in general, involves comparing an individual's drawings to the designs displayed on the cards. For example, the Global Scoring System (GSS) rates each drawing on a scale

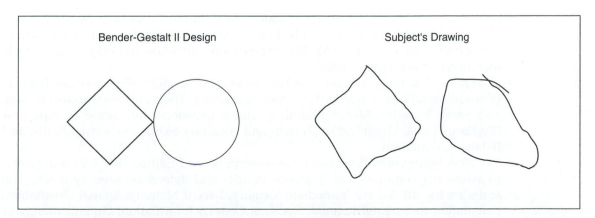

| Bender-Gestalt II Design | Subject's Drawing |

FIGURE 13.4   Design similar to Bender-Gestalt II stimulus card.

of 0 to 4, with 0 being equivalent to scribbles or a complete lack of accuracy and 4 being equivalent to perfect accuracy. It specifically evaluates such deviations as misalignment (rotations), reduction of elements, increase of elements, simplification of elements, omission of elements, substitution of elements, and integration of elements. The Koppitz Developmental Scoring System, Second Edition (KOPPITZ-2) also focuses on errors in the examinee's drawings. The assessor examines each card for four types of error: distortions, rotations, errors of integration, and errors of perseveration (i.e., repetition of the elements of some designs). The system provides standard scores, percentile ranks, specialized scores, and age equivalents.

Koppitz (1975) also described the practice of using the Bender-Gestalt to screen for *emotional indicators*, which are defined as drawing characteristics that are associated with specific types of emotional-behavioral problems in children, such as impulsivity, mental confusion, and low frustration tolerance. Emotional indicators are as follows:

1. *Confused Order* Sign of mental confusion, lack of planning ability, and poor organizational skills
2. *Wavy Line* Poor motor coordination and/or emotional instability
3. *Dashes Substituted for Circles* Impulsivity or lack of interest
4. *Increasing Size of Figures* Low frustration tolerance and explosiveness
5. *Large Size* Impulsivity and acting-out behavior
6. *Small Size* Anxiety, withdrawal, constriction, and timidity
7. *Fine Line* Timidity, shyness, and withdrawal
8. *Careless Overwork or Heavily Reinforced Lines* Impulsivity, aggressiveness, and acting-out behavior
9. *Second Attempt at Drawing Designs* Impulsivity and anxiety
10. *Expansion (Using Two or More Sheets to Complete the Nine Drawings)* Impulsivity and acting-out behavior
11. *Box around the Design* Attempt to control impulsivity, weak inner control, and need for outer limits and structure
12. *Spontaneous Elaboration and/or Additions to Designs* Unusual preoccupation with own thoughts, fears, and anxieties; serious emotional problems

Other tests used for neuropsychological assessment include the following:

- The Kaufman Short Neuropsychological Assessment Procedure (K-SNAP) was developed by H. S. Kaufman and N. L. Kaufman to measure the cognitive functioning of individuals ages 11 to 85. The test measures attention and orientation, simple memory, and perceptual skills.
- The Quick Neurological Screening Test, Second Edition (QNST-II) assesses 15 areas of neurological integration as they relate to learning. The scales are Control of Large and Small Muscles, Motor Planning, Motor Development, Sense of Rate and Rhythm, Spatial Organization, Visual and Auditory Skills, Perceptual Skills, and Balance Orientation.
- The Ross Information Processing Assessment, Second Edition (RIPA-2) is designed to assess any cognitive and linguistic deficits and determine severity levels. The scales on the RIPA-2 are Immediate Memory, Recent Memory, Spatial Orientation, Orientation to the Environment, Recall of General Information, Organization, and Auditory Processing and Retention.

CULTURAL CONSIDERATIONS IN CLINICAL ASSESSMENT

Cultural competence is essential for counseling practice and should be a consideration for your work with every client. It is important to recognize that assessment procedures are used throughout the world and that counseling is a global profession. As counselors in a global world, you are entrusted to use assessment instruments with consideration of the cultural implications for your clients. Whether you are practicing counseling in the United States or in the United Kingdom, you will assess clients from different ethnic groups and cultural backgrounds. During the assessment process, it will be important to take into account your client's cultural frame of reference when evaluating behaviors. The consequence of lack of multicultural perspectives in assessment is identifying culturally normal behaviors as pathological. For example, certain cultures believe in connections with the spirits of those who are deceased. If a client from that culture reported hearing or seeing a deceased relative during bereavement, it would be imperative to evaluate that report in light of the cultural lens. Failure to consider culture in this case would likely lead to a misdiagnosis of a psychotic disorder (American Psychiatric Association (APA), 2013).

As you have learned or will learn, being comfortable discussing cultural issues is one of the most important steps toward cultural competency. In a clinical assessment situation, you may have to respectfully ask about cultural differences with your client. These questions could be about differences in gender, age, race, ethnicity, religion, or other cultural factors. For example, imagine that you have a client who is struggling with drug use and reported on his or her intake paperwork that he or she is Amish. It would be important to explore the client's connection to Amish culture and traditions. It would also be important to understand the perspective of the Amish community on drug use and on counseling. Sommers-Flanagan and Sommers-Flanagan (2013) suggest a variety of techniques to use when exploring cultural differences, such as asking for clarification, accepting cultural norms for behaviors and verbalizations, accepting beliefs in causes of crisis, and not diagnosing prematurely.

Summary

The term *clinical assessment* generally refers to applying assessment procedures to (a) diagnose a mental disorder, (b) develop a plan of treatment, (c) monitor treatment progress, and (d) evaluate treatment outcome. Traditionally employed in mental health settings, clinical assessment involves the counselor determining the information that is needed to answer the referral question, organizing and integrating the data, and using his or her clinical judgment in forming an opinion about a client's diagnosis.

Interviews are widely used in clinical assessment to help determine an individual's diagnosis. Interview techniques include unstructured, semistructured, and structured interviews, as well as the MSE. In addition, many formal instruments are used in clinical assessment. Most of these instruments have a pathological focus and are closely aligned to symptoms of disorders listed in the DSM-5. Instruments may assess a broad array of symptoms or a specific set of related symptoms. Formal and informal observations are also used in clinical assessment to help make an accurate diagnosis and in developing a treatment plan.

Questions for Discussion

1. What is the purpose of clinical assessment in mental health settings?
2. Which assessment method (e.g., interviews, tests, observations) provides the most important information in clinical assessment? Explain your reasoning.
3. What are the advantages and disadvantages of using behavioral observation in clinical assessment? In what types of situations would observations be more appropriate than standardized tests?
4. What are the advantages and disadvantages of using the interview in clinical assessment?

Suggested Activities

1. Interview psychologists and counselors working in the mental health field, and find out what tests and assessment procedures they use and why. Report your findings to the class.
2. Critically review a test used in clinical assessment. Read the reviews of the test in different journals and yearbooks.
3. Design an interview schedule, and try it out on several individuals. Write an analysis of the results.
4. Write a review of the literature on a topic such as behavioral assessment, intake interviews, use of tests in counseling practice, or neuropsychological testing.
5. Review the following case study and answer the questions at the end:

   Karen calls the suicide hotline number Friday night at 9 P.M. and speaks to an on-call crisis counselor. Karen says that she is depressed and wants to kill herself. She has been drinking vodka and has obtained several Valium tablets from a neighbor. She says she is lonely and has wasted her life. She has the tablets in her house and is thinking about taking them. After further discussion, the counselor finds out that Karen will be turning 40 next week. She lives alone, has no friends, and has no family members who live nearby. She used to be quite religious but stopped attending church last year. Karen has been previously involved with mental health services, having been treated at an inpatient psychiatric hospital several times over the years for depression and suicidal ideation.

   a. Identify the factors and warning signs associated with suicide risk.
   b. How would you describe Karen's overall risk for suicide?
   c. To further assess suicide risk, what questions would you like to ask Karen?

References

Achenbach, T. M., & Rescorla, L. A. (2001). *Manual for the ASEBA school-age forms & profiles*. Burlington, VT: University of Vermont, Research Center for Children, Youth, & Families.

American Psychiatric Association (APA). (2013). *Diagnostic and statistical manual of mental disorders* (5th ed.). Washington, DC: Author.

Beck, A. T., & Steer, R. A. (1993). *Manual for the Beck Hopelessness Scale*. San Antonio, TX: Psychological Corporation.

Beck, A. T., Steer, R. A., & Brown, G. K. (1996). *Manual for the Beck Depression Inventory-II*. San Antonio, TX: Psychological Corporation.

Carlat, D. J. (2011). *The psychiatric interview: A practical guide* (23rd ed.). Philadelphia, PA: Lippincott, Williams & Wilkins.

Cohen, R. J., Swerdlik, M. E., & Sturman, E. D. (2012). *Psychological testing and assessment: An introduction to tests and measurement* (8th ed.). Boston, MA: McGraw-Hill.

Demyttenaere, K., Bruffaerts, R., Posada-Villa, J., Gasquet, I., Kovess, V., Lepine, J., . . . Morosini, P. (2013). Prevalence, severity, and unmet need for treatment of mental disorders in the World Health Organization World Mental Health Surveys. *Social Psychiatry and Psychiatric Epidemiology, 48*(1), 137–149.

Derogatis, L. R. (1994). *SCL-90-R: Symptom Checklist 90-Revised: Administration, scoring, and procedures manual* (3rd ed.). Minneapolis, MN: Pearson.

First, M. B., Spitzer, R. L., Gibbon, M., & Williams, J. B. W. (2012). *Structured Clinical Interview for*

DSM-IV Axis I disorders (SCID-I), Clinician Versions. Washington, DC: American Psychiatric Press.

Foa, E. B. (1995). *The Posttraumatic Diagnostic Scale manual.* Minneapolis, MN: Pearson Assessments.

Folstein, M., Folstein, S. E., & McHugh, P. R. (1975). "Mini-Mental State": A practical method for grading the cognitive state of patients for the clinician. *Journal of Psychiatric Research, 12*(3), 189–198.

Gilliland, B. E., & James, R. R. (1997). *Theories and techniques in counseling and psychotherapy* (4th ed.). New York, NY: Allyn & Bacon.

Granello, D. H. (2010). A suicide crisis intervention model with 25 practical strategies for implementation. *Journal of Mental Health Counseling, 32*(3), 218–235.

Granello, D. H., & Granello, P. F. (2006). *Suicide: An essential guide for helping professionals and educators.* Boston, MA: Pearson.

Hawton, K., Casañas i Comabella, C., Haw, C., & Saunders, K. (2013). Risk factors for suicide in individuals with depression: A systematic review. *Journal of Affective Disorders, 147*(1), 17–28.

Ivanoff, A., Jang, S. J., Smyth, N. F., & Linehan, M. M. (1994). Fewer reasons for staying alive when you are thinking of killing yourself: The Brief Reasons for Living Inventory. *Journal of Psychopathology and Behavioral Assessment, 16*, 1–13.

Jones, K. D. (2010). The unstructured clinical interview. *Journal of Counseling & Development, 88*(2), 220–226.

Koppitz, E. M. (1975). *The Bender Gestalt Test for Young Children* (Vol. 2: Research and applications, 1963–1973). New York, NY: Grune & Stratton.

Lambert, M. J., Lunnen, K., Umphress, V., Hansen, N., & Burlingame, G. M. (1994). *Administration and scoring manual for the Outcome Questionnaire (OQ-45.1).* Salt Lake City, UT: IHC Center for Behavioral Healthcare Efficacy.

Louisiana Mental Health Counselor Licensing Act. (1987). Acts 1987, No. 892 §1, eff. July 20, 1987.

Mitchell, M. B., & Atri, A. (2014). Dementia Screening and Mental Status Examination in Clinical Practice. *Dementia: Comprehensive Principles and Practices, 461.*

O'Donohue, W. T., Cummings, N. A., & Cummings, J. L. (2006). *Clinical strategies for becoming a master psychotherapist.* Burlington, MA: Academic Press.

Remley, T. P., & Herlihy, B. (2013). *Ethical, legal, and professional issues in counseling* (4th ed.). Upper Saddle River, NJ: Prentice Hall.

Sadock, B. J., & Sadock, V. A. (2007). *Kaplan and Sadock's synopsis of psychiatry: Behavioral sciences/ clinical psychiatry* (10th ed.). Philadelphia, PA: Lippincott Williams & Wilkins

Seligman, L., & Reichenberg, L. W. (2014). *Selecting effective treatments: A comprehensive, systematic guide to treating mental disorders* (4th ed.). San Francisco, CA: Jossey-Bass.

Sommers-Flanagan, J., & Sommers-Flanagan, R. (2013). *Clinical interviewing* (4th ed.). Hoboken, NJ: John Wiley & Sons.

Whitbourne, S. K. (2013). What the DSM-5 changes mean for you. *Psychology Today.* Retrieved from http://www.psychologytoday.com/blog/fulfillment-any-age/201305/what-the-dsm-5-changes-mean-you

Assessment in Education

Counselors who work with children, adolescents, college students, parents, or families require a thorough understanding of assessment in educational systems. Regardless of work setting, the results of educational assessment inform the counseling process. Educational assessment, a primary function for school counselors and school-based mental health counselors, encompasses many of the types of assessment reviewed throughout this textbook (e.g., achievement, aptitude, career assessment, observation). The purposes of assessment in educational systems varies and can include tasks such as identifying students with special needs, determining whether students have mastered the requirements for graduation, determining appropriate accommodations for a college student with a learning disability, advocating for a child with unmet educational needs, coaching a parent on their rights under the Individuals with Disabilities Education Act (IDEA), and evaluating the effectiveness of a comprehensive school counseling program. Assessment in education is a broad practice that includes the use of a wide variety of instruments (e.g., achievement tests, ability tests, aptitude tests, career assessment instruments) and assessment procedures (e.g., functional behavior assessment, observation, interpretation, report writing).

School counselors, school-based mental health counselors, and college counselors play an important role in assessment programs and are often involved in collecting and using assessment data; regularly monitoring student progress; and communicating the purposes, design, and results of assessment instruments to various parties. To practice effectively, counselors need specific knowledge and skills about the assessment instruments and strategies used in the schools. Because the scope of educational assessment is broad, it is difficult to capture the roles and activities of all counseling professionals who interact with educational systems in one chapter. Thus, we will focus primarily on the roles and functions of school counselors in this chapter, but we stress that the material herein is relevant to all counselors and helping professionals.

After studying this chapter, you should be able to:

- Discuss the goals of school assessment programs.
- Explain the common assessment activities of counselors.
- Define *specific learning disabilities* (SLDs).
- Describe the assessment process related to specific learning disability determination and Responsiveness to Intervention (RTI).

- Describe the process and procedures for assessing giftedness.
- Discuss the use of test preparation and performance strategies in increasing achievement test scores.
- Describe the purpose of environmental assessment in the schools.
- List and explain the competencies in assessment and evaluation for school counselors.
- Discuss the issue of high-stakes testing in education.

SCHOOL ASSESSMENT PROGRAMS

Teachers, counselors, administrators, and parents need all types of information about students. They need to know about their cognitive and scholastic abilities, their interests, their achievement, and their problems. Schools implement assessment programs to provide information needed to improve the public schools by enhancing the learning gains of all students and to inform parents of the educational progress of their children. School assessment programs may consist of several diverse instruments used for a variety of purposes, such as the following:

- Identifying the readiness of kindergarten and first-grade students.
- Determining whether students have mastered the basic and essential skills required by the school system.
- Placing students in educational programs.
- Identifying students with special needs.
- Evaluating the curriculum and specific programs of study.
- Helping students make educational and vocational decisions.
- Assessing the intellectual ability and aptitude of individual students.
- Measuring achievement in specific courses and subject areas.

School counselors are actively involved in school assessment programs. They may administer, score, and interpret assessment instruments themselves, or they might be asked to coordinate an entire testing program. School counselors are also frequently called upon to disseminate assessment results that have been collected by other professionals to students, parents, teachers, and administrators.

Planning a School Assessment Program

Planning a school assessment program is a complex process that requires cooperation among a diverse group of stakeholders. In order to ensure the development of an assessment program that is best practice and comprehensive, the planning process should involve the superintendent's staff, principals, school counselors, teachers, parents, community leaders, representatives from local postsecondary institutions, and other administrative leaders in the school district. Involvement by a diverse group of stakeholders promotes acceptance of the assessment program and helps each group understand its role in the process. For example, through participation in the planning process, teachers might contribute information about their needs for being able to use assessment information for instructional decisions; principals might help formulate the plan so that assessment data can aid in the evaluation of the curriculum; and the team might determine methods for allowing students to use assessment information to guide their educational and vocational decision making. A number of steps should be followed in designing a school assessment program:

1. Identify the goals and purposes of the assessment program.
2. Identify the types of information needed to make decisions.
3. Identify the types of instruments to be given and establish procedures for selecting them.
4. Identify the responsibilities of the staff in the assessment program.
5. Develop procedures for disseminating assessment results to appropriate individuals.
6. Develop an evaluation strategy to continuously monitor the assessment program.

Instruments Used in School Assessment Programs

School assessment programs encompass several different types of assessment instruments used at different grade levels (see Figure 14.1). For example, *state achievement tests* are given to students in grades 3 through 8 and one grade in high school to assess students' progress in achieving their state's educational standards. Readiness tests may be administered to preschoolers to determine their readiness to enter kindergarten or first grade. As students reach the middle and high school years, instruments assessing interests, abilities, and values may be utilized to obtain information for post–high school planning. The following is a list and brief description of the types of assessment instruments and strategies used in school assessment programs.

Test/Inventory	Grade Level												
	K	1	2	3	4	5	6	7	8	9	10	11	12
Readiness test	X												
State achievement test				X	X	X	X	X	X		X		
NAEP					X				X				X
Subject area tests										X	X	X	X
General aptitude battery								X					
Career development/ maturity										X			
Career interest/values											X		
ASVAB											X		
PSAT/PLAN											X		
SAT												X	X
ACT												X	X
National Merit													X

FIGURE 14.1   Sample school assessment program.

ACHIEVEMENT TESTS Every state requires schools to administer *achievement tests* that are aligned with their educational standards. As we addressed in the chapter on assessing achievement (Chapter 9), states may develop their own standardized achievement test or use a commercially developed achievement test battery, such as the Stanford Achievement Test (Stanford 10). On these examinations, students must earn a minimum test score to prove mastery in order to be promoted to the next grade or graduate high school. Schools may also administer the National Assessment of Educational Progress (NAEP), which tracks student achievement in 4th, 8th, and 12th grades. Many elementary schools administer diagnostic reading tests to screen and monitor student progress in learning reading skills. Other forms of achievement assessment include curriculum-based assessment, curriculum-based measurement, and performance-based assessment.

INTELLECTUAL ABILITY TESTS Test that measure intellectual ability are used in the schools for a variety of purposes. They may be used to help identify students with intellectual disabilities or learning disabilities or to place students into specialized academic or vocational programs. Most schools administer ability tests such as the Cognitive Abilities Test (CogAT) or the Otis–Lennon School Ability Test (OLSAT 8) to screen students for placement in gifted and talented programs.

READINESS TESTS Schools frequently use the scores from readiness tests to determine whether children are "ready" for kindergarten or are "ready" for promotion to first grade. Readiness tests assess whether children have the underlying skills deemed necessary for school learning. As we indicated previously, school readiness tests should be used with caution and careful examination of normative groups. There is a strong potential for cultural bias with these types of instruments.

APTITUDE TESTS Four of the most widely used aptitude tests are the Armed Services Vocational Aptitude Battery (ASVAB), the General Aptitude Test Battery (GATB), the Differential Aptitude Test (DAT), and the Career Aptitude Placement Survey (CAPS). Some school districts administer an aptitude test in the 10th grade. Civilian counselors working with the ASVAB will visit high schools and administer the test to all high school students who want to take the test for educational and vocational guidance purposes. Students meet with armed services personnel only if they request an interview.

ADMISSIONS TESTS Most high school counselors are in charge of coordinating programs to administer the PSAT, PLAN, SAT, ACT, or other college admissions tests to students in the 10th, 11th, and 12th grades. Coordinating the administration of admissions tests can include providing orientation about admissions tests to students and parents, having information about prep classes, and ensuring that students meet the necessary deadlines for complete test registrations.

CAREER ASSESSMENT INSTRUMENTS Various career assessment instruments are used in the schools, especially at the middle school and high school levels. General interest inventories are often given at both levels. In addition, school counselors often administer career development inventories that help the school district evaluate the educational and vocational needs of the students. Popular career assessment systems include the COPSystem, the Kuder Career Planning System, and the College and Career Readiness System.

ASSESSMENT ACTIVITIES OF SCHOOL COUNSELORS

In order to illustrate assessment in educational systems, we profile the assessment activities of school counselors. School counselors are actively involved in assessment in the schools and are frequently engaged in selecting, administering, scoring, and interpreting various assessment instruments for diverse purposes. For example, school counselors are involved in the administration and interpretation of standardized achievement test results at all levels; use formal and informal assessment measures to identify students' career choices, interests, and attitudes; conduct *needs assessments* to determine the focus of comprehensive school counseling programs; and conduct evaluations of program and intervention effectiveness. School counselors need knowledge of the process of identifying students with learning disabilities as well as students who qualify for gifted and talented programs. Furthermore, teachers and administrators often rely on school counselors as a resource to provide them with information about assessment instruments, to answer measurement-related questions, and to interact with parents on assessment issues (Young & Kaffenberger, 2011)

In addition to student assessment, school counselors are responsible for evaluating the effectiveness of comprehensive school counseling programs (Dahir & Stone, 2011). Various assessment instruments are used to show the impact of a school counseling program on school improvement and student achievement. School counselors must show that each activity or intervention they implement was developed from a careful analysis of students' needs, achievement, and/or other data. School counselors must also report on immediate, intermediate, and long-range results, showing how students are different as a result of the school counseling program. This aspect of the school counselor role is directly related to the concept of accountability. Under the ASCA National Model, school counselors must be able to demonstrate that they have an impact on student success (American School Counselor Association (ASCA), 2012).

Assessment is one of the biggest workload demands of a professional school counselor (McCarthy, Van Horn Kerne, Calfa, Lambert, & Guzmán, 2010). Whether engaged in assessment to evaluate student performance or to evaluate a comprehensive school counseling program, school counselors play a primary role in school assessment programs. Thus, counselors need knowledge and training in a wide range of diverse assessment activities. In a survey of professional school counselors, Ekstrom, Elmore, Schafer, Trotter, and Webster (2004) found that 80% of the 161 respondents indicated performing assessment-related activities such as reading about ethical, special needs, and multicultural issues; communicating assessment information to parents, school administration and teachers, and other professionals; and integrating test and nontest data when making decisions.

Ekstrom et al. (2004) also found that the assessment activities performed by school counselors may vary according to the educational level (elementary, middle, or high school) at which they work. For example, high school counselors were more likely to be involved in administering standardized tests than counselors in elementary schools. High school counselors also used assessment instruments more often for helping students with career planning. Middle school counselors spend more time designing or adapting assessment instruments for use in planning or evaluating school counseling programs and spend more time reading professional literature about assessment. Elementary school counselors were less likely to schedule testing, to interpret results from assessment instruments, or to use assessment information in counseling or in making placement decisions. Of counselors in all three educational levels, high school counselors had more responsibility for selecting, administering, and interpreting assessment instruments. Although no studies have been conducted to validate that these assessment tasks remain the same today, they are clearly aligned with the accountability requirements of the ASCA National Model (American School Counselor Association (ASCA), 2012) and the Standards for Educational and Psychological Testing (American Educational Research Association (AERA), American Psychological Association (APA), & National Council on Measurement in Education (NCME), 2014). These tasks are considered common for school counselors, but there is a degree of concern about the competency of school counselors to perform the tasks (Maras, Coleman, Gysbers, Herman, & Stanley, 2013). We stress that competency requires practice under supervision and extended study through continuing education and thorough review of assessment materials.

Needs Assessments

Assessment of students' counseling needs is a crucial component of implementing an effective school counseling program. *Needs assessment* is a formal process of gathering information from a range of sources (e.g., students, parents, teachers, administrators) about their perceptions of the needs of the student population. Needs assessments determine the students' needs or desired outcomes and, in doing so, identify the priorities of the school counseling program within the philosophical framework of the school and community. According to Sink (2009), school counselors conduct needs assessments as part of the accountability dimension of the ASCA National Model. Sink indicated that school counselors must take accountability leadership and evaluate their comprehensive school counseling programs for missing or underutilized elements, student learning progress, service improvement efforts, to evaluate concerns, and to guide school program changes. Most needs assessment instruments are informally constructed to assess students' needs in three broad areas: academic, career, and personal or social. Figure 14.2 shows an example of a career development needs assessment instrument. As another example, you might consider conducting a needs assessment among parents and teachers to determine the types of services you should provide in your comprehensive school counseling program. Items on the needs assessment might ask participants to rate various service needs on a Likert scale (e.g., bully prevention, multiculturalism, social skills, conflict resolution).

Assessing Specific Learning Disabilities

School counselors work individually and with other school personnel to meet the developmental needs of all students, including those with specific learning disabilities. A *specific learning disability* (SLD) is a neurological disorder that severely impairs children's ability to learn or to demonstrate skills in several academic areas:

1. *Oral Expression* Ability to convey ideas and information verbally
2. *Listening Comprehension* Ability to listen to and understand words, questions, and instructions presented through spoken words and sentences
3. *Written Expression* Ability to convey ideas and information in written form
4. *Basic Reading Skill* Ability to decode (read) words
5. *Reading Comprehension* Ability to make sense of and understand written or printed information

> Read each phrase and then decide the importance of that activity to you. Circle the appropriate number to the right of each phrase using the following scale.
>
> 0 if you feel the item is not important
> 1 if you feel the item is of some importance to you
> 2 if you feel the item is of moderate importance to you
> 3 if you feel the item is of great importance to you
>
> | | | | | |
> |---|---|---|---|---|
> | 1. Knowing what jobs are available locally that I can enter immediately after graduating from high school | 0 | 1 | 2 | 3 |
> | 2. Knowing how to apply for a job | 0 | 1 | 2 | 3 |
> | 3. Knowing how to write a résumé | 0 | 1 | 2 | 3 |
> | 4. Knowing how to dress for and what to say in an interview | 0 | 1 | 2 | 3 |
> | 5. Learning more about my career interests | 0 | 1 | 2 | 3 |
> | 6. Learning more about the training and education required in my career interest areas | 0 | 1 | 2 | 3 |
> | 7. Talking with people employed in my career interest areas | 0 | 1 | 2 | 3 |
> | 8. Arranging for work experience in my career interest fields | 0 | 1 | 2 | 3 |
> | 9. Learning more about my values and the way they relate to my career choice | 0 | 1 | 2 | 3 |
> | 10. Learning about what courses I should take if I want to enter certain career fields | 0 | 1 | 2 | 3 |

FIGURE 14.2   Example of a career-development needs-assessment instrument.

6. *Mathematical Calculation* Ability to learn basic math facts and perform basic math operations, such as addition, subtraction, multiplication, and division
7. *Mathematical Reasoning* Ability to apply mathematical techniques, concepts, or processes to solve problems

Students with an SLD may have difficulty listening, thinking, speaking, reading, writing, spelling, or doing math problems. They usually have average to above-average intelligence, but may have difficulties demonstrating academic knowledge and understanding. They will show intraindividual differences in their academic skills and abilities; in other words, they often do well in some school subjects, but usually have extreme difficulty with certain skills, such as decoding (reading) words, calculating math facts, or putting their thoughts and ideas into writing. SLDs are believed to be caused by some kind of neurological condition that affects information processing, which means that although students with SLDs almost always hear and see normally, they have trouble understanding what they see or hear. SLDs can be caused by such conditions as perceptual (visual or auditory) disabilities, brain injury, minimal brain dysfunction, dyslexia, and developmental aphasia (language impairment). SLDs do not encompass learning problems that are primarily the result of visual, hearing, intellectual, or motor disabilities; emotional disturbance; environmental, cultural, or economic factors; or limited English proficiency. Although the true prevalence rate of SLDs is not known, it is estimated that approximately 5% of students have an identified SLD, but that as many as 15% more of students remain unidentified (Cortiello, 2014).

An important practice for schools is to identify students with SLDs to ensure that the students receive appropriate services to meet their educational needs. Historically, the most common method schools have used to identify students with SLDs is the *ability-achievement discrepancy model* (also called the *IQ-achievement discrepancy model*), which was a component of the Individuals with Disabilities Education Improvement Act (IDEA) of 1997. This model identifies students as learning disabled when there is a *severe discrepancy* between their scores on an ability (i.e., intelligence) test and their scores on an achievement test. A discrepancy of 1 to 1.5 standard deviations between the scores generally qualifies as severe. Thus, if a student's achievement test scores are well below his or her ability test scores in at least one area (such as reading), then the student can be classified as having a specific learning disability. There have been many concerns cited about the use of the ability-achievement discrepancy approach (National Association of State Directors of Special Education's IDEA Partnership, 2007). First, critics have described the ability-achievement discrepancy approach as a *wait-to-fail* approach, because intervention is withheld until a discrepancy can be demonstrated, which often does not occur until the student has experienced several years of academic failure. Second, the information gathered from the ability and achievement assessments does not indicate each student's specific learning needs. Third, the discrepancy model can create inequitable treatment for students; that is, disproportionate numbers of students from culturally and linguistically diverse backgrounds have been identified as having SLDs via the ability-achievement discrepancy approach. Contemporary cognitive assessment involves more than just standardized testing. Today, evidence-based procedures that include standardized assessment are required for the identification of SLDs (Decker, Hale, & Flanagan, 2013).

RESPONSIVENESS TO INTERVENTION The IDEA of 2004 changed the evaluation process by which schools identify students with SLDs. Schools are no longer required to use the ability-achievement discrepancy model; rather, schools should use a combination of research-based instruction, intervention, and assessment procedures for determining whether students have SLDs. As a result, many states and school districts have adopted an alternative model called *Responsiveness to Intervention* (RTI). RTI is a comprehensive, multistep approach to identifying students with SLDs in which services and interventions are provided to at-risk students at increasing levels of intensity based on progress monitoring and data analysis. The RTI process includes the following tasks:

1. Universal screening of all students to identify those who are at risk for academic failure
2. Providing and monitoring the effectiveness of research-based instruction and other interventions for at-risk students
3. Providing special education services to those students who are achieving below age or grade expectations and fail to make adequate progress (having been provided research-based instruction and interventions)

Although no universally accepted approach currently exists, Table 14.1 provides a description of a three-tiered RTI model as conceptualized by the National Joint Committee on Learning Disabilities (NJCLD; 2005, p. 3). Assessment occurs at all tiers, and a wide variety of formal assessment instruments (e.g., achievement test batteries, diagnostic achievement tests, school readiness tests, state achievement tests) and informal instruments (e.g., curriculum-based measurement) are used for screening, progress monitoring, and diagnostic purposes. For example, in Tier 1, screening tests are administered school-wide to identify

TABLE 14.1 Responsiveness to Intervention Three-Tier Model

Tier Level	Approach	Tasks
Tier 1	Instruction	The goal of tier one is to provide appropriate screening, instruction, and behavior supports. Differentiated instruction is a primary component of this tier level
Tier 2	Intervention	Identified students receive a higher level of attention. Intervention occurs based on research. Students are monitored for progress and additional interventions are determined based on data. Parents are incorporated into the process.
Tier 3	Special Education	Evaluation is more comprehensive to determine the need for special education services. Numerous student observations occur at this tier. Procedural safeguards are implemented.

Source: From *Responsiveness to intervention and learning disabilities: A report prepared by the National Joint Committee on Learning Disabilities.* Copyright 2005 by the National Joint Committee on Learning Disabilities (NJCLD). Reproduced by permission.

students who are not meeting grade-level expectations so that instructional or behavioral interventions can be implemented. Progress monitoring (using curriculum-based assessment) occurs at Tier 2 to identify students who continue to need assistance and to evaluate the effectiveness of instructional and behavioral interventions. In Tier 3, diagnostic assessment is conducted as part of a comprehensive evaluation for students who fail to make sufficient progress in Tier 2 in order to determine their eligibility for special education.

INDIVIDUALIZED EDUCATION PLAN If a student is diagnosed as having a specific learning disability, then schools are required to develop an *Individualized Education Plan* (IEP). An IEP is a written document created by a team of teachers, parents, and other school staff (e.g., school counselors, school psychologists) that contains a statement of the student's present level of educational performance, a list of annual goals and objectives, and a description of the special education and related services (e.g., speech therapy, counseling, parent training, rehabilitation counseling) to be provided to the student. The IEP is reviewed at least once per year to examine the student's progress toward those goals.

In many cases, school counselors are directly involved in the IEP process. The American School Counselor Association (2012) views individual advocacy during IEP meetings as an appropriate activity for school counselors and also views advocacy as part of a comprehensive school counseling program. In addition to attending IEP meetings, they may consult with teachers, intervene with students, and support parents.

Assessing Giftedness

When considering the concept of Giftedness, it is important to note that numerous definitions exist. Although states may differ in how they define giftedness, there is a federally legislated definition that guides the conceptualization of giftedness in educational settings. The United States federal government views the gifted and talented classification as encompassing those students who demonstrate potential for high achievement in a range of areas (e.g., academics, performance, arts, creativity) and who need support services to realize their potential. (No Child Left Behind Act, 2004). These children demonstrate high performance capability in intellectual, creative, or artistic areas, as well as strong leadership ability. The National Association for Gifted Children (2008) reported that nearly three million children (i.e., 5% of the U.S. student population) are considered gifted and talented. However, this may not be a reliable estimate. Researchers conducting the National Surveys of Gifted Programs (Callahan, Moon, & Oh, 2014) reported that there was a high degree of variance in the percentage of identified gifted children from district to district and that some districts didn't identify gifted students at all.

Although we can't identify the exact percentage of gifted children, we do have research-based approaches for assessment and intervention for that population. Gifted children require services or activities not typically provided in a regular classroom setting; thus, most schools have *gifted and talented programs* that provide unique educational opportunities for children who have been identified as gifted and talented. These programs can include modifying or adapting regular curriculum and instruction; accelerated learning opportunities, such as independent study and advanced placement; opportunities for subject and grade skipping; and providing differentiated learning experiences. To qualify for participation in a school's gifted and talented program, students must meet certain minimum standards.

The process of assessing students for giftedness usually entails two phases: screening and identification. To *screen* for giftedness, most districts conduct annual school-wide screening using standardized ability or achievement tests. Students may also be referred or nominated for giftedness screening by their teacher, school counselor, or parent. Students must meet a set cutoff score on the screening test to continue to the *identification phase*. In the identification stage, further assessment is conducted, focusing on four areas:

1. *Cognitive Ability* Ability to perform at an exceptionally high level in general intellectual ability, which may be reflected in such cognitive areas as reasoning, memory, nonverbal ability, and the analysis, synthesis, and evaluation of information
2. *Academic Ability* Ability to perform at an exceptionally high level in one general academic area or a few specific academic areas significantly beyond others of one's age, experience, or environment
3. *Creative Thinking Ability* Ability to perform at an exceptionally high level in creative thinking, as evidenced by creative or divergent reasoning, advanced insight and imagination, and solving problems in novel ways
4. *Visual or Performing Arts Ability* Ability to perform at an exceptionally high level in the visual arts, dance, music, or drama

To assess these four areas, a variety of assessment instruments and strategies may be used (see Table 14.2). Cognitive ability and academic ability are typically evaluated using standardized ability tests and standardized achievement tests. To be placed into a gifted and talented program, students must meet or exceed minimum cutoff scores as defined by state laws. For example, in some states, students must either score at least two standard deviations above the mean minus the standard error of measurement or at or above the 95th percentile on an approved cognitive ability test and an achievement test. For assessing academic achievement, states may require scores only for specific subtests or scales of the test, such as reading comprehension, written expression, and mathematics.

Creative thinking ability can be assessed by using intelligence tests, general giftedness screening instruments, or instruments designed specifically to appraise creativity. An

TABLE 14.2 Instruments and Strategies for Assessing Giftedness

Cognitive Ability	Creative Thinking Ability
• Cognitive Abilities Test (CogAT) • Cognitive Assessment System-Second Edition (CAS2) • Differential Ability Scales (DAS-II) • Kaufman Brief Intelligence Test, Second Edition (KBIT-2) • Raven's Progressive Matrices (APM and SPM) • Otis–Lennon School Ability Test, Eighth Edition (OSLAT 8) • Stanford–Binet Intelligence Scale, Fifth Edition (SB5) • TerraNova 3 • Wechsler Preschool and Primary Scales of Intelligence, Third Edition (WPPSI-III) • Wechsler Intelligence Scale for Children (WISC-IV) • Woodcock–Johnson Tests of Cognitive Abilities, Fourth Edition (WJ-IV)	• Cognitive Abilities Test (CogAT) • Cognitive Assessment System-Second Edition (CAS2) • Differential Ability Scales (DAS-II) • Gifted & Talented Evaluation Scales (GATES) • Kaufman Brief Intelligence Test, Second Edition (KBIT-2) • Raven's Progressive Matrices (APM and SPM) • Otis–Lennon School Ability Test, Eighth Edition (OSLAT 8) • Scales for Rating Behavior Characteristics of Superior Students (SRBCSS) • Stanford–Binet Intelligence Scale, Fifth Edition (SB5) • Torrance Tests of Creative Thinking (TTCT) • Wechsler Preschool and Primary Scales of Intelligence, Third Edition (WPPSI-III) • Wechsler Intelligence Scale for Children (WISC-IV) • Woodcock–Johnson Tests of Cognitive Abilities, Fourth Edition (WJ-IV)

Academic Ability	Visual and Performing Arts Ability
• Basic Achievement Skills Inventory (BASI) • California Achievement Tests (CAT 6) • Grade Point Average • Iowa Test of Basic Skills (ITBS) • Kaufman Test of Educational Achievement (KTEA-II) • PSAT • SAT • TerraNova 3 • Wechsler Individual Achievement Test—Third Edition (WIAT-III) • Woodcock–Johnson III Tests of Achievement	• Gifted & Talented Evaluation Scales (GATES) • Gifted Rating Scales • Rubric for Scoring Dance Performance • Rubric for Scoring Drama Performance • Rubric for Scoring Music Performance • Rubric for Scoring Display of Work—Visual Art • Scales for Rating Behavior Characteristics of Superior Students (SRBCSS)

example of a well-known instrument developed specifically to evaluate creative thinking is the Torrance Tests of Creative Thinking (TTCT) developed by E. Paul Torrance (1974). Constructed for individuals from kindergarten through graduate school and beyond, the TTCT consists of two different tests: the Figural TTCT and the Verbal TTCT. The Figural TTCT contains abstract pictures, and the examinee is asked to state what the image might be. The Verbal TTCT presents the examinee with a situation and gives the examinee the opportunity to ask questions, to improve products, and to "just suppose." The tests yield results in several subscales, including *Fluency*, the number of relevant ideas; *Originality*, the rarity and unusualness of ideas; *Elaboration*, the amount of detail in the responses; *Abstractness of Titles*, the degree to which a picture title is expressed beyond simple labeling; and *Resistance to Premature Closure*, the degree of psychological openness. Torrance also developed *Thinking Creatively in Action and Movement*, a nonverbal movement assessment of creativity; *Thinking Creatively with Sounds and Words*, which measures an individual's ability to create images for words and sounds; and *Thinking Creatively with Pictures*, which uses picture-based exercises to measure creative thinking.

Visual or performing arts ability is usually demonstrated through a display of work, a performance, or an exhibition. For example, students may submit portfolios containing artistic samples; perform a musical recital; provide evidence of placing first, second, or third in a music or art contest; or perform a series of drama or dance sessions. Trained examiners evaluate the products or performance using an approved rubric or checklist.

Instruments are also available that were developed specifically for assessing characteristics of giftedness. For example, the *Scales for Rating the Behavioral Characteristics of Superior Students, Revised* (SRBCSS; Renzulli et al., 2010) is a widely used rating scale that can be completed by school personnel who are familiar with the student's performance. It is comprised of 14 scales associated with the characteristics of gifted students: Learning, Motivation, Creativity, Leadership, Art, Music, Drama, Planning, Communication (Precision), Communication (Expressiveness), Mathematics, Reading, Science, and Technology. Score reports include raw scores, grade-level means, and percentile ranks that are calculated based on the particular group of students taking the test; there are no published national norms for the scale. Each of the 14 scales represents relatively different sets of behaviors; therefore, the scores obtained from the separate scales should *not* be summed to yield a total score (Renzulli et al., 2010). Test users may select from among the 14 scales only those scales appropriate to both the purpose of the test and the requirements or needs of the school; for example, schools may use only the Artistic, Creativity, and Musical scales as part of their giftedness assessment program. Each scale consists of several items in which raters evaluate student behaviors using a scale from 1 (never) to 6 (always). The SRBCSS authors did not establish cutoff scores for identification of gifted children, based on the assumption that there would be variations in student populations. Instead, they recommended that test users calculate local cutoff scores. An online version of the SRBCSS is available, and summary reports include raw scores and percentile ranks. Other instruments designed for identifying gifted and talented students include the *Gifted Rating Scales—School Form* (GRS-S), *Gifted and Talented Evaluation Scale* (GATES), and the *Screening Assessment for Gifted Elementary and Middle School Students* (SAGES-2).

Standardized assessment instruments are useful for screening and identifying giftedness in students and for designing programs and services based on these needs. Despite their potential usefulness, tests also have limitations. The technical inadequacy of tests can result in bias against certain populations of gifted students, especially those from racial, cultural, and ethnic minority populations, those from low socioeconomic environments, and those with disabilities or for whom English is a second language. Thus, although standardized tests are critically important in the assessment process, careful attention is critical to the selection of appropriate assessment instruments when assessing underserved gifted students. Furthermore, a score from a single instrument should never be the sole basis for placement decisions for gifted and talented programs. In order to further your understanding of assessment for giftedness, complete Exercise 14.1 and then respond to the exercise questions.

Exercise 14.1
Assessment of Giftedness

Gayle began taking piano lessons at age 4. By the time she was 10 years old, she was a proficient pianist, had completed in several statewide youth piano competitions, and had recently won the prestigious national Chopin Youth Piano Competition. Gayle has already decided that she wants to be a professional musician.

In school, Gayle performs well academically. Her fifth grade teacher believes that Gayle's musical ability as well as her high level of academic performance dem-

onstrates gifted characteristics, so the teacher decides to refer Gayle to be screened for the gifted and talented program. Gayle passed the screening test and was assessed for identification of giftedness. In Gayle's school, to qualify for the gifted and talented program students have to meet specific criteria for superior cognitive ability, specific academic ability, creative thinking ability, and visual or performing arts ability, as indicated in the following table:

	Instrument	Cutoff Scores
Superior Cognitive Ability	Cognitive Abilities Test	Minimum standard score of two standard deviations above the mean, minus the standard error of measurement on the Composite Score and on at least one of the batteries.
Specific Academic Ability	Woodcock–Johnson IV Tests of Achievement	Minimum 95% percentile on all the following subtests: 1. Passage Comprehension 2. Applied Problems 3. Writing Samples
Creative Thinking Ability	Scales for Rating the Behavioral Characteristics of Superior Students	Minimum raw score of 32 on the Creativity Scale.
Visual or Performing Arts Ability	1. Scales for Rating the Behavioral Characteristics of Superior Students 2. Display of work in art or music	1. SRBCSS Minimum raw score on one of the following scales: a. Art Scale = 53 b. Music Scale = 34 c. Dramatics Scale = 48 2. Evidence of art display or musical performance

The following are Gayle's test scores:

Cognitive Abilities Test

Batteries and Composite	Standard Score	Stanine	Percentile	Descriptors
Verbal	132	9	98	Very High
Quantitative	129	9	97	Very High
Nonverbal	126	8	96	Above Average
COMPOSITE	129	9	97	Very High

Note: SEM = 3

Woodcock–Johnson IV Tests of Achievement

Standard Battery Tests	Standard Score	Percentile	Descriptor
Oral Vocabulary	124	95	Superior
Number Series	127	96	Superior
Verbal Attention	121	92	Superior
Letter Pattern Matching	124	95	Superior
Phonological Processing	120	91	High Average
Story Recall	121	92	Superior
Visualization	119	90	High Average
General Information	124	95	High Average
Concept Formation	120	91	High Average
Numbers Reversed	125	95	Superior

Scales for Rating the Behavioral Characteristics of Superior Students

Scales	Raw Score	Percentile
Artistic	48	85
Communication expressive	42	75
Communication precision	37	64
Creativity	55	95
Dramatics	50	65
Leadership	37	58
Learning	58	90
Mathematics	58	93
Motivation	50	95
Musical	52	98
Planning	45	60
Reading	52	95
Science	35	75
Technology	30	79

Exercise Questions

1. How would you describe Gayle's overall level of intelligence based on the CogAT scores?
2. How would you describe her overall level of achievement based on her scores on the WJ-IV ACH?
3. How would you interpret the comparison of Gayle's CogAT scores to her WJ-IV ACH scores?
4. How would you interpret Gayle's SRBCSS scores on the Creativity and Musical subtests?
5. Based on Gayle's scores, she is *not accepted* into the gifted and talented program. Why was she not accepted?
6. Write a letter to the Gifted Program Administrator appealing this decision. In your letter, make sure you reference all the relevant assessment about Gayle, including her academic grades, scores on the assessment instruments (e.g., WJ-IV ACH, CogAT, and the relevant SRBCSS subtest scores), as well as any other evidence related to creative, artistic, or music ability.

Consulting with Teachers

Because school counselors are trained in tests and measurement, they are frequently called upon by teachers to help interpret a student's assessment results. Teachers may lack knowledge about basic measurement concepts and not understand what a student's test score means, not be familiar with a new edition of a standardized test, or need to understand the implications of a student's test results for classroom instruction. School counselors can provide in-service trainings or workshops to educate teachers about measurement concepts in general or about new editions of standardized tests. School counselors may also consult with teachers individually to review and interpret a student's test scores.

ENVIRONMENTAL ASSESSMENT IN THE SCHOOLS

Assessment in the schools often focuses almost exclusively on academic achievement and learning outcomes. Although student outcomes provide valuable information, they cannot give a complete picture of the educational process. A critical determinant of student outcomes is the classroom environment, which is evaluated through the process of environmental assessment. *Environmental assessment* involves appraising specific environmental factors that interact with and predict behavior. The environment includes everything that surrounds us and experiences to which we are exposed, including the following:

1. *Physical Space* Amount of space that is available and the way the space is arranged
2. *Organization and Supervision of Space* The organization of the space according to use or function
3. *Materials* The materials required by the individual who will be using the environment
4. *Peer Environment* The number and type of people who are going to share the environment
5. *Organization and Scheduling* The level of organization of the environment, how activities are scheduled, and the roles of the people involved
6. *Safety* An environment that is free of hazards and has adequate supervision
7. *Responsiveness* An environment that provides opportunities to enhance feelings of competency and independence

Many environmental factors with schools can be associated with students' academic problems, such as the physical setting, teacher/student relationship, curricular and educational materials, and other students' behaviors. Other variables, such as attendance, social interaction, and class interruptions, can also impact student performance.

Assessment of the classroom environment needs to focus on (a) physical and structural dimensions, (b) interactional dimensions, and (c) instructional dimensions. *Physical and structural dimensions* include seating position, classroom design and furniture arrangement, spatial density, and crowding, noise, and lighting. *Interactional dimensions* involve the extent to which students interact with materials, people, and activities in the environment. *Instructional dimensions* refers to teacher behaviors that are related to student achievement. Strong, Gargani, and Hacifazlioğlu (2011) identified several effective teacher behaviors, such as accessing students' prior knowledge, active interaction, moving around the classroom, enabling students to generate ideas, creating a stimulating classroom environment, using visuals and manipulatives, checking for student understanding, having clear objectives, presenting concepts clearly, exhibiting equity, and differentiating instruction.

Person-environment fit theories stress the need to study the congruence between the client's needs, capabilities, and aspirations and environmental demands, resources, and response opportunities (Holland, 1997). Counselors look for ways that different environmental arrangements and conditions force accommodations in behavior and study the individual/environment interactions. Person-environment fit has wide application and is especially important when working with preschool children and students with disabilities who are placed in regular classrooms.

Several assessment instruments have been developed to measure aspects of the classroom school environment at all levels. Instruments measure the perceptions of various groups, such as parents, teachers, students, and administrators. Some of the major instruments are as follows:

- The Classroom Environment Scale, Third Edition (CES; Trickett & Moos, 1995) assesses perceptions of the learning environment of middle and high school classrooms. The instrument evaluates the effects of course content, teaching methods, teacher personality, class composition, and characteristics of the overall classroom environment. The student form contains 90 true/false items and takes 20 to 30 minutes to complete. Students rate their perceptions of the classroom climate from using a 5-point scale from 1 (almost never) to 5 (very often). There are nine subscales grouped into three major dimensions: relationship, personal growth/goal orientation, and system maintenance and change. The subscales are involvement, affiliation, teacher support, task orientation, competition, order and organization, rule clarity, teacher control, and innovation.
- The Effective School Battery (ESB) assesses school climate and provides a portrait of the attitudes and other characteristics of a school's students and teachers. It measures and reports on school safety, staff morale, administrative leadership, fairness and clarity of school rules, respect for students, classroom orderliness, academic climate, school rewards, student educational expectations, attachment to school, and other aspects of school climate as reflected in teachers' and students' perceptions, behavior, and attitudes.
- The School Environment Preference Survey (SEPS) measures work-role socialization as it occurs in the traditional school. SEPS has four scales: self-subordination, traditionalism, rule conformity, and uncriticalness. The test is helpful in planning instructional strategies for students or as an aid for placement in alternative learning environments.
- The Responsive Environmental Assessment for Classroom Teaching (REACT) evaluates student perceptions of the classroom environment. The instrument results in a single factor score (i.e., classroom teaching environment) and six subscale scores: positive reinforcement, instructional presentation, goal setting, differentiated instruction, formative feedback, and instructional enjoyment (Nelson, Demers, & Christ, 2014).

COMPETENCIES IN ASSESSMENT AND EVALUATION FOR SCHOOL COUNSELORS

A joint committee of the American School Counselor Association (ASCA) and the Association for Assessment in Counseling (AACE; 2000) developed a document describing the assessment and evaluation competencies school counselors need. This document identifies nine competencies that school counselors should meet:

1. School counselors are skilled in choosing assessment strategies.
2. School counselors can identify, access, and evaluate the most commonly used assessment instruments.
3. School counselors are skilled in the techniques of administration and methods of scoring assessment instruments.

4. School counselors are skilled in interpreting and reporting assessment results.
5. School counselors are skilled in using assessment results in decision making.
6. School counselors are skilled in producing, interpreting, and presenting statistical information about assessment results.
7. School counselors are skilled in conducting and interpreting evaluations of school counseling programs and counseling-related interventions.
8. School counselors are skilled in adapting and using questionnaires, surveys, and other assessment instruments to meet local needs.
9. School counselors know how to engage in professionally responsible assessment and evaluation practices.

ASSESSMENT ISSUES IN EDUCATION

The primary issue in school assessment today is the widespread compulsory testing of public school students. Standardized achievement tests have long been part of the U.S. education system. Caldwell (2008) described the traditional process involved in testing in the schools as a cycle, with days set aside for standardized testing. Once tests were returned, usually months later, from being scored by the publishers, it was generally too late to make changes to classroom instruction. A frenzy of school administration meetings and newspaper articles would occur before things would normalize until the next cycle.

All this changed after the No Child Left Behind (NCLB) Act, passed in 2001 and signed into law in January 2002. This law contains the most sweeping changes to the Elementary and Secondary Education Act (ESEA) since ESEA was enacted in 1965. Emphasizing educational *accountability*, NCLB requires America's schools to describe their success in terms of what each student accomplishes—the belief being that through accountability, schools and parents can receive the information needed to identify and focus attention and resources on children who need help. Thus, in order to receive federal funding, school districts in all 50 states are required to administer tests that measure student progress toward *state achievement standards*. Each state has identified educational standards that specify the skills and knowledge that students are expected to master in a given subject area at a specific grade (e.g., Mathematics, Grade 5). Under NCLB, all states must test in reading, mathematics, and science in grades 3 through 8 and one grade in the high school span. Students must earn a minimum test score to prove mastery in order to be promoted to the next grade or graduate high school.

This type of testing program has been labeled *high-stakes testing*. Stakes and consequences of assessment are important considerations. The term *stakes* refers to the impact that test results may have on a student, group, or organization (American Educational Research Association (AERA), American Psychological Association (APA), & National Council on Measurement in Education (NCME), 2014). High-stakes tests can directly affect a student's educational paths or choices, such as whether a student is promoted or retained at a grade level, graduated, or admitted into a desired program. *Low-stakes tests*, on the other hand, are used for monitoring and providing feedback to students, teachers, and parents on student progress. High-stakes testing also involves judging schools according to their students' test performance. For example, high-performing schools may receive financial rewards, such as bonuses or merit pay, whereas low-performing schools may receive sanctions, which can include developing or implementing improvement plans, being placed on probation, losing accreditation, losing funding, relocating children to better-performing schools, and even closing the school. Schools are generally ranked (i.e., school report card) according to their students' test scores, with the implication that a school's ranking reflects the effectiveness or quality of teaching.

Proponents of NCLB believe that testing assists in identifying and providing resources for children who need help, holds schools accountable for student progress, and provides parents with choices when their school ranking falls to unacceptable levels, and in 2006, the U.S. Department of Education reported that that since NCLB's inception, student achievement has risen across America. However, many critics believe the act is failing; they identify the following concerns (Adrianzen, 2010; Frey, Mandlawitz, & Alvarez, 2012; Kieffer, Lesaux, & Snow, 2008; Ott, 2008; VanCise, 2014):

- School curriculum has narrowed to basic reading, writing, and arithmetic, excluding subjects (e.g., art, music, social sciences, physical education) that are not tested.
- Schools with children from diverse backgrounds or who have diverse learning skills are being penalized.
- High-stakes testing has created an atmosphere of greed, fear, and stress in schools, none of which contribute to learning.
- Extremely high stakes encourage schools to cheat and to urge low-achieving students to drop out.
- School counselors spend more time coordinating achievement test administration, reducing their ability to provide services to students, teachers, and administrators.
- There is no consistency among states as to which standardized achievement tests they use, which means that there is no way to compare the performance of students from state to state.

The American Educational Research Association (AERA) is the leading organization that studies educational issues. The organization has acknowledged that although policymakers instituted high-stakes tests with the good intention of improving education, they need to carefully evaluate the tests' potential to cause serious harm. For example, policymakers and the public may be misled by spurious test score increases unrelated to any educational improvement; students may be placed at increased risk of educational failure and dropping out; teachers may be blamed or punished for inequitable resources over which they have no control; and curriculum and instruction may be severely distorted if high test scores per se, rather than learning, become the overriding goal of classroom instruction (American Educational Research Association (AERA), 2000). The organization recommends validating test scores and individual uses, providing resources and opportunities for students to learn the materials, and stating explicitly probable negative consequences as well as the rules used to determine test-taking individuals. The association's full policy on high-stakes testing is available online at aera.net/AboutAERA/AERARulesPolicies/AERAPolicyStatements/PositionStatementonHighStakesTesting/tabid/11083/Default.aspx.

Although NCLB has been due for reauthorization, there has been continued debate in Congress over the changes in the law. Partisan politics have been a continued issue in changing the law to address some of the concerns identified by AERA.

TEST PREPARATION AND PERFORMANCE

Because scores on achievement tests can be critical for attaining access to and succeeding in educational programs or occupational opportunities, students must perform well on achievement tests. As such, there has been an increase in interest regarding test preparation and performance strategies that students can use to increase their test scores. These strategies can include coaching, increasing test wiseness, and reducing test anxiety.

Coaching

Coaching is a method used by administrators, teachers, and counselors to help test takers improve their test performance. Although there is no universally accepted definition for coaching, the term is popularly used to mean training test takers to answer specific types of questions and provide the information required by a specific test (Hardison & Sackett, 2008). Coaching programs usually focus on test familiarization, drill and practice on sample test items, or subject matter review. Coaching programs are provided through classes offered in public schools; private classes; private tutors; and test books, software programs, or videos. Probably the best example of a coaching program is an SAT prep class. Thousands of high school students take SAT prep courses each year, hoping to increase their scores on the college entrance exam. The results from a recent nationwide study showed that students who took private SAT prep classes scored an average of 60 points higher on their SAT tests compared to students who didn't take the classes (Grabmeier, 2006).

Of significance are concerns about the social, philosophical, and ethical aspects of coaching. Research studies have found that students from less-advantaged families—those with lower family incomes and with parents who have less education and lower-level jobs—are less likely to use any form of test-preparation program (Grabmeier, 2006).

Test-Wiseness

Test-wiseness refers to an individual's ability to utilize the characteristics and formats of a test to receive a high score. Test-wiseness is independent of the student's knowledge of the subject matter that the test is designed to measure. Skills involved in test-wiseness include strategies for time use, error avoidance, guessing, and use of deductive reasoning.

Strategies to increase test-wiseness include becoming familiar with the test before test day. It is always best to know as much as possible about what to expect before arriving at the test center. Once students know what to expect on the test, they should practice taking the test. In general, test takers feel more knowledgeable and have less anxiety when they receive instructions about how to take a test. This reduces errors caused by unfamiliarity with test procedures and leads to scores that better reflect an examinee's knowledge and abilities.

Special strategies apply to each type of item format. For example, on multiple-choice tests, test takers should examine carefully all of the options or responses before attempting to choose the correct answer. If the student stops when she sees a correct answer—say, option A—then she could miss reading options B, C, D, and E, which might also be correct. Some options on multiple-choice items may be similar and vary only slightly; usually, these options can be eliminated. The examinee has a better chance of getting a higher score if options known to be incorrect can be eliminated and the choice is made from among the remaining alternatives. Sometimes, an option resembles the stem—that is, it uses the same names, words, or phrases. Usually, such options should be selected. Correct answers are often longer and perhaps stated more precisely or specifically than the other alternatives.

Simmonds, Luchow, Kaminsky, and Cottone (1989) designed the SPLASH test-taking strategy for multiple-choice tests. SPLASH is an acronym that stands for the following:

1. *Skim the Test* Skim the entire test to get a general idea of the number of items, the types of questions, and areas of proficiency and deficiency.
2. *Plan Your Strategy* This includes knowing time constraints of the test and where to begin.
3. *Leave Out Difficult Questions* Students should leave difficult questions for the end.
4. *Attack Questions You Know* Students should first answer all questions they are sure of.
5. *Systematically Guess* After completing all questions they know, students should make their best guess on the questions they don't know.
6. *House Cleaning* A few minutes should be left prior to the end of the exam to fill in all answers, double-check forms, and clean up erasures.

Test Anxiety

With the increased use of high-stakes tests throughout K–12 education, test anxiety has become a common issue confronted by school counselors. *Test anxiety* is the general feeling of uneasiness, tension, or foreboding that some individuals experience in testing situations. Test anxiety can cause a host of problems in students, such as upset stomach, headache, loss of concentration, fear, irritability, anger, and even depression. Students with test anxiety typically worry about not doing well on a test. This mind-set inhibits their ability to absorb, retain, and recall information. Students with low test anxiety, on the other hand, do not worry and are able to focus on their test performance. There are some controversies about test anxiety. Some researchers debate the idea that anxiety interferes with test performance. In other words, there is some belief that those with lesser ability would have higher incidence of anxiety and that deficits in test performance are based on skill rather than anxiety. Sommer and Arendasy (2014) concluded that test anxiety is a situation-specific trait based on existing deficits.

There are few published inventories with strong psychometric properties that assess test anxiety. Only one specific instrument, the Test Anxiety Profile, is reviewed in the *Mental Measurements Yearbook*, and the reviews suggest extreme caution in using this instrument. Other instruments, such as the Test Anxiety Inventory (TAI) and the Test Anxiety Scale for Children (TASC), are available from various publishers, but we also suggest caution in using these inventories. The TAI consists of 20 items in which respondents are asked to report how frequently they experience specific symptoms of anxiety before, during, and after examinations using a 4-point scale from 1 (almost never) to 4 (almost always). The TASC is a 30-item instrument that assesses test anxiety, remote school concerns, poor self-evaluation, and somatic signs of anxiety.

Students should be motivated to do their best on tests but should not be made anxious. Sometimes, however, pressure comes not from the counselor or teacher but from the parents. Currently in our educational system, tests have assumed too much importance in some states. They are used as the sole criterion to judge whether a student should be promoted to the next grade or allowed to move from one level to another. Counselors should consider these strategies in test administration:

1. Make sure students understand test instructions; check with them, asking whether they understand. In a group test, circulate around the room to see if students are following directions and recording their answers properly.

2. Establish rapport and an environment that is as relaxed and stress-free as possible. Before the test, create a learning-oriented environment. Students may need to be taught more effective study habits and may need more time to prepare for tests. Tests can be an interesting learning experience as well as a motivational one. At test time, be friendly and positive, but follow standardized procedures. Ensure that students have the proper physical facilities, space to work, proper lighting, adequate ventilation, and so on.

3. To remove some of the pressure from major tests and exams, conduct group or class sessions on how to take a test, give the students practice tests, and provide a list of guidebooks and study guides that are available for an upcoming test.

Relaxation exercises are often used in reducing test anxiety. The object of *relaxation exercises* is to help students practice mind calming. The following is an example of what a counselor might say before a test:

> Sit down and get very comfortable. Close your eyes and take a deep breath. Exhale and let your body and mind relax completely. Breathe in again, and as you breathe out, feel even more relaxed. Forget about everything except what I am saying. Listen carefully. Continue to breathe deeply and slowly. You should begin to feel more and more relaxed.
>
> You are sitting in a lounge chair on the beach. It is not too warm or too cold. The temperature is just right. Everything is very peaceful and pleasant. You see the waves coming onto the beach. They are a beautiful blue, and the sun is a brilliant yellow. You feel nice and warm and relaxed all over. Take a deep breath in the nice clear air. You lose track of time. The sky becomes a deeper blue.
>
> Now that you are relaxed, think positively of yourself. Say, "I can remember all I need to know on the test." Say it several times. Say, "I will know the right answers." Say, "I am alert; my mind is powerful."

Summary

Assessment instruments and strategies are used extensively throughout children's educational experience and play a major role in their life decisions, ranging from grade promotion and graduation to college admission and entry into certain vocational or educational training programs. School counselors play an active role in school assessment programs and may administer, score, and interpret various assessment instruments; communicate assessment results to students, parents, teachers, and administrators; or coordinate an entire assessment program. Counselors need knowledge about the process of designing school assessment programs, the various types of assessment instruments and strategies used, and the assessment activities they will most often engage in. They should also be aware of other assessment-related issues in education, such as assessing giftedness, assessing learning disabilities, test preparation and performance, environmental assessment, and high-stakes testing.

Questions for Discussion

1. Study Figure 14.1, a sample school assessment program. What tests would you add or drop? Why?

2. Should intelligence tests be given to students every 2 to 3 years along with achievement tests? Why or why not? Should all students be required to take some type of personality test, such as the Myers–Briggs Type Indicator? Why or why not?

3. Describe Response to Intervention, and explain why it is important for students with learning disabilities.

4. Do you agree with the view that the ability-achievement discrepancy model is a wait-to-fail approach? Explain your response.

5. Should counselors and teachers make sure that sessions on test-taking skills are conducted prior to all major examinations? Why or why not?

6. Do you think that anxiety plays a significant role in test performance? Should we try to assess anxiety before and during testing situations? Why or why not?

7. Teachers may feel that they are under tremendous pressure because of achievement testing. They may dislike the standardized achievement test used in their state because it does not measure what they are teaching. In such a situation, what steps should the district administrators take to gain the support of district teachers?

Suggested Activities

1. Interview a school counselor to find out what tests are part of that school's assessment program. Report your findings to the class or in a written paper.

2. Write a position paper on one of the issues related to school assessment programs.

3. Prepare an annotated bibliography of sources to help an individual prepare to take one of the major college admissions tests.

4. Administer a test designed to measure test anxiety, and discuss the results with the class.

5. Read the following brief cases and answer the questions at the end of each.

Case of Kent

Kent needs to take the SAT to complete his file so that he can be considered for admission to the college for which he is applying. He says, "I don't have time to go to the test prep sessions at school. It's just an aptitude test, and either I have it or I don't."

a. Do you agree with Kent?
b. What approach would you use to help him?

Case of Letitia

Letitia, a high school senior, is taking an honors class in chemistry. She has a 3.0 grade point average on a 4-point system. Whenever she has a test in class, she becomes nauseous and faints. She does not report the same feeling when she takes tests in other courses.

a. What do you think is Letitia's problem?
b. What approach would you use to help her?

References

Adrianzen, C. A. (2010). *A critical examination of equity issues associated with the implementation of the Title III components of the No Child Left Behind Act on bilingual students*. (70), ProQuest Information & Learning, US. Retrieved from http://libproxy.lamar.edu/login?url=http://search.ebscohost.com/login.aspx?direct=true&db=psyh&AN=2010-99011-429&site=ehost-live Available from EBSCOhost psyh database.

American Educational Research Association (AERA). (2000). *AERA position statement on high-stakes testing in pre-k–12 education*. Retrieved from http://www.aera.net/?id=378

American Educational Research Association (AERA), American Psychological Association (APA), & National Council on Measurement in Education (NCME). (2014). *Standards for educational and psychological testing*. Washington, DC: Authors.

American School Counselor Association (ASCA). (2012). *The ASCA national model: A framework for school counseling programs* (23rd ed.). Alexandria, VA: Author.

American School Counselor Association (ASCA) & Association for Assessment in Counseling (AACE). (2000). *Competencies in assessment and evaluation for school counselors.* Alexandria, VA: Author.

Caldwell, J. S. (2008). *Reading assessment: A primer for teachers and coaches* (2nd ed.). New York, NY: Guilford.

Callahan, C. M., Moon, T. R., & Oh, S. (2014). *National surveys of gifted programs: Executive summary.* Charlotesville, VA: University of Virginia.

Cortiella, C., & Horowitz, S. H. (2014). *The state of learning disabilities: Facts, trends, and emerging issues* (3rd ed.). New York, NY: National Center for Learning Disabilities. Retrieved from http://www.ncld.org/types-learning-disabilities/what-is-ld/state-of-learning-disabilities

Dahir, C. A., & Stone, C. (2011). *The transformed school counselor.* Boston, MA: Cengage Learning.

Decker, S. L., Hale, J. B., & Flanagan, D. P. (2013). Professional practice issues in the assessment of cognitive functioning for educational applications. *Psychology in the Schools, 50*(3), 300–313.

Ekstrom, R. B., Elmore, P. B., Schafer, W. D., Trotter, T. V., & Webster, B. (2004). A survey of assessment and evaluation activities of school counselors. *Professional School Counseling, 8,* 24–30.

Frey, A. J., Mandlawitz, M., & Alvarez, M. E. (2012). Leaving NCLB behind. *Children & Schools, 34*(2), 67–69.

Grabmeier, J. (2006, August 7). *SAT test prep tools give advantage to students from wealthier families.* Retrieved from http://researchnews.osu.edu/archive/satprep.htm

Hardison, C. M., & Sackett, P. R. (2008). Use of writing samples on standardized tests: Susceptibility to rule-based coaching and the resulting effects on score improvement. *Applied Measurement in Education, 21*(3), 227–252.

Holland, J. L. (1997). *Making vocational choices: A theory of vocational personalities and work environments* (3rd ed.). Upper Saddle River, NJ: Prentice Hall.

Kieffer, M. J., Lesaux, N. K., & Snow, C. E. (2008). Promises and pitfalls: Implications of NCLB for identifying, assessing, and educating English language learners. In G. L. Sunderman (Ed.), *Holding NCLB accountable: Achieving, accountability, equity,* & *school reform* (pp. 57–74). Thousand Oaks, CA: Corwin Press.

Maras, M. A., Coleman, S. L., Gysbers, N. C., Herman, K. C., & Stanley, B. (2013). Measuring evaluation competency among school counselors. *Counseling Outcome Research and Evaluation, 4*(2), 99–111.

McCarthy, C., Van Horn Kerne, V., Calfa, N. A., Lambert, R. G., & Guzmán, M. (2010). An exploration of school counselors' demands and resources: Relationship to stress, biographic, and caseload characteristics. *Professional School Counseling, 13*(3), 146–158.

National Association for Gifted Children. (2008). *Definitions of giftedness.* Retrieved from http://www.nagc.org/index.aspx?id=574

National Association of State Directors of Special Education's IDEA Partnership. (2007). *Dialogue guides: What is the IQ-achievement discrepancy model?* Alexandria, VA: Author.

National Joint Committee on Learning Disabilities (NJCLD). (2005). *Responsiveness to intervention and learning disabilities.* Retrieved from http://www.ldonline.org/about/partners/njcld#reports

Nelson, P. M., Demers, J. A., & Christ, T. J. (2014). The Responsive Environmental Assessment for Classroom Teaching (REACT): The dimensionality of student perceptions of the instructional environment. *School Psychology Quarterly, 29*(2), 182–197.

Renzulli, J. S., Smith, L. H., White, A. J., Callahan, C. M., Hartman, R. K., Westberg, K. L., . . . Sytsma, R. E. (2010). *Scales for Rating the Behavioral Characteristics of Superior Students: Technical and administration manual.* (Rev ed.). Mansfield Center, CT: Creative Learning Press, Inc.

Simmonds, E. P. M., Luchow, J. P., Kaminsky, S., & Cottone, V. (1989). Applying cognitive learning strategies in the classroom: A collaborative training institute. *Learning Disabilities Focus, 4,* 96–105.

No Child Left Behind Act. (2004). P.L. 107–110 (Title IX, Part A, Definition 22, 2002); 20 USC 7801(22).

Ott, E. M. (2007). *Schools Left Behind: Statistical Issues with NCLB (No Child Left Behind).* ProQuest.

Sink, C. A. (2009). School counselors as accountability leaders: Another call for action. *Professional School Counseling, 13*(2), 68–74.

Sommer, M., & Arendasy, M. E. (2014). Comparing different explanations of the effect of test anxiety on respondents' test scores. *Intelligence, 42,* 115–127.

Strong, M., Gargani, J., & Hacifazlioğlu, Ö. (2011). Do we know a successful teacher when we see one? Experiments in the identification of effective teachers. *Journal of Teacher Education*, doi: 10.1177/0022487110390221

Torrance, E. P. (1974). *Torrance Tests of Creative Thinking, figural form A*. Bensenville, IL: Scholastic Testing Service.

Trickett, E., & Moos, R. (1995). *Classroom Environment Scale manual* (3rd ed.) Redwood City, CA: Mind Garden.

U.S. Department of Education. (1994). *National excellence: A case for developing America's youth.* Washington, DC: U.S. Government Printing Office.

VanCise, S. A. (2014). A descriptive study of the impact of the highly qualified teacher requirement of NCLB on the attrition of special education personnel. *Dissertation Abstracts International Section A, 74.*

Young, A., & Kaffenberger, C. (2011). The beliefs and practices of school counselors who use data to implement comprehensive school counseling programs. *Professional School Counseling, 15*(2), 67–76.

15 Assessment Issues with Diverse Populations

Fairness in testing is an essential component of the *Standards for Educational and Psychological Testing*. According to the AERA et al. standards (American Educational Research Association (AERA), American Psychological Association (APA), & National Council on Measurement in Education (NCME), 2014), the concept of fairness to all test takers is foundational to the assessment process and deserves specific attention and evaluation. Fairness in testing is a complex construct that includes issues related to measurement bias, accessibility, universal design, responsiveness to individual characteristics and testing contexts, treatment during the testing process, access to constructs being measured, and validity of individual test score interpretation for the intended test uses (AERA et al., 2014). Counselors who conduct assessment must do so with consideration of the characteristics of diverse subgroups of people (e.g., race, gender, ability, language).

Cultural competence is critical for all professional counselors. Thus, counseling professionals who use assessment strive to ensure fair and equitable treatment of diverse populations. Diverse populations can be defined as "persons who differ by race, ethnicity, culture, language, age, gender, sexual orientation, religion, and ability" (Association for Assessment in Counseling (AAC), 2003). In this chapter, we will divide our discussion of assessing diverse populations into two sections: (1) multicultural assessment, which will refer to the competencies required for assessing individuals from various cultural groups that are distinguished by race, ethnicity, age, language, gender, sexual orientation, religious or spiritual orientation, and other cultural dimensions, and (2) assessment of individuals with disabilities, which will center on the competencies and standards necessary for assessing individuals with significant limitations in physical or cognitive functioning.

After studying this chapter, you should be able to:

- Define *multicultural assessment*.
- List and describe the major sources of test bias.
- Describe the issues involving the use of standardized tests with diverse populations, including psychometric properties, administration and scoring procedures, and test use and interpretation.
- Describe assessment issues related to test-taker and examiner bias.
- Describe ethical principles and other issues relevant to multicultural assessment.

- Define *disability*, and explain standards for assessing individuals with disabling conditions.
- Describe assessment issues for individuals with visual impairments, hearing impairments, intellectual disabilities, communication disorders, and other disorders.

MULTICULTURAL ASSESSMENT

Cultural diversity among the U.S. population continues to grow. In 2014, the U.S. Census Bureau reported that as many as one-third of the total 31,600 million U.S. residents now claim "minority" heritage. Undoubtedly, counselors and other helping professionals will work with individuals with differing cultural backgrounds, customs, traditions, and values. As such, counselors need to be prepared to work with individuals from diverse backgrounds and must recognize and appreciate the differences that exist among people and clients. *Multicultural assessment* refers to competencies and standards necessary for assessing individuals who differ on various aspects of cultural identity, such as race, ethnicity, age, language, gender, sexual orientation, religious or spiritual orientation, and other cultural dimensions. Each cultural dimension has unique issues and concerns. Thus, to be effective, counselors must possess a depth of knowledge concerning the culture of clients as well as an awareness of available resources for acquiring information about persons of diverse cultures (Huey, Tilley, Jones, & Smith, 2014).

Standardized tests are frequently used in the assessment process, and many professionals rely on the scores of standardized tests to make important decisions or inferences about a client. Nonetheless, the use of standardized tests has been criticized for being biased and unfair for use with diverse populations. Multicultural assessment focuses on the extent to which assessment instruments and procedures are appropriate, fair, and useful for accurately describing abilities and other traits in individuals from a given culture. We will focus our discussion on several issues pertinent to using standardized tests in multicultural assessment, including test bias, psychometric considerations, test-taker factors, examiner bias, etic and emic perspectives, and acculturation.

Measurement Bias

According to the *Standards for Educational and Psychological Testing* (AERA et al., 2014), one of the principal threats to fairness is measurement bias. There are two primary components of measurement bias: accessibility and universal design. These two components of measurement bias are evolutions of concepts from earlier versions of test standards. The concept of accessibility relates to the extent to which all individuals are given an equal chance to demonstrate their capabilities or level of functioning during the assessment process. For example, imagine that a client who speaks English as a second language is taking the MMPI-2-RF as part of your clinical assessment process. It would be difficult to use the results of the assessment instrument to accurately formulate a diagnosis if the client was not proficient enough in English to fully understand the questions.

Universal design is purposeful test design aimed at maximizing accessibility for the population of intended test takers. The process of universal design involves a test developer giving consideration to the various processes that may impede access to a test and attempting to minimize any challenges that may be related to those processes. More simply stated, test developers must put themselves in the shoes of test takers and imagine the various facets of a test that might block performance unnecessarily. For example, imagine that you are taking a scenario-based exam aimed at evaluating your ability to accurately diagnose an individual client. In the exam, you are given a case study and a time limit of 20 minutes to arrive at a diagnosis. What relevance does 20 minutes have to the ability to diagnose? Is a 20-minute time limit part of competency in diagnosis, or does the time limit create construct-irrelevant variance (i.e., an incorrect inflation or deflation of test scores due to measurement error)?

When some aspect of an assessment instrument does not allow for accessibility or is not designed for universal access, the instrument is viewed as being biased. *Measurement bias* can be defined as "construct underrepresentation or construct-irrelevant components of tests that differentially affect the performance of different groups of test takers and consequently the reliability/precision and validity of interpretations and uses of their test scores" (AERA et al., 2014, p. 216). In other words, a test is labeled as biased when individuals with the same ability perform differently on the test because of their affiliation with a particular group. It's important to note that test bias is not the same as group differences; groups that differ on test results in a way that is consistent with the research is evidence of the validity of test results (e.g., individuals with depression scoring higher on the Beck Depression Inventory). Fairness in measurement is a new way of conceptualizing measurement bias. According to AERA et al., fairness in measurement quality can be examined from three different perspectives: fairness as the lack or absence of measurement bias, fairness as access to the construct being measured, and fairness as validity of the individual test score interpretation.

FAIRNESS AS THE LACK OR ABSENCE OF MEASUREMENT BIAS Do groups perform differently when examining patterns of relationships between test scores and other variables? If so, the phenomenon is called *differential prediction* or *predictive bias*. This is a primary question when considering fairness in light of measurement bias. In practice, this means that professional counselors must look not only at a summary of the psychometric data when evaluating a test but also the research on the test related to group performance and potential for bias. For example, imagine that you are asked to determine an appropriate test to measure the potential for success in technical school. However, when examining the research on this instrument, you discover that women have patterns of lower scores in relation to auto mechanics, plumbing, or other stereotypically masculine activities. You must then determine if there is a potential for measurement bias in this case and if this would be a fair measurement for your particular needs. The question in this case is whether or not the scores provide an inaccurate prediction for success in technical school simply because of group membership (e.g., gender).

Another aspect of fairness in relation to measurement bias is *differential item functioning* (DIF), or the difference in scores on particular items by examinees of equal ability who are members of different groups (commonly gender or ethnicity). Differential item functioning occurs if items are interpreted differently by members of different groups. In order to avoid DIF, test designers should include words in general use, not words and expressions associated with particular disciplines, groups, or geographic locations. If evidence of item bias is apparent, then flagged items are further scrutinized, and a subjective determination is made as to whether DIF is occurring (Suzuki & Ponterotto, 2008). For example, imagine an IQ test with the following question aimed at examining fund of knowledge: "What is a toboggan?" Although some of you who live in New England may recognize the term as a type of snow sled, others from Tennessee or Appalachia may consider the term as a type of knit cap. Still others from Arizona may have never been exposed to the term. Performance on this item may simply be a result of geographic differences rather than intelligence.

If a test is full of items that result in different groups of equal standing having overall differences in test scores, then there may be bias related to differential test functioning. This type of bias may also result from a lack of clarity of test instructions or from faulty scoring procedures. For example, for non-English-speaking individuals, the failure to perform on a task may simply be the result of not understanding test directions.

FAIRNESS IN ACCESS TO THE CONSTRUCT AS MEASURED When examining a test for fairness, it is important to determine if the population for which the test is intended has equal opportunity to access the construct being measured. Measurement bias can occur when the knowledge, skills, and abilities needed to access the test differ from those being measured in the test. For example, imagine that a state mandates the use of the paper-and-pencil version of the MMPI-2 for determination of fitness for the death penalty in a capital murder case. Having reviewed the MMPI-2 in Chapter 12, you might see this as a reasonable measure considering the amount of research available, the scales that measure malingering, and the level of training involved in accurate interpretation of scores. However, the reading level of the MMPI-2 is fifth grade, and many individuals on death row are considered illiterate. Providing an audio version of the instrument might result in a more valid picture of personality than the paper-and-pencil version.

FAIRNESS AS VALIDITY OF INDIVIDUAL TEST SCORE INTERPRETATION Examiners need to recognize personal bias and how it may influence interpretation of results. Reducing examiner bias requires treating each individual with dignity and respect and pursuing the best interests of the examinee. For example, imagine a counselor education program that enrolls an international student who speaks English as a second language and is interested in becoming a professional counselor in his or her home country. Would it be a fair comparison to examine that individual's scores on a comprehensive exam in English and to compare those scores to individuals whose primary language is English? Because English proficiency is not the construct being measured on this exam, the correct procedure in this situation would be for the counselor education program to administer the test in such a way as to minimize the language barrier. One strategy might be to provide a dictionary and

FIGURE 15.1   Equal vs. fair.

additional time. It is important to note that there are many other accommodations that could be made to increase fairness in the interpretation of test scores in this scenario. The key is for testing coordinators to consider these factors and to take appropriate steps to increase fairness.

Baruth and Manning (2011) identified several barriers to effective multicultural counseling that may be applied to the issue of examiner bias:

1. Differences in class and cultural values between counselor and client.
2. Language differences between counselor and client.
3. The counselor believes stereotypes about culturally different people.
4. The counselor fails to understand his or her own culture.
5. Lack of counselor understanding about the client's reluctance and resistance in counseling.
6. Lack of understanding of the client's worldviews.
7. Labeling cultural groups as mentally ill when their behaviors vary from so-called norms.
8. Expecting all clients to conform to the counselor's cultural standards and expectations.

In addition, the *Standards for Educational and Psychological Testing* (AERA et al., 2014) explain that in educational, clinical, and counseling situations, test users should not attempt to evaluate test takers whose special characteristics—such as age, disability, or linguistic, generational, or cultural backgrounds—are outside the range of their academic training or supervised experience.

Multicultural Perspectives in Assessment

Fairness is a key component of the standards for educational and psychological testing (AERA et al., 2014). It is impossible to fully review the nature of fairness in assessment without paying specific attention to multicultural issues. Many of the legal issues in assessment have been related to fairness and culture (e.g., *Larry P. v. Riles*, *Diana v. State Board of Education*, *Griggs v. Duke Power*). In order to illustrate the interrelatedness of assessment and culture, we review some common principles (i.e., etic and emic perspectives). The *etic perspective* emphasizes the universal qualities among human beings by examining a phenomenon that has common meaning across cultures. The *emic perspective* is culture specific and examines behavior from within a culture, using criteria relative to the internal characteristics of that culture (Kelley, Bailey, & Brice, 2014).

From the etic perspective, assessment involves comparing individuals' scores to those of a norming group and comparing different individuals from different cultures on a construct assumed to be universal across all cultures. Dana (2005) included as etic measures a broad spectrum of instruments to measure psychopathology, personality measures, and major tests of intelligence and cognitive functioning. Included as etic personality measures are the California Psychological Inventory and the Eysenck Personality Questionnaire. Included in the intelligence or cognitive functioning area are the Wechsler Intelligence Scales, the System of Multicultural Pluralistic Assessment, the Kaufman Assessment Battery for Children, the McCarthy Scales of Children's Abilities, and the Stanford–Binet Intelligence Scale. Other single-construct tests for identification of psychopathology are the State-Trait Anxiety Scale, the Beck Depression Inventory, and the Michigan Alcoholism

Screening Test. The MMPI is also on this list; it has been translated into 150 languages and has reported applications in 50 countries. The other tests listed have also been translated into other languages, mainly Spanish.

Emic methods include behavior observations, case studies, studies of life events, picture story techniques, inkblot techniques, word association, sentence-completion items, and drawings. Most of these methods are classified as *projective*. These tests can provide a personality description of the individual that reflects the data and mirrors the culture and ethnic group (Dana, 2005). The analysis requires the examiner to have more knowledge of the culture but aids the understanding of the individual in a cultural context. Thematic Apperception Test versions include the *Tell Me a Story Test*, designed for Spanish-speaking populations, and the *Thompson Modification of the Thematic Apperception Test*, a 10-card version of the TAT for African Americans. Sentence-completion methods have also been used, and items can be designed to assess the social norms, roles, and values of clients from different cultures. Here are examples of some of the items:

The thing I like most about America is _____.

Anglos _____.

If I could be from another culture or ethnic group, _____.

Acculturation

The degree of acculturation to the dominant society and the extent to which the original culture has been retained provide valuable information in interpreting assessment results. Assessing acculturation can help assessment professionals understand the unique challenges and transformations experienced by racial and ethnic minorities exposed to a new culture (Zhang & Tsai, 2014). An examiner can get an idea of whether the client is identifying with a culture of origin rather than with the dominant Anglo-American culture by asking questions such as those shown in Figure 15.2. In addition, several instruments are available that evaluate cultural and racial identity, including the following:

- Acculturation Rating Scale for Mexican Americans (ARSMA-II)
- African American Acculturation Scale (AAAS)
- The East Asian Acculturation Measure (EAAM)
- Bicultural Involvement Questionnaire (BIQ)
- Cross Racial Identity Scale (CRIS)
- Multigroup Ethnic Identity Measure (MEIM)
- Racial Identity Attitude Scale (RIAS)

Strategies

Because each client is unique, the examiner needs to be alert to important behavioral signals during the assessment process. Certain behaviors may affect the reliability and validity of the assessment procedure. Appropriate examiner responses are summarized in Table 15.1.

Assessment of Linguistically Diverse Individuals

Demographic data clearly show that the number of individuals from diverse linguistic backgrounds in the U.S. is increasing. In 2011, nearly 20% of U.S. residents ages 5 and older

---

1. What is your country of origin?
2. What was your reason for coming to the United States?
3. How long have you been in the United States?
4. Was any parent, grandparent, or relative in this country before you came?
5. What language do you speak in your home?
6. What languages can you speak? How well?
7. Is your family in the United States?
8. Do you have friends from your country here?
9. Are there people from your country living near you?
10. Where do you live? A house, apartment, room?
11. What education or schooling did you complete?
12. Are you currently going to school or taking classes somewhere?
13. Are you currently working? Where? What do you do on the job?
14. What type of work did you do before coming to this country?
15. Have you had any problems since coming here?
16. Have you had any conflicts on the job, at school, or at home?
17. What kind of problems have you had adjusting to life in the United States?

FIGURE 15.2   Questions for assessing acculturation.

spoke a language other than English (Ryan, 2013). Because the diversity of language is now becoming a clear trend in the United States, it is imperative that U.S.-based assessment practices include a more global perspective and attend to language-based issues in the assessment process.

Tests written in English may become tests of language proficiency for these individuals, rather than measures of other constructs. Of course, it is sometimes important and necessary to have tests that measure English proficiency—especially for educational assessment and placement. Tests not meant to measure proficiency in English are sometimes translated into the appropriate native language. However, there may be problems in translation, and the content and words might not be appropriate or meaningful to the group being tested.

The *Standards for Educational and Psychological Testing* (AERA et al., 2014) includes several standards relating to the testing of linguistically diverse populations. A number of standards are intended primarily for the test authors and publishers, but should be taken into consideration by the test user. If the test is modified for individuals with limited English proficiency, then the changes should be presented in the manual. The reliability and validity of the test for the intended linguistic group are also important. If two versions of dual-language tests exist, then evidence of the comparability of the forms should be included. The *Standards* also caution users not to require a greater level of English proficiency for the test than the job or profession requires—a significant concern in developing and selecting employment, certification, and licensing examinations. Another standard cautions test users to not judge English-language proficiency on the basis of test information alone. Many language skills are not adequately measured by multiple-choice examinations. The examiner needs to use observation techniques and perhaps informal checklists to assess proficiency more completely.

TABLE 15.1 Critical Behavior Indicators and Possible Examiner Responses

Behavior	Response
Is silent	Establish rapport. Give nonverbal and performance test first, get other indexes of individual behavior.
Says "don't know"	Don't assume client cannot respond.
Is shy and reserved; lowers eyes	Observe client in other situations, spend time establishing rapport, start with nonverbal and untimed tests, provide reinforcement, try to motivate client.
Uses wit or popular language	Be firm and positive; be sure examinee knows why the test or instrument is being given.
Interrupts the test or asks questions	Be firm, but allow some dialogue; be sure the examinee knows the purpose of the test.
Is inattentive and restless	Structure test environment; keep examinee involved.
Is uncertain about how to respond	Rephrase question; make meaning clear.
Watches the examiner rather than listening to the questions	Be firm; be sure questions are clear; be sure there are no distractions in test situation. If the responses are inappropriate, question further.
Performs poorly on timed tests	Recognize a culture not oriented to the value of time; avoid drawing conclusions about individual performance until untimed measures have been tried.
Shows poor knowledge of vocabulary	Try other ways of measuring the examinee's expressive vocabulary; question individual in primary language.
Is unmotivated to take test	Explain purpose and value of test to client and family; try techniques to motivate client performance.
Scores poorly on information items	Recognize that some items might be biased and not a part of the examinee's culture; ask examinee to clarify any unusual responses.
Is afraid of embarrassing or dishonoring family	Initiate test-wise session, practice session, or some type of warm up.
Is quiet and does not ask questions or interact	Establish rapport; explain examiner's role and purpose of the test; ask client to repeat the question if no answer is given or the answer is inappropriate.
Is afraid of a male examiner	Observe examinee; establish rapport before testing.

ASSESSMENT OF INDIVIDUALS WITH DISABILITIES

More than 56 million Americans (19% of the population) report some level of disability (Brault, 2012). A *disability*, as defined by the Americans with Disabilities Act (ADA), is "a physical or mental impairment that substantially limits a major life activity" (U.S.C. Title 42 Chapter 126 Section 12102 [2]). The American Association on Intellectual and Developmental Disabilities (AAIDD) further elaborates that a disability "should be considered within the context of the individual's environmental and personal factors, and the need for individualized supports" (2008, p. 2). The Individuals with Disabilities Education

---

TABLE 15.2 IDEA Disability Categories for Children

1. Autism	8. Orthopedic impairment
2. Deaf-blindness	9. Other health impairment
3. Deafness	10. Specific learning disability
4. Emotional disturbance	11. Speech or language impairment
5. Hearing impairment	12. Traumatic brain injury
6. Mental retardation	13. Visual impairment, including blindness
7. Multiple disabilities	

Improvement Act of 2004 (IDEA) lists 13 specific disability categories under which children may qualify for special education and related services (see Table 15.2).

Although not listed in the IDEA disability categories, the term *developmental disabilities* is widely used to describe a diverse group of severe, lifelong disabilities attributable to mental and/or physical impairments, which manifest prior to age 22. People with developmental disabilities have problems with major life activities, such as language, mobility, learning, self-care, and independent living. Autism, cerebral palsy, hearing loss, intellectual disabilities, and vision impairment are examples of developmental disabilities.

Assessment of individuals with disabilities is conducted for a variety of reasons: to diagnose or determine the existence of disability, to determine intervention plans, for placement or selection decisions, and/or for monitoring performance in an educational setting (AERA et al., 2014). With regard to ability/disability assessment, instruments are often designed to measure skills that should be mastered at certain stages across the life span:

- *Communication Skills* Verbal and nonverbal, receptive and expressive, listening and comprehension
- *Cognitive Skills* Reasoning, thinking, memory; basic achievement in reading, writing, and mathematics; problem solving
- *Physical Development* General growth; motor and sensory; balance, locomotion, walking
- *Emotional Development* Temperament, adjustment, emotional expression, self-concept, attitudes
- *Social Development* Peer and family relationships, friendships, interpersonal relationships
- *Self-Care Skills* Basic self-care needs, such as drinking, eating, toileting, dressing
- *Independent Living Skills* Functioning independently in the home and community, including clothing care, cooking, transportation, shopping, money management
- *Work Habits and Adjustment Skills* Working independently, maintaining proper work habits, working with employers and employees, seeking and keeping jobs
- *Adjustment Problems* Aggression, hyperactivity, acting out, withdrawal, delinquency, stress, depression

A major issue in assessing individuals with disabilities concerns the use of accommodations or modifications that minimize the impact of the individual's attributes that are not relevant to the construct that is being measured. Most assessment instruments are designed for use with the general population and may not be appropriate for use with individuals with specific disabilities. For example, a person who is blind and reads only Braille cannot complete a traditional written exam. Thus, modification of tests and test administration procedures is necessary to make an accurate assessment. Examples of test-modification strategies include the following (AERA et al., 2014):

- Modifying the presentation form
- Modifying the response format
- Modifying timing
- Modifying test setting
- Using only portions of a test
- Using substitute or alternate tests

The *Standards for Educational and Psychological Testing* (AERA et al., 2014) established several standards for instruments designed to assess people with disabling conditions. Test developers are required to have psychometric expertise and experience in working with individuals with disabilities, and test publishers should caution examiners about the use and interpretation of the test with clients with special needs until it has been fully validated. Test developers should conduct pilot tests on people who have similar disabilities to check on the appropriateness and feasibility of test modifications and should include a careful statement of steps taken to modify the test so that users will be able to identify any changes that may alter its validity. They should use empirical procedures to establish time limits for modified forms and explore the effects of fatigue. They also should provide validity and reliability information on the modified forms and on the unmodified forms.

Clearly, it is important for test users to study the test manual and evaluate the technical information to determine whether the modifications are valid and reliable for the group in question. In addition, practitioners working with clients who have special needs should know what alternate tests and methods are available and appropriate for these persons. Those who are interpreting the test results need to know which set of norms should be used. Regular norms are used when the examiner needs to compare the test performance of the individual with disabilities with that of the general population. Special norms are appropriate when the examiner is looking at how the individual performs in relation to peers with the same disabling condition.

Assessment of Individuals with Visual Impairment

Visual impairment may be caused by injury or disease that reduces the individual's central vision, accommodation, binocular vision, peripheral vision, or color vision. The impairment affects normal patterns of cognitive, affective, and psychomotor development. Assessment professionals assess individuals with visual impairments by using instruments to meet their needs, such as tests with large-print versions, Braille forms, and forms on audio recorders. Because many tests have not been normed on those with visual impairments, assessment professionals must pay close attention to fairness in terms of measurement bias, access, and interpretation. Steer, Gale, and Gentle (2007) highlighted the complexity of test accommodations for those individuals with visual disorders. According to the researchers, accommodations for individuals with visual impairment fall into five broad categories:

- Presentation related
- Time related

- Setting related
- Response related
- Aids related

Counselors who conduct assessment on individuals who experience some form of visual impairment must become familiar with the various accommodations that are related to each category. For example, many assessment instruments have audio recorded materials for administration to those with visual impairment. Providing an audio presentation would make an appropriate accommodation. As another example, consider a student who is completing an online program in counselor education and must take exams as part of the training program. It may be an appropriate accommodation to provide the individual with a screen reader.

Determining appropriate accommodations in the assessment process is a critical element of fairness in testing. However, a more appropriate path is to select a test that is normed on the population for which it is intended. There are specialized tests available for assessing children and adults with visual impairments. The Hill Performance Test of Selected Positional Concepts measures the spatial concepts of children aged 6 to 10 with visual impairments. The Reynell–Zinkin Scales provide a profile of six areas for children up to 5 years old: social adaptation, sensorimotor, exploration of environment, response to sound/verbal comprehension, expressive language, and nonverbal communication.

Assessment of Individuals with Hearing Impairment

Individuals differ in their degree of hearing impairment as well as the age of onset of the impairment. Audiologists screen individuals with hearing losses that range from mild to profound; such losses can be caused by a number of factors. Normally, examinees with hearing deficits have had a pattern of delayed speech and language development and problems in social development.

During the assessment process, individuals with hearing impairments need interpreters who sign the instructions and items for them. Some tests have DVDs or videos with the directions and items presented in sign language. Examiners must be careful in reaching conclusions during observations. Individuals who exhibit behavior characteristic of people with learning disabilities, behavior disorders, or intellectual disabilities may be suffering from a hearing loss that leads to those similar behaviors. Simeonsson (1986) identified three major purposes of assessment of individuals with hearing impairments:

1. To assess the cognitive competency and achievement discrepancy
2. To assess the cognitive and linguistic discrepancy
3. To assess personal and social functioning

Many individual differences exist within this group, and it is important to take into consideration both the etiology of the impairment and the developmental history of the individual. The following guidelines pertain to assessment of individuals with hearing impairments:

- Be sure that any individual with problems speaking or understanding spoken language has a hearing evaluation.
- Keep the test environment controlled and free from distraction; an individual with a mild hearing loss may be distracted by extraneous noise.

- Avoid visual distractions, especially if the examinee is reading lips.
- If necessary, have an interpreter help communicate with the examinee.
- Allow the interpreter and the person with a hearing impairment to arrange seating to enhance the lines of communication.
- Have more than one assessment approach to measure the construct in question.

Sattler and Hoge (2006) recommended assessing adaptive behavior of all students with disabilities or suspected disabilities along with observations conducted in different settings.

Assessment of Individuals with Intellectual Disability

Intellectual disability is a developmental disability characterized by significant limitations in intellectual functioning and in adaptive behavior as expressed in conceptual, social, and practical adaptive skills; the disability originates before the age of 18 (Luckasson et al., 2010, p. 1). The term *intellectual disability* is currently preferred to what historically has been referred to as "mental retardation" (AAIDD, 2008). In a child, intellectual disability can be caused by injury, disease, or a brain abnormality, which can happen before a child is born or during childhood. For many children, the cause of their intellectual disability is not known. Some of the most commonly known causes of intellectual disability occur before birth, including Down syndrome, Fragile X syndrome (a genetic syndrome), fetal alcohol syndrome, infections, or birth defects. The symptoms of intellectual disability usually appear early in life. Children with the disorder tend to develop more slowly than normal. They may learn to sit up, crawl, or walk later than other children, or take longer to develop speech or have trouble speaking. Both adults and children with intellectual disability may experience one or more problems in the following areas: learning, communication, social skills, academic skills, vocational skills, and independent living.

To assess for an intellectual disability, instruments are used to evaluate two general areas: (1) cognitive or intellectual ability and (2) adaptive behavior. Intelligence tests, such as the Wechsler scales and the Stanford–Binet, are the primary instruments used to assess intellectual ability. Limitations in intellectual ability are generally thought to be present if a child has an IQ score of about 70 or below. In the *Diagnostic and Statistical Manual of Mental Disorders, Fifth Edition* (American Psychiatric Association (APA), 2013) intellectual disability is divided into four levels of severity (based on intelligence test scores) indicating the degree of intellectual impairment: mild, moderate, severe, or profound.

In contrast to earlier versions of the *Diagnostic and Statistical Manual*, intellectual disability is not identified solely by IQ score. *Adaptive functioning* is now a central component in identifying the severity of the intellectual disability. *Adaptive functioning* refers to conceptual, social, and practical skills that people have learned to be able to function in their everyday lives. It can include such skill areas as communication, self-care, home living, social or interpersonal skills, use of community resources, self-direction, functional academic skills, work, leisure, health, and safety (APA, 2013). Adaptive functioning is assessed by using standardized tests, and a widely used instrument is the Vineland Adaptive Behavior Scales (Vineland-II).

VINELAND ADAPTIVE BEHAVIOR SCALES, SECOND EDITION The Vineland-II (Sparrow, Cicchetti, & Balla, 2005) is an individually administered instrument that measures personal and social skills needed for everyday living. It was designed to identify individuals, from birth to age 90, who have intellectual disabilities, developmental delays, autism spectrum disorders, and other impairments. The instrument contains five domains, each with two or three subdomains (see Table 15.3). The Vineland-II is available in four formats: a Survey Interview Form, a Parent/Caregiver Rating Form, an Expanded Interview Form, and a Teacher Rating Form. The instrument yields standard scores (M = 100, SD = 15), V-scale scores (M = 15, SD = 3), percentile ranks, age equivalents, stanines, adaptive levels (i.e., low, moderately low, adequate, moderately high, and high), and maladaptive levels (i.e., average, elevated, clinically significant).

TABLE 15.3 Vineland-II: Domains and Subdomains

Domain	Communication
Receptive Language	How the individual listens and pays attention, and what he or she understands
Expressive Language	What the individual says, how he or she uses words and sentences to gather and provide information
Written Language	What the individual understands about how letters make words, and what he or she reads and writes
Domain	**Daily Living Skills**
Personal	How the individual eats, dresses, and practices personal hygiene
Domestic	What household tasks the individual performs
Community	How the individual uses time, money, the telephone, the computer, and job skills
Domain	**Socialization**
Interpersonal Relationships	How the individual interacts with others
Play and Leisure Time	How the individual plays and uses leisure time
Coping Skills	How the individual demonstrates responsibility and sensitivity to others
Domain	**Motor Skills**
Gross	How the individual uses arms and legs for movement and coordination
Fine	How the individual uses hands and fingers to manipulate objects
Maladaptive Behavior Domain (OPTIONAL)	
Internalizing Behavior	Examples: sad, avoids others, lacks energy, anxious or nervous, sleeping and eating difficulties
Externalizing Behavior	Examples: impulsive, defies authority, temper tantrums, lies, physically aggressive, bullies
Other	Examples: sucks thumb, wets bed, bites nails, runs away, truant, uses drugs or alcohol

Source: Vineland Adaptive Behavior Scales, Second Edition (Vineland-II). Copyright © 2008 by NCS Pearson, Inc. Reproduced with permission. All rights reserved.

Assessment of Individuals with Neuropsychological Impairment

A major assessment area related to intellectual disability is *neuropsychological assessment*, which involves assessing for impairment caused by a brain injury or damage. A wide variety of cognitive and intellectual abilities is typically assessed during a neuropsychological evaluation, including attention and concentration, learning and memory, sensory-perceptual abilities, speech and language abilities, visuospatial skills (ability to perceive spatial relationships among objects), overall intelligence, and executive functions. In addition, psychomotor speed, strength, and coordination all would be addressed in some fashion. Three well-known neuropsychological instruments are the Halstead–Reitan Neuropsychological Test Battery, the Luria–Nebraska Neuropsychological Battery (LNNB), and the Bender Visual-Motor Gestalt Test, Second Edition (Bender-Gestalt II). These tests are described in Chapter 13, Clinical Assessment.

Assessment of Individuals with Communication Disorders

Communication disorders are problems that affect an individual's speech or language functioning. They are among the most common disorders in childhood; approximately 40 million people have communication disorders, and the cost of providing services for these disorders can be up to $186 billion dollars annually (Tanner, 2007). Although the number of individuals impacted by communication disorders is vast, there are limited services available for these individuals (Roth, 2013). *Speech disorders* generally include problems with producing speech sounds (articulation), controlling sounds that are produced (voice), and controlling the rate and rhythm of speech (fluency). *Language disorders* include problems using proper forms of language, using the content of language (comprehension), and with the use and functions of language (i.e., social conversational rules; Ysseldyke & Algozzine, 2006). Communication disorders can result in significant problems in school, work, and social functioning.

Speech-language pathologists are responsible for assessment of individuals with communication disorders and may use a number of different assessment approaches. Psychologists and counselors testing these individuals may find that examinees are unable to say words correctly or to formulate ideas according to accepted standards. Examiners need to concentrate their attention on what these clients have to say and reward client efforts with warmth and positive reinforcement. The following are some other good practices:

1. Demonstrate acceptance and positive regard for the client as an individual.
2. Try to remove any distracting stimuli from the testing environment.
3. Keep instructions and directions simple. Repeat or rephrase questions when appropriate.
4. Be alert to facial expressions, gestures, and tone of voice.
5. Allow the examinee to nod, point, or otherwise indicate the answer in a nonverbal manner.

Assessment of Children with Disabilities

When children have the potential to have a disability, an accurate assessment process is critical. In many cases, early assessment can impact the outcome of treatment and can help design the appropriate treatments. We review assessment procedures for Autism Spectrum Disorders, ADHD, and general developmental disabilities. Counselors should note that assessment of children with special needs can be a difficult process. All counselors conducting assessment should have supervision of their assessment practice until they gain competence, but such supervision is especially important when working with children. In order to be effective, counselors should also consider attending additional training for each particular disorder.

AUTISM SPECTRUM DISORDERS *Autism spectrum disorders* (ASDs) include those disorders characterized by impairment in several areas of development, including social interaction skills, communication skills, or the presence of stereotyped behavior, interests, and activities. The revision to the diagnosis of Autism Spectrum Disorder in the DSM-5 now encompasses several specific disorders from the DSM-IV-TR (i.e., Rhett's Disorder, Childhood Disintegrative Disorder, Asperger's Disorder, Pervasive Developmental Disorder Not Otherwise Specified). Autism is a complex spectrum of symptoms that is usually evident in the first years of life. One of the issues that makes diagnosis complex is that individuals may range from gifted intelligence to some degree of cognitive impairment. Regardless of intellectual functioning, children with ASDs display difficulties in the following areas:

1. *Social Interaction* Appear aloof, want to spend more time alone than with others, show little interest in making friends, and lack emotional reciprocity
2. *Communication* Show a significant delay in or absence of speech
3. *Repetitive Behaviors* Become intensely preoccupied with one toy or activity, or engage in rituals or routines
4. *Senses* Demonstrate extreme overreaction or underreaction to sensory (e.g., sight, hearing, touch, smell, taste) information

Assessing children with an ASD should include, at minimum, a parent or caregiver interview, a medical evaluation, direct behavioral observation, a cognitive assessment, and an assessment of adaptive functioning (Sheperis, Mohr, & Ammons, 2014). No assessment instrument or procedure can be used in isolation to make a diagnosis of autism, but the combined use of evidence-based assessment methods is recommended. Formal assessment instruments are often best for determining risk of autism rather than for making a specific diagnosis. Examples of these instruments include the following:

- Autism Behavior Checklist (ABC)
- Autism Screening Instrument for Educational Planning, Third Edition (ASIEP-3)
- Autism Diagnostic Interview, Revised (ADI-R)
- Behavior Observation Scale for Autism (BOS)
- Childhood Autism Rating Scale, Second Edition (CARS-2)
- Gilliam Autism Rating Scale, Third Edition (GARS-3)

ATTENTION-DEFICIT/HYPERACTIVITY DISORDER Although its cause is unknown, attention-deficit/hyperactivity disorder (ADHD) is a chronic condition that becomes apparent in some children in preschool and the early school years, and the disorder can continue on to adulthood. Individuals with ADHD have problems with inattention, hyperactivity, and impulsivity. The assessment of ADHD requires multiple methods and multiple sources of information. These include parent and child interviews, teacher and parent rating scales, direct observation, and school reports. Professionals who usually perform evaluations for ADHD are clinical psychologists, school psychologists, psychiatrists, neurologists, and pediatricians.

Behavior checklists and rating scales play a prominent role in assessment of children with ADHD. They provide important information about a child's behavior in different settings and how it is judged by significant others (Hersen, 2006). Some checklists or rating scales assess broad dimensions of child behavior but can be used to assess ADHD, including the following:

- Child Behavior Checklist (CBCL/6-18)
- Behavioral Assessment System for Children (BASC-2)
- Conner's Rating Scales, Third Edition (Conners 3)

Checklists and rating scales that focus more narrowly on ADHD characteristics or symptoms include the following:

- ADHD Symptom Rating Scale (ADHD-SRS)
- Attention Deficit Disorder Evaluation Scale (ADDES-2)
- Attention Deficit Hyperactivity Rating Scale (AD/HD-RS-IV)
- Barkley Home Situation Questionnaire (HSQ-R)
- Strengths and Weaknesses of ADHD Symptoms and Normal Behavior (SWAN)
- Swanson, Nolan, and Pelham Rating Scale (SNAP-IV)
- Development and Well Being Assessment (DAWBA)
- Diagnostic Interview Schedule for Children (DISC-IV)

DEVELOPMENTAL DELAYS *Developmental delay* is a term that means a child is developing slower than normal in one or more areas and is at risk of academic failure (Glascoe, Marks, & Squires, 2012). These delays may occur in one or more of the major areas of development, including physical abilities (gross or fine motor skills), cognitive development, language, or personal or social skills development. In recent years, there has been an effort to identify children with developmental delays prior to kindergarten. The Early Intervention Program for Infants and Toddlers with Disabilities (Part C of IDEA) is a federal grant program that assists states in providing early intervention services for infants and toddlers (ages birth through 2 years) with disabilities and their families. In order to be eligible for services, a comprehensive, multidisciplinary evaluation and assessment of the child and family must be conducted. The evaluation of the child involves assessing the following areas of child development:

- Physical (reaching, rolling, crawling, walking)
- Cognitive (thinking, learning, solving problems)
- Communication (talking, listening, understanding)
- Social/emotional (playing, feeling secure and happy)
- Adaptive (toileting, eating, dressing, personal hygiene)

Various instruments are available to help assess these developmental areas. An annotated list of these instruments is provided as follows:

- The Bayley Scales of Infant and Toddler Development, Third Edition (Bayley-III) are used to assess the cognitive, language, and psychomotor development of children from 2 to 30 months of age and to aid in the diagnosis of normal or delayed development.
- The Battelle Developmental Inventory, Second Edition (BDI-2) was designed to assess five domains of development in infants and children through age 7: adaptive behavior, personal/social skills, communication, gross and fine motor ability, and cognitive skills.

- The Cattell Infant Intelligence Scale measures the intellectual development of children from 3 to 30 months by assessing verbalizations and motor control.
- The Dallas Preschool Screening Test (DPST) is used to assess the learning disabilities of children between the ages of 3 and 6; it measures auditory, language, motor, visual, psychological, and articulation development.
- The Denver Developmental Screening Test, Second Edition (DDST-II) is used to evaluate a child's personal, social, fine motor, gross motor, language, and adaptive abilities. The test is appropriate for use as a screening tool with children from birth to age 6.
- The Kent Infant Development Scale, Second Edition (KID Scale) uses a 252-item inventory to assess infants from birth to 15 months and children up to 6 years with developmental ages of less than 15 months. The test measures cognitive, language, motor, self-help, and social skills.

STANDARDS FOR ASSESSMENT WITH DIVERSE POPULATIONS

Ethical standards require assessment professionals to have specific knowledge and expertise related to working with individuals from diverse cultural backgrounds and with individuals with disabilities. Counselors must respect the diverse values, beliefs, and experiences of clients, which affect clients' view of the world and psychosocial functioning. They must also be aware of the impact of social, environmental, and political conditions on problems and interventions. In assessing diverse populations, the need for multiple methods and multiple sources of information is even more important to accurately assess an individual's capabilities, potentials, and limitations (APA, 2002).

In 2012, the Association for Assessment and Research in Counseling (AARC) published *Standards for Multicultural Assessment* that addresses many of the challenges that are specifically related to the assessment of diverse populations (see Appendix I). These standards are a compilation of standards from five sources:

1. *Code of Fair Testing Practices in Education*
2. *Responsibilities of Users of Standardized Tests*
3. *Standards for Educational and Psychological Testing Multicultural Counseling Competencies and Standards*
4. *Code of Ethics* and *Standards of Practice* of the American Counseling Association (2014)

Summary

Fairness in measurement is a primary consideration for all assessment. Counselors and other helping professionals must recognize and appreciate the differences that exist among people who differ in terms of race, ethnicity, age, language, gender, sexual orientation, religious or spiritual orientation, ability, and other cultural dimensions.

Multicultural assessment encompasses assessment procedures that are appropriate, fair, and useful for accurately describing abilities and other traits in individuals from diverse populations. Professionals are aware of the important issues related to the use of standardized tests, such as test bias, psychometric properties, administration and scoring procedures, test use and interpretation, and test-taker and examiner bias. Furthermore, they have knowledge of the ethical principles, etic and emic perspectives, and the issue of acculturation.

Assessment of individuals with disabilities is conducted to diagnose or determine the existence of disability, to determine intervention plans, for placement or selection decisions, or for monitoring educational performance. Examiners have knowledge of the assessment standards and procedures for working with individuals with disabilities. They understand the importance of using test accommodations or modifications that reduce testing of the individual's attributes that are not relevant to the construct being measured.

Questions for Discussion

1. Compare and contrast your culture with that of another culture. What are the similarities? What are the differences? What are the different dimensions of bias that an examiner must be alert to?
2. How might the following examiner variables affect the validity of the test results?
   a. Personal bias and expectation
   b. Difficulty in understanding what the examinee says
   c. Lack of knowledge of the particular disability
   d. Lack of experience testing and working with the particular exceptionality
   e. Lack of special communication skills (e.g., American Sign Language)
   f. Lack of knowledge of the client's first language
   g. Lack of knowledge of the specific ethnic group
3. Do you think it is acceptable to adapt and modify a standardized test to accommodate an individual's disability? Why or why not?
4. How important do you feel the environment is in assessing individuals with disabilities? How would the following factors affect the validity of the test results?
   a. Lighting in the test environment
   b. Noise level
   c. Physical features of the test environment
   d. Positioning needs of the examinee

Suggested Activities

1. Interview professionals who assess diverse populations and find out what tests they use and why. Report your findings to the class.
2. Review a video of a test administration of an individual with a disability. Did the examiner modify test procedures? If so, how?
3. Interview individuals with disabilities and find out their experiences and reactions to testing. Report your findings to the class.
4. Review the legislation and judicial decisions related to assessing individuals from different cultural groups and individuals with disabilities. Write a summary of what you find.
5. Locate a test that has been adapted and standardized for use with a specific cultural group or diverse population. Compare the adaptation with the original version. How was the test modified? How do the two sets of norms compare?

References

American Association on Intellectual and Developmental Disabilities (AAIDD). (2008). *Frequently asked questions on intellectual disability and the AAIDD definition*. Washington, DC: Author.

American Counseling Association (ACA). (2014). *ACA Code of Ethics*. Alexandria, VA: Author.

American Counseling Association and Association for Assessment in Counseling. (2003). *Responsibilities of users of standardized tests*. Alexandria, VA: Author.

American Educational Research Association (AERA), American Psychological Association (APA), and National Council on Measurement in Education (NCME). (2014). *Standards for educational and psychological testing*. Washington, DC: Authors.

American Psychiatric Association (APA). (2013). *Diagnostic and statistical manual of mental disorders* (5th ed.). Washington, DC: Author.

Americans With Disabilities Act of 1990, Pub. L. No. 101-336, 104 Stat. 328 (1990).

Association for Assessment in Counseling (AAC). (2003). *Standards for multicultural assessment* (2nd ed.). Retrieved from http://aarc-counseling .org/assets/cms/uploads/files/multicultural.pdf

Baruth, L. G., & Manning, M. L. (2011). *Multicultural counseling psychotherapy* (5th ed.). Upper Saddle River, NJ: Merrill/Prentice Hall.

Brault, M. W. (2012). *Americans with disabilities: 2010 Household economic studies*. U.S. Department of Commerce: Economics and Statistics Administration, Washington, DC.

Dana, R. H. (2005). *Multicultural assessment: Principles, applications, and examples*. Mahwah, NJ: Lawrence Erlbaum Associates.

Glascoe, F. P., Marks, K. P., & Squires, J. (2012). Improving the definition of developmental delay. *Journal of Developmental and Behavioral Pediatrics, 33*(1), 87–87.

Hersen, M. (2006). *Clinician's handbook of behavioral assessment*. Burlington, MA: Elsevier/Academic Press.

Huey, S. J., Jr., Tilley, J. L., Jones, E. O., & Smith, C. A. (2014). The contribution of cultural competence to evidence-based care for ethnically diverse populations. *Annual Review of Clinical Psychology, 10*, 305–338.

Joint Committee on Testing Practices. (2004). *Code of fair testing practices in education*. Washington, DC: Author.

Kelley, L., Bailey, E. K., & Brice, W. D. (2014). Teaching methods: Etic or emic. *Developments in Business Simulation and Experiential Learning, 28*, 123–126.

Luckasson, R., Borthwick-Duffy, S., Buntinx, W. H. E., Coulter, D. L., Craig, E. M., Reeve, A., … Tassé, M. J. (2010). *Mental retardation: Definition, classification, and systems of supports* (11th ed.). Washington, DC: American Association on Mental Retardation.

Roth, K. (2013). *Understanding and managing the growing SLP shortage*. San Fransisco, CA: Presence-Learning, Inc. Retrieved from http://www .slideshare.net/presencelearning/understanding-and-managing-the-growing-slp-shortage

Ryan, C. (2013). *Language use in the United States: 2011.* US Department of Commerce: Economics and Statistics Administration. Washington, DC.

Sattler, J. M., & Hoge, R. D. (2006). *Assessment of children: Behavioral, social, and clinical foundations* (5th ed.). San Diego, CA: Jerome M. Sattler Publisher Inc.

Sheperis, C. J., Mohr, J. D., & Ammons, R. (2014). Best practices: Autism spectrum disorder. *Center for Counseling Practice, Policy, and Research*. Retrieved from http://www.counseling.org/knowledge-center/center-for-counseling-practice-policy-and-research/practice-briefs

Simeonsson, R. J. (1986). *Psychological and developmental assessment of special children*. Boston, MA: Allyn & Bacon.

Sparrow, S. S., Cicchetti, D. V., & Balla, D. A. (2005). *Vineland Adaptive Behavior Scales, second edition: Survey forms manual*. Minneapolis, MN: Pearson Assessment.

Steer, M., Gale, G., & Gentle, F. (2007). A taxonomy of assessment accommodations for students with vision impairments in Australian schools. *British Journal of Visual Impairment, 25*(2), 169–177.

Suzuki, L. A., & Ponterotto, J. G. (2008). *Handbook of multicultural assessment: Clinical, psychological, and educational applications* (3rd ed.). San Francisco, CA: Jossey-Bass.

Tanner, D. C. (2007). *Medical-legal and forensic aspects of communication disorders, voice prints, & speaker profiling*. Tuscon, AZ: Lawyers & Judges Publishing Company.

U.S. Census Bureau (2014). *State & Country QuickFacts, 2014.* Retrieved from http://quickfacts .census.gov/qfd/states/00000.html

Ysseldyke, J. E., & Algozzine, R. (2006). *Teaching students with communication disorders: A practical guide for every teacher*. Thousand Oaks, CA: Sage.

Zhang, Y., & Tsai, J. (2014). *The assessment of acculturation, enculturation, and culture in Asian-American samples: Guide to psychological assessment with Asians*. New York, NY: Springer.

16 Communicating Assessment Results

Once the assessment process is complete and results are analyzed and interpreted, counselors have the responsibility to communicate the results to those individuals entitled to the information. Communicating results in an appropriate manner is as essential as following appropriate procedures in conducting assessment (see Figure 16.1). We place this chapter toward the end of the book to allow for developmental learning about the assessment process. However, the process of communicating results is an integral component in assessment and should not be considered something that happens after assessment is completed.

When communicating the results of the assessment process, you may include more than just the person being assessed. Communication of results may involve the client, parents (if the examinee is a minor), and other professionals involved with the examinee (i.e., teachers, school administrators, mental health professionals). In cases in which clients are mandated for assessment by the court system, you may have to communicate results to the court or court officials. It is important to clearly state that results are communicated to others only with the explicit permission of the client or guardian. In some cases, you will have to determine who the appropriate person is to receive this information. For example, in court-mandated cases, the client may actually be the court system, and the results are only reported to the court. As you can see, the process of communicating results is more complex than it may appear. This chapter will present information about communicating assessment results using feedback sessions and written reports.

After studying this chapter, you should be able to:

- Describe the use of feedback sessions in orally communicating assessment results.
- Describe the potential problems and issues associated with feedback sessions.
- Describe the process of feedback sessions with parents.
- Explain the purpose of written assessment reports.
- Describe each section of the assessment report.
- Describe the qualities of a well-written assessment report.
- List and discuss the guidelines for reporting assessment results to other professionals and the public.

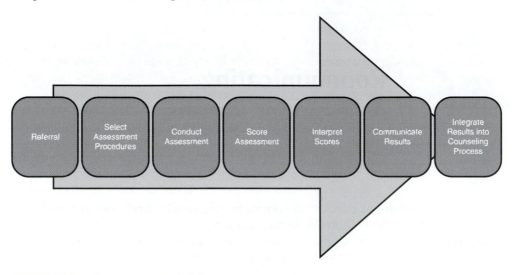

FIGURE 16.1   The assessment process.

FEEDBACK SESSIONS

In most instances, the assessment process ends with an oral or written report, whereby counselors communicate assessment results to clients (or other relevant parties) in a comprehensible and useful manner. Assessment results are of direct interest to clients. Depending on the reason for assessment, they may be concerned about what the results mean in terms of their academic standing or goals, career decisions, abilities, or emotional problems. In some cases, the results of assessment have high stakes associated with them. For example, assessment is required to determine competency to stand trial in forensic settings and for competency to be sentenced to death in capital punishment cases. Being able to communicate fair and valid interpretations of test results can be as serious as life and death. Even in cases in which the stakes are not as high as life or death, the results can have lasting implications. Imagine being a counselor in a school setting and having to explain to parents that their child's assessment results do not qualify them for gifted education. In a real example, a parent had two older children who were involved in the gifted education program at a local school. The parent asked that their youngest child also be tested for inclusion in the program. After completing a multifaceted and multidimensional assessment, it was determined that the child did not qualify. It was important to communicate to the parent the procedures followed and the meaning of the test scores. In this case, the student had an IQ of 110 and had similar achievement scores. His grades were also average, and his teachers viewed him as comparable to other children at the same grade level. The parent was certain that the child was gifted and asked for an additional assessment. As part of communicating the results of this assessment process, the standard error of measurement was explained to the parent in a manner she could understand. With regard to IQ tests, there is a band of error (e.g., $+/-3$) that predicts what a test score would be if a person was tested over and over. In this case, we could predict that if the child was tested again, his scores might improve or they might go down. Either way, the change would only be slight, because intelligence is something that doesn't change very much across testing occasions. If the child was tested again, he would likely score between 107 and 113 and still would not qualify for the gifted education program. By taking the time to explain the results in an understandable manner, the parent was able to accept the results and realize that the youngest child did not qualify for the additional program. Effective communication also saved the district the time and money involved in additional testing.

Hopefully, you can see that counselors and other helping professionals use *feedback sessions* with clients to orally communicate their assessment results. During feedback sessions, counselors can review and clarify assessment results, acquire additional information relevant to the assessment process, educate the client (and family members, if relevant) about what their results mean, and provide recommendations regarding interventions or educational services. Furthermore, feedback sessions can be a vehicle for establishing good rapport with clients and to help them understand why treatment is being recommended.

The feedback session is usually scheduled soon after the assessment, and spouses and primary caregivers may be invited to attend. If the examinee is a child, then teachers, school administrators, and other professionals may be included with the family's permission. Counselors should begin feedback sessions by describing the purpose of the assessment. They should be prepared to explain difficult concepts and the limits of a test. Counselors may also wish to explain the various sources of test bias that may affect the interpretation of the scores. The client also needs to understand that test data represent just one source of information and are not sufficient for fully assessing an individual's abilities, skills, or traits.

After explaining the purpose of the test, counselors should report test results in a manner that clients (and family members) can understand. Most people, professionals and laypersons alike, find that percentile ranks can be the easiest types of scores to understand (Lichtenberger, Mather, Kaufman, & Kaufman, 2004). When explaining percentile ranks to clients, it is easy for them to see that being #1 is not the best outcome. If you are in the 1st percentile, then that means that out of 100 people your score is equal to or higher than one score. In other words, your score is probably the lowest out of the 100. Hopefully, as a professional counselor you won't have to tell someone they are number 1, but you can see the utility of explaining assessment results in terms of percentile rank. Standard scores can easily be converted to percentile ranks using a conversion table. Some professionals prefer using qualitative descriptions of scores rather than the scores themselves. When appropriate, the standard error of measurement can help to emphasize that the test results are not absolute; results provide approximations of where true scores might fall. The following are examples of how to orally communicate various types of scores with a hypothetical client named Ellis, who is 10 years old and in the fifth grade as well as with Ellis's parent (Miller, Linn, & Gronlund, 2011):

- *Percentile Ranks* "With regard to math, Ellis scored in the 95th percentile. This means that she performed very well compared to others in her grade. In fact, her score was equal to or better than 95% of children her age who have taken the test.
- *Deviation IQ* Ellis is also above average in her ability to understand verbal concepts. She performs much higher than most of her peers.
- *T Scores* Ellis did demonstrate some areas for concern on the Child Behavior Checklist/6-18 Withdrawn/Depressed syndrome scale. The results indicate that she may be having some problems with adjustment. According to her scores on the CBCL, she may be experiencing some aspects of depression. Overall, the scores suggest that she is somewhat withdrawn and lacks energy. She also seems to be experiencing a sense of sadness.

- *Stanines* Ellis received a stanine score of 9 on her testing. Basically, a 9 indicates that Ellis is performing at a higher level than her peers. Her score is in the above-average range (e.g., stanine scores from 7 to 9).
- *Grade Equivalent Scores* Ellis' performance on the math computations test was also above average. It is important to note that these scores are only comparing her to others her age. Because she is performing at a higher level may not mean that she should be promoted to a new grade level. Although a score of 6.3 might suggest the need to move ahead to the sixth grade, such an assumption is not correct. The only comparison group is same age peers. However, the 6.3 intimates that she should be moved forward in a grade. However, the only comparison is with peers. As such, she has no exposure to advanced materials. She is simply doing better than most of her peers
- *Age Equivalent Scores* Age equivalent scores are also important to discuss. Ellis scored an 11-2. This simply means that Ellis' performance equals or exceed other children's performances in the 11th year.

Because clients are often nervous or anxious about receiving their assessment results, counselors should focus on the clients' thoughts and feelings about their scores and interpretations. Thus, the feedback session itself can become a therapeutic experience for the client. The client's reaction to results also may provide professionals with new insight about the individual. Furthermore, by participating in the discussion and interpretation of assessment results, the client may become more accepting of the findings, gain more self-awareness, and be more willing to use the information in decision making. Counselors should consider the guidelines shown in Figure 16.2 for interpreting results in feedback sessions (Reynolds, Livingston, Willson, & Willson, 2010).

Group Feedback Sessions

Group feedback sessions are frequently used to communicate test results. Clients with particular learning or personality styles may prefer group and social interaction; such clients often learn from each other as well as from the counselor. Most tests now provide interpretive material that the counselor can highlight effectively and efficiently in group sessions. This approach is usually more economical. The counselor can work with a small or large group and can use overhead transparencies, filmstrips and tapes, or videotapes to present material. Such aids are less likely in a one-on-one situation. The use of group sessions does not preclude offering individual sessions if a client needs further help processing the information.

Problem Areas

Counselors may face some issues when disseminating information during feedback sessions. We present some of the more common problems here, including acceptance of results, client readiness, negative results, flat profiles, and client motivation and attitude.

ACCEPTANCE The goal of the feedback session is often to get clients to accept assessment results and incorporate that information into their decision making. Negative results fre-

_____ Review the purpose of the instrument.

_____ Explain how the instrument is scored and interpreted.

_____ Clearly define all terms.

_____ Discuss who receives the results and how they are used.

_____ Report results in a manner that is easily understood by the client.

_____ Use percentile ranks when reporting quantitative data.

_____ Be tactfully honest.

_____ Avoid jargon. If you must use technical terms, take time to explain their meaning.

_____ Emphasize the positives and objectively discuss the negative aspects of the assessment results.

_____ Avoid terms such as "abnormal," "deviant," or "pathological." Simply explain the characteristics of these terms or other symptoms without using the labels.

_____ Do not discuss every test or subtest score. Limit your interpretation to a few of the most important assessment results.

_____ Check to see whether the examinee understands the test results.

_____ Encourage clients (and parents) to ask questions, offer corrective feedback, and provide more information.

_____ Avoid making global or negative future predictions.

_____ Schedule sufficient time for clients to process the results and reach closure.

_____ Do not try to convince clients to accept that your interpretations of the results are correct.

_____ Use good counseling skills with clients to listen attentively, observe nonverbal cues, validate their opinion (even if they disagree with assessment results), and reflect their feelings about assessment results.

_____ Encourage client to further research or study the meaning of the results.

_____ Schedule follow-up sessions, if needed, to facilitate understanding, planning, or decision making.

FIGURE 16.2   Checklist for feedback sessions.

quently prompt test takers to resist accepting valid and genuine information about themselves. Counselors can enhance acceptance of test results by doing the following:

1. Involve the clients in decision making and general selection of tests prior to the testing.
2. Establish rapport with the clients so that they trust the counselor and are relaxed in the sessions.
3. Spend sufficient time interpreting the results to test takers, but do not overwhelm them with too much data.
4. Translate the results into language that the clients can understand.
5. Show the validity of the information for the decision(s) to be made.

READINESS   The critical factor in the acceptance of the test results is the examinee's _readiness_ to hear it. How one presents test results has a substantial effect on an individual's ability to accept the results. If the information is damaging to an examinee's self-concept, then the counselor might have to work on getting that individual to extend his or her acceptance. The following techniques can help increase an examinee's readiness level:

1. Have several sessions prior to the feedback session to build rapport.
2. Allow the client to bring up the topic of test results; don't immediately begin the feedback session with test interpretation.

3. Focus on the test rather than on the client.
4. Reflect the examinee's responses to feedback.

NEGATIVE RESULTS Often, the results are not what the test taker wanted, desired, or expected. The individual may have failed to pass a certification or licensing examination or failed to achieve the minimum score for admission to college. On a clinical test, a client may become defensive after being informed that he or she scored high on scales assessing substance-abuse problems, or an individual may score high on the validity scales on a personality test and be told that his or her test was invalid. The test administrator must know how to appropriately communicate negative test results to individuals. The following are several recommendations:

1. Explain the rationale for cutoff scores and the validity of the established procedures.
2. Avoid using negative terms or labels, such as "abnormal," "deviant," or "pathological."
3. Gain an understanding of the test taker's perceptions and feelings.
4. Accept the test taker's right to argue with test implications, without necessarily agreeing with the test taker.
5. Identify other information about the individual that supports or does not support the test data.
6. Discuss the implications of the data and the importance of that information for decision making.

FLAT PROFILES Many times, an individual's pattern of scores has no highs or lows, but is just a flat profile. On aptitude and achievement tests, this would indicate a similar level of performance in all areas. On interest or career inventories, flat profiles may indicate that the client is undecided about future goals. Response set might be a factor on a test, with the individual ranking everything high, average, or low. In the case of flat profiles on interest and career guidance tests, counselors can ask clients to read the descriptions of the six Holland types and rank the three types most characteristic of themselves (Gati & Amir, 2010) and discuss the clients' expectations, relevant past experiences, previous work activities, and misconceptions and stereotypes. In the case of flat profiles on aptitude and achievement tests, counselors can look at the interests, values, and career goals and assure the clients that their profiles are not abnormal. The counselor should discuss what an individual considers his or her goals to be and what he or she can do acceptably. A good procedure is to investigate the individual's performance on previous tests to determine whether this pattern is typical.

MOTIVATION AND ATTITUDE Test results are more significant to clients who are motivated to take a test, come in and discuss the results, and have a positive attitude toward the value of the data. Some clients have a negative attitude toward testing prior to the test and maintain that attitude afterward. Some clients become negative after they see that the test results are not what they expected.

Counselors should recognize that tests can aid clients in developing more realistic expectations about themselves and can be valuable in decision making. However, some clients put too much weight on the results and become overly dependent on test data to solve their problems. Other clients use test results as a way of escaping from their feelings and problems. Counselors interpreting test results need to be aware not only of a client's motivation to take or not take a test but also his or her attitude toward the test. Other important information is the immediate goal for the interpretation of the test results and the client's desire to be involved in decision making about the type of test to be taken and the dissemination of test results.

Feedback Sessions with Parents

Almost all children today take some form of standardized test throughout their school careers. Although most will take group achievement tests that all students complete, some will be referred for individual assessment because of a suspected problem. All parents want to know how their child is performing in school, yet parents may feel apprehensive about test findings and fearful of the impact the test results may have on the child's future. In feedback sessions with parents, counselors can explain the child's assessment results and help parents understand the purpose of assessment, what test scores mean, whether their child is meeting school standards, and if their child has any other concerns or issues that need to be addressed. The ultimate purpose of assessment is to help the child; thus, providing specific test information can help parents make informed decisions about any concrete steps that should be taken for their child (Reynolds et al., 2010).

The first step in the parent feedback session is describing what the test measures. For example, the examiner can simply inform parents that the math computation subtest of the Wide Range Achievement Test (WRAT4) measures an individual's ability to perform basic mathematics computations without using long, technical descriptions of the subtest. The examiner then discusses the child's scores, avoiding scientific jargon and providing meaningful information to parents (Miller, Linn, & Gronlund, 2011). The examiner should walk the parent through the interpretation, being patient and understanding but honest. In general, percentile ranks, grade equivalent scores, and stanines are easy to explain and are less likely to be misinterpreted. Actual test results may be presented visually through the use of graphs and profiles to help parents understand the results. Oral feedback needs to be comprehensible as well as informational. However, in general, it is best to keep explanations brief and simple and not overwhelm parents with more information than they can grasp in a short period of time.

The *Code of Fair Testing Practices in Education* (Joint Committee on Testing Practices, 2004) states that parents or guardians should be informed about how test scores will be stored and to whom and under what circumstances scores will be released. Parents should also be informed of how to register complaints and have testing problems resolved. Parents and guardians should also be informed about the rights of test takers, whether they can obtain copies of their child's tests and completed answer sheets, and if their child can retake tests, have tests rescored, or cancel scores.

Sattler and Hoge (2006) provide a four-phase model for presenting assessment findings to parents:

Phase 1: Establish Rapport Arrange to meet with parents in a private setting, and make every effort to have both parents or guardians present at the interview. Examiners should help parents feel comfortable during the session and encourage them to talk freely and ask questions.

Phase 2: Communicate Assessment Results Assessment results and their implications should be summarized as clearly as possible, in a straightforward, detailed, and unambiguous manner. Examiners should be prepared that some of the information shared might at times arouse conflict, hostility, or anxiety in parents. They need to help parents express their feelings and have their feelings acknowledged by the examiner. The hope is that the parents will develop realistic perceptions and expectations for their child.

Phase 3: Discuss Recommendations Examiners need to allow time for parents to assimilate assessment results and help them formulate a plan of action. The parents may want specific recommendations or program suggestions, and the examiner should be prepared to provide these.

Phase 4: Terminate the Interview Examiners should summarize the assessment results and recommendations and encourage parents to ask any additional questions. Examiners should also inform parents that they are available for additional meetings.

In responding to parents' concerns, examiners should be prepared to answer many questions about testing. Table 16.1 provides a list of frequently asked questions.

According to Miller, Linn, and Gronlund (2011), counselors should take some proactive steps to prevent misinterpretation of results by clients or parents. Based on the work of Miller, Linn and Gronlund, we recommended that counselors keep the following points in mind:

1. Be conscious of the potential negative stigma surrounding intelligence tests. Be sure to describe the tests in a way that is understandable to the receiver of the information.

TABLE 16.1 Frequently Asked Questions from Parents

- Why are you testing my child?
- Why do you test so much?
- What is a standardized test?
- How was the test administered?
- What do my child's test scores mean?
- How is my child performing compared with other children of the same age or grade?
- What is wrong with grade equivalent scores?
- Why are our school's scores below the national norms?
- How do you use the scores?
- Why do students take a state achievement test? What does it measure? When do students take it?
- How can my child prepare for taking the state achievement test?
- What is the passing score on the test?
- What kinds of questions were asked on the test?
- Who will see the test results?
- Can I see a copy of the test?
- Can I get a copy of my child's test results?
- Can test scores be improved with coaching?
- How do my child's test scores affect his or her future choices?
- How accurately do the tests predict success?
- Is the test fair to members of my race, gender, or ethnic group?

---

2. Be sure to point out that ability or aptitude test scores may change over time because the abilities measured are learned.
3. Present the results of ability tests in a way that helps parents to understand that scores do not equal school performance. Many factors impact performance, and the results of an ability test only indicate the potential for a certain level of performance.

During a feedback session, parents may express concerns about a variety of aspects of their child's assessment. A common question is what to do if they disagree with the results of the testing—for example, if assessment results indicate that the child is not ready for kindergarten, yet the parents think the child is, or if the parents think their child should be placed in the gifted program, but assessment results show that the child doesn't qualify for placement. Parents should be advised of avenues they might take, such as pursuing an independent evaluation on their own, while recognizing that the school district may not reimburse them for the evaluation and that it may be difficult to have the client tested with the same tests.

Parents may want to know whether test results really matter. Professionals can explain the objectives of assessment programs and the issue of accountability to help parents understand why assessment results are important. They should also emphasize to parents that many placement and selection decisions are based on the outcome of the assessment process; thus, parents should encourage children to take the assessment process seriously and do their best.

Parents might ask whether the tests are culturally biased. Examiners can discuss with parents the procedures that many standardized tests use to reduce test bias, such as using panels of experts to review test items or comparing test results among various groups to see if score differences occur because of affiliation with a particular group. It is important to explain that even with these attempts, some bias might still be operating in the testing situation and may distort a person's true score.

Parents may be concerned about whether scores are fixed or changeable. They need to be reminded that a test measures a sample of behavior at a particular time, using items from a given domain. Tests scores do change; they can go up and down, and their child's scores may vary from year to year. Sometimes, poor performance happens because a student may not be skilled in the areas measured by the test. Most children perform better in some areas than in others. Parents need to understand the dynamics at work and refrain from hasty value judgments.

Parents may ask whether children should be informed about their own test results. In most cases, students should be provided feedback on their performance in words and terms they can understand. The information can help them understand their own strengths and weaknesses and make more realistic educational and vocational choices.

ASSESSMENT REPORTS

In addition to oral feedback, counselors may communicate findings in a written *assessment report*, often called a *psychological report* or a *psychoeducational report*. These reports summarize the data collected from interviews, tests, and observations that directly addressed the reason for assessment. Professionals from various disciplines write assessment reports, including school psychologists, clinical psychologists, neuropsychologists, counselors, and speech and language therapists. Although their professional roles may differ, all engage in the process of report writing. The central purposes of assessment reports are fourfold: (a) to describe the client, (b) to record and interpret the client's performance on assessment instruments, (c) to communicate assessment results to the referral source, and (d) to make recommendations or decisions regarding educational programs, therapy, or other appropriate intervention (Cohen, Swerdlik, & Sturman, 2012; Engelhard & Wind, 2013; Urbina, 2014). Reports also create a record of the assessment for future use and may serve as a legal document (Gunn & Taylor, 2014).

The content of written reports addresses the specific concerns (e.g., psychological, behavioral, academic, linguistic) of the referral source (Goldfinger & Pomerantz, 2013). For example, a teacher may request information about whether a child's learning progress differs from peers or why a child is having difficulty in a particular subject area, such as reading (Schwean et al., 2006). Parents might request an assessment to determine if their child meets the school's criteria for inclusion in the gifted and talented program. A judge may need to know the best placement for a child in a child custody dispute. A probation officer might want to know an adolescent's psychological functioning to determine whether any mental health needs should be addressed. Each referral source has different information needs. Assessment reports are tailored to address the referral questions and the intended audiences.

Written reports should *integrate* information from multiple assessment methods, including interviews, observations, tests, and records. The extent to which reports integrate assessment information varies greatly. Reports that are low on integration generally focus more on test scores, neglect inconsistent results between various methods, ignore the overall context of the client, and do not discuss the meaning of the scores for the client. An integrated report carefully blends assessment findings so that they have specific meaning for the client (Goldfinger & Pomerantz, 2013).

The length of written reports can vary substantially. Although the average report is between five and seven single-spaced pages (Donders, 2001), no universal agreement on length is recommended (Groth-Marnat & Horvath, 2006). For forensic evaluations, Ackerman (2006) distinguishes between reports that are brief (1–3 pages), standard (2–10 pages), and comprehensive (10–50 pages). Length is based on the purpose of the report, the context (i.e., educational, mental health, medical, or vocational settings), the expectations of the referral source, the importance and impact of the assessment, and the complexity and quantity of information to be reported.

Qualities of Well-Written Reports

The success of the assessment process requires that assessment results be communicated effectively. Written reports are read not only by other mental health professionals, but also by clients, parents, teachers, court systems, and other professionals. Thus, reports need to be written in a language that is understandable by a fairly wide audience. However, several major problems are frequently encountered in written reports, such as the use of jargon, poorly defined terms, and abbreviations; poor or illogical explanations of results; vague or inappropriate recommendations, poor organization; emphasis on numbers rather than explanations; and the exclusive use of computer-generated test reports (Carr & McNulty, 2014). Overuse of jargon was the most frequent complaint cited from clients, parents, teachers, and even mental health professionals (Lichtenberger et al., 2004).

To keep written reports clear and understandable, the language should be specific and concrete rather than abstract and ambiguous. Abstract statements may be difficult for readers to interpret, and ambiguous sentences are often misinterpreted, because they imply different meanings to different individuals. The sentence, "John lacks mechanical aptitude" leaves the reader to interpret "lacks" and "mechanical aptitude." It would be better to say, "John is unable to use the screwdriver or put washers on the bolts." Similarly, in the sentence "Mary is an extrovert," who is to define an *extrovert*? It would be better to say, "Mary likes to be with people and be the center of attention. She talks and laughs loudly and makes sure she introduces herself to everyone in the room."

When writing assessment reports, counselors should consider the following recommendations (Carr & McNulty, 2014; Goldfinger & Pomerantz, 2013; Lichtenberger et al., 2004; Wiener & Costaris, 2012):

- Avoid jargon and abbreviations.
- Refer to yourself in third person (e.g., "the examiner found" instead of "I found").
- Use simple words and concise sentences.
- Avoid using needless words and phrases.
- Avoid redundancies.
- Begin paragraphs with a strong declarative sentence followed by information that supports the declarative statement.
- Write background information and observations in the past tense.
- Write assessment results in the present tense.
- Information irrelevant to the purpose of the assessment generally should not be included.
- Capitalize test titles.
- Pay attention to punctuation, capitalization, spelling, and grammar.

The Assessment Report Format

There is no single, optimal report format suitable for every setting and assessment (Wiener & Costaris, 2012). The exact format of an assessment report depends on the audience, referral questions, and the assessment instruments and strategies administered. In general, a written assessment should discuss the reason for referral, the assessment procedures used, the client's background information, behavioral observations, assessment results and interpretation, the examiner's interpretation and conclusion, and recommendations (see Table 16.2). Because some assessment professionals use tests as one data collection method, some assessment reports (particularly comprehensive

---

TABLE 16.2 Sections of a Typical Report

   I. Title and identifying information

  II. Reason for referral

 III. Background information

 IV. Behavioral observations

  V. Assessment instruments and procedures

 VI. Assessment results and interpretation

 VII. Summary

VIII. Recommendations

---

psychological evaluations) will contain a list of the tests that were used during the assessment process. However, when tests are *not* used in the assessment process, they are not listed or discussed in the written report. We will describe each of the sections of an assessment report. As an example, we have provided an abbreviated assessment report later in the chapter.

TITLE AND IDENTIFYING INFORMATION Most reports begin with a title that is followed by important identifying information. The title is typically centered across the top of the first page (e.g., Mental Health Evaluation, Psychoeducational Assessment, Psychological Evaluation). Identifying information is generally recorded underneath the title as follows:

- Examinee's name
- Date of birth
- Chronological age
- School and grade (if assessing a student)
- Date(s) of assessment
- Report date (date written)
- Examiner's name

REASON FOR REFERRAL The first substantive section of the report contains the reasons that the individual is being referred for assessment. This section is crucial, because the reason for referral determines the focus of an evaluation and provides the rationale for the assessment; all other sections of the report should be written with the referral question in mind (Lichtenberger et al., 2004). Writers must also assume that the referral source is not the only individual who will read the report; other individuals, such as other mental health professionals, attorneys, case managers, parents/spouses/children of the examinees, and even examinees themselves, may read the report.

BACKGROUND INFORMATION This section provides a context for understanding the client (Goldfinger & Pomerantz, 2013). In this section, counselors give a brief description of the individual's personal history, which may include a chronological summary of the client's social and developmental history, medical history, education, family constellation, and employment information (if relevant). This information is typically obtained through interviews (with the client and relevant collateral sources) and records (e.g., school records, previous assessment results, intervention plans, court documents, health records). Although this section provides the context in which assessment results are interpreted, if the background information is not relevant to the referral problem and it is very personal, then counselors should consider carefully whether or not to include it in the report (Kamphaus & Frick, 2005). The report should not include hearsay, unverified opinions, generalized statements, or potentially harmful or damaging information.

BEHAVIORAL OBSERVATIONS This section covers observations that occurred during the assessment process and/or observations that occurred in other settings (e.g., the classroom, waiting room, playground, at home; Lichtenberger et al., 2004). Behaviors can be observed directly by the counselor, or observations can be provided indirectly by reports from teachers, parents, and others who have contact with the client. Examples of observations made during the assessment include physical appearance, ease of establishing and maintaining rapport with the client, language style (e.g., speed, pitch, volume, and rhythm of speech), attention span, distractibility, activity level, anxiety level, mood, attitude toward the assessment process, attitude toward the examiner, and unusual mannerisms or habits (Lichtenberger et al., 2004). Typically, behaviors are presented in the report if they had a positive or negative impact on the individual's performance during the assessment or on the individual's academic, social, or emotional functioning.

ASSESSMENT INSTRUMENTS AND PROCEDURES This section provides a brief description of the instruments and procedures used in the assessment process. Usually written in list form, reports may also identify the dates that the client and other relevant collateral sources (e.g., parents, teachers) were interviewed. This is followed by the names of any tests that were administered, including any formal methods of observation.

ASSESSMENT RESULTS AND INTERPRETATION The results of the instruments administered should be presented descriptively in this section. Only include results that are relevant to the assessment; it is not mandatory to describe every test score in this section of the report. In terms of format, assessment results can be organized by (a) domain, (b) ability, or (c) test. Using a *domain-oriented* approach, separate paragraphs are written on each domain of interest, such as intellectual ability, achievement, adaptive behavior, social or emotional functioning, and the like. Each paragraph may include data from multiple instruments and strategies. An *ability-oriented* format is similar to a domain-oriented approach, except that assessment results are organized based on specific abilities (e.g., memory, reasoning, visual-spatial ability, expressive language) rather than on general domains. The *test-oriented* format, the most commonly used organizational format, includes separate paragraphs that describe the results of each individual assessment instrument. In addition to reporting results using one of the three formats, counselors may also provide instrument data in a chart or graph format as an appendix.

　　After the assessment results are presented, they should be interpreted in a manner that is meaningful and relevant to the client, the referral source, and other relevant collateral sources. Discuss clinically significant findings, such as test scores that fall in the "clinical range." Report results that are supported by (a) scores on other assessment instruments, (b) behavioral observations that occurred both during the assessment and in other contexts, or (c) background information obtained from interviews with the client and collateral sources and/or from any documents or records (Lichtenberger et al., 2004). Try to explain any discrepancies across assessment instruments and strategies. Factors that may affect the validity or reliability of assessment results should also be addressed in this section, such as cultural differences, language factors, disabilities, health problems, and so on. It is important to remember that the focus of this section is on the individual being assessed, not simply the scores on assessment instruments.

　　Advancements in computer technology are changing the way professionals conduct assessments, including incorporating computer-based test interpretations (CBTIs) into the results and interpretation section of the written report. CBTIs convert an individual's test results into extensive narrative reports, which can provide several advantages to examiners: The reports may be more comprehensive than an individual examiner's reports, CBTIs save the examiner time in preparing reports, and CBTIs may provide more objective information. However, a central issue in the use of CBTIs is the accuracy of these interpretations. Another concern is that many of the lengthy narratives often appear valid (even if they are not valid) to untrained consumers and even to some professionals (Goldfinger & Pomerantz, 2013). Unqualified counselors may use these reports to compensate for a lack of training and experience. In addition, counselors may come to depend more on the CBTIs than on their own clinical judgment. There can be numerous problems with the interpretations made using CBTIs (Lichtenberger, 2006). Counselors should view CBTIs as a valuable adjunct to, rather than a substitute for, clinical judgment. In this light, counselors can incorporate the information from CBTIs into the results and interpretation section of the written report in the context of their own clinical judgment.

SUMMARY This section of the report integrates key information from each part of the report as well as the counselor's hypotheses or clinical impressions about the client. This section is particularly important; some may read only this section out of the entire written report. Counselors briefly restate the reason for referral, pertinent background information, behavioral observations, and test results and interpretations. The hypotheses or clinical impressions are a key element of this section because they help describe and clarify the nature of and reasons for the client's particular problems or concerns. All hypotheses and clinical impressions are based on and supported by multiple pieces of assessment information. A clear summary of the assessment is then provided that answers the referral questions using connections among the examinee's background information, behavior observations, and test results. Summaries are concise and should rarely exceed one page. New information is never included in the summary.

Abbreviated Assessment Report

Student: Sean
Date of Birth: 10/8/2006
Chronological Age: 8 years, 11 months
School: Middletown Elementary School
Grade: 1st grade
Date of Evaluation: 9/15/2015
Evaluator: Catherine Ramirez

Reason for Referral

Sean was referred for an evaluation to determine if he meets the criteria for a specific learning disability. Sean's teacher is concerned about whether Sean possesses adequate oral language skills.

Background Information

Sean's teacher indicated that he has difficulty expressing himself in class. When asked a question, he often has difficulty thinking of the appropriate word to use and struggles putting sentences together. In regards to behavior, Sean is generally well behaved and has no record of conduct problems.

Sean says that he enjoys school, and mathematics is his favorite subject. When not attending school or playing with friends, he spends time watching TV with his older brother.

Behavioral Observations

During the assessment, Sean was shy at first but quickly warmed up. His effort and cooperation during the assessment process were good.

Assessment Instruments

Wechsler Intelligence Scale for Children (WISC-V)
Expressive Vocabulary Test, Second Edition (EVT-2)
Peabody Picture Vocabulary Test (PPVT-4)

Assessment Results and Interpretation

Wechsler Intelligence Scale for Children (WISC-V)

Composite	Standard Score	Percentile Rank
Verbal Comprehension Index	96	39
Visual Spatial	95	37
Fluid Reasoning	103	58
Working Memory	95	37
Processing Speed Index	97	42
Full Scale IQ	97	42

The Wechsler Intelligence Scale for Children, Fifth Edition (WISC-V) was administered to assess Sean's general intellectual abilities. Sean's Full Scale IQ (97) and the Verbal Comprehension (96), Perceptual Reasoning (95), Working Memory (103), and Processing Speed (97) index scores are all within the average normal range. There are no significant differences between index scores, indicating no significant areas of cognitive strengths or weaknesses.

Expressive Vocabulary Test (EVT-2)

	Standard Score	Percentile Rank
EVT-2 Score	98	45

The Expressive Vocabulary Test, Second Edition (EVT-2) was administered to assess expressive language and word retrieval. Items consist of tasks in which the examiner presents a picture to the test taker, makes a statement or asks a question, and the test taker responds with a one-word answer. Sean obtained a standard score of 98, which is in the average range. This indicates that he is able to use a range of words typical of children his age. During the testing, he displayed some difficulty with word retrieval and struggled to recall the exact word he was looking for.

Peabody Picture Vocabulary Test (PPVT-4)

	Standard Score	Percentile Rank
PPVT-4 Score	90	25

The Peabody Picture Vocabulary Test, Fourth Edition (PPVT-4) was administered to measure Sean's receptive (hearing) vocabulary. The test consists of items that require test takers to select one picture (from a group of four pictures) that best represents the meaning of a word. Sean obtained a PPVT-4 standard score of 90, which is in the low average range for his age. This indicates that Sean has knowledge of basic vocabulary.

Summary

Sean was evaluated for a possible learning disability. In terms of cognitive abilities, Sean's scores are in the average range; there appears to be no cognitive issues interfering with his ability to learn. Sean performed in the low average to average range on tests assessing expressive and receptive language. He exhibits some weakness in rapid word retrieval, which is consistent with teacher reports and observations made during the assessment. However, he does not meet the criteria for a learning disability.

Recommendations

Sean's difficulty with recalling words may interfere with his ability to manage classroom assignments. He would benefit from regular classroom supports, such as allowing ample time when Sean is required to respond to questions, allowing Sean to speak without feeling rushed or being interrupted, and offering Sean prompts when he is struggling to recall a word.

Some reports written for medical or forensic settings often require evaluators to record a formal diagnosis from the *Diagnostic and Statistical Manual of Mental Disorders, Fifth Edition* (DSM-5; American Psychiatric Association (APA), 2013). The diagnosis can be written in sentence format.

RECOMMENDATIONS In this section, specific suggestions are offered regarding programs, strategies, and interventions that address the referral questions and improve outcomes for the individual being assessed. Recommendations vary based on the reason for referral as well as the setting where the assessment takes place. For example, recommendations for students in K–12 schools typically focus on behavioral interventions, instructional strategies, or other appropriate educational services (Lichtenberger et al., 2004). Recommendations for clients assessed in mental health clinics usually center on treatment recommendations based on the client's diagnosis. Note that some assessment reports also contain an appendix that includes any additional information or readings that the counselor wishes to share to help implement the recommendations—for example, information about a particular learning or emotional disorder, the pharmaceutical treatment of a particular disorder, or a specific technique to use for spelling instruction.

COMMUNICATING ASSESSMENT RESULTS TO OTHER PROFESSIONALS

Many times, a counselor is required to communicate test results to other professionals, such as teachers, principals, correctional officers, and judicial staff members. Not all of these professionals understand test information. Again, it is important to work cooperatively to establish good rapport and a working relationship based on mutual respect and recognition of joint proficiencies. Communication skills remain an important variable. Explanations should be clear and unambiguous. The American Counseling Association's Code of Ethics (American Counseling Association, 2014) calls for the examiner to understand the psychometric properties of instruments and to be able to interpret the results in light of those properties. Counselors are cautioned to ensure that the results of assessment are reported accurately and to the correct parties. Goldfinger and Pomerantz (2013) provided some basic guidelines for presenting assessment information to other professionals:

1. Find out exactly what information the recipient needs, what he or she plans to do with it, and what qualifications he or she has.
2. Make sure ethical and legal procedures are followed, such as securing a client's written permission to release information.
3. Check to see whether procedures have been established for test information. Normally, a policy is already in force.
4. Aim the report as directly as possible to the particular question asked. This practice saves time and provides clear communication of needed information.

COMMUNICATING ASSESSMENT RESULTS TO THE PUBLIC

When test results are released to the news media, those responsible for releasing the results should provide information to help minimize the probability of misinterpretation. The current movement toward accountability has influenced the use and reporting of test data by the schools. Administrators like to use norm- and criterion-referenced test data to show that the schools are accomplishing the educational goals of society. However, many people have trouble understanding the concepts used in measurement and the many different types of derived scores test makers report. Test data, when properly presented, can be a useful tool in interpreting the school system for the community.

Dear Parents,

Within the next few weeks, your child will be taking the Stanford Achievement Test Series, Tenth Edition (Stanford 10). The Stanford 10 is a norm-referenced standardized test. This means that your child's scores will be compared to the scores of thousands of other children in the same grade who also took the test. The Stanford 10 includes many of the subjects that your child is taught in school. Please note that a student does not pass or fail the Stanford 10. Test results help show what a student knows about a subject and how the teacher can best help the student to learn.

Included in this letter are several sample test items. We recommend that you share these sample questions with your child so he or she will know what to expect. The teacher will also be reviewing sample questions before the Stanford 10 is given.

You can help your child prepare for the test-taking experience by following some simple suggestions:

1. Each child should have a good night's sleep prior to a testing day. We suggest 10 hours of sleep.
2. Each child should have a good, well-balanced breakfast before coming to school on a testing day.
3. Conflicts and arguments should be avoided. A child's emotional state has great influence on performance.
4. Make sure your child understands that the Stanford 10 scores simply provide information. Scores will not be used to reward or punish students.

If you have any questions or suggestions, please do not hesitate to contact the school office, in person or by telephone. We have appreciated your assistance and support throughout the year.

Sincerely,
School Counselor

FIGURE 16.3   Sample letter of information for parents.

Communication with the public should follow these general procedures:

1. Communication should take place before and after testing. News releases can announce a test, and letters and cards can be sent to the parents or guardians. An example of such a letter is shown in Figure 16.3. Reports of test results can be made through the local media or can be presented at PTA or community meetings.
2. Because most citizens are not familiar with test jargon and statistical terms, the results should be presented as simply as possible while still remaining accurate and honest.
3. Percentile bands or stanines can be reported graphically or visually using handouts, transparencies, or slides.
4. Data should be presented in summary form—for example, by grade rather than by teacher.
5. Statistical and measurement terms can be defined in nontechnical language, with examples provided.
6. The public is not stupid and should not be treated with condescension.

Any oral or written communication should include the following components:

1. A general description of the tests or testing program
2. Uses of the test results
3. Types of skills and competencies measured
4. Types of scores reported and the meaning of those scores
5. Type of norms used

6. Definitions and examples of the summary statistics and measurement concepts needed to understand the presentation
7. The results with appropriate comparisons (national, state, district, and school; year-to-year changes; or grade by grade)
8. Factors that might have influenced the results

An oral presentation requires time for questions. The examiner should be prepared to answer the following types of questions about major issues:

- Are these tests biased against minority and disadvantaged students?
- Why do we test so much?
- Why are some schools in the system achieving higher results than others in the system?
- Are teachers influenced by the test results?

Summary

Communicating assessment results is the final step of the assessment process. Once the assessment process is complete and results are analyzed and interpreted, professionals have the responsibility of communicating the results to those individuals entitled to the information, such as the client, parents (if the examinee is a minor), and other professionals involved with the examinee (e.g., teachers, school administrators, mental health professionals).

Feedback sessions are meetings that counselors schedule with the client to disclose assessment results. The sessions serve to review and clarify assessment results, to acquire additional information relevant to the assessment process, to educate the client (and family) about what the results mean, and to provide recommendations. Written assessment reports are also used to communicate assessment findings. Reports integrate information obtained from interviews with the client, test results, observations, and any information obtained from collateral sources. The central objectives of assessment reports are to describe the individual being assessed, answer the referral questions, organize and interpret the data, and recommend interventions related to the original reason for referral.

Questions for Discussion

1. What are the major problem areas in disseminating results to the test taker? To parents?
2. How would you improve a client's readiness to hear test results?
3. How would you explain negative test results to a client?

4. Do you agree that professionals should be extremely careful about interpreting test results for individuals from diverse backgrounds? Why or why not?
5. If you could choose the way you were to receive your test results, what approach would you choose? Why?

Suggested Activities

1. Interview school counselors, mental health counselors, career counselors, or psychologists who use tests frequently. Find out how they communicate assessment results to their clients and their approaches to problems such as client acceptance of results, examinee readiness, negative results, flat profiles, and examinee motivation and attitude. Report your findings to class.

2. Conduct simulated feedback sessions in which a student portrays a "counselor" communicating test results to (a) a "parent" (also played by a student) and then to (b) an adult "client." Videotape the sessions.

3. Devise a workshop for a group of individuals in your field who need help in communicating test results.

4. Role-play a situation in which you have to consult a helping professional on testing problems or results. For example, a teacher might want to know how she can help her students improve their test scores because she is afraid that she will lose her job if the class does not do well on achievement tests, or a doctor might want to know whether a child shows any signs of learning disabilities and how that information could be relayed to the child's parents.

5. Read the following case study and answer the questions at the end:

Mary's mother was very concerned when she received her second grader's scores on the Stanford Achievement Test. Mary scored at the 99th percentile on Total Mathematics but only at the 81st on Total Reading. Mary scored at the 95th percentile on Spelling but at the 45th on Language and 54th on Science. She had been tested for the gifted program and was accepted by virtue of a 133 score on the Stanford–Binet Intelligence Scale. Mary's mother can't make any sense out of the test scores and wants the teachers and counselors to help her daughter improve her scores.

a. How would you approach a feedback session with Mary's mother?
b. What would you tell her about the test results?

6. Read the following case study and answer the questions at the end:

Albert, a 23-year-old male, would like help in understanding his results on the Self-Directed Search (SDS) and the Myers–Briggs Type Indicator (MBTI). You find out that Albert dropped out of school in the 10th grade and is enrolled in a high school equivalency program. He's held numerous jobs in the food service industry but has been unable to keep them. He has a wife and three children and realizes that he needs further training and education to support his family. He is an ISFJ on the MBTI and an ARS on the SDS.

a. How would you communicate Albert's assessment results to him?
b. What would you tell him about the test results?

References

Ackerman, M. J. (2006). Forensic report writing. *Journal of Clinical Psychology, 62*, 59–72.

American Counseling Association. (2014). *ACA Code of Ethics*. Alexandria, VA: Author.

American Psychiatric Association (APA). (2013). *Diagnostic and statistical manual of mental disorders* (5th ed.). Washington, DC: Author.

Carr, A., & McNulty, M. (2014). Intake interviews, testing, and report writing. In A. Carr & M. McNulty (Eds.), *The Handbook of Adult Clinical Psychology: An Evidence Based Practice Approach* (pp. 253–288). New York, NY: Routledge.

Cohen, R. J., Swerdlik, M. E., & Sturman, E. D. (2012). *Psychological testing and assessment: An introduction to tests and measurement* (8th ed.). Boston, MA: McGraw-Hill.

Donders, J. (2001). A survey of report writing by neuropsychologists, II: Test data, report format, and document length. *The Clinical Neuropsychologist, 15*, 150–161.

Engelhard, G., Jr., & Wind, S. A. (2013). Educational testing and schooling: Unanticipated consequences of purposive social action. *Measurement: Interdisciplinary Research and Perspectives, 11*(1–2), 30–35.

Gati, I., & Amir, T. (2010). Applying a Systemic Procedure to Locate Career Decision-Making Difficulties. *The Career Development Quarterly, 58*(4), 301–320.

Goldfinger, K., & Pomerantz, A. M. (2013). *Psychological assessment and report writing*. Thousand Oaks, CA: Sage.

Groth-Marnat, G., & Horvath, L. W. (2006). The psychological report: A review of current controversies. *Journal of Clinical Psychology, 62*, 73–81.

Gunn, J., & Taylor, P. (2014). *Forensic psychiatry: Clinical, legal, and ethical issues*. Boca Raton, FL: CRC Press.

Joint Committee on Testing Practices. (2004). *Code of fair testing practices in education*. Washington, DC: Author.

Kamphaus, R. W., & Frick, P. J. (2005). *Clinical assessment of child and adolescent personality and behavior* (2nd ed.). New York, NY: Springer.

Lichtenberger, E. O. (2006). Computer utilization and clinical judgment in psychological assessment reports. *Journal of Clinical Psychology, 62*(1), 19–32.

Lichtenberger, E. O., Mather, N., Kaufman, N. L., & Kaufman, A. S. (2004). *Essentials of assessment report writing*. Hoboken, NJ: John Wiley and Sons.

Miller, M. D., Linn, R. L., & Gronlund, N. E. (2011). *Measurement and assessment in teaching* (11th ed.). Upper Saddle River, NJ: Pearson.

Reynolds, C. R., Livingston, R. B., Willson, V. L., & Willson, V. (2010). *Measurement and assessment in education*. Upper Saddle River, NJ: Pearson.

Sattler, J. M., & Hoge, R. D. (2006). *Assessment of children: Behavioral, social, and clinical foundations* (5th ed.). San Diego, CA: Jerome M. Sattler Publisher Inc.

Schwean, V. L., Oakland, T., Weiss, L. G., Saklofske, D. H., Holdnack, J. A., & Profitera, A. (2006). Report writing: A child-centered approach. In L. G. Weiss, D. H. Saklofske, A. Prifitera, & J. A. Holdnack (Eds.), *WISC-IV advanced clinical interpretation* (pp. 371–420). Boston, MA: Academic Press.

Urbina, S. (2014). *Essentials of psychological testing* (Vol. 4, 2nd ed.). Hoboken, NJ: John Wiley & Sons.

Wiener, J., & Costaris, L. (2012). Teaching psychological report writing: Content and process. *Canadian Journal of School Psychology, 27*(2), 119–135. doi: 10.1177/0829573511418484

17 Ethical and Legal Issues in Assessment

Professional standards and codes of ethics express the values on which counselors build their practice and provide a framework for responsible test use. There are probably as many codes of ethics as there are professional societies, but to become effective helping professionals, individuals must be committed to the ethical standards of their profession and follow them in their practice. In addition to ethical codes, a number of laws at both the state and national level affect assessment and testing practices. Counselors need to be familiar with the statutes, regulations, and court decisions that have implications for assessment. Although this is the final chapter in the textbook, it is a topic that is integral to each and every chapter. We considered placing this chapter toward the beginning of the book, but we believe that you must develop an understanding of the basics of assessment before you can understand how to ethically and legally apply your understanding. Some of you may read this chapter earlier in a course on measurement and assessment, whereas others will read it at the end of a graduate course. Regardless of when you read the chapter, we strongly suggest integrating the material into your understanding of the assessment process.

After studying this chapter, you should be able to:

- Identify and describe the ethical standards of professional organizations related to assessment.
- Explain the importance of professional training and competence in assessment and summarize the guidelines for the competencies of test users.
- Summarize the professional standards for test-user qualifications.
- Discuss the issue of client welfare in assessment.
- List and describe the statutes and regulations that impact assessment practice.
- List and describe the judicial decisions affecting employment and educational assessment.

PROFESSIONAL STANDARDS AND CODES OF ETHICS

Because of the impact of assessment on society and lives, professional standards and ethical codes have been developed to promote responsible professional practice in psychological testing and assessment. Ethics can be viewed as moral principles adopted by an individual or group that provide the basis for right conduct. Most governing bodies associated with psychological and educational assessment have established codes of ethics for their members to follow. These codes provide guidelines for professionals but do not provide answers to *all* ethical dilemmas. Thus, it is up to individual professionals in the field to reflect on their behavior and assess whether what they're doing is in the best interest of their clients. Several professional organizations have ethical standards that relate specifically to assessment. Our discussion will center on the following:

- American Counseling Association—*Code of Ethics*
- American Educational Research Association (AERA), the American Psychological Association (APA), and the National Council on Measurement in Education (NCME)—*Standards for Educational and Psychological Testing*
- American Psychological Association (APA)—*Ethical Principles of Psychologists and Code of Conduct*
- Association for Assessment in Counseling (AAC)—*Responsibilities of Users of Standardized Tests, Third Edition (RUST)*
- Joint Committee on Testing Practices—*Code of Fair Testing Practices in Education*
- National Council on Measurement in Education—*Code of Professional Responsibilities in Educational Measurement*

American Counseling Association Code of Ethics

The ACA is a professional organization with members who work in a variety of settings and serve in multiple capacities. The *ACA Code of Ethics* (American Counseling Association (ACA), 2014) serves to clarify the ethical responsibilities of its members as well as describe best practices in the counseling profession. The *Code* is divided into eight main sections that address key ethical issues; Section E, Evaluation, Assessment, and Interpretation, focuses specifically on assessment (see Table 17.1 for a portion of this section of the code. For a full version, see counseling.org/resources/aca-code-of-ethics.pdf). The ACA emphasizes that counselors should use assessment instruments as one component of the counseling process, taking into account the client's personal and cultural context.

AERA, APA, and NCME Standards for Educational and Psychological Testing

One of the most comprehensive documents on assessment standards is the *Standards for Educational and Psychological Testing* (American Educational Research Association (AERA), American Psychological Association (APA), & National Council on Measurement in Education (NCME), 2014). This document—which we will refer to as the *Standards*—represents the seventh in a series of publications that originated in 1954. It provides test developers and test users with assistance in evaluating the technical adequacy of their instruments for educational and psychological assessment. The intent of the *Standards* is to promote the sound and ethical use of tests and to provide criteria for the evaluation of tests, testing practices, and the effects of test use. We recommend that anyone who routinely engages in any form of testing—from test design and implementation to assessment and evaluation—obtain a copy of the *Standards* and become

TABLE 17.1 ACA Code of Ethics Section E.1 to E.4: Evaluation, Assessment, and Interpretation

Counselors use assessment as one component of the counseling process, taking into account the clients' personal and cultural context. Counselors promote the well-being of individual clients or groups of clients by developing and using appropriate educational, mental health, psychological, and career assessments.

E.1. General

E.1.a. Assessment

The primary purpose of educational, mental health, psychological, and career assessment is to gather information regarding the client for a variety of purposes, including, but not limited to, client decision making, treatment planning, and forensic proceedings. Assessment may include both qualitative and quantitative methodologies.

E.1.b. Client Welfare

Counselors do not misuse assessment results and interpretations, and they take reasonable steps to prevent others from misusing the information provided. They respect the client's right to know the results, the interpretations made, and the basis for counselors' conclusions and recommendations.

E.2. Competence to Use and Interpret Assessment Instruments

E.2.a. Limits of Competence

Counselors use only those testing and assessment services for which they have been trained and are competent. Counselors using technology-assisted test interpretations are trained in the construct being measured and the specific instrument being used prior to using its technology-based application. Counselors take reasonable measures to ensure the proper use of assessment techniques by persons under their supervision.

E.2.b. Appropriate Use

Counselors are responsible for the appropriate application, scoring, interpretation, and use of assessment instruments relevant to the needs of the client, whether they score and interpret such assessments themselves or use technology or other services.

E.2.c. Decisions Based on Results

Counselors responsible for decisions involving individuals or policies that are based on assessment results have a thorough understanding of psychometrics.

E.3. Informed Consent in Assessment

E.3.a. Explanation to Clients

Prior to assessment, counselors explain the nature and purposes of assessment and the specific use of results by potential recipients. The explanation will be given in terms and language that the client (or other legally authorized person on behalf of the client) can understand.

E.3.b. Recipients of Results

Counselors consider the client's and/or examinee's welfare, explicit understandings, and prior agreements in determining who receives the assessment results. Counselors include accurate and appropriate interpretations with any release of individual or group assessment results.

E.4. Release of Data to Qualified Personnel

Counselors release assessment data in which the client is identified only with the consent of the client or the client's legal representative. Such data are released only to persons recognized by counselors as qualified to interpret the data.

Source: Reprinted from the ACA *Code of Ethics.* Copyright © 2014 The American Counseling Association. Reprinted with permission. No further reproduction authorized without written permission from the American Counseling Association.

familiar with the guidelines. The current edition of the *Standards* is organized into three parts:

1. *Foundations* This section contains standards for validity, reliability/precision and errors of measurement, and fairness in testing. The subsections discuss standards related to test development and revision; scaling, norming, and score comparability; test administration, scoring, and reporting; and supporting documentation for tests. According to the *Standards*, "validity is … the most fundamental consideration in developing tests and evaluating tests" (AERA et al., 2014, p. 11). As such, the *Standards* addresses the different types of validity evidence needed to support test use. In addition, standards on reliability and errors of measurement address the issue of consistency of test scores. Although the *Standards* supports standardized procedures, it recognizes the need to consider fairness and testing. According to the *Standards*, special situations may arise in which modifications of the procedures may be advisable or legally mandated; for example, a person with a vision impairment may need a larger print version of a standardized test. Standards for the development and revision of formal, published instruments, an often overlooked area of importance, describe criteria important for scale construction.

   The first section of the *Standards* focuses heavily on fairness and bias, the rights and responsibilities of test takers, testing individuals of diverse linguistic backgrounds, and testing individuals with disabilities. This section emphasizes the importance of fairness in all aspects of testing and assessment. According to the standards, fairness is a foundational construct that impacts validity. Fairness should be considered in all aspects of test use. Special attention to issues related to individuals of diverse linguistic backgrounds or with disabilities may be needed when developing, administering, scoring, interpreting, and making decisions based on test scores.

2. *Operations* The second section of the standards relates to test design and development; scores, scales, norms, score linking, and cut scores; test administration, scoring reporting, and supporting documentation for tests; the rights and responsibilities of test takers; and the rights and responsibilities of test users. This section of the *Standards* addresses the more technical and psychometric aspects of assessment. As professional counselors, it will be important to carefully review Part II and to develop a strong understanding of how these standards apply in practice.

3. *Testing Applications* The third section of the *Standards* provides an overview of psychological testing and assessment; workplace testing and credentialing; educational testing and assessment; and uses of tests for program evaluation, policy studies, and accountability. This section provides specific guidance on the general responsibilities of test users in each area. One of the new elements of the *Standards* is accountability. This final section provides specific guidance for test users on evaluation of programs and policy initiatives, test-based accountability systems, and issues in program and policy evaluation and accountability.

American Psychological Association Ethical Principles of Psychologists and Code of Conduct

The *APA Ethical Principles of Psychologists and Code of Conduct* (American Psychological Association (APA), 2002) consists of several ethical standards set forth as rules of conduct for psychologists. Section 9 specifically addresses 11 issues related to assessment.

The first standard (Standard 9.01) states that psychologists should base recommendations on information and techniques sufficient to substantiate their findings. Standard 9.02 addresses the importance of using valid and reliable assessment techniques as evidenced by research. The third standard states that psychologists must obtain informed consent when using assessment techniques; this includes explaining the nature and purpose of the assessment, fees, involvement of third parties, and limits of confidentiality. The fourth standard asserts that psychologists must not release a client's test results unless the client gives permission; in the absence of client permission, psychologists provide test data only as required by law or court order. Standard 9.05 refers to ethical procedures involved in test construction. The sixth standard addresses test interpretation and psychologists' need to explain results in the language that can be understood by the individual being assessed. The seventh standard emphasizes psychologists' responsibility of not promoting the use of psychological assessment techniques by unqualified examiners. Standard 9.08 emphasizes the importance of not using obsolete tests or outdated test results; that is, psychologists must refrain from basing their assessment, intervention decisions, or recommendations on outdated test results and measures that are not useful for the current purpose. Standards 9.09 and 9.10 refer to scoring and interpreting tests and explaining assessment results. Individuals offering assessment or scoring services to other professionals have the obligation to make sure their procedures are appropriate, valid, and reliable. In explaining assessment results, psychologists must ensure that explanations are given by appropriate individuals or services. The 11th and final standard holds the psychologist responsible for making reasonable efforts to maintain the integrity and security of tests and other assessment techniques consistent with the law, contractual obligations, and the code of ethics.

Association for Assessment and Research in Counseling Responsibilities of Users of Standardized Tests, Third Edition

The Association for Assessment in Counseling (AAC; now called the Association for Assessment and Research in Counseling [AARC]), a division of the ACA, is an organization of counselors, counselor educators, and other professionals that provides leadership, training, and research in the creation, development, production, and use of assessment and diagnostic techniques in the counseling profession. The organization is responsible for developing the *Responsibilities of Users of Standardized Tests* (RUST; AARC, 2003), which promotes the accurate, fair, and responsible use of standardized tests by the counseling and education communities, including counselors, teachers, administrators, and other human service workers (see Appendix II). RUST addresses several areas related to test-user qualifications, including the following: qualifications of test users, technical knowledge, test selection, test administration, test scoring, interpreting test results, and communicating test results. RUST emphasizes that qualified test users (a) have appropriate education, training, and experience in using tests and (b) adhere to the highest degree of ethical codes, laws, and standards governing professional practice. Lack of qualifications or ethical and legal compliance can lead to errors and subsequent harm to clients. Individual test users are responsible for obtaining appropriate education, training, or professional supervision when engaged in testing.

Joint Committee on Testing Practices Code of Fair Testing Practices in Education

The *Code of Fair Testing Practices in Education* (2004) is a guide for professionals who engage in testing in education. It was prepared by the Joint Committee on Testing Practices, which includes members from the ACA, the AERA, the APA, the American Speech-Language-Hearing Association (ASHA), the National Association of School Psychologists (NASP), the National Association of Test Directors (NATD), and the National Council on Measurement in Education (NCME). The code emphasizes *fairness* as the primary consideration in all aspects of testing. Professionals are obligated to provide and use tests that are fair to all test takers, regardless of age, gender, disability, race, ethnicity, national origin, religion, sexual orientation, linguistic background, or other personal characteristics. In this regard, the *Code* provides guidance for test developers and test users in four areas:

1. Developing and selecting appropriate tests
2. Administering and scoring tests
3. Reporting and interpreting test results
4. Informing test takers

National Council on Measurement in Education Code of Professional Responsibilities in Educational Measurement

The NCME published its *Code of Professional Responsibilities in Educational Measurement* (CPR) in 1995. The council developed the CPR to promote professionally responsible practices in educational assessment. The CPR provides a framework of eight major areas of assessment standards that focus on the responsibilities of those who do the following:

1. Develop assessment products and services
2. Market and sell assessment products and services
3. Select assessment products and services
4. Administer assessments
5. Score assessments
6. Interpret, use, and communicate assessment results
7. Educate others about assessment
8. Evaluate educational programs and conduct research on assessments

Each section includes more specific standards. In Section 6, for example, those who interpret, use, and communicate assessment results are to provide all needed information about the assessment, its purposes, and its uses for the proper interpretation of the results; provide an understandable discussion of all reported scores, including proper interpretations; promote the use of multiple sources of information about persons or programs in making educational decisions; communicate the adequacy and appropriateness of any norms or standards being used in the interpretation of assessment results and any likely misinterpretations; and protect the rights of privacy for individuals and institutions.

ETHICAL ISSUES IN ASSESSMENT

Currently, ethical issues receive widespread attention from professionals who use psychological and educational tests. Similar themes are contained in all of the codes—for example, professional training and competence, test-user qualifications, client welfare issues, and fairness in assessment.

Professional Training and Competence

One of the most important ethical issues is the competency of the professional in the use of available assessment instruments. Professionals must be qualified to select, administer, score, and interpret tests. Different tests require different levels of competency. Some tests that require a high level of skill include the Wechsler scales, the Thematic Apperception Test, and the Rorschach. The professional standards of several professional associations have set explicit guidelines for the competencies of tests users; the following is a summary of these guidelines:

1. Understand basic measurement concepts, such as scales of measurement, types of reliability, types of validity, and types of norms.
2. Understand the basic statistics of measurement and define, compute, and interpret measures of central tendency, variability, and relationship.
3. Compute and apply measurement formulas, such as the standard error of measurement and the Spearman–Brown prophecy formula.
4. Read, evaluate, and understand test manuals and reports.
5. Follow exactly as specified the procedures for administering, scoring, and interpreting a test.
6. List and discuss major tests in their fields.
7. Identify and locate sources of test information in their fields.
8. Discuss and demonstrate the use of different systems of presenting test data in tabular and graphic forms.
9. Compare and contrast different types of test scores and discuss their strengths and weaknesses.
10. Explain the relative nature of norm-referenced interpretation and the use of the standard error of measurement in interpreting individual scores.
11. Help test takers and counselees to use tests as exploratory tools.
12. Aid test takers and counselees in their decision making and in their accomplishment of developmental tasks.
13. Pace an interpretative session to enhance clients' knowledge of test results.
14. Use strategies to prepare clients for testing to maximize the accuracy of test results.
15. Explain test results to test takers thoughtfully and accurately and in a language they understand.
16. Use the communication skills needed in test interpretation and identify strategies for presenting the results to individuals, groups, parents, students, teachers, and professionals.
17. Shape clients' reaction to and encourage appropriate use of the test information.
18. Be alert to the verbal and nonverbal cues expressed by clients, not only in the testing situation but also during feedback situations.
19. Use appropriate strategies with clients who perceive the test results as negative.
20. Be familiar with the test interpretation forms and computerized report forms in order to guide clients through the information and explanation.
21. Be familiar with the legal, professional, and ethical guidelines related to testing.
22. Be aware of clients' rights and the professional's responsibilities as a test administrator and counselor.
23. List and discuss the current issues and trends in testing.
24. Present results from tests both verbally and in written form, and know what types of information should be presented in case studies and conferences.
25. Discuss and utilize strategies to assist an individual in acquiring test-taking skills and in lowering test anxiety.
26. Identify and discuss computer-assisted and computer-adaptive testing and show application to their fields.

Test-User Qualifications

According to the International Test Commission (2013), competence is a key facet in qualifying individuals for test use. The concept of *test-user qualifications* refers to the necessary knowledge, skills, abilities, training, and credentials for using tests (Oakland, 2012). The issue of test-user qualifications remains controversial. Although some professional groups advocate restricting the use of psychological tests to psychologists only, others believe firmly that one's qualifications to use tests is directly related to competence, not to a specific professional field, and competence can be achieved through various means, such as education, training, and experience in the use of tests. Internationally, competence-based assessment practice is considered the standard over specific licenses or degrees. According to the International Test Commission (ITC), responsible test users work within the limits of scientific principle and substantiated experience; set and maintain high personal standards of competence; know the limits of their own competence and operate within those limits; and keep up with relevant changes and advances relating to the tests they use and to test development, including changes in legislation and policy, which may impact on tests and test use (2013). The ACA (2003) also developed a set of standards for test user qualification, the *Standards for the Qualifications of Test Users*, which states that professional counselors are qualified to use tests and assessments in counseling practice to the degree that they possess the appropriate knowledge and skills (see Table 17.2).

The purchase of tests is generally restricted to persons who meet certain minimum qualifications. Most test publishers rely on a three-level system for classifying test-user qualifications that was first developed by APA in 1950. The APA later dropped the classification system in 1974, but many publishers continue to use this or a similar system. The classification includes the following levels:

A Level Test users are *not* required to have advanced training in the test administration and interpretation to purchase A-level tests. They may have a bachelor's degree in psychology, human services, education, or related disciplines; training or certification relevant to assessment; or practical experience in the use of tests. Examples of A-level tests include some aptitude and career exploration tests.

B Level To use B-level tests, practitioners typically have a graduate degree in psychology, counseling, education, or related disciplines; have completed specialized training or coursework in testing; or have licensure or certification documenting training and experience in testing. In addition, being a member of a professional organization, such as ASHA or the American Occupational Therapy Association (AOTA), may make one eligible to purchase B-level products. Examples of B-level tests include general intelligence tests and interest inventories.

C Level C-level tests require users to have B-level qualifications plus a doctorate degree in psychology or a related discipline (that provides appropriate training in the administration and interpretation of tests), licensure or certification, or to be under the direct supervision of a qualified professional in psychology or a related field. Examples of C-level tests include intelligence tests, personality tests, and projective measures (e.g., the Wechsler Intelligence Scale for Children [WISC-IV], the Minnesota Multiphasic Personality Inventory [MMPI-II], the Rorschach Inkblot Test).

TABLE 17.2 ACA Standards for the Qualifications of Test Users

1. Skill in practice and knowledge of theory relevant to the testing context and type of counseling specialty

Assessment and testing must be integrated into the context of the theory and knowledge of a specialty area, not as a separate act, role, or entity. In addition, professional counselors should be skilled in treatment practice with the population being served.

2. A thorough understanding of testing theory, techniques of test construction, and test reliability and validity

Included in this knowledge base are methods of item selection, theories of human nature that underlie a given test, reliability, and validity. Knowledge of reliability includes, at a minimum, methods by which it is determined, such as domain sampling, test-retest, parallel forms, split-half, and interitem consistency; the strengths and limitations of each of these methods; the standard error of measurement, which indicates how accurately a person's test score reflects their true score of the trait being measured; and true score theory, which defines a test score as an estimate of what is true. Knowledge of validity includes, at a minimum, types of validity, including content, criterion-related (both predictive and concurrent), and construct methods of assessing each type of validity, including the use of correlation; and the meaning and significance of standard error of estimate.

3. A working knowledge of sampling techniques, norms, and descriptive, correlational, and predictive statistics

Important topics in sampling include sample size, sampling techniques, and the relationship between sampling and test accuracy. A working knowledge of descriptive statistics includes, at a minimum, probability theory; measures of central tendency; multimodal and skewed distributions; measures of variability, including variance and standard deviation; and standard scores, including deviation IQs, z scores, T scores, percentile ranks, stanines/stens, normal curve equivalents, and grade and age equivalents. Knowledge of correlation and prediction includes, at a minimum, the principle of least squares, the direction and magnitude of relationship between two sets of scores, deriving a regression equation, the relationship between regression and correlation, and the most common procedures and formulas used to calculate correlations.

4. Ability to review, select, and administer tests appropriate for clients or students and the context of the counseling practice

Professional counselors using tests should be able to describe the purpose and use of different types of tests, including the most widely used tests for their setting and purposes. Professional counselors use their understanding of sampling, norms, test construction, validity, and reliability to accurately assess the strengths, limitations, and appropriate applications of a test for the clients being served. Professional counselors using tests also should be aware of the potential for error when relying on computer printouts of test interpretation. For accuracy of interpretation, technological resources must be augmented by a counselor's firsthand knowledge of the client and the test-taking context.

5. Skill in administration of tests and interpretation of test scores

Competent test users implement appropriate and standardized administration procedures. This requirement enables professional counselors to provide consultation and training to others who assist with test administration and scoring. In addition to standardized procedures, test users provide testing environments that are comfortable and free of distraction. Skilled interpretation requires a strong working knowledge of the theory underlying the test, the test's purpose, the statistical meaning of test scores, and the norms used in test construction. Skilled interpretation also requires an understanding of the similarities and differences between the client or student and the norm samples used in test construction. Finally, it is essential that clear and accurate communication of test score meaning in oral or written form to clients, students, or appropriate others be provided.

(continued)

TABLE 17.2 ACA Standards for the Qualifications of Test Users   (*Continued*)

6. Knowledge of the impact of diversity on testing accuracy, including age, gender, ethnicity, race, disability, and linguistic differences

Professional counselors using tests should be committed to fairness in every aspect of testing. Information gained and decisions made about the client or student are valid only to the degree that the test accurately and fairly assesses the client's or student's characteristics. Test selection and interpretation are done with an awareness of the degree to which items may be culturally biased or the norming sample not reflective or inclusive of the client's or student's diversity. Test users understand that age and physical disability differences may impact the client's ability to perceive and respond to test items. Test scores are interpreted in light of the cultural, ethnic, disability, or linguistic factors that may impact an individual's score. These include visual, auditory, and mobility disabilities that may require appropriate accommodation in test administration and scoring. Test users understand that certain types of norms and test score interpretation may be inappropriate, depending on the nature and purpose of the testing.

7. Knowledge and skill in the professionally responsible use of assessment and evaluation practice

Professional counselors who use tests act in accordance with the ACA's *Code of Ethics* and *Standards of Practice* (1997), *Responsibilities of Users of Standardized Tests* (AAC, 2003), *Code of Fair Testing Practices in Education* (JCTP, 2002), *Rights and Responsibilities of Test Takers: Guidelines and Expectations* (JCTP, 2000), and *Standards for Educational and Psychological Testing* (AERA et al., 1999). In addition, professional school counselors act in accordance with the American School Counselor Association's (ASCA's) Ethical Standards for School Counselors (ASCA, 1992). Test users should understand the legal and ethical principles and practices regarding test security, using copyrighted materials, and unsupervised use of assessment instruments that are not intended for self-administration. When using and supervising the use of tests, qualified test users demonstrate an acute understanding of the paramount importance of the well-being of clients and the confidentiality of test scores. Test users seek ongoing educational and training opportunities to maintain competence and acquire new skills in assessment and evaluation.

Source: Reprinted from *Standards for the Qualifications of Test Users,* Copyright © 2003 The American Counseling Association. Reprinted with permission. No further reproduction authorized without written permission from the American Counseling Association.

Client Welfare Issues

A major concern is whether the welfare of the client is taken into consideration in the choice and use of tests. Lack of confidentiality and invasion of privacy in testing are viewed as minor problems in the field of education but are seen as a more serious problem in psychology. It is important for professionals to have informed consent before testing the individual or releasing the results to a third party. Individuals have become suspicious about the possible "downloading" of information by unauthorized users.

LEGAL ISSUES IN ASSESSMENT

In addition to ethical codes, state and national laws also regulate assessment. There are several sources of laws:

- *Statutes* Laws written by legislative bodies
- *Regulations* Laws created by government agencies
- *Judicial Decisions* Laws created by opinions from the court, often in litigation cases

Professionals need to stay informed of the major laws that affect assessment. We will begin by presenting statutes and regulations that have implications for assessment and several judicial decisions brought about from cases involving litigation.

Statutes and Regulations

Assessment is a regulated professional activity, and counselors using assessment should be aware of the laws and rules that impact the practice of assessment. Both federal and state laws govern the practice of assessment and the use of assessment results. As such, counselors should be fully aware of the legal guidelines for assessment and take extreme care to practice within those guidelines. Although we review several statutes and regulations related to assessment, there are many more. Counselors are responsible for knowing all legal requirements for assessment practice and should recognize the potential for serious consequences related to violation of any laws or regulations.

AMERICANS WITH DISABILITIES ACT OF 1990 The Americans with Disabilities Act (ADA) was passed by Congress and signed into law on July 26, 1990. The law was passed for the purpose of reducing discrimination and making everyday life more accessible to the over 43 million Americans who have some form of disability. The ADA defines a disability as a physical or mental impairment that substantially limits a major life activity (U.S.C. Title 42 Chapter 126 Section 12102 [2]). The ADA states that an employment agency or labor organization shall not discriminate against individuals with a disability. This applies to job application procedures, hiring, advancement and discharge of employees, worker's compensation, job training, and other terms, conditions, and privileges of employment.

The law has certain provisions related to employment assessment. Under the reasonable accommodations section, it states the following:

> A private entity offering an examination is responsible for selecting and administering the examination in a place and manner that ensures that the examination accurately reflects an individual's aptitude and achievement level, or other factors the examination purports to measure, rather than reflecting an individual's impaired sensory, manual, or speaking skills, except where those skills are factors that the examination purports to measure. (Section III.4.6100)

In other words, employers cannot select and administer an employment test if a particular disability adversely affects an individual's performance on that test. This means that to comply with the ADA, individuals with disabilities must be assessed using "reasonable accommodations"—that is, appropriate changes and adjustments in test-administration procedures. It is important to remember that when any modification is made to a standardized test, results should be interpreted cautiously, recognizing that modification can jeopardize validity. Examples of modifications include the following:

- Extending testing time
- Providing written materials in large print, Braille, or audiotape
- Providing readers or sign language interpreters
- Holding test administration in accessible locations
- Using assistive devices

CIVIL RIGHTS ACT OF 1991 Title VII of the Civil Rights Act of 1964—amended in 1971, 1978, and 1991—outlaws discrimination in employment based on race, color, religion, gender, pregnancy, or national origin. The original legislation created the Equal Opportunity Commission (EEOC), which was charged with developing guidelines to regulate equal employment. In the 1970s, the EEOC developed strict guidelines involving the use of employment tests. The guidelines stated that all formal assessment instruments used for employment decisions that may adversely affect hiring, promotion, or other employment opportunity for classes protected by Title VII constitutes discrimination unless the test can demonstrate "a reasonable measure of job performance" (i.e., validity).

An example of problems with employment tests and potential discrimination is the landmark case of *Griggs v. Duke Power Company* (1971). The case involved African American employees of a private power company who filed suit against the company, claiming that the criterion for promotion, such as requiring high school diplomas and passing scores on standardized tests (i.e., the Wonderlic Personnel Test and the Bennett Mechanical Comprehension Test), were discriminatory. The U.S. Supreme Court decided that Duke Power violated Title VII of the Civil Rights Act because the standardized testing requirement prevented a disproportionate number of African American employees from being hired by, and advancing to higher-paying departments within, the company. Validity of the tests was a key issue in this case, because neither of the tests was shown to be significantly related to successful job performance; as a result, the case spurred stronger focus on the validity of employment tests.

FAMILY EDUCATIONAL RIGHTS AND PRIVACY ACT OF 1974 The Family Educational Rights and Privacy Act (FERPA) of 1974 is a federal law that protects that privacy of student records. FERPA gives parents certain rights with respect to their children's education records, such as the right to examine their children's academic records and stipulate the terms under which others may have access to them. If there is assessment information in the records, then parents have a right to see these results as well.

INDIVIDUALS WITH DISABILITIES EDUCATION IMPROVEMENT ACT OF 2004 The Individuals with Disabilities Education Act (IDEA) was originally signed into law in 1975. Its purpose was to ensure that children with disabilities throughout the nation were provided with appropriate services and educational opportunities. The law requires that each state have a comprehensive system for identifying, locating, and evaluating children of ages birth through 21 who have disabilities. The IDEA defines "child with a disability" as a child who has been evaluated as having autism, deafness, deaf-blindness, emotional disturbance, hearing impairment, mental retardation, multiple disabilities, orthopedic impairment, other health impairment, specific learning disability, speech or language impairment, traumatic brain injury, and visual impairment (including blindness). Schools are required to provide children with disabilities with special education services. Special education instruction may take place in a general education classroom, special education classroom, specialized school, home, hospital, or institution and may include academic or behavioral support, speech and language pathology services, vocational education, and many other services.

In 2004, IDEA was reauthorized and renamed the Individuals with Disabilities Education Improvement Act. This latest version of IDEA greatly impacted assessment in education and the process by which schools determine whether students have specific learning disabilities (SLDs). School districts are no longer required to use the traditional *ability-achievement discrepancy model*, which was a component of IDEA of 1997. IDEA now mandates that schools utilize several scientifically based assessments and instructional and behavioral interventions to determine whether students have SLDs, thereby qualifying them for special education services. As a result, many states and school districts have adopted an alternative model called *Responsiveness to Intervention*, or RTI. RTI is a comprehensive, multistep approach to providing services and interventions to students at increasing levels of intensity based on progress monitoring and data analysis. RTI is fully described in Chapter 14.

HEALTH INSURANCE PORTABILITY AND ACCOUNTABILITY ACT OF 1996 The Health Insurance Portability and Accountability Act (HIPAA) was enacted by the U.S. Congress in 1996. The act has three main purposes: to guarantee insurance portability, to increase protection against fraud in the insurance industry, and to institute new regulations regarding the security and privacy of health information.

The HIPAA Privacy Rule (CFR 42. Cite. 42 CFR Part 2. §164.501) establishes a minimum level of privacy protection for health care information. For professionals involved with assessment, the new privacy regulations are most relevant. The privacy regulations establish that personal health information (which includes assessment information) must be kept confidential. The regulations are designed to safeguard the privacy and confidentiality of an individual's health information, particularly in this age of electronic transmission of information (U.S. Department of Health & Human Services, 2014). The regulations define the rights of individuals, the administrative obligations of covered entities (i.e., health-care providers, health plans, health-care clearinghouses), and the permitted uses and disclosures of protected health information. In general, the privacy rule requires practitioners to act as follows:

- Provide clients with information about their right to privacy and how any information collected may be used.
- Adopt and follow procedures for protecting privacy
- Conduct training of all staff to ensure that they understand and can accurately apply the privacy standards.
- Appoint a designated individual to monitor adherence to the adopted privacy standards and HIPAA.
- Ensure that patient records are maintained in compliance with HIPAA standards.

NO CHILD LEFT BEHIND ACT OF 2001 No Child Left Behind (NCLB) contained the most sweeping changes to the Elementary and Secondary Education Act (ESEA) since it was enacted in 1965. It changed the federal government's role in K–12 education by requiring America's schools to describe their success in terms of what each student accomplishes. The NCLB contains four basic education reform principles: stronger accountability, increased flexibility and local control, expanded options for parents, and an emphasis on teaching methods that have been proven to work. NCLB significantly raises expectations for states, local school systems, and individual schools, in that all students are expected to meet or exceed state standards in reading and mathematics within 12 years. NCLB requires all states to establish state academic standards and a state testing system that meet federal requirements.

As a result of NCLB, states have created policies to reward schools that score well on high-stakes tests. Merit-based awards, clear accountability and public visibility, and financial incentives for educators are purported benefits of high-stakes tests. However, many criticize the use of these tests in education (further discussion in Chapter 14).

CARL D. PERKINS VOCATIONAL AND TECHNICAL EDUCATION ACT OF 2006 The Carl D. Perkins Vocational and Technical Education Act provides federal funding and guidance for career and technical education, with a focus on student achievement and preparing students for careers and postsecondary education. The 2006 reauthorization called for increased focus on the academic achievement of career and technical education students, strengthened the connections between secondary and postsecondary education, and improved state and local accountability. The accountability aspect of this new law means that, for the first time, career and technical education programs will be held accountable for continuous improvement in performance, measured by the academic proficiency of their students. Success will be determined through valid and reliable tests, including No Child Left Behind assessments in reading, math, and science.

Judicial Decisions

Judicial decisions are laws created by opinions from the court, often in litigation cases. Most of the judicial decisions affecting assessment involve employment and educational tests.

JUDICIAL DECISIONS INVOLVING EDUCATIONAL ASSESSMENT The following is a list of noteworthy judicial decisions related to educational assessment:

- *Larry P. v. Riles* (1974, 1979, 1984) involved as plaintiffs African American elementary school students from a California school district who claimed that they had been improperly placed in Educable Mentally Retarded (EMR) classrooms. The placement had been made on the basis of their scores on an intelligence test that they claimed was inappropriate for use with African American students. The district EMR students were 28.5% White and 66% African American. The court concluded that the schools had been using an inappropriate test for the placement of African Americans in EMR programs and that the test could not be used. In the future, the school would have to submit a written statement declaring that tests were not discriminatory and had been validated for EMR placement decisions and provide statistics on the scores of both White and African American students.
- *Diana v. California State Board of Education* (1973, 1979) concerned the appropriate use of intelligence tests with Mexican American students. These students tended to score poorly and were placed in EMR classes. The out-of-court agreement required the schools to test students both in their first language and in English and restricted the administration of many of the verbal sections of the tests.
- *Debra P. v. Turlington* (1979, 1981, 1983, 1984) questioned the fairness of the Florida State Student Assessment Test. The plaintiffs, 10 African American students, argued that they had been denied due process because they had not been given adequate time to prepare for the test and that the test was used to segregate students by race. The court found the test was not discriminatory. The court concluded that it was the responsibility of the school system when using a test for granting high school diplomas to show that the test covers only material that was actually taught to the students.

- *Sharif v. New York State Educational Department* (1989) concerned the use of Scholastic Aptitude Test (SAT) scores as the sole basis for awarding state merit scholarships. The plaintiffs claimed that the state was discriminating against girls who were competing for the award. The court ruled that New York could not use the SAT scores alone as a basis for awarding scholarships and needed to have other criteria, such as grades or statewide achievement test data.

JUDICIAL DECISIONS INVOLVING EMPLOYMENT TESTS Employment is another area that has received legal attention for assessment practices. The following is a list of noteworthy judicial decisions related to employment assessment:

- *Griggs v. Duke Power Company* (1971) decided that Duke Power Company violated Title VII of the 1964 Civil Rights Act by requiring a high school diploma and two written tests of applicants for jobs as laborers. The U.S. Supreme Court decided that Duke Power violated Title VII of the Civil Rights Act because the standardized testing requirement prevented a disproportionate number of African American employees from being hired by, and advancing to higher-paying departments within, the company. Validity of the tests was a key issue in this case, because neither of the tests was shown to be significantly related to successful job performance.
- *Washington v. Davis* (1976) was a case that dealt with the issue of bias in selection tests. In this case, two African Americans filed suit against the District of Columbia's police department for using a selection test (a test of verbal skills) that disproportionately screened out African American applicants. The U.S. Supreme Court ruled against the workers and stated that an official action (in this case, the use of a selection test) could not be determined unconstitutional solely because it results in a racially disproportionate impact. The Court instead relied on whether or not the police department intended to discriminate against African American job applicants. The Court found no intent to discriminate; therefore, it ruled in favor of the police department.
- *Bakke v. California* (1978) was a landmark decision by the U.S. Supreme Court on affirmative action. It ruled that the use of racial "quotas" for university admissions was unconstitutional, but approved affirmative action programs that give equal access to minorities.
- *Golden Rule Insurance Company v. Richard L. Mathias* (1984) was a landmark lawsuit that charged that the insurance agent licensing exam made by the Educational Testing Service (ETS) was racially biased and not job related. The case was settled out of court when ETS agreed to construct future tests by (a) including items for which the percentage of correct responses for all test takers is at least 40% and (b) considering any item biased if the difference in the percentage of correct answers between White and African American test takers exceeded 15%.
- *Contreras v. City of Los Angeles* (1981) held that the employer's burden is satisfied by showing it used professionally acceptable methods and that the test was predictive or significantly correlated with important elements of work behavior that comprised or were relevant to the job.
- *Berkman v. City of New York* (1987) struck down an arbitrary conversion process to enhance scores for female firefighter applicants, even though the underlying tests did not predict job performance.

- *Watson v. Fort Worth Bank and Trust* (1988) ruled that adverse impact does not apply to subjective criteria. The plaintiff must identify a specific criterion as producing an adverse impact and show reliable and probative statistical evidence to support an inference of discrimination. The employer needs only to offer a legitimate business reason for the criterion. Employers are not required, even when defending standardized tests, to introduce formal validation studies showing that particular criteria predict actual on-the-job performance.
- *Ward Cover Packing Company v. Antonio* (1989) reversed the impact of *Griggs v. Duke Power* (1971). A much more conservative Supreme Court agreed that, yes, employment tests must be substantially job related, but that employers could require tests that went beyond what was essential for the job as part of "business necessity."

Summary

Professional standards and codes of ethics ensure ethical and professional behavior by counselors and other helping professionals who engage in assessment. Laws and court decisions have had an impact on assessment practice. The overall effect has been fairer tests and testing practices for diverse groups. The role of tests is constantly being redefined by the courts. Professionals need to be guided by the code of ethics of their organization, be familiar with laws and court interpretations relating to testing, and be careful, critical consumers of assessment practices and procedures.

Codes of ethics and standards of practice are essential elements of fair assessment. There are similarities among the codes. Some of the common principles are competence, integrity, treating clients with respect and dignity, accepting responsibility, and concern for the welfare of others. Those involved in testing need to have competency in administering the test selected, provide an explanation for using the test, and discuss the test results in a language test takers can understand. They must get informed consent prior to administering the test. Counselors need to be familiar with techniques and procedures that are appropriate for use with clients from other ethnic and cultural groups. Practitioners also need to be aware of and respect the beliefs, attitudes, knowledge, and skills of all individuals they work with. This requires counselors to understand their own assumptions, biases, and values.

Questions for Discussion

1. Who should be allowed to purchase psychological tests? What should their qualifications be?
2. Many employment test experts believe that the guidelines from the courts and legislature are outdated and make costly demands on employers

that are not justified by the latest research. Do you agree or disagree with this position? Why?

3. What position would you take if your code of professional ethics conflicted with a recent court ruling?

Suggested Activities

1. Conduct a content analysis of two or three of the codes of ethics as they relate to testing. How are they alike? How are they different?
2. Stage a mock trial on one of the major issues in testing, such as due process, appropriateness of

certain tests for a particular function, misuse of tests, appropriateness of a certain test for a minority group, and the like.

3. Discuss some of the cases presented in the section on responsible test use.

4. Research to see if any cases in your local court system have involved assessment issues.
5. Read the following case study and answer the questions at the end:

   A private liberal arts college was working toward getting regional accreditation. The school had usually admitted a large percentage of students that were lower performers in their high school class, including any student who had a 2.0 grade point average (GPA) on a 4.0 scale. The college did not require the SAT or ACT. The admissions committee was under pressure to increase the academic respectability of the college by changing the standards to require a minimum score of 900 on the SAT Reasoning test. The committee was told that enrollment would increase if the school used an established assessment test and that fewer students would drop out.

   a. What are the assessment issues in the situation?
   b. What factors or assessment practices are involved?
   c. If you were a consultant invited by the college to help the admissions committee in the selection and retention of students, what would you advise?

6. Read the following case study and answer the questions at the end:

To remain competitive, Memorial Hospital has decided it needs to cut its budget by downsizing semiskilled workers, such as orderlies, custodians, cafeteria personnel, stockroom clerks, file room clerks, and so on. The hospital would like to help these workers qualify for higher-level jobs so that they can remain with the organization. From the attrition rate, the hospital administrators know they will need workers with advanced technical skills and will have to recruit from the outside to fill these positions if they have no one qualified internally. The personnel department has decided to give all the targeted workers who will lose their positions the Wide Range Achievement Test (WRAT-III) and the Wonderlic Personnel Test-Revised (WPT-R) and select those with the highest scores to be retrained. Of the workers, 80% are women and minority group members.

a. What are the ethical and legal issues related to this case?
b. If you were a consultant hired by the hospital to help identify workers to be retrained and conduct outplacement counseling for those who are to be let go, what would you advise Memorial to do?

References

American Counseling Association. (2014). *ACA Code of Ethics*. Alexandria, VA: Author.

American Counseling Association. (2014). *Standards for qualifications of test users*. Alexandria, VA: Author.

American Educational Research Association (AERA), American Psychological Association (APA), & National Council on Measurement in Education (NCME). (2014). *Standards for educational and psychological testing*. Washington, DC: Authors.

American Psychological Association (APA). (2002). *Ethical principles of psychologists and code of conduct* (Rev. ed.). Washington, DC: Author.

Americans With Disabilities Act of 1990, Pub. L. No. 101-336, 104 Stat. 328 (1990).

Association for Assessment and Research in Counseling (AARC). (2003). *Responsibilities of users of standardized tests* (RUST). Alexandria, VA: Author.

Code of Fair Testing Practices in Education. (2004). Washington, DC: Joint Committee on Testing Practices.

International Test Commission (ITC). (2013). *International Guidelines for Test Use*. Retrieved from http://www.intestcom.org/itc_projects.htm

National Council on Measurement in Education (NCME). (1995). *Code of professional responsibilities in educational measurement*. Washington, DC: Author.

Oakland, T. (2012). Principles, standards, and guidelines that impact test development and use and sources of information. In Leach, M.M., Stevens, M. J, Ferrero, A., Korkut, Y., & Lindsay, G. (Eds.), *Oxford international handbook of psychological ethics* (pp. 201–215). Oxford, UK: Oxford University Press.

U.S. Department of Health and Human Services (2014). HIPPA privacy rule and sharing information related to mental health. Retrieved from http://www.hhs.gov/ocr/privacy/hipaa/understanding/special/mhguidance.html

APPENDIX I

STANDARDS FOR MULTICULTURAL ASSESSMENT
FOURTH REVISION, 2012

The Association for Assessment in Counseling and Education (AACE) is an organization of counselors, educators, and other professionals that advances the counseling profession by providing leadership, training, and research in the creation, development, production, and use of assessment and diagnostic techniques. The mission and vision of AACE drives the continuing effort to create awareness of the importance of assessment and diagnostic techniques for an increasingly diverse population, to promote better training in the uses and development of assessments, and to advocate for social justice concerns in counseling and educational assessment.

In 1992, the Committee on Diversity in Assessment under the direction of the Association for Assessment in Counseling (now AACE) Executive Council created the first set of standards addressing cultural diversity and the impact on assessment in counseling and education. In 2003, the Executive Council of the Association for Assessment in Counseling (AAC) appointed a committee to expand and update the original set of standards.

During the past decade, the Council for Accreditation of Counseling and Related Educational Programs (CACREP) emphasized the centrality of diversity in our profession by including language regarding diversity and advocacy throughout every aspect of the 2009 CACREP Standards. The Council on Rehabilitation Education (CORE) has also acknowledged in its 2010 Standards the importance of cultural and individual diversity and has incorporated cultural competence into standards for rehabilitation counseling programs.

This revision of the Multicultural Assessment Standards addresses more specifically the role of social advocacy in assessment. Further, they speak to the importance of effectively selecting, administering, and interpreting assessments and diagnostic techniques while providing training standards in multicultural assessment. The intent of the revision is to enhance counseling professionals' knowledge of as well as the public's awareness and support for culturally appropriate assessment. This is particularly salient as assessment is an individual and system interventions useful for client/student and community empowerment, advocacy, collaboration, to change systems, and inform public opinion and policy.

DEFINITION OF MULTICULTURAL AND DIVERSE POPULATIONS

We define multicultural populations broadly to recognize persons who differ by race, ethnicity, culture, language, age, gender, sexual orientation, religion, and ability. Today counselors consider during the assessment process the impact of age, color, culture, ability, ethnic group, gender, gender identity, race, religion, sexual orientation, linguistic background, socioeconomic status or other personal characteristics. Counselors are also challenged to advocate for culturally diverse individuals from marginalized populations. To this end, this revision of the Multicultural Assessment Standards offers an introductory section on Advocacy, however, we assert that advocacy be infused throughout the Standards.

THE STANDARDS

Advocacy

Culturally competent professional counselors recognize the importance of social justice advocacy; they integrate understanding of age, gender, ability, race, ethnic group, national origin, religion, sexual orientation, linguistic background, and other personal characteristics in order to provide appropriate assessment and diagnostic techniques.

Professional counselors should:

- Recognize in themselves and others, subtle biases and the way these biases influence and impact the assessment process for marginalized populations.
- Seek opportunities for learning by immersion into marginalized populations in order to gain understanding of clients' worldview and the impact on the assessment process.
- Support use of assessments with psychometric properties appropriate for individuals and vulnerable groups and create awareness about assessment of culturally diverse clients.
- Provide culturally competent and effective practices in all areas of counseling and assessment in individual, family, school, and community settings.
- Work collaboratively with community leaders to understand and address the needs of diverse clients providing opportunities to access services if needed.
- Address systemic barriers and consider how these barriers impact the interpretation and use of assessment results.
- Be knowledgeable of potential bias in assessment instruments and use procedures that comply with ethical guidelines when assessing marginalized populations.
- Are responsible for the appropriate applications, scoring, interpretations, and use of assessment instruments relevant to the needs of clients, whether they score and interpret such assessments themselves or use technology or other services.
- Take reasonable measures to ensure the proper use of psychological and assessment techniques by persons under their supervision, that results are kept confidential and that results are not misused by others.

Selection of Assessments: Content and Purpose, Norming, Reliability and Validity

Culturally competent professional counselors select assessments and diagnostic techniques that are appropriate and effective for diverse client populations.

Professional counselors should:

- Understand and follow the standard development procedures utilizing accepted research methods when developing new instruments to ensure technical quality of the content domains evaluated.
- Be knowledgeable of the technical aspects of assessments, including the importance of reliability, validity, measurement error and scores and norms when selecting assessments.
- Evaluate representative samples of test questions or practice tests, directions, answer sheets, manuals, and score reports before selecting a test.
- Understand how to review information on the performance of test takers of diverse subgroups, using appropriate norming information to ensure adequate subgroup analyses.

- Understand how to select and utilize appropriate modified forms of tests for test takers with disabilities who need special accommodations.
- Select assessments that help identify client needs, strengths and resources for client empowerment and self-advocacy.
- Select instruments with which they are trained and are competent to use and adhere to the ethical standards for the administration, scoring, interpretation, or reporting procedures and ensure that persons under their supervision are aware of these standards.
- Recognize the impact of cultural identity on test administration and interpretation, and place test results in proper perspective with other relevant factors.

Administration and Scoring of Assessments

Culturally competent professional counselors recognize challenges inherent in assessment of persons and seek to provide administration and scoring of assessment to clients respecting age, gender, ability, race, ethnic group, national origin, religion, sexual orientation, linguistic background, and other personal characteristics.

Professional counselors should:

- Obtain, understand and follow all established protocol for administering standardized test instruments to clients with diverse linguistic backgrounds utilizing a competent and bilingual translator to address cultural identity throughout the assessment process including informed consent or other procedural directives.
- Become familiar with test question format and procedures for answering test questions as well as understand additional materials or needed equipment.
- Understand the nature and importance of test security, copyright, and ramifications of cheating and maintain confidentiality of scores using adequate security procedures.
- Be knowledgeable with procedures, materials and directions for scoring tests and/or monitoring scoring process to ensure accuracy of test scores, promptly reporting any errors and communicating corrected results promptly.
- Administer assessments only within the context of a defined professional relationship and utilize tests for their recommended purpose only
- Obtain informed consent from clients regarding the nature and purpose of assessment methods to be used and ensure that the test taker has the opportunity to become familiar with test question format.

Interpretation and Application of Assessment Results

Culturally competent professional counselors acknowledge the importance of social justice advocacy in interpretation and communication of assessment results with diverse populations.

Professional counselors should:

- Understand the normative groups, technical information, benefits and limitations of assessments and potential for bias in scoring and interpretation of assessment instruments.
- Provide a holistic appraisal of clients by creating a strong foundational evaluation respecting the influence of culture, background, and individual characteristics.
- Understand the influence of culture, background, and individual characteristics when designing and implementing interventions to achieve effective counseling outcomes.

- Recognize how the effects of stigma, oppression, and discrimination impact the interpretation and application of assessment results for culturally diverse clients.
- Recognize and collaborate with others to eliminate biases, prejudices, and discriminatory contexts in conducting evaluations, interpretations and providing interventions.
- Explain the nature and purpose of assessment and specific use of results in an understandable, developmental level of the client or the client's legally authorized representative providing information about the impact of culture on assessment results and interpretation.
- Consider other factors present in the client's situation (e.g., disability or cultural factors or systematic or internalized oppressing) before making any recommendations, when relevant.
- Do not use data or results from assessments that are obsolete or outdated and make every effort to prevent the misuse of obsolete measures and assessment data by others.
- Release assessment data in which clients are identified only with the consent of clients or their legal representatives, or court order and only released to professionals recognized as qualified to interpret the data.

Training in the Uses of Assessments

Culturally competent professional counselors seek training and supervised experience to ensure they provide appropriate assessment and diagnostic techniques for diverse client populations.

Professional counselors should:

- Understand the test's characteristics and receive guidance on the levels of skills, knowledge and training required to administer.
- Understand individual and group approaches to multicultural assessment.
- Receive training in how assessment data can be used to develop client action plans to make systemic changes that benefit disadvantaged individuals and vulnerable groups.
- Gain knowledge in how to collaborate with allies and policy makers to develop assessment practices that empower clients and educate the general public about culturally appropriate assessment of culturally diverse individuals and groups.
- Engage in continuous education to increase knowledge of assessment and enhance job performance.
- Have training and expertise in the use of traditional assessment and testing instruments including technical aspects of the instruments as well as cultural limitations to use test instruments for the welfare of culturally different clients.

References

American Art Therapy Association. (2011). *Art therapy multicultural/diversity competencies*. Retrieved from http://www.arttherapy.org/upload/multiculturalcompetencies2011.pdf

American Counseling Association. (2005). *Code of ethics and standards of practice of the American Counseling Association*. Retrieved from http://www.counseling.org/resources/codeofethics/TP/home/ct2.aspx

Association for Lesbian, Gay, Bi-Sexual, Transgender Issues in Counseling. (2010). *Competencies for counseling LGBTQ clients and competencies for counseling transgender clients*. Retrieved from http://www.algbtic.org/resources/competencies.

Association for Multicultural Counseling and Development. (1996). *AMCD multicultural counseling competencies*. Retrieved from http://www.multi culturalcounseling.org.

American Psychological Association. (2004). *Code of Fair Testing Practices in Education*. Retrieved from http://www.apa.org/science/programs/test ing/fair-testing.pdf.

Council on Accreditation of Counseling and Related Educational Programs. (2009). *2009 standards*. Retrieved from http://www.cacrep.org /doc/2009%20Standards%20with%20cover.pdf.

Counselors for Social Justice Position Statement on Academic Achievement Gap and Equity on Educational Services. (2008). Retrieved from http:// counselorsforsocialjustice.com/CSJ_Position_-_ Academic_Achievement_Gap.pdf.

Council on Rehabilitation Education. (2012). *Accreditation manual for masters' level rehabilitation counselor education programs*. Retrieved from http:// www.core-rehab.org/Files/Doc/PDF/CORE-StandardsPrograms.pdf.

Commission on Rehabilitation Counselor Certification. (2009). *Code of professional ethics for rehabilitation counselors*. Retrieved from http://www .crccertification.com/filebin/pdf/CRCCodeOf-Ethics.pdf.

Lewis, Arnold, House, and Toporek. (2003). *ACA advocacy competencies*. Retrieved from http:// www.counseling.org/resources/competencies /advocacy_competencies.pdf.

National Association of Alcoholism and Drug Abuse Counselors. (2011). Code of ethics. Retrieved from http://www.naadac.org/membership/code-of-ethics.

National Association of School Psychologists. (2010). *National Association of School Psychologists' model for comprehensive and integrated school psychological services*. Retrieved from http://www.nasponline .org/standards/2010standards/2_PracticeModel .pdf.

National Board for Certified Counselors. (2005). *Code of ethics*. Retrieved from http://nbcc.org/Assets /Ethics/nbcc-codeofethics.pdf.

National Career Development Association. (2010). *Career counselor assessment and evaluation competencies*. Retrieved from http://associationdatabase .com/aws/NCDA/asset_manager/get_file /18143/aace-ncda_assmt_eval_competencies.

Association for Assessment and Counseling. (2003). *Responsibilities of users of standardized tests*. Retrieved from http://www.theaaceonline.com /rust.pdf.

Texas Professional Educational Diagnosticians Board of Registry. (2010). *Best practice guidelines*. Retrieved from http://regped.com/pdf/TPED-BestPract.pdf.

2011–2012 Executive Council:

- President: Danica G. Hays, Old Dominion University, dhays@odu.edu
- President-Elect: Carl Sheperis, Lamar University, csheperis@gmail.com
- Past President: Joshua Watson, Mississippi State University-Meridian, jwatson@meridian.msstate.edu
- Secretary: Casey Barrio-Minton, University of North Texas, casey.barrio@unt.edu
- Treasurer: Stephanie Crockett, Oakland University
- Governing Council Representative: Joshua Watson, Mississippi State University-Meridian, jwatson@meridian.msstate.edu
- MAL Publications: Dale Pietzrak, University of South Dakota, dale.pietrzak@usd.edu
- MAL Awards: Susan Carmichael, susan.eaves@gmail.com
- MAL Membership: Amy McLeod, Argosy University- Atlanta, amymcleod1@gmail.com
- Graduate Student Representative: Jayne Smith, Old Dominion University, j5smith@odu.edu

Multicultural Assessment Standards Revision Task Force: Dr. Linda Foster, Chair (Foster_lh@mercer. edu , Mercer University); Members: Dr. Gabriel Lomas (lomasg@wcsu.edu), Danica Hays (DHays@ odu.edu), Michael Becerra (mbecerra@bamaed.ua. edu), and Anita Neuer Colburn (aneuer@regent.edu)

APPENDIX II

RESPONSIBILITIES OF USERS OF STANDARDIZED TESTS (RUST; 3RD ED.)

Prepared by the Association for Assessment in Counseling (AAC)

QUALIFICATIONS OF TEST USERS

Qualified test users demonstrate appropriate education, training, and experience in using tests for the purposes under consideration. They adhere to the highest degree of ethical codes, laws, and standards governing professional practice. Lack of essential qualifications or ethical and legal compliance can lead to errors and subsequent harm to clients. Each professional is responsible for making judgments in each testing situation and cannot leave that responsibility either to clients or others in authority. The individual test user must obtain appropriate education and training, or arrange for professional supervision and assistance when engaged in testing in order to provide valuable, ethical, and effective assessment services to the public. Qualifications of test users depend on at least four factors:

- *Purposes of Testing* A clear purpose for testing should be established. Because the purposes of testing direct how the results are used, qualifications beyond general testing competencies may be needed to interpret and apply data.
- *Characteristics of Tests* Understanding of the strengths and limitations of each instrument used is a requirement.
- *Settings and Conditions of Test Use* Assessment of the quality and relevance of test user knowledge and skill to the situation is needed before deciding to test or participate in a testing program.
- *Roles of Test Selectors, Administrators, Scorers, and Interpreters* The education, training, and experience of test users determine which tests they are qualified to administer and interpret.

Each test user must evaluate his or her qualifications and competence for selecting, administering, scoring, interpreting, reporting, or communicating test results. Test users must develop the skills and knowledge for each test they intend to use.

TECHNICAL KNOWLEDGE

Responsible use of tests requires technical knowledge obtained through training, education, and continuing professional development. Test users should be conversant and competent in aspects of testing, including:

- *Validity of Test Results* Validity is the accumulation of evidence to support a specific interpretation of the test results. Since validity is a characteristic of test results, a test may have validities of varying degree for different purposes. The concept of instructional validity relates to how well the test is aligned to state standards and classroom instructional objectives.

- *Reliability* Reliability refers to the consistency of test scores. Various methods are used to calculate and estimate reliability depending on the purpose for which the test is used.
- *Errors of Measurement* Various ways may be used to calculate the error associated with a test score. Knowing this and knowing the estimate of the size of the error allows the test user to provide a more accurate interpretation of the scores and to support better-informed decisions.
- *Scores and Norms* Basic differences between the purposes of norm-referenced and criterion-referenced scores impact score interpretations.

TEST SELECTION

Responsible use of tests requires that the specific purpose for testing be identified. In addition, the test that is selected should align with that purpose, while considering the characteristics of the test and the test taker. Tests should not be administered without a specific purpose or need for information. Typical purposes for testing include:

- *Description* Obtaining objective information on the status of certain characteristics, such as achievement, ability, personality types, and so on, is often an important use of testing.
- *Accountability* When judging the progress of an individual or the effectiveness of an educational institution, strong alignment between what is taught and what is tested needs to be present.
- *Prediction* Technical information should be reviewed to determine how accurately the test will predict areas such as appropriate course placement; selection for special programs, interventions, and institutions; and other outcomes of interest.
- *Program Evaluation* The role that testing plays in program evaluation and how the test information may be used to supplement other information gathered about the program is an important consideration in test use.

Proper test use involves determining if the characteristics of the test are appropriate for the intended audience and are of sufficient technical quality for the purpose at hand. Some areas to consider include:

- *The Test Taker* Technical information should be reviewed to determine if the test characteristics are appropriate for the test taker (e.g., age, grade level, language, cultural background).
- *Accuracy of Scoring Procedures* Only tests that use accurate scoring procedures should be used.
- *Norming and Standardization Procedures* Norming and standardization procedures should be reviewed to determine if the norm group is appropriate for the intended test takers. Specified test administration procedures must be followed.
- *Modifications* For individuals with disabilities, alternative measures may need to be found and used and/or accommodations in test-taking procedures may need to be employed. Interpretations need to be made in light of the modifications in the test or testing procedures.

- *Fairness* Care should be taken to select tests that are fair to all test takers. When test results are influenced by characteristics or situations unrelated to what is being measured (e.g., gender, age, ethnic background, existence of cheating, unequal availability of test preparation programs), the use of the resulting information is invalid and potentially harmful. In achievement testing, fairness also relates to whether or not the student has had an opportunity to learn what is tested.

TEST ADMINISTRATION

Test administration includes carefully following standard procedures so that the test is used in the manner specified by the test developers. The test administrator should ensure that test takers work within conditions that maximize opportunity for optimum performance. As appropriate, test takers, parents, and organizations should be involved in the various aspects of the testing process, including the following:

Before administration, it is important that relevant persons

- are informed about the standard testing procedures, including information about the purposes of the test, the kinds of tasks involved, the method of administration, and the scoring and reporting;
- have sufficient practice experiences prior to the test to include practice, as needed, on how to operate equipment for computer-administered tests and practice in responding to tasks;
- have been sufficiently trained in their responsibilities and the administration procedures for the test;
- have a chance to review test materials and administration sites and procedures prior to the time for testing to ensure standardized conditions and appropriate responses to any irregularities that occur;
- arrange for appropriate modifications of testing materials and procedures in order to accommodate test takers with special needs; and
- have a clear understanding of their rights and responsibilities.

During administration, it is important that

- the testing environment (e.g., seating, work surfaces, lighting, room temperature, freedom from distractions) and psychological climate are conducive to the best possible performance of the examinees;
- sufficiently trained personnel establish and maintain uniform conditions and observe the conduct of test takers when large groups of individuals are tested;
- test administrators follow the instructions in the test manual; demonstrate verbal clarity; use verbatim directions; adhere to verbatim directions; follow exact sequence and timing; and use materials that are identical to those specified by the test publisher;
- a systematic and objective procedure is in place for observing and recording environmental, health, and emotional factors, or other elements that may invalidate test performance and results; deviations from prescribed test administration procedures, including information on test accommodations for individuals with special needs, are recorded; and

- the security of test materials and computer-administered testing software is protected, ensuring that only individuals with a legitimate need for access to the materials/ software are able to obtain such access and that steps to eliminate the possibility of breaches in test security and copyright protection are respected.

After administration, it is important to

- collect and inventory all secure test materials and immediately report any breaches in test security; and
- include notes on any problems, irregularities, and accommodations in the test records.

These precepts represent the basic process for all standardized tests and assessments. Some situations may add steps or modify some of these to provide the best testing milieu possible.

TEST SCORING

Accurate measurement necessitates adequate procedures for scoring the responses of test takers. Scoring procedures should be audited as necessary to ensure consistency and accuracy of application:

- Carefully implement and/or monitor standard scoring procedures.
- When test scoring involves human judgment, use rubrics that clearly specify the criteria for scoring. Scoring consistency should be constantly monitored.
- Provide a method for checking the accuracy of scores when accuracy is challenged by test takers.

INTERPRETING TEST RESULTS

Responsible test interpretation requires knowledge about and experience with the test, the scores, and the decisions to be made. Interpretation of scores on any test should not take place without a thorough knowledge of the technical aspects of the test, the test results, and its limitations. Many factors can impact the valid and useful interpretations of test scores. These can be grouped into several categories, including psychometric, test taker, and contextual, as well as others.

- *Psychometric Factors* Factors such as the reliability, norms, standard error of measurement, and validity of the instrument are important when interpreting test results. Responsible test use considers these basic concepts and how each impacts the scores and hence the interpretation of the test results.
- *Test-Taker Factors* Factors such as the test taker's group membership and how that membership may impact the results of the test are critical factors in the interpretation of test results. Specifically, the test user should evaluate how the test taker's gender, age, ethnicity, race, socioeconomic status, marital status, and so forth, affect the individual's results.
- *Contextual Factors* The relationship of the test to the instructional program, opportunity to learn, quality of the educational program, work and home environment, and other factors that would assist in understanding the test results is useful in interpreting test results. For example, if the test does not align with curriculum standards and how those standards are taught in the classroom, the test results may not provide useful information.

COMMUNICATING TEST RESULTS

Before communication of test results takes place, a solid foundation and preparation is necessary. That foundation includes knowledge of test interpretation and an understanding of the particular test being used, as provided by the test manual.

Conveying test results with language that the test taker, parents, teachers, clients, or general public can understand is one of the key elements in helping others understand the meaning of the test results. When reporting group results, the information needs to be supplemented with background information that can help explain the results with cautions about misinterpretations. The test user should indicate how the test results can be and should not be interpreted.

CLOSING

Proper test use resides with the test user—the counselor and educator. Qualified test users understand the measurement characteristics necessary to select good standardized tests, administer the tests according to specified procedures, assure accurate scoring, accurately interpret test scores for individuals and groups, and ensure productive applications of the results. This document provides guidelines for using tests responsibly with students and clients.

RUST Committee

Janet Wall, Chair	Brad Erford
James Augustin	David Lundberg
Charles Eberly	Timothy Vansickle

Source: Association for Assessment in Counseling, 2003. All rights reserved.

NAME INDEX

A

Achenbach, T. M., 39, 320
Ackerman, M. J., 384
Ackerman, P. L., 159
Adrianzen, C. A., 349
Aiken, L. A., 34, 196, 234
Algozzine, B., 214
Algozzine, R., 369
Allalouf, A., 111
Allard, G., 153
Allport, G. W., 271–273, 275
Alonso-Arbiol, I., 276
Alvarez, M. E., 349
American Association on Intellectual and
    Developmental Disabilities (AAIDD),
    363, 367
American Counseling Association (ACA), 148, 390,
    396, 397, 402, 403–404
American Educational Research Association
    (AERA), 2, 32, 91, 110–114, 117, 118, 121, 125,
    136, 195, 337, 348, 349, 356–358, 360, 362, 364,
    365, 396, 398
American Psychiatric Association (APA), 4, 42, 116,
    140, 282, 305–307, 309, 313, 320, 329,
    367, 372
American Psychological Association (APA), 2, 32,
    91, 110, 136, 195, 337, 348, 356, 396,
    398–399, 402
American School Counselor Association (ASCA),
    336, 337, 340, 347
Amir, T., 380
Amirjani, N., 234
Ammons, R., 370
Anastasi, A., 14, 119, 126
Angoff, W. H., 72
Arendasy, M. E., 351
Aron, A., 68
Aron, E. N., 68
Aronow, E., 288
Arulmani, G., 253
Ashworth, N. L., 234
Association for Assessment and Research in
    Counseling (AARC), 140, 372, 399,
    412–416
Association for Assessment in Counseling (AAC),
    10–11, 155, 347, 356, 399
Atri, A., 310
Austin, W. G., 42

Aydlett, L. A., 239
Ayeni, E., 100

B

Bacharach, V. R., 98
Bagby, R. M., 4
Bailey, E. K., 360
Balla, D. A., 367
Balluerka, N., 276
Barbuti, S. M., 237
Barclay, S. R., 257, 258
Bardos, A. N., 74
Barnick, M. J., 259
Barry, C. T., 35, 37
Barton, P. E., 216
Baruth, L. G., 360
Beck, A. T., 22, 74, 85, 122, 312,
    313, 319
Becker, K. A., 180
Beckstead, J. W., 100
Beier, M. E., 159
Bennett, G. K., 231
Ben-Porath, Y. S., 276
Berg, C. A., 159
Bergeron, R., 169
Bergman, H., 276
Beutler, A., 272
Beutler, L. E., 8, 23
Bierman, K. L., 240
Binet, A., 14
Boan, C., 239
Boekhorst, J. A., 259
Bonner, M., 286
Boo, J., 33
Borgen, F. H., 246
Boyd, D., 93
Bracken, B. A., 104, 215, 239
Breaugh, J. A., 260
Brice, W. D., 360
Briggs, K. C., 283
Brown, C., 97
Brown, G. K., 22, 74, 85, 122, 312
Brown, S. D., 256
Buchanan, T., 16
Buck, J. N., 291
Burlingame, G. M., 319
Burns, R. C., 294
Buros, O. K., 133

SUBJECT INDEX

Kuder Preference Record–Vocational, 244
Kuder–Richardson formulas, 97, 100–103
Kuder Skills Assessment (KSA), 255
Kuhlmann–Anderson Intelligence Tests, 186
Kurtosis, 55
Kwalwasser Music Talent Test, 235

L

Language disorders, 369
Larry P. v. Riles (1974), 408
Latent variables, 47, 112
Latino/Latina clients, 73
Law School Admissions Test (LSAT), 239
Lead poisoning, impact on achievement, 216
Learning, impact on reliability, 94, 97
Learning disabilities, 205, 335, 337–340
Legal considerations, 404–410
    ADA, 261, 363, 405
    Carl D. Perkins Vocational and Technical
        Education Act, 408
    Civil Rights Act, 406
    FERPA, 406
    HIPAA, 407
    IDEA, 205, 332, 339, 363–364, 406–07
    judicial decisions, 404, 408–410
    NCLB, 71, 213, 214, 341, 348, 349, 407–08
    statutes and regulations, 404, 405–08
Leiter International Performance Scale, 187, 188
Length of test, impact on reliability, 95, 107
Leniency errors, 40
Leptokurtic distributions, 55, 56
Likert scales, 38, 39, 64
Linear regression, 66
Linear transformations, of raw scores, 77
Line of best fit, 66, 67
Linguistically diverse individuals, 361–362
Linguistic intelligence, 167
Locus of control, 50
Logical errors, 40
Logical/mathematical intelligence, 167
Lohman, 185
Long-term storage and retrieval, 164
Low birth weight, impact on achievement, 216
Low-rate behaviors, 36
Low-stakes tests, 348
Luria–Nebraska Neuropsychological Battery
    (LNNB), 326–327, 369
Luria's model of information processing, 166, 182

M

Magnitude, 48–50
Mandated testing programs, 125
Manifest variables, 112
Manuals, 134, 135–136, 138, 139

Matching questions, 27
Mathematical intelligence, 167
Maturation, impact on reliability, 94, 97
Maximum-performance tests, 30–31, 87
Mean, 56, 57
Measurement bias, 139, 357–360
Measurement error, 93–95, 139
Measurement invariance, 117
Measurement movement, 11
Measurement scales, 48–50
Measures of central tendency, 55–58
Measures of relationship, 61–68
Measures of variability, 57–60
Mechanical abilities, 231–232
Mechanical Aptitude Test (MAT 3-C), 232
Median, 56, 57
Medical College Admissions Test (MCAT), 239
Meier Art Test of Aesthetic Perception, 235
Meier–Seashore Art Judgment Test, 234–235
Memory ability, 163
Mental disorders
    defined, 4, 305
    diagnosing, 304–08
    prevalence of, 304
Mental Measurements Yearbook (MMY, Buros
    Institute), 133–134, 137, 198, 351
Mental Processing Index (MPI), 182
Mental quotient, 170
Mental status exams (MSEs), 310–311
Mesokurtic distributions, 55, 56
Metacognition, 159
Methods of assessment, 20–41
    formal vs. informal, 5, 22–23
    interviews (*See* Interviews)
    observations (*See* Observations)
    overview, 5–7, 20–21
    tests (*See* Tests and testing)
Metropolitan Readiness Tests, 240
Midpoints, 54
Military employment assessment, 14, 16, 185, 262
Military Entrance Score, 226
Miller Analogies Test (MAT), 238–239
Millon Clinical Multiaxial Inventory (MCMI-III),
    122, 276, 277, 280, 282, 311, 312
Mini Mental Status Examination (MMSE), 311
Minimum-level skills tests, 211, 212–213
Minnesota Clerical Test (MCT), 231
Minnesota Importance Questionnaire (MIQ), 252
Minnesota Multiphasic Personality Inventory
    (MMPI-2), 79, 81, 153, 275–281, 298, 312
Mode, 56, 57
Most recent performance errors, 40
Motivation, for taking tests, 380–381
Multiaxial diagnostic system, 306